THE
SPIRITS
AND THE
LAW

Jacqueline Stewart
Reno
2011

THE
SPIRITS
AND THE
LAW

VODOU AND POWER IN HAITI

Kate Ramsey

THE UNIVERSITY OF CHICAGO PRESS

Chicago and London

KATE RAMSEY is assistant professor of history at the
University of Miami.

The University of Chicago Press, Chicago 60637
The University of Chicago Press, Ltd., London
© 2011 by The University of Chicago
All rights reserved. Published 2011
Printed in the United States of America

20 19 18 17 16 15 14 13 12 11   1 2 3 4 5

ISBN-13: 978-0-226-70379-4 (cloth)
ISBN-10: 0-226-70379-7 (cloth)

Library of Congress Cataloging-in-Publication Data

Ramsey, Kate.
The spirits and the law : vodou and power in Haiti /
Kate Ramsey.
p. cm.
Includes bibliographical references and index.
ISBN-13: 978-0-226-70379-4 (cloth : alk. paper)
ISBN-10: 0-226-70379-7 (cloth : alk. paper)
1. Haiti—Religion. 2. Religion and law—Haiti—History.
3. Nationalism—Haiti—Religious aspects—History.
I. Title.
BL2530.H3R25 2011
306.6′99675097294—dc22
2010043112

♾ The paper used in this publication meets the minimum
requirements of the American National Standard for
Information Sciences—Permanence of Paper for Printed
Library Materials, ANSI Z39.48-1992.

For my parents,
and for those working to build *yon lòt Ayiti*

CONTENTS

List of Illustrations ix

Acknowledgments xi

Note on the Spelling and Use of Terms in Kreyòl xix

Introduction 1

1

Crimes of Ritual Assembly and
Assemblage in Colonial and
Revolutionary Saint-Domingue

24

3

Penalizing Vodou and Promoting
"Voodoo" in U.S.-Occupied Haiti,
1915–1934

118

2

Popular Spirituality and
National Modernity in
Nineteenth-Century Haiti

54

4

Cultural Nationalist Policy and
the Pursuit of "Superstition" in
Post-Occupation Haiti

177

Epilogue 248

Notes 257

Bibliography 369

Index 405

ILLUSTRATIONS

FIGURE 1   Map of Saint-Domingue. 2

FIGURE 2   Map of Haiti. 3

FIGURE 3   Anténor Firmin. 93

FIGURE 4   Louis-Joseph Janvier. 96

FIGURE 5   Drum confiscated in 1916. 163

FIGURE 6   Ti Memenne and Faustin Wirkus. 168

FIGURE 7   Wirkus and a collaborator filming *Voodoo* on La Gonâve, 1932. 169

FIGURE 8   Image from reissue of pressbook for *White Zombie*. 171

FIGURE 9   Jean Price-Mars. 179

FIGURE 10   Rural police officer, Plaisance, Haiti, 1937. 192

FIGURE 11   Dantès Bellegarde, Camille Lhérisson, and Jacques Roumain, Port-au-Prince, 1941. 214

FIGURE 12   Lina Fussman-Mathon, in background, watching an informal performance at her home in the mid-1940s. 217

FIGURE 13   "The prisoner who drummed." 219

FIGURE 14   Madame Ti-Nomme, Plaisance, Haiti, 1937. 223

FIGURE 15   Altar in Madame Ti-Nomme's home, Plaisance, Haiti, 1937. 224

FIGURE 16   Jean-Léon Destiné in 1946. 225

FIGURE 17   Members of the troupe Mater Dolorosa performing in Pétionville, 1945. 226

FIGURE 18   Katherine Dunham with friends in Haiti, 1936. 227

FIGURE 19   The troupe of Lina Fussman-Mathon before their trip to Washington, D.C., to perform at the 1941 National Folk Festival. 233

FIGURE 20   Jean-Léon Destiné and Gladys Hyppolite rehearsing in preparation for their performances at the National Folk Festival in Washington, D.C. 234

ACKNOWLEDGMENTS

I owe an enormous debt of gratitude to everyone who has contributed to the evolution of this book. Its first incarnation was as a dissertation, and thus I begin with my Ph.D. advisors at Columbia University, Michael Taussig and Rosalind Morris, who inspired me through their writing and teaching and guided my work wisely and generously throughout. They always asked in advance the questions that proved most important in the end. John Szwed's influence spans every stage of my higher education, from college through graduate school, and I have been the recipient of his scholarly generosity many times over the years. J. Michael Dash's scholarship on Haitian literary history and politics has been a touchstone for my work as long as I have been engaged in these studies, and I have valued greatly his guidance along the way. Although Laënnec Hurbon was not a formal advisor for my doctoral thesis, his writing and input have critically shaped the way I think about these histories, as is reflected in the pages that follow. I would also like to thank Barbara Kirshenblatt-Gimblett and Karen McCarthy Brown for their intellectual generosity and mentoring at different points during my development of this study. Sterling Stuckey has encouraged my research since the very first time I presented it publicly, and I am deeply grateful for our scholarly exchange over the years. Finally, I wish to express my gratitude for Cynthia Jean Cohen Bull's intellectual nurturing from the first moments of my graduate education until her passing in 1996. I miss her as a teacher, mentor, and friend.

I am extremely grateful to those who discussed their perspectives on these histories with me, both in Haiti and in the United States. My deepest appreciation goes to Jean-Léon Destiné, who for seventeen years has generously shared his memories and analyses of the *mouvement folklorique*, along with his friendship. In addition, I extend my gratitude to Jean-Yves Blot, Jean Coulanges, Pierre Desrameaux, Etienne Germain, Michel Lamartinière Honorat, Alphonse Jean, Louines Louinis, and Emerante de Pradines Morse. I also wish to acknowledge and honor the contributions of five remarkable women who are gone, but whose inspiration and influence carries on: Katherine Dunham, Lina Mathon-Blanchet, Carmencita Romero, Odette Latour Wiener, and Lavinia Williams.

The debt I owe to those who supported my research in Haiti is enormous. I thank Marvel Dandin and Yanick Guiteau Dandin for their friendship—weekly meetings in Kreyòl and English at Radio Kiskeya with Marvel, and afternoon dances classes with Yanick—and for their serious engagement and invaluable assistance with my research. In 1991 and again in 1996–1997 I relied on the everyday support and guidance of the extended Jean-Charles family, with special thanks to Claudie and Antoine for making me feel so at home, and to Glarsnell, Gutteridge, Henseler, Hervé, Monge, Nadie, Nadige, and Shirley. I am grateful for the equally generous hospitality of Jacques Bartoli during a shorter period of research in the spring of 1998. I want to thank Florencia Pierre and the members of the folklore troupe Djaka for welcoming me into the community of their company classes several afternoons a week. My thanks as well to Kathie Klarreich and Georges Venel Remarais for the opportunity to work for a time as a translator with L'Agence Haïtienne de Presse, which supported an extended stay in Haiti. Now that we both live in Miami, more thanks to Kathie for her moral support as I completed the manuscript. I am very grateful to Henry-Robert Jolibois for his generous material support of my research by providing office space at ISPAN, for his help with research questions over years, and for his friendship today. It was my good fortune to overlap in Port-au-Prince with Sara Lechtenberg, who generously shared her own research with me. I am grateful to Eileen Herzog-Bazin for co-organizing a stimulating conference on the history of Haitian folklore dance that advanced my research considerably. Sympson Rinvil was a wonderful partner for language exchange. For their friendship and/or input on the project, I would also like to acknowledge Tamara Apollon, Sharon Bean, Amelia Burgess, Marjorie Celestin, Stania Celestin, Brian Concannon, Laurence Durand, Marie-Lourdes Elgirus, Lucien Maurepas, Donna Plotkin, Nadege Robertson Tippenhauer, and Mushi Widmaier.

One of my greatest debts is to the librarians and archivists who aided my research at collections in Haiti and the United States. In Port-au-Prince, my gratitude goes to Ephèle Milcé, director at that time of the Bibliothèque Haïtienne des Pères du Saint Esprit, and to his assistant Sabrina Réveil; to Frère Ernest Even at the Bibliothèque Haïtienne des Frères de l'Instruction Chrétienne, whose generosity and support he demonstrated by opening the library for me on a weekend morning so that I could hand-copy a few remaining materials before leaving town; to the staff of the Bibliothèque Nationale, particularly Nadège Constant; and to Eleanor Snare, former director of the Institut Haïtiano-Américain, who made her own extensive library available to me at the start of my research in Port-au-Prince, thereby orienting the project in crucial ways.

In the United States, I wish first to thank for their invaluable assistance the staffs of the interlibrary loan offices of New York University, Columbia University, Ohio State University, Brown University, Princeton University, the University of Pennsylvania, and the University of Miami. My archival research had a fortuitous beginning in the Melville J. Herskovits Papers at Northwestern University. I would like to thank the archivists and librarians there, and also those who supported my research on a short-term research fellowship in the Department of Anthropology, National Museum of Natural History, Smithsonian Institution, especially Jake Homiak; in the National Museum of African Art, also at the Smithsonian; in the Manuscripts, Archives, and Rare Books Division of the New York Public Library's Schomburg Center for Research in Black Culture, especially Andre Elizee; in the General Research Division of the New York Public Library; in Special Collections, George A. Smathers Libraries, University of Florida, Gainesville, where I was fortunate to make the acquaintance of Keith Manuel, who continued research that I was not able to complete during my visit; at the U.S. Marine Corps History and Museums Division in Washington, D.C., especially Robert Aquilina; in the National Archives and Records Administration, especially Trevor Plante; in Special Collections at Morris Library, Southern Illinois University, Carbondale; at the University of Pennsylvania Museum of Archaeology and Anthropology; at the New York Public Library for the Performing Arts; at the Manuscript Division, Library of Congress; at the Florida International University Green Library Special Collections; by mail, at the Gray Research Center, and the Reference Branch, History Division, U.S. Marine Corps at Quantico; and last but certainly not least, I would like to thank Cristina Favretto, Beatrice Skokan, and Rochelle Pienn in Special Collections at the University of Miami Libraries. Thanks to Katherine Carroll Davis for compiling a helpful inventory of works held by the University of Miami that were relevant to this project.

I am likewise extremely grateful for the funding that has made this research and writing possible over the years. The Tinker Foundation through New York University's Latin American and Caribbean Studies Program supported my earliest work in this area. I was fortunate also to receive Tinker Foundation summer funding at Columbia through the Iberian and Latin American Studies Center there. I was the grateful beneficiary of a Columbia University Traveling Fellowship and a Lindt Dissertation Fellowship, as well as funding from the Sheldon Scheps and the Firestone Family Funds through the Department of Anthropology. My work benefited enormously from two visiting fellowships and two postdoctoral fellowships. In the spring of 1998 I was invited to take part in a research seminar entitled "Race and Representation in Dance" sponsored by the Department of Dance at the University of California, Riverside. Many thanks to Susan Leigh Foster for organizing this program, to Jacqueline Shea Murphy for leading a dynamic seminar, to Sally Ann Ness for her hospitality and dialogue, and to the entire working group of graduate students and visiting scholars assembled, especially Celeste Fraser Delgado and Richard Green. In the spring of 2001 I had the chance to spend ten weeks as a visiting fellow at the Ohio State University's Institute for Collaborative Research and Public Humanities, as part of its "Performances of Culture/Cultures of Performance" seminar. My great thanks go to the institute's directors, Christopher Zacher and Rick Livingston, as well as to Erika Bourguignon, Steven Conn, Jill Lane, Dorothy Noyes, Amy Schuman, and especially Laura Chrisman for making my time at the institute and in Columbus so productive and enjoyable.

In 2002–2003 I was very grateful to have the support of a nonresidential postdoctoral fellowship at the Center for Religion and American Life, Yale University. Many thanks to Jon Butler and Harry Stout for this opportunity, as well as to the other fellows for their collegiality and engaging work. The following year I was thrilled to receive the support of an Andrew W. Mellon Postdoctoral Fellowship at the Penn Humanities Forum, University of Pennsylvania. Many thanks to Jennifer Conway for making the forum such a hospitable space for the visiting researcher, and to Carol Muller, Peter Stallybrass, Wendy Steiner, and all of the participants for making the weekly "Belief" seminar so productive. I would like to thank my fellow "Mellons" Andreas Andreopoulos, Michael Bailey, Sidney Boquiren, and Yaakov Mascetti for many stimulating conversations over the year. In completing the research and writing of this book, two Max Orovitz Summer Awards in the Arts and Humanities from the University of Miami and a 2007 Franklin Research Grant from the American Philosophical Society were indispensable.

It has been enormously helpful to present parts of this study along the way, including on panels at multiple Haitian Studies Association and American Anthropological Association annual meetings; as well as at meetings of the Society for the Anthropology of Religion, the American Studies Association, and the Society for Dance History Scholars. I also greatly valued being able to present my work in the 1997 symposium "La

Danse Haïtienne: Histoire et Traditions" in Port-au-Prince; the University of Pennsylvania Department of Anthropology 2004 Colloquium Series; the 2004 Center for French Civilization and Culture symposium "Michel Leiris: Miroir des Antilles/Caribbean Reflections" at New York University; the 2007 Brown Bag Series, Department of History, Florida International University; the 2008 Atlantic Studies Interdisciplinary Research Group, University of Miami; the 2008 Distinguished Speaker Series, Center for Latin American Studies, University of Miami; the 2008 symposium entitled "Obeah and Other Powers: The Politics of Caribbean Religion and Healing," School of Historical Studies, Newcastle University; the 2009 "Haitian Vodou, History, and Culture" symposium organized by the Afro-Romance Institute of the University of Missouri–Columbia; and the 2010 conference "Haiti's History: Foundations for the Future" at Duke University.

I am also grateful to have been able to publish pieces of this study in earlier forms. A much shorter version of chapter 4 appeared in *Radical History Review* 84 (Fall 2002) on "the uses of the folk"; my thanks to Regina Bendix for alerting me to the theme; and to the issue's editors, Karl Hagstrom Miller and Ellen Noonan, and an anonymous reviewer for their extremely helpful input. I am grateful to the journal and to its publisher, Duke University Press, for granting me permission to use parts of that article in chapter 4. Many thanks as well to the editors Henry Goldschmidt and Elizabeth McAlister for including my article "Legislating 'Civilization' in Postrevolutionary Haiti" in their anthology *Race, Nation, and Religion in the Americas* (Oxford University Press, 2004) and for their very helpful feedback during the editorial process. I appreciate Oxford University Press's permission to draw from that piece in chapter 2. My great thanks go to Carlo Avierl Célius for editing the landmark special 2005 issue of the journal *Gradhiva*, entitled *Haïti et l'anthropologie*, in which my article "Prohibition, Persecution, Performance: Anthropology and the Penalization of Vodou in Mid-20th-Century Haiti" appeared. I am grateful for their permission to reproduce parts of that article in chapter 4.

With my graduate training in anthropology, having the opportunity to teach courses in Caribbean history proved to be extremely productive and stimulating during the final stages of this book. I thank all of my colleagues in the Department of History at the University of Miami for their support and input during this process, especially Ashli White for discussions about eighteenth-century Saint-Domingue, and Robin Bachin, Hermann Beck, Richard Godbeer, Mary Lindemann, Michael Miller, Guido Ruggiero, Don Spivey, and Hugh Thomas for their advice and encouragement throughout. The graduate and undergraduate students with whom I have worked over the past four years in courses such as "Haiti in History," "Afro-Caribbean Religion and the Law," and "Magical Modernities" have taught me much about the questions that lie at the center of this study. I am also grateful for my nondepartmental homes at the University of Miami, including the support and input of Steve Stein and Tiffany Madera at the Center for Latin American Studies, that of Lillian Manzor and other colleagues in the Latin American Studies Program, and that of Edmund Abaka in the Africana Studies Program. The Atlantic Studies Interdisciplinary Research Group has been a continuously stimulating forum for discussion. I am grateful to be able to collaborate with my colleague Louis Herns Marcelin on both the programs of the University of Miami's Haiti Research Group and the work of the Haiti-based Interuniversity Institute for Research and Development (INURED). I much appreciate the chance to work with Guerda Nicolas, Pierre-Michel Fontaine, and Rose Glemaud on these initiatives as well. I am grateful for support from the dean's office of the University of Miami College of Arts and Sciences toward publication costs associated with this book. My thanks to Perri Lee Roberts in particular.

One of my greatest resources throughout this project has been the support of close friends, some of whom, as colleagues too, have read parts or all of the manuscript. I am particularly grateful to Gina Athena Ulysse, who read nearly everything, whose questions and comments proved invaluable as I revised, and whose moral support since my ABD days has meant the world. Cynthia Oliver's input on chapter 4 was incisive, and our reality checks have been essential, if never frequent enough. Kevin Yelvington's and Gérarde Magloire-Danton's comments on an earlier version of that same chapter helped shape its current form, and I will be forever in debt to both of them for the countless articles they have sent in the spirit of pure scholarly generosity. I am thankful for Anne-Maria Makhulu's great support and input across the years and miles. Chantalle Verna has been one of my most important interlocutors in Miami since we both arrived, and I am grateful for her collegial friendship. Tracy Devine-Guzman and Bianca Premo are my wonderful writing group partners; their comments helped me so much in the final stages of revision that I only wish we could have been working together all along. For her wisdom, sanity, and support all these years, many thanks to Radhika Subramaniam. I am happy to be collaborating with Elizabeth Chin once again, thanks to her initiatives on the work of Katherine Dunham. I am grateful to Erik Davis for encouraging me to attend the Haitian dance class where in some sense this all began, and to Pat Hall, a remarkable dancer and teacher. I would also like to thank friends not mentioned above who sustained me through graduate school, whether they were themselves enrolled or, in most cases, not: Sue Beddoe, Betsy Cooper, Cathy Edwards, Patricia Hoffbauer, John Jackson, Esther Kaplan, Jody Lester, Eleni Myrivili, Pepón Osorio, Mark Shapiro, Merián Soto, Pam Thompson, and Mike Wishnie. I first talked and thought through many of the questions and ideas discussed here with Joe Wood. While the unending tragedy is that Joe is gone, his inspiration and example are abiding.

For their support and/or input at different stages of this project, I would also like to thank Robert Adams, Aurelio Alonso, Gage Averill, Ruth Behar, Patrick Bellegarde-Smith, Amy Borovoy, Alejandra Bronfman, Sandra Brown, Vincent Brown, Marc Brudzinski, Jean Casimir, Vèvè Clark, Marlene Daut, Colin Dayan, Watson Denis, Charlene Desir, Bernard Diederich, Brenda Dixon-Gottschild, Laurent Dubois, Brent Hayes Edwards, Sibylle Fischer, Gerdès Fleurant, Carolyn Fluehr-Lobban, Anne Flynn, Carl Fombrun, Peter Frisch, Alejandro de la Fuente, Amitav Ghosh, Michelle Gonzalez Maldonado, Steven Gregory, Leonie Hermantin, Deborah Jenson, Valerie Kaussen, Jennifer Lambe, Alex Lichtenstein, Ira Lowenthal, David Luis-Brown, Susan Manning, Claudine Michel, William Nelson, Stephan Palmié, Frank Palmeri, Diana Paton, Alasdair Pettinger, Mary Renda, Terry Rey, Vanessa Reynaud, Karen Richman, Reinaldo Román, Nina Schnall, Matthew Smith, Edward Sullivan, Deborah Thomas, Michelle Warren, Lois Wilcken, Brooke Wooldridge, and Flore Zéphir. My special thanks to Rachel Beauvoir-Dominique for the gift of *Savalou E* at the moment when, as it turned out, I most needed it. The exchange on the Haiti-focused listserv moderated by Bob Corbett has shaped and enriched my thinking about this project for over a decade.

The maps and images that appear in these pages deserve their own acknowledgments section. I am particularly indebted to Jean-Léon Destiné for sharing photographs from his personal collection; to Daniel Métraux for permission to reproduce photos from the album of his parents' first visit to Haiti in 1941; to Frantz Voltaire, Jancy Bolté, and Peddy Multidor at the Centre International de Documentation et d'Information Haïtienne, Caribéenne et Afro-Canadienne (CIDIHCA) for their extensive photographic research and permission to reproduce several portraits that appear in these pages; to Bryan Senn for generously sending me a copy of an illustration that appeared in his book *Golden Horrors*; to Linda Chapin for her photographic help; and to Erin Greb for the masterful maps that she created. My special thanks go to Eddy Jacques for his painting *Campagne antisuperstitieuse* and to Culturesfrance for permission to feature a detail from it on the cover. I would also like to thank the New York

Public Library; the University of Pennsylvania Museum of Archaeology and Anthropology; the National Anthropological Archives, Smithsonian Institution; the Special Collections Research Center, Morris Library, Southern Illinois University Carbondale; Getty Images; and the George A. Smathers Libraries, University of Florida, Gainesville.

I am extremely grateful to T. David Brent of the University of Chicago Press for his support and extraordinary patience as I completed the manuscript, and for his guidance during the editorial process. My great thanks as well go to Laura Avey for her assistance in preparing the manuscript for publication, and to Barbara Norton for her meticulous copyediting. My gratitude goes in addition to Erik Carlson for shepherding the book through the production process and to Robert Hunt for his work in marketing it. I deeply appreciate the intellectual and scholarly generosity of the two anonymous readers, now revealed as Robin Derby and Michael Largey, who reviewed the manuscript and critically shaped my revisions through their comments, questions, and suggestions.

My parents, Dorothy and Jarold, have aided and supported my work in every conceivable way, from talking over ideas, to encouraging writing retreats at their home, to tracking down articles and books for me, to being there always. I am incredibly grateful for the constancy of their faith and encouragement, which has sustained me through the ups and downs of the research and writing. Likewise, my sister, Sophie, my brother, John, and their families have been nothing but supportive and encouraging, never once asking the dreaded question, "Aren't you finished yet?" I have also deeply appreciated the support of Pat and Roger Watson and my entire England-based family. Various sections of the manuscript were written, in fact, at Pat and Roger's kitchen table. Leo has only ever known his mother to be working on this book. I thank him for his passionate curiosity and patience, and for always finding ways to remind me that the stakes of the project were not simply academic. My gratitude goes to the caregivers and teachers who both nurtured him and supported the completion of the book. Tim Watson has shared this project with me (and me with this project) from its very beginnings. He has read everything, been my most important interlocutor, and shown me again and again the ways of my own arguments. My greatest thanks, and much more, go to him.

My spelling of Kreyòl words in this text follows the orthography standardized by the Haitian government since 1979. I am indebted to Albert Valdman, Yves Joseph, Craige Roberts, and Sarah Yoder for their two-volume resource *Haitian Creole-English-French Dictionary* (Indiana University, Creole Institute, 1981). In quoting other writers, however, I preserve their choice of spelling. Because words in Kreyòl are not pluralized by adding *s*, I have chosen not to tack on -*s* to signal multiplicity. I hope that the context will make clear when nouns are plural and when they are singular.

Between 1835 and 1987 many popular ritual practices in Haiti were officially prohibited, first as *sortilèges* (spells) and later as *pratiques superstitieuses*
(superstitious practices). This study asks several key questions about the
institutional and social histories of this legislation. Why was the ban on
popular ritual maintained as a fixture of the Haitian Code Pénal (penal
code) for over 150 years when, for the most part, the sustained application of these laws was politically impossible for the Haitian government?
What was the significance of these laws for popular religious communities both at times when they were strictly enforced and also, as was more
generally the case, when they were not? How did local communities interpret these laws and shape their application, and what does this reveal
about the relationship of the Haitian state to the rural majority at different
points in the country's history? What role did these laws play in producing the object of "*le vaudoux*" or "voodoo," particularly in foreign imag-
inings about Haiti, and how did such figures, in turn, impact the penal regime against popular ritual practices in Haiti?

   This book situates these questions in relation to the long history of
Euro-American denigration of African and African diasporic spiritual and
healing practices. As the nation born of the world's only successful slave
revolution, Haiti was the preeminent locus for nineteenth-century debates about whether peoples of African descent had the capacity for self-
government. Detractors of the "Black Republic" pointed to the persistence and prevalence of what they called "the *vaudoux* cult" as primary
evidence to the contrary. Arguably no religion has been subject to more
maligning and misinterpretation from outsiders over the past two centuries. In his 1928 book *Dra-Po*, written in the midst of the first United
States occupation (1915–1934), the Haitian esotericist Arthur Holly argued that the "accusations according to which our African Fathers have

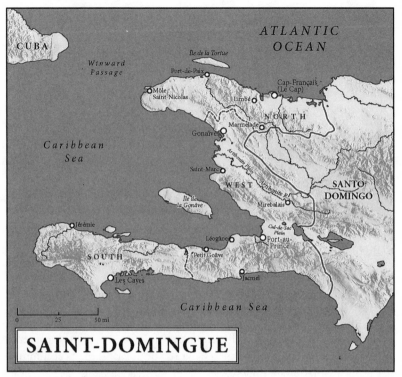

FIGURE 1. Map of Saint-Domingue.

bequeathed to us a degrading and 'diabolic cult' . . . have very much contributed to maintaining the black race in a deplorable state of social segregation in Haiti as elsewhere."[1] Holly spoke to the social force of these ideologies and implicitly raised the question of how they were materialized and made effective in law. Because the barbarism relentlessly attributed to Haiti by imperial denigrators during the mid- to late nineteenth century was consolidated in the figure of *vaudoux*—this one word, as Hannibal Price wrote, from which sprang "all the misunderstandings, sincere or not, spread against the Haitians in the world"—a key focus of this study has been the extent to which different Haitian governments relied upon the penal prohibition of *le vaudoux* to repudiate foreign charges that "civilization" was regressing in independent Haiti.[2]

The question, though, is not only to what extent these laws were intended to defend against European and North American anti-Haitianism (and other variants), but also what the internal political stakes of their promulgation and enforcement were at particular historical conjunctures. This is an especially important problem in light of the role attributed to

FIGURE 2. Map of Haiti.

African-based magico-religious practices, organization, and leadership in unifying enslaved, maroon, and free rebels in northern Saint-Domingue in 1791, and ultimately in propelling the revolutionary overthrow of French colonialism and the founding of independent Haiti in 1804. To what extent were penal laws against *le vaudoux*—enacted and maintained by the postcolonial state—designed to contain and control a potential parallel political power in Haiti? If these statutes became part of the battery of laws that specifically targeted the Haitian rural population, to what extent and in which ways did the prohibition of many family- and temple-based ritual practices classified as *sortilèges* and *pratiques superstitieuses* contribute to the political marginalization, economic exploitation, and social stigmatization of this population over the course of the nineteenth and twentieth centuries?

My conceptualization of this study is indebted to the pathfinding work of several scholars on the history and legacy of these laws, and most particularly to that of Jean Price-Mars and Laënnec Hurbon.[3] One reason these laws have received little attention, apart from such notable exceptions, in the voluminous ethnographic literature on popular religious practice in Haiti is, again, that they tended not to be consistently or rigorously enforced over the course of their 152-year history. At times during my research in Haiti, this was reflected in responses to my description of the project, usually from those who, on account of class standing, religious affiliation, and/or age, had never themselves been immediately affected by the laws. Some, for example, expressed surprise to hear that such laws had existed, asserting that it was the Roman Catholic church, not the state, that had been most active in repressing these practices. More commonly, interlocutors acknowledged the laws but cautioned me not to read them too literally, given their infrequent application against Vodou. These responses were extremely valuable, for they raised crucial points concerning (1) the ambivalent relationship of the Haitian state to practices it officially prohibited, yet, on political grounds, necessarily tolerated or sought to co-opt; (2) the role assigned to the Catholic church after its 1860 Concordat with the Haitian state in enforcing this regime; and (3) the nature of the customary regulation to which popular religious practice was subject.

Perhaps most important, such responses propelled me to think seriously about how to understand the historical significance and contemporary legacy of these laws, if they usually were not strictly enforced against socially sanctioned family or temple-based religious practices. This book is an extended attempt to answer that question, taking into account its complexity and, oftentimes, its uncertainty, given the fragmentation and silences that mark archival research on subaltern histories.[4] It is critical to remember that these laws always retained the potential to be enforced, and at times were violently so. The book is organized around several notable cases when the official prohibitions of *sortilèges* or *pratiques superstitieuses* served as the authorizing basis for the repression of communities of Vodouizan (practitioners of Vodou). Given that it was politically impossible for any Haitian government to sustain such an offensive, it is unsurprising that three out of four of the campaigns against *le vaudoux* or "voodoo" examined below were instigated by foreigners in Haiti: namely, the French-dominated Roman Catholic church hierarchy in the late 1890s and early 1940s and the U.S. military during its occupation of Haiti between 1915 and 1934. These cases most powerfully bear out Jacques Derrida's caveat in his essay on legal authority that if there are, "to be sure, laws that are not enforced, . . . there is no law without enforceability, and no applicability of the law without force."[5]

Yet over the course of my research on the social histories of these laws, it became clear that local communities also played a significant role in shaping their enforcement according to popular interpretations of what their just object should be. Thus, people whose own spiritual practices may have been officially criminalized by the inclusion of *vaudoux* in the law against *les sortilèges* seem to have taken the state's apparent will to forbid "spells" at its word, and pressured local authorities to apply this statute against alleged crimes of "sorcery." As long as they were interpreted in this way and enforced against alleged malicious magic and not against socially sanctioned ritual practices, there even seems to have been a level of popular investment in these laws.[6] The effectiveness of popular influence on their local enforcement is an ambivalent dimension of this history, on the one hand ensuring that for the most part those rituals considered essential to maintaining mutually sustaining relations with the spirits could still be performed. At the same time, the archival record is largely silent about what local hierarchies and power relations conditioned the direction of these laws against those accused of malicious "spells."

That Vodouizan, quite understandably, interpreted the law against *les sortilèges* as prohibiting malicious magic also points to the perversely affirmative nature of these prohibitions. The intermittent efforts to see these laws strictly applied on the parts of state authorities, the Roman Catholic church, and U.S. marines in Haiti often seemed to more powerfully confirm and instantiate the reality of "superstitious" beliefs than to undermine them. In other words, as enforced under these regimes, the laws tended to affirm beliefs that they were meant ostensibly to eliminate. At the same time, the Catholic church's campaigns against what it called *le mélange* (the mixture) inevitably culminated in acts of self-destruction and self-interdiction given the interpenetrations of Catholicism and Vodou in popular practice, and the tenet among Vodouizan that to serve the spirits well, one must be a good Catholic. In the late nineteenth century, the law against *les sortilèges* was also relentlessly read against its intended grain by foreigners hostile to Haiti's existence as positive proof of the persistence of the "barbarism" that the state sought, perhaps in part through the prohibition of "spells," to repudiate. If the great post-Enlightenment rationale for legislation against "pretended" magic, divination, and enchantment was to protect the public from the "tricks" of charlatans, these laws proved to be extremely tricky themselves for different Haitian governments and for any other entity that sought their enforcement.

Such paradoxical effects bring to mind a Haitian saying that comments on the potential "trickery" of law more generally, but from a subaltern perspective: *lwa toujou genyen yon zatrap ladan* (law always has a trap inside of it).[7] It is a succinct commentary on the long history of ruling-class and foreign manipulation of the Haitian legal system to exploit peasants and, particularly, to appropriate their lands.[8] In light of that history, the potential trickiness of the law might seem analogous to that of magic it-self.[9] Do not magic and the law share a common potential for mobiliz-ing power toward good and for ill, as relatively defined? Cannot law, like magic, be engaged to produce, in Theophus Smith's terms, either "tonic" or "toxic" effects? Smith, in his book *Conjuring Culture: Biblical Formations of Black America*, examines "how black Americans have attempted to ren-der American law as a social curative or *pharmakon* (Greek: medicine, poi-son) for transforming the destructive reality of slavery."[10] This study like-wise documents and analyzes how the Haitian peasantry and urban poor engaged with juridical law and attempted to shape its enforcement as a potential social curative even as they opposed and resisted its toxic provi-sions, such as the penalization of family-based, socially sanctioned ritual practices.

Serving the Spirits

Vodou is the name by which Afro-Haitian spiritual beliefs and ritual prac-tices are today known in official Kreyòl orthography and most scholarly writing.[11] Yet practitioners have tended not to objectify the religion in this way, but rather say in Kreyòl that they *sèvi lwa* (serve the spirits).[12] References to Vodou across colonial and postcolonial histories often take this object for granted, obscuring an important genealogical question: if, in popular usage, the word Vodou has traditionally referred only to one way of ritually serving the spirits, among others, when and how did it (in its various orthographies) come to be figured by outsiders as the meto-nymic sign for a demarcatable "whole," whether this has been ascribed a "superstitious" or a religious character?

That question revives an etymological debate that was conclusively settled over eighty years ago. In the inaugural issue of the *Journal of American Folk-Lore* (1888), the American folklorist William W. Newell wrote an article exonerating Haitian peasants of the ritual crimes then re-lentlessly attributed to them by tracing how many of these charges par-alleled those made against the Vaudois, a heretical sect in late medieval France and elsewhere: child sacrifice and cannibalism, the ability to take on monstrous forms, and disinternments.[13] Newell's theory that the word Vaudoux was derived from Vaudois won a number of prominent converts at the turn of the century, including the young W. E. B. Du Bois, who cited it in his study *The Negro Church* (1903).[14] This derivation was defini-tively countered in 1928 by the founder of Haitian ethnology, Jean Price-Mars, who argued in *Ainsi parla l'oncle* (So Spoke the Uncle), his classic study of Haitian folklore, that the word actually came from the former

Dahomey, where "Vôdoun" signified spirit or deity.[15] However, as Price-Mars himself acknowledged, what this authoritative etymology did not fully explain was why the name *vaudoux* became appropriated by foreigners as the encompassing sign for all African-based spiritual beliefs and ritual practices in Haiti, thereafter taking on a powerful life of its own.[16]

In Haiti the word Vodou has traditionally referred to a particular mode of dance and drumming, and has generally not been figured as an inclusive term for the entire range of spiritual and healing practices undertaken within extended families and through relationships with male and female religious leaders, called, respectively, *oungan* and *manbo*. As Rachel Beauvoir and Didier Dominique note, when reference is made to a "Danhomen-Vodoun dance," the word holds a "very specific sense," evoking the West African roots of the important Rada spirit nation.[17] For many practitioners, the encompassing term is not Vodou, but rather Ginen, a powerful moral philosophy and ethical code valorizing ancestral African ways of serving the spirits and living in the world.[18] The Rada spirits are particularly identified with the ethos of Ginen, but the concept can also be invoked more inclusively, in reference to the broader range of popular spiritual practices in Haiti.[19] These include rituals serving other *nanchon* (nations) of *lwa*, including the Nago, the Ibo, and the Petwo, as well as *lemò* (the dead) and *lemarasa* (the sacred twins); baptism, initiation, and death rites; and, with *manbo* and *oungan*, individualized client consultations focusing on healing, divination, and the creation of charms for specific ends such as protection, health, prosperity, and love. Gran Mèt or Bondye (French Bon Dieu, or God), the creator of the universe and the spirits, is a remote and transcendent figure, for whom the *lwa* serve as intermediaries through their interventions in worldly affairs. However, as the frequently heard expression *si Bondye vle* (if Bondye is willing) reflects, there is no eventuality outside of God's will.[20]

Regional variations as well as differences in rural, urban, and diasporic religious organization, ritual, and nomenclature complicate attempts to generalize about Vodou translocally as much as transhistorically. Families in rural Haiti who have lived on or maintained a relationship to a piece of land for several generations are tied through their *zansèt* (ancestors) to a venerated *prenmye mèt bitasyon* (original founder), from whom they inherited not only the physical estate, but also a spiritual heritage encompassing familial spirits and the ritual knowledge of how properly to serve them.[21] The involvement of ritual specialists such as *oungan* and *manbo* may have been peripheral to the religious practice of such families during the nineteenth and early twentieth centuries. Oral historical and archival evidence suggests that their role intensified over the course of the twen-

tieth century in parts of the country where economic pressures, dispossessions, and displacements forced migrations to other regions, to cities,
across the border to the Dominican Republic, and to Cuba and beyond.
Today, what has been called "temple Vodou" is more commonplace in the
countryside than it once was.[22]

In Port-au-Prince and other cities, including those in the diaspora,
voluntary congregations are likewise family based, but in a more expansive sense, incorporating members into fictive kinship networks in relation to a religious elder, whether *manbo* or *oungan*. As Karen McCarthy Brown has observed, "The relationship between devotees and spirits
is . . . characterized by reciprocity and mutual dependence," and in both
rural and urban settings *sèvis* (services) are the occasions for mutually sustaining communions with the spirits.[23] Ceremonies in honor of major
lwa are timed to coincide with the feast days for the Catholic saints with
whom they are iconically or otherwise characteristically associated. For
example, St. Peter holding the keys to the gates of heaven evokes Legba,
guardian of the crossroads and all barriers (thus also the *lwa* of communication); Azaka, *lwa* of agriculture, is associated with St. Isadore the
Farmer; Ezili Frida, Creole goddess of love and lover of luxury, is a Rada
lwa identified with the bejeweled Mater Dolorosa, or Mother of Sorrows;
her rival, Ezili Dantò, a Petwo spirit, has darker skin and is fiercely ma-
ternal, and is thus linked with Our Lady of Czestochowa, Our Lady of
Mount Carmel, Mater Salvatoris, Our Lady of Perpetual Help, and Our
Lady of Lourdes.[24] *Lwa* of the same "family" can belong to different *nanchon* and perform, like these two Ezilis, the ideological complementarity
of the Rada and Petwo pantheons—the august authority, tradition, cool-
ness, and benevolence of the Rada posed against the innovative individu-
alism, transformative potency, efficiency, and sometime hot violence of
the Petwo.[25] The Petwo are magically identified *lwa*, and their proximity
to the Rada spirits is always well buffered and marked off, whether spa-
tially, in terms of the placement of altars, or temporally, in terms of the
sequence of ritual.

During large-scale ceremonies spirits are invited through sacred de-
signs called *vèvè* drawn on the ground with cornmeal; by drum rhythms,
songs, prayers, and dances in their honor; and by libations and offerings
of favorite foods, including, when appropriate, sacrificed animals that
are cooked and shared with the group. The order and protocol through
which different spirits are greeted are called, notably, the *reglemam*, presumably deriving from the French *règlement*, meaning (in one sense) regulation or statute. Once a *lwa* has "mounted a horse," that is, has spiritually embodied or "possessed" a devotee, she or he may counsel, comfort,

chastise, bless, and otherwise communicate with those present and also perform cures or characteristic physical feats. The *lwa* might have messages of advice or complaint for her or his *chwal* (horse), whose *gwo bon anj* (in Gerdès Fleurant's words, "big consciousness") is displaced by the spirit and thus has no memory of what occurs during the trance.[26] These performances (the word does not imply pretense) and the distinct personalities and relationships of the *lwa* themselves—codified in mannerisms, dress, speech, and general comportment—can be understood to comment on, analyze, and reinterpret not only familial and local matters, but also memories of ancestral Africa, enslavement and revolution, postcolonial militarism, foreign occupation and dictatorship, and social relations across such histories.[27] In earlier ethnographic literature the "hot" Petwo *nanchon* of spirits were believed to have been Creole *lwa*, emerging under slavery and revolution, as evoked in the cracking whips, small explosions of gunpowder, and piercing police whistles that are hallmarks of their ritual service. Now the Petwo *lwa* are recognized as having deep roots in Kongo (West Central African) culture, but their iconography and performances can still be seen as indexing and commenting on multiple histories and relations to power.[28] As Brown writes, "One Petwo ritual gesture could . . . evoke, at once, the magical power often attributed to Kongo religion, the social power of colonial slave holders, the financial and technological powers of American tourists and politicians, and the destructive potential of one's own inner rage."[29]

Foreigners have long taken "voodoo" (and its various Francophone and Anglophone cognates) to be synonymous with Haitian "sorcery" and with "black magic" more generally. The image of pins stuck in dolls is a product of the colonial and imperial histories that this book studies, one that lamentably shows little sign of becoming history itself in European and American fantasies of African diasporic religion. In fact, though, for its self-definition Ginen tradition relies in part on the critique of self-seeking and malevolent *maji* (magic), considered the business of specialists who "work with the left hand" dealing in spirits that have been stolen from the dead or purchased and can thereafter be made to perform magical works for their owners. Of course, what constitutes immoral magic is ambiguous, subjective, and indefinable in absolute terms; as Karen Richman has analyzed based on her research in Léogâne, spirits purchased for protection or as an instrument of self-gain in one generation may be ritually "incorporated into the descent group's Guinea legacy" in the next.[30] What is particularly striking, though, in light of past and persistent Hollywood images of "voodoo" is that malicious magic has long been constructed as a constitutive outside of socially sanctioned belief and ritual, morally repudiated by those who identify their religious practices with Ginen.[31] It is particularly ironic, then, that the word that came to signify the "whole" of malevolent Haitian "sorcery" among often hostile outsiders has in popular usage been figured by servants of the Ginen *lwa* as antithetical to such practices.[32]

The gloss of Haitian popular spiritual practice by outsiders as *vaudoux* or "voodoo" will be situated at the center of this study. The questions raised by this objectification become particularly salient with regard to colonial and postcolonial legal texts, as statutes prohibiting *le vaudoux* further reified "it" as a politically and perhaps also magically threatening entity existing in the world.[33] My research suggests, however, that the reality of such an object, legally defined as a form of witchcraft under the category of *sortilèges*, would have been refuted and repudiated by the great majority of the Haitian population after the revolution. Thus, throughout this book, I want to think about what the historic incommensurability between such laws and their purported object has meant for the potential freedom of popular religious practice in Haiti, and for the potential success of state and, after 1860, Roman Catholic church attempts to apply those laws given the strength of popular opposition and everyday practice set against them.

"The Instrument to Make Us Legal and Legitimate"

Throughout his writings, Jean Price-Mars examined the ways in which the official criminalization of Vodou contributed to the social and political marginalization of the peasantry and urban poor. In his 1951 address *Folklore et patriotisme*, for example, he asserted that Haitian elites had long relied upon the Code Pénal to deliver them from any association with the barbarism that Haiti's detractors often generalized to the entire population: "Ah! you do not wish to hear talk of Vodou, your ears are offended by the raucous sound of the drums, the dynamic and rhythmic intermingling of steps in the vodouesque dances confuse your conception of choreography, your academicism revolts against the syncopated assonance of the chants, you feel only shame and scorn for this form of barbarity and it is the Code Pénal that you call upon for help to end this disgrace that contrasts so strongly with the degree of civilization that you pride yourself on having attained."[34] Such laws, he argued, not only stigmatized the peasantry and urban poor as a class apart. At one time or another, in their ever-expanding sweep, they potentially criminalized the majority of the Haitian population. Thus, because this regime was a key factor in the subjugation of the masses, its lifting—or, as Price-Mars suggested more precisely in this essay, its reform—had to be considered a critical prerequisite for their empowerment.

Price-Mars's consideration of the social and political force of these laws and the liberatory potential of their repeal strongly resonates with the Trinidadian writer Earl Lovelace's analysis in his novel *The Wine of Astonishment* (1982) of the significance of a similar set of laws passed in 1917 against the "Shouters" or Spiritual Baptists in British colonial Trinidad and Tobago. As narrated by Eva, wife of the novel's protagonist, Bee: "One day it was in the papers. They pass the law against us that make it a crime on the whole island for people to worship God in the Spiritual Baptist religion. . . . One day we was Baptist, the next day we is criminals."[35] Bee and other members of his church resolve to organize against the law by "put[ting] a man of our own in the Legislative Council to speak for us, to make the law protect us as the law is suppose to and to keep the police from brutalising our people."[36] Once in office, this representative, Ivan Morton, born into the community but educated out of it, chooses not to identify with or politically assist their struggle. Bee's incomprehension and exasperation in the face of Morton's inaction and seeming indifference is explained by Eva in an extraordinary passage: "Bee say the church is the key to everything, that if Ivan Morton can't understand that to free the church is to free us, if he can't understand that the church is the root for us to grow out from, the church is Africa in us, black in us, if he can't understand that the church is the thing, the instrument to make us legal and legitimate and to free him, Ivan Morton, himself too, if he can't understand that, Bee say, then he don't have any understanding of himself or of black people."[37] Lovelace's novel diagnoses not only, then, how the banning of Spiritual Baptism in Trinidad or of Vodou in Haiti rendered practitioners perennially delinquent before the law. Because such religions permeated every aspect of believers' lives, and because their practice was officially constructed, not least of all through such laws, as the principal sign of popular backwardness in need of civilizing reform, they became, to Bee's mind, "the key to everything." Through this passage Lovelace suggests that the right to serve the *lwa* or worship as a Spiritual Baptist freely was not simply connected to other socioeconomic and political struggles, but rather had the potential to be an instrument through which a wider social liberation and legitimacy could be achieved.

A similar analysis seems to have propelled the coming together of thousands of Vodouizan and their supporters in the wake of the period of *dechoukaj* (uprooting) that followed the ousting of Jean-Claude Duvalier and the end of the twenty-nine-year Duvalier dictatorship in February 1986. *Oungan, manbo,* and *bòkò* (ritual specialists who work with "both hands"), members of their families, and other Vodouizan were among those attacked by crowds across the country after Duvalier's flight, identified as *sorciers* (sorcerers) and/or as members of the *tonton makout* (secret police) forces that had terrorized Haiti since the beginning of François Duvalier's regime.[38] This violence can be attributed partly, though not solely, to the fact that the elder Duvalier was well-known for his efforts to iconographically appropriate, ideologically manipulate, and institutionally co-opt the popular powers of Vodou.[39] There were, indeed, prominent Vodouizan affiliated with the Duvaliers' paramilitary apparatus, alongside well-known Catholic and Protestant *makout.* However, as Laënnec Hurbon has argued, any analysis of why so many *oungan* and *manbo* became targets of *dechoukaj* in the days following the overthrow of the dictatorship must also take into consideration the long history of clerical discourses demonizing *oungan* as agents of Satan, a label that, in preceding years, fundamentalist Protestants in Haiti had particularly exploited in their missions.[40]

Rachel Beauvoir and Didier Dominique document and analyze the 1986 violence against Vodouizan in their *Savalou E.* They recount the visit of an American pastor with his Christian music group that year who broadcast an anti-Vodou message in a nationally televised presentation, and they report that leaflets repudiating Vodou in "the New Haiti" were left on houses and cars. In recording the testimonies of many who witnessed and were themselves victims of the anti-Vodou violence, Beauvoir and Dominique also document the inaction and silence of the interim government and of the political class more generally in the face of these crimes. Significantly, their analysis, like that of Hurbon, connects the atrocities against Vodouizan in 1986 to the long history of repression of popular religious organization and practice in colonial Saint-Domingue and postcolonial Haiti, one that encompasses, but also exceeds, the "missions" of Catholic and Protestant clergy.[41] The fact that in one way or another Vodou was criminalized in the Haitian Code Pénal from 1835 forward was the authorizing basis for such campaigns.

In the face of the 1986 anti-Vodou *dechoukaj,* two groups, Zantray and Bòde Nasyonal, formed to demand that the religious rights of Vodouizan be officially recognized and protected. That year rallies, demonstrations, and open meetings were held across the country.[42] In early February 1987, the Association des Vodouisants et Défenseurs du Vodou submitted a declaration to the Assemblée Constituante (Constituent Assembly) calling for the abrogation of the 1935 law prohibiting *les pratiques superstitieuses* on the grounds, in part, that it served as the basis for "certain imported sects . . . to preach intolerance, racism and the suppression of liberty of conscience and of religion." They also called for the recognition of Vodou as a national religion, just as Kreyòl had been recognized as a national language.[43] The first demand was met by Article 297 of the new Haitian Constitution of 29 March 1987, which abrogated the *décret-loi* against *les pratiques superstitieuses*. Article 30 of the new constitution stated: "All religions and faiths shall be freely exercised. Everyone is entitled to profess his religion and practice his faith, provided the exercise of that right does not disturb law and order."[44]

Sixteen years later, on 4 April 2003, President Jean-Bertrand Aristide signed a decree granting official recognition to the Vodou religion for the first time in the nation's two-hundred-year history. Describing Vodou as an "essential constitutive element of [Haitian] national identity," the decree authorized religious leaders to register with the government and become licensed to officiate at civil ceremonies such as baptisms, marriages, and funerals. It noted the increasingly public role that Vodouizan were claiming in Haitian civil society and politics as a key factor in the government's decision to extend official recognition.[45] For Vodouizan and their supporters in this cause, the decree was the vindication of a long and ongoing struggle for religious rights. For individuals, it meant that they would no longer be required to affiliate with other religions, and thus generally to conceal that they served the *lwa*, in order to baptize a child, marry, or bury a loved one. The decree also meant that Vodou-based organizations could seek government aid for initiatives in public health, education, and other social services.[46] In the days following the government's announcement, testimonies from popular religious leaders about the importance of the decree appeared in the Haitian and foreign press. One *oungan* noted that the decree "allows us to emancipate our culture, to practice in the open."[47]

Significantly, this decree granted national status, recognition, and protection to Vodou, an objectification that, as Brown notes, was first used by "outsiders . . . to name the whole of Haiti's traditional religious practice."[48] Arguably, it was partly because the sign of Vodou (and its cognates) had long been constituted as a demarcatable "whole" by outsiders that it could be converted into, in Lovelace's words, an "instrument" for the demand of religious rights. In making *vaudoux* a metonymic gloss for Haitian "sorcery" and *pratiques superstitieuses*, Haiti's nineteenth-century detractors unwittingly paved the way for the word's resignification, by defenders (such as Jean Price-Mars), over the last century in religious terms, and for the emergence of the sign of Vodou as an indispensable object of political identification and struggle.[49] I hope that my focus on the construction and contestation of Vodou as an object of the law in the pages that follow will illuminate the complex processes through which several of these conversions have taken place.

Outline of the Book

The core chapters of this book (2–4) are framed by the promulgation of the Haitian penal law against *les sortilèges* under the government of Jean-Pierre Boyer in 1835, and the replacement of this prohibition (revised in 1864) with a new law against *les pratiques superstitieuses* under Sténio Vincent in 1935. However, the repression of African-based ritualism in colonial Saint-Domingue and the role that magico-religious practice, organization, and leadership played in the overthrow of first slavery and ultimately French colonialism are crucial reference points for that postcolonial history. Chapter 1 thus focuses on the statutes that criminalized particular ritual practices and forms of assembly on the part of slaves and free *gens de couleur* in late colonial Saint-Domingue.[50] It examines how, in the four decades prior to the 1791 uprisings in the northern province, crimes of "poisoning," "profanation," and "sorcery" came increasingly to be merged together in white dread of black resistance. During these years, the law prohibiting gatherings of slaves from different plantations, first codified in the 1685 Code Noir (the legal basis for slavery in the French Caribbean colonies), was the object of repeated elaborations, each of which seemed designed to expand the field of prohibition through ever increasing specificity. The chapter also analyzes recent historical debates over the role Vodou played in the revolutionary struggle in Saint-Domingue, and it briefly examines the policies of the revolutionary leaders Toussaint Louverture, Jean-Jacques Dessalines, and Henry Christophe toward popular religious practice and organization.

Chapter 2 examines the legal categorization and prohibition of Vodou as a form of *sortilège* (spell) in the 1835 and 1864 Haitian penal codes. It argues that from the standpoint of those dedicated to serving the *lwa*, the inclusion of "vaudoux" confounded the law, given that such rituals were viewed as constitutively opposed to forms of malicious magic. In considering why the law was framed in this way, the chapter evaluates the extent to which Haitian governments after 1835 relied upon this penal prohibition to reform popular "backwardness" and repudiate foreign charges that "civilization" was declining in the independent "Black Republic." It also considers the extent to which these laws were promulgated and maintained in order to check the potential political threat of popular religious organization and leadership. I also examine how practitioners reinterpreted these laws and directed their local enforcement against alleged cases of malicious sorcery, rather than against family-based, communally sanctioned ritual practices. I go on in this chapter to argue that the legal assimilation of *vaudoux* to the category of *sortilèges*, in defiance of popular understandings of both of these terms, ultimately preordained the failure of any attempt on the part of the state or, after Haiti's 1860 Concordat with the Vatican, the French-dominated Roman Catholic church to sustain the strict enforcement of these laws. The second half of the chapter analyzes two such episodes, the first launched in the mid-1860s under the presidency of Fabre Nicolas Geffrard, and the second led by the Catholic church in northern Haiti between 1896 and 1900.

Chapter 3 focuses on the U.S. marines' enforcement of the legal regime against *les sortilèges* during the American occupation of Haiti between 1915 and 1934. It argues that the United States consolidated its military and financial control of Haiti not only by revoking Haitian laws and passing new ones, but also by selectively exploiting certain existing statutes with opportunistic disregard for customary legal precedent. The law against *les sortilèges*—which U.S. officials understood to prohibit "voodoo"—was one of those prioritized for enforcement, both in keeping with the American paternalist mission to establish "moral decency" in Haiti, and because of the close association that military personnel drew between Haitian "sorcery" and popular insurgency. In examining the severity of the regime against Vodou over the course of the occupation, I also examine how popular pressures shaped the marines' application of the law against *les sortilèges* in ways completely at odds with official U.S. military rationales for enforcing it. The chapter concludes by examining the seemingly impossible charge, made by a number of Haitian writers who opposed the occupation, that marines were actually "encouraging Vodou" through their policies for the purpose of denigrating Haiti's reputation abroad. The logic of those charges, I argue, lay in the role that the marines' penalization of Vodou played in the international construction, proliferation, and commoditization of images of "voodoo" during the 1920s and thereafter.

Chapter 4 studies official cultural-nationalist policy in Haiti during the late 1930s and early 1940s in relation to the post-occupation legal regime against *les pratiques superstitieuses*. This was a new penal category instituted by President Sténio Vincent a year after the departure of U.S. troops from Haiti in 1934. Having repealed the existing statute prohibiting *les sortilèges*, the Vincent government promulgated a new *décret-loi* that made ritual animal sacrifice the primary litmus test of prohibition. The prologue to the new law justified its tightening of the penal regime with reference to the state's responsibility to protect the "good name" of the country from harmful association with "superstitious beliefs." As much as this law was compelled by the pressure of imperial sensationalism around "voodoo" during and after the U.S. occupation, I argue that it was also shaped by the pressure of Haitian cultural nationalism at this time. The prologue to the 1935 law affirmed the right of citizens, and particularly "country dwellers," to organize popular dances and entertainments in accordance with popular custom. The chapter explores the implications of this legal formulation, focusing on the initial support of Vincent's successor, Élie Lescot, for the Catholic church's *campagne anti-superstitieuse* (antisuperstition campaign) in the early 1940s as his government simultaneously constructed and promoted folklore performance as an official national sign.

The lwa *and the* loi

How do Afro-Haitian spiritual formations themselves encompass, incorporate, and/or embody conceptions of law and justice? How might the ethos of Ginen be understood to internalize a moral order akin to law? Although to some extent these questions lie beyond the scope of this book, they also connect directly to the history and nature of the penal regime against Vodou and suggest directions for future study. To pose such questions is to underscore that for practitioners, Vodou is not a discrete aspect of social life, bounded off from realms such as healing and law. Rather, Vodou encompasses and internalizes legal concepts and processes in complex ways that defy compartmentalization.[51] There is already a rich foundation of research in this area, beginning with Jean Price-Mars's contention in 1928 that the "web of interdictions" to which Vodouizan must adhere should be recognized as an ethic: "If, instead of considering [Vodou morality] in comparison with Christian morality, we judged it by its intrinsic value, it would be seen by the severity of the sanctions to which the adept who transgresses *la loi* exposes himself, how it commands a discipline of private life and a conception of the social order which lacks neither sense nor suitability." More recently, Kesner Castor has comparatively analyzed what he likewise defines as the ethics of the Rada and Petwo rites against persistent images of *le vaudou* or "voodoo" as a sign and source of immorality. Jacquelin Montalvo-Despeignes, Martial Celestin, and others have examined the ways in which such values shape and inform Haitian informal law.[52]

The weakness of the judiciary and of the rule of law in Haiti has been widely discussed in the past two decades, with the independence of judges thrown into question, the administration of criminal justice seen as dysfunctional, and the confidence of the public in the entire system reported as low.[53] For the Haitian majority and their advocates, these problems are not new; rather, as noted above and discussed in the pages that follow, the legal system has long seemed mined with more traps and tricks than with protections for the disenfranchised. Yet, as this study also shows, in spite of skepticism about the likelihood of obtaining justice through the formal legal system, ordinary Haitians have still sought recourse to the courts for a range of reasons over the course of these histories.[54] Across the country alternative judicial orders have also long existed. As Jennie Smith notes, among "the oldest civic organizations in Haiti" are the *sosyete* that collectivize agricultural labor, function as mutual benefit associations, and "often provide members and their larger communities with an informal judicial system as well, thereby allowing locals to regulate interpersonal disputes without having to appeal to the state court system—renowned for humiliating and exploiting poor Haitians."[55] There has also long been a "nighttime" legal system organized through networks of *sosyete sekrè* (secret societies)—Bizango, Chanpwèl, Vlengbedeng, Zobòp, and others. With roots in similar West and West Central African associations, these *sosyete* evolved in slave resistance, *marronage* (flight from slavery), and revolutionary struggle, and because they assert themselves still as forces of community protection and defense, they are both relied upon and feared.[56] Laënnec Hurbon has analyzed the dread that outsiders associate with *sosyete sekrè* and the way in which rumors of their imputed supernatural criminality mediate the social and political influence of these groups in certain regions.[57] At the same time, in their rich ethnography of, particularly, the Chanpwèl, Rachel Beauvoir and Didier Dominique have examined how these societies base their claim to authority in the ethos of Ginen and may share membership and leadership with local *ounfò* (Vodou temples).[58] In their hierarchy, the Chanpwèl societies evoke a parallel governmentality, encompassing an emperor, several presidents and queens of different ranks, administrators of various functions, army officers, and soldiers. "Passports" that *sosyete sekrè* issue for nighttime travel, perhaps written on paper stamped with Haiti's official seal, seem to index and invert the history of state restrictions on peasant mobility.[59]

In considering what the existence of this parallel "nighttime" legal order says about popular attitudes toward the courts and the formal legal system more generally, a comparative historical perspective may prove helpful. Diana Paton has examined the recourse of enslaved and freed people in nineteenth-century Jamaica to obeah, which was colonially constructed as witchcraft, but which she and other scholars see as having functioned, in part, as an alternative legal resource for enslaved and poor Jamaicans. Paton argues that obeah, along with other competing methods for pursuing justice, "made it difficult for the [British colonial] state to naturalize its own judicial and penal systems as the common-sense answer to problems of wrongdoing."[60] There are significant contrasts between obeah, worked by individual practitioners, and Haitian *sosyete sekrè*, which function as groups, voluntary but exclusive, and which in their legal processes—encompassing investigation, tribunals, testimony, deliberation, sentencing, and potentially punishment—more closely resemble the formal judicial and disciplinary institutions that they supplement and in some cases altogether supplant. However, as Paton writes, obeah, like these associations, operated "as a way of mobilizing power that partially overlapped with the formal state system of justice . . . , disciplin[ing] people involved in practices recognized by the state as criminal, such as theft, but also those who transgressed community norms in ways that were not defined by the state as criminal."[61] If there have been broad areas of overlap, as well as divergence, in how the Haitian state and these *sosyete* defined an offense, when was one legal process pursued in favor of the other, by whom, against whom, and toward redressing what kinds of allegations of harm?

It seems striking that the judicial processes and punitive actions (usually spiritual) of these *sosyete* were never specifically named as a target of the laws against *les sortilèges* and *les pratiques superstitieuses*, or of the two major campaigns against Vodou that the Roman Catholic church mounted with initially strong government support. Were the disciplinary practices of these groups implicitly subsumed under the ambit of those laws? Might the challenge they posed to the authority of the state and the hegemony of formal law have been a factor in the penalization of popular ritualism in the first place? To my knowledge, no national campaigns were ever waged explicitly against these *sosyete* as such; so how did local rural police and *juges de paix* (justices of the peace) across the country regard and relate to these alternative judicial and disciplinary organizations in the midst of their jurisdictions?[62] How has the Haitian state contended with, attempted to co-opt, or, as a president of one Bizango society insisted, "cooperated" with this "nighttime" legal order at different historical junctures?[63]

Such questions grow out of this study and—in their particular relevance to the Duvalier regime—also exceed its scope.[64] Even so, they do not begin to exhaust the possible ways to think about how principles and processes of law and justice are internalized in Afro-Haitian spiritual cultures and organizations. Indeed, that question raises another intriguing etymological problem insofar as one of the primary words for the Haitian spirits, taken individually or as a collectivity, is *lwa*, which is phonetically indistinguishable from one of the French words for law (*loi*) and one of the Kreyòl words for law (likewise spelled *lwa*).[65] In fact, although the American anthropologist Melville Herskovits rendered this word as *loa* in his influential work on the religion in the mid-1930s, early twentieth-century Haitian writers on these practices, such as Price-Mars, usually spelled it *loi*. Price-Mars is one of the few scholars to have pondered the derivation of this word, suggesting in *Ainsi parla l'oncle* that the spirits were thus popularly identified with the laws of the Roman Catholic church.[66] The American sociologist George Eaton Simpson, who conducted field-work in northern Haiti in the late 1930s, noted in a 1945 article that an *oungan* had once told him that Vodouizan must follow both the laws of God and the laws of the *lwa* (which, after Herskovits, he spelled *loa*), without commenting on the pun that structured that statement in Kreyòl.[67] More recently, Colin Dayan has discussed this problem, suggesting key direc-tions for its future study: "When pronounced in Creole, lwa sounds like *loi* in French. It would be interesting to know what those possessed by the *loi d'état* (law of state) thought that slaves were doing when they prayed to and served their lwa."[68]

That the repression of popular ritual practice, organization, and, espe-cially leadership, became the crucible for such semantic confusions can be attested by the English transcript of an exchange between the judge ad-vocate and a witness for the prosecution during the military trial, under the 1915–1934 U.S. occupation of Haiti, of a reputed *oungan* suspected of aiding the insurgency:

Q: Where were you on November 1, 1919?
A: Assisting a ceremony at Cadeus' house.[69]
Q: What kind of ceremony?
A: A ceremony of the vodoo laws.
Q: What did this ceremony consist of?
A: It was a ceremony of giving the laws something to eat.[70]

In disorienting and defamiliarizing any available conception of "law," this mistranslation points to the importance of thinking more about the historical implications of the *loi/lwa* homology. Linguists now trace the etymology of *lwa*, meaning spirit, to a family of Yoruba words including *oluwa* (god) and *babalawo* (diviner or priest).[71] I would suggest, however, that its phonetic affinity with the French word for "law" ought not to be dismissed as mere linguistic coincidence, and that this likeness might in fact raise far-reaching questions about the social history of African dia-sporic religions under colonial, ecclesiastical, and postcolonial regimes of the Atlantic world. At the least, the homology invites further inquiry into the complex historical relationship of Haitian popular spiritual forms to the colonial ordinances, canonical statutes, and postcolonial Haitian juridical and customary laws that constrained, and thereby shaped, their practice over the course of four centuries. Such research holds the promise of shedding further light on the ways in which, as I examine here, Vodouizan themselves significantly altered the nature and application of these regimes, in part through direct political pressure, and in part through subversive appropriations. It is now more than seventy years since C. L. R. James in *The Black Jacobins* first argued that the events of the Haitian Revolution must be taken into account as a supplement to and transformation of the traditional understanding of Enlightenment modernity based on the models of the American and French Revolutions.[72] One way to build on James's now widely accepted historiographical reversal is to ask how the *"lois* of the *lwa"* can be understood to transformatively reinterpret and supplement Western models of law—precisely those through which African diasporic spiritual practices were constructed, interdicted, and persecuted as sorcery or superstition throughout the colonial and postcolonial Americas.

★   ★   ★

On 12 January 2010, as I was completing final revisions to this book, a magnitude 7.0 earthquake struck Haiti, its epicenter southwest of Port-au-Prince. It took an estimated 300,000 lives, injured as many more, displaced 1.5 million people, and caused unfathomable physical destruction across the impacted regions.[73] The international response was strong, but in the days and weeks that followed, it became clear that the greatest initiative and leadership in the face of this unparalleled catastrophe were coming not from the Haitian government, nor from international relief agencies and organizations, but from the survivors themselves, particularly in poor areas in and outside of the capital where aid was slow to arrive, if it ever did so at all. Stories of self-organization, mutual aid, and solidarity became a mainstay of international reporting on the disaster and a welcome counterpoint to the disempowering and patronizing images of the Haitian poor that were ubiquitous, including in fund-raising solicitations and other well-intentioned appeals.

In the early days following the earthquake, there was renewed interest outside of Haiti in a question that the U.S. media often posed thus: Why is Haiti so poor? Alongside the analysts who addressed that problem in its complexity,[74] there were also commentators who in high-profile editorials located the root of Haiti's poverty in its "culture," and particularly in the religion that they called "voodoo." David Brooks in the *New York Times* contended that Haiti suffered from "a complex web of progress-resistant cultural influences," including "the voodoo religion, which spreads the message that life is capricious and planning futile." He cited as an authority a former United States Agency for International Development official in Haiti named Lawrence Harrison, who now runs the Cultural Change Institute at Tufts University.[75] A few weeks later, Harrison made his own intervention on the subject in the pages of the *Wall Street Journal*, declaring that Haiti had "defied all development prescriptions" because its "culture is powerfully influenced by its religion, voodoo," which he described as devoid of "ethical content." Both Brooks and Harrison asserted in their respective editorials that "voodoo" was a progress-impeding force, and Brooks made that contention the partial basis for his conclusion that a more "intrusive paternalism" was called for on the parts of the United States and the international community toward Haiti, asserting that this would represent a break with the "same old, same old" approaches to development.[76]

In fact, of course, there was nothing new in Brooks's prescription of such a solution, nor in his and Harrison's claim that "voodoo" obstructed progress and contributed to or even produced poverty in Haiti. To take a few examples, in 1796, five years after the start of the massive slave revolts in northern Saint-Domingue and three years after general emancipation, France's commissioners in the colony legally prohibited for the first time what they called "the dance known by the name of *Vaudou*" on the grounds that it was contrary to republican institutions, good morals, public health, public safety, and, implicitly, the strict plantation labor regime to which most of the formerly enslaved were subject.[77] In the late 1890s the French bishop of Cap-Haïtien, who led the first major Roman Catholic "crusade" against *vaudoux* in Haiti after the return of the church in 1860, anticipated both the assertions of Brooks and Harrison and the televangelist Pat Robertson's much-publicized interpretation of the 2010 earthquake as the consequence of a revolutionary-era "pact with the devil." The bishop charged that *le vaudoux* both cursed Haiti in the eyes of God and was impeding national economic progress: "a dancing people," he warned, "degraded by savage orgies, will never be a working people."[78] During the U.S. occupation of Haiti between 1915 and 1934, American civil and military officials claimed at one time or another that "voodoo" was an obstacle to the rule of law, foreign investment, economic prosperity, and the moral and physical welfare of the Haitian population. "It" served as both an explanation for Haiti's problems and a pretext for an earlier "intrusive paternalism" that disrupted the lives of the Haitian rural poor in myriad ways, not least through the repression of their religious practices.[79]

As these historical antecedents make clear, Brooks's and Harrison's pronouncements were rooted in the long-standing assumption that (among other ills) Vodou is not just unmodern (and thus, in the logic of modernist development, destined to decline), but actively anti-modern, obstructing the linear course of progress in Haiti. Both assumptions have been challenged by a host of scholars and practitioners in recent years who argue that Vodou and other African diasporic religions were born of the forces and processes of modernity under slave regimes across the Americas and are today, as Stephan Palmié has put it, as "modern as nuclear thermodynamics."[80] The idea that Vodou is a chief cause of poverty in Haiti depends for any semblance of plausibility on the denigrating ways the religion has long been represented by outsiders, the political force of which is clearly far from being exhausted and, as this book examines, has always materially impacted the Haitian majority. That in the immediate wake of the January 2010 catastrophe the charge was given new credibility in the pages of two of the world's most widely circulated newspapers is a sign that the scapegoating of the religion could become stronger in the present conjuncture unless vigilantly challenged.

Beyond perpetuating falsehoods about Vodou, the most immediate problem with the assertion that "voodoo" keeps Haiti poor is, of course, that it effaces the complex of geopolitical factors that actually have impoverished the country at the same time that it conveniently absolves or minimizes any international role in that historical process. However, depictions such as Brooks's and Harrison's are arguably even more insidious in that they also work to authorize and empower the externally imposed development policies and programs that many on the receiving end of aid regard as having exacerbated the desperate conditions they were ostensibly meant to alleviate.[81] In this light, the contention that the Haitian poor are cultural agents of their own immiseration could not be more serious for the course of Haiti's post-quake recovery. If the Haitian majority are held responsible for the country's low standing in human development indexes on account of (at least in part) their deficient or actively pernicious religious culture, then clearly they cannot be entrusted with setting the terms of development agendas in their own communities, much less with helping to shape the vision of a new Haiti. Such logic is particularly egregious in the face of the self-determinism to which impoverished communities have owed their survival before and certainly since the earthquake. Many commentators in Haiti and beyond have argued that the catastrophe of 12 January 2010 must be made into an opportunity to "build Haiti back better."[82] One prerequisite of such a project, this book contends, is deconstructing images of Haitian popular religion that have long served as a pretext for denying the Haitian majority full civil capacity and agency.

CHAPTER ONE

Crimes of Ritual Assembly and Assemblage in Colonial and Revolutionary Saint-Domingue

In 1685 the government of Louis XIV issued its Code Noir, which provided an official legal basis for slavery in the French Caribbean colonies. Described by Louis Sala-Molins as "the most monstrous juridical text produced in modern times" and by Colin Dayan as "the most barbaric product of the Enlightenment," these laws were drafted by top colonial officials in the Caribbean at the behest of Jean-Baptiste Colbert, the influential controller-general of finance and secretary of state for the navy.[1] The drafters may have consulted Roman law in preparing the Code, but they based it primarily on slave laws already in effect in the French colonies of Martinique, Guadeloupe, and Saint-Christophe, especially those concerning policing and public order.[2] Promulgated for the colonies and not applicable in France, the Code recognized slavery as a local "domestic institution" while at the same time asserting the metropolitan government's ultimate authority in regulating the treatment of enslaved workers, a tension that, as Malick Ghachem has analyzed, set the Crown on a collision course with Caribbean planters, who claimed "absolute sovereignty" in the management and disciplining of slaves.[3]

It is striking that while the first eight articles of the Code Noir directly concern religious conformity in the French colonies, this document contains no explicit interdiction of African-based ritual practice. Although a broad reading of its article 3, prohibiting the "public exercise" of any religion other than *la catholique, apostolique et romaine*, might seem to implicate such practices, it was more in keeping with the overall logic of the Code that this article targeted Protestantism and Judaism.[4] Article 1, in fact, banished Jews outright, and article 5 stipulated that those of the "reformed" religion were banned from impeding "our other subjects, even their own slaves, in the free exercise of the Catholic, Apostolic, and Roman religion." The Code's article 2 required all slaves to receive Catholic baptism and instruction, a provision that served as an ideological justification for their enslavement but that, as this population in Saint-Domingue grew dramatically over the course of the eighteenth century and relations between planters and clergy progressively deteriorated, came to be followed irregularly.[5] African and African diasporic spiritualities were, moreover, rarely classified as "religious" in European colonial documents and writings at this time; rather, as David Chidester has argued, such texts figured what they termed African "fetishism" and "sorcery" as evidence of the "absence of religion."[6]

Although the heterodox practices of enslaved Africans went unmentioned in the Code Noir, over the course of next century they were subject to an increasing number of prohibitions in what became France's most profitable colony, Saint-Domingue. This chapter examines that legislative history, tracing the evolution of these laws in connection with larger social and political forces in the colony and analyzing how particular popular practices came to be interdicted (and thus objectified) under the law, for what reasons, and with what effects. The seeming redundancy of the succession of laws against, in particular, different forms of slave healing, assembly, and ritual "profanation" was in part a sign of their inefficacy: enslaved people, as individuals and communities, continued to perform (and, in the process, transform) magico-religious practices that were officially prohibited, either surreptitiously or with the tacit consent of planters and their agents. The ambivalence that Michel-Rolph Trouillot has analyzed as characteristic more generally of the Saint-Dominguan colonial establishment spotlights a crucial dynamic of this legal history. On the one hand, planters downplayed slave resistance and pointed to dances and other performative "customs" as evidence of "the contentment of slaves"; on the other, colonials promulgated "a plethora of laws, advice, measures, both legal and illegal . . . to curb the very resistance denied in theory."[7] That slaves, *marrons*, and free people of color continued to hold the nighttime assemblies banned by the Code Noir and multiple statutes thereafter up to the literal eve of the insurrection in August 1791 is testimony to the "unthinkability," as Trouillot puts it, of such a conspiracy for the white establishment; and, no less, to the resourcefulness of conspirators who made such gatherings a cover, locus, and impetus for organizing against extraordinary odds.

The chapter goes on to examine debates over the role that popular religious organization, leadership, and belief played during the Haitian Revolution of 1791–1804, which culminated in the overthrow of French colonialism and the founding of Haiti, the second independent state in the Americas and the only universally free one. The chapter closes with a brief look at the continuities and departures of early post-revolutionary regimes against popular religious practices and organizations. These were shaped by a new order of ambivalence in which the Haitian elite saw such communities as, on the one hand, an essential base for popular political power and, on the other, a potential locus for popular resistance, as well as a manifestation of popular "backwardness" in need of "civilizing" reform.[8]

The chapter also examines the early literary and legal life of the word that eventually came to subsume these formations in both foreign and Haitian writings, *le vaudoux*. During the late colonial period and over the course of the revolution, that usage had not yet stabilized, and hostile yet fascinated commentators employed the term both to index particular sets of religious practices, types of organization, and/or identities, which may or may not have been popularly so designated, and also to gloss a range of practices that participants would likely not have objectified in such a way. As subsequent chapters examine, the referential uncertainties and ambiguities of this word as a term of legal prohibition would continue to have far-reaching implications for the regimes to which practitioners were subject well beyond the final years of colonial rule.

Law and Labor in Eighteenth-Century Saint-Domingue

When the Code Noir was drafted, the western third of Hispaniola was not yet officially a French colonial possession. The island of Hispaniola had been under Spanish jurisdiction since Columbus's first voyage, but in the centuries that followed Spain's claim to the western regions became increasingly notional. Indigenous Taíno populations were decimated within decades of contact by massacre, forced labor, physical and cultural dislocation, malnutrition, and, particularly in conjunction with these other factors, waves of disease. Although there is evidence that both free and enslaved men of African descent had been part of the Columbian voyages, with the precipitous decline of Amerindian populations in the Greater Antilles Spain began to grant licenses for captives to be brought directly from Africa to work in the failing mines and on sugarcane plantations. In spite of the increasing focus of Spanish imperial attention on the extraction of precious metals from New Spain and Peru, the sugar industry in Hispaniola briefly thrived, only to decline by the end of the sixteenth century. Beyond the cities of Santo Domingo and Havana, the Caribbean colonies became to greater or lesser degrees colonial backwaters, a situation exacerbated by Spain's restrictive trade system and the infrequency of stops made by Spanish fleets at most Caribbean ports. Santo Domingo, on the southeastern coast of Hispaniola, remained a seat of administrative and judicial power in the Spanish empire, given that the first *audiencia* (royal high court) in the Americas was established there. However, even this city's fortunes declined with the emergence of Havana as the primary stopover port for the heavily guarded annual convoys between the mainland colonies and Seville, combined with frequent attacks on the colony by pirates.[9]

Cut off from administrative oversight by Hispaniola's rugged mountain ranges, the population in the western regions of the island raised livestock and traded smoked meat and hides with the Dutch merchants who became ubiquitous in the Caribbean in the early seventeenth century and were instrumental in enabling British and French merchant groups to occupy and establish settlements in the Lesser Antilles. As a measure to end this illegal trade, in 1605 the governing authority in Santo Domingo burned northern and western Hispaniola's remaining coastal towns and forced their inhabitants to relocate around Santo Domingo. The deserted northwestern coastal region of the colony was thereafter populated by newcomers who continued to live off the herds of wild livestock roaming these lands. The term "buccaneer" (French *boucanier*, from the Taíno *boucan*, or grill) may have derived from the smoked meats they produced for trade and survival, but it came to be more strongly associated with their piratical adventures targeting Spanish ships and ports, though not exclusively. Meanwhile, *flibustiers* (freebooters) established an independent international pirate base on the tiny island of Tortuga off the northwestern coast. Given that these populations were made up largely of former indentured servants (in French, *engagés*) and deserters from navy and merchant vessels, many forswore allegiance to any and all imperial powers, unless they were commissioned as privateers, as was frequently the case when the Caribbean became a battlefield during the European wars of the second half of the seventeenth century.[10]

Nonetheless, the predominantly French origin of the buccaneers in the northwestern coastal regions of Hispaniola and on Tortuga became a ground on which France staked its claim to these territories, sending a governor in 1664. The authorities sought to make what they now called Saint-Domingue more stable and profitable by encouraging French colonists to immigrate as *habitants* and establish plantations, growing tobacco and indigo to begin with, and as time went on, sugarcane.[11] At the same time, France heavily relied on buccaneers to defend the fledgling colony, and during the Nine Years' War (1688–1697), the Crown appointed as governor a buccaneer captain and slave trader, Jean-Baptiste du Casse, who led devastating attacks in Jamaica and Cartagena. After the Treaty of Ryswick ended the war in 1697, Spain formally ceded the western third of Hispaniola to France. As Peter Linebaugh and Marcus Rediker have examined, colonial powers increasingly regarded pirates as obstacles to the expansion of the slave trade and the development of profitable agricultural colonies in the Caribbean and greater Atlantic world and sought to rout them.[12] Some buccaneers in Saint-Domingue invested the wealth from their plunder in plantations; but for the rest, increased investment in the production of tropical commodities spelled the end of independent pirate culture in the colony.[13]

Saint-Domingue was divided by mountain ranges into three provinces, that of the north, which encompassed the port city of Le Cap (or Cap-Français), the largest and most important commercial center in the colony; that of the west, with Port-au-Prince becoming the colony's official capital with a royal order in 1749; and the southern peninsula, which was the most isolated and least economically developed region in the colony because of its mountainousness (including the highest peaks in Saint-Domingue) and its remoteness from the Atlantic shipping lanes that served Le Cap and Port-au-Prince.[14] The northern plains around Le Cap featured the largest and most profitable sugarcane operations in the colony, as well as smaller indigo plantations and, in the mountains, coffee estates. The two plains of the western province, that of the Cul-de-Sac east of Port-au-Prince and, further north, that of the Artibonite, were both arid but made to some extent viable for sugarcane cultivation by France's investment in extensive irrigation systems; indigo, cotton, and coffee were important export crops on these plains as well. The southern province, whose commercial center was the town of Les Cayes, produced sugarcane, indigo, and coffee, much of which it traded illegally with the British and Dutch.[15] Of the principal tropical commodities produced in Saint-Domingue in the eighteenth century, coffee was the latest to have a boom, with exports rising in the 1760s. Many of the newly founded estates were established by free people of color.[16]

A governor and an intendant, both appointed directly by the king, were responsible for different aspects of the colony's administration—the governor in charge of military matters, and the intendant, civilian affairs.[17] Both of these figures were empowered to issue ordinances enforceable across the colony. There were two Conseils Supérieurs (high courts), the first of which moved from Petit-Goâve to Léogâne until its permanent transfer to Port-au-Prince in the mid-eighteenth century, and the other established in Le Cap. The Crown appointed the members of these bodies, which included the governor and intendant, high-ranking officials, and, in each case, six judges representing, generally, the regions' largest planters. In addition to serving as courts of appeal, one of the functions of the Conseils Supérieurs was to "register" royal laws, this becoming, as the century wore on, a mechanism of planter protest against what they regarded as the Crown's overreaching intrusions into, most sensitively, the treatment of their enslaved workforce. The high court in Le Cap, in particular, delayed or refused to register laws they considered objectionable.[18] In addition to what Malick Ghachem characterizes as the quasi-legislative function of registering royal laws, the two Conseils also issued their own locally applicable decisions.[19] Below the high courts there were ten *sénéchaussées*, or local courts of first instance, dispersed across the three administrative departments; they handled both civil and criminal cases.[20]

During the early years of plantation agriculture in Saint-Domingue, centered on tobacco and indigo cultivation rather than on sugarcane, indentured servants contracted for three years, working alongside enslaved Africans. Indeed, French colonial authorities at first attempted to restrict the numbers of enslaved Africans who could be brought to the colony: a 1686 royal ordinance required that their population not exceed that of indentured servants.[21] This was never enforced, and the African slave trade to the colony escalated as the number of indentured workers dwindled and large-scale, labor-intensive sugar operations proliferated.[22]

Over the course of the eighteenth century it is estimated that 685,000 women, men, and children were brought as captives to Saint-Domingue from the West African regions of Senegambia, the Windward Coast, the Gold Coast, the Bight of Benin, the Bight of Biafra, and West Central African Kongo and Angola.[23] Tracing the ethnicities of Africans who arrived in Saint-Domingue through the Atlantic trade is extremely difficult. Slavers often identified them by their port of embarkation, which may have been far from their birthplace, especially given the number of prisoners of war who were trafficked. That said, it seems that early on in Saint-Domingue's sugar boom, captives from the Bight of Benin predominated, especially those from the port of Allada, called Arada, and those from Yoruba regions, called Nagô. However, over the course of the eighteenth century this shifted, so that by the eve of the revolt of 1791, enslaved West Central Africans, known as Kongos, had become the largest population in the colony.[24]

By then Saint-Domingue was the leading producer of sugarcane and coffee in the world through the labor of at least 500,000 slaves, two-thirds of whom, according to the colony's most prominent Creole commentator, were African born.[25] It has been estimated that the mortality rate of Africans within the first three to five years of arriving in the colony was 50 percent.[26] That the enslaved population in Saint-Domingue (as in other Caribbean "sugar colonies") never reproduced themselves bears out what numerous observers contended at the time: namely, that the ostensibly "protective" provisions of the Code Noir went unheeded by planters and their surrogates. Many planters subscribed to the infernal logic that the highest levels of production and profit could be attained by working enslaved laborers even to the point of death and then replacing them. Resentful of any official or ecclesiastical encroachment on their private authority in the "domestic sphere" of their plantations, they and their agents observed those provisions of the Code that promoted production or heightened the security of their regime and ignored the others.[27] Although article 42 of the Code Noir prohibited masters from torturing or mutilating slaves, and article 43 authorized the Crown's officers to "criminally pursue" those who killed a slave under their "power or direction," officials were ultimately reluctant to impose penalties that could incur the wrath of wealthy slaveholders in the colony.[28] Thus, planters, managers, and overseers enforced what Colin Dayan terms the colony's "law of terror" with impunity, enacting exemplary punishments, tortures, and executions for "crimes," or suspicions thereof, ranging from "insolence" to sabotage, poisoning, conspiracy, and revolt.[29] As Ghachem has examined, when some colonial officials and commentators began to argue more forcefully in the 1770s and 1780s that the "excesses" of such brutality undermined the security of the colony, planters and their advocates insisted that, to the contrary, any legal check on the powers they held over those they enslaved threatened not just their individual operations, but the entire colonial order.[30] The Crown attempted to buttress the restraining aspects of the Code Noir with "reforms" in 1784, providing for inspections of slave living conditions and threatening planters and agents who exceeded the limits on corporal punishment (now set at fifty lashes) with deportation, and any master or agent who killed a slave, with the death penalty. Because plantation owners, agents, and their advocates vociferously protested the ordinance, the high court of Le Cap refused to register it for months. In the meantime, the Crown issued another ordinance, appeasing those interests to the extent that the court eventually registered them both.[31] In a high-profile case four years later, in 1788, fourteen slaves reported a coffee planter named Nicolas Le Jeune in Plaisance near Le Cap for atrocities that were subsequently corroborated by a judicial commission, including the killing of four suspected poisoners and the torture of two enslaved women, who later died from the burns they had suffered. Le Jeune was charged by one of the lower courts but ultimately acquitted, the governor and the intendant of the colony concluding in their remarks on the verdict, "in a word, that the security of the colony depends upon" it.[32]

Sorcerers, Seducers, Profaners, and Poisoners

Louis Sala-Molins has argued that, if not legally objectified by the Code Noir, the collective spiritual practices of slaves were still subject to a sweeping penalization under it, encompassed, without being named, by article 16, which prohibited the assembly of slaves belonging to different masters, "during the day or the night, under the pretext of wedding or otherwise, whether on their master's property or elsewhere, and still less on roads or in isolated places." Slaves who took part in such gatherings were to be punished, at minimum, by the whip and *fleur-de-lis* (branding iron); in the case of recidivism or "other aggravating circumstances," they could be executed at the discretion of a judge.[33] The severity of this ban was reinforced by its succeeding article, which held accountable planters who permitted or tolerated such assemblies on the part of slaves through a penalty of fines.[34]

If, as Sala-Molins has argued, article 16 sought to cover, in its generality, all "black subversive practices," the omission of any explicit mention of African ritual practices here or elsewhere in the Code Noir can be read as reflecting the relative unconcern of colonial authorities for such acts at the time of its promulgation.[35] As the enslaved population grew dramatically in Saint-Domingue in the decades thereafter, and as greater numbers escaped to the mountains to form *marron* communities, such gatherings and also the individual client services that specialists in healing, divination, and spiritual protection provided to other slaves, free people of color and not a few whites became the targets of ever more elaborate and stringent legislation.[36] In August 1704 the governor of Saint-Domingue issued an ordinance forbidding "the Dances and Assemblies of Blacks during the night on Sundays and on holidays during the Divine Service." In recapitulating the proscriptions of the Code's articles 16 and 17, the ordinance added several new provisions: slaves were prohibited from beating drums or holding *assemblées tumultueuses* (raucous assemblies) between sunset and sunrise, and all "Officers and Commanders in our Government, officers of troupes and militias, planters, and whatever other persons" were enjoined to "take a hand in executing the present Order," with members of the militia commanded to form "a detachment to go in the night to places where they hear the drum beaten or the noisy gatherings of Blacks."[37]

Not named in the Code Noir, the complex threat that the figure of the black *sorcier* represented to the planter establishment registers in the colonial legal record as of 1727. That September the Secrétaire d'État de la Marine et des Colonies addressed a letter to the royal governor and intendant of Saint-Domingue concerning reports that certain planters in the colony who suspected slaves of being "sorcerers," "give themselves the license to put them to death by their own authority, some by fire, and the others in breaking their bones with blows . . . , without obtaining for them Baptism or other Sacrament." Although the phrasing might make it seem that the minister's primary objection was to the neglect of these sacraments, he broadened the scope of his condemnation a few lines later, writing that it was not acceptable "that masters themselves exercise a justice so severe, even if the crime of *sortilège* is as real as it appears imaginary; this is against the law, religion, good order and humanity; you should repress these excesses with all the severity that Justice demands."[38]

In legally restricting planters' punishment of slaves to the whip and *fleur-de-lis*, colonial authorities in Saint-Domingue reserved the "excesses" the minister described to themselves, and publicly administered them as rumors of poisoning and revolt on the parts of the enslaved, *marrons*, and free people of color swept Saint-Domingue in the mid- to late 1750s. These caused particular panic in the northern province, where in 1755 the public prosecutor in Le Cap was instructed to "seek out and pursue all persons having the reputation of being diviners or sorcerers; although that person's smallest crime might be that of pickpocket or petty thief. Still there were blacks that placed great confidence in his [*sic*] abilities. More often, such persons were profaners that committed sacrilege because they mixed holy things in their preparations. Naturally because of that we suspected him of evil doing. Such a person was a corrupter of good order who made the other blacks think that they could act with impunity and cause all manner of disorder."[39]

This directive condenses a good deal about how the mid-eighteenth-century colonial regime in Saint-Domingue constructed the enslaved, *marron*, or free "sorcier" of color, and why the white establishment considered this figure so menacing more than seven decades after *la sorcellerie*, as a form of diabolism, had been decriminalized in France.[40] Note that the targets of the above instruction are not simply sorcerers and diviners, but those who have the "reputation" of such abilities, in which others "placed great confidence." On the one hand, this careful wording adhered to the official French skepticism toward such claims or attributions; on the other, it was precisely the reputation of spiritual and magical empowerment that threatened law and order if such figures then emboldened others to "think that they could act with impunity and cause all manner of disorder." The "profanations" committed by these "sorcerers" when they employed "holy things" in their preparation of magical works were objectionable not only on ecclesiastical grounds, but also because they could intensify the ritual potency of those assemblages. For the thousands of enslaved Africans brought to Saint-Domingue from the kingdom of Kongo, where the Catholic church had been well established since the turn of the seventeenth century, such incorporations of Christian substances and iconography were likely not recent appropriations.[41]

The numerous late colonial ordinances targeting *sorciers* and *devins* (diviners) focused on how such figures exploited the supposed credulity of the enslaved population in ways that could threaten the colonial order. These laws never acknowledged the extent to which white colonists themselves feared the efficacy of black "sorcellerie" along with the political resistance it could inspire, for they brought to Saint-Domingue their own strong occult beliefs and traditions that cross-fertilized with those from West and West Central Africa.[42] Indeed, some analysts have argued that the greater portion of this inheritance came from France; for example, Jean Kerboull, a Catholic priest and ethnographer writing in the 1970s, characterizes malicious magic as a "legacy from colonial days, . . . a poisoned gift from the white masters to their slaves and their children."[43] Thus, when white fear of poisoning by enslaved, maroon, and free people of color reached its height in the late 1750s, particularly in Le Cap, some saw both natural and occult forces at work.[44]

This dread became embodied in the figure of the African-born, possibly Muslim *marron* leader François Makandal, who had once been enslaved on a plantation owned by Lenormand de Mézy in Limbé in the northern province. Makandal lost his hand in a mill accident on the plantation, at some point after which he became a fugitive for more than a decade.[45] Already well-known as an herbalist among black populations in this region, Makandal and his reputed botanical and magical knowledge inspired widespread panic as deaths on plantations, both of livestock and humans, mounted during 1757, blamed, with increasing indiscriminateness, on enslaved, *marron*, and free "poisoners" of color. Many more of these fatalities were suffered by slaves and free people of color than by whites; in January 1758 the intendant and governor attributed (rightly or wrongly) the deaths of more than six thousand blacks in and around Le Cap in a three-year period to poisoning.[46] Partly on this basis, they decided that the poisoners did not "nourish any 'project of conspiracy' against the colony"—a conclusion that may or may not have been correct, but, either way, was indicative of the colonists' more general will to deny the possibility of such a conspiracy, as Trouillot has argued.[47] Slaves and free people of color, who were themselves the most frequent victims of poisoning, were also suspected of being its agents. The terror intensified as authorities detained those under suspicion, tortured them to confess and implicate others, and gave wide latitude to planters pursuing the same ends through the same means on their plantations. By the end of the month, the state had executed nearly thirty people, with the numbers of those imprisoned, according to the intendant, rising "each day by new denunciations made by those who are interrogated."[48]

Arrested by colonial authorities that month, Makandal was sentenced to be burned at the stake in the public square of Le Cap, having been convicted of a litany of charges, including but, significantly, not limited to the manufacture, sale, and distribution of "poisons of all kinds." The first-mentioned charge in the decree issued by the Conseil of Le Cap on 20 January 1758, in fact, was that he was "guilty of making himself formidable among Blacks, and of having corrupted and seduced them by marvels." Next, he was guilty of making those under his sway "indulge in impieties and profanations . . . , [of] mixing holy things in the construction and use of allegedly magical packets," and of making and selling "evil spells to the Blacks." On the day of his execution, Makandal was forced to wear placards on his front and his back inscribed "Seducer, Profaner, and Poisoner," a sequence that followed the logical progression of the indictment. The *marron* leader was guilty first for his influence among other blacks, which enabled his "corruption" of them through various forms of profanation—whether the performative power of "evil spells" or the distribution of protective packets known also as *makandal*, a word of Kikongo derivation that seems to have been in use before the fame of François Makandal gave it new significance.[49] These small charms, which many wore or carried as a shield against harm, were considered threatening enough to warrant their own prohibition by the Conseil of Le Cap two months after the *marron* leader's capture. Again, according to the decree, this was principally on the grounds that such packets profaned sacred things, being coated with a mixture of holy water and incense smuggled out of local chapels.[50] Given the often difficult relations between the planter establishment and the French Catholic religious orders in Saint-Domingue (particularly the Jesuits in the northern province), one might doubt that profanation and sacrilege were the primary concerns behind this ban. However, if the framers of the decree recognized that the use of holy water, incense, and crucifixes augmented the powers attributed to such packets, then the act of "profanation" might well have seemed particularly threatening in this context. The statute also prohibited *tous nègres* (all blacks) from making and distributing medicines to other blacks without the permission of their masters.[51]

In April 1758, the Conseil of Le Cap issued another ordinance that both recapitulated and significantly elaborated upon the Code Noir's blanket prohibition of slave gatherings, legally naming and prohibiting specific forms of ritualism practiced by slaves, *marrons*, and free people of color.

Planters were prohibited from tolerating "the superstitious assemblies and ceremonies that certain Slaves are accustomed to holding at the death of one of them"; notably, free people of color as well as slaves were forbidden from "creating, selling, distributing, or buying Garde Corps and Macandals, on the penalty of being extraordinarily pursued, as profaners and seducers"; slaves from different plantations were again prohibited from "assembling in the Churches after sunset," as well as from gathering together virtually anywhere else during the day or night under the threat of whipping and branding, and in cases of recidivism, death; and planters or, if absentee (as many were), their agents were to be punished by a fine and the payment of restitution to their neighbors if they allowed any slaves, their own or "foreign, to beat the drums during the night, or during the holy service."[52]

This decree cited general negligence of existing laws as necessitating their consolidation and republication. However, the new law was not simply a recapitulation; its elaboration upon existing statutes suggests that the calculated generality of the Code Noir's article 16, which had aimed at comprehensiveness through a single sweeping prohibition, was now seen as insufficient. In issuing the decree, the Conseil of Le Cap announced that it was compelled "to pronounce judgment on cases that prudence could not have foreseen." The *sénéchal* of Le Cap, Sébastien Courtin, one of the interrogators during the witch hunt for enslaved, *marron*, and free poisoners of color in 1758, wrote a summary statement for his colleagues that year concerning the "alleged magical practices" of these populations and their connection to the poisonings under investigation. He warned that although colonists had long "made light of all the superstitions of the *nègres*, their *garde-corps*, their fetishes, and the rest," the interrogations of Makandal and his "accomplices" had proved that blacks in the colony were progressing from these *pratiques superstitieuses* to serious crimes of profanation, sacrilege, and poisoning, and thus that, "far from regarding their alleged superstitions with indifference," colonial authorities must act to repress them.[53] Basing his information on the interrogations of Makandal and those charged with being his clients or agents, Courtin described the ritual making, feeding, and use of *garde-corps* (literally, "bodyguards"), and specifically *macandals* (in his spelling) in close detail, so that the colony's official personnel might know, in order to suppress, the seemingly innocuous ritual practices that, he contended, were serving as a gateway to more serious crimes.

Henceforth, too, supplements to the Code's ban on slave gatherings would also take the form of more detailed legal inventories, often with attention to precise naming. Thus an ordinance of the *juge de police* in

Le Cap on 5 August 1758 sentenced the manager of a plantation in Bois de l'Anse to pay the required fine for having permitted not only "an assembly of Blacks," but also "a *Calenda*." References to these gatherings (also spelled *kalenda*) in ordinances from this point on often seem generic, glossing any illicit "night dances." However, a prominent colonial commentator described the *calenda* as a specific type of "dance" performed by slaves and free people of color.[54] This was Médéric-Louis-Élie Moreau de Saint-Méry, a Martinican lawyer and longtime resident of Le Cap who published an exhaustive compendium of the laws and constitutions of the French Caribbean colonies through 1785 (from which I am drawing here), as well as a wide-ranging profile of the colony, parish by parish, entitled *Description topographique, physique, civile, politique et historique de la partie française de l'isle Saint-Domingue*. The detail with which Moreau describes the *calenda* in the latter work reflects that these gatherings continued to take place in late colonial Saint-Domingue, in spite of the legal regime set against them. That conclusion is borne out as well by the frequency with which *calenda* were targeted in the laws Moreau codified in his other volumes.[55]

In the meantime, northern churches and chapels were themselves coming under increasing surveillance by planters and colonial authorities, partly because they seemed to be sites in which slaves were able to evade the proscription of gatherings from different plantations. As Dayan notes, the atmosphere of suspicion was such that what seemed to be the "most devoted Catholic worship" came to be interpreted as "a cover for deadly magic."[56] In February 1761 the Conseil of Le Cap issued a decree on suspected abuses, banning slaves from gathering in churches or chapels not only after sunset, but also between the hours of noon and 2 p.m., when "Citizens retire to their homes." However, the decree also charged that certain clerics in the city, particularly some of the Jesuit order, were abetting these contraventions through the nature of their work with slaves and free people of color. At this time the Jesuit order was ensconced in the north, while the Dominicans were established in the west and south, with a single *curé des nègres* responsible for all people of African descent, enslaved and free, in a given parish.[57] The "zeal" of one of these figures in evangelizing among such communities in Le Cap came in for particular reproach because those with whom he worked seemed to consider themselves "a body of Faithful distinct and separate from the others." According to the decree, these *fidèles* (faithful) had the custom of gathering in church in the absence of clergy and were catechized on such occasions by one of their own. Even more alarming, such catechists sometimes traveled to the countryside without authorization to evangelize among slaves on plantations. Given that, according to the decree, "the truths and dogma of our Religion could be altered in the mouth of a Missionary of this kind, good order and public security is necessarily harmed by it." Thus "all Free Blacks or Mulattos and Slaves" were henceforth forbidden from "catechizing in houses and plantations, under penalty of the whip."[58]

Nearly three years later, in November 1763, the Conseil Supérieur of Le Cap expelled the Jesuits from Saint-Domingue. There had long been resentment against the order among planters, some of it stemming from the belief that Jesuit evangelization curtailed plantation productivity.[59] During the poisoning panic in and around Le Cap from 1757 to 1759, the Jesuits who worked with enslaved and free people of color came under increasing scrutiny, especially when an enslaved woman named Assam, interrogated and tortured in September 1757, revealed that the Jesuit *curé des nègres*, Father Duquesnoy, had enjoined her during a prison visit not to "reveal the names of her accomplices, advising her that it was far better to endure the torments that could be inflicted upon her rather than . . . risk the torments of eternal damnation."[60] Although the Jesuits (along with the Dominicans) were themselves large slaveholders and relied on profits from their plantations to finance their missions in Saint-Domingue, the Conseil accused them of "teaching false doctrines and favoring the desertion of the slaves. . . . Indeed they are guilty of enormous crimes, especially the great number of profanations and poisonings of their slaves."[61]

During the remaining years of the colonial regime in Saint-Domingue, the Code Noir articles against unlawful gatherings continued to be elaborated upon in new statutes that seemed designed to expand the field of prohibition through greater specificity.[62] Increasingly, as reflected in the 1761 decree, these laws targeted not only the enslaved, but also the growing population of free people of color, who after the Seven Years' War (1756–1763), and in spite of their military service during that conflict, saw the institution of a battery of new legislation that discriminated against them on racial grounds.[63] This was a break with the Code Noir, which likened manumission to free birth in the French colonies and stipulated that freed slaves would not need "our letters of naturalization in order to enjoy the advantages of our natural subjects."[64] The Code Noir, however, also included provisions prohibiting planters (and free people more generally) from manumitting the children they fathered by enslaved women, and colonial administrators attempted to restrict this custom as well, to little avail. Against the dictates of the Code, but according to social expectation, such children were often manumitted and to some degree supported by their fathers.[65] Their sometime inheritances, combined with their own success and that of their descendants in plantation agriculture, particularly coffee and indigo production, made them, along with black *affranchis* (freed persons) and their descendants, an increasingly formidable political and economic force in the colony.

Yet from the 1760s on, free people of color were increasingly subject to legal disabilities and social exclusion.[66] Over the next three decades, this discrimination would propel them to organize with advocates in Paris to fight for political representation and citizenship, a struggle that intensified in the context of the revolutionary openings and upheavals in France during the mid- to late 1880s. There were laws that interdicted them from holding office in the colony, from adopting a white father's surname unless their parents were married, and from dressing, wearing their hair, or carrying themselves (whatever this meant) as whites.[67] The new legislation both conscripted free people of color as the guardians of the colony's security and figured them as its potential domestic enemies. On the one hand, because white colonists resisted serving in the colony's military and police organizations, these units had long relied on free people of color; on the other hand, the degree to which the colony depended upon them to police enslaved populations and pursue *marrons* did not mitigate the suspicion that increasingly targeted them, alongside slaves, in colonial legislation. Thus, a royal ordinance in April 1764 forbade any person of color, enslaved or free, from practicing medicine or surgery and from treating the sick more broadly. This signaled, as Paul Brodwin notes, how "slaves' skills as healers and poisoners were linked in the colonial imagination," and also the extent to which the medical abilities of free people of color were likewise considered suspect.[68] In May 1772 an ordinance directed to "the police of the city of Port-au-Prince" and focusing principally on the enslaved population included an article prohibiting specifically free people of color from holding *les danses de nuit ou Kalendas*.[69]

In May 1786 a judgment by the Conseil Supérieur of Le Cap renewed the interdiction on assemblies in banning anyone of African descent, free or enslaved, from practicing what it termed *magnétisme* in the colony. It reported that the area around Marmelade in the northern province had become a "theater" for such nighttime gatherings, in which great numbers were submitting themselves to "magicians" whose powers produced convulsions in some and reduced others to a stupor, and who then "desorcelled" those affected through profanations involving holy water. Such practices, the decree specified, were known among the participants as *bila* and posed the threat of "contagion": "Who knows and who could say where either the initiators or the 'convulsioners,' of the class of Macandals, could one day take the fanaticism and delirium."[70]

The use of the term "magnetism" to identify the illicit gatherings and rituals held in Marmelade and other locations in the region cannot be taken at face value. As Karol Weaver discusses, the extended visit of a prominent French disciple of mesmerism to Saint-Domingue in 1784 generated great debate, with enthusiasts and detractors holding forth on the wonders or deceptions of Anton Mesmer's therapies.[71] The extent to which the latter bore any resemblance or direct relation to the rituals suppressed in Marmelade two years later is unclear. The official indictments do not explain on what grounds the authorities were assimilating *bila* to "magnetism," nor whether practitioners were using this terminology themselves. In the view of the biomedical establishment, both represented forms of charlatanry, and in identifying *bila* with "magnetism," officials in Le Cap likely aimed to discredit both.

In November 1786 the Conseil Supérieur of Le Cap convicted three men of having held "superstitious and tumultuous nocturnal meetings of slaves, on several plantations in the district of Marmelade and neighboring places," during which profanations and illicit practices took place "under the pretense of magnetism, and under the names of *mayombo* and *bila*."[72] Two "authors of these assemblies" were by that point fugitives, a *mulâtre* (mulatto) named Jérôme (or Poteau) and a black man named Télémaque, both formerly enslaved on a plantation in Islet à Cornes. A third man, named Jean, enslaved on a plantation in Souffrière, had been arrested in late August, and a fourth, named Julien, was also detained. Marmelade was a mountainous section of the northern province that had recently become a center for coffee production, a boom that coincided with the arrival in the colony of large numbers of African captives from West Central Africa.[73] It is unsurprising, then, that the healing, divinatory, and protective rituals and objects that Jérôme, Télémaque, and Jean offered clients, as alleged and described in the indictments against them, reflect strong West Central African roots. The testimonies of witnesses in these cases focus on the creation and uses of *garde-corps* sold by the collaborators, in the form of little sacks called *fonda* containing small calcareous stones known as *maman-bila*, and also of hollow sticks, called *mayombo*, filled with a powder made from these stones, which, according to Moreau de Saint-Méry, rendered those who wielded them invincible.[74] A number of the practices described in the indictments resemble ways that *lwa* of the Petwo spirit *nanchon*, with strong roots in Kongo culture, have long been served, including the use of pepper, other hot spices, and gunpowder in ritual preparations, performance, and therapies.[75] In the case of one treatment, for example, Jérôme was reported to have placed *maman-bila* stones in a glass of *tafia* (unrefined rum) then mixed in gunpowder "to make them furious [*furieux*]," reminding of the way the "hot," powerful, volatile Petwo *lwa* are today "offered rum mixed with ingredients such as coffee, hot pepper, blood, and gunpowder."[76]

The most extensive testimonies cited in the November 1786 judgment focus on the figure of Jean (perhaps because, unlike Jérôme and Télémaque, he was in custody), and reveal that he was armed upon his arrest with a hunting knife and what appears to have been a *mayombo* fitted with a bayonetlike attachment. The May 1786 testimony on which Moreau de Saint-Méry based his account of this case, from a Marmelade colonist named Gressier de la Jalousière, concluded that "Jérôme and his followers preached independence."[77] Yet after reviewing the various testimonies collected against these men, the ruling concluded that if the gatherings and practices were to be judged purely in themselves they would not be found to represent "a very great offense." What would be regarded elsewhere only as a form of charlatanry, a "swindle," and punished accordingly, took on an altogether different significance in a slave society where the population of "nègres" so exceeded that of whites.[78] Indeed, he went on, according to the Code Noir and the above-discussed law of April 1758, instead of a minor infraction, the organization of such assemblies became a capital offense: "These two laws . . . authorize the judges to pronounce the death penalty in cases of recidivism and of aggravating circumstances," such as *marronage* (flight from slavery). On these grounds, Jean was condemned to be hanged; Julien, to attend Jean's execution and then be returned to his master; and the *marrons* Jérôme and Télémaque, to be hanged in effigy.[79]

Although laws against the gatherings and ritual practices of enslaved and free people of color became ever more precise in naming what they prohibited over the course of the eighteenth century, none of those codified by Moreau de Saint-Méry through 1785 mention *le vaudoux*. This is particularly striking given that Moreau discussed what he called this "superstitious institution" at length in his famed contemporaneous *Description* (completed in 1789 and published in 1797–1798) and stressed that planters and authorities considered it a grave threat to colonial order.[80] He described in detail a set of rites "known for a long time, principally in the Western part" of the island, particularly among "Arada blacks" (that is, taken from the port of Allada), to whom, he writes, "Vaudoux" signified "an all-powerful supernatural being" embodied in the "nonvenomous snake, a species of the grass-snake."[81] At times during his description, Moreau refers to these practices as *la danse du Vaudoux*; but in order to highlight the "superstitious" character of such meetings in contrast to other popular dances (i.e., the *chica*), he more often referred to them as *le Vaudoux*.[82] Not only did his account of these rites go on to become the template for subsequent colonial representations of such rituals, heavily emphasizing the role of snakes; but this gloss, le Vaudoux, was itself eventually adopted by outsiders as the generic and encompassing sign of African-based magico-religious belief and practice in Saint-Domingue and subsequently Haiti.

This is not, of course, to suggest that Moreau originated the usage, but rather to underscore the role that his influential account played in extending it beyond the colony.[83] While Moreau identified le Vaudoux as a specific ritual complex, Jean Price-Mars argued that this term was also used generically by colonists, in a way analogous to their pejorative gloss of "les nègres," effacing all ethnic diversity.[84] In general, however, as Pierre Pluchon notes, the "colonial literature of the Old Regime rarely utilizes" the term at all, a silence that starkly contrasts with the proliferation of sensationalist Euro-American references to le vaudoux from the mid-nineteenth century onward.[85]

How is it that le vaudoux seems not to have had a juridical existence when Moreau de Saint-Méry was codifying his Loix et constitutions des colonies françaises de l'Amérique sous le vent in the mid-1780s, yet in 1789, only four years after that left off, he reports in his Description that colonial police had "sworn war upon le Vaudoux"? He even notes that members of this culte mystérieux attempted to evade the police by pretending le Vaudoux was a dance like any other, performing some version of it in public, "to the noise of drums and with hand-clapping . . . to escape the vigilance of the magistrates, and better ensure the success of these mysterious secret meetings."[86] Pluchon argues that the juridical silence around le vaudoux reflected the more general "refusal of magistrate-landowners to admit publicly the existence of African rites."[87] However, the overall trend since the 1750s had been against such reticence, as witnessed in the statutory naming and detailed descriptions of makandal, bila, mayombo, and so forth discussed above. There appears not to have been a high-profile criminal case against practitioners of le vaudoux during these years, so perhaps the blanket law against slave assemblies was deemed sufficiently prohibitive, especially as supplemented by various corollaries further restricting where, when, and how enslaved and free people of color could congregate.[88] Still, the absence of any mention of le vaudoux in the laws Moreau codified is striking given the extent to which the dangers he attributes to the leadership of this "sect" in his Description echo those embodied by the specter of Makandal. He warns in particular of the sway that le Roi et la Reine Vaudoux (the Vaudoux king and queen) held over the other members of the sect: "There are not any of the latter who would not prefer anything to the misfortunes with which he is menaced, if he does not go as-

siduously to the gatherings, if he does not blindly obey what *Vaudoux* demands of him. . . . In a word, nothing is more dangerous from all reports,
than this cult of *Vaudoux*, founded on this extravagant idea, which can be
made into a very terrible weapon, that the ministers of the being that is
decorated with this name, are omniscient and omnipotent."[89]

Ritual and Revolution

The role that subaltern spiritual leadership, organization, and belief
played in empowering the slave insurrection that began on plantations
near Le Cap on 22 August 1791 has proved a highly contested question in
recent scholarship on the Haitian Revolution. The debate has partly centered on the historical basis for the event long narrated as inaugurating
the revolutionary struggle on the part of slaves—the ceremony of Bwa
Kayiman (Bois Caïman).[90] The multiple published versions of this history
have synthesized into a more or less standard textbook account, according to which, on the stormy night of Sunday, 14 August 1791, enslaved
representatives from all of the major plantations in the colony's northern province met in a secluded, wooded spot on the Lenormand de Mézy
plantation in Morne Rouge, ten miles from where Makandal had once la-
bored, to finalize plans for the revolt that was to begin a week later. The
rebel leader Boukman presided over this gathering, joined by a priestess
who consecrated his oath to take up arms against the whites by sacrificing
a black pig, the blood of which everyone imbibed.[91]

The scholarly controversies around the Bwa Kayiman ceremony distill
the quandary at the heart of subaltern historical research more generally.
As Laurent Dubois writes, "The social context that produced the revolt
a priori excluded the voices of slave insurgents from the very documents
that have been used to write its history."[92] One can appreciate the questions that the literary scholar Léon-François Hoffmann has raised about
the evolution of published versions of the story, beginning with the colonist and plantation physician Antoine Dalmas's 1814 report (apparently
written in 1793–1794), without accepting Hoffman's contention that "it is
very probably a question not of an historic event, but rather of a myth, the
origin of which is paradoxically attributable to the ill-will of a French-
man of Saint-Domingue" (i.e., Dalmas).[93] David Geggus reads the same
set of early accounts and concludes that a ceremony did take place just before the insurrection.[94] However, he argues that it was probably held on
the night of 21 August (just before the revolts began), and not in Morne
Rouge, but rather, according to Dalmas's account, likely on the Choiseul plantation, "ten kilometers to the east, at a place still called Caïman."
Drawing further on Dalmas's account, Geggus and other historians have

argued that there were, in fact, two meetings, one held on the Lenormand de Mézy plantation on Sunday, 14 August, during which the rebellion was planned, and the second, a week later, which "served to sacralize a political movement that was then reaching fruition."[95]

One feature of this history that is not in question stands out in light of the legal regimes examined above: that despite multiple interdictions over the course of the eighteenth century, slaves from different plantations across the region were assembling at night to plan the insurrection in the weeks leading up to its intended start on Wednesday, 24 August, the day before a meeting of the Colonial Assembly in Le Cap. Many if not most of the delegates seem to have been "elite" slaves—Boukman was himself a coachman—who, far from serving as lackeys to the enslaving order, exploited their privileged status and relative mobility to fly under the radar of colonial surveillance. Indeed, colonists reported that many of the slaves had permission from their plantations to attend a *repas* (meal) on the evening of 14 August.[96]

In 1999 Rachel Beauvoir-Dominique, Eddy Lubin, and a team of researchers conducted oral historical interviews about Bwa Kayiman in the Morne Rouge area, Choiseul, the historic Nan Kanpèch (Nan Campeche) sanctuary, and other sites.[97] They argue that the scholarly debate over Bwa Kayiman is illuminated and complicated by consideration of how those with a lengthy ancestry in the region remember and narrate this history, and understand its symbolism and legacies in relation to specific physical sites and through particular spiritual practices. In this light, they question the "Cartesian logic" of Dalmas's report that the political organization and religious consecration of the conspiracy took place at separate meetings, the former on 14 August and the latter a week later.[98] Beauvoir-Dominique and Lubin point out that 14 August is the eve of the annual celebration of Ezili Kawoulo, a spirit who is "before all the appanage of secret societies" and is popularly believed to have spiritually embodied the woman who partnered with Boukman at the ceremony "all the night of the 14th, which is to say until the 15th." That night, 14 August, was also the eve of one of the most important religious holidays in Saint-Domingue's Catholic calendar—the feast day of Notre-Dame de l'Assomption, patron saint of the colony, after whom the cathedral in Cap-Français was named in 1718. This feast day was significant to many enslaved and free people of color in the colony, and among enslaved Kongolese Catholics the cult of the Virgin was particularly strong. Today, 15 August is also the occasion for annual rituals honoring Kongo *lwa* at the historic *lakou* Nan Soukri, in the area of Gonaïves.[99] In highlighting the layered religious significance of these dates, Beauvoir-Dominique and Lubin caution against parsing too discretely the "political" from the "spiritual" in attempting to distinguish myth from reality in the case of the Bwa Kayiman ceremony and Haitian revolutionary history more generally.

However contentious the historiographical debate over Bwa Kayiman has been in recent years, there is wide scholarly consensus that, as Geggus puts it, "during the Revolution magico-religious beliefs served to mobilize resistance and foster a revolutionary mentality" and, in Pluchon's words, provided "networks of information and action."[100] The personalized protective assemblages, or *garde-corps*, that had incited so much legal attention in mid-eighteenth century Saint-Domingue were frequently referenced in first-person accounts of the revolution as well. That they served as a powerful political resource might be gathered by the "little sack full of hair, herbs, bits of bone, which they call a fetish" found on the chest of an insurgent captured and shot in the north in 1791, who was also discovered to have been carrying "pamphlets printed in France, filled with commonplaces about the Rights of Man and the Sacred Revolution" in one pocket, and "a large packet of tinder and phosphate of lime" in another.[101] Pierre Joinville-Gauban reported that the possession of protective talismans empowered soldiers to take incredible risks in battle, "in the faith that this object would shelter them from all attack."[102] Charles Malenfant was pursuing rebels in the plain of Cul-de-Sac in February 1792 as part of the colonial army when his division came upon arrangements of dead birds along the way, some surrounded with stones, and finally a collection of broken eggs, "also encompassed by great circles in zig-zag." Continuing on, they found the camp they had been tracking, in which a ceremony seemed to be in progress, led by a "great priestess of *Vaudou*": "What was my astonishment when we saw all the blacks who were jumping, and more than two hundred black women dancing and singing with security." Over twenty were killed in the attack that ensued, including the "priestess." Under interrogation, several other women expressed disbelief that the troops could have passed through "the obstacles that the great mistress of *Vaudou* had multiplied along our way."[103]

The extent to which the chief political leaders of the insurrection were themselves considered (and considered themselves) spiritually empowered has proved to be a more contentious question among scholars. However, even those who downplay this connection acknowledge the extensive documentation, particularly from early in the revolts, linking political and religious leadership. Boukman, one of the most important figures of the first months of the insurrection, may or may not have been a spiritual leader himself; the earliest accounts of Bwa Kayiman do not mention him, and even Céligny Ardouin's oral-historically informed description of the ceremony in which he does figure represents the ritual as being led by a woman.[104] Georges Biassou, who with Jean-François was one of the most important insurgent leaders in the north in the months thereafter, is described by the Haitian historian Thomas Madiou (1814–1884) as having been attended by "sorcerers [and] magicians," who formed "his Council," and as having his tent covered with "symbols of African superstition." Moreover, he and other rebel leaders were said to motivate his troops by assuring that if they fell in battle, they would be reborn in their African homelands.[105] Near Léogâne a landowner of color, possibly of Spanish descent, who was named Romaine Rivière but called himself Romaine la Prophétesse attracted a following of thousands of rebels when he announced that the king had already emancipated the slaves and that he himself was the godson of the Virgin Mary, with whom he was in direct communication.[106] Known as a healer, Romaine installed himself in an abandoned church near Léogâne, where he received personal communications in writing from the Virgin herself.[107] It was upon her orders, according to Romaine, that he and his band waged a campaign of terror against the planter establishment and its military forces in the region between Léogâne and Jacmel until March 1792.[108] Terry Rey underscores "the extremity of this subversive appropriation of the Mary symbol" in light of the degree to which "European conquest of the Caribbean and Latin America . . . [was] legitimized by Catholic Europe through reference to the Blessed Mother." Rey argues that whether or not Romaine was himself of Kongo descent, the fact that he seemed to draw upon Kongolese religious and philosophical traditions, including Marianism and prophecy, was likely key to his charismatic authority and appeal.[109]

As the slave insurrections spread from the northern province across the colony, France came to see an alliance with free *gens de couleur* as its best hope for repressing the revolts and reestablishing the old order. This meant that French legislators were now more receptive to the cause of free people of color, who had been struggling for full citizenship in Saint-Domingue for years, most intensely during the period leading up to and following the passage of the Declaration of the Rights of Man in August 1789. Only months before the insurrection began in the north, the National Assembly decreed that "people of color born of free fathers and mothers" who held sufficient property would be admitted to the "Parish Assemblies and future Colonial Assemblies," a limited enfranchisement that was fiercely protested by white planters and rescinded that September.[110] By April 1792, with French control of the colony hanging in the balance, the Legislative Assembly in Paris guaranteed full citizenship for all free men of color. Paris sent two commissioners, Léger-Félicité Sonthonax and Étienne Polverel, accompanied by troops to see that the decree was enforced and that the insurgency would be put down with the backing of newly enfranchised free people of color.

By the time the commissioners and forces arrived in September, France had become a republic. When Louis XVI was executed in January, Britain and Spain declared war, and the Caribbean became a major battleground. The informal support that Spain had been providing some rebel groups thereafter expanded, with Jean-François and Biassou recruiting thousands to the Spanish side. One of their most valuable officers was named Toussaint, who had been born into slavery but freed before the insurrection, and on its eve was cultivating a small coffee plantation near Le Cap; he would soon take the surname Louverture. Sonthonax and Polverel increasingly saw winning the support of the insurgents and enslaved populations—long figured as the actual or potential "internal enemies" of the colony—as the only way to avert takeover by another imperial power. At the end of August 1793, Sonthonax declared general emancipation in the northern province; and as British troops invaded the colony in September 1793, eventually taking control of parts of the west, the south, and the strategically important Môle Saint-Nicolas near the tip of the northwestern peninsula, Polverel followed suit in the other provinces.[111] The National Convention ratified these decisions in early February 1794, abolishing slavery in all the French territories. That May, Toussaint Louverture switched sides and became an increasingly powerful political and military figure for France in the colony, leading the routing of the Spanish in the north by 1795 and, with André Rigaud, ultimately Toussaint's rival, weakening British control in the western province and southern peninsula. When Sonthonax and Polverel were recalled to France to face trial for treason in 1794, they appointed Rigaud commander of the south, which he governed as a de facto autonomous state. In 1796 Louverture became commander of the western province and, in 1797, the preeminent French officer in the colony.[112]

Beyond waging military campaigns against the Spanish and British, Louverture and Rigaud were charged with enforcing the labor policies implemented by Sonthonax and Polverel in order to restore productivity on plantations (which in thousands of cases had been burned and/or abandoned) and revive the colony's export economy. For the majority of the recently emancipated (unless they were serving in the army), this meant that they were required to continue working on the plantations where they had been enslaved, though they would now be compensated according to task, age, and gender, with women paid two-thirds as much as men.[113] The application of these regulations against the freedom dreams of so many inspired uprisings, *marronage*, and sabotage; yet, in suppressing the revolts and attempting to mediate conflicts on plantations, Louverture was apparently convinced that freedom could only be guaranteed and preserved in Saint-Domingue as long as it remained a colony and regained agricultural prosperity.[114]

When in May 1796, after two years during which Paris paid little attention to Saint-Domingue, the exonerated Sonthonax arrived back in Le Cap as head of another civil commission, restoring and reorganizing the plantation economy was the first mission. Although the commission saw delivering the parts of the colony still under British occupation as critical for the success of this agricultural revitalization, they seemed to consider instilling republican values and virtues in the formerly enslaved no less important. Robert Louis Stein writes that Sonthonax was determined that emancipation entail not only a change in legal status, but a "moral" evolution as well, transforming the former slaves into republican citizens.[115] To that end, the commission took steps to intensify the penal regime against what was now juridically objectified as *le Vaudou*, or more precisely, "the dangerous assemblies" known as such.[116] They issued a law on 21 November 1796 banning *la danse connue sous le nom de Vaudou* on the grounds that it "is contrary to good morals, to republican institutions, to decency, and even to the health of the participants in these scandalous scenes; that frightful oaths, which can compromise public safety, are sworn between the hands of those who preside at these orgies, as frightening as [they are] ridiculous, and which are always followed by prostitution; that these infamies take place under the eyes of the young and even of children, who are admitted, without shame, to a spectacle as disgusting as it is pernicious for their education."[117] Charged with corrupting republican morality and institutions, and with compromising public health as well as security, *le Vaudou* was interdicted, with penalties ranging from a month in prison for participation to three months' imprisonment and a fine for those organizing such assemblies. Yet, beyond the reference to pernicious oaths and the charges of prostitution and "orgies," the law never explained precisely what practices it prohibited. Did the commissioners who signed the law, including Sonthonax, employ this word with precision, distinguishing "the dance known as *Vaudou*" from others, such as those Moreau highlighted in his *Description*? Or did they use it more generically to apply to any gatherings focused around African-based ritual performance? The more specific reading might be suggested by the fact that the very next day, the commissioners issued another law regulating popular assemblies and dances in particular. By a decree of 22 November 1796, the latter had to end within two hours of sunset, and anyone who desired to attend was required to seek permission from the local military commander or justice of the peace of their jurisdiction.[118] In light of the strict labor policies under enforcement in Saint-Domingue, alongside concerns over public morality and colonial security, it seems possible that these laws were also economically motivated—the assumption being that such gatherings would distract and enervate the disciplined republican worker-in-training. More generally, with Spanish troops gone and the British occupation considerably weakened (it would end in 1798), the commissioners seemed focused on identifying and combating France's "internal enemies" in the colony. Three months after the law against *le Vaudou* was issued, Sonthonax wrote to a justice of the peace in Le Cap ordering the arrest of a "witch" named Maman Dio, leader of a "band of freedman," whom he charged with "terrifying the weak-minded and . . . propagating the type of fanaticism abused to lead into disorder all the Africans who allow themselves to be taken by these hallucinations."[119]

By the time Toussaint Louverture promulgated his own ordinance against *le Vaudoux* and "all dances and all nocturnal assemblies" in January 1800, he had successfully consolidated not only military but also political power in Saint-Domingue. He had forcefully persuaded Sonthonax, with whom he was increasingly in conflict, to return to France in 1797 and was prevailing in a devastating civil war against the considerably outnumbered forces of André Rigaud, commander of the southern province.[120] David Geggus's archival research suggests that one reason he issued his ordinance was that these assemblies were being associated "with talk of massacring *anciens libres* (the former free coloreds)," a sensitive point in the midst of a civil war caricatured as a battle of formerly enslaved blacks versus landed *mulâtres*.[121] Yet Louverture's ordinance also seemed to figure *le Vaudoux* as another internal parallel political power to be contained, if not eliminated. He charged that "the leaders of these dances have no other end than that of disturbing the order and spoiling anew the peacefulness that is beginning . . . to reestablish itself in the cities and in the countryside, and of giving to the people who listen [to them] principles absolutely contrary to those which the man who is the friend of his country ought to profess." Thus, to "cut the roots of the incalculable ills to which the propagation of such a depraved doctrine would lead, since it only gives birth to disorder and idleness," he called upon local military authorities to arrest, corporally punish, and imprison anyone who held such dances or nighttime gatherings.[122]

As with the decree of the French commissioners in 1796, it is also appropriate to read this ordinance (and especially the excoriation of "idleness") in relation to Louverture's determined, and increasingly successful, efforts to restore agricultural productivity, which he saw as the key safeguard of liberty in the colony. With the conservative drift in French politics in the late 1790s, and particularly with Napoleon Bonaparte's rise to power by coup d'état in 1799, France's commitment to freedom in the empire was increasingly thrown into question. Indeed, Bonaparte's colonial ministry was dominated by apologists for slavery, including Moreau de Saint-Méry, one of the Creole lawyers and jurists who had long advocated for "particular laws" in the colonies, sometimes invoking in their defense Montesquieu's theories of *mœurs* in *De l'esprit des lois* in spite of that work's antislavery argument. It was not long before Bonaparte's Consulate produced a new constitution stipulating that law would not be universal throughout all of continental France and its territories; rather, each of the colonies would be subject to its own "special laws."[123]

Foreseeing the threat to liberty encoded in the discourse of "special laws," Louverture issued his *Règlement de culture* in October 1800. It reinforced and bolstered Sonthonax and Polverel's labor policies under a regime of military discipline, meaning that just as officers and soldiers were punished for neglecting their responsibilities, so would managers, drivers, and cultivators be if they failed in their duties.[124] The historian Thomas Madiou, writing in the 1840s, suggests that popular religious organization and congregations were targeted in the enforcement of these policies. He notes that Jean-Jacques Dessalines, who ultimately led Haiti to independence, was inspector-general of agriculture in the west in 1800 and "pursued relentlessly all the secret societies in which African superstitions were practiced." Having heard reports that "many of these sorcerers named *Vaudoux* were meeting in the Cul-de-Sac plain, that the head of this band was an old black woman, and that a great number of cultivators abandoned the fields in order to travel to the place where these sorceries were performed," Dessalines raided the assembly with a battalion, killing fifty of those gathered.[125] Yet as Colin Dayan has examined, accounts of Dessalines's brutality against popular religious leaders and societies prior to 1804 coexist in popular telling and recorded history with stories of the revolutionary leader who made himself emperor and was assassinated in 1806, serving the spirits himself. Odette Mennesson-Rigaud noted that "none of the heroes of Independence left behind him as many traces in the popular and Vodou traditions" as Dessalines, and as others have pointed out, he seems to be the only revolutionary leader reborn as a *lwa*.[126]

Ultimately Louverture's reply to Bonaparte's institution of "special laws" for the colonies came in the promulgation of his own constitution for Saint-Domingue in 1801, which affirmed the permanent abolition of slavery, maintained the agricultural labor laws in effect, declared Roman

Catholicism "the only publicly professed religion," and appointed him governor-for-life, with the right to choose his successor.[127] This was not a declaration of independence, given Louverture's persistent belief that the survival of Saint-Domingue depended on the maintenance of the colonial relationship, a conviction that underscores Michel-Rolph Trouillot's contention that the revolution was "at the limits of the thinkable . . . even among its own leaders."[128] Yet Bonaparte took the promulgation of the Constitution of 1801 as an affront to his authority, especially coming on the heels of Louverture's takeover of the formerly Spanish part of the island without authorization from Paris. In late 1801 Bonaparte sent his brother-in-law Charles Victor Emmanuel Leclerc to Saint-Domingue at the head of an expedition totaling some fifty ships, with additional troops arriving in the colony over the next year, for a total of some eighty thousand soldiers and sailors.[129] Louverture resisted the invasion until May 1802, when, not long after the defection of one of his key generals, Henry Christophe, and then another, Dessalines, he surrendered after reaching an agreement whereby he would retire and his troops would be assimilated into the French army. The next month Leclerc had Louverture arrested and sent to France in chains, where he died in April 1803, imprisoned in the Jura Mountains.

However, other rebel officers—such as the African-born leaders Jean-Baptiste Sans Souci, Makaya, and Sylla—and soldiers had refused to capitulate. They waged guerilla attacks on the French forces, which were already in a precipitous decline in part because of the yellow fever that killed Leclerc himself in early November 1802.[130] Reports of the Consulate's restoration of slavery in Guadeloupe and French Guiana (it had been maintained in Martinique, which was controlled by Britain until March 1802) intensified the desertions, as did the escalation of French brutality not only against insurgents, but also increasingly against colonial troops, massacred under suspicion of sedition.[131] The atrocities heightened under Leclerc's successor, Donatien-Marie-Joseph de Vimeur, comte de Rochambeau. By this point Louverture's former officers had rejoined the side of the revolutionary forces, with Dessalines heading an alliance between formerly enslaved and mulâtre generals such as Alexandre Pétion.[132] Calling their force the "indigenous army" and eventually eliminating or incorporating unaligned rebels, the revolutionary forces prevailed with a fortitude, skill, and self-sacrifice that stunned their French adversaries and other observers, as the archives reveal. A desperate Leclerc, in a letter dated September 1802, only weeks before his death, pleaded for Bonaparte to send ten thousand more troops and warned that racism would cost France its most valuable colony: "Unfortunately the condition of the colonies is not known in France. We have there a false idea of the Negro," and then the next day, with emphasis, "*We have in Europe a false idea of the country in which we fight and the men whom we fight against.*"[133] Even a year later, Trouillot writes, "as late as the fall of 1803," the possibility of former slaves overthrowing colonialism and founding "an independent state was still unthinkable in Europe and North America."[134]

The revolutionary forces defeated France that November, and on 1 January 1804 in Gonaïves, Jean-Jacques Dessalines proclaimed the independence of "Haïti," an indigenous name that, as Laurent Dubois notes, signaled that the new nation "was to be the negation not only of French colonialism, but of the whole history of European empire in the Americas."[135] Dessalines became the first chief of state and later that year named himself Emperor Jacques I. Reports of his order of the massacre of unknown numbers of whites who were suspected of complicity with Leclerc's and Rochambeau's campaigns of extermination became, as C. L. R. James and others have argued, the constant touchstone of apologists for slavery and colonialism in denouncing Haiti's "barbarity" and a sometime alibi for the international diplomatic isolation to which Haiti was subject for decades thereafter.[136]

Postrevolutionary Parallel Powers

Writing in the late 1920s, the Haitian ethnologist Jean Price-Mars noted that "if, during the thirteen years of violence, privations, and torture, the blacks drew from their faith in the gods of Africa the heroism that enabled them to confront death and achieve the miracle of 1804—the creation of a black nationality in the Antilles—it is curious to note with what zealousness the leaders, in the dawn of victory, declared war upon the old ancestral beliefs."[137] To my knowledge, Dessalines's government did not promulgate laws against popular religious assemblies: indeed, the Constitution of 1805 declared that the law recognized no "dominant religion" and allowed "freedom of worship." Yet at the end of 1805 Henry Christophe, whom the emperor had appointed commander-in-chief of the Haitian army, instructed the military leadership stationed in the north to suppress the "danses de vodou" that were being held in northwestern Haiti and arrest their organizers, on the grounds that these gatherings, which had "always been forbidden by every government," were "so detrimental to tranquility."[138] Here the colonial ban on such assemblies is figured as an authorizing precedent for Christophe's action, premised on the abiding threat that such dances would disrupt the public order.

The political nature of that menace was more explicitly defined in a proclamation issued on 3 February 1814 by Alexandre Pétion, president of the southern republic after Dessalines's assassination, that prohibited "all dance groups [*corporations*] . . . or associations which foster an *esprit de corps* and a hierarchy of position in their denominations." In other words, the object of prohibition shifted from the assemblies themselves to the groups that organized them. The Haitian historian Beaubrun Ardouin (1796–1865) explained that this decree targeted the "sociétés" that people had been forming, particularly in Port-au-Prince, "under the pretext of indulging in the dances of the country" and were directed by groups of women and men who "mimicked the civil and political hierarchy" in taking on official administrative and military titles such as "*président, sénateur, général de division, commandant de la place, de l'arrondissement*. Others had kings, queens, etc. and all these individuals made themselves obeyed in their meetings or outside of them, in the same manner as the public authorities of the State. Such ideas could have disturbing consequences for the public order."[139]

Pétion's law likely targeted a range of popular organizations that were structured according to such hierarchies, and that, in any given locale, may have had overlapping officers and memberships. Moreau de Saint-Méry's description of the religious organization and complex he objectified as *le Vaudoux* prominently featured a king and queen, and today in temple Vodou congregations, the *laplas* (from the French *commandant de la place*—commander of a military zone) is the ritual assistant and sword bearer, a figure whom Alfred Métraux describes as a kind of master of ceremonies, responsible in part for "keeping good order" during the *sèvis*.[140] As Rachel Beauvoir and Didier Dominique have examined, the hierarchy of individual Chanpwèl *sosyete* (*sekrè*) features an emperor, presidents, queens, various administrators, army officers, and soldiers.[141] Jennie Smith has studied the organization of agricultural labor collectives and mutual aid societies known as *sosyete* in the Grand'Anse (on the southern peninsula) into offices of president, governor of the people, army general, secretary, treasurer, flag queen, and soldiers, among others.[142]

In its apparent concern that popular groups were organizing themselves locally as "shadow governments," Pétion's law seems to bear out Laënnec Hurbon's argument that the early Haitian state continued to penalize popular religious organization in part "to deliver the country from uncontrollable parallel powers."[143] It was not, then, in spite of the fact but to some extent precisely because popular religious organization and leadership played a role in empowering rebels who first overthrew slavery, and ultimately French colonialism, that the new authorities placed them outside of the law.[144] When not figured explicitly as political threats, these groups, and, particularly their leadership, were represented as impediments to the moral reform and industry of the peasantry. Officially, then, and in the writings of elites, they were forces of disorder, indecency, and idleness that successive Haitian governments vowed, and to varying degrees acted, to repress. Unofficially, their sociopolitical importance and power meant that prominent sanctuaries which formed after independence were beneficiaries of surreptitious (albeit storied) political patronage; and, more generally, as analyzed in the next chapter, that local communities under these regimes themselves shaped the customary enforcement of such statutes at the margins of the law.

CHAPTER TWO

Popular Spirituality and National Modernity in Nineteenth-Century Haiti

In a fascinating semantic history, Jean Starobinski reveals that the French word *civilisation* first emerged as a term of jurisprudence, the noun form of the verb *civiliser* that meant "to change a criminal case into a civil one," as well as "to make manners civil and mild."[1] By the end of the eighteenth century, the legal sense of *civilisation* had fallen away, supplanted by a set of new meanings derived from the second sense of *civiliser*. "The word *civilisation* flourished," Starobinski writes, "to such an extent during the [French] Revolution that it was easy to attribute to the revolutionary spirit a neologism that in fact belonged to an earlier period."[2] By then the verb *civiliser* was being used as a kind of figurative equivalent of the verb *polir* (to polish), which had close semantic, as well as phonetic, affinities with the adjective *policé* (orderly).[3]

Haiti's independence was won by former enslaved and free revolutionaries of color just as the word *civilisation* was taking on its modern sense, signifying both a progressive historical process and the end result of that process. In both cases, if we are to follow Starobinski, the word was endowed with "a sacred aura, owing to which it could sometimes reinforce traditional religious values and at other times supplant them."[4] Postrevolutionary language, he writes, "naturally identified the sacred values of the Revolution with those of civilization and therefore claimed for France, the fatherland of revolution, the privilege of leading civilization's advance guard, of serving as its beacon."[5] Although the overthrow of first slavery and then colonialism in Saint-Domingue between 1791 and 1804 was inspired, in part, by these same "sacred" republican values, independent Haiti was immediately and relentlessly figured by apologists for those institutions as a site of civilization's demise—not its beacon, but rather its extinguishing.[6] This was their defensive narrative against the mounting moral and political pressures of abolitionism and, above all, against the fear that a contagion of rebellion would spread across the slave-holding world. Haiti, after all, was a powerful beacon itself, as well as a sometime refuge, for enslaved and otherwise oppressed peoples throughout the Americas and beyond.[7]

It seems fitting to foreground the originally juridical sense of the word *civilisation* and its semantic affinities with the adjective *policé*. This chapter will examine how certain Haitian penal laws were figured by the postcolonial Haitian state as both an index and a force of civilization: that is, as a sign of a condition already achieved among the republic's governing class, and as a process of reform to which its peasantry would be subjected. In his 1885 *De l'égalité des races humaines*, a founding text of antiracist scientific argument and pan-Africanist thought, the Haitian lawyer, anthropologist, and diplomat Anténor Firmin diagnosed the way in which nineteenth-century "defamers of the black race," for whom Haiti was a constant touchstone, defended their claims of black intellectual and moral inferiority on two principal grounds: first, that people of African descent were incapable of administering justice (demonstrating "an habitual contempt for the law"), and second, that they were incapable of true religion (that is, "unable to rise above fetishism and totemism").[8] As his contemporary Louis-Joseph Janvier observed in *La République d'Haïti et ses visiteurs, 1840–1882*, these two cornerstones of racist thought were frequently worked together in the writings of detractors of the "Black Republic" who figured the persistence and prevalence of what they called the "*vaudoux* cult" as proof of Haitians' incapacity for self-government, and that of peoples of African descent more generally.[9] In fact, those arguments had become so conflated in anti-Haitian rhetoric by the end of the nineteenth century that Monsignor François-Marie Kersuzan, the French bishop in northern Haiti, attempted to rally support from Haitian elites for the church's first sustained campaign against the practice of *vaudoux* in 1896 by declaring: "It is a question, let us not forget any longer, of . . . knowing if a black people can civilize themselves, govern themselves, and, finally, form a nation worthy of this name."[10]

This chapter focuses on the penal prohibitions promulgated by the Haitian state against Vodou over the course of the nineteenth century. It begins by examining the anomalous construction and criminalization of "vaudoux" as a class of *sortilèges* in the 1835 Code Pénal under the government of Jean-Pierre Boyer. This statute was revised and tightened in 1864 under the presidency of Fabre Nicolas Geffrard. The extent to which these laws were pressured by foreign denigration of the state of "civilization" in postcolonial Haiti and functioned, along with other legal disabilities, to contain and marginalize the subaltern rural majority are questions foregrounded throughout the chapter. Just as important to this analysis is how local communities shaped the enforcement of these laws to ensure that, in general, they were not applied against family-based religious practices. Yet the statutes nevertheless retained that potential. The second part of the chapter examines two significant episodes in which the law against *vaudoux* was applied strictly and at times violently following the return of the Roman Catholic church to Haiti in 1860. At this point, popular ritual practice fell, in effect, under a second punitive regime, even as the newly arrived foreign clergy also pressed the Haitian state for stricter enforcement of the penal laws already in place.

However, the sustained application of what were frequently consolidated after 1860 as *les lois divines et humaines* (divine and human laws) against *le vaudoux* repeatedly proved impossible for both state and church. On the one hand, the government's enforcement of laws that did not distinguish between popularly sanctioned and popularly repudiated practices was politically unsustainable. On the other hand, the continuities and commonalities between institutional Catholic practices and popular ritual ways of serving the *lwa* meant that any *campagne anti-superstitieuse* led by the church against *le vaudoux* could only culminate in acts of self-annihilation. At the heart of this study lies the question of precisely what the word *vaudoux* (or Vodou) encompassed. Ironically, the term that came to signify the "whole" of Haitian "sorcery" among frequently hostile outsiders over the course of the nineteenth century has long been figured in popular Haitian usage as contrary to those practices. The disparity between how this word was constructed through penal and ecclesiastical laws and how it was popularly understood thus became, I will argue, the key point on which both the state's and the church's campaigns against popular ritual invariably foundered.

PART I

"The Nature of the Offenses to Which They Are Most Inclined"
Upon taking office as president of the Haitian southern republic in 1818, General Jean-Pierre Boyer instituted a commission for the consolidation of Haitian laws into an ensemble of legal codes. The Haitian legal historian Thalès Jean-Jacques describes this project as having been propelled by a sense of urgency stemming from the "incoherence" of the laws then in effect, which, he writes, threw "judicial decisions into confusion rather than clarifying them." The situation was exacerbated by the fact that soon after Emperor Jean-Jacques Dessalines was assassinated in 1806, the country divided into a state in the north and Artibonite (eventually monar-

chical) ruled by Henry Christophe, and a republic in the south and west governed by Alexandre Pétion.[11] Boyer succeeded Pétion upon the latter's death in 1818 and reunited these polities in 1820 after Christophe's suicide. The work of Haitian legal "unification," then already under way, came to be incorporated into the larger project of centralizing the state apparatus, which took place in the political and economic interest of elites aligned with the president.[12] In 1822, several weeks after Santo Domingo's declaration of independence from Spain, Boyer's troops invaded and annexed the eastern part of Hispaniola with support there from the enslaved population, the poor majority of color, and ranchers who wished to trade freely with Haiti. Slavery was abolished, and the entire island of Hispaniola remained under Haitian rule until 1844.

Over the course of his commission's work on legal codification, Boyer expressed concern, as he put it in an 1822 dispatch to Haiti's *grand juge* (chief justice), that "foreign laws" continued to be "the guide of judges" and thus, he charged, "the source of public discord and disasters." Specifically, Boyer sought to overturn Pétion's 1816 decree that France's Napoleonic Code should serve as a legal supplement to fill in the gaps of Haitian civil law. As a "temporary remedy" to combat the ills that afflicted the courts until a Haitian Code Civil could be promulgated, Boyer decreed that Haitian courts should base their decisions strictly on the Haitian Republic's own laws or, where the law was silent, on arbitration between contending parties.[13]

The president's dispatch appears never to have reached the courts to which it was directed, perhaps explaining, in part, why French civil and other laws continued to be applied in many jurisdictions until the Haitian codes framed by his commission were promulgated successively between 1825 and 1835. Boyer's earlier dismay over the influence of the Napoleonic Code on Haitian juridical practice is striking, however, given the extent to which the Haitian Code Civil that went into effect in 1825 resembled its French counterpart. The legal scholar Clovis Kernisan notes that, save for certain "indispensable modifications in detail," this first Haitian code to be adopted was "an almost complete reproduction of the . . . French *Code civil* of the same period."[14] To greater and lesser degrees, this also proved true of the other codes published thereafter—the Code de Commerce and Code Rural in 1826, the Code d'Instruction Criminelle (code of criminal procedure) and Code Pénal in 1826, and the Code de Procédure Civile in 1834. The 1826 Code Pénal and Code d'Instruction Criminelle were revised in 1834 by a commission under the presidency of Joseph Balthazar Inginac, secretary general in Boyer's government, and the new codes were promulgated the following year. Thalès Jean-Jacques notes that the commission, "finding a certain affinity between French and Haitian temperament and character," adopted the French codes "almost in their entirety."[15] In fact, among the controversies that surrounded the promulgation of the codes, the objection, particularly on the part of political and economic nationalists, that the laws codified by Boyer's commission "slavishly" imitated those of another country proved to be one of the most enduring.[16] Although Boyer had himself once deplored the application of foreign laws in Haiti, ordering, if not effecting, their suspension, one critical commentator on the codes promulgated by his government later charged that the laws which, in some cases, these codes supplanted rather than incorporated had been better suited "to meet the particular social realities of the new nation."[17]

Thalès Jean-Jacques documents that, in the cases of the Code Pénal and Code d'Instruction Criminelle, Boyer had instructed his commission to be sure to "consult the spirit and the particular character of the people; experience will show the nature of the offenses to which they are most inclined, those calling for the most prompt repression and the most decisive measures."[18] The Code Pénal defined crimes and indexed their punishments, and the Code d'Instruction Criminelle regulated the arrest, investigation, and prosecution of those accused of breaking a penal law. If in the end, as Jean-Jacques notes, the Haitian Code Pénal promulgated soon after the Code d'Instruction Criminelle in the summer of 1835 "hardly differ[ed]" from its French counterpart (dating from 1810), it did feature one anomalous section.[19] The 1835 Haitian Code Pénal was divided into five laws, which were, in turn, subdivided into chapters, sections, paragraphs, classes, and articles.[20] The penultimate section of the final law, covering "Contraventions de Police" (or minor offenses judged by the Tribunaux de Paix—Tribunals of the Peace—with one located in each commune) was entitled "Des sortilèges":[21]

ART. 405

All makers of *ouangas*, *caprelatas*, *vaudoux*, *donpèdre*, *macandals*, and other *sortilèges* will be punished by one to six months of imprisonment, and a fine of 16 to 25 gourdes; without prejudice to the stronger sentences that they might have incurred for misdemeanors or felonies committed in preparing or carrying out their evil spells.

ART. 406

People who make a trade of fortune-telling, or of divination, of foretelling dreams or of reading cards, will be punished by six days to one month of imprisonment and a fine of 16 to 25 gourdes.

ART. 407

Furthermore, the instruments, utensils, and costumes used or destined to be used in the acts referred to in the two preceding articles will be seized and confiscated.[22]

This section of the law appeared between those defining *le vagabondage* (vagrancy) and *le larcin* (petty theft). The maximum penalties that article 405 assigned to the making of "spells" were the highest allowed under the misdemeanor classification.[23] Léon Nau, an early twentieth-century annotator of the Haitian codes, linked article 406 of the Code Pénal to the French criminal code's prohibition of divination, fortune-telling, and dream explication.[24] Otherwise, "Des sortilèges" was a section of the Haitian criminal code that had no direct analog in the French code on which it was modeled. It also departed from the original 1826 Haitian Code Pénal, which had not constituted a category of crime under the heading of *sortilèges* but only criminalized, as a minor offense, the selling of *macandal*, a particular type of magical work.[25]

The antecedents of this law lay more in the proliferation of ordinances promulgated in late colonial Saint-Domingue interdicting, in ever more specific and strenuous terms, the ritual practices of slaves, *marrons*, and free *gens de couleur* that were considered potentially subversive of the colonial order. Yet when compared with the severity of those laws and of contemporaneous laws against African-based ritual practices in the British Caribbean colonies, one of the most striking features of the 1835 Haitian law was its relative mildness. *Les sortilèges* were classified as a minor offense in Haiti's 1835 Code Pénal, whereas in Barbados in 1818, anyone who "willfully, maliciously, and unlawfully pretend[ed] to any magical or supernatural charm or power in order to promote the purposes of insurrection or rebellion of the slaves . . . or who willfully and maliciously . . . use[d] or carr[ied] on the wicked and unlawful practice of obeah," was punishable by transportation or death.[26] Also noteworthy from a comparative-historical perspective is that corporal punishment was not prescribed for infractions of articles 405–406 of the Haitian Code, whereas in post-emancipation Jamaica by 1860, as Diana Paton has examined, those convicted of practicing obeah could be sentenced to flogging.[27]

However, like the French colonial statutes against various forms of pretended sorcery and profanation, and like the statutes against obeah in the British Caribbean, article 405 of the 1835 Code Pénal reflected an investment in precise nomenclature. *Les sortilèges* were not simply prohibited categorically, but were inventoried as a class of offense encompassing a range of specific practices. *Ouangas, caprelatas, vaudoux, donpèdre,* and *macandals* were codified as distinct sorts of *sortilèges*, their naming here the only moment in the Code Pénal where French (the new state's juridico-administrative language) gave way to popular terminology. Article 405 did not preclude the possibility, and prohibition, of *autres sortilèges* (other forms of spells), but rather, through a strategic economy of specificity and generalization, aspired to criminalize an entire field of ritual practices. This is especially striking in light of the absence of both a categorical ban and a series of specific names in the earlier 1826 Code Pénal, which again prohibited only the "*métier* of Macandals." If, as Thalès Jean-Jacques notes, the revision of the Code Pénal in 1834–1835 was motivated by the discovery of certain *lacunes* (gaps) in the existing legislation, perhaps this was an area targeted by Boyer's commission for expansion.[28]

Yet, the precision that seemed to characterize the law against *les sortilèges*, and particularly its article 405, belied an ambiguity that stemmed from that same listing of names. In the absence of definitions or descriptions of the acts designated by these names, could the law know for certain to what practices it referred? Were such references stable over time? Were they even self-evident to begin with? Such questions suggest the extent to which *les sortilèges* was itself a problematic legal classification.[29] Nowhere did the law define what constituted a *sortilège*, except through the listing of names that appeared under its heading; and these names, in turn, were defined only by their categorization as *sortilèges*, a circularity that introduced still other problems. Namely, *les sortilèges* was not a popular category or classification, and the practices that the Haitian state sought to subsume comprehensively by this penal category were, in popular understanding, neither necessarily objectified as such nor grouped together in such a way.[30]

One might object that, with a significant exception, all the names constructed and prohibited as *sortilèges* in article 405 bore some relation to popular conceptions of *maji* (magic). For example, *ouanga* (or *wanga*) was defined in much the same way by nineteenth-century Haitian writers as it is understood today: as a magical work or charm.[31] Drouin de Bercy, a former Creole estate owner in Saint-Domingue, described *le Caprelata* in 1814 as one who impersonated and mimicked "sorcerers," emphasizing an element of fraudulence in this designation that seems to have persisted over the nineteenth century. In his 1885 *Esquisse ethnographique* on *le vaudoux*, the Haitian lawyer Duverneau Trouillot identified *caprelata* as a popular term of derogation, signifying "charlatan," which *oungan* applied to colleagues whom they considered unworthy of their own title. It is striking that they both define the word as referring to a figure, a person, rather than, as the law implies, a type of "spell."[32] *Macandal* (or *makan-*

dal) likewise seems to have had a double sense in popular usage during the late colonial period; according to Moreau de Saint-Méry, it signified, "at once, a poison and a poisoner"—both a magical work and its worker. As discussed in chapter 1, it seems that the famed *marron* leader Makandal derived his name from the eponymous protective packets that he constructed and distributed, rather than the other way around. In their 1955 study of African survivals in Haitian popular religious vocabulary, Suzanne and Jean Comhaire-Sylvain defined *makandal* as *gad-kò* (i.e., *garde-corps*), derived from the Kikongo word *makwanda*, also designating a type of charm. Today in Haiti the ritual texts in which *pwen* (concentrations of magical energy) are "thrown" to another in song are referred to as *makanda*.[33] Again according to Moreau de Saint-Méry, the *danse à Dom Pèdre* was originated by and named after "un nègre" of Spanish descent in Petit-Goâve, in which participants drank rum mixed with gunpowder. The Comhaire-Sylvains define *dompedre* as an outdated word that at one point meant *sortilège*. "Petwo" (or "Petro") became the designation for one of the principal divisions of *lwa* and the ritual repertoire through which they are served. They are a magically identified pantheon, with strong Kongo roots.[34]

However ambiguous for not explicitly defining the practices it banned by name, the 1835 statute against *les sortilèges* might nevertheless have achieved a certain coherence had it not been for the inclusion of the word *vaudoux* in this inventory. Again, without definition or description, this reference is a node of uncertainty: what acts were implicated by the state's banning of *le vaudoux*? In fact, the assimilation of this word as popularly understood to the register of *les sortilèges* confounded the law, given that *vaudoux* (or Vodou) has been traditionally figured by practitioners as antithetical and even constitutively opposed to practices of malicious *maji*.

In an influential 1977 essay entitled "The Meaning of Africa in Haitian Vodu," Serge Larose draws on his research in the plain of Léogâne to examine how contemporary Vodouizan "take much pain to point out the differences between them and other groups mainly pre-occupied with other sets of powers, all more or less related with the practices of sorcery." He notes that this is a moral distinction generally figured "in terms of fidelity to *l'Afrique Guinée*," standing for "tradition, unswerving loyalty to the ancestors and through them to the old ways and rituals they brought from overseas" and opposed to "innovations" that were "judged morally wrong."[35] Of course, magical work is a morally complex and ambiguous terrain, and, as Larose writes, "everyone is Guinea in his own way and everyone denigrates his neighbor for having added to and thus diluted the inheritance."[36] He thus acknowledges that the categorization of that which qualifies as Ginen versus that which is considered "sorcery" is not absolute, nor is it stable from one generation to the next or from one person to another. What might be regarded, and disapproved of, as "innovation" in one generation can be "inherited" by descendants in subsequent ones and thus constructed as traditional, that is, in keeping with the ethos of Ginen.[37] Although the practices classified as Ginen or *maji* are relative and cannot be defined absolutely, the moral opposition of such categories (however named) in the service of particular kinds of social legitimation and authority seems to be of long standing.[38]

In drawing on recent ethnographic writing in this way, I do not mean to suggest that contemporary analyses of the nature and scope of the particular ritual practices referred to as Vodou among practitioners in one region of rural Haiti today can be unproblematically ascribed to their ancestors of generations ago. Indeed, Karen Richman's work goes far to historicize the Ginen/*maji* dialectic by examining its apparent intensification in the Léogâne region with American agroindustrial land takeovers during the 1915–1934 U.S. occupation and the shift from sharecropping to wage labor on sugarcane estates.[39] However, I want to take seriously Larose's proposition that "Guinea needs and always needed magic as its ground-figure." That is, as I understand his meaning, the Vodou rites now associated with Ginen have been historically valued and shaped in constitutive relation to the figure and practices of *maji*, however these were defined at a given point and by a given party.[40] For this reason, and based on particular cases to be discussed below, I would suggest that from the viewpoint of those dedicated to serving familial spirits, article 405's incongruous classification and prohibition of *le vaudoux* as a form of *sortilège* would have appeared to lack not only justice, but also intelligibility. The law made a category mistake.

The Concert of Civilized Nations

What motivated the Boyer government's promulgation of the law against *les sortilèges* and its framing in this way? One way to approach that question is to consider the place of the Haitian codes more broadly in efforts by the state and Haitian elites to assert Haiti's "civilization" and "progress" in the face of the republic's diplomatic isolation and exclusion following independence.[41] Haiti's self-deliverance from slavery and ultimate overthrow of French colonialism made it a pariah among the powerful states whose economies still depended on those institutions. On the one hand, the existence of Haiti was an "inconceivable embarrassment" and an "impossible contradiction" for colonial and enslaving powers that premised their subjugation of peoples of color on increasingly scientized theories of "racial" inferiority.[42] At the same time, defenders of those regimes also saw the existence of Haiti as a grave threat. Writing in the mid-1840s, the Haitian historian Thomas Madiou noted the frequency with which Haiti was accused of fomenting slave revolt across the Caribbean in the first decades of the nineteenth century. In 1823, for example, Boyer was compelled by external pressure to prohibit any commercial relations between Haiti and nearly all of the European colonies of the Caribbean, as well as North and South Carolina.[43] When Britain and the United States extended official recognition to the newly independent Central and South American republics in the mid-1820s, Haiti remained shut out. What is more, although Pétion in 1816 had provided Simón Bolívar refuge and arms during the latter's anticolonial struggle, these new Latin American republics did not immediately recognize Haiti after their own independence had been won. Haiti was thus excluded from the Panama Congress in 1826.[44]

In the context of this climate of foreign hostility, suspicion, exclusion, and denigration, the government of Boyer and sectors of the elite sought to assemble a dossier of evidence asserting Haiti's rightful place among the ranks of "civilized" nations. Formal recognition of this status would alleviate, first and foremost, the threat of military takeover by France or other colonial powers, as well as open new markets for Haiti's agricultural exports.[45] It would also advance what many elite writers, both those who supported and those who opposed Boyer's regime, saw as the nation's special vocation in a world structured by racism, as materialized in legal systems and foreign policies: to refute the contention that people of African descent could not govern themselves or develop a "civilized" society, and to work for the advancement of black peoples worldwide.[46]

In 1825 the Boyer government justified in these terms its agreement to pay France, as the condition of official recognition, an indemnity of 150 million francs in reparation for the loss of colonial property. In establishing commercial relations, moreover, the former colonial power would pay only half duties on imported and exported goods.[47] Unable to produce the first installment of the indemnity payment, the government was forced to seek a loan from a French bank, beginning a cycle of foreign indebtedness that marked, as Mimi Sheller notes, "the first major debt-repayment crisis of a 'Third World' nation."[48] Opposition to the cost of France's recognition, which Madiou described as "extraordinarily too heavy for the people," was especially strong in the north, where it was protested that "the whites had been indemnified enough by the servitude of blacks which had lasted more than two centuries."[49] Madiou writes that one of Boyer's allies, General Guy Joseph Bonnet, sought to promote a counter-interpretation of the indemnity in his jurisdiction in the Artibonite, acknowledging that although "the conditions of the ordinance" might feel "onerous," French recognition ought to be seen "as the consecration of the work of Dessalines and the end of apprehensions of a new barbarous and semi-savage existence in the plains and the mountains."[50]

In one sense, the codification of Haitian law on French models during these same years can be understood as a benchmark in the Boyer government's assertion of Haiti's official national modernity and "civilization."[51] As Carlos Aguirre and Ricardo Salvatore have discussed, Haiti was by no means alone in following French juridical models during this era. Across post-independence Latin America, as legislators "enacted an array of new laws, codes, and constitutions. . . . many legislative pieces were (selectively) cloned from French, British, and other European sources which were usually considered the *non plus ultra* of juridical science and progress."[52] Madiou notes that the Boyer government made sure to distribute the published codes to foreign consuls and prominent friends of Haiti abroad, one of whom, an influential lawyer in Paris, wrote to J. B. Inginac, the secretary-general under Boyer, about the importance of legal historiography in publicizing the progress of civilization in Haiti: "It is in spreading the knowledge of its laws that a free country establishes its superiority."[53]

The extent to which the 1835 penal law against *les sortilèges* should be understood as a key part of this dossier, though, is a complicated matter. On the one hand, rather than asserting Haiti's juridical modernity, might not the inclusion of a statute against "spells" have risked being read abroad as itself regressive, insofar as a number of European powers had decriminalized "witchcraft" altogether at this point or redefined the crime to target those who "pretended" to practice any form of magic, enchantment, divination, and so on?[54] Such a shift was sometimes figured as a measure of civilized enlightenment itself, however much the coherence of that new legal order was undermined by the harsh ambiguities of mid-eighteenth century colonial statutes in the British and French Caribbean against, for example, obeah men and women and the makers of *macandals*.

Yet in the face of relentless reports by hostile foreign writers that civilization was in decline and atavism ascendant in Haiti, might the law against *les sortilèges* have been intended to serve, in part, as an official repudiation of practices that Haiti's detractors constructed as backward and/or barbaric? And in that case, would the name *le vaudoux* have been a particularly important constituent of the list of *sortilèges* banned by article 405, given its late colonial notoriety? This word had been first introduced to a French colonial readership through the writings of Moreau de Saint-Méry, who wrote two years before the 1791 slave revolts that "nothing is more dangerous from all reports, than this sect of *le Vaudoux*." In an 1814 work, the ex-colonial Drouin de Bercy outlined specific steps toward retaking "Saint-Domingue" and personified *le Vaudou* (here an identity) as "the most dangerous of all the blacks . . . ; he is a thief, liar, and hypocrite; he gives bad advice to the blacks, and distributes subtle poisons to them with which they destroy imperceptibly livestock, poultry, whites and blacks who displease them."[55]

Yet the proposition that *le vaudoux* was listed among the prohibited *sortilèges* in Boyer's Code Pénal, in part, because it was already the foremost sign of a menacing barbarism attributed to Haiti by racist denigrators requires qualification and complication. In works published by French authors on Haiti in the first few decades of the nineteenth century, *le vaudoux* was not yet the ubiquitous racial signifier and generic gloss for Haitian "sorcery" that it would later become, but was more, as Alasdair Pettinger notes, the object of a "somewhat patronising curiosity, flavouring a more or less ordered classification of customs." In Michel Étienne Descourtilz's *Voyages d'un naturaliste en Haïti, 1799–1803* (1809) and Colonel Charles Malenfant's *Des colonies, et particulièrement de celle de Saint-Domingue* (1814), both of which "narrate episodes of the protracted and violent struggle against slavery and colonial rule," the practitioners of *le vaudoux* are not singled out as a particular threat or as "proof" of independent Haiti's barbarism.[56] It is striking to note that for the most part, in fact, neither foreign sympathizers with nor denigrators of Haiti invoked this word much at all from the 1820s through the mid-1840s.[57] When the French abolitionist Victor Schoelcher published an excoriating attack on the autocratic tendencies and racial exclusions of the Boyer government based on his 1841 visit to Haiti, he deplored the state of religion in the island, placing the corruption of the clergy and the prevalence of "makers of *wangas, grisgris, sortilèges*," and diviners at Boyer's feet. Yet he never consolidated those figures under the catch-all heading *vaudoux*, as later writers would.[58] The early and mid-nineteenth-century literature on Haiti in English follows suit. The British merchant James Franklin's *The Present State of Hayti* (1828) figured the republic as the negative example of why emancipation was "absolutely impracticable" in the British colonies:[59] Yet for all his claims about the regressive moral state of the population in Haiti, Franklin never referred to *vaudoux*. In his *The History and Present Condition of St. Domingo* (1837), Jonathan Brown, a physician from New Hampshire who lived in Haiti in 1833–1834, condemned the Haitian peasants' intermixture of "the legitimate ritual of the Catholic faith with the mysterious adoration paid to their national Fetishes" without once mentioning *vaudoux*.[60] The British Quaker and abolitionist John Candler, who traveled across Haiti in 1841, likewise deplored the "heathen superstition" that he found pervasive, but did not objectify this as *vaudoux*.[61] In foreign accounts during these decades, the word *vaudoux* was, for the most part, neither marshaled as proof of the regression of "civilization" by Haiti's detractors nor cited as evidence of the urgent need for Protestant missionaries to evangelize the Haitian population. In fact, it was usually not mentioned at all. Thus, if the 1835 statute against *les sortilèges* was framed, in part, to signal the Haitian state's commitment to eradicating "uncivilized" popular practices, it seems unlikely that *le vaudoux* would have been prioritized in terms of how this law would be read abroad. Neither would the other names listed in article 405 have been familiar to most foreign observers a generation after the overthrow of French colonialism.

This suggests that although it is crucial to consider how the prohibition of *les sortilèges* was pressured by unremitting white Western hostility toward and maligning of Haiti in the mid-nineteenth century, it would be a mistake to read this law as simply an official disavowal directed abroad. To do so would be to disregard the local stakes and effects of the law, both at times when the prohibition against *le vaudoux* was strictly applied and also when, as seems to have been more generally the case, it was not. Laënnec Hurbon makes this point in arguing that beyond "safeguard[ing] a façade of 'civilization,' in order to avoid the denigration of Haiti in the eyes of the foreigner," these laws functioned "to deliver the country from uncontrollable parallel powers, and to reduce to a delinquent or marginal state the most exploited social groups."[62] The revolution had amply demonstrated that popular spiritual belief, practice, leadership, and organization were a potent resource and force for political mobilization. Joseph Balthazar Inginac, who headed Boyer's commission to revise the Code Pénal and Code d'Instruction Criminelle in 1834, became commandant of the arrondissement of Léogâne at about the time that the new Code Pénal criminalizing *le vaudoux* as a form of *sortilège* was promulgated the following year. He wrote in his 1843 memoir of his efforts to "maintain order and discipline, to end thievery, disorders of any type, and especially the dangerous superstitions of *vaudoulx* [*sic*] and others of which the place was a center."[63]

At the same time, the scope of articles 405, and particularly its technical criminalization of family-based ritual practice, reinforced the peripheral political status of the peasantry as, in Hurbon's words, "a population of foreigners, of exiles at the very heart of the nation, which was then identified with the 'elite,' with the class of privileged citizens."[64] Beyond signifying the government's commitment to "civilizing" the popular classes through the law's punitive pedagogy, the criminalization of *le vaudoux* can be seen as one of the legislated "checks" on the full citizenship of the *moun andeyò*, or people of the countryside, in post-independence Haiti. In this respect it correlated with the ensemble of agricultural laws comprising the 1826 Code Rural, which had already been in effect in Haiti for nearly a decade when the 1835 Code Pénal was promulgated.[65] One might even suspect that the ban against *le vaudoux* was likewise partially motivated by state concern with intensifying peasant labor, as frequent rural dances were believed to diminish agricultural productivity. Indeed, article 190 of the 1826 Code Rural stipulated that, except on weekends and holidays, peasants were forbidden to take part in either daytime or nighttime dances or parties, transgressors of this law being subject to arrest and imprisonment for three days, and double that for recidivists.[66]

Rural Law and the Customary Order

Given that early to mid-nineteenth-century patterns of peasant landholding shaped both the codification of this legislation and the development of the Vodou religion, a brief discussion of postrevolutionary land tenure is in order before I turn to the question of the regulative force of unpopular rural laws. Boyer's Code Rural had several precedents, beginning with the system of forced agricultural labor that the French commissioners Léger-Félicité Sonthonax and Étienne Polverel imposed in Saint-Domingue after abolishing slavery in 1793.[67] In 1800 Toussaint Louverture issued his own Règlement de Culture, which placed agricultural production in the colony under a regime of military discipline.[68] After independence, with many colonial plantations (along with uncultivated land) reverting to state property, first Dessalines and then Christophe in the northern kingdom imposed their own versions of militarized agriculture that were likewise met with popular resistance and *marronage*. Christophe feudalized the system and in the process created a new black landed nobility by placing large estates under the control of generals and functionaries in his royal government; his Code Henry severely restricted the mobility of the agricultural workers on those plantations. In the southern republic, Pétion's more liberal land and labor policies were shaped, in part, by the ongoing pressures of civil war with the north and a strong peasant rebellion in the southwest beginning in 1807 and lasting until 1819.[69] As an elite *mulâtre* and *ancien libre* (free person of color in the era before emancipation), Pétion sought to win support for his government from the black majority by breaking up plantations through land concessions, both grants and sales. Paul Moral estimates that between 1807

and 1817 Pétion distributed between 150,000 to 170,000 hectares in concessions among some 10,000 beneficiaries.[70] The largest and most desirable of
the plantations went to loyal army officers and government functionaries;
but enough soldiers and other people of lower social standing benefited
from his agrarian policies that by the time of his death in 1818 his popular
moniker was *papa bon kè* (father with a good heart).[71] Speculators bought
state lands and parceled them out in resale, often to those of lesser economic means, thus, as Drexel Woodson notes, "amplif[ying] the democratic effects of the Pétion regime's concession policy" which was born
of political expediency.[72] Late in his regime, Christophe also made concessions of some smallholdings (in the form of grants and sales) to lower-
ranking army officers, soldiers, government administrators, and members
of the general public.[73] Boyer temporarily maintained Pétion's land tenure
policies upon taking office and, with the reunification of the country, extended them to the Artibonite and north, thus continuing concessions of
state lands during the early years of his government.[74]

With the breakup of the plantation system and the proliferation of
smallholdings (titled and otherwise) across much of the country, sugarcane production declined, and coffee became Haiti's principal export
crop, supplemented by foreign trade in cotton, cacao, logwood, and ma-
hogany.[75] The agricultural economy also became more centered on sub-
sistence farming and supplying domestic markets. The range of legal and
customary relationships to the land across the country included ownership of small or large holdings, leasing of lands, sharecropping (*demwatye*),
squatting on state lands in more remote areas (especially in the mountains), overseeing and driving, and field labor on large plantations in the
parts of the country where they were maintained.[76]

Jean Casimir has analyzed the predominant socioeconomic organization of post-revolutionary rural Haiti (and other parts of the Caribbean)
as "the counter plantation," encompassing the "variety of techniques" by
which peasants sought to maintain autonomy over their labor and lives:
"Specific norms governed the establishment and the organization of families, land ownership and access to property, the administration of the domestic economy and peasant mutual aid, the development of rural communities . . . , religion and language. A system of life flourished without
the peasants concerning themselves unduly about the patronage of the
metropolis and its lieutenants."[77] By the mid-nineteenth century, one
of the predominant institutions organizing social and economic life in
rural Haiti was the *lakou*, a group of conjugally related families occupying their own dwelling places on an inalienable piece of land (often part
of a larger holding) inherited by all the descendants of a *prenmye mèt bita-*

syon (an original founder).[78] The nineteenth-century history of the *lakou* is fragmentary, but its ritual remembrance is a central feature of contemporary Vodou practice in some parts of rural Haiti. Recent ethnographic studies of land tenure in the Léogâne and the Cul-de-Sac plains, centers of colonial sugarcane production, note that *eritaj* (rural descent groups) sometimes trace their lineage to such an original nineteenth-century figure, through whom they have collectively inherited not only the inalienable, sacred homestead on which this ancestor resided (the *demanbre*, or original *lakou*), but also reciprocal relationships to the family's spirits, and the rituals through which they are served on this piece of the property.[79] Scholars such as Rémy Bastien and Paul Moral have emphasized the relationship of the *lakou* to the host of agrarian societies that emerged in postrevolutionary rural Haiti, collectivizing agricultural labor and organizing other forms of mutual aid and religious service, including burial rituals.[80] These analysts also document the decline of the *lakou* after three generations because of soil exhaustion and the demographic pressures resulting from the division of the land into smaller plots with each passing generation.[81] Serge Larose contrasts the apparent self-sufficiency of *lakou* in the nineteenth century with the late twentieth, when many of those in Léogâne had "been more or less stripped off from their productive functions" and were primarily residential units, with members sharecropping other properties, working for wages, or, especially in the case of women, working as small traders.[82] It is important to emphasize that there was always wide diversity in peasant socioeconomic circumstances, stemming in part from hierarchies that were a legacy of slavery and that conditioned differences in access to land thereafter.[83] However, the proliferation of smallholdings and the emergence of the *lakou* and cooperative agricultural societies in rural Haiti in the mid-nineteenth century meant that many families across the country worked their own land (whether legally or customarily defined as such), rather than that of a large landowner.

As a consequence, estate owners, many of them absentee, some of them government or military officials, found it increasingly difficult to maintain a workforce to keep their plantations functional and profitable.[84] Saddled with massive foreign debt as the price of diplomatic recognition in 1825, Boyer's government promulgated its Code Rural the next year in order to intensify agricultural production for export.[85] To that end, the Code Rural's third article prescribed "cultivation of land" for any citizen not otherwise employed in civil service or the military, licensed for another profession, or already working as a laborer, domestic, or woodcutter. The Code's fourth article stipulated that *les citoyens de profession agricole* (citizens engaged in an agricultural profession) could not move to a city or town without authorization from the *juges de paix* of both the commune that they desired to leave and the commune where they sought to settle. Anyone who relocated without such documentation risked arrest by the officers of the rural police for vagrancy.[86] The Code Rural also militarized the administrative organization of the countryside by stipulating that rural police appointed from the peasantry and endowed with a military commission would supervise each commune's *sections rurales* (rural sections).[87] Assisted by three *gad chanpèt* (*gardes champêtres*), also appointed from the local population, the rural police officer was responsible for enforcing the laws of agriculture set down in the Code Rural, apprehending "vagrants," and generally pursuing anyone suspected of minor offenses (along with more serious crimes) in the section—including, after 1835, the making or performance of *sortilèges*. More than a century later, the sociologist Jean Comhaire aptly characterized this rural officer, by then known as the *chèf seksyon* (*chef de section*, or section chief), as representing, "for all practical purposes, . . . the state within the section."[88] Indeed, the broad civil and military powers conferred on this figure, along with the abuses they sometimes committed, prompted repeated calls throughout the nineteenth and twentieth centuries for the reform of the institution.

However, the most intolerable features of the Code Rural and Code Pénal were also tempered in the face of popular pressure under the authority of local rural police and the *juges de paix* appointed to the *tribunal de paix* (the local court in each commune).[89] This meant that like the most unpopular articles of the Code Rural, the penal prohibition of *les sortilèges* seems not to have been consistently applied against socially sanctioned familial and temple-based ritual practices.[90] Yet, the technical criminalization of *le vaudoux* meant that such practices were subject, at the very least, to "informal" regulation by rural authorities, who derived from them a source of revenue.[91] By the early twentieth century a practice had developed, at least in certain regions of the country, in which people were customarily obliged to request and/or purchase permits from rural police to mount particular ceremonies, without which they would be subject to disciplinary measures.[92] At the same time, it is important to note that many of those officers themselves would have been servants of the *lwa*, along with the laws of the state. Indeed, given that appointees were usually local figures of some influence, wealth, and/or prestige, it is likely that some of them were *oungan*.

How the law against *les sortilèges* contributed to the political marginalization, social stigmatization, and everyday economic exploitation of the rural majority in Haiti even when it was not being strictly enforced against *le vaudoux* is a question to which this study repeatedly returns. Of equal importance, however, is the question of how local people shaped the enforcement of these regimes and attempted to harness the laws to their own ends as forms of defense and empowerment. This dialectical relationship, and not simply the way in which elite Haitians used these laws to serve their own class interests and political purposes, is crucial for understanding the social significance and legacies of these laws. Fragmentary evidence from the late nineteenth and early to mid-twentieth centuries suggests that there was actually some popular investment in the penal laws against *les sortilèges*, in that articles 405–407 were seen as a juridical bulwark against malicious manipulations of supernatural forces and charlatanism.[93] Rather than (or perhaps in some cases in addition to) seeking justice through the juridical processes of a *sosyete sekrè* or otherwise retaliating with exclusively supernatural means, those who suspected themselves to be victims of "sorcery" sometimes pressed to have their charges publicly adjudicated. By their very formulation, these laws were always already implicated in the social logic of "sorcery," the existence and supernatural efficacy of which their prohibition seemed, paradoxically, to confirm. Thus, the history and legacy of these laws cannot be understood outside of the complex ways in which they have been interpreted through and incorporated into popular struggles against the threat of supernatural harm. Why would a statute against "spells" be interpreted in any other way?

In short, popular pressures (which the government sometimes affirmed as "public clamor") shaped the enforcement of these laws away from widely sanctioned ritual practices and toward the alleged agents of malicious *maji*. This underscores that the penal regime against *les sortilèges* ought to be regarded not simply as a top-down apparatus of state control, but rather as a site of negotiation in which subaltern groups exerted pressure on the evolution of a customary legal order. Such communities, however, were of course not homogeneous, but were structured by their own internal hierarchies and power relations along lines of class, color, gender, age, literacy, "respectability," and so on. This meant that popular calls for the enforcement of the law had the potential to be repressive in their own right, particularly against marginal and structurally weak members of a given community. As Laënnec Hurbon has found, suspicion of "sorcery" tended to fall on "two poles of the social scale: on the one hand, politicians and the rich, and on the other, the poor and the weak." And it was the latter—"those who have every reason to be envious"—who "in ordinary times (as opposed to times of crisis)" were most often accused of malicious sorcery.[94]

Saints *and* guyons

The complexities of the relationship between legal authority and subaltern religious agency under the regime of the law against *les sortilèges* were
particularly striking during the popular political and religious mobilizations in Haiti in the mid-1840s. Upon the bloodless revolution (inaugurated at Praslin in the south) that ousted Boyer in March 1843, the provisional government that took over, dominated by liberal *milat* (*mulâtres*),
moved quickly to abrogate both the Code Rural and the Code Pénal, replacing the latter with its 1826 forerunner, which, as might be recalled,
had not criminalized the practice of *le vaudoux*.[95] In January 1844 the revolutionary general Charles Rivière-Hérard was named president, but he
soon revealed himself to be antagonistic to the liberal constitution that
the Assemblée Constituante had passed, and particularly to the con-
straints that it placed on presidential power.[96] His government itself then
became the target of waves of mobilization by groups from the south
pressing for the expansion of black civil, political, and economic rights.[97]
First the landholding Salomon family led smallholders and coffee grow-
ers to protest persistent color prejudice, initially through civil means
and then in rebellion, for which people were armed mostly with *piquets*
(wooden pikes), from which the Piquet Rebellion took its name. The revolt was put down, and the Salomons went into exile in Jamaica; but as
the provisional government attempted unsuccessfully to suppress the independence movement in the Spanish-speaking eastern part of the island,
a charismatic peasant leader named Louis Jean-Jacques Acaau emerged
from Les Cayes in the south to lead an armed peasant movement known
as the Armée Souffrante (Army of Sufferers). They pressed the government to honor the constitution and the calls of the black rural majority
for land and economic reform, universal education, and the end of martial law, and they demanded, as Leslie Manigat notes, "what they proudly
called their rights."[98]

Although the extent to which the Armée Souffrante mobilized for
greater religious freedom is unclear, the organization and self-fashioning
of this movement can be read as assertions of popular religious agency
and empowerment.[99] Gustave d'Alaux, the *nom de plume* of Maxime Raybaud, the French consul-general to Haiti, gives one of the most detailed
accounts of the movement (if also one of the most disparaging, thus the
need for caution in mining it as a historical source). D'Alaux notes that
Acaau announced at the *calvaire* (open-air crucifix) in his parish that "'divine Providence' ordered poor people, first to pursue *mulâtres* and secondly to share the properties of the *mulâtres*."[100] The religious dimension
of what d'Alaux characterized as Acaau's "black communism" was en-

dorsed that day by a *guildive* (rum distillery) worker who became a popular spiritual and political leader known as Frère Joseph. As Mimi Sheller has examined, he clarified that the movement Acaau announced was not waged simply against *milat*, since social hierarchies in Haiti were not organized purely by color: "'Acaau is right,'" d'Alaux reports him as explaining that day at the *calvaire*, "'because the Virgin said: The rich black who knows how to read and write is *mulâtre*; the poor *mulâtre* who does not know how to read nor write is black.'"[101] Thereafter, according to d'Alaux, he dressed entirely in white, wrapped his head in a white scarf, and "walked, a candle in hand, in the midst of the bands of Acaau, whom he edified by his novenas to the Virgin, and whom he mastered by his well-known favor with the *Vaudoux* god."[102]

The Piquet Rebellion in the south, in combination with military backing of the black general Philippe Guerrier for president in the north and the loss of what became the independent Dominican Republic, culminated in 1844 in the fall of the provisional government and Guerrier's coming to power. He was the first of three elderly black generals installed as president over the next several years, with elite factions attempting to maintain oligarchic control behind the scenes through what became known as the *politique de doublure* (the politics of the understudy). He died in office a year later. In 1845 Boyer's Code Pénal, with the law criminalizing the practitioners of *le vaudoux* intact, was reimposed under the government of Jean-Louis Pierrot, like Guerrier an octogenarian general from the north.[103]

Yet, again, this codified penal prohibition gave way to a much more complicated situation on the ground. Pierrot's short term in office (April 1845 to March 1846, when he was ousted) was characterized by d'Alaux as a period when practitioners of *le vaudoux* were "emboldened," and the Roman Catholic church historian Adolphe Cabon cites a letter from 1845 regretting that "all the old superstitions that the strong government of M. Boyer was able to contain, that it had nearly suppressed, have appeared again with more ardor than ever."[104] It was during Pierrot's tenure that the antagonism that historian Thomas Madiou describes between two sects, the *saints* and the *guyons*, "the one as dangerous as the other," erupted in violence in rural areas of Haiti's Western department. The *saints*, according to Madiou, practiced *le vaudoux* in the name of Roman Catholicism, and fanatically pursued the *guyons*, also known as *lougawou*— shape-shifting, vampirelike beings especially feared for attacking small children.[105] According to Cabon's *Notes sur l'histoire religieuse d'Haïti*, one of the leaders of the *saints* was the same Frère Joseph who had played a key role in mobilizing popular support for Acaau's Armée Souffrante a year earlier.[106] Madiou notes that the *saints* were armed with sticks from the *médicinier* tree, and the *guyons* were reputed to carry pouches "containing fetishes, human bones, and even snakes." Although it seems clear that the *saints* constituted themselves as a sect in opposition to those they characterized as *guyons*, the historical accounts of this episode are ambiguous as to whether *guyon* was itself a form of self-identification on the part of a similarly constituted group or an epithet thrown at suspected individuals, with violent consequences. The latter seems more likely to have been the case, given the contemporary meaning of *giyon* (jinx, bad luck).[107] Madiou describes the *saints* as fanning out across the countryside in organized bands, pillaging the homes of those identified as *guyons* and beating those unable to escape. When an elderly woman was killed by one of these vigilante groups, who accused her of "eating" a child and maintaining custody over his or her soul, the authorities stepped in and arrested not just the *saints* suspected of murder, but also a number of those identified as *guyons*, on charges of anthropophagy.[108] According to Madiou, the arrival of those arrested in Port-au-Prince produced a "great commotion" among the local population; however, he notes that both *saints* and *guyons* were soon freed because the government was concerned that holding the trial would heighten charges "abroad that there were anthropophagists in Haiti." Significantly, several nights after their release, members of the *saints* mounted a public ceremony directly opposite the prison in which they had been held. There was ritual drumming and dance, and a goat was sacrificed in offering. Madiou notes that the local authorities made no effort to disperse, much less arrest, the congregants, and police officers even mixed with the crowd, joining in the dancing and singing.[109]

The fragmentary reports of this episode raise more questions than they answer. However, Madiou's and Cabon's accounts illuminate, at the very least, the complicated relationship of popular religious practice to law and legal authority. Madiou is careful to distinguish the "fanatical" sect of the *saints* from other *sectateurs du vaudoux* (Vodouizan) who "dreaded" the *guyons* and considered them "damned" but did not join the violence against them.[110] The construction and repudiation of the *guyons* as malevolent sorcerers again suggests the way in which moral opposition to malicious *maji* was constitutive of popular religious identity and authority. As I have argued, this powerful opposition shaped the way that articles 405–407 of the 1835 Code Pénal were enforced and seems in this case to have propelled those who self-identified as *saints* to take the law into their own hands, pursuing a violent form of divinely sanctioned moral justice in the name of Roman Catholicism.

Both Madiou and Cabon stress the audacity of the *saints* in their campaign and in their public staging of the ceremony across from the prison in which they had so recently been incarcerated. Cabon interprets this boldness as reflecting their sense of empowerment, one that we might understand, especially given Frère Joseph's apparent leadership role, as both spiritual and political. One could analyze the *saints'* choice to stage this ritual outside the prison as a defiant assertion of religiopolitical power against that of penal law and state authority, a taunting of the official justice system and performative challenge to its hegemony. However, the disclosure that they were joined in this performance by members of the local police force complicates such a reading. If the ceremony that they performed was legally prohibited under article 405 of the Code Pénal, their apparent sense of impunity or immunity in mounting it speaks to the complicated relationship of local authorities to subaltern religious communities of which they themselves may have been a part. Jean Comhaire, writing in the mid-1950s, notes that President Pierrot himself was "said to have protected Voodoo so long as it was pure Rada," and Étienne Charlier, writing at about the same time, mentions that the president was married to a *manbo*, Cécile Fatiman, who "had participated in the ceremony of Bois-Caïman," according to their grandson.[111]

Above all, the case of the *saints'* pursuit of the *guyons* points again to the fallacy of analyzing the penalization of *les sortilèges* as simply a top-down repressive regime without considering the local relations of power, hierarchies, and antagonisms that divided subaltern communities, shaped the enforcement of these laws, and, in the case of the *saints*, seems to have propelled a violent attack on the *guyons*.[112] The paucity of archival sources that speak to such localized power relations, structures, and struggles in nineteenth-century Haiti is the most challenging dimension of this study and makes the accounts of the *saints* and the *guyons* that much more significant. It is a truism of anthropological theories of magic that an inverse relation has often obtained between attributed supernatural power and socioeconomic and political power; that is, those reputed to be the most powerful "sorcerers" are often the most socially marginal and structurally weak.[113] One therefore wonders how the *guyons* targeted by the *saints* were marked along lines of class, gender, age, and propriety; what was the social standing of the elderly woman whom Madiou identified as one of the victims? As the *saints'* vigilantism against the *guyons* demonstrated, popular justice could be no less and sometimes even more oppressive than the state's own regime. Likewise, the social pressures that directed the enforcement of articles 405–407 against those suspected of malicious *maji* held their own repressive potential.

Laënnec Hurbon has analyzed how rumors of sorcery and in this case, anthropophagy, often attributed to secret societies, "without a doubt came from the African heritage, but are no less rooted in the language of the diabolization of Vodou (and thus of the barbarization of the black) which appeared from the first moments of the slave trade and which continues to have effects on the practices and discourses of the Vodouisants themselves."[114] That is, many of the historically most feared forms of supernatural aggression in Haiti—including anthropophagy and the transformation of humans into animals—strongly resemble the supernatural crimes attributed to "sorcerers" in Europe in the late Middle Ages, and later to African and African-descended ritual specialists in the context of the slave trade and colonization. Hurbon argues that this imaginary was reinterpreted in conversation with West and West Central African "witchcraft" beliefs and became the extreme constitutive "outside" of socially sanctioned religious practice.[115] There was considerable circularity (and irony), then, in the fact that Haiti's nineteenth-century European detractors seized upon such rumors as proof of the regression of civilization in the "Black Republic." These writers frequently literalized as actual cases of "cannibalism" accounts that were, to say the least, much more ambiguous in their particulars: for example, rumors that a victim was transformed by a secret society into a goat, pig, or cow, then eaten by unsuspecting consumers; or that a woman in a community was a *lougawou* who made nocturnal excursions to drain the blood of small children. As Jennie Smith notes, based on recent ethnography in the southwestern Grand'Anse region, although the expression *manje moun* may literally mean "'eat people,' this term refers to killing through sorcery."[116]

"Passing Storms"

Hénock Trouillot aptly characterized the intermittent episodes of persecution to which Vodouizan were subject on the part of the nineteenth-century state as "passing storms," thus making the point that as long as articles 405–407 were on the books of the Code Pénal, they always retained the potential of being strictly enforced, albeit temporarily, for various political ends and purposes.[117] Jean-Baptiste Riché, Pierrot's successor and the third in the succession of elderly *nwa* (*noir*) generals installed as presidents by elite *milat* politicians in the mid-1840s, is reputed to have been particularly insistent that the law prohibiting *les sortilèges* be applied against ritual *sèvis* for the *lwa*. That reputation, which seems all the more notable given that Riché died after less than a year in office (March 1846–February 1847), is based both on the ways in which his government reinforced the existing legal prescriptions against *les sortilèges* and on apocryphal reports of his own personal zeal in tracking down offenders. In a presidential circular concerning agriculture dated September 1846, Riché asked arrondissement commanders for assurance that "all these forbidden dances such as *le vaudou*, etc. are completely abolished" and that "all these makers of *ouangas* and of *macandats* [*sic*] are sought out and delivered to justice to be punished in conformity with the law."[118] The government's secretary of state for the interior, Céligny Ardouin—who, with his brother, the politician and historian Beaubrun Ardouin, and other members of the elite *milat* oligarchy, effectively ruled Haiti by *la politique de doublure* during these years—issued a circular from his office the next day to the same recipients, reinforcing that they must put a stop to "*le vaudou* and superstitious sects. . . . Honest dances can take place, but only on Sundays and Friday evenings, and Sundays only until eight o'clock at night, outside of extraordinary cases and according to an explicit permit."[119] Later on that year, a new law was passed specifying that those convicted of *les sortilèges* would face hard labor in maritime prisons.[120]

Over the course of his year in office, Riché acquired a reputation for regarding these popular practices with such antipathy that, according to apocryphal accounts, he took the enforcement of the law into his own hands. The Haitian writer and surveyor Justin Bouzon reported in an 1894 work that Riché was "excessively severe" in his pursuit of the "coarse superstitions of *Vaudoun* or *Vaudoux*" and recounted a story of the president's being awakened one night at the national palace in Port-au-Prince by the sound of far-off drumming, summoning his aide-de-camp, and heading off to the hills above the city to arrest those violating the prohibition of rites defined by the law as *sortilèges*.[121]

Riché died almost a year after taking office, but it is unlikely that his offensive against *le vaudoux* would have been sustainable had he lived to continue his term. Any prolonged assault on family rituals, or on the range of private cliental practices that *oungan* and *manbo* provided Vodouizan—such as divination, healing therapies, the creation of protective charms—would have jeopardized his government's longevity. There is today a considerable body of folklore in Haiti about presidents who fell because of their interference with popularly sanctioned traditional practices, as well as about those who cultivated particularly close ties with popular spiritual and/or magical societies.[122] Laënnec Hurbon argues that successive Haitian postrevolutionary states were torn between "maintaining Vodou as an inadmissible support to their power, and appealing to the Catholic Church as [Haiti's] sole official religion."[123]

Les lois divines et humaines

Roman Catholicism did not always enjoy the official status Hurbon describes in independent Haiti. The 1805 Constitution promulgated by the imperial government of Jean-Jacques Dessalines forbade the establishment of any such "dominant religion" (article 50), specifying that the state would "not provide for the expenses of any form of religion or ministry" (article 52).[124] Furthermore, Dessalines's constitution made marriage a "purely civil deed that is authorized by the government" and legalized divorce—provisions that the Vatican viewed as provocative and pernicious.[125] During Haiti's "schism" with Rome, *la religion catholique, apostolique et romaine* was identified as the state's own by nearly every government after Dessalines's assassination in 1806. Of course, in the absence of a concordat, the state could control the religion it declared official, an arrangement that the Vatican considered a usurpation of ecclesiastical power.[126] Pétion and Christophe sought to establish new church hierarchies, appointing the few priests who remained in the country to elevated positions as bishops and, in the case of the Capuchin prefect Father Corneille Brelle in the north, to the title of "Archbishop of Haiti and Grand Almoner to the King." That Brelle served in this capacity during Christophe's coronation ceremony points to the way in which early heads of state sought to legitimate their power through the "schismatic" church, even as they sought recognition from Rome.[127]

By the mid-1820s, however, the Vatican had its own reasons for pursuing negotiations with Haiti. In 1822 Boyer's troops had taken over Santo Domingo, the church's oldest see in the Americas. After Don Pedro Valera, the archbishop of Santo Domingo, refused to move his residence to Port-au-Prince as Boyer requested, the Haitian government passed a law in 1824 nationalizing church land and property in the eastern part of the island.[128] There was also concern at the Vatican about those serving as priests in Haiti, some of whom, Cabon charged, were deliberately sent by the "liberal camp" in France, whose "zeal for Haiti" was particularly strong when "mixed with their hate of the church."[129]

Vatican concern over the negative examples for the population that were set by such priests was particularly high in the context of the Boyer government's intermittent openness to Protestant missionary work in Haiti—especially in the context of its efforts to recruit African American emigrants—and the strong influence of freemasonry among the ruling classes.[130] In fact, although Boyer actively sought negotiations with the Vatican and received several papal legations between 1834 and the fall of his government in 1843, some of his supporters, and many of the opposition, were against pursuing a concordat with Rome on the grounds that it would undermine Haitian national sentiment and patriotism and potentially lead to the republic's domination by a foreign power.[131] The contestation that surrounded the Haitian concordat at every stage of its negotiation must be emphasized, particularly given the reverberations of such debates for years thereafter. However, in the decades of diplomatic isolation that followed Haitian independence, the establishment of a concordat assumed a vital political and economic significance for its elite advocates. Such an agreement promised further international recognition, the expansion of education, and "definitive proof" of the republic's rightful place among the ranks, again, of "civilized nations."[132]

By the mid-nineteenth century this status had been thrown repeatedly into question in the writings of Haiti's foreign detractors, among them scientific racists such as Joseph Arthur de Gobineau, who in his *De l'inégalité des races humaines* (1853–1855) deplored the "retrogression" of civilization in Haiti since the overthrow of French rule and slavery. Gobineau was writing during the government of Faustin Soulouque (1847–1859), who became president through the machinations of the *politique de doublure* upon Riché's death in 1847 but soon threw off his elite handlers and installed himself as emperor of Haiti (Faustin I) in 1849. Thereafter he and his government became the object of foreign denigration and ridicule for, according to such accounts, combining delusions of imperial grandeur with close ties to "*vaudoux* societies."[133] Particularly influential in this genre were the aforementioned writings of Maxime Raybaud, the French consul-general during Soulouque's government. Under the pseudonym Gustave d'Alaux, he serialized an exposé of the regime in the *Revue des deux-mondes* in 1850–1851, then expanded these articles into his *L'Empereur Soulouque et son empire* (1856). Drawing heavily on Moreau de Saint-Méry's representations of *le Vaudoux*, d'Alaux painted a picture of a government in the thrall of this "African free-masonry, of which Soulouque is one of the high dignitaries."[134] He ridiculed Soulouque's rumored fear of being ensorcelled and his wife's supposed consultations with a well-known "sorceress" in Port-au-Prince, who, according to d'Alaux, determined that Boyer, upon his overthrow, had buried in the gardens of the national palace a *fétiche* (fetish) that cursed all subsequent holders of the presidential office.

Such depictions need to be examined first and foremost in terms of what they reveal about the shifting strategies of foreign denigration of Haiti—more on this shortly. Yet it may still be possible to glean points of social historical interest from d'Alaux's account. One of the few insights d'Alaux offers about Soulouque's relationship to these religious communities was that he "knew how to strengthen himself through these influences, without strengthening them" in turn.[135] In oral tradition, in fact, Soulouque's otherwise despotic regime is remembered for its open association with popular religious practice and organization, even if article 405 of the Code Pénal remained in place throughout his twelve years in power. According to d'Alaux, the same Frère Joseph who was Acaau's close associate and who was also reportedly a leader of the *saints* in their violent pursuit of *guyons* during Pierrot's government, played an advisory role in the early part of Soulouque's regime as well before falling from favor.[136] He also notes that that the government issued a circular on 18 October 1847 that "enjoined the authorities, in severe terms, to maintain the interdiction which pressed hard on *le vaudoux* and *le don Pèdre*." However, a few weeks later "another circular forbade, in terms no less severe, the same officers from molesting the good people who wanted to enjoy dancing the *arada* [Rada], official euphemism of *le vaudoux*." This report suggests that in maintaining the Code Pénal's articles 405–407, the government of Soulouque, like that of Pierrot before him, sought to exempt such forms of religious expression from the criminalized category of *sortilèges*, thus officially observing and honoring a distinction that, I have argued, was effaced in the text of the law itself.[137]

It was during and after Soulouque's regime that specific references to *le vaudoux* (in English-language writings, simply *vaudoux*) began to proliferate in accounts by foreigners continuing to announce the decline of "civilization" in Haiti.[138] It is not incidental, of course, that the international ascendance of this figure coincided with what David Scott has characterized as the shift in "raced discourse" in the 1850s and 1860s from "the optimism and humanitarianism of the abolitionists and philanthropists of the early decades of the nineteenth century . . . to an aggressive and openly derogatory racialism undergirded by the new science of anthropology and espoused by travel writers, scholars, missionaries, and politicians."[139] To this list I would also add, in the case of Haiti, foreign ministers. Indeed, the French consul-general's book was particularly influential in this regard and was brought out in English in 1861 by a Virginia-based publisher. In his introduction, the translator advocated the forced colonization of Haiti by free black Americans, who would "be made the medium through which the reforming power of our civilization can be brought to bear on the social condition of Hayti."[140] Increasingly, the proof of Haiti's lapse into barbarism had a specific, subsuming name, *vaudoux*, under which the entirety of Haitian "fetishism," "sorcery," and "black magic" was consolidated in such accounts. The word was used in ways as various as its spellings. It not only referred to a practice, but also named an identity ("the Vaudoux"), described an event ("to give a *vaudoux*"), or, in its Anglicized form, became a verb (to "voodoo" someone). The proliferation of disparaging references to this word in foreign accounts of Haiti during and after Soulouque's regime raised the stakes for those members of the Haitian ruling class who supported a concordat with the Vatican. It also impacted those who served the *lwa* when, in the mid-1860s and then again during the mid-1890s, as examined below, the international restoration of "national honor" became a rallying cry for the repression of *le vaudoux*.

Soulouque was overthrown in 1859 by General Fabre Nicolas Geffrard (1859–1867), a strong Catholic from the south, who proclaimed Haiti's return to republicanism yet, in practice, reproduced the oligarchic power base of his predecessors. Rather than requesting another papal legation to Haiti, Geffrard sent delegates to Rome, where negotiations took place over a period of four months, concluding in March 1860 with the document that became the Concordat.[141] In its article 1 it established that Roman Catholicism, as "the religion of the great majority of Haitians, will be especially protected, along with its ministers, in the Republic of Haiti, and will enjoy the rights and attributes which are its own." Article 3 stipulated that the Haitian government was obligated to support the Catholic clergy based there with a suitable annual salary from the public treasury. The state, in turn, received the right, subject to approval from the Holy See, to appoint archbishops and bishops, who, upon assuming these positions, were required to take an oath swearing their "obedience and fidelity to the Government established by the Constitution of Haiti, and never to undertake, either directly or indirectly, anything contrary to the rights and interests of the Republic."[142] This pledge took on particular significance in light of rumors that certain French clergy in Haiti were colonial agents, and that France sought to repossess the country gradually through Catholic missions.[143]

Although the pursuit and eradication of "superstition" were not explicitly mentioned in the convention signed by the representatives of Pope Pius IX and President Geffrard on 28 March 1860, these goals, along with the allied project of expanding a system of primary instruction across the country, seem to have been understood by both parties as a principal function of the church's work in Haiti.[144] Some eighty-two years later, upon the failure of the church's last major campaign against "superstition" in 1941–1942, the archbishop of Port-au-Prince, Joseph Le Gouaze, wrote a confidential pastoral letter to clergy in Haiti stating that "our antisuperstition Crusade continues and cannot not continue" because "it is the *raison d'être* of the Church."[145] That statement might suggest the extent to which the Catholic church in Haiti historically defined itself in opposition to the popular practices it constructed as superstition.[146]

Shortly after the Concordat was signed, Geffrard exhorted his compatriots to "hasten to remove from our land these last vestiges of barbarism and slavery, superstition and its scandalous practices."[147] Laënnec Hurbon has argued that the role that the Haitian state assigned to the

Catholic church upon the institution of this convention was that of "an apparatus destined to produce an inquisitional discourse against Vodou," yet without the practical means or political mandate to "result in its eradication."[148] The impossibility of such a project was preordained at the time of the signing of the Concordat, given the political power of popular will and the extent to which Catholicism was already internalized in and transfigured by popular belief and ritual. The incorporation and transformation of Catholic liturgy in popular ritual seems to have intensified after the Haitian Revolution, when, according to the reports of certain visitors and elite writers, there was little or no effort on the part of priests to police the boundaries of Roman Catholicism as popularly practiced.[149] Terry Rey has argued that the importance of the cults of the Virgin Mary and St. Jacques le Majeur (Saint James the Greater) during the Haitian schism suggests the postrevolutionary significance of Kongolese Catholicism, for these devotions had also been prioritized in the kingdom of Kongo.[150] One might remember Frère Joseph's invocation of the Virgin in endorsing Acaau's movement in 1844, and sightings of apparitions of the Virgin in 1849 under Soulouque were also endowed with national political significance.[151] Hein Vanhee argues that the *pè savann* (lay priest), counted on by rural communities to recite prayers and songs in French and Latin at moments during devotional *sèvis* and other rituals when Catholic liturgy was required, similarly had roots in eighteenth-century Kongolese Christianity.[152]

"With the Concordat a new order of things was established in Haiti," wrote Carl Edward Peters, a Haitian priest who championed the church's campaign against "superstition" in his numerous writings during the mid-twentieth century.[153] When this convention was signed in 1860, popular ritual practice in Haiti fell, in effect, under a second legal regime. Henceforth, the popular practice of "superstition" would be denounced by both church and state with reference to *les lois divines et humaines* (divine and human laws). The church's periodic campaigns against "superstition" took Haitian penal laws against *les sortilèges* as their authorizing basis, but they also became the occasion for the promulgation of new sets of disciplinary measures emanating from the ecclesiastical power and exercised by the clergy. Classifying attendance at *sèvis* as a "crime of idolatry," such *statuts synodaux* (synodal statutes) and *ordonnances épiscopales* (episcopal ordinances) established rigorous sanctions against those reputed to be *oungan*, *manbo*, or *magiciens* (the latter assimilated to heretics) that included the denial of baptism, communion, the right to be godparents or witnesses to marriage, and the right to a Catholic burial.[154]

That the blessing of *rad penitans* (penitential clothes) was itself banned by church authorities in 1898, because priests suspected that this Catholic practice had been incorporated into the expansive repertory of what they called superstition, draws attention to how problematic the church's campaigns and sometimes self-proclaimed "crusades" against *le vaudoux* were when laws of the church were either already embodied in or potentially assimilated into Haitian popular ritual practice.[155] Joseph Roach has argued that law itself, "as a cultural system dedicated to the production of certain kinds of behaviors and the regulation or proscription of others, . . . functions as a repository of social performances, past and present."[156] If, after the Concordat, French priests in Haiti discovered that Catholic protocols of penitence had themselves been incorporated into the rituals the church constructed as superstition, then we need to think more not only about law as a repository of performances, but also about such performances as transformative repositories of law.[157] Popular ritual in Haiti may have fallen under a new legal regime with the signing of the Concordat, but the fact that church authorities in Haiti were soon compelled to ban one of their practices points to the complexities surrounding clerical efforts to enforce it.

PART II

"La tolérance coupable"

The first Catholic clergy authorized by the Concordat arrived in Haiti in 1864, the same year that an alleged case of ritual anthropophagy that became known as the *affaire de Bizoton* took place.[158] As Alfred Métraux writes, this episode "warrants our attention only because of its repercussions, which . . . threw on *Vaudou*—and on Haiti—a completely unjustified disrepute."[159] In his *De la réhabilitation de la race noire par la République d'Haïti* (1900), Hannibal Price argues that the arrival of the French priests in the midst of the public uproar surrounding this case predisposed them to "believe themselves transported into an absolutely savage milieu, among wild men whom they were called to civilize."[160] If, as Price suggests, this timing sheds light on the nature of the clergy's subsequent missions in Haiti, one might also wonder how the arrival of the priests may likewise have conditioned the government's response to the events that allegedly took place in Bizoton, on the outskirts of the capital city, early that year.

According to the criminal charges, a *cultivateur* (farmer) in Bizoton named Congo Pélé wished to improve his "miserable position" and "appealed to the *vaudoux* god," who demanded a human sacrifice. The man enlisted his sister, Jeanne Pélé (also spelled Pellé) and eventually six others and allegedly killed a child, a girl named Claircine, identified as their niece.[161] Tried and convicted for *sortilèges*, premeditated murder, and torture, the eight conspirators were publicly executed by firing squad in Port-au-Prince on 13 February 1864 before, reportedly, a cheering crowd of spectators. However, even Spenser St. John, the British minister to Haiti at the time, whose infamous account of this trial in his *Hayti, or The Black Republic* (1884) would for years thereafter associate "Vaudoux worship" with cannibalism in the imperial imaginary, at one point cast doubt on the justice of the guilty verdict: "The prisoners were bullied, cajoled, cross-questioned in order to force avowals; in fact, to make them state in open court what they were said to have confessed in their preliminary examinations. I can never forget the manner in which the youngest female prisoner, Roséïde Suméra, turned to the public prosecutor and said, 'Yes, I did confess what you assert, but remember how cruelly I was beaten before I said a word.'"[162]

St. John intended such disclosures to throw into question the Haitian government's official commitment to the "principles of justice," and perhaps its capacity for justice as well. Certainly he did not mean to question the guilt of the eight accused, of which he had no doubt. My aim here is not to establish what actually took place in the town of Bizoton in late December 1863; no such transcript is even recoverable. Rather, I am interested in examining the government's reconstruction and explanation of those events and how the Haitian official response was read by imperialists such as St. John as evidence for the regression of civilization in Haiti, rather than for its defense by the country's elite.

The account published in *Le Moniteur* a week after the executions already reflected state concern over how reports of the crime abroad would be misconstrued by those "having no knowledge of the country," who, "reading from afar about what just happened, will see a fact from which to generalize."[163] This report's author, whose name was Monfleury, noted that the "abominable crime" was committed not in some remote section of the countryside, but at the very "doors of the Capital." The perpetrators had mingled in society and were even churchgoers, prompting the question, what could have induced them to commit such an atrocity? It is striking, as Léon-François Hoffmann has noted, that neither this account nor those published in the government's subsequent circulars raised the possibility that "the assassins could have been a 'bad lot' or mentally ill."[164] The disclosure by the *commissaire du gouvernement* in the transcript of the trial itself that "nearly all of the accused" were "habitual criminals," seems not to be taken into consideration. Nor, it appears, was the testimony of one of the accused, Jeanne Pélé, who, when asked whether "the death of this child was indispensable to the requirements of *vaudoux*," replied, "No"; when further asked whether, "ordinarily, your *vaudoux* god requires human sacrifices," she again replied, "No."[165] Yet the account in *Le Moniteur* attributes the crime entirely to the persistence of "idolatry" and "superstition" in Haiti, and specifically to "le vaudoux," this "barbaric form of worship imported to us from some corner of Africa." In this conception, *le vaudoux* is figured not as a symptom of peasant barbarism, but rather as a unique source and encompassing term: "Their anthropophagy is only the result of idolatry; thus, destroy the cause, and you destroy the effect."[166]

This was a departure from the classificatory scheme of article 405 of the Haitian Code Pénal, in which *le vaudoux* was only one of several crimes listed under the heading *les sortilèges*. In these writings, "it" now seemed to gloss all the practices subsumed under the generic term "superstition." Notably, this usage was consonant with the way that *vaudoux* (and its various cognates) had come increasingly to be constructed in imperial discourses since the Soulouque regime—as encapsulating all of the barbarous rites attributed to Haitians. In likewise consolidating all "superstition" under the sign of *le vaudoux*, the author of the account in *Le Moniteur* effectively isolated "it" as the sole source of the barbarism imputed to Haiti by the hostile West. The extirpation of this *culte barbare* through "zealous" missionary work, and its replacement by Roman Catholicism, becomes all that stands in the way of "civilizing" the Haitian masses and preventing future depravities.

However, if, according to Monfleury, "the moral state of the masses undeniably leaves much to be desired," their response to the execution of the eight convicted anthropophagists in Port-au-Prince should prove to the world that a "notion of good and evil" is not entirely foreign to them. The author had walked among the crowds that day and was heartened by the cheers of "Vive le Président d'Haïti! Vive la civilisation!" that greeted the spectacle, despite, as he notes, the highly unusual circumstance that four of those executed were women. If many of those gathered at the execution still lived under the baleful influence of *le vaudoux*, he reasoned, such expressions of popular outrage, and not the crimes against which they were directed, should be the point on which foreign observers generalized about Haiti.[167]

It is striking that the author of this official account does not attempt to reconcile the horror popularly expressed against the alleged crimes in Bizoton with his proposal that they were propelled, in the first place, by the idolatrous *culte du vaudoux*. In constructing *vaudoux* as the source of such barbaric criminality, he cannot acknowledge that the public furor he finds so heartening might itself have been born of popular religious belief and feeling itself. In that case, the expressions of outrage at the crime and acclamation for the punishment that reassured the author about the morality of the Haitian masses would need to be understood as emerging, at least in part, *from* popular spiritual convictions, not in spite of them. As Hurbon observes, "Would it not be on the very basis of Vodou beliefs that the public supports such a condemnation?"[168]

This was not a conclusion that the Geffrard government entertained, at least publicly, what with the arrival of the Concordat clergy and reports of the Bizoton crime circulating internationally. Hénock Trouillot once observed that the degree to which popular religious practices were persecuted under nineteenth-century Haitian governments depended, on the one hand, on "the religious faith of the holders of power" and, on the other, on "what foreign writers were saying at the time."[169] In a report to the British Foreign Office ten days after the executions, Spenser St. John wrote that "within the last few days, the police have arrested a large number of persons connected with the Fetish worship and have seized the contents of their temples."[170]

Then, on 5 March 1864, Geffrard issued a circular to arrondissement commanders warning them that it was not enough to have punished the crimes committed in Bizoton. Rather, it was the "imperative duty" of authorities to prevent them from taking place at all, "because a crime so horrible, if it does not stay isolated, would be a disgrace for the Haitian name."[171] The circular then reviewed the relevant Code Pénal articles: "The law punishes those who indulge in practices or spells . . . ; it also punishes those who illegally exercise medicine; finally it also punishes unauthorized meetings and nighttime disturbances of the peace. Most of those who indulge in practices, spells, meetings, and dances of the *vaudoux* sect fall under the application of these dispositions of the penal law."[172] He ordered the local authorities across the country to "pursue severely all those who, in the reach of your command, indulge publicly or secretly in practices of *vaudoux*, to arrest them and deliver them to the judicial authority to be tried." They were also instructed to conduct searches to seize "the objects and instruments used in such practices and spells" and deposit them as evidence at the office of the civil court of that jurisdiction. Interestingly, Geffrard exhorted them to show "the most rigorous severity in executing these orders" not simply because such practices were a sign of barbarism, but because they were one of the "last vestiges of slavery and barbarity. . . . introduced and propagated under the colonial regime, in order to stupefy and better enslave the populations." If not many followed Geffrard in attributing the existence of the practices he objectified as *vaudoux* to a colonial strategy, their identification with slavery, both historically and ontologically, became one of the great themes of "antisuperstition" rhetoric, particularly, in later years, on the part of foreign clergy. Haiti might be free and independent, these appeals to national pride and patriotism went, but its masses were still enslaved to the *oungan*.[173] In Geffrard's text, the overthrow of superstition by *le vrai culte du vrai Dieu* was figured as fulfilling the promise of the revolution, freeing the population from this remnant of colonialism, which perpetuated its own regime of subjugation.

Hannibal Price describes the campaign launched by Geffrard's circular and implies that it enabled his own ethnographic investigations of several *ounfò* in the area of La Plaine, just outside the capital. His account is critical of the violent and arbitrary way in which these raids were carried out, in which "flags, drums, all the material of the societies" were seized and burned, and "all individuals reputed, wrongly or rightly, to be *papa-loi* or *maman-loi*" were arrested and imprisoned "as cannibals, as anthropophagists." Price argues that such persecution drove the targeted practices underground in a way that was in certain cases, paradoxically preservative: "The rare *hounfors* that could escape the active surveillance of the police therefore came to be sacrosanct places where the proscribed fetishism would be conserved in all its primitive purity."[174]

Yet it seems that Geffrard's campaign against *le vaudoux* soon crashed on the rocks of its own political impossibility. Just two months after Geffrard issued his circular to the arrondissement commanders, on 2 May 1864, his secretary of state for justice and religions (an interesting conjunction of appointments, in this context) sent a circular concerning "the shameful practices of *vaudoux*" to the government commissioners to the civil courts. It reviewed the circumstances and motivations that had compelled Geffrard to issue his earlier orders, which had resulted in the "arrest of a throng of individuals prevented from indulging in spells, *vaudoux*, and other infamous practices derived from superstition." Significantly, *vaudoux* is no longer figured here as the encompassing term, but rather is distinguished from *sortilèges* and inventoried as only one manifestation of "superstition" among others. The reasons for this subtle, yet significant reclassification, along with its implications, might be read between subsequent lines. Among the many imprisoned, whether convicted or still awaiting trial, the circular continued, nearly all bemoaned *la tolérance coupable*, which meant that in the past, what was formally forbidden by divine and human laws had in practice been permitted. They swore to the error of their ways and sought repentance. Given that the chief of state subscribed to the "maxim that it is better to prevent errors than to have to punish them," he was ordering the local courts "to grant full and entire clemency. . . . [to] all the individuals arrested for having practiced *vaudou*, and even those already tried and convicted for offenses of this nature."[175]

It seems to me that this reversal speaks to the political force of popular belief and will in the face of the state's disciplinary regime against Vodou. Read against its grain, the reference to the prisoners' "bemoaning" the "tolerance" that, until then, led them to believe in the permissibility of these prohibited practices might prove particularly suggestive. If there was an outcry among those imprisoned on the subject of such "tolerated illegalities" (in Foucault's formulation), is there not ample evidence, particularly in the action of the government's second circular itself, that this more likely took the form of protest rather than repentance?

Foucault argues in *Discipline and Punish* that in prerevolutionary France, "the least favored strata of the population did not have, in principle, any privileges," but "benefited, within the margins of what was imposed on them by law and custom, from a space of tolerance, gained by force or obstinacy; and this space was for them so indispensable a condition of existence that they were often ready to rise up to defend it."[176] If Haitian peasants were subject to an arbitrary and inherently exploitative regime of local regulation on the part of some rural police, popularly sanctioned ritual practices nonetheless attained a measure of protection from any sustained attack on the part of Haitian authorities because their status was that which Foucault describes. With its abrupt decision to free all those who had been arrested and imprisoned for practicing *le vaudoux*, even those already convicted and sentenced in the local courts, the Geffrard government may have conceded the political untenability of its campaign in the face of public pressure to end it.

Through his minister, Geffrard exhorted local magistrates not to "relax the active surveillance prescribed by the aforementioned circular," as the government persisted "in its unshakable resolve to combat the errors that endangered the future of the country." However, in perhaps the most revealing instruction of all, the president requested that those authorities particularly focus their surveillance "on the individuals designated by public outcry as being the heads of the sect, and as pursuing these practices toward a criminal or self-seeking end."[177] Thus, it was not simply that this circular ordered the sudden release of all of the prisoners. What was even more significant was that local authorities were instructed to follow *la clameur publique* in enforcing the penal laws reprised by the earlier circular. Henceforth, in other words, the popular sense of justice was to be the arbiter of the application of these laws. This amounted to a hardly surreptitious official acknowledgment, and even endorsement, of the constitutive popular distinction between, on the one hand, rituals allegedly employed for criminal ends, and thus properly subject to punishment, and those, on the other, whose toleration by the authorities constituted, in Foucault's words, an "indispensable . . . condition of existence" for the majority of the population. If, as the second circular suggested, a conversion had taken place as a result of Geffrard's campaign, did it not seem more likely that it was the law that had been chastened by the force of popular will, rather than the people who had been chastened by the force of the law?

Of course, the government's directive that authorities henceforth return to customary practice and follow public outcry in enforcing articles 405–407 of the Code Pénal did not make this regime just. As Sherry Ortner has examined, beliefs, practices, and movements that seem fundamentally resistant in the face of institutionalized structures of power may generate repression *within* local groups, given internal divisions and hierarchies.[178] Thus, although the Geffrard government's about-face and abrupt release of all of the Vodouizan arrested and convicted under article 405 of the Code Pénal during this two-month window in 1864 represented, in my reading, a victory in the ongoing struggle for religious and other civil liberties in Haiti, this was undermined by the prescription that authorities return to the customary legal order and make "public outcry" their legal litmus test in enforcing the law against *sortilèges*.[179]

The concessions that Geffrard's instructions to local authorities in early May 1864 seemed to signal were not recognizable in the government's revisions to the Haitian codes several months later. In October 1864 Geffrard promulgated a new Code Rural and expanded and tightened the existing Code Pénal in three significant respects. First, to article 246 of the Code Pénal, defining the crime of poisoning, was added a corollary: "The use of substances that, without leading to death, produce a more or less prolonged lethargic state is also qualified as an attempt on the life of a person through poisoning. . . . If, as a result of this lethargic state, the person was buried, the attempt will be defined as an assassination."[180] Second, the two articles on vagrancy that appeared in the 1835 Code Pénal (articles 403–404) were abrogated and replaced by five new articles (articles 228–232) that expanded the potential field of vagrancy, increased its minimum prison sentence and range of possible fines, and stiffened the penalties for recidivism. Finally, articles 405–407, which covered *les sortilèges* in the 1835 Code Pénal, were substantially modified: minimum prison stays were lengthened and fines were raised severalfold.[181] In proposing these revisions to the Chambre des Representants on 6 October 1864, Geffrard's secretary of state for justice and religions noted that "it is necessary . . .

that energetic means be employed to put an end to all these *pratiques super-stitieuses* that dishonor the nation."[182] Notably as well, in the wake of Bizoton, a second paragraph was added to article 405 that seemed calculated to further expand its field of prohibition and make it that much more comprehensive: "All dances and any other practices that are of a nature to maintain the spirit of fetishism and superstition in the populations will be considered *sortilèges* and punished with the same penalties."[183] A century later Alfred Métraux argued that even though this added paragraph had "often been invoked against the practice of *Vaudou*[,] . . . it is clear that in the minds of the men who drew it up, it was aimed at sorcery.[184] Yet, to me, this conclusion is far from obvious. Of all the revisions to "Des sortilèges," it is this extension that is most antithetical to the government's instructions to local magistrates six months earlier. Rather than bringing the law more in step with popular definitions and local regulatory customs, the addition of this paragraph seems to pull the continuum of popular spiritual practices further into the domain of *sortilèges*.

The first paragraph of article 406, criminalizing fortune-telling, prognostication, the explication of dreams, and the reading of cards, was kept intact, but minimum penalties for these offenses were increased.[185] Last among the revisions to this section of the Code Pénal, it was no longer adequate for authorities merely to seize the "instruments, utensils, and costumes used or destined for use" in the execution of *sortilèges*, as article 407 had formerly specified. Now, such items were confiscated in order to be "burned or destroyed."[186]

That this section of the Code Pénal was singled out for expansion and tightening in the wake of the alleged events at Bizoton, and in spite of the government's hasty abandonment of its subsequent campaign against *le vaudoux*, again raises the question of how such laws were meant to function as systems of signification, no less than as prescriptions for punishment. Pierre Buteau has suggested that the trial of the alleged Bizoton anthropophagists, "attended by a good number of representatives from the diplomatic corps of the epoch," can be understood as "an effort to show the international community that the Haitian Government really wanted to insert itself in the 'civilized' world."[187] Likewise, the expansion of the category of *sortilèges*, and its placement under a harsher penal regime through these penal revisions, can be understood, at least in part, as an effort on the part of Geffrard's government to repudiate the barbarism relentlessly attributed to Haiti by foreign detractors. Because *vaudoux* was now figured as the primary sign of that barbarism in such literatures, penal laws and criminal procedures against those identified as its practitioners became an increasingly important space of defense and disavowal for the nineteenth-century Haitian state. Read in a certain way, such laws not only signaled the state's will to "civilize" and modernize rural Haiti, but, as performatives, seemed to back this authorizing intention with force.

"Law Always Has a Trap Inside of It"

Yet prohibition has a dual and paradoxical nature: as much as it negates, it also affirms. Or, as Jacques Derrida once enigmatically observed, "the essence of law is not prohibitive but affirmative."[188] In prohibiting *les sortilèges*—a colonial construction, not a popular category—the Haitian state sought, in part, to provide evidence of its own civilizing offensive and political modernity. Yet, because prohibition is a Trojan horse that affirms what it negates, these laws and the court proceedings through which they were sometimes enforced were paradoxically seized upon by Haiti's late nineteenth- and early twentieth-century detractors as positive, even official, proof of the reality and existence of practices that the Haitian state, through interdiction, sought to disavow.

As mentioned earlier, there is a Haitian proverb which observes that *lwa toujou genyen yon zatrap ladan*—law always has a trap inside of it. It is a saying born of a history in which juridical law has provided more grief than protection to the Haitian poor, particularly around land ownership and tenure. The ethnologist J. B. Romain, in his monograph *Quelques mœurs et coutumes des paysans haïtiens*, interprets the proverb as reflecting the suspicion of peasants that lawyers, notaries, surveyors, and other purveyors of legal documents "can always lay a trap to dispossess" them.[189] Yanick Guiteau Dandin, a public health advocate in Port-au-Prince with whom I discussed the proverb's meaning, emphasized more precisely that the trap should be understood as embedded in the *language* of the law: "there is always a little nuance that you must interpret carefully if you don't want to fall into the trap."[190] Might this saying, particularly as explicated by Dandin, help explain how Haitian legal discourses and proceedings that placed *les sortilèges* in general and *le vaudoux* in particular under an ever-tightening regime of penalization wound up being deployed by late nineteenth-century imperialists such as St. John and James Anthony Froude as positive evidence of a residual or regressive barbarism that ultimately subsumed the state itself? Paul de Man has argued that laws, as performatives, never refer "to a situation that exists in the present," but point "toward a hypothetical future." In this sense, "laws are future-oriented and prospective; their illocutionary mode is that of the *promise*."[191] Thus there is a temporal delay between the law's descriptive (or "constative") moment, when it states what it prohibits, and its performative moment, when that ban is enforced.[192] This lag, de Man suggests, makes laws "promissory notes in which the present of the promise is always a past with regard to its realization."[193]

This temporal gap was precisely the trap that late nineteenth-century defamers of Haiti exploited in their perverse interpretations of the legal regime against *les sortilèges*. The fact that the application of the law is not simultaneous with its promulgation enabled detractors such as St. John and Froude to read these prohibitions as descriptive statements of the existence of barbarism in Haiti, rather than as performative texts signaling the state's will to eliminate *pratiques superstitieuses* through the force of law. Such writers often took their conclusions even further, proposing that the law against *les sortilèges* was actually arrested in this constative state and almost never had a performative moment. The charge that the law was rarely enacted, remaining in de Man's formulation an empty promise, could then be deployed as evidence of the state's own tolerance for or implication in the practices that it banned.

The Haitian state's supposed nonenforcement of the laws against *les sortilèges* became one of the great themes of late nineteenth- and early twentieth-century anti-Haitian propaganda, whether interpreted as a politics of appeasing the masses or as a strategy of ameliorating the country's image abroad by avoiding negative publicity.[194] This trope had been anticipated by Joseph Arthur de Gobineau, who, in arguing for the permanence and fixity of "racial" characteristics, maintained that there was a wide discrepancy between Haitian legal discourse and penal practice. After stressing the European derivation of Haitian political institutions and noting, for example, that "nothing African has remained in the written laws," he asserted that such pretensions of civilization were but a façade. While the institutions "sleep harmlessly upon the paper on which they are written," he wrote, a hypothetical "high official" had "ultimately no serious worry except chewing tobacco, drinking alcohol, disemboweling his enemies, and conciliating his sorcerers."[195] It was not a far cry from discourses of conciliation and appeasement to charges, frequently made during and after the reign of Soulouque, that the Haitian political class was itself thoroughly implicated in the "*vaudoux* crimes" that, according to these accounts, were so irregularly punished.[196]

"Haiti Is an Argument"

The charge that civilization was declining in Haiti did not go unchallenged by Haitian writers across the liberal–nationalist political spectrum in the later decades of the century, whose published rebuttals, addressed to specific defamers, became the occasion for broader statements about racial equality and the exemplary status of Haitians as, in J. Michael Dash's

FIGURE 3. Anténor Firmin. Courtesy of Archives CIDIHCA.

formulation, "the avant-garde that would rehabilitate the black race" internationally.[197] Anténor Firmin's landmark study, *De l'égalité des races humaines (anthropologie positive)* (1885), uses evolutionary anthropology to refute the claims of scientific and particularly anthropological racists. (See fig. 3.) As might be gathered from Firmin's revisionary title, Gobineau's tract was a key target of this treatise, particularly his statements about the "natural" tendency toward tyranny in black political leadership and social organization, evidenced, Gobineau claimed, by Haiti's history of "massacres," blacks against mulattoes, while the republic's democratic institutions remained "dormant on the piece of paper on which they were conceived."[198]

One of the critical contributions of Firmin's pioneering work was his analysis of the different points on which humanity was hierarchically ranked according to "race" in such literatures. He identified as a key tenet of scientific racist theory the claim that blacks were "unable to rise above fetishism and totemism" and had never developed "a superior conception of divinity."[199] Firmin's rebuttal of the thesis that fetishism was "a special product of the African mind" underlines the importance of evolutionary theory for late nineteenth-century antiracist theorists, Haitian and others, in scientifically contesting racial hierarchies.[200] If all human societies were understood to follow the same laws of development, scale the same "rungs of progress," as he puts it, then polygenetic divisions of the human species into superior and inferior races were clearly insupportable. Thus the so-called fetishistic practices that figured so prominently in racist statements about Haitian and, more generally, black incapacity for "civilization" were, according to Firmin, "found until recently among the peoples who are considered today the most worthy representatives of modern civilization."[201]

However, Firmin goes further, positing that religious faith more generally was in global decline, particularly in its institutionalized Christian forms.[202] Although this "revolution" was extremely difficult and painful for Europeans, Firmin notes, it would pose no hardship or exigency for those of African descent: "Never having experienced the sort of religious fanaticism and dogmatism now choking the Caucasian race, Blacks are ready to evolve toward rational and positivist conceptions which are consistent with the workings of the universe and with its attendant moral order." Firmin cites Comte's proposal that "the fetishistic stage is more conducive to the development of positivist philosophy than the theological stage, or even the metaphysical stage." Thus, rather than providing proof of African inferiority, it was precisely this "indifference to the more external aspects of religious worship" that made African peoples' "mental disposition" ideally suited for "the emancipation of reason."[203] The remote conception of a superior divinity on which European travelers to Africa so often commented was, by this argument, a prototype for the God of the future—a distant "constitutional sovereign, who looks on science as His minister and allows it the freedom to do its job."[204]

If those of African descent had the potential to be exemplary rationalists, in Firmin's argument, Haitians had not just the potential but the duty to be the exemplary representatives of all African-descended people. This is a point to which Firmin returns throughout his work. "Haiti must serve to the rehabilitation of Africa," he writes in his preface. In spite of the degradations of slavery, their ancestors had "managed to conserve in their heaving chests the sacred fire that was to spark the epic explosion which would lead to our freedom and independence." In the two generations since, in spite of the unremitting hostility of the white Western world, "a tremendous transformation occurred in their very nature."[205] This was the effect of liberty and, Firmin suggests, of climate—conditions in Haiti being "less harmful to their higher faculties" than those that their pro-

genitors had known in Africa. These factors made Haiti the ideal labora-
tory for disproving theories of racial inequality; they also made Haitians
the natural leaders of blacks internationally, its "avant-garde," who, according to Firmin, had the responsibility to work for the progress of all
peoples of Africa and its diaspora.

Haiti was figured ubiquitously during these years in the works of
scientific racists and colonial apologists as proof of black incapacity for
self-government, but Firmin and other Haitian intellectuals of his generation turned that logic on its head. Haiti was exemplary, yes—exemplary
of black equality, achievement, and potential. Hannibal Price opposed
his portrait of Haiti as "the providential agent of the rehabilitation of the
black race" to Spenser St. John's image of Haiti as "the sign of the eternal
damnation of the black race."[206] Louis-Joseph Janvier, leading figure of
the "ultranationalist" wing of the Haitian National Party (see fig. 4), formulated the idea in this way in his La République d'Haïti et ses visiteurs, 1840–
1882 (1883): "Haiti is an argument . . . that disturbs and displeases. But we
cannot change any of that. We are at least 200,000 men, prepared to die if
need be, so that Haiti might exist."[207]

While Firmin focused his illustrations of black progress in Haiti since
the revolution on the accomplishments of distinguished poets and writers, magistrates, historians, medical doctors, and politicians, Janvier located proof of this evolution in the peasantry and working classes. His
two-volume study, published, like Firmin's work, in Paris, addressed itself less to anthropological purveyors of scientific racism than to the travel
writers of anti-Haitian tracts. The author of the account that catalyzed
Janvier's response was, in fact, not a European, but a black Martinican
named Victor Cochinat who, "until now, had always passed . . . as the
friend of Haitians."[208] Cochinat had published a number of articles chronicling his travels in Haiti in a Parisian daily newspaper called La Petite presse
between September and December 1881. Entitled "De Paris à Haïti," the
series included, among other defamations, a harsh attack on the Haitian
laborer, whom Cochinat characterized as lazy and devoid of a work ethic.
Janvier devoted a chapter to rebutting those claims.[209] It was the Haitian
worker, he wrote, who, with the institution of universal primary education, had the potential to be exemplary: "one of the first workers not
only of his race, but of all America, and he will even be superior to the
Anglo-American worker because of his Latin blood and spirit—this artistic, refined, original and charming spirit." Most significantly, in light
of larger themes of Cochinat's account: "All the old African dances: le
banda, le madouk, l'arada, le congo, le séba, l'ibo, etc., have completely disappeared as much in the towns as in the countrysides. The pleasant tonnelle

FIGURE 4. Louis-Joseph Janvier. Courtesy of Archives CIDIHCA.

[a type of outdoor shelter] under which *la martinique* used to be danced is less and less frequented, and for the Port-au-Prince worker, carnival itself is only a too tiring and too expensive pleasure from which he increasingly abstains."[210]

Janvier's testimony draws attention to the way in which popular dance was stigmatized in nineteenth-century imperial and ecclesiastical pronouncements on Haiti, both on account of its association with Vodou ritual and as a blight on worker productivity. Some fifteen years later, in calling for greater government enforcement of laws against "fetishism," Monsignor François-Marie Kersuzan, bishop of Cap-Haïtien, noted that "this would be in the interest of the country, because a dancing people, degraded by savage orgies, will never be a working people."[211] By such logic, the decline of "old African dances" was a sign of national progress. Hannibal Price likewise asserted that the "creole dances" which "the more enlightened of the poor people in Haiti" used to enjoy, had all but disappeared "before the progress of civilization." The dance to the drum was, in general, "dead in Haiti," although not because of the heightened industry of peasants and urban workers; rather, according to Price, it was "killed by the development of the taste for dressing up among women."[212]

The decline and demise of the popular practices that d'Alaux, St. John, Cochinat, and others indexed as evidence for the regression of civilization in Haiti was a theme of late nineteenth- and early twentieth-century Haitian writing against such charges. However, if such defenses were inscribed by an evolutionary logic in which the persistence of "old African dances" was assumed to be incompatible with or antithetical to the progress of civilized modernity in Haiti, this did not necessarily mean that they were devoid of nuanced insights about the practices whose imminent doom they foretold. It is fitting that mid-twentieth-century Haitian ethnologists were to claim several of these writers as intellectual forebears, given the degree to which their representations of popular beliefs and practices seem to have been ethnographically informed. Indeed, to the extent that writers such as Hannibal Price and Duverneau Trouillot, in particular, were concerned with problematizing foreign constructions of *vaudoux* with reference to popular understandings, their studies should be read as works of reconceptualization, rather than simply of repudiation.

Price ridiculed the credulity of those detractors, and particularly St. John, who assumed that the persistence of "superstitious" beliefs in Haiti corresponded to the practice of actual barbaric crimes. In the course of critiquing the effacement of that distinction by such writers, Price took particular care to identify ethnographic inaccuracies and imprecisions in St. John's representations. His foremost objection, interestingly, was to St. John's use of the term *vaudoux* itself: "there is not, and there has never been in Haiti . . . either a *vaudoux* cult, nor *vaudoux* priests."[213] On the latter count he notes: "In their capacity as savants, doctors, or sorcerers," the true title of such figures, "according to our peasants, would be that of *houngan*, a word which came, it is believed, from an African dialect in which it was equivalent to expressions of *doctor* or *scientist*."[214] He later returns to this point: "St. John himself, who collected so many notes to transform all these superstitious beliefs into barbarous practices, into African fetishism, seems not to have known the word *houngan*, unless he willfully substituted that of *vaudoux*, to which Haitians have never attached the meaning that he gives it in his book."[215]

The significance of this critique might be appreciated in light of the Geffrard government's initial direction of local authorities in 1864 to pursue and arrest practitioners of *le vaudoux*, and then its subsequent order, two months later, to release all of these prisoners and henceforth follow public outcry in enforcing articles 405–407 of the Code Pénal primarily against those thought to practice ritual for "criminal or self-seeking ends." In critiquing meanings attributed to the word *vaudoux* that were unknown in or antithetical to popular usage, Price observed that, contrary to St. John's representations, the popular masses in Haiti felt "not admiration but a veritable horror . . . against those who make a profession of exploiting the superstitious terrors of others."[216] He writes that as a young man in the plain of Cul-de-Sac he had known "an infinity of people . . . who held *vaudou* dances at their homes out of pure love of this dance, without any pretension of passing themselves either as doctors or as priests of any sort of rite."[217] Thus he affirmed the status of *vaudou* (his spellings shift throughout the text) as "a simple dance of African origin, not very attractive, even repellent if you wish, but innocent, and which only owes its bad reputation, its sad celebrity to the *houngans* who have used it to obscure their charlatanism, to attract clients, by exploiting the taste of women of the poor people of the towns and countrysides for this tiring dance."[218]

In arguing that *le vaudou*, thus understood, posed no "obstacle to the civilization of this country," Price invokes another major theme of late nineteenth- and early twentieth-century Haitian writing on this topic: namely, that *oungan* were "swindlers" of the clients who sought their services. Such pretenders, Price contended, had cynically exploited the one-time popularity of the dance to expand their client base and in the process perverted the image of what was in fact only a form of rural recreation. Interestingly, the construction by elites of *oungan* and *manbo* as imposters, much exploited by the church in its "antisuperstition" missionizing during these years, paralleled what Price himself identified as a popular discourse of charlatanism, in which *oungan* and *manbo* referred disdainfully to their competitors as *caplatas* to undermine their credibility.[219] However, such epithets belonged to a world that was rapidly vanishing, according to Price, who claimed that all dances to the drum, including *vaudou*, were condemned by "popular sentiment" at the time he wrote.[220]

Duverneau Trouillot, also a lawyer, painted a similar portrait of decline in his monograph *Esquisse ethnographique: Le vaudoun; Aperçu historique et évolutions* (1885; Ethnographic Sketch: Vodou; Historical Overview and Evolutions), which mid-twentieth-century ethnologists cite as Haiti's first ethnography.[221] Trouillot's brief study includes a discussion of Vodou's historical roots in West and West Central African traditions; the first published listing, to my knowledge, of principal Vodou spirits along with their characteristics; detailed and apparently ethnographically informed descriptions of several ceremonies; and a glossary of "Vaudoux Vocabulary."

Trouillot's law practice was based in Port-au-Prince; five years after the publication of his sketch he was appointed secretary of state for justice and religions under the government of Florvil Hyppolite (1889–1896), in which Anténor Firmin also served.[222] I have not been able to determine where in Haiti Trouillot conducted his ethnographic study, nor what prompted him to undertake it. His monograph is fascinating in light of the internal tensions that structure it. It rehearses a number of the elite discourses on Vodou that Price and others later advanced as well, most particularly that the religion was in an advanced state of decline, extinguished by the "laws of evolution," along with the force and spread of Enlightenment thought, scientific rationality, and Christian conversion. Much like Price, Trouillot depicts le vaudoux as only, at that point, a form of coarse recreation, in which "the spirit of sugarcane is the great generator of spirits, lois, and saints," while "papas and mambos . . . smile up their sleeves." Thus, Trouillot concludes, "cane alcohol on the one hand, and the greed of papas on the other are the most powerful stimuli of the current dance of vaudoux."[223]

However, Price also emphasizes that this had not always been the case. If his study is underwritten by the same logic of decline-as-progress that Price's later would be, Trouillot's ethnographic sketch is exceptional among similarly focused late nineteenth-century Haitian writings for the powerful sense of loss he seems to attach to that process, despite its inevitability. Haitian "superstitions," he writes, had their roots in "a well of belief that was far more elevated."[224] Drawing on the writings of the nineteenth-century French monogenist anthropologist Armand de Quatrefages and the accounts of several European explorers, he observes that the so-called cult of the serpent in Haiti, the favorite "hobbyhorse of fantasizing travelers," had "fallen far from its primitive splendor." What had once been an elaborate, unified faith—one that, contrary to those who derided it as fetishism, had at least an "unconscious intuition" of a supreme divinity—was now only a "vulgar entertainment, having preserved the empty envelope of a vanished belief."[225] Rituals that were once full of meaning had lost their former significance. The great pantheon of gods that had distinguished "true vaudoux" had dissipated, replaced by countless "subaltern lois," which could be "acquired at will," as long as one had the means to purchase them.[226]

Again, one has the sense that elite discourses of the decline of vaudoux mimicked popular analogs.[227] Serge Larose notes the rhetoric of decline that pervaded communities of Vodouizan in Léogâne, where he worked in the 1970s, and the way that evidence for this trend was located in the proliferation of magic associations in the region. His analysis is particularly intriguing in that it suggests that this sense of decline, or falling away, consolidated a yet stronger sense of Ginen as an originary tradition, embodied in the family *lwa* passed down from generation to generation. In effect, Larose proposes that the popular rhetoric of decline might be understood as internal to and constitutive of the idea of a Ginen tradition, reinforced by the notion that *maji* was perennially in the ascendance.

In documenting the inevitable corruption and slow demise of what, "in its . . . splendor," had been an elaborate and noble, albeit "primitive" religion, Duverneau Trouillot's ethnographic sketch constructs, perhaps in spite of itself, a sense of nostalgia for the integrity of those lost origins. The ambivalence of Trouillot's narration is best encapsulated by what he characterizes as Vodou's "regressive evolution," whereby deterioration and dissolution actually signify progress: "regressive with regard to the superstitious beliefs . . . which enveloped the religion at the time when it flourished in its native setting; but this evolution is progressive, from the point of view of Christian civilization, toward which it tends."[228] As a result of such inevitable historical processes and the "syncretism," as he puts it in an early use of the term, that contributed to their course, he writes, "it is certain that if an old Guinéan passed by, he would no longer recognize himself in the middle of the dance and ceremonies of *vaudoux* today."[229]

Like Price, Trouillot emphasized the error of representations that collapsed such practices with those of *sorcellerie*, a heritage as much European as African. In fact, he argues, sorcery was universally condemned and repudiated, "as much by those who are adepts of *vaudoux* as by all those who are not."[230] The confusion, he suggested, lay in the fact that practitioners of *sortilèges* tried to "take the mantle of *vaudoux* in order to perpetrate their crimes."[231] However, according to Trouillot, the popular distinction between *vaudoux* and *sorcellerie* had serious implications for how each set of practices should be combated institutionally. Trouillot is, to my knowledge, the only prominent writer of his generation to critique explicitly the collapse of *vaudoux* into the penal regime against *les sortilèges*. Sorcery, not Vodou, was properly "the business of civil authority, armed for the repression of the penal law applied mercilessly." The degree to which "sectarians of *vaudoux*" incorporated Catholic belief and ritual into their practices signaled that its "disappearance depends on an active, intelligent religious propaganda, which is the business of Christian missionaries," not of civil or military authorities.[232] There was no question, he wrote, that *vaudoux* would fall away in the face of such missionary efforts, "directed carefully, and with tact; because it is worn, it is even out of fashion for a great number."[233]

La Ligue Contre le Vaudoux

Yet, when the church in northern Haiti organized its first sustained anti-*vaudoux* "crusade" in the mid-1890s, a decade after Trouillot's ethnography was published, the rhetoric mobilized to justify the missions was one not of decline but of recrudescence. Philippe Delisle argues that it was not just the Haitian state, but the Catholic clergy as well, who felt pressured by the proliferation of denigrating foreign accounts that constructed the "vaudoux cult" as proof of the decline of civilization in Haiti.[234] This was intensified by frequent references (often in the writings of Protestant missionaries) to the internalization of Catholic belief, iconography, and liturgy in Haitian popular ritual practices.

In July 1895 Monsignor François-Marie Kersuzan, bishop of Cap-Haïtien since 1886, circulated a survey among his clergy requesting information on the prevalence of "superstition" in their parishes and asking to what extent church faithful might themselves be implicated in such practices.[235] Six months later Kersuzan issued a pastoral letter reporting that "superstitious and pagan ceremonies, degrading dances desolate our countrysides, and our cities themselves are far from being sheltered. These practices, which in former times hid themselves in shadowy dens in the mountains and were only carried out under the darkness of night, now display themselves in broad daylight . . . , and what can only be said with tears in the eyes, the very people who claim themselves Christians and who frequent the sacraments are not afraid to participate in them, as if they could serve Jesus Christ and the devil at once."[236] In an address later that year, Kersuzan again emphasized that although some twenty years earlier most of his audience only knew of *le vaudoux* as "something savage, criminal, monstrous," now almost everyone at one time or another had "been witness to hideous exhibitions of this crude fetishism," and even "children, in running errands, hum songs of *vaudoux*."[237]

Kersuzan never addressed the most striking implication of this narrative: namely, that the escalation he alleged would have taken place, according to his chronology, on the church's watch. His reports seem to suggest that since the signing of the Concordat and the arrival of Catholic clergy, the practice of *vaudoux* had become more public and pervasive in Haiti. The rhetoric of recrudescence was by this time an established convention of Haitian official discourse. The announcement that "superstitious practices" were sweeping the country had often served as a pretext justifying the reinforcement of the penal regime (as in 1864) or the intensification (always temporary) of its enforcement. Kersuzan also made it a call to action, one addressed not just to clergy, but to the Haitian government, the elite, and society at large.

Marc Péan, who has written a thorough account of the church's late nineteenth-century "crusade" (as Kersuzan characterized it) against "idolatry" and "superstition," suggests that the bishop's call found fertile ground in the social milieu of fin-de-siècle Cap-Haïtien elite society, focused as it was on the pursuit of "progress."[238] Péan connects elite support for the bishop to what he sees as multiple manifestations of a modernizing and reformist drive in Haiti's second city, ranging from major public works projects to the founding of the École Libre de Droit du Cap-Haïtien, the dynamism of the city's press, and the popularity of salons focused on social issues. A lawyer, newspaper editor, and journalist named J. Adhémar Auguste, who was one of the foremost figures in Cap-Haïtien's multiple-front urban awakening, became one of the key lay leaders of the church's campaign as well.[239]

That elite Capois across the political spectrum initially rallied to the bishop's call suggests the importance of situating this campaign in relation to other progressive-era movements across the Atlantic world, and perhaps particularly to those underwritten by theories of "social hygiene." Comparisons with urban campaigns in republican Brazil in the 1890s against *feitiçaria*—glossing as "witchcraft" Afro-Brazilian religious practices, folk healing, and Kardecian spiritism—might prove particularly productive. Dain Borges has analyzed how the church's long-standing project of Romanizing popular Catholicism "intertwined" during this decade in the cities of Salvador and Rio "with new policies of social control" that, coming only a few years after emancipation, "fell particularly hard on Afro-Brazilians."[240] As Borges and other scholars have examined, the burgeoning fields of criminal anthropology and psychiatry in republican Brazil in the 1890s and also in early twentieth-century republican Cuba pathologized African diasporic religious practices as a symptom of racial degeneracy and force of criminality in these places. In fact, the medicolegal construction of *feitiçaria* in Brazil and *brujería* (witchcraft) in Cuba as urgent social threats to national order and progress was constitutive of these fields, along with those of anthropology and sociology.[241]

Here lie rich points of comparison and contrast with the case of late nineteenth-century Haiti, to which I can only gesture. Vodou was likewise an object of Haitian medical study and discourse at the turn of the century, most notably in the work of Élie Lhérisson, who, in articles that appeared in the Haitian journal *La Lanterne médicale* and in the French weekly *Semaine médicale*, wrote of the *culte* as a form of neurosis.[242] Yet, I have found little evidence to suggest that the Haitian medical and legal professions were fixated at this moment on researching "African atavism" as one of the most urgent social problems facing the nation, or on clinically studying the Vodou practitioner as a distinct racial and criminal type—that is, as a force of contagious social corruption who must be subjected to the analysis and therapies of modern science.[243] Indeed, the foremost legal journal in turn-of-the-century Haiti, the *Revue de la Société de législation*, mentions Vodou only rarely in the issues that I have been able to examine, and then primarily in reviewing vindicationist books by Haitian authors, which, as we have seen, tended to downplay its import.[244] One of the more sustained discussions of the religion in this journal appeared in the publication of a talk given by a distinguished medical doctor, Léon Audain, to the society in April 1904, which later became a chapter of his book *Le mal d'Haïti: Ses causes et son traitement* (1908). Audain deplored the drunkenness and "nervous excitation" that he once witnessed while attending a *sèvis* and concluded that it was necessary to "purify the dance of *vaudou* of all that which can carry the mind back to the barbarism of past times, to suppress the ceremony that precedes the sacrifice, to prohibit the public bloodshed of animals, to check the tafiatic [rum-induced] passion of initiates, to reduce, in a word, *vaudou* to a simple popular dance, joyful and decent."[245] However, the overriding tenor of his address to the society was to minimize and relativize the significance of these rituals in the face of racist foreign sensationalism, much as Firmin, Janvier, Duverneau Trouillot, and Price had done in their earlier works. Early Haitian scientific writing on *le culte du vaudou* was not fixated on "materializing its object, only to annihilate it," as Stephan Palmié has characterized Cuban criminological work on *brujería* at the turn of the century.[246] Although Kersuzan and his lay supporters invoked social-reformist ideas and language in an attempt to galvanize wider support among elite Capois society, and although the campaign that the bishop launched was supported by a number of Cap-Haïtien physicians and lawyers, the church's "crusade" in northern Haiti at the turn of the century seems not to have been reinforced by major allied programs of "social hygiene" against Vodou across the Haitian legal and medical professions.

Two months after Kersuzan wrote his pastoral indictment of the moral and spiritual condition of northern Haiti, on 14 March 1896, he founded a new Catholic weekly based in Cap-Haïtien entitled *La Croix*, which became the principal mouthpiece for the movement against both *le vaudoux* and, significantly as well, the growing social and political influence of Protestants in Haiti.[247] At this point, Haitian Protestantism encompassed Methodist (including African Methodist Episcopal), Baptist, and Episcopalian congregations.[248] Although I will not be focusing here on the anti-Protestant articles published in the pages of *La Croix*, their number suggests that the church and its lay supporters saw the campaigns against *le vaudoux* and against Protestantism as closely interconnected.[249] Kersuzan was apparently especially concerned about the educational inroads that Protestants were making in the north, predicting in an 1892 letter that "the Protestants will soon be the masters everywhere through their schools."[250]

Directed by Élie Benjamin, a former member of the Haitian legislature, and edited by Adhémar Auguste and a lawyer and poet named J. F. Thalès Manigat, both of whom became well-known public speakers on the topic of *vaudoux* practices over the next few years, the newspaper announced its intention to lead "a vigorous campaign" not simply for the health of souls, but also for the honor and development of the country.[251] This message targeted the middle classes and elites who were the primary focus of the church's campaign and the intended audience of the newspaper. "The existence of *Vaudoux* is a dishonor for us all," an editorial of 16 May 1896 read, noting that hostile white foreigners, despising the black race and the Haitian nation, figured such practices as proof of the incapacity of Haitians to assume their place "in the concert of nations." Thus, the editorial went on, "the responsibility of the patriot is to erase this stain from the face of the homeland. Let us prove to the foreigner that we are a civilized people."[252]

La Croix also justified its call for a "merciless" struggle against *le vaudoux* on the grounds that it fostered internal social ills by attributing misfortune or success to supernatural forces and by depriving workers of the fruits of their labors through the demands of offerings. Thus, the paper's denunciations of Vodou were frequently couched in a populist mode, defending the exploited Haitian peasantry against one of the agents of their oppression, embodied in the figure of the "papaloi" or "bocor."[253] One article, by a frequent writer named Alexis (Péan identifies him as Alexis Alphonse), blamed "the Bocors" for the decline of Haitian agriculture over the past decade, and specifically for their role in pressing the peasantry to maintain "a rigorous level of equality among all. If one has harvested a great deal and made money, he must spend a great deal" on ceremonies: "No agriculture as long as the influence of the Bocors endures; consequently, no future for Haiti if the race of these vampires is not made to disappear."[254]

It is important to note here that Kersuzan's colleagues in the church hierarchy elsewhere in the country did not universally endorse his polemical tactics in leading a "crusade" against *le vaudoux*. For example the bishop of Les Cayes never joined Kersuzan in calling for denunciations and the organization of lay pressure groups. Likewise, the bishop of Port-au-Prince reportedly hoped that Kersuzan would not become archbishop because he "feared the 'religious war'" that the bishop of Cap-Haïtien could foment with his newspaper *La Croix*.[255] Nevertheless, although *La Croix* was distributed principally in the north, it soon established a national profile and readership, particularly in the capital, where it came to the attention of the government of President Tirésias Simon Sam (1896–1902). Sam had just come to power, succeeding Florvil Hyppolite, a black general associated with the Liberal Party who had suffered a heart attack and died after falling from a horse. Hyppolite was rumored to have been a frequent patron of the well-known northern sanctuary Nan Kanpèch, and following his death this affiliation and his association with Vodou more generally became the subject of veiled denunciations by members of both Catholic and Protestant clergies.[256] An article in *La Croix* in late July 1896, again by "Alexis," excoriated the elite "pilgrims" to Nan Kanpèch, likening it to Mecca and calling upon newspapers to publish the names of these "enemies to our honor"; another article argued that during the past decade (that is, principally under Hyppolite's government) "*Vaudoux* govern[ed] us."[257] Notably, this association was also the subject of international press coverage, with the *New York Times* devoting an article to the topic in 1895 and then repeating the assertion in Hyppolite's obituary.[258]

Perhaps Sam saw the campaign beginning to mobilize in the north as a means by which to distance himself preemptively from rumors attached to his predecessor and other politically powerful figures. In late May 1896 the minister of the interior, General Buteau, issued what became a widely publicized circular to arrondissement commanders across the country, ordering stricter enforcement of laws against *la danse du vaudoux*, which had reemerged with an "unaccustomed recrudescence in our cities." Attributing this trend to the inattention of authorities who were distracted by other political matters, it called on commanders to pass on to their subordinates, both in the cities and in the countryside, "the most formal instructions to the end that delinquents are delivered to Justice and punished in conformity with the law."[259]

According to Monsignor J. M. Jan, in his multivolume chronicle of the religious history of the diocese of Cap-Haïtien, this circular was precisely the expression of government support that the clerical and lay proponents of the burgeoning movement had sought: "Magnificent result: alliance of the religious authority and of the civil authority against fetishism. What relief for national pride! What encouragement for the continuation of the struggle! What hope for tomorrow."[260] A series of public lectures were then convened, the first given by Kersuzan himself on Sunday, 2 August 1896, at the Cap-Haïtien marketplace before, according to *La Croix*, a large audience.[261] He began by applauding the voices, "vibrant with indignation, demanding grace for the honor of the nation," that had finally broken the "fearful silence" which had heretofore met the "retreat of morality and civilization" from Haiti. But, he exhorted the crowd, speaking was not in itself enough, and so he identified the purpose of his talk as "provok[ing] action against the scourge that overwhelms Haiti."[262] Kersuzan charged that those who practiced *vaudoux* were not simply superstitious, but idolatrous, in endowing "saints, images, [and] relics with exaggerated or ridiculous attributes." The label of idolatry enabled him at a later point in the speech to remind the audience that "death is the punishment to which the Lord condemns the idolatrous, the diviners, those who throw evil spells." If such a penalty was no longer exacted from individual offenders, Haitian society was still paying a high collective price "for its cowardice in allowing itself to be exploited by pagan priests." He argued that the political and civil conflicts that had rocked the country over the past twenty-five years were divine retribution for such tolerance: "A death sentence presses on us because of our idolatries. . . . It is my conviction that the radical abolition of *vaudoux* would make one of the principal causes of our revolutions disappear."[263]

Kersuzan's choice of the term "abolition" in this context was, of course, a calculated one; his talk was laden with metaphors of slavery, revolution, and emancipation. Practitioners of *vaudoux* were oppressed "under the yoke of *bocors*," who exploited their credulity with swindling ways; they were also enslaved to the "demons" they served as gods, unable, as individuals, "to break their chains."[264] But in joining the crusade the bishop heralded, they would find the power to "achieve the conquest of [their] independence."[265] Kersuzan appealed yet more explicitly to elite Haitian patriotism in emphasizing the high stakes of establishing national honor: "it is a question of rehabilitating ourselves in the eyes of the civilized world, it is a question of saving our very existence gravely compromised by the vampires who suck our fortune." The end of *vaudoux* would prove to the world that an African-descended people could indeed "civilize themselves, govern themselves, and, finally, form a nation worthy of this name."[266]

Such petitions to patriotic feeling might be considered particularly strategic and, at the same time, particularly incongruous points in Kersuzan's speech, given the frequency with which the Catholic church had itself been accused of interfering in Haiti's political affairs and undermining national sentiment since the signing of the Concordat. The wing of the National Party sometimes known as the ultranationals had repeatedly called for the revocation of the Concordat on those grounds, and in 1881 the National Assembly even passed a resolution to that effect, which, however, went no further under President Salomon (1879–1888). Louis-Joseph Janvier leveled some of the most vehement accusations against the church and its attempt, as he characterized it in his writings, to subordinate the national state to a foreign power. The church's ultranational critics charged that this clergy was making Haitians "slaves of the priests, who with their holy water and their false blessings were robbing the poor people of the country."[267] Janvier characterized Catholicism itself as "only a more purified, fine, artistic form of paganism from antiquity and primitive fetishism" and called on "all men who have African blood under their skin" to be free-thinkers or Protestants.[268]

Reading Kersuzan's August 1896 address in light of this history of contestation, one is struck by the way the bishop's arguments against *le vaudoux* often seem to replicate charges that had been leveled against the church itself.[269] Kersuzan's speech reads as a series of substitutions and displacements that recast the church as the guardian of Haitian national honor and the bishop himself as its committed patriot.[270] Heightening those claims to patriotism in an address delivered later in the campaign, Kersuzan responded to the "ignorant critics" who "accuse us of wanting to innovate and sow division in the Country, under the pretext of doing better than our ancestors." Indeed, he protested, "it is exactly the opposite that is true. In combating *le vaudoux* we walk in the tracks of founders of the Haitian nationality. . . . Not only were Toussaint Louverture and Dessalines not adepts of *vaudoux*, but they pursued it with a perseverance, with a severity that we would tend to call cruelty."[271] Thus, Kersuzan argues, the church's crusade followed a tradition of repression established in the founding moments of the nation.

It seems clear that Kersuzan capitalized on the campaign inaugurated in 1896 to counter charges that the Roman Catholic church was weakening Haitian nationalism and threatening the nation's autonomy. However, at least one auditor during his conference wondered if parts of his speech that August might not serve to tarnish Haiti's national honor rather than burnish it. This interlocutor was Anténor Firmin, who directed a letter to Kersuzan the following day, congratulating him on a *belle Conférence*, but expressing concern over one of its sections: that in which the bishop targeted those among *la classe dirigeante* who patronized *vaudoux* sanctuaries while pretending to be good Catholics.[272] Kersuzan had cited, anonymously, several cases personally known to him, including two medical doctors who sought treatment for their own maladies from a "papaloi," and a lawyer who traveled yearly to another *ounfò*, "accompanied by all that he needed for a sacrifice." Kersuzan excoriated such "false Christians" as "particularly harmful to our honor . . . in that their example tends to make the simple folk believe that *vaudoux* is not only not criminal, but is very well allied to Religion."[273] Firmin, however, wondered why the bishop did not denounce these figures by name, since this was what he called upon his audience to do as one of the tactics of the campaign. In suppressing the identities of those "aimed at by these allusions," did he not cast suspicion "on each of the first families, each of the educated people, lawyers, or doctors, belonging to Haitian society, especially abroad, where the true state of things is ignored"?[274]

In his response, Kersuzan assured Firmin that no one would ever conclude that *he* was the "famous lawyer" to whom the speech referred, a personalization that deflected the larger question Firmin had raised. In proposing that such veiled accusations could be generalized by Haiti's detractors, further compromising the nation's honor in the name of rehabilitating it, Firmin pointed to the potential for the campaign's "antisuperstition" rhetoric to intensify the ascription of backwardness and barbarism to Haiti. Rather than proving the ruling class's determination to eliminate the "scourge" of *vaudoux*, as Kersuzan put it, might not the "principles of action" for which the bishop called at the end of his first lecture only serve to reinforce the identification of Haiti with such practices? These were: "(1) To combat, by all the means in their power, all superstitious practice, all commerce with *bocors, chapiteurs, devineurs*, etc.; (2) To never hesitate to bring justice against the *faiseurs de caprelatas*; [and] (3) To denounce to the authorities and, when necessary, public opinion, by means of newspapers, all public practice of *le vaudoux*, and the existence of all places consecrated to *vaudoux* meetings."[275]

Thus *La Croix* began publishing the names of "bocors" (the church's gloss for all popular ritual specialists) who practiced in the department, along with the locations of their sanctuaries, and also occasionally the identities of prominent people who consulted them. Supporters sent in information about ceremonies (often referred to as *gombos*) that had been held in their localities, and *La Croix* exhorted public authorities to "do their duty" in enforcing the laws against *les sortilèges*.[276] Some followed suit, and not only in the north. In the months thereafter, the newspaper reported raids, arrests, the destruction of temples, and the widespread confiscation and burning of drums and other sacred objects across the country. Sometimes local *curés* accompanied police and took part in the pillage—as, for example, when a few days after a group of "bocors" was arrested in the hills northwest of Saint-Marc in a stronghold intriguingly named (in English) Black House, the *curé* of the parish joined military, police, and judicial authorities in demolishing the little room in which they had met.[277] Often a great mass of objects was accumulated from multiple raids and then burned publicly in the marketplace on the occasion of anti-*vaudoux* lectures or on Sundays following mass. Occasionally *La Croix* published inventories of objects confiscated in raids, perhaps in the spirit of one general in the southwest, in Jérémie, whom the newspaper celebrated for having "assembled in the offices of the arrondissement, a very curious museum . . . of drums, flags, and *pierres tonnerre* [Taíno ax heads]. All this was thrown into the fire and into the sea, the shacks for the *mystères* were also burned."[278]

However, a series of complaints soon began appearing in the pages of *La Croix* against rural police officers and local agents of the judiciary for failing to enforce articles 405–407 of the Code Pénal according to the church's interpretation of these laws. An article in mid-October 1896 warned against the lack of uniformity in the application of the statutes, some military authorities enforcing them "to the letter" and others applying them partially or not at all: "this difference emboldens the *papas-bocors* and their clique; they see themselves as testing the authorities; in some places the dances resume, without drums at first, then with new types of drums."[279] Such complaints become a major editorial theme of *La Croix* during the latter months of 1896, reflecting two interconnected social realities: first, that *oungan* and *manbo* were finding ways to circumvent the law, and second, that certain local military and judicial authorities were inadvertently or willfully enabling them to do so. The *truc* (trick), as one article put it, that practitioners were exploiting was to hold *sèvis* under the cover of authorized *bal* (dances) and avoid using conical drums; instead, other instruments were played, and people also simply clapped their hands.[280] Certain authorities, according to *La Croix*, mistakenly considered the use of drums the legal litmus test in determining whether or not article 405 had been violated. Those military chiefs who failed to make arrests because no drums were used and those *juges de paix* who released those detained on the same grounds, the newspaper argued, were either ignorant of the actual terms of the law or were themselves complicit in the *truc*. A series of articles sought to clarify any misconception along these lines, with one entitled "Le vaudoux et l'honneur national" emphasizing, in an almost ethnographic mode, that "the drum is no more *le vaudoux* than the bell is the mass," and "the dance is no more all of *vaudoux* than the procession is the Catholic worship." It continued: "It is therefore not enough to have suppressed the drum and the dance. Oh! It is enormous, certainly, and it would be an injustice to want everything done at once. But it would also be an illusion, a dangerous illusion, to imagine that all is said because the drum is no longer played and people no longer dance. The enemy remains, it is only wounded, it must be killed."[281]

There were also instances of open defiance of the church's interpretation of the law, as reported in *La Croix*. In one highly publicized case, a "grand Vaudoux" was held in Hinche by the former commandant of that place, O. Zamor. This was probably Oreste Zamor, who went on to become president of Haiti for nine months in 1914.[282] When military authorities arrived there were cries of "À bas Monseigneur!" and "Vive le Vaudoux!," which, given the penal prohibition of the latter as a form of *sortilège*, the newspaper argued, was tantamount to crying, "Down with the law, down with order, down with the government itself." The general himself remained defiant, telling the colonel who led the military detachment, "I am on my own property . . . I have the right to do what I want." When the colonel threatened to arrest him, Zamor fired shots in the air.[283] In another case, a well-known *manbo* named Olivine Pierre sought, according to *La Croix*, to further augment her prestige and powers by receiving her first communion. Interestingly, she seems to have pursued this plan under the cover of the church's campaign, insisting to a *curé* in Milot that she had reformed and "renounced her infamous profession" and sought now to become a good Catholic. Two days later she was arrested with eight others in Plaine-du-Nord for giving *un grand Vaudoux* and sent to the local *juge de paix*, who declined to try them locally and dispatched the group to Cap-Haïtien. Determining that this was not the proper jurisdiction, the authorities in Cap-Haïtien had them sent back to Plaine-du-Nord. Throughout much of this journey, *La Croix* reported, the group defiantly played their drums, and spirits mounted Olivine: "the police who escorted [them] failed their duty in not preventing this scandal."[284]

Further signaling the divergence between the church's interpretation of the Code Pénal and that of some local authorities, *La Croix* reported that at Quartier-Morin, on Haitian Independence Day, 1 January 1897, "soldiers danced *le vaudoux* for a quarter of an hour, to the sound of military drums, before the altar of the fatherland, a moment before the Te Deum," without interference from their superiors. "Beautiful way to celebrate our independence!" the newspaper commented, thus acknowledging the possibility, even the likelihood, that whatever the nature of these dances, they were indeed expressions of national pride on the occasion of Independence Day. In the face of the church's campaign, they bespoke a countersentiment of national honor, one that was affirmed and celebrated, not disgraced, by the dances of Vodou.[285]

Such reports in the pages of *Le Croix* might have alerted the bishop and lay campaign promoters to conflicts of interpretation upon which their movement would eventually founder. However, if anything, the crusade gained momentum in late 1896 and early 1897 with the founding of the Ligue Contre le Vaudoux under the presidency of Kersuzan, backed by a *comité d'action* (action committee) that included well-known members of Capois elite society such as General Annibal Béliard, Cincinnatus Leconte, and the editors of *Le Croix*, J. F. Thalès Manigat and J. Adhémar Auguste, among others. Its mission was to "support the government in its action against *le Vaudoux*," working by "all the means in its power" to achieve its "annihilation." President Sam sent a "very warm telegram" to the group endorsing their efforts.[286] The Ligue moved swiftly to expand and broaden its base. Although the series of lectures before elite audiences in Cap-Haïtien continued, the *comité d'action* focused a greater effort on generating support for the Ligue in other communities, and particularly among rural populations throughout the region and nationally. In February 1897 Adhémar Auguste gave a talk before a group of delegates from across the northern department to discuss the organization of regional and national anti-*vaudoux* congresses, and in April he traveled to Limonade to address a "popular audience" in Kreyòl on the campaign that was under way.[287] The bishop himself spoke at, "in all, seventeen meetings against fetishism" in 1897, with open-air missions at Perches and Fort-Liberté, as well as across the diocese of Port-de-Paix, where a second branch of the Ligue was established. Kersuzan reported: "We made a point of giving popular conferences on fetishism outside of churches and chapels, most often in open-air locations."[288] Soon after the news of President Sam's official endorsement appeared in the Cap-Haïtien press, the two principal governmental representatives of the northern department, General Nord Alexis (who later became president, 1902–1908) and his deputy, Albert Salnave, wrote to the *comité d'action* as well, offering their support "with a view to the triumph of this generous campaign."[289] Thereafter, Kersuzan reported, rural populations were "prepared" for each of his talks by local military commanders, who "reinforced our speech and outdid our curses against fetishism."[290]

That division of labor again draws attention to the way in which, following the Concordat, practices of popular ritual fell under a double legal regime—*les lois divines et humaines*, as the expression went. Shortly after the founding of the Ligue, the church published an *ordinance episcopale*, which expanded and tightened the *statuts synodaux* that had been promulgated in 1872 by Monsignor Guilloux. Although these earlier laws had established sanctions for "magicians" (assimilated to the category of heretics), the clients who frequented them, and those who otherwise engaged in "superstitious rites," the statutes had never classified such figures or practices under the sign of *vaudoux*. By contrast, the disciplinary measures issued by church authorities in 1897 were specifically addressed to those who presided over or took part in "cérémonies du Vodou," who were guilty of "the crime of idolatry, the greatest crime of all."[291]

During his missions across the northern region in 1897, the bishop announced and publicized these new sanctions, which subjected those who took part in a "*vaudoux* ceremony or dance" to "severe penitence" and a "deprivation of communion." That such measures were indeed applied by clergy during the period of "antisuperstition" proselytizing which followed their promulgation might be inferred from the fact that, a year later, church authorities were compelled to revise these statutes, banning one of the penitential practices they had originally prescribed. As noted earlier, clergy had discovered to their dismay that the blessing of "penitential clothes" was itself incorporated into the repertoire of "superstitious practice."[292] This instance of the church's being forced to turn the regime of prohibition back on its own punitive practices was symptomatic of the impossibility of this and every subsequent anti-*vaudoux* or "antisuperstition" mission it undertook in Haiti. The clergy's attempts to exercise penalties against "superstitious" or "idolatrous" practices always seemed to end in acts of self-proscription and/or self-destruction.

As for the application of *les lois humaines* against the practices objectified in articles 405–407 of the Code Pénal as *sortilèges*, Péan reports that it was common to find notices in the Cap-Haïtien press announcing arrests for contraventions of article 405.[293] However, even as a new chapter of the Ligue Contre le Vaudoux was being organized in Haiti's southern department, conflicts were developing in the north between the Ligue's *comité d'action* and the region's military authorities precisely around the enforcement of these laws. Again the problem centered on different perceptions of what their proper object should be. Significantly, it was the government's representatives, Nord Alexis and Albert Salnave, who emerged as the most prominent antagonists of the Ligue's interpretation of these laws and defenders of popular views of their legitimate application. Thus, for example, the generals balked when the Ligue's *comité d'action* called for a ban on the dances performed in the streets during Carnival on the grounds they were manifestations of *vaudoux*; on the contrary, they insisted, these were merely "traditional dances for that time of the year." The controversy finally had to be arbitrated by Haiti's minister of the interior, who decided in favor of the Ligue's position, outlawing such performances that year.[294]

This incident, among others with similar stakes, fueled resentment against the Ligue and its apparent determination to repress practices that, in the view of the vast majority, presented no justifiable cause for penalization. In September 1897, as public officials somewhat muted their

support, the newspaper *La Croix*, which had moved its operations to
Port-au-Prince in April, ceased publication, citing "insurmountable difficulties." Péan interprets the newspaper's folding as an act of deliberate
"self-sabotage" in the midst of growing popular and political dissent over
the course of the campaign.[295] Polemics against the tactics employed by
the church in its crusade had been appearing in local and national newspapers.[296] Monsignor Jan indexed a number of these in chronicling the
history of the campaign:

> If We called upon public powers and if We received from the government
> this so loyal, so attentive, and so effective assistance to which we must at-
> tribute, to be fair, the serious and solid establishment of the Ligue Contre
> le Vaudou, we are accused of meddling in politics, of wanting to dominate
> the country. . . . [When] We went so far as to denounce magicians as crim-
> inals . . . , and We provoked all honest people to unite to defend themselves
> against these public enemies and to force them to renounce their odious
> practices: then, oh! then especially, what cries of indignation! what scan-
> dal! the Minister of God[,] of peace and of charity preached hate, sowed
> division, armed one citizen against another![297]

He further regretted that "during the antisuperstition campaign, the
societies of the countryside were permitted to come into the city for certain national holidays. . . . The instructions of the Buteau circular were
not everywhere observed. In the public, a certain indulgence manifested
itself for ancestral customs, too old not to be tolerated."[298]

Yet clergy in the north continued to enlist the backing of local military and police, both in evangelizing among rural populations and also,
at times, in raiding suspected "superstitious" sites. In 1899 Father Bertin,
the *curé* of Déréal, confronted a "bocor" named Valbrun with an armed
guard drawn from local civil and military authorities. Valbrun, according to Jan's recounting of the incident, denied having anything to do with
vaudoux. Others present "let out a stream of recriminations" against the
curé, charging that "the priest had overstepped his rights in wanting to
take away from them the freedom of doing what to them seemed good."
Jan reports that they even threatened Bertin's life, declaring "that if the
Father had been alone, he would have been assassinated."[299]

If the church considered the strict enforcement of *les lois humaines et divines* against *le vaudoux* to be the aim and means of its crusade, it was precisely the application of such laws upon which the campaign consistently
foundered and ultimately self-destructed. The coup de grâce played out
in late 1899 and early 1900 in the Plaine-du-Nord, a commune of the ar-

rondissement of Cap-Haïtien, which Péan identifies as "at once a high place of Catholicism and of Vodou." The patron saint of this parish, Saint-Jacques (in English, St. James), whose images adorned the local church, was identified in popular belief as the *lwa* Ogou. One priest appointed to this diocese noted, "I do not like to attend the feast day of St. Jacques. I dislike finding myself mingling with worshippers of Papa Ogou. . . . In rubbing shoulders with this large crowd, I ask myself, where are the Catholics? Where are the *vodouyeurs*?"[300]

Clerical concern over such identifications frequently centered on what clergy viewed as excessive popular attachment to pieces of religious statuary representing the Virgin or particular saints that, it was suspected, were worshipped as "pagan idols."[301] There were two statues of Saint-Jacques at the Church of Plaine-du-Nord. One, called *le petit Saint-Jacques* even though it was full-sized, was a recent gift to the parish from former President Hyppolite.[302] The other, known as *le grand Saint-Jacques*, was a plaster tableau, sculpted in relief, which had hung above the high altar of the church since colonial times and was the object of "extraordinary veneration" on the part of local parishioners. One evening in late December 1899, the cord from which *le grand Saint-Jacques* had long hung snapped and the sculpture fell to the ground, breaking into pieces.[303]

Kersuzan reportedly regarded the event as a welcome accident. However, two months later General Nord Alexis requested an audience with Kersuzan. He informed the bishop of his intention to have the statue repaired. The bishop proposed sending the statue to France for restoration and wrote a letter to the *curé* of Plaine-du-Nord instructing him to relinquish the fragments of statuary to this end. These were collected by the communal magistrate, who set out en route to Cap-Haïtien and became the center of a high-spirited procession, during which, according to Jan's history, stops were made at various *ounfò*, where "there were songs, *vaudoux* drums, [and] dances."[304] The fragments of the statue were never sent to France; instead, they were pieced back together in Cap-Haïtien by a local sculptor. On 19 July 1900 the restored *grand Saint-Jacques*, mounted on a huge stretcher and held up from behind by two wooden triangles, was carried to Plaine-du-Nord on the shoulders of members of a large crowd. Although neither Jan nor Péan mentions this in their respective accounts, the canonical feast day for Saint-Jacques is 25 July, and it seems likely that the return of the statue was timed accordingly.[305] This procession was more on the order of an organized political parade than the spontaneous popular pilgrimage of several weeks before. Nord Alexis led the escort himself, accompanied by other notables from Cap-Haïtien. The statue was restored to its place of glory over the altar, and then, according to Jan and in his words, an "orgy" took place in the church: "crying, singing, drinking, a veritable sabbath."[306]

When Kersuzan heard of these events and of the restoration of *le grand Saint-Jacques* above the altar, he notified the government in Port-au-Prince. Two months later, still waiting for their intervention, he traveled to Plaine-du-Nord himself on the morning of Sunday, 30 September, surrounded by an entourage of priests. There the bishop told the assembled parishioners that he had come to remove the tableau of Saint-Jacques from above the high altar in order to place it at the back of the church. According to Jan's account, Kersuzan was in the midst of his explanation when the protests started. As the unrest grew, he warned the congregation that he was prepared to close the church if it continued. When the *curé* of the parish, Père Lacrampe, began removing sacred ornaments and vases for safeguarding in the presbytery, a "riot" broke out, from which, according to Jan, the clergy narrowly managed to escape.[307]

Two days later, back in Cap-Haïtien, Kersuzan announced the excommunication of those who had been involved in the "sacrilegious scenes" of 19 July and 30 September and placed the church of Plaine-du-Nord under an order of interdiction. However, because the second measure could not be a permanent one, the bishop was still no closer to resolving the problem of the placement of the statue. Thus, during his annual courtesy visit to the chief of state in Port-au-Prince in January 1901, he took up the problem with President Sam, who promised that the government would oversee the exchange of the statues and proposed that this be planned to coincide with his upcoming tour of the northern department. However, Sam cautioned, in order avert further confrontation and strife, some concession would have to be made to Nord Alexis. It was decided that the *curé* of the church in Plaine-du-Nord, about whom the general had complained on several occasions, would be reassigned to another parish.

One problem remained: who would actually perform the potentially dangerous task of removing the statue? Cincinnatus Leconte, the minister of public works and agriculture, one of the founding members of the Ligue Contre le Vaudoux, and a future president of Haiti, volunteered. Thus, during Sam's trip to Cap-Haïtien in early April, Leconte embarked for Plaine-du-Nord, accompanied by a minimal escort. They had only traveled six kilometers when they met gunfire and were forced to turn back. The next day, Leconte set out again, this time with "imposing forces," and accomplished his mission without interference. As Péan notes, the fusillade that greeted the group's first attempt to reach Plaine-du-Nord was widely interpreted as a warning from Nord Alexis, and soon thereafter "La Ligue Contre le Vaudoux, already put on hold since the first moments of the affair, ceased all activity for good."[308] Thus, the statue was successfully moved at the expense of the continuation of the campaign.

★   ★   ★

I have discussed this episode at some length not only because it culminated in the demise of the Ligue, but more particularly because it illuminates the ultimate impossibility of Kersuzan and his supporters' crusade to eliminate *le vaudoux* through the application of *les lois divines et humaines* against "its" practice. It is striking that the church's efforts to see these prohibitions enforced finally ended in self-interdiction, with Kersuzan imposing a ban on the church in Plaine-du-Nord itself. Far from being an exceptional or extraordinary step, this action was representative of the kinds of self-destructive measures in which the church's campaigns against *le vaudoux* or "superstition" often seemed to culminate. As the lengths which the bishop took to have *le grand Saint-Jacques* removed from above the high altar reflect, the church always suspected and feared that it would be taken over for "superstitious" purposes. However, as Laënnec Hurbon has written, the "osmosis" of Catholicism into popular services for the *lwa* meant that "all 'antisuperstition' crusades could only lead to an impasse: each high place of Catholic pilgrimage is already at the same time a Vodou sanctuary. . . . It would be necessary . . . for the church to fight against its own traditional liturgical practices."[309] Thus, any attempt to attack the "contaminating" belief, the "idolatrous" practice, or the "superstitious" site placed the church in the paradoxical position of shutting itself down, banning its own rites, and destroying its own iconography.

The confrontations at the Plaine-du-Nord church underscore the ultimate political impossibility of a campaign that initially inspired expressions of governmental support and congratulations at every level. One need not doubt the sincerity of Nord Alexis's earlier offer of assistance to the Ligue in order to understand his later forceful opposition to their efforts. The problem, again, was one of legal interpretation. As had been the case under Geffrard in 1864, any attempt to strictly enforce these laws that did not follow popular consensus on what their proper object should be was destined to fail. It was not that most people were opposed to the application of laws against *les sortilèges*; indeed, given the popular dread and condemnation of malicious *maji*, the announcement of a tightened regime of penalization against "spells" was usually met, as it seems to have been in this case, with acclamation. Hence Cap-Haïtien newspapers in late 1896 reported that the trials against several notorious alleged "sorcerers" were followed "passionately" by sectors of the local populace. Yet the church's insistence that this legal regime encompassed popular celebrations of *fèt chanpèt* (French *fêtes champêtres*, or country fairs) honoring town or village patron saints, Carnival traditions, and, of course, devotional *sèvis* for *lwa* such as Ogou/Saint-Jacques was met with outrage and protest on the part of affected communities, and recalcitrance and sabotage on the part of the local authorities who not only policed, but also politically represented them. This case spotlights the extent to which many of these appointees, whether arrondissement commanders or rural police, were themselves invested in maintaining the customary status quo on these laws, and not only because they relied on the fees generated by informal regulation. As Geffrard's hasty reversal in 1864 made clear, the sustained enforcement of these laws against practices sanctioned by the vast majority of the population was politically untenable. Furthermore, many if not most of the members of the local military and police apparatus were themselves engaged in the continuum of practices that the church sought to repress.

Although mediated by multiple narrations and translations, including my own, there still seems to be a powerful clarity in the way those who confronted Father Bertin on his raid in Déréal in 1899 formulated their protest. In charging, according to church history, that he had "overstepped his rights in wanting to take away from them the freedom of doing what to them seemed good," they foretold the ultimate impossibility of successfully carrying out any clerical or official campaign that made *vaudoux* the object of its repression. Such campaigns rallied Haitians to defend the honor of both nation and race against the barbarism imputed to Haiti and Haitians by imperial denigrators through the figure of *vaudoux*. Yet each of these campaigns eventually foundered in the face of popular understandings of Vodou that were antithetical or even constitutively opposed to the definitions of "witchcraft" and "sorcery" that had long circulated in colonial and ecclesiastical discourses. In such cases, popular religious practices and organization served as a key locus and instrument of political struggle through which and in defense of which state and church regimes were brought in line, however ambivalently, with popular conceptions of justice.

CHAPTER THREE

Penalizing Vodou and Promoting "Voodoo" in U.S.-Occupied Haiti, 1915–1934

The U.S. occupation of Haiti must be situated in the larger history of U.S. military intervention and territorial acquisition (or attempts thereof) in the Pacific, the Caribbean, and Latin America following the Civil War. In the Caribbean this intensified after 1898, with the Spanish cession of Puerto Rico and the first U.S. occupation of Cuba, and even more after 1903, with the Roosevelt administration's "taking" of Panama and take-over of the construction of the isthmian canal. In 1904 Roosevelt announced his famous corollary to the Monroe Doctrine, asserting the right and responsibility of the United States to intervene as an "international police power" in the affairs of its "southern neighbors" in cases of foreign debt delinquency and/or the "general loosening of the ties of civilized society."[1] The United States occupied Cuba for a second time between 1906 and 1909, where American investment in the sugarcane industry had grown steeply. It invaded Nicaragua in 1909, Haiti in 1915, and the Dominican Republic in 1916, and it purchased the Danish Virgin Islands in 1917.

Washington's foremost strategic concern in Haiti (as elsewhere in the region) was over what it perceived as growing European and particularly German influence on Haitian affairs in the context of the country's mounting foreign indebtedness and internal political instability.[2] The latter were not unrelated conditions, for the turnovers in government that U.S. military officials, in justifying the 1915 invasion, would characterize as Haiti's "chronic revolutions" were often bankrolled by different Western European powers in the late nineteenth and early twentieth centuries. As of 1910, U.S. interests controlled the Banque Nationale de la République d'Haïti. However, when successive Haitian governments refused to grant the United States a customs receivership, the Woodrow Wilson administration began to plan for armed intervention. The justificatory pretext the United States was waiting for came in late July 1915, when an enraged mob killed President Vilbrun Guillaume Sam in retribution for the massacre of 167 political prisoners as the opposition leader Rosalvo Bobo's forces approached the capital. Within a week 1,100 U.S. marines and sailors had landed in Haiti.[3]

The extent to which the United States achieved military and financial control of Haiti between 1915 and 1934 by revoking existing Haitian laws and enacting new ones is well documented in the historical literature on the occupation.[4] The most prominent example of this was the 1918 U.S.-sponsored Haitian Constitution, which lifted the interdiction of alien landholding that had been in place since Haitian independence. When the Haitian legislature, the only body with the legal power to revise the constitution, refused to approve the version drafted by U.S. civil and military authorities in 1917, it was dissolved by the marines under the nominal authority of the client government. This charter was later "passed" by an extraconstitutional plebiscite, in which it is estimated that less than 5 percent of the Haitian population participated, under an armed guard of marines.[5] As historical studies of the occupation have further shown, the legalization of foreign land ownership became the condition of possibility for the subsequent passage of a series of new laws that empowered U.S. corporate interests and disrupted the already precarious existence of Haitian peasants in the agriculturally richest regions of the country.[6]

Journalistic and scholarly attention has thus focused on how U.S.-sponsored laws consolidated Washington's control over Haiti and, through the detentions, displacements, dispossessions, and taxations that they authorized, worsened conditions of life for large sectors of the peasant population.[7] In the pages that follow, however, I will argue that the effects of such legal revisions need to be understood in light of the strategic and opportunistic uses that U.S. military and civil officials also made of existing Haitian laws, and particularly those that, although codified, were not consistently applied by Haitian authorities.

In her *Les paysans haïtiens et l'occupation américaine d'Haïti, 1915–1930*, Kethly Millet argues that the occupation strengthened what had been, as she puts it, "the unsteady governmental hold on the peasant world."[8] Other analysts have emphasized the ways in which the occupation weakened regional institutions and local economies, reinforcing Haiti's political, military, and socioeconomic centralization in Port-au-Prince.[9] Millet's work points to the corollary effect of this centralization: namely, how U.S. military presence and policy in Haiti heightened state intervention in rural peasant life, particularly through legal means.[10] One of the most striking features of the occupation's administration is that as much as U.S. control in Haiti was guaranteed by the imposition of martial law, press censorship, and efforts to alter the country's legal apparatus, it was perhaps even more pervasively effected through the enforcement of selected Haitian laws, with opportunistic disregard for customary legal practice.

The U.S. military imposition of the *kòve* (French *corvée*, or forced-labor crew) for road construction across central and northern Haiti in 1917–1918 was the most prominent and, in many ways, disastrous example of the latter. However, its revival was relatively short-lived in comparison with that of other customarily modified or neglected laws. Among those singled out for enforcement over the course of the occupation were articles 405–407 of the Code Pénal prohibiting *les sortilèges* and understood by U.S. military officials to target the popular practice of *le vaudoux*, or, as Anglophone foreigners increasingly rendered this word, "voodoo." Such officials readily acknowledged that these laws had not been strictly applied by Haitian authorities. In fact, they made this a point of self-congratulation when defending U.S. military policy on the grounds that it was establishing both "law and order" and "moral decency" in Haiti.

My analysis here will focus, to begin with, on why the application of this particular section of the Code Pénal was so prioritized by the U.S. military regime, especially at the beginning of the occupation. This question is particularly illuminated by the 1921–1922 U.S. Senate inquiry into reports of atrocities committed by U.S. marines in suppressing popular insurgency in Haiti and the Dominican Republic.[11] The testimony of military officials during these hearings reveals the close association U.S. military personnel in Haiti drew between popular rebellion and "native sorcery," while also suggesting the effect that the marines' assumptions about "voodoo" had on the forms that counterinsurgency took.

The second part of the chapter considers the effects of this penal regime, both materially and otherwise, over the course of the occupation's later years. If Vodouizan developed tactics to resist and evade repression of their ritual practices, they also sometimes insisted that marines apply article 405 in ways consistent with popular consensus about the just object of these laws (malicious magic), but antithetical to U.S. military rationales for enforcing them. Elite Haitian opponents of the occupation, on the other hand, at times accused U.S. military forces of "promoting" prohibited ritual practices through their policies in order to denigrate the reputation of the country abroad. I analyze the multiple senses in which this latter charge can be understood to be true, not in spite of marine enforcement of the law against *sortilèges* but rather, in some

sense, because of it. This involves analyzing how the campaign against
"voodoo" played a key role in the construction, proliferation, and com-
moditized circulation of imperial images of Haitian ritualism during and
after the occupation. I conclude by considering to what extent the regime against *les sortilèges*, in the context of the other profound socioeconomic disruptions produced by the occupation, may have intensified
local rumors of supernatural aggression in particularly impacted parts of
the country.

PART I

"My First Real Experience Running Part of Another Man's Country"
The marines' application of customarily disregarded laws was enabled by
the U.S. military's decision to dissolve the Haitian army, dismantle local
structures of law enforcement, and take over rural and urban policing
across Haiti through the newly formed Gendarmerie d'Haïti in 1916. The
creation of this force was written into the 1915 Haitian-American Treaty
legalizing the occupation, article 10 of which prescribed that the Haitian
government organize "without delay an efficient constabulary, urban and
rural, composed of native Haitians."[12] The gendarmerie assumed military
and police functions throughout Haiti in February 1916, under the command of Lieutenant Colonel Smedley Butler. With the abrogation of existing Haitian municipal and rural police structures in early July of that
same year, the 1,300-member gendarme force, officered by 115 U.S. marines, took over the policing of the entire country.[13]

From its inception, the gendarmerie was characterized by what seemed
to critical commentators, Haitian and American alike, to be a troubling
ambiguity of identity. On the one hand, the gendarmerie supplanted the
existing law-enforcement apparatus and served the function of a civil
force, as prescribed in the 1915 treaty; on the other hand, it was structured
and trained along military lines and was commanded by U.S. marine officers. Emily Greene Balch, editor of *Occupied Haiti*, a volume of critical
essays on the occupation published in New York in 1927, took note of the
frequency with which "one meets the complaint in Haiti that the Americans are training not police, but soldiers."[14] The force's military nature
and profile were officially sanctioned in 1928, when, as the gendarmerie
historian James McCrocklin explains, "the new and more descriptive
title, 'Garde d'Haïti,' was conferred on the organization after agreement
between the Haitian and American Governments."[15]

As officers of the gendarmerie, marines were posted throughout the
country in what U.S. military officials, for administrative and strategic

purposes, classified as the departments of Port-au-Prince in the west, Cap-Haïtien in the north, and Les Cayes in the southwest peninsula. To these were added in 1922 the central department, comprising the districts of Hinche, Las Cahobas, and Belladère (areas formerly administered as part of the military department of the north).[16] Each department was commanded by a colonel and subdivided into several territorial districts commanded by gendarmerie captains; those districts were in turn broken down into three to five subdistricts, each commanded by a gendarmerie lieutenant; each subdistrict was made up of several remote outposts commanded, for the most part, by noncommissioned marines.[17] Haitians who enlisted in the gendarmerie were initially provided some instruction in their local districts and then transferred, according to policy, to posts well outside their home districts to serve under American gendarmerie officers at each level of the chain of command.[18] Most of these recruits came from the peasantry and urban poor. Ranked as privates, they were paid $10 per month and a daily ration allowance for food. As the occupation went on, a very few of these gendarmes (later called *gardes*) were promoted to levels of command as corporals, sergeants, and first sergeants.[19] In 1922 there were five Haitian officers in the entire gendarmerie force; their ranks grew slightly that year with the graduation of the first class of the country's newly established military school. In 1927, at the moment when American gendarmerie officials began a more concerted program of "indigenization" of the force's middle ranks, Haitians still only accounted for 25 percent of the total corps of officers.[20]

Throughout the occupation, then, the vast majority of these posts were commanded by marine officers and noncommissioned enlisted men, who, as gendarmerie officers, were elevated in status by one rank and issued two salaries: one from the Haitian government, and one from the U.S. Marine Corps.[21] At the time there was much commentary, both complimentary and critical, in U.S. writing on the reach of these officers' powers in the local areas they oversaw as civil-military administrators. Their functions were expanded in 1917, when U.S. military officials, through the client government of President Sudre Dartiguenave, endowed gendarmerie officers with advisory authority in the commune in which they were stationed. Thus, beyond counterinsurgent operations and general law-enforcement duties, and in spite of what must have been, in most cases, considerable linguistic difficulty, American commanders thereafter had the right and responsibility to supervise local government, particularly its fiscal administration. As "communal advisers," these officers sat in on meetings of the communal board, possessed the deciding voice in questions of budgetary allocations, and audited the commune's books on a monthly basis.[22] Frederic May Wise, who was stationed as an officer in the southwestern peninsular city of Jérémie early in the occupation, said of the experience: "This was my first real experience running part of another man's country. I'd had a little taste of it at Sancti Spiritus in Cuba, during the second Intervention, but in Cuba we didn't have the absolute authority we had here. It was a liberal education."[23]

Such statements by former U.S. gendarmerie officers on the novelty of virtually unlimited power were, of course, implicitly racialized and gendered. They reprised the rhetoric of the Haitian need for democratic "tutelage" that served as the preeminent U.S. official justification for the occupation and its prolongation over nineteen years.[24] Wise wrote on becoming commander of the entire gendarmerie force in 1919, "I knew that black troops had always fought well when they had a white officer to lead them."[25] Such logic, which permeated and structured every aspect and level of the occupation's administration, ensured the virtual exclusion of Haitians from the gendarmerie's upper chain of command, with the inevitable consequence that the majority of local offices of the newly created position of "communal adviser" would be filled by enlisted marines. This, in effect, replicated the occupation on a miniature scale in every locality.

Indeed, Emily Balch notes that communal advisors stationed at remote posts were supposed to act as representatives of the occupation's different departments or treaty services (customs receiver, public works, public health), in addition to their military and police duties as officers in the gendarmerie. She reported of her own investigative travels in Haiti: "Americans who are simple enlisted men are sometimes elevated to these positions of supreme local authority, demanding to say the least many sided competence, tact, and good feeling. . . . It seems to be a marvel that these young marines, recruited as they are, with very commonly the extreme Southern attitude towards negroes [sic], trained as they are, isolated in black villages, do as well as they do, but this does not mean that it is a proper system!"[26] James Weldon Johnson wrote more strongly against the overreaching authority of the gendarmerie officers in local settings: "Many of these men are rough, uncouth, and uneducated, and a great number from the South, are violently steeped in color prejudice. They direct all policing of city and town. It falls to them, ignorant of Haitian ways and language, to enforce every minor police regulation. Needless to say, this is a grave source of continued irritation."[27]

I want to connect Johnson's concern over American officers applying "every minor police regulation," outside of an understanding of "Haitian ways" or custom, with Kethly Millet's insight that such legal enforcement tightened what had been "the unsteady governmental hold on the peasant world." In dismantling long-standing structures of law enforcement, the occupation also disrupted the diffuse economy of local "customary law," which sometimes worked in the interest of the peasantry and urban poor. President Fabre Nicolas Geffrard's 1864 Code Rural, which remained in effect during the occupation, carried over most of the repressive provisions of the Code Rural originally promulgated under Boyer in 1826. Yet, many of its articles, in practice, had either never been strictly enforced, or had fallen into disuse on account of the strength of local opposition, customary precedent, and everyday practice against them.

That the rigorous enforcement of selected Haitian laws contributed greatly to peasant struggles under—and against—the occupation thus stemmed not only from the often repressive and abusive nature of their application, but primarily from the fact that these statutes had not been consistently or strictly applied under Haitian authority. Tax collection was a case in point. U.S. officials insisted upon the exact payment of all applicable agrarian taxes to government authorities; but "the small farmer had developed a network of loopholes that the occupier was bent on dismantling," Millet writes, whether "family relations, false declarations, corruption on the part of local functionaries, [or] falsification of the instruments of measurement."[28] Thus, Michel-Rolph Trouillot's argument that the Haitian peasantry and lower classes were taxed more heavily during the occupation than they had ever been before is borne out in part with regard to increased import and export duties during this period and the imposition in 1928 of a tax on the production of alcohol that was particularly burdensome for small sugarcane farmers and distillers.[29] Also, however, as U.S. gendarmerie officers became tax collectors in the different communes in which they were stationed throughout the country, the economy of tolerated and necessary illegalities was suspended; those who refused or were unable to pay their taxes were penalized through the confiscation of livestock and other property.[30] Millet makes the crucial point that as "the vise tightened around the peasant," the "occupier seemed not to be worried about their reaction. . . . He could apply in all its rigor the agrarian policy installed by the national bourgeoisie who dared not always exploit it fully for fear of losing power; and affirm that all was well since the streets were clean, the market prosperous, and the communal revenues rising."[31]

The kòve

In a summary report on the occupation issued just prior to the marines' withdrawal from Haiti in 1934, Major Franklin A. Hart wrote: "Although possessed of excellent laws, based on the *Code Napoléon* of

France, Haiti possessed no means of enforcing them."[32] Marines' self-congratulation about enforcing customarily disregarded laws drew upon paternalist rhetorics of order and clean-up that underwrote U.S. military interventions elsewhere in the Caribbean, Latin America, the Pacific, and beyond. Yet, Dantès Bellegarde, who became a prominent elite opponent of the occupation, argued in a 1929 monograph addressed to U.S. President Herbert Hoover that, in fact, far from establishing the "rule of law," "one of the most disastrous moral consequences of the Occupation is the general scorn for the *law* to which it has given birth. The law, having become a simple 'instrument of rule' made by an absolute power, undone and modified to its liking, no longer imposes any respect: it is only obeyed in order to escape its severe sanctions, decreed and applied by brutal force."[33]

There was considerable opportunism in U.S. military enforcement—or sometimes the nonenforcement—of Haitian laws. The implementation of the *kòve* for road construction across Haiti in 1916–1918 is a particularly salient example of the strategic selectivity that characterized U.S. applications of Haitian law. Although the French word *corvée* did not appear in the 1864 Code Rural then in effect, its principle was delineated by articles 53–65 of that document, which provided for the upkeep and repair of stretches of communal roads by a rotation of residents from the rural sections(s) that the roads crossed.[34] During the late nineteenth and early twentieth centuries, calls for legal reform in Haiti spotlighted these provisions as symptomatic of the injustices that pervaded the Code Rural, which many observers viewed as a special set of laws applying only to the peasantry.[35] Although the *kòve* law had been enforced intermittently during the nineteenth century, by the early 1900s it seems to have fallen into disuse in many parts of the country, on account of its unpopularity among those it conscripted.[36]

In 1916, when Major Smedley Butler, the American commander of the newly formed Haitian gendarmerie, determined that the construction and repair of a network of roads across Haiti was necessary for military control of the country, he found articles 53–65 of the Code Rural to be a kind of legal *prêt-à-porter*.[37] Although U.S. officials credited this massive project with advancing overland communication and connecting markets, the routes they prioritized reflected the military imperatives driving it: large farming areas were left outside of the network. The centerpiece of the project was the creation of a passable road between Port-au-Prince and Cap-Haïtien, completed in December 1917.[38] Franklin D. Roosevelt, who was then the assistant secretary of the U.S. Navy, sent a letter congratulating Butler on this feat, to which the marine officer replied in a letter of 27 December 1917, "It would not do to ask too many questions as to how we accomplish this work."[39]

Gaillard makes the point that if the enforcement of the *kòve* in 1917–1918 was the most salient example of how U.S. military officials selectively and opportunistically adopted obsolete Haitian laws in order to further the occupation, it was also representative of the way in which, as he puts it, some laws were "denatured" and others circumvented in the process.[40] For example, the Code Rural provided only for the repair and upkeep of existing routes, not for the construction of new roads using conscripted labor. Such violations of the letter of a law that had, in any case, long fallen into customary disuse "seemed not, at the start and among 'people of means,' to have shocked anyone"; it was not disturbing, at first, to most of the elite, "if the 'progress' of the nation required an aggravation of [the peasant's] servitude."[41]

The U.S. officers of the Haitian gendarmerie stationed in each region dictated quotas for "recruiting" laborers that Haitian gendarmes were expected to meet. When peasants resisted conscription, they were forcibly taken from their homes at night, and from the fields they tended during the day. Gaillard notes that such abductions generated some of the first objections in the elite press, but more in defense of the rights of Haitian plantation owners than those of the laborers.[42] Rather than working in their own locality for the period of four days prescribed by law, some were made to labor for months at a time in distant districts. In his testimony to the Senate Committee, Lieutenant Colonel Alexander Williams, who succeeded Butler as commander of the Haitian gendarmerie in May 1918, acknowledged cases of entire work crews—the personnel of a brickyard, the crew of a small fishing schooner—being summarily "collected" for labor crews.[43] That such conscriptions were not restricted to the countryside is documented by the brief arrest in July 1918 of the medical doctor, statesman, and pioneer ethnologist Jean Price-Mars in Pétionville, who was returning home on horseback after making house calls on the outskirts of the city.[44]

Conscripted workers were roped together to travel to and from the *kòve* camps, and they worked under armed guard. Those who attempted to escape were fired upon and, according to the testimony of marines involved, many were killed.[45] Witnesses and former laborers described the camp compounds themselves as prisons. Kethly Millet notes that during the construction of the road between Gonaïves and Cap-Haïtien, workers at the particularly infamous Chalbert camp (housing at one time nearly 5,500 laborers) died "at a rate of five per day, whether by epidemics, malnutrition, or maltreatment."[46] James Weldon Johnson and other occupation opponents argued that the *kòve* represented the temporary enslavement of those it subjugated: "The Occupation seized men wherever it could find them, and no able-bodied Haitian was safe from such raids, which most closely resembled the African slave raids of past centuries. And slavery it was—though temporary."[47] Of course, such analogies were not at all lost on Haitian rural populations, particularly in the central and northern regions of the country where the impact of the *kòve* was felt most strongly and where the insurgency after 1918 was concentrated. When Gaillard asked one of his informants from this generation, Stéphen Gautier, why he insisted on calling the *kòve* slavery, Gautier replied: "First, the work is not paid. Second, you work with your back to the sun. . . . Third, this work does not have an end; you can only leave if you are sick. Fourth, you ate badly, *mayi moulin* and *poi congo*. Fifth, you sleep in prison or at the work site. Six, if you try to save yourself the gendarmes shoot you. So, what is that? Is it not slavery?"[48]

The comparison of the *kòve* to slavery became a rallying cry for popular armed resistance. Officially abolished in August 1918 after months of protest, the *kòve* was illegally continued in the Maïssade-Hinche district in central Haiti for several months beyond that date.[49] This was under the direction of Major Clarke Wells, who was later accused of, but never court-martialed for, ordering or condoning the widespread summary execution of Haitian prisoners without trial during what became known in U.S. military parlance as the "*caco* war."[50] Prior to the U.S. intervention, *kako* (in Kreyòl orthography) was the term used in Haiti to refer to soldiers who sold their services to presidential aspirants; during the occupation, this word was used interchangeably by U.S. military officials and marines with the imperial term "bandit" to refer to insurgents.[51] In his statement to the Senate committee, the Baptist field secretary and former missionary to Haiti Reverend L. Ton Evans testified regarding the popular perception of the *kòve* as well as what he viewed as its effects: "The forced and slavish labor on the roads, and catching, roping, brutal treatment, and killing of those who tried to escape, not merely doubled, trebled, and multiplied many folds the number and strength of the cacos by way of recruits, but it was, in my opinion, the clenching nail and proof positive at last not simply that Americans took all their lands but had come there to bring them all back to slavery with all its horrors."[52] Bearing out James Weldon Johnson's trenchant observation in 1920 that "the military Occupation has made and continues to make military Occupation necessary," a project originally instituted by military officials to secure the "pacification" of the country through the creation of a system of passable roads became the most immediate catalyst for the mobilization of armed rebellion.[53]

Law and Labor

The institution of the *kòve* was the most prominent and widely publicized case of marines in Haiti selectively and opportunistically deploying laws toward military ends in disregard of their customary modification or obsolescence. However, the *kòve* generated such massive opposition across rural Haiti, culminating in armed insurgency, that its imposition was relatively short-lived. Early on, marines instrumentalized a number of other customarily disregarded laws that remained a legal means of repression and object of peasant resistance over the entire course of the occupation.

In 1916 U.S. gendarmerie officers stationed at posts across the country were provided an English-language version of the Haitian Code Rural, translated by Captain R. S. Hooker. This edition was most notable for its addenda. A complete English edition of the Haitian Code Pénal would not be completed and distributed to U.S. officers in Haiti until 1922, but three of its sections were translated and compiled with the 1916 Code Rural.[54] These were the articles prohibiting vagrancy, poisoning to produce a deathlike state, and *les sortilèges*. They had been revised and published together in the 1864 Code Pénal and had also been included as an annex to certain editions of the Code Rural since then; yet it is notable that, out of the 413 articles that made up Haitian penal law at that time, it was these three alone that were translated and included in the only legal handbook distributed to U.S. forces in Haiti during the first seven years of the occupation.

In attempting to account for the prioritization of these laws, one might begin by considering their potential utility for the "ends" of occupation, which, though seldom coherently formulated as such, might be understood in the broadest strokes as securing U.S. military and financial control of Haiti.[55] Certainly, the statute prohibiting vagrancy was serviceable for marines, who, facing insurgency throughout the interior early on in the occupation, sought to limit the free mobility of peasants. However, like its analogs among laws targeting African Americans in the postbellum U.S. South, the Haitian law against vagrancy was also enforced by marines in order to exact labor.[56] Posted between 1925 and 1929 as resident subdistrict commander of the island of La Gonâve, Faustin Wirkus became an international celebrity after W. B. Seabrook depicted him in his travelogue *The Magic Island* (1929) as "the white king of La Gonâve."[57] In 1931 Wirkus published a coauthored account of his experiences as a marine in Haiti. One chapter, called "Vagabond Labor," described how, with the cooperation of the rural police and a *juge de paix* in La Gonâve, he established a virtually unlimited "reserve of labor at hand in the different sections of the island" through opportunistic enforcement of the law against vagrancy.[58]

According to marine reports and oral historical accounts, the law against *les sortilèges* was applied to compel peasant labor as well. As roughly translated by Captain Hooker, this statute read:

ART. 405. All persons practicing "ouangas," "caprelatas," "vaudoux," "donpedre," "macandals," and other sorceries, will be punished with imprisonment of from three to six months, and a fine of from sixty to one hundred and fifty gourdes, adjudged by an ordinary police court; in case of a second ofense [sic], imprisonment of from six months to two years and a fine of from three hundred to one thousand gourdes, adjudged by the Court of Correction, without prejudice to the most severe sentences they may have incurred, through offenses or crimes commited [sic] by them in preparing or accomplishing their sorceries.

All danse [sic] and other practices of any kind likely to foster in the people a spirit of fetishism and superstition, will be considered sorceries and will receive the same punishments.

ART. 406. People who have as a trade fortune telling, divining, foretelling, explaining dreams, or telling fortunes with cards, will be punished by imprisonment of not less than two months or more than six months, and a fine of from one hundred to five hundred gourdes.

In addition, after the expiration of their sentences, they will be placed under the surveillance of the police, on account of their conviction, if for no other reason.

ART. 407. Instruments, utensils and costumes, serving or destined to serve at the rites covered in the two preceeding [sic] articles, will be seized and confiscated for burning or destruction.[59]

Étienne Germain, whose father had been an *oungan* in the area of Tabarre, just outside of Port-au-Prince, told me in a 1997 interview that he had heard that one of the reasons marines imprisoned those who "played the drums" was because they "wanted Haitians to work."[60] Wirkus's memoir corroborates Germain's account. Notably, he writes that it was a Haitian *juge de paix* in the central town of Petite Rivière who first proposed the arrangement to him in the early 1920s, before he was posted to La Gonâve.[61] In their discussion of the insufficiency of public funds for the construction of a subdistrict headquarters, the *juge de paix* informed him that there was to be "a small voodoo ceremony" that night at the home of a local stonemason named Cambon. If Wirkus raided the ceremony and brought "'Cambon and his two helpers . . . before me in the morning for indulging in forbidden practices, why should I not sentence them to six months at hard labor under your direction?'"[62] In the end, this was how the gendarmerie headquarters at Petite Rivière were built. Wirkus notes that he would have employed the same scheme for construction projects on La Gonâve, save for the reluctance of the local *juge de paix* to apply it. In a sense, the prohibition against *sortilèges* was the most effective penal law to enforce to such ends. Read as targeting family- and temple-based religious ritual, and applied by foreigners who, as Millet noted, had little concern for the political consequences of its strict enforcement, this statute could incriminate much of the rural Haitian population at one time or another.

"Voudauxism Was Rampant"

However, the enforcement of labor for military projects was not the only, or even the most significant reason why this law was prioritized by marine authorities in Haiti. Testifying during the U.S. Senate hearings in November 1921, General Eli Cole was asked to describe what factors had justified the landing of marine forces in Haiti on 28 July 1915. He replied with a list of internal conditions prevailing in Haiti on the eve of the invasion that compelled U.S. intervention, the penultimate of which was: "Voudauxism was rampant."[63] This is by no means the only moment over the course of the nearly two thousand pages of testimony and reports on the occupation when the practice of "voudauxism" (or, increasingly, "voodooism" or "voodoo") is officially invoked to serve as a kind of ultimate symptom of Haitian "disorder," in need of American military "cleaning up"—a metaphor literalized in sanitary code regulations and applied much more broadly.[64] However, Cole's testimony is probably the most clear-cut instance of this sign being marshaled to justify the military invasion and occupation of Haiti in moral terms. Asked what Washington's "object" had been in landing forces in Haiti in 1915, Cole replied: "Well, my own opinion is that its objects or object was to eliminate a state of chaos, and replace it by a condition wherein the Negro Republic of Haiti could continue to exist as an independent State and exercise its own functions of government. In other words, I believe it had a moral duty to clean that place up and establish decency down there, because it did not exist."[65]

The oxymoronic logic of the United States safeguarding Haiti's independence—or as James Weldon Johnson put it, "self-determining Haiti"—through military occupation depended for its coherence and force on the paternalistic premise of a "moral mission," which, I would argue, relied, in turn, on certain fictions of Haitian ritualism. During the Senate hearings, marine pursuit and penalization of practitioners of the "voodoo cult" were cited as exemplary ways in which the occupation was upholding the rule of law and establishing "order" in Haiti. As noted above, this rhetoric was often couched in terms of the failure or reluctance of Haitian authorities to enforce the prohibitions prescribed by articles 405–407 of the Code Pénal. In the Senate committee hearings in 1921, Walter Bruce Howe, counsel for the committee of senators, asked General Littleton Waller, "Did the practice of voodoo have any influence in the course of events down there during the occupation, or was it a thing to be reckoned with?" Waller replied: "It is against the Haitian law, this practice, but they never enforced the law. We did, and we broke up all their meetings, seized all their drums, etc., and wherever a voodoo drum was heard we immediately got on the trail and captured it, and broke it up, as far as we could."[66] The general mistook the implication of the question, perhaps strategically, so that rather than addressing what influence "voodoo" was having on the course of the occupation, he testified instead to what impact the occupation was having on the practice of "voodoo." The reversal allowed him to continue his narration of the ameliorative effects of American "uplift" in Haiti, in which marine enforcement of the official Haitian prohibition against "voodoo" became that narrative's culminating term. Howe, undeterred, pursued his initial question through a succession of others:

MR. HOWE: What was the voodoo drum used for, in connection with what?

GEN. WALLER: In calling them to these meetings, in the first place, and also in the dances that they had. They used three or four or five drums. Some of the drums were 5 feet high, and as big around. It is a wooden log, hollowed out, with a cowhide over the top.

MR. HOWE: What is voodoo?

GEN. WALLER: It is very difficult to say exactly what it is. It comes really from the West Coast of Africa originally.

MR. HOWE: Of what does it consist?

GEN. WALLER: There it consists in the belief that human sacrifice was a cure for all evils, but I do not think that human sacrifice had been resorted to in Haiti for some years, but they do sacrifice the goat and sheep, and they do it in a very cruel way.

MR. HOWE: In general, with respect to the material side of life down there, what was the effort of the American occupation?

GEN. WALLER: Uplifting in every direction. That was our attitude toward them.[67]

These questions recur in different configurations and registers over the course of the Senate hearings. What is voodoo? Of what does it consist?

How prevalent is it in Haiti? What is the function of the drum? They draw attention to the fact that much of the military and official testimony on "voodoo" during the hearings was given at the behest of Senate committee members (or their counsel) who seemed determined to establish a positive knowledge about "its" practice through the persistent questioning of those, as one marine later put it, "sworn to suppress [it]."[68]

Waller's responses were consistent with the testimony of his colleagues as well as a wellspring of colonial folklore, particularly centering, since the publication of Spenser St. John's *Hayti, or The Black Republic*, on tales of human sacrifice and ritual anthropophagy.[69] Of course, the imperial ascription of cannibalism to the Caribbean has a much longer history; the two words, in fact, have a common etymological root in the name Carib. Peter Hulme has argued that the cannibalism attributed to Amerindians who resisted Spanish conquest in the late fifteenth- and sixteenth-century Caribbean might better be understood as a metaphor for the engulfment by the colonial power that they were experiencing.[70] Several centuries later, Haitians who mounted armed resistance to U.S. military and economic encompassment were likewise suspected of cannibalism, which, thanks to St. John and his successors, was now figured in imperial texts not simply as a tactic of "savage warfare," but also a sometime rite of "voodooism."

My first concern is what such ideologies meant for the regime of repression to which Haitian peasants were subjected under U.S. military control between 1915 and 1934, and particularly during the uprisings of 1918–1920, when marines drew a strong connection between popular insurgency and "native sorcery." Unquestionably, popular spiritual beliefs, magical works, and religious leadership and organization were a key locus and force of peasant opposition during the occupation. This is a point of consensus among marine accounts, anti-imperial historiography, and Haitian popular memory of the occupation. Because marine chroniclers were often so fixated on constructing a relationship between sorcery and insurgency, their texts, read against the grain, have represented a key, if historically complicated, source of documentation for scholars attempting to reconstruct the role that such beliefs and practices played in impelling popular armed resistance against the occupants.[71] Military reports and marine accounts consistently cite the prestige of insurgent leaders, such as Benoît Batraville, who were reputed to be *oungan*, and the courage of rebels who considered themselves invulnerable owing to the powers of protective *pwen*—concentrations of magical energy in the form of words, gestures, herbs, or talismans.[72] Almost all of the marine accounts speculate that insurgents used drum rhythms for communication, as when Wirkus, pursuing a group of rebels near the gendarmerie base at Perodin, describes having heard drumming that was "plainly a signal to another force on another mountain."[73] They also detail the discovery of apparent magical works against the U.S. military regime and their Haitian collaborators.[74]

U.S. military identification of the 1918–1920 rebellion with popular magicoreligious practice and organization, then, was not necessarily misplaced. The question is rather how imperial fantasies about "voodoo" shaped the enforcement of the Haitian Code Pénal articles against *sortilèges* and became an alibi for the brutal forms that the counterinsurgency took. The Senate hearings are a particularly important site in which to examine the force of such constructions and associations, given that, over their course, a recurrent slippage took place in the object under official inquiry. The committee, which was convened to investigate reports of atrocities committed by marines against Haitians, repeatedly turned to stories of Haitian atrocities committed against marines. At the center of these lay mythologies of ritual cannibalism, presumed to be a sacrament of "voodoo" worship. This turnaround produced dramatic shifts in testimony during the hearings, when the sober formulaicism of questions and responses regarding marine policy and conduct in Haiti gave way to hearsay, rumor, speculation, and innuendo in which "voodoo priests" were figured as a primary force behind Haitian insurgency.

Facticity and Fantasy

Nowhere is this shift in the tone of the hearings more striking than in the testimony of General George Barnett, who played a precipitous, if inadvertent, role in the unfolding of events leading up to the convening of the Senate inquiry. Accounts of marine brutality against Haitian insurgents, prisoners, and civilians had been circulating in the opposition press for months and came to national attention in the fall of 1920 with the disclosure of a "personal and confidential" letter, dated 2 October 1919, from Barnett, who was then major general commandant of the Marine Corps, to John Russell, the brigade commander in Port-au-Prince, ordering the immediate cessation of the "practically indiscriminate killing of natives," which, Barnett had cause to believe, had been "[going] on for some time."[75] Barnett's alarm, as he related during his testimony before the Senate committee two years later, was triggered by his reading of the transcript of the court-martial of Private Walter Johnson, one of two marines (the other was Private John McQuilkin Jr.) charged with executing Haitian prisoners at Croix-des-Bouquets, northeast of Port-au-Prince, upon the order of a superior, Lieutenant Louis A. Brokaw. According to military records, two Haitian prisoners had been forced to dig their own graves, were ordered to stand alongside them, and were shot by a firing squad that included Johnson and McQuilkin. The transcript of the court-martial reflected that Lieutenant F. L. Spear, serving as counsel for John-son, had defended his client on the grounds that the private had simply been following orders and "general custom." In fact, Spear disclosed, he himself had "seen many similar cases of executions of that kind" while serving as second-in-command of a marine detachment near Mirebalais, in a region then considered "a trouble center for bandits."[76]

Barnett's letter to Russell, written in the strongest language and charac-terizing the case as "the most startling thing of its kind that has ever taken place in the Marine Corps," was leaked to the press in October 1920 and widely exploited by the Republican presidential candidate, Warren G. Harding, who had already made the occupation of Haiti an election issue against the incumbent, Woodrow Wilson.[77] By this time Barnett had been dismissed as major general commandant of the Marine Corps, and a Haiti veteran, John A. Lejeune, was appointed in his place. What had been widespread mainstream journalistic indifference toward, if not endorse-ment of, the military occupations of Haiti and the Dominican Republic during World War I shifted with the politicization of reported condi-tions, especially in Haiti, during the 1920 presidential campaign.[78] The *Nation*, a center of oppositional coverage through the writings of James Weldon Johnson, Herbert Seligmann, and Ernest Gruening, the manag-ing editor, editorialized that September: "Haiti is getting into the news-paper headlines at last." The magazine renewed its call for a bipartisan congressional investigation.[79]

Shortly after Barnett's letter was publicized, the secretary of the Navy, Josephus Daniels, dispatched a naval court of inquiry to Haiti headed by Admiral Henry Mayo to investigate the allegations. When the Depart-ment of the Navy released strategically selected portions of the testimony several months later, readers of major U.S. newspapers might have been excused for understanding the Mayo inquiry to have been an investigation into alleged Haitian atrocities against U.S. marines, rather than the other way around.[80] As it was, the inquiry resulted in the disclosure of "two un-justifiable homicides" and "16 other serious acts of violence" committed by marines in which disciplinary action had already been taken, and the culminating report stressed that these ought not be given "any consid-erable weight in forming a conclusion as to the general conduct of such personnel."[81] In spite of extensive testimony gathered in earlier investi-gations about summary executions of Haitian prisoners in the Hinche-Maïssade region between 1918 and 1920, including by marines who them-selves admitted to killing prisoners, the report concluded that the orders to court-martial those implicated should be withdrawn because there was insufficient evidence to prosecute them.[82] Barnett was indirectly censured in the report, which found that there had been "no proper grounds" for his widely publicized alarm over the "practically indiscriminate killing of natives" in Haiti.[83]

Given this official reprimand and his dismissal from the rank of major general commandant in June 1920, Barnett was a particularly defensive witness during the Senate hearings, which convened a year later. Questioned by the committee at length about the extent and nature of the abuses that had been reported in Haiti, including the summary execution of prisoners, attacks on private citizens, the high Haitian casualty statistics from marine offensives against insurgents, and mistreatment of workers under the *kòve*, Barnett disclaimed firsthand knowledge of any of the allegations. Throughout his testimony, he seemed most intent on clearing his name vis-à-vis the Mayo inquiry, and at one point, late in the day, he protested the "faulty wording of their report": "It was worded so badly that everybody misunderstood it. I do not say a few people, but I say that everybody misunderstood it, and thought it was a severe censure of me."[84]

It was at this moment, that Senator William King, Democrat of Utah, who had been either silent or absent for much of the proceedings that afternoon, made a startling intervention. Taking advantage of a momentary pause in the testimony as Ernest Angell, counsel for the coalition of Haitian and American opposition groups participating in the hearings (the Haiti–Santo Domingo Independence Society, the NAACP, and the Union Patriotique d'Haïti), rifled through his notes, King announced that he "would like to ask a question": "When I was in Haiti a little over a year ago I was told that a number of marines had been butchered, and their bodies had been devoured, in part at least, by the natives. Did you, when you went down there, learn anything of that?" Barnett responded: "I did not. I heard nothing up to the time I left. I do know that there was a report that two American engineers down there were tied up to trees and hacked to pieces by the natives." What is striking about the exchange that follows is not merely the single-mindedness of King's pursuit of testimony from Barnett on this subject, but also that Barnett's professed ignorance of such cases seems irrelevant to King's desire to hear them narrated. Thus, as he pressed on with this line of questioning, King increasingly took over the subject position of witness, providing the testimony he was attempting to elicit from Barnett: "This was told me by the natives as well as by Americans, that one marine in particular had his head cut off, and his skull had been used in some of their incantations there; did you hear of that?" Barnett replied, "I did not hear of it," then added more cooperatively, "but I can well understand it might be true." King continued: "I was told also that there were a number of natives in the prison at Port-au-Prince— possibly in some other city, I am not sure which—awaiting trial for the butchery of one or more little children, whose blood was necessary in their rituals, in their pagan religious ceremonials." Barnett, his testimony now fully subsumed by the senator, replied, "Yes." Then King, as if catching himself in his own excess, asked: "Did you learn what became of those natives that were held awaiting trial?" To this Barnett responded, "No, sir; I did not; I have no report on that subject at all."[85]

How do we understand this exchange, which reverses the object of official inquiry from allegations of the "practically indiscriminate killing" of Haitians by marines to stories of the "butchery" of marines and children by Haitians, presumed to be a function of "incantations" and "pagan religious ceremonials"? It would not pay to be too quick to explain King's line of questioning in terms of the ultimate utility of such charges for official propaganda in defense of the occupation. Such an explanation might be problematized, to begin with, by the fact that King was a persistent critic of the occupation and probably its strongest and most vocal opponent in Congress. Well-known for his anti-imperialist stance, King drafted an amendment to a military appropriations bill in 1922 stipulating that no further support be provided to maintain marine forces in Haiti, the Dominican Republic, or Nicaragua.[86] The motion was defeated forty-three to nine, but King continued his public criticism of U.S. policy and military presence in Haiti throughout the 1920s, and in a much-publicized incident in 1927 was barred from entering Haiti by client president Louis Borno on account of his record of opposition to the occupation.[87]

Such biographical information might begin to complicate any simple explanation of King's questioning of Barnett on the grounds that it served official justificatory propaganda about the United States' "civilizing mission" in Haiti. There is an excessive and gratuitous quality to King's stories, a will to have them narrated that exposes the insufficiency of arguments for the pure instrumentality of such images in the service of imperial power. The exchange between King and Barnett spotlights how fantasies of Haitian ritualism became a vortex of imperial fear and fascination early in the occupation, readily displacing the "atrocity" under official investigation during the hearings from marine abuses in Haiti, discussed under the regime of facticity, to stories of "voodoo"-inspired mutilation and anthropophagy. An investigation by Major General Commandant John Lejeune and Brigadier General Smedley Butler just prior to the Mayo inquiry in October 1920 reported allegations of abuses by marines in Hinche as horrific as the stories that King recounted during the hearings. For example, an ex-marine testified that another member of the force claimed he and a superior officer had crucified people; a gendarme reported that he had witnessed an American lieutenant summarily execute prisoners by machine gun and electrocute another prisoner by attaching him to a radio plant; a priest who was sympathetic to the occupation reported that a captain had the skeleton of a onetime prisoner hanging in his house.[88] Such stories were not subject to repeated telling during the subsequent Senate inquiry; in fact, they seem not to have been narrated at all during the hearings or in any of the subsequent marine memoirs of these years of the occupation. In contrast, the killing and possible mutilation of two marines by rebels in November 1919 and April 1920 became the space for extravagant fabulation during the hearings and in this literature about the insurgency's being fired by "voodoo," with ritual mutilation figured as both a high rite of that "cult" and a tactic of "savage warfare."[89]

If the summary executions and other abuses against Haitians uncovered in these investigations could be ultimately dismissed as the isolated misdeeds of a small number of individual malefactors, the atrocities allegedly committed against these marines by Haitian insurgents were not treated in the same way. Rather than figured as "isolated" and "exceptional," such cases were taken, partly because of their presumed connection to "voodoo," as an extreme sign of a more generalizable racial atavism.

What was the relation of imperial myths about "voodoo" to the "barbarism," as the Reverend L. Ton Evans put it in his testimony before the Senate committee, of the marines' efforts to "pacify" Haitian rebels when it seemed at times, particularly during the insurgent rebellion of 1918–1920, that marines mimetically enacted the violence that they attributed to Haitians?[90] In considering that question, it is important to note that according to at least one marine account, the case that eventually brought what General Barnett characterized as the "practically indiscriminate killing of natives" in Haiti to widespread public consciousness was the summary execution of two Haitian men, one of whom was believed to be an *oungan*, by marines in May 1919.[91] This was the case at the center of Barnett's testimony during the Senate hearings, the specifics of which had been eclipsed by the court-martial argument of Lieutenant Spear, who had attempted to relativize his client's crime by contending that he had just been "following general custom."[92] Frederic May Wise was about to take over as commander of the Haitian gendarmerie from his predecessor, Colonel Alexander Williams, when this court-martial took place on 26 June 1919.[93] In his memoir, Wise recounts that the marine in charge of the gendarmerie post at Croix-des-Bouquets, Lieutenant Louis A. Brokaw, "and two of the three Marines of the telephone detail got drunk with a native one night. They had in jail an old Haitian they had put there, claiming he was a 'Papaloi'—a Voodoo priest. It was supposed to be against the law."[94] According to military records, the two privates, Johnson and McQuilkin, were charged with assaulting Leonard Placide, absence from the station and duty without leave, and "conduct to the prejudice of good order and discipline," obliquely referring to the firing-squad shooting of Placide and the killing of "another native named Destine Jean, a native prisoner."[95] During their trials, Johnson and McQuilkin claimed that when Brokaw ordered them, along with three Haitian gendarmes, to shoot the two prisoners "they, doubting his authority to order such an execution, but fearing to disobey orders, shot 'wide' so as not to kill, and that, seeing the prisoners were still alive, Brokaw with his own pistol shot and killed them."[96] Brokaw was diagnosed with dementia, hospitalized, and discharged from the Marine Corps without being court-martialed. Johnson was found guilty only of the "assault" of Placide. The other charges were "held to be not proved," and he was sentenced to six months' confinement and dishonorable discharge.[97] I have not been able to determine whether McQuilkin was also found guilty, and in fact both of these court-martial files are missing from the record series in which they should appear at the U.S. National Archives, having been pulled, it seems, for the Senate hearings in 1921 and never returned.[98]

The reasons for the imprisonment of Leonard Placide and Destine Jean may not have mattered to the court charged with investigating their executions; nor was this a question or concern for the members of the Senate committee, who were less interested in the particulars of the case than in the possibility that it might be representative.[99] Yet, Wise's disclosure that one of these men had been taken prisoner because he was believed to be an *oungan* cannot be regarded as incidental, in light of the force of rumors about "voodoo" that circulated among marines during the occupation and propelled a campaign against "papaloi" and "mamaloi" that military officials and occupation apologists touted for its severity. As protests of marine tactics in Haiti and the Dominican Republic became louder in the United States, Brigade Commander John H. Russell's son-in-law, J. Dryden Kuser, published a defense of the occupation in the form of a travelogue entitled *Haiti: Its Dawn of Progress after Years in a Night of Revolution* (1921). It included a particularly stark statement about the threat of the "Vaudoux priest" in the context of the insurgency: "It is Vaudouxism . . . which makes more difficult the fighting of the cacos; for Vaudoux priests have, through their hold upon the religious fear of the Vaudouxists,

tremendous power over all their doings. Upon the sounding of a Vaudoux drum the priest can very often do about what he wants with his followers. Probably all of the caco chiefs are Vaudoux priests and thus hold
together bands which, freed from religious scruples, would abandon their
purpose of brigandry."[100] The association of ritual with revolt meant that
oungan, bòkò, "papaloi" (identifications that were used interchangeably by
occupation officials and marines), and *manbo* (also called *mamaloi* by the
same) who were particularly well-known in communities and regions
were targeted for arrest on account of their prestige and influence.[101] Significantly, although there was no testimony given during the Senate hearings implicating Jean and Placide in the insurgency, the final report published on this inquiry in 1922 identifies them as two "Caco prisoners."[102]

"Savage Warfare"

Throughout the Senate hearings, marine misconduct so well documented
in the military record that it could not be refuted was frequently explained
and justified on the grounds that Haitian insurgents practiced "savage
warfare," which warranted the suspension of protocols of "regular" or
"civilized" warfare. This argument received its most sustained elaboration in the testimony of Spear, who, as counsel to Johnson, had argued
for leniency on behalf of his client based on what he characterized as the
unexceptional nature of the charges. Spear was questioned by Ernest Angell about his unwavering sense of justification for orders and actions that
were among those under investigation as atrocities by the Senate committee. Angell probed: "Was it your understanding of the general situation
in Haiti, at the time of the instances referred to, that our forces there were
engaged in regular warfare against the Cacos in the hills?"

MR. SPEAR: Yes.

MR. ANGELL: And that the rules and customs of regular modern warfare
prevailed.

MR. SPEAR: Not entirely.

MR. ANGELL: In what respects did they not prevail?

MR. SPEAR: Well, those Cacos were very savage men, and if they had captured one of our marines they would probably have skinned him alive.

MR. ANGELL: Did you ever know of such circumstances?

MR. SPEAR: No; I never knew of such.

MR. ANGELL: Did you ever hear of any such instances?

MR. SPEAR: It was reported to me that one of the native guides was found
neatly stacked up by the road one morning in pieces this long.

MR. ANGELL: You mean cut into pieces?

MR. SPEAR: Yes; I knew what to expect from them.

MR. ANGELL: That was hearsay, so far as you were concerned?

MR. SPEAR: Yes; of course, I had viewed those Cacos, too, at close range. I knew what kind of men they are.[103]

What stands out here is how the "savagery" attributed to the insurgents becomes the basis, and indeed the imperative, for the "barbarization" of "the rules and customs of regular modern warfare." Michael Taussig has described such displacements as a form of mimesis, "a colonial mirroring of otherness that reflects back onto the colonists the barbarity of their own social relations, but as imputed to the savagery they yearn to colonize."[104] The powers of this "colonial mode of production of reality" are sustained and felt through narration, the telling of stories like those alluded to in the exchange above, which Angell attempts to qualify as "hearsay" and which Spear affirms as such without in any way diminishing his conviction in the truth of their "fictional realities."[105] Smedley Butler's account in his memoir of being terrorized by a group of insurgents while on patrol overnight reads like a case study of the mirroring that Taussig analyzes and, at the same time, suggests how such stories could be dialogically constructed in spaces of colonial and imperial domination: "The cacos tried to chill our hearts by blowing incessantly on their conch shells. They called out to us, and our interpreter explained that they intended to chop us into small pieces when they caught us. . . . At daylight we knocked hell out of them. . . . You never heard such a damned racket. We killed about seventy-five Cacos and the rest took to the bushes. But the Marines went wild after their devilish night and hunted the Cacos down like pigs."[106] The wildness attributed to—and in this case, according to Butler, strategically claimed by—the rebels was enacted by his troops the next morning in a massacre that reproduced the savagery they feared and, as Taussig puts it, fictionalized.

Mary Renda has argued that the paternalist fiction that ideologically underwrote the occupation "could [only] be kept alive if a clear distinction was drawn between the peaceful inhabitants and the bad cacos."[107] As she discusses, however, and according to the testimony and writings of those who served in Haiti, these populations were not readily distinguishable. Accounts of the size and number of the insurgent troops mobilized varied widely, ranging by marine estimates from 5,000 to 15,000.[108] The disparity of such figures and the inability of U.S. military officials to fix statistically an estimate of the strength of the insurgency draws attention to crucial features of the popular support behind it. There were core groups of rebels fighting under the leadership of the nationalist hero Charlemagne Péralte, who led the resistance in central and northern Haiti until his assassination by marines in November 1919. Other insurgent groups fought under the leadership of Benoît Batraville, who operated in the Plateau Central region and was considered the preeminent rebel leader after the assassination of Péralte. There were also lesser leaders operating regionally, such as Adhémar Francisma, Papillon, Ectraville, Estraville, and Oliver, who attacked gendarmerie outposts and mobile patrols and also took part in larger-scale mobilizations directed by Péralte or Batraville.[109] Beyond this was also a vast reserve of "occasional" insurgents, peasants who could be counted on to join the armed resistance for short periods or specific actions when troops were operating near their homes. Informal popular intelligence networks tracked marine and gendarmerie movements across the central and northeastern regions of Haiti as they pursued insurgent "bands." Suzy Castor notes that these were principally organized around the women market vendors known as *madanm sara*, who, given their daily circulation between town and countryside, were ideally positioned to collect and pass on intelligence to insurgents based in their area.[110] In addition to this kind of reconnaissance and the auxiliary military support provided by temporary fighters, rebel forces also relied on peasant settlements for provisions and shelter when operating in remote parts of the country.

The possibility that such communities could effectively absorb insurgents, making them indistinguishable from local populations, was a source of continual concern for U.S. military officials. In his memoir, Frederic May Wise reported that "instantly they could disband, hide their weapons, and become peaceful inhabitants." The fluidity and elasticity of these boundaries, peasants temporarily becoming bandits and bandits instantly becoming peaceful peasants, meant, in Wise's words, that "all over the island, there were thousands of Haitians who were good citizens most of the year and bad Cacos every now and then." Wise's vision of a rebel force with "literally no beginning or no end" points to the uncertainties of recognition.[111] Kethly Millet argues that the imposition of martial law reinforced "the tendency of the occupants to see in all adult peasants a bandit or a caco" and notes that U.S. Secretary of State Robert Lansing "avowed, voluntarily, that all adult males could be suspected of being part of the guerillas."[112] In his Senate inquiry testimony, Barnett invoked this fluidity to explain the high casualty statistics during the insurgency in Haiti, in comparison with other interventions: "There were a great many natives down there who would be friends today and so-called Cacos tomorrow. They had no uniform, and it was hard to distinguish one from the other, and they were not well armed. They were brave, but they would have no show against well-armed troops, especially with machine guns, and it is perfectly natural to suppose that the contrast would be very marked and that a very great number should be killed in comparison with the number of white people who were killed."[113]

Wise's suspicion that peasants were constantly slipping back and forth between a state of childlike innocence and grace and the no less mytholo-gized horrors of *kako* banditry draws attention to the way in which, rather than corresponding to different sectors of the peasant population, this di-chotomy was imagined as a dual nature.[114] The potentialities claimed for this split figure oscillated constantly between two mutually constitutive extremes: never was there a people so gentle, docile, pleasure-loving, and peaceful; never was there a people capable of such brutality.[115] In the chal-lenge to U.S. policy in Haiti after 1915, that dichotomy also framed the imperial argument against the ability of Haitians for self-government, re-hearsed by U.S. officials and occupation supporters throughout the Sen-ate hearings.[116] On the one hand, General Barnett averred: "I do not think the mass of the people have any more thought on the subject [of gover-nance] than children would. . . . They should be given every consider-ation compatible with good government, and should be given every fa-cility for improving and possibly in the future coming into control, but the people are certainly, in my opinion, not fitted for it yet."[117] By the same token, occupation defenders narrated Haitian postindependence history as a succession of revolutions, conducted, as Admiral William B. Caper-ton noted in his testimony, through "savage warfare, that is uncivilized warfare."[118] No matter that, as Dantès Bellegarde argued, "Portugal had eighteen revolutions in the space of sixteen years," or that "many of these so-called 'revolutions' [in Haiti] were simple mutinies or insurrections that did not even have the seriousness of a strike in Chicago or certain lynchings in Alabama."[119] Bellegarde's pointed comparison drew atten-tion to how official defenses of the occupation relied on a long history of racist argument in which political upheaval in postindependence Haiti was marshaled as proof of the inability of blacks to be self-governing.[120]

Defenses of the continued occupation on the grounds that, as one ac-ademic expert warned, "immediate revolution" would be the result of a premature U.S. military pullout relied on a paternalist rhetoric of tu-telage that implicated both aspects of the double figure of the Haitian peasant.[121] On the one hand, subjugation to the white occupant would have a pacifying and "civilizing" effect, as Smedley Butler writes in his memoir about the "domestication" of a captured rebel who thereafter be-came his faithful servant and the trusted caretaker of his children. On the other hand, there is the testimony of Roger Farnham, president of the American-owned National Railway of Haiti and vice president of National City Bank, which controlled the Banque Nationale of Haiti. Unsurpassed in his influence as a state department advisor on Haiti in the years leading up to and during the U.S. occupation, Farnham maintained during his Senate testimony that the "child-like" nature of the Haitian peasant made tutelage not just a necessity, but also a business opportunity: "I think that the Haitian can be taught to become a good and efficient laborer. If let alone by the military chiefs, he is as peaceful as a child, and as harmless."[122] It finally came down to the same point, which Colonel Wise summed up in explaining that, under his leadership, the marines' counterinsurgency focused on assassinating rebel leaders such as Charlemagne Péralte and Benoît Batraville rather than going after the rank and file, "who would eventually make good laborers."[123] In an August 1920 report, Brigade Commander Russell highlighted that such conversions were already taking place, with the Haytian American Sugar Company "employing a few hundred surrendered bandits for the cultivation of their cane . . . under the charge of their chief" and "the United West Indies Corporation [hiring] many ex-bandits . . . working under the command of a former powerful bandit chief of the north, named Papillon (the butterfly)."[124]

Once the essential "goodness" of the Haitian peasantry was established and defined here, as elsewhere, in terms of their potential as laborers, the question was what could drive such a gentle and amenable people to commit the acts that had been attributed to them over the course of the hearings. It made a certain kind of sense that it would be Brigadier General Smedley Butler who most prominently took up and attempted to account for such transformations in the course of his testimony during the Senate hearings. "Ninety-nine per cent of the people of Haiti," he told the committee, "are the most kindly, generous, hospitable, pleasure-loving people I have ever known. They would not hurt anybody. They are most gentle when in their natural state."[125] He described this idyllic condition as a world apart, untouched by modernity, and yet entirely welcoming of the American military sojourner: "I went all over Haiti, living with them in their shacks, and they always gave you the best they had—food and anything they had in the world."[126] However, "When the other one per cent that wears vici [sic] kid shoes with long pointed toes and celluloid collars stirs them up and incites them with liquor and voodoo stuff, they are capable of the most horrible atrocities; they are cannibals. They ate the liver of one marine. But in their natural state they are the most docile, harmless people in the world."[127]

Butler scorned the Haitian elite, derisively referring to them as "the shoe class" and caricaturing them here, as elsewhere in his testimony and writings, through tropes of blackface minstrelsy.[128] In Butler's vision, elite Haitians were the agitators whose political machinations incited the peasantry to commit barbaric acts against the occupying forces. Yet by what means did they catalyze such dramatic conversions among the otherwise peaceable peasants? It was only when fired "with liquor and voodoo stuff" that this population became capable of the atrocities that the senators had heard so much about.

Mutually constitutive and covertly complicitous, the colonial discourses of child and barbarian required a mediating factor. Butler's recourse to "voodoo" in accounting for the atrocities he attributed to the otherwise innocent and harmless Haitian peasant diverged only slightly from Kuser's aforementioned supposition that "upon the sounding of a Vaudoux drum the priest can very often do about what he wants with his followers."[129] Although Butler, given the structure of his racial feelings, combined the figure of the elite politician with Kuser's priest, both imagined "voodoo" as the means and medium through which such revolutionary instigators incited the ever malleable and "amenable" peasantry to insurgency and atrocity against occupying forces. Such narrations of popular rebellion, of course, stripped all agency from the peasantry, making the mounting of armed opposition to U.S. military presence and policy in Haiti an irrational thing, "external to the peasant's consciousness," as opposed to a movement that was mobilized by conscious collective self-interest and nationalist conviction and empowered, in part, by popular magicoreligious belief, ritual, organization, and leadership.[130]

"Father of the Law"

In a confidential report written to the chief of Naval Operations in March 1920, as the insurgency was weakening, Colonel John Russell, then brigade commander in Haiti, warned that the pernicious effects of "Vaudoism" for U.S. interests in Haiti were not restricted to the military realm. He argued that in spite of the 1918 constitutional revision permitting foreign nationals to own property in Haiti, American businessmen who purchased land there could never be assured of justice in Haitian courts under current conditions on account of antiwhite prejudice and "the hold of Vaudoism."[131]

Beyond the other branches of government, the Haitian courts were able to maintain a degree of independence during the occupation, thanks to judicial tenure. Occupation officials considered them intractably opposed to U.S. military and commercial interests in Haiti, despite an article written into the 1918 Constitution suspending for six months the irremovablility of judges in order to purge their ranks of those hostile to the occupation.[132] According to Russell, "The men appointed by the President to replace those removed are Haitiens [sic] indoctrinated with the old system of graft, hatred of the white and his methods, converts to Vaudoism and are now beyond removal from office except by impeachment, an almost impossible method in this country of racial prejudices and superstitions." He recommended that a "separate agreement . . . be made between the United States and Haiti concerning the re-organization of Haiti's courts and remedying the present unsatisfactory condition," ideally with the provision that Americans "be required to sit on the bench with the Haitien [sic] judges and assist and guide them in their work."[133]

If Russell was principally concerned in this report with the establishment of a favorable legal and juridical environment for American corporate investment in Haiti, particularly in large-scale agroindustrial enterprises, his extended arguments regarding the dangers of Haitian "superstition" for the Haitian judicial system suggest that it was not only justice for American businessmen, but justice, period, that was unattainable in Haiti as long as the population and courts remained in the thrall of "Vaudoism," the "true religion of the Haitien [sic]." Russell, whose views were clearly echoed in his son-in-law Kuser's writing, depicted the Haitian peasant as "the easy prey of the PAPALOI," whose name he translated as "Father of the Law," further emphasizing the threat that this figure represented to the rule of law in Haiti.[134]

Russell based his argument in part on the case of Cadeus Bellegarde, a wealthy landowner and reputed *oungan* who, perhaps more than any other figure, embodied the specter of the powerful "voodoo priest" who could manipulate ignorant, malleable peasants into joining the insurgency.[135] A sometime informant for the occupation himself, Bellegarde was arrested in February 1920 near Mirebalais and charged with arson, aiding and abetting an armed uprising against the U.S. forces in Haiti (including providing assistance to Benoît Batraville), murder, and cannibalism. The written-up charges identified him in each case as "a Voodoo priest and citizen of the Republic of Haiti."[136] Russell's "Daily Diary Reports" at the end of March note that he had initially approached President Dartiguenave about turning Bellegarde over to the Haitian authorities so that he could be tried in the Haitian courts. The president, according to Russell, demurred and asked "the Occupation" to handle it.[137] A military commission was then convened in Port-au-Prince to try Bellegarde, who was found guilty on all charges and sentenced to death pending approval by Washington. The judge advocate for the military, Captain Bruce Mac-

Arthur, who was charged with making the case against Bellegarde focused his opening argument almost exclusively on the threat of "Vodooism," as personified by the accused: "The foundation stone of the present uprising is undoubtably [sic], Vodooism [sic], and the retrograding of the Haitien [sic] Republic under its own administration is logically traceable to this same barbaric and inhuman perversion of the natural instinct in all men to worship something." Bellegarde testified during the proceedings that he had supported the marines' efforts to end the insurgency, but MacArthur asserted that "the possibility of a Vodoo Priest aiding the United States forces is not only ridiculous and absurd but is wholly contrary to the rules of logic," because the occupiers were actively working against the interests of men like the accused in attempting to advance civilization in Haiti. "Gentlemen," he read, "today you have it in your power to aid in ridding humanity of one of its most dangerous and degrading elements; You have it in your power to aid in delivering the Republic of Haiti from a curse which has been on it from the time of its foundation."[138]

Upon reviewing the case back in Washington, however, the Navy's judge advocate general issued a scathing opinion which he turned into an extended treatise on the legal basis for the occupation and the proper bounds of martial law (in effect since September 1915), especially when it came to the Haitian courts.[139] According to U.S-Haitian treaty agreements legalizing the occupation, a military court could be convened to try a Haitian citizen only for "offenses which interfere with the exercise of military authority," and thus, because Bellegarde's alleged victims were not U.S. military personnel and no U.S. property was damaged, the convictions on the counts of murder, cannibalism, and arson were illegitimate. The opinion further stated that the findings on the charge that Bellegarde had aided and abetted the armed insurgency against the U.S. forces in Haiti should be disapproved on account of the "highly unsatisfactory character and inadequacy of the evidence upon which a conviction was reached." The testimony of Second Lieutenant Louis Cukela, "in which a commissioned officer of the Marine Corps, under oath, swears emphatically to the existence of facts which, as appeared from his later testimony on cross-examination, he could have had no knowledge by reason of the times and places of their occurrence," came in for particular censure. These "facts," according to the judge advocate general, included testimony "at great length and in detail as to alleged Voodoo ceremonies conducted by Cadeus, including the sacrifice of children, as to all of which he had no personal knowledge at all."[140]

Although Russell had invoked the Bellegarde case as evidence of the impossibility of justice in Haiti, especially for the white American businessman, given the "hold of Vaudoism," the opinion of the Navy's own judge advocate general turned this indictment back on itself, casting doubt on the possibility of justice for Haitian civilians under U.S. military courts, which were used more in 1920 than any other year during the occupation.[141] Upon learning that the military convictions of Bellegarde had been disapproved, President Dartiguenave again declined to prosecute Bellegarde in a civil court "for the reason that it would acquit him." Russell noted in his daily diary report of 1 December 1920 that this "confirms absolutely my remarks on the judicial system of Haiti, as contained in my memorandum of 16 March 1920."[142] U.S. Navy Rear Admiral H. S. Knapp sent a letter to the Secretary of State a few days later saying that he "greatly fear[ed] that the action of the President of Haiti in connection with the decision of the Navy Department . . . [would] result in a strengthening of voodooism in Haiti."[143]

As Russell's memorandum reveals, it was not simply the role of "voodooism" in propelling popular revolt that became the grounds for "its" repression through the enforcement of penal laws against *sortilèges*. "Voodoo" was figured as a prime factor in a host of other social, political, and economic ills diagnosed by U.S. civil and military authorities in Haiti. Haitian "superstition," especially through the nefarious influence of the "papaloi" and "mamaloi," was charged with corrupting the judiciary and obstructing the pursuit of justice, undermining fair elections and well-functioning republican institutions, and impeding progress in the areas of sanitation and public hygiene. At one time or another "voodoo" was figured as anathema to civil peace, good government, foreign investment, and the economic, physical, and moral well-being of the population.[144] With the waning of popular armed opposition to the occupation, then, other compelling rationales emerged for prioritizing the enforcement of the laws against *sortilèges*, making this regime a key aspect of the occupation's ideology of "uplift" in Haiti and of its own self-justification even after the end of the insurgency.

PART II

"A Wizard Attached to the Police Station"

I want to turn now to the enforcement of the penal law against Vodou over the course of the entire occupation, and to the ways in which Vodouizan evaded, resisted, redirected, and reinterpreted this regime. In December 1915 August Montas, the Dartiguenave government's commissioner to the Tribunal Civil in Port-au-Prince, sent a circular to the members of the judiciary recommending that they "lend a strong hand to the execution

of articles 405 and 406 of the Code Pénal, relating to *Vaudou*, . . . 'ignorance and superstition being the two ills which have hindered the Haitian
people from evolving.'" Then, in March 1916, the year that the penal laws
against *sortilèges* were published in the English-language edition of the
Code Rural, Haiti's minister of justice and religions, Étienne Dornéval,
issued a circular announcing the government's will to overthrow "all the
altars of fetishism" and "destroy superstitions as quickly as possible."[145] A
rare account of the anger and outrage of those who were themselves or
whose loved ones were targeted by the ensuing offensive appears in Monsignor J. M. Jan's redacted history of the diocese of Cap-Haïtien. One of
the monsignor's colleagues encountered a woman later that year whose
husband had been arrested and imprisoned for having "given a *vaudou*":
"What a woman! And what fury against the Dartiguenave government,
against the *magistrat communal*, against the Americans and all the whites
and all the priests and the gendarmes."[146] That she held these multiple parties accountable for her husband's imprisonment, not simply the marines,
underscores the extent to which U.S. military repression of Vodou during the occupation was endorsed and supported by the Roman Catholic
and growing Protestant clergies, as well as by the client government and
many elites.

The Dartiguenave government's call for the repression of "fetishism" and "superstition" at the outset of the U.S. occupation was by no
means unprecedented. Similar circulars had announced Geffrard's campaign against *le vaudoux* in 1864, Tirésias Simon Sam's endorsement of the
church's anti-*vaudoux* crusade in 1896, and Cincinnatus Leconte's dictate
to arrondissement commanders in March 1912 that they must strictly enforce the penal law against *vaudoux*.[147] However, the 1916 circular took
on particular force, given imperial associations between ritual and revolt,
between "sorcery" and sedition, especially in the context of insurgency.
Homer Overley, a nineteen-year-old private when he landed in Haiti in
1920, warned a group of Haitians on their way to a dance in honor of "the
Grande Mamalie [*sic*] of their church" that he had orders from President
Dartiguenave himself "to shoot all Cacos and Voodoes."[148] Whether or
not it was strictly true, what is significant is that he felt empowered to
make the claim. Faustin Wirkus reports that district commanders "had
orders to suppress forbidden ceremonies, raid the temples, [and] furnish
complete lists of all 'Voodoo artists' in their regions," and details his role
in leading an attack, on Christmas Eve 1922, when he was the assistant
chief of police in Port-au-Prince.[149] Having received a tip that an important annual ceremony was to take place that night on the outskirts of the
capital, he organized an expedition "as secretly as possible," only to learn

that evening that "the natives had been warned of our intended raid and had postponed their services."[150] However, later that night a messenger arrived with the news that the ceremony had actually been transferred to another *ounfò* northeast of the capital. Wirkus set out with five Haitian gendarmes and found the gathering. After watching for two or three hours, he directed his force to lay siege. His narrative recounts the violence of the attack.[151] In the end, the gendarmes arrested fifty-four prisoners, including the "priest and priestess," who appeared before the *juge de paix* of that district and, according to Wirkus, were sentenced to between one and three months in jail. Two truckloads of ritual objects were confiscated as "evidence."[152]

There seems to have been nothing particularly unusual about this raid, except for the keen interest of the white officer in observing the rituals performed before enforcing the law that prohibited them. Raids such as the one Wirkus describes were then taking place on a regular basis (he notes at one point "the constant raids on the temples"), particularly near the coastal cities and towns where marines were concentrated after their "pacification" of the interior.[153] However, the importance of Wirkus's account lies not only in its narrative of one of these attacks, indicating the military surveillance, harassment, and violent repression to which Vodouizan were subject by occupying forces at this time. It is also noteworthy for detailing strategies by which Vodouizan attempted to evade this regime, beginning with the counterintelligence that advertised a false postponement of the ceremony, which was instead moved surreptitiously to another *ounfò* that night.[154] If gendarmerie headquarters had informants, so did *oungan* and *manbo*, through whom they kept track of police actions and could even, as in this case, publicize a deceptive tip to elude detection.

Wirkus also notes that the drums used during the *sèvis* had been stuffed with cotton fiber, "except for an inch or two beneath the leather tops," in order to muffle their volume.[155] Drumming, of course, presented a particular problem for evading pursuit by the marines because even when muted it was a means by which *sèvis* could be located. Wirkus later describes a towering drum, presumably the *tanbou asòtò*, which marines frequently confiscated in raids during the early years of the occupation but "passed out of use" over its course on account of "the continuous hunting down of voodoo gatherings."[156] At its height, the repression seems to have led to innovations in the forms of percussion used for particular ceremonies. W. B. Seabrook reported that while visiting an *ounfò* between Gonaïves and Ennery, he had been shown "a curious set of Rada drums, or rather a substitute therefor, made simply of three unequal lengths of a big bamboo, tubes about four inches in diameter without heads, on the sides of which the drummers tapped with soft wooden sticks. These had been used, I was told, in 1919 when the Marines were more active in suppressing Voodoo ceremonies."[157] Harold Courlander likewise describes "the bamboo stamping tube, called the *ganbo* or *ti kanmbo*," which was "a length of bamboo, open at one end and closed at the other by a natural joint membrane. The closed end is struck sharply upon the ground, and the tone comes from the open top. . . . A battery of four or five *ganbos* may provide the percussion music otherwise played by drums." Courlander, who made his first field trip to Haiti in 1937, three years after the marines were withdrawn from Haiti, notes that these instruments were widely used during the occupation because "drums could not easily be hidden, but the *ganbos* were simply slipped into the straw roofs and thus put out of sight. Moreover, by some strange process of reasoning, military authorities regarded the bamboos as 'harmless,' though they were used for the same purposes as the contraband drums."[158]

Marines stationed in Haiti over the course of the occupation seemed to pride themselves on being able to distinguish between the rhythms of ritual drumming and those played for nonceremonial social gatherings. In an oral-history interview Merwin H. Silverthorn, onetime chief of police in Port-au-Prince, recalled both arresting "any number of those voo-doo people" and granting permissions on the weekend for dances, "'bambush' [*banbòch*], I guess they called it. That was a regular social event."[159] However, the sociologist George Eaton Simpson, who traveled to Haiti on an SSRC fellowship in 1937, was told by informants that during the occupation, such dances were sometimes a cover for *sèvis*.[160] This might be borne out by a 1922 report in the *New York Times* that marines had "raided an unusually boisterous dance on a Saturday night in the central part of the city [Port-au-Prince]" and found evidence of offerings to the *lwa*.[161]

As the occupation wore on, some *oungan* found yet more reliable ways to evade harassment and persecution by gendarme troops: they became part of the policing structure themselves. There is no doubt that the gendarmerie's ranks were filled with Vodouizan from the beginning, as perhaps reflected in the agonizing reluctance of some gendarmes, in cases described by Wirkus and other marines, "to enter a *houmfort* and confiscate the Voodoo fittings."[162] Roger Gaillard interviewed the son of Médard Saint-Pré, who had served as an auxiliary under the commander of the station at Maïssade and was also a *doktè fèy* ("leaf doctor"), one "initiated in the curative virtues of plants and often as well, an 'hougan' [*sic*], *vaudou* priest."[163] Under the command of American gendarmerie officers, who had strict orders to arrest all "voodoo artists" in their areas and who often assumed a close identification between practitioners of popular religion and insurgents, Haitian gendarmes could presumably do little to soften the regime that the occupation imposed during its early years. However, the structure of rural policing changed in the early 1920s—or rather, to some extent, reverted back to preoccupation norms. During the early years of the occupation, rural districts had been patrolled by gendarmes sent out by the nearest station. However, according to James McCrocklin, a localized rural police force was organized in 1923: "The 551 sections of Haiti were canvassed, and a prominent citizen in each section was selected to serve as the chief of that section. The men enlisted as members of the Rural Police, Gendarmerie d'Haïti were required to provide themselves with neat blue denim uniforms and were issued Krag rifles, ammunition, and staffs denoting their office. . . . They were to enforce the Code Rural, a copy of which was furnished them, encourage the inhabitants in their work, and see that law and order was maintained in their respective sections."[164]

Thus the institution of the rural police officer that had been dissolved by the Dartiguenave government at the direction of the U.S. military in early 1916 was restored following the "pacification" of the country. The section chief was assisted by two auxiliaries called *chanpèt* (French *champêtres*). Although, again according to McCrocklin, "gendarmerie officers maintained close supervision over the chiefs of section, requiring each to report to the subdistrict headquarters weekly, and themselves making an inspection of each section frequently," there is evidence that at least in some sections of the country, the regulation of popular religious practice began thereafter to return to customary forms.[165] This process may have been furthered by the "indigenization" of the gendarmerie hierarchy in the later 1920s. Seabrook, for example, writes of the tolerance of a gendarme he refers to as Kebreau (Jean Price-Mars identifies him as Lieutenant Kébreau Devésin), stationed in the subdistrict of Croix-des-Bouquets, for the work of *oungan* and *manbo* based in his jurisdiction: "Kebreau knew that Dort was a *papaloi*, Dieron a *hougan* [*sic*]. Kebreau knew the location of their *houmfort* and knew that from time to time ceremonials technically against the law occurred there. Kebreau knew everything. But Kebreau was not active in persecuting the religion of his own devoted peasants."[166]

Yet more significant, a number of the "prominent citizens" selected to serve as local rural police officers after 1923 seem themselves to have been religious elders. This is hardly surprising given that, according to McCrocklin, U.S. military officers specifically sought to appoint men (I have found no cases of women being appointed) who already had influence and prestige in their sections. Wirkus, for example, recounts his decision to name Zule Prezeau—whom he knew as "a *gros nègre*, an important man in his district, owning a large place"—as *chèf seksyon* in the La Gonâve interior. Only later did he learn that Prezeau was also an *oungan*.[167] A similar system of local policing had been established earlier in Port-au-Prince. According to McCrocklin, a small detective force was organized in the capital in 1921 made up of plainclothesmen who "drew no regular pay." Rather, "in most cases they were chiefs in the different sections of town who performed this duty in return for favors granted them by the police, such as permission to hold cockfights and dances in their respective areas."[168] Again, the likelihood that *oungan* would have been included among the ranks of this force seems high, particularly given that, at least in the beginning, permission to hold "dances" was a principal form of compensation. In fact, John Houston Craige observed in his first of two infamous occupation memoirs, *Black Bagdad*, that during his tenure as Port-au-Prince's police chief one of his most valued detectives was a "bocour" and suggests that by the mid- to late 1920s such appointments were sometimes more strategic than inadvertent on the part of marine officers: "It was convenient to have a wizard attached to the police station. He was a back-stairs link with the powerful voodoo fraternity. He interpreted the law to his fellow *bocours* and told them what they could do and what they must not attempt."[169] A letter to the director of the Port-au-Prince newspaper *La Presse* in February 1930 complained that in the neighborhood of Bas-Peu-de-Chose a detective named Timagène was organizing Vodou dances at his home attended by "agents attached to the secret police." The next day *Le Nouvelliste* published a notice reporting that in Portail Léogâne there was a "headquarters of these sorts of dances directed it is said by agents of the Police themselves."[170]

Through this "indigenization" of rural and, to a lesser extent, urban policing, the legal regime against the practices that marines constructed as "voudauxism" or "voodoo" shifted over the occupation's course and varied from place to place. The unevenness of enforcement of articles 405–407 of the Code Pénal is evident in data collected in response to a November 1924 confidential intelligence order by the chief of the gendarmerie, Lieutenant Colonel Douglas C. McDougal, to department commanders across the country. "As a result of several conferences with the President [Louis Borno, Dartiguenave's successor] on the subject of voodooism," this memorandum requested that the department commanders organize the secret collection of "a complete list of the names and addresses of the following voodoo people: Houngan (Papa Loi), Mambo (Mamma Loi), Houngsi [*ounsi*, members of a religious *sosyete*], Bocors, also the location of Humforts, or other meeting places." The rationale for this clandestine census was McDougal's concern that too many of those arrested for violations of articles 405–407 were ultimately acquitted owing to insufficient evidence and "the faulty procès verbaux prepared by the judges [*sic*] de paix, either purposely or through ignorance." The memo specified that offenders should be caught *en flagrant délit* (in the act): "It is believed that when a correct list of voodoo people is in the hands of officers they can keep more or less in touch with the activities of these people and make arrests that will result in convictions."[171]

The reports filed by district and subdistrict officers (mostly Americans, but some Haitians as well) across the country over the course of the following year attest to wide disparities in the local enforcement of these laws and the degrees of surveillance to which suspected practitioners were subjected. For example, the district commander of Jérémie, in the southwest, submitted a report in February 1925 listing 123 persons arrested and brought to trial between January 1924 and January 1925 for infractions of articles 405–407 of the Code Pénal. Of these, approximately 80 were convicted and sentenced, for the most part, to between one to three months in prison and a fine of 60 gourdes. The commander of the subdistrict of Croix-des-Bouquets (who seems to have been Haitian) submitted a report in late December 1924 listing 159 people who "have the reputation of Hougan and Mambo"; and in the subdistrict of Port-à-Piment in the district of Cayes, on the southern peninsula, 183 names were listed as "Voodouism people."[172] On the other hand, in the neighboring subdistrict of Aux Cayes, two reports in 1925 concluded that "so far as is known there is no Voodooism being practiced . . . at the present time." The subdistrict commander of Anse-à-Veau, on the northern coast of the southern peninsula, likewise reported in April 1925 that he had been unable to locate any information about the "voodoo people" in the area. This report was deemed "of no value" by the department commander and sent back; another report was submitted a few weeks later stating that local judicial officials and priests stationed in and around this district had all confirmed that "there were no dances or forms of voodooism held in their parts of the country."

A number of district and subdistrict commanders submitted lengthy rosters of reputed practitioners of "voodooism" but reported that they seemed no longer to be active in the area because of police surveillance and prosecution. Several reports refer to the displacement of *oungan, manbo,* and *bòkò* whose homes and temples were burned earlier in the occupation or who had retreated to the mountains or across the Dominican border. Other commanders suspected that illicit rituals were still being conducted surreptitiously in their districts and subdistricts but cited the near

impossibility of tracking such events, given that drums were no longer
being used. For example, when submitting his roster of twenty names in
January 1925, the district commander of Hinche wrote that "it is reported
that at the ceremonies the necessary rhythm is created by the clapping of
hands or the beating of hands upon banana leaves. By this procedure it
is very difficult to locate any gatherings by the noise created as was formerly done." On the other hand, the subdistrict commander of Arcahaie
revealed in his 9 February report that drums were still very much in use
in *ounfò* in his district. Of the gatherings held weekly at the *ounfò* Bassy
Marie by a "Papa Loi" named Thelisma, he wrote: "This dance is run
strictly on a three drum affair and to no persons' knowledge has anything
farther than a straight dance of voodoism been indulged in. No sacrificial
dances of any kind have been seen there." The report dated 21 April from
the commander of the northern subdistrict of Le Trou likewise suggested
that the regulation of ritual practice may have been turning back to customary norms there, with authorities focusing more on adjudicating the
claims of disgruntled clients: "Most cases that have arisen where the suspect has been condemned by the Justice Courts is [*sic*] where a person has
taken advantage of the superstitious belief of the inhabitant and charged
him money for treatment. Then when the desired result was not obtained
the inhabitant made a complaint."[173]

The confidential order from the chief of the gendarmerie that prompted
the compilation of this "Voodoo census" seemed to intensify the surveillance and repression of Vodouizan in certain parts of the country. An intelligence report from the American district commander of Saint Marc
in early December 1924 (a few weeks following the request from Gendarmerie headquarters for intelligence on "voodoo people") noted that
"in the Communes of Verrettes and Dessalines action was started to suppress Vaudooism. In the former Commune there were ten arrests made
for this crime and seven convictions. In the latter commune there were
three arrests and two convictions. All convictions received the limit of
G-[gourdes]150.00 fine and Six Months Hard Labor." This report also
recommended that "one additional Unit of the Police Rurale, consist-
ing of a Chief and two champetres, be authorized" for duty in the commune of La Chapelle, where "reports have been received that many illegal acts and Vaudo Ceremonies have been carried on . . . and Gendarmes
stationed there have been unable to suppress them."[174] As was so often
the case in these histories, the perception of recrudescence may well have
been an effect of increased penal attention.

The *chèf seksyon* and *chanpèt* were themselves under intense scrutiny in
some districts and faced severe consequences if they failed to enforce the

law against public ceremonies, as well as the individual client services of *oungan* and *manbo*. The American district commander of Cerca la Source in the central department raised concern in December 1924 about a *chèf seksyon* who "half-heartedly" reported the "Manger les Morts" that two hundred people attended in his section the month before: "[He] seemed to be wavering between fear of imprisonment if he did not report the fact and his superstitious fears."[175] The former fear was by no means idle. In Mirebalais a *chanpèt* arrested on 31 December 1924 "for having permitted an inhabitant to carry on a voudoo ceremony" was court-martialed in the district and sentenced "to be confined at hard labor for a period of thirty days, and to lose all pay and allowances due him . . . and at the expiration thereof to be dishonorably discharged from the Gendarmerie d'Haiti."[176] Although it was not prescribed in articles 405–407 of the Code Pénal, imprisonment at hard labor was frequently specified in convictions of "voodoo people" during the occupation.[177]

What is also clear, though, is that throughout the waves of repression to which Vodouizan were subject during the occupation, stories were constantly circulating not of defeat, but of the resilience and transcendence of the spirits in the face of their persecutors; of their retribution against the same, whether marines, gendarmes, Catholic or Protestant clergy, or some combination thereof; and of the punishment, affliction, capitulation, or conversion of those who attempted to suppress popularly sanctioned religious practices. Jean Price-Mars and Melville Herskovits both recount popular narratives of occupation-era conflicts during the annual pilgrimage to the sacred falls of Sodo (Saut d'Eau) near the town of Ville Bonheur, southwest of Mirebalais, honoring Our Lady of Mount Carmel and Ezili Dantò. Visions of the Virgin had been appearing in the plumed branches of a palm grove in Ville Bonheur since the mid-nineteenth century, and, as Price-Mars wrote, "this first miracle led to other minor miracles. The deaf heard, the blind saw, the paralyzed walked. But here at the foot of the trees, among the candles of Christian penitence, other candles burned illuminating other orders and amidst the sparkling dew of the thick grass the offerings of food to the *Vaudou* gods multiplied."[178] The long-simmering dispute with Roman Catholic clergy over the annual July festival erupted again during the occupation, according to Herskovits, when a local priest closed two of the sacred spots in Ville Bonheur, including the palm grove, to pilgrims. Yet the Virgin again appeared on a palm tree: "The people, on their knees worshipping, sent to the priest to come and pray. He declared it merely superstition, however, and called an American Marine captain stationed at Mirebalais to help him suppress this worship. The captain ordered a Haitian sergeant to shoot the vision, but the Virgin merely moved to another tree; another shot, and she moved again. They cut down the tree, and those who looked on with terror saw the vision slowly ascend to the sky."

Then came reports of the priest's house burning down, the American captain falling ill and having to return to the U.S., the Haitian sergeant losing his mind and asking pardon of the Virgin. In the face of such apparent retributions, "'public clamor' became so strong" that both of the interdicted sacred sites were reopened.[179]

Milo Rigaud reports another story that circulated in which marines "bothered by the authority of a *oum'phor* located in Digneron, in the plain of Cul-de-Sac," raided the site and confiscated a towering *asòtò* drum, the most prestigious of the Rada battery, and the most desirable object of plunder for marines. According to Rigaud, as soon as the drum was brought back to the occupation headquarters in Port-au-Prince, it began to boom on its own without being struck, eventually forcing the astonished marines to return it. Rigaud also recounts stories of marines charged with suppressing Vodou being drawn to the religion and initiated during their stay, including one who was himself apotheosized after his death: "Captain Daybas" (or "Déba"), a spirit whose possession performance mimetically evoked, according to Alfred Métraux, who also wrote about him, the salty persona of an American sailor. He spoke only English and craved corned beef, ham, and oatmeal.[180] Such stories tell a counternarrative of the marines' repression of popular religious practice during the occupation in which the *lwa* are consistently ascendant over the law, and its would-be enforcers are ultimately forced in the face of their confrontation with these higher powers to soften their regime, or even to honor those powers themselves—the "*loi* of the *lwa*," as one *oungan* put it.

"The Law Wrote Itself Down an Ass"

In examining the severity with which marines enforced the Code Pénal's articles 405–407, it would be a mistake to underestimate the extent to which popular pressures shaped their application, sometimes in ways completely at odds with how the occupation defined its "civilizing mission." Just as article 405 assimilated Vodou to the category of *les sortilèges*, so the law itself was assimilated into popular defenses against malicious magic. Some marines complained that they were being called upon to apply the law in ways that seemed more to reinforce "superstitious" beliefs than to undermine them—in other words, in ways that were antithetical to U.S. military rationales for enforcing them in the first place.

Sometimes, for example, peasants complained to local gendarme stations about the ineffectiveness of a requested magical work. Blair Niles, whose travelogue *Black Haiti: A Biography of Africa's Eldest Daughter* documents her journeys throughout the country in the mid-1920s, reported hearing from the wife of a U.S. gendarme that her laundress had just received a prison sentence of three months' hard labor "for taking five gourdes from a woman who had come to consult her as to how to make money." The latter had been instructed to dig in a particular spot near her home, and when she found nothing, "the victim defied the rage of the sorceress by carrying her complaint to the Gendarmerie."[181]

A good deal more troublesome to marines stationed across Haiti were accusations from community residents that someone in their midst, often an older woman, was a *lougawou* (from the French *loup-garou*, or werewolf), a vampirelike being who traveled by air at night to extract the soul and blood of small children.[182] While stationed on La Gonâve, Faustin Wirkus was drawn into the case of a woman named Vernélie Cherisier, accused by people in Pointe à Raquette of being a *lougawou*. She arrived under guard at his headquarters one day with a report from the Haitian gendarme who policed that area. The report explained that "this Vernélie is unbearable in this town of Pointe à Raquette. All the people complain against her on this score of the sorcery of *loupgarou*. I send her to you for such treatment as her acts merit." The woman was eventually convicted and sentenced to the maximum term of six months' imprisonment. Wirkus noted that he was principally interested in her case because she was reputed to be connected with a "high priest" he hoped to meet and thus "was willing to let the law take its course, even if by doing so . . . the law wrote itself down an ass."[183]

Marines in Haiti thus discovered that the enforcement of the law prohibiting *les sortilèges* was mined in ways that implicated them in the local logics of sorcery belief. That marines during the occupation were popularly pressured to apply this prohibition in ways that seemed to legitimate the reality and efficacy of criminal magic is another dimension of the law's paradoxical potential to affirm what it negated. The strict enforcement of the law could ultimately serve to instantiate belief in "superstition" rather than, as occupation apologists defensively claimed, to weaken or undermine it. As the law of the state was drawn into the customary order, it became ensorcelled itself. It also worked its own sorcery by playing a central role in the production of "voodoo" as an imperial object that, as I will examine below, took on a life of its own in foreign fantasies about Haiti during and after the occupation.[184]

Such cases draw attention to the U.S. military investment in enforcing the law against *les sortilèges* in light of alternative policies that could have been pursued. In the early years of the occupation, certain marine officials researched different models for the U.S. administration of Haiti, the most frequently cited of which were the British occupation of Egypt and, to a somewhat lesser extent, rule in India.[185] Given the attention paid to such comparisons, the disparity between U.S. policies toward *les sortilèges* in Haiti and contemporaneous British policies on "witchcraft" in central Africa seems particularly notable. As Karen Fields discusses in her study *Revival and Rebellion in Colonial Central Africa*, the Witchcraft Ordinance that British officials imposed in Malawi and Zambia in 1914 "systematically attacked the whole complex of witch belief," removing "the offense of witchcraft from the purview of the law altogether."[186] In fact, this statute criminalized not the performance of sorcery, but rather its diagnosis and accusation, prescribing severe penalties that included imprisonment, fines, and flogging for offenders.

However, this British policy proved to be mined with its own set of traps, stemming first and foremost from the fact that, in turning custom on its head, the Witchcraft Ordinance was popularly viewed as a perversion of justice: "It put the regime that claimed to uphold law and order in the position of shielding known criminals. It put customary upholders of justice in the position of outlaws. And it made the ordinary villager who obtained a charm for self-defense . . . subject to prosecution."[187] What is more, the enforcement of the Witchcraft Ordinance seemed destined to threaten British colonial power in central Africa, because the administration of indirect rule was founded on maintaining the authority of customary leaders. Fields examines the antiwitchcraft movement, led by medicine men called Bamucapi, that spread throughout Malawi and Zambia between 1930 and 1934. British administrators initially opposed this revival through the Witchcraft Ordinance but were forced into a position of toleration when it became clear that the tribal chiefs upon whose authority British control rested were under popular pressure to allow the Bamucapi to distribute their cleansing medicines.[188] The Witchcraft Ordinance thus proved untenable: the British could not impose this law without undermining the authority of the chiefs, and thus their own power. The British acquired the reputation of being "soft" on sorcery in colonial central Africa on account of their promulgation of the Witchcraft Ordinance and, once officials realized its unenforceability, their policy of leaving the detection and deterrence of such crimes in the hands of customary rulers.[189]

Promoting "Voodoo"

Interestingly, from time to time marines in Haiti faced similar accusations from urban elites of being "soft"—not on "sorcery," but on familial and temple-based Vodou. As Léon-François Hoffmann notes, opponents of the occupation charged "the American authorities with encouraging Vodou, to the end of giving the country a pejorative image and thus disarming the campaign of protest . . . in the progressive press."[190] This was the argument, in particular, of the nationalist daily newspaper, *Le Courrier haïtien*, which repeatedly ran afoul of occupation authorities and the client government in the early 1920s for its "seditious" content.[191] In February and March 1921 the newspaper ran a series of articles in response to a report on Haiti issued by Rear Admiral Knapp shortly after the Mayo inquiry, excerpts of which were published in the *Christian Science Monitor* along with, according to *Le Courrier haïtien*, an engraving of a "scene of Haitian cannibalism."[192] By this point it had become clear that each new investigation by the U.S. Department of the Navy into misconduct by marines against Haitians was destined to be spun into another opportunity to spotlight alleged "voodoo"-inspired atrocities committed by Haitians against occupation forces.[193] In condemning the attribution of cannibalism to the Haitian peasantry in these reports, the anonymous author of one of the articles in *Le Courrier haïtien* defined *Vaudou* as "only an African dance," but one "ruinous for our poor peasants" in light of the offerings they were obliged to make each year "to appease the Saints and merit their protection." The article went on, with emphasis: "One of my principal grievances against the AMERICAN OCCUPATION and THE OFFICERS OF THE GENDARMERIE D'HAITI is that after six years of their governing us, THEY THE CIVILIZERS have done nothing to combat the practice of *Vaudou*, but that to the contrary, they have done everything to spread and diffuse it."[194] A little more than a week earlier, a front-page article reported that a *juge d'instruction* in Port-au-Prince had discovered several *danses de Vaudou* taking place in the center of the capital, organized by Haitian gendarmes and local police representatives with the authorization of their *chefs américains*, or even, it was suggested, upon their orders. The report concluded: "When one reminds oneself that the Americans associate cannibalism with the practice of *Vaudou*, one understands that they are trying to spread *Vaudou* among us in order to try to say that we are cannibals."[195]

The charges made in these articles—and in other elite and ecclesiastical writings from the occupation—raise a number of difficult questions.[196] On the one hand, the report in *Le Courrier haïtien* suggests again that Vodouizan were integrated into every level of the military and police structures: those involved included a sergeant, an enlisted man, an urban police officer, and two detectives. On the other hand, the circumstances under which U.S. military personnel authorized or even ordered the mounting of these dances are uncertain. Was this a case of an opportunistic relaxation of the penal regime against Vodou for specific political or military ends (perhaps ones more immediate and local than those which the newspaper charged)? More broadly, on what possible grounds could the occupation have been accused of "encouraging" or "spreading and diffusing" prohibited ritual practices, given the severity with which marines enforced the laws against *les sortilèges*? Indeed, in what ways and in what sense could that policy itself be understood to have had such an effect?

Moving beyond the scope of the specific accusations in *Le Courrier haïtien*, the remaining pages of this chapter examine the affirmative logic and productive effects of the marines' enforcement of the law against *les sortilèges*. As examined in the previous chapter, the penal pursuit and prosecution of *le vaudoux* by the Geffrard government paradoxically drew more international publicity to such practices (or, rather, fantasies thereof) than to the fact of their prohibition and repression. Likewise, during the occupation, the marines' penalization of "voodoo" was partly driven by and, in turn, further incited foreign fascination with Haitian ritualism. What is more, how such audiences constructed the object of "voodoo" during and following the occupation was crucially shaped, I would argue, by the penal regime enforced by marines between 1915 and 1934.

In imperial writing during the occupation, much was made of the positivism of the law, which seemed to provide undeniable proof in both its text and its application that "voodoo" flourished in Haiti. W. B. Seabrook capitalized on both of these evidentiary regimes in *The Magic Island*. At one point, for example, he recounts a meeting with the physician Antoine Villiers, who, in response to his guest's questions about the possibility of "zombies" (*zonbi*) in Haiti, replied, "I will show you . . . a thing which may supply the key to what you are seeking." Then, according to Seabrook, he pulled down a copy of the Code Pénal from one of his shelves in order to point out article 246. This was one of the three penal laws included in the 1916 marine-translated Code Rural and prohibited poisoning to produce a deathlike state.[197] An adaptation of this scene was staged in the American horror film *White Zombie* (1932), set in Haiti, and highlighted in posters promoting the film. The latter featured a translation of article 246 under the heading "Actual Extract from the Penal Code of Haiti," next to a "Note" in smaller print (see fig. 8 below): "The practice of Zombiism is punishable by death in Haiti! Yet, Zombiism is being practiced in this country."[198]

The marines' enforcement of these laws yielded an even more indisputable form of evidence, as far as Seabrook was concerned. His book is laden with references to military reports, the official provenance of which served to authorize his representations.[199] At one point, for example, he claims: "The necromantic uses which [Haitians] make of various parts of the corpse are thoroughly authenticated in many verifiable cases. The facts have appeared even in American military reports of the Caco guerilla uprisings."[200] In discussing the presence of Catholic iconography in popular religious assemblages, Seabrook notes: "I am contributing nothing new in telling that a crucifix stands today on every Voodoo altar in Haiti. That fact is well known, for *houmforts* have been raided."[201] At another point he cites the contents of a *"ouanga* bag confiscated by Marines in 1921 near Gonaïves": "'It was a hide bag, and in it were these objects: luck stones, snake bones, lizard jaws, squirrel teeth, bat bones, frog bones, black hen feathers and bones, black lamb wool, dove hearts, mole skins, images of wax and clay, candy made of brown sugar mixed with liver, mud, sulphur, salt, and alum, and vegetable poisons.'"[202]

The remarkable detail of the inventory Seabrook cites suggests the ambivalent fascination of military personnel in Haiti with the practices they constructed as "voodoo," one that the mandate of penalization both indulged and further charged.[203] As reflected in published marine accounts, surveillance of ritual practices became the opportunity for voyeurism; confiscation of sacred objects, the pretext for personal appropriation. Wirkus was particularly forthright about such relationships. He wrote in prefacing his narration of the 1922 Christmas Eve raid: "As an enforcer of the law it was for me to learn all I could about these rites which I was sworn to suppress. In honesty I must admit that it fitted very well with my urgent curiosity about these secretive people that such was my duty. To satisfy my personal curiosity I preferred gaining friendly admission into voodoo ceremonies, but by raiding them I found out a great deal that would otherwise have taken many months and infinite patience."[204] On a similar note, and with particularly circular logic, John Houston Craige regretted that while stationed in Hinche, where repression of peasants during the 1918–1920 uprising had been particularly severe, he had "found little information" about the ritual practices that U.S. troops were focused on suppressing.[205] And Merwin Silverthorn, onetime chief of police in Port-au-Prince, recalled his frustration when Haitian gendarmes in his "secret service"

would make arrests over the weekend for a voo-doo ceremony. . . . And I would say, "How would you know this was coming off? . . . Why didn't you let me know? You know I want to be present at some of these and be in on the arrests." I didn't say I wanted to see what was going on. "Oh, well, we didn't have time. We just happened to stumble on it." And all the time I was in Aux-Cayes. I could hear the drums on the weekends of the voo-doo ceremonies, but you never could get to them. I attempted even to go out in the direction of the drums and find my way and stumble on one of these things. I never even located where this drum noise was originating from.[206]

The desire to see and become knowledgeable about "voodoo" was both enabled and thwarted, and either way incited, by the penal regime that marines were, as Wirkus wrote, "sworn to enforce."

According to Article 407 of the Code Pénal, any ritual "instruments, utensils and costumes" were supposed to be confiscated during raids of *ounfò* "for burning or destruction." However, proof that not everything seized reached its legally prescribed end can be found both in the memoirs of individual marines and in the storage spaces of major U.S. museums and ethnographic collections.[207] The accusation in *Le Courrier haïtien* that marines were "encouraging" Vodou to denigrate Haiti's image resonates with the Haitian esotericist Arthur Holly's characterization of the collection and export of such objects in *Les daïmons du culte vodu* (1918): "One recalls with what heroic zeal the Occupation assaulted the peaceful sanctuaries of African temples (houmfors), with what energy it sacked them. Under the inoffensive aspect of sacred objects and ritual accessories (drums, *canaris-zin*, collections of thunderstones, etc), the plunder was packed up . . . for the destination of the Unites States of America, to the end of proving and illustrating the *inferior mental state* in which the people of Haiti live and thereby justify the application of the most extraordinary measures."[208]

Drums were the marines' most highly prized trophies. Believed to be a means of insurgent communication as well as popular control, the drum was fetishized by marines as an instrument of both ritual and revolution.[209] Many of the officers and enlisted men who served in Haiti during the occupation and who wrote diaries and published memoirs or gave oral-historical accounts of their experiences mention the drums that they confiscated and took into their personal possession. Lieutenant Adolph B. Miller describes a raid on a "Caco village" only a few months after the beginning of the occupation somewhere near Ouanaminthe, when he and a fellow marine "each brought a tom-tom along as a souvenir." Merwin Silverthorn refers in his oral history to the "voo-doo drum that I got when I was out in the hills," one of three that he kept in his basement after returning home.[210] The first Haitian drums acquired by the Smithsonian Institution were a set of three (presumably Rada drums) donated by Captain R. O. Underwood in September 1916, along with a one-page "outline" on "vaudouism" that rehearsed one imperial myth after another and concluded: "The practice of vaudouism has been the means of degrading

FIGURE 5. Drum confiscated in 1916. Courtesy of the Penn Museum, film NC35-21128.

the population, and of frightening the ignorant people into the influence of tricky and unscrupulous Haitian politicians."[211] Marines donated and sold drums and other ritual objects to the Smithsonian over the course of the occupation and in the decades thereafter, a number of pieces having been "collected" in Hinche and Maïssade during the counterinsurgency.[212]

In *Black Bagdad,* Craige at one point inventories the altarlike assemblage of confiscated sacred objects and weaponry he had constructed in a corner of his Philadelphia home since returning from Haiti, the centerpiece of which was a "big drum, a genuine Arada nearly six feet tall," and three smaller drums.[213] Craige donated these drums some two decades later to the museum of the University of Pennsylvania. The accession card for the four drums identifies them as having been "confiscated at illegal voodoo ceremonies by donor when he was Chief of Police in Port-au-Prince, with U.S. Marines, ca. 1924–1928."[214] There they joined another drum from occupation-era Haiti, this one confiscated in 1916 by then-Major Alexander S. Williams during the first wave of rebellions that followed the U.S. invasion (see fig. 5). It was during Williams's tenure as gendarmerie commander in Haiti that the worst abuses associated with the *kòve* took place, particularly in Hinche and Maïssade. Perhaps because of its topical currency and tropical novelty (this was the museum's first drum from Haiti), the acquisition warranted an article in the university's *Museum Journal*, which compiled, in the name of contextualization, many of the most lurid fantasies that had circulated about Haitian ritualism since the mid-nineteenth century. The article began by explaining that the head of the donated drum had been punctured by marines "because the beating of a drum was the signal to assemble the Voodoo devotees and to incite them to a religious race war" and closes three pages later by affirming the "importance attached to the drums" by Haitians and thus "the wisdom of the present day authorities in removing them."[215] A photograph of the artifact from the museum reveals that the drumhead had indeed been slashed at its center. One of the older Haitian drums in the Smithsonian's collection is likewise punctured.[216]

The rending of these drumheads raises many questions. In particular, why would this have been considered necessary once the drums were already in marine custody and, as prescribed by law, destined to be destroyed? Was the laceration of the drums in the course of a raid calculated to heighten the terror of these assaults? Was it spurred by the threatening powers that some marines attributed to Haitian drums, powers intensified by the regime that they enforced?[217] We might remember the way that General Littleton Waller seemed to anthropomorphize the drum in his Senate testimony, describing how as soon as voodoo drums were heard his troops would "get on the trail" to "capture" them. Of course, these particular drums were not fated for destruction, but rather "collection"; and so, although they were irreparably damaged through the tearing of their heads, they were at the same time, paradoxically, preserved.

The puncturing of these drumheads literalized what Stephan Palmié has analyzed with regard to the confiscation of Afro-Cuban *batá* drums by U.S. occupying forces and Cuban authorities in early republican Cuba as "the violent and religiously highly problematic severance of an animated object or, rather, objectified being from the only context in which it could fulfill its divine purpose."[218] Any speculation about what the confiscation of and violence against these drums meant for those who made them, those who played them, and those who were spiritually embodied by the *lwa* called through them must begin with the fact that, as Alfred Métraux noted, the Haitian drum "is not only a musical instrument, it is also a sacred object and even the tangible form of a divinity."[219] According to mid-twentieth-century ethnographic accounts, with the first moments of a drum's creation—indeed, of its conception—a process of consecration began that endowed it with a spirit called the *outò*.[220] The drum is baptized and given names by a *pè savann* in the presence of its human godmothers and godfathers, and in that sense, as the drummer Coyote (Philoclès Rosenbère) told the ethnomusicologist Gerdès Fleurant, "it is like a person." It is also "like a *lwa*," he noted, because it must be fed with offerings in special ceremonies that renew and/or augment its powers.[221] One wonders if the attenuation of the rituals of consecration since the early 1930s that Fleurant observes in his ethnography might be connected to the widespread confiscation, destruction, and in certain cases "exile" of drums, as Milo Rigaud puts it, during the occupation and then again during the church's *campagne anti-superstitieuse* in the early 1940s.[222] In the course of his work in Haiti between the 1930s and 1950s, Harold Courlander likewise noted the disappearance of the elaborate carvings that once illustrated Haitian drums. He saw this as a direct consequence of the occupation and antisuperstition raids: "Drums had become expendable, hence they were made simpler. The carved decorations disappeared. Paint was substituted and less attention was given to detail."[223]

If the enforcement of penal laws against popular ritual in Haiti produced positive disciplinary knowledge about "voodoo," one of the ways this was popularized and circulated in the U.S. (and elsewhere) was through the construction of the marine as "expert." It was precisely because penalization seemed to afford marines a proximity to, even intimacy with the practices they were "sworn to suppress," that their authority on such subjects was publicly conferred. Early instances of marines claiming or being endowed with an almost ethnographic authority about "voodoo" can be found in testimony during the 1921–1922 Senate hearings, as when Walter Bruce Howe, counsel for the committee of senators, pressed General Littleton Waller to explain what "voodoo" is and "of what it consists." However, the assumption that marines held specialized knowledge about such practices intensified in the later years of the occupation and thereafter, as they returned home to recount their experiences in lectures, newspaper and magazine articles, and, in a few cases, best-selling books.

This popularization of the figure of the marine as an authority on "voodoo" took place just before Haiti became a major destination for North American and other foreign anthropological researchers interested in studying, in Melville Herskovits's formulation, "New World Africanisms." Indeed, the extent to which the occupation and such literatures stimulated the dramatic turn of U.S. anthropological interest toward Haiti during the mid- to late 1930s is a question that warrants further study.[224] Herskovits and his wife, Frances, first passed through Haiti in 1928 on their way to Dutch Guiana (now Suriname) and were hosted in the capital by John Houston Craige, then the police chief in Port-au-Prince. The six-year correspondence between the two men thereafter points to how the burgeoning American anthropological focus on Haiti emerged in quite literal conversation with the disciplinary knowledge and imperial images of Haitian popular cultures produced by the American occupation. Craige was a self-acknowledged believer in white racial superiority who fashioned himself as an amateur anthropologist, a hobby stimulated by his time in Haiti. During the Herskovitses' first stopover in Port-au-Prince, Craige apparently offered to serve as a kind of long-distance research assistant for the studies on physical anthropology in which Melville was then engaged. He wrote to Herskovits upon his return to the United States in 1928 about his own ethnographic aspirations: "I really believe that I am the best generally-equipped person who has ever studied the Haitian at close range. The result has been a mass of material, social, political, linguistic, literary, musical, anthropological—well I have twelve good-sized cases full of stuff that will take a year or two to get acquainted with."[225]

In the meantime, Craige was working on a book about his own experiences in Haiti, which at first took the form of a political exposé of the occupation. The publishers "said it would be a knock-out," but Craige confided to Herskovits: "On reading it over I decided that it would knock me out of the Marine Corps because it was brutally frank about political matters." Thus, by early 1932 he had "decided to eliminate all reference to official action of any kind and do the whole thing over as a local color book."[226] Soon after their correspondence began, Craige and Herskovits had written a series of letters to one another in which each disparaged W. B. Seabrook's *The Magic Island*, which had just been published and which Herskovits reviewed negatively in the *Nation*.[227] Whatever his reservations about Seabrook's literary choices, Craige clearly took note of their financial success, for the two books he thereafter published in rapid succession, *Black Bagdad* and its sequel, *Cannibal Cousins* (1934), were at least as indebted to such genres as Seabrook's book had been.[228] Indeed, one could argue that Craige raided the archive of colonial tropes far more exhaustively than had Seabrook. In one of his last letters to Herskovits, shortly after the publication of *Black Bagdad*, Craige explained the calculation of its sensationalism, complaining that while the book "continues to sell well," he was feeling "disappointed, as I hoped some of the Haitians would attack it." He continued, "This would be grand, as it would sell a lot of books."[229] Craige was tapped as a public speaker on Haiti even before the publication of *Black Bagdad*, writing to Herskovits in later 1929: "I have had quite a bit of success as a lecturer, of late, and am going down, January 3rd, to talk on the Haitian situation to the National Geographic Society in Washington."[230] His report that the Society had already sold over four thousand seats might suggest the public interest in such events at this time and the way in which particular marines were seen as privileged informants on Haitian topics.

The most celebrated of these was Faustin Wirkus, whose billing by W. B. Seabrook as the "white king of La Gonâve" led to the marine's international celebrity, and, in 1931, the publication of his own memoir, written in collaboration with a journalist named Taney Dudley. In an introduction to this latter work, Seabrook explained the international fascination with the story of the "white king" as having its roots in a white masculinist, paternalist fantasy: "Every boy ever born, if he is any good, wants, among other things, to be king of a tropical island. . . . Every man (who isn't dead on his feet like a zombie) perhaps wants to be God." He concluded, "I think that is why his story . . . took wings and flew round the world."[231]

One wonders how the narration of Wirkus's heroic ascendance "from the coal-mines of Pennsylvania to the throne of a tropical isle" might stand in relation to Eugene O'Neill's tale of Brutus Jones in his occupation-era play *The Emperor Jones* (1920).[232] Drawing from legends surrounding Haiti's revolutionary and post-independence leaders, O'Neill's drama tells the story of the improbable rise and ignoble fall of a black American who escapes a chain gang, stows away to a tropical island, and becomes emperor there. While press accounts of the "white king" focused on Wirkus's efforts to eliminate graft, judicious collection of taxes, and benevolent rule of grateful "natives" on La Gonâve, O'Neill's Emperor Jones is a tyrant, whose taxation of his subjects "squeezed 'em dry," as he is reminded at one point. Taken together, the famous figures of Brutus Jones and Faustin Wirkus, one fictional, the other fictionalized, seem to stand as inverted doubles of one another, complicitously reinforcing the themes of black despotism and paternalist white tutelage through which American apologists continued to justify the nineteen-year military occupation.[233]

In actual fact, though, it seems clear that Wirkus's influence on La Gonâve was brokered by his good relations with the predominantly female leadership, known as *renn yo* (French *les reines*, or the queens), of the cooperative agricultural labor and mutual aid societies on La Gonâve collectively called *sosyete kongo*.[234] In particular, the goodwill between Wirkus and Ti Memenne, the queen of several of these societies, proved to be of considerable mutual benefit during the years he was stationed there (see fig. 6). If he was indeed inducted as "king" into these societies, the calculation on the part of their female-dominated leadership was surely that there would be political advantages to the incorporation of a sympathetic member of the U.S. military into their organizations during the occupation, particularly in terms of relations with the mainland.

FIGURE 6. Ti Memenne and Faustin Wirkus. From *The White King of La Gonave*.

Upon returning to the United States from Haiti in 1930, Wirkus temporarily left active military duty, in order, as the press reported at the time, to devote himself full-time to writing and lecturing. His memoir was a great popular and critical success, even praised by longtime antioccupation activists such as Ernest Gruening.[235] Wirkus published magazine articles and, like Craige, was invited to speak before the National Geographic Society.[236] What has not been widely recognized, however, is that after his book appeared he returned to La Gonâve in 1931 and 1932 to shoot a short film, with sound, that he planned to show during his lecture tours (see fig. 7).[237] Completed in 1933, Wirkus's *Voodoo* was distributed as a "Principal-Adventure Production" through Sol Lesser's Principal Distributing Corporation and screened in theaters in New York, Los Angeles, and elsewhere, as well as by Wirkus in his public appearances across the country. It has since been lost—one of many ephemeral independent cinematic productions of that time.[238]

The few descriptions of Wirkus's film signal the multiple senses—generic and otherwise—in which it was a hybrid production. On the one hand, *Voodoo* seems to have been fashioned as a kind of documentary travelogue showing, as one reviewer noted, "in some detail the surviving rituals of voodoo as practiced by the natives of this island." This reviewer concluded that "so far as the straight shots of assemblages, dances and ceremonial preparations is [*sic*] concerned, [the film was] obviously authentic."[239] George Turner, who saw the film during its brief cinematic release as a child, remembers it as having been primarily ethnographic, focused on a "remarkable study of Voodoo practices."[240] One key dimen-

FIGURE 7. Wirkus and a collaborator filming *Voodoo* on La Gonâve, 1932. Frank R. Crumbie Papers, Special and Area Studies Collections, George A. Smathers Libraries, University of Florida, Gainesville, Florida.

sion of what I am calling *Voodoo*'s hybridity is the role that religious practitioners on La Gonâve played in its filming, the exact nature of which is unknowable at this point. Yet fragmentary evidence gleaned both from reports on the "raw" footage and from reviews of the completed film suggests that one or more of the *sosyete kongo* into which Wirkus was inducted organized their members to stage decontextualized ritual performances, including the sacrificial offering of fowl and a goat, as the camera rolled.

Their participation as performers and, perhaps, in some cases as behind-the-scenes consultants, choreographers, and even directors raises many questions, most of them unanswerable at this point. Under what conditions did they agree to be involved in the film, and to what degree was their participation coerced? If they were told to "perform themselves" in scenes depicting ritual preparations and processes, what did they choose to depict, and how did they objectify these sacred practices? What kind of "feedback loops" emerged through their work on the film, with imperial

narratives of "voodoo" framing the production but perhaps not overde-
termining it on account of their participation? What were local interpretations of the film's final scene, universally lambasted by reviewers, which
enacted "the escape into the jungle of an intended human victim who, but
for the intervention of the adventurer . . . would have been offered upon
the altar of the serpent god"?[241]

Fatimah Tobing Rony has examined the relation between the wave
of ethnographically informed "racial films" produced during the 1920s
and early 1930s and presenting, as one critic noted in 1928, "the daily life
of out-of-the-way minorities" and the emergence of Hollywood horror
movies, often themselves narratively structured on the model of scientific-
expedition films.[242] Wirkus's *Voodoo* seems to have straddled these genres
with particular self-consciousness, given that it was framed as a tour of
"native" religious practices on the already famous island of La Gonâve
by a guide whose attributed ethnographic authority on such topics derived
directly from his former military authority there. An advertisement for
the film that appeared in the *New York World Telegram* on 22 March 1933
billed *Voodoo* as the "First Authentic Film Record of the Forbidden Ritual
of Voodoo Held by Primitives of Haiti." It featured a diaphanously clad
woman, apparently white, with one arm halfway sucked into the maw of
an amorphous, wild-eyed monster, and a masked figure who seems to direct the scene from below with ritual gestures. *Voodoo* may indeed have been
the first filmed representation of ritual staged by Vodouizan. But surely
one reason it is unknown in the ethnographic film archive on Haiti today is
that it was automatically assimilated, as its backers seem to have hoped,
into the burgeoning horror genre on account of its subject matter.[243]

Zonbi *Working in the Canefields*

Only a year earlier, the director Victor Halperin's classic *White Zombie*,
starring Bela Lugosi, had instantiated "voodoo" sorcery, and particularly
the figure of the living dead, as fixtures of the cinematic horror imaginary. In his book *Golden Horrors: An Illustrated Critical Filmography of Terror
Cinema, 1931–1939*, the horror-film historian Bryan Senn devotes eleven
pages to *White Zombie*, calling it "the most atmospheric independent
horror film of the decade."[244] Although, as Mary Renda notes, "zombie
flicks" would proliferate over the course of the 1930s and lose their specific referentiality to Haiti, Halperin's film, produced by his brother Edward, was set there explicitly.[245] The Halperins' "Haiti" was constructed
on the back lot of Universal Studios largely from the standing sets of earlier horror films. It is a gothic landscape populated mostly by white char-
acters, although no direct reference is made in the film to the ongoing oc-

FIGURE 8. Image from reissue of pressbook for *White Zombie*. Courtesy of Brian Senn.

cupation. By this point, however, merely identifying the setting as Haiti carried its own atmosphere, and United Artists focused on this angle in publicizing the film. According to the pressbook for *White Zombie*, "The story . . . is based upon personal observation in Haiti by American writers and research workers, and, fantastic as it sounds, its entire substance is based upon fact." As noted earlier, cinema owners were urged to hang blown-up posters of what was mistakenly identified as "article 249" of the Haitian Code Pénal (actually article 246), with the word "zombie" inserted strategically into the translated text (see fig. 8).[246]

The key source for *White Zombie* was Seabrook's *The Magic Island*, the book responsible for first animating the figure of the "zombie," which, with the assistance of the Halperins' film, took on a cinematic life of its own. The Halperins seem to have discovered Seabrook's work through a short-lived Broadway play called *Zombie* that opened on 10 February 1932 and ran for twenty performances to poor reviews before moving west.[247] The scene that Senn describes as the film's "eeriest sequence" is adapted and brought to life directly from the pages of Seabrook's book. This occurs early on, when a wealthy white American plantation owner, Charles Beaumont (Robert Frazer), seeks out the assistance of the malevolent Murder Legendre (Bela Lugosi) at the latter's sugar mill in his desire to win the affections of Madeline (Madge Bellamy), who has just arrived from New York to marry her fiancé, an American banker (John Harron) stationed in Port-au-Prince. The scene is dominated by the mill itself, operated entirely by Legendre's crew of shuffling, vacant-eyed zombies, the picture of alienated labor.[248]

At the center of the chapter that he devotes to such beings and the beliefs surrounding them, Seabrook recounts an elaborate rumor that he reported hearing from a landowning farmer and tax collector named Constant Polynice during his visit to the island of La Gonâve.[249] Insisting on the reality of *zonbi*, Polynice noted that sometimes they were even discovered close to the cities: in 1918 a team of them reportedly toiled for several months at the newly opened Haytian American Sugar Company (HASCO), a large American-owned sugar operation, with its factories, railway, and plantations (mostly under long-term lease arrangements) situated on the Cul-de-Sac and Léogâne plains.[250] According to Seabrook, Polynice explained that the company had offered "a big bonus on the wages of new workers" that season, and among those drawn by this prospect was a Ti Joseph of Colombier, who arrived at HASCO's registration office with a "band of ragged creatures who shuffled along behind him, staring dumbly, like people walking in a daze." Although Ti Joseph claimed that his companions, whose work in the fields he would supervise, were mountain people from the Dominican-Haitian border region who did not understand plains Kreyòl, they were actually *zonbi* under his mastery. The scheme enriched Ti Joseph and his wife Croyance for months until she made the fatal error of giving them a candy that had salt in it, an ingredient that must be withheld from *zonbi* because it has the effect of awakening them.

Seabrook writes of his astonishment at hearing such events associated with HASCO, which he describes as "perhaps the last name anybody would think of connecting with either sorcery or superstition." He elaborates: "The word is American-commercial-synthetic, like Nabisco, Delco, Socony. It [is] an immense factory plant, dominated by a huge chimney, with clanging machinery, steam whistles, freight cars. It is like a chunk of Hoboken. . . . Hasco makes rum when the sugar market is off, pays low wages, twenty or thirty cents a day, and gives steady work. It is modern big business, and it sounds it, looks it, smells it."[251] Yet the association of HASCO with sorcery was by no means as incongruous as Seabrook insists. As the largest American-owned enterprise in Haiti and foremost icon of the agribusiness that was steadily displacing peasant sharecroppers across these regions by means of land appropriations, HASCO was, to the contrary, a highly likely object of sorcery discourse in early-occupation Cul-de-Sac and Léogâne. Indeed, that this course of events was said to have taken place in 1918 is noteworthy in itself: that was the year the HASCO factory in the Cul-de-Sac opened and the company marked its first harvest. It was also in 1918 that popular outrage over the *kòve* system of forced labor reached its height, and in June of that year the new U.S.-sponsored Haitian constitution authorizing foreigners to own land was put into effect by the marine-enforced "popular plebiscite."[252]

Karen Richman has examined how even though HASCO only minimally exploited the right to foreign land ownership after that constitutional revision, ultimately purchasing 2,600 *carreaux* in the Cul-de-Sac and almost none in Léogâne, the arrival of American agribusiness was profoundly disruptive for those who had long farmed the land on these fertile plains, whether independently or working for elite landowners through the *demwatye* (sharecropping) system.[253] Through this latter arrangement in Léogâne, cultivators received 60–75 percent of the harvest and could "interplant" food crops for themselves amidst the cash crop. Once regional elites leased their lands to the American company for sugar production, however, the sharecroppers were expelled. They were then invited to return to work as day laborers on the "modernized" plantations for one-fifth of the wages that migrant workers (predominantly Haitians and Jamaicans) were paid at that time on American sugar plantations in Cuba.[254] Candelon Rigaud, who was himself a HASCO administrator, confirmed that sharecroppers were also displaced in the Cul-de-Sac after the company established its operations there. Emphasizing the longtime entrenchment of the system of *demwatye* throughout the region, he writes that he was himself an agent of its suppression on behalf of HASCO: "[A] Foreign Agricultural Company took upon itself to dismiss all the share-

croppers on all of the properties that entered into the circle of its administration . . . . And who was charged with this fine job? Me! Your faithful
servant."[255]

The figure of Ti Joseph in Seabrook's story seems quite plausible given
that, as the occupation historian Hans Schmidt notes, HASCO "absolved
itself of all responsibility for its [wage] workers by subhiring through native gang bosses." Candelon Rigaud emphasized that the company had
"no control" over laborers in the Cul-de-Sac and that, "naturally," the
more productive a contractor's *équipe*, the better he was remunerated by
the company.[256] In examining the stigmatization of wage labor in parts of
Léogâne once dominated by HASCO, Karen Richman notes that those
kiltivatè (independent farmers) who at some point in life were forced to
perform day labor usually left the community to pursue this. Thus, it
was generally "outsiders" and "mountain people" who performed agricultural day labor in the area—and, she notes, locals derisively referred to
them as *zonbi*, among other epithets.[257]

Just as Michael Taussig once asked about the "relationship between the
image of the devil and capitalist development" among plantation workers and miners in South America, so we might ask about the relationship
between the image of the *zonbi* and capitalist development in occupation-
era Haiti.[258] Could there have been a more fitting image of and incisive
commentary on the proletarianization of the displaced Haitian peasant
sharecropper than a crew of *zonbi* toiling in the HASCO cane fields? That
story could be read productively alongside the letter, signed "OUVRIERS,"
that a group of HASCO wage workers sent to the director of the company
in late 1917 demanding a workday of eight hours instead of ten, a short-
ened day on Saturday, and a 10 percent wage increase and warning that
"otherwise, we will all be forced to abandon this Company to go to the
Dominican Republic for better conditions." Roger Gaillard describes the
collective spirit of this letter as "unprecedented" and sees the document
as marking a "turning point" in the history of Haitian social struggle.[259]
Never forgetting its mediation by an author whom Alfred Métraux aptly
characterized as a kind of sorcerer himself, "[drawing] with both hands"
on such tales, the account of *zonbi* slaving at HASCO can likewise be
read as relating a powerful social analysis and indictment of the encompassing of rural life in these plains by North American capitalist enterprise after 1915.[260] Indeed, I would posit a connection between these two
texts, both of which critically evaluate the experience of proletarianization under the occupation.[261] As Stephan Palmié, also reading Seabrook,
has analyzed: "Far from representing a mistaken interpolation of archaic
fantasy into the rational script of agroindustrial labor relations, the image

of the zonbi and the reduction of humans to commodified embodiments of labor power to which it speaks are cut from the cloth of a single social reality long in the making, a reality deeply riven with a sense of moral crisis unleashed by a predatory modernity and experienced, chronicled, and analyzed by its victims in the form of phantasmagoric narratives about how even the bodies of the dead, bereft of their souls, do not escape conscription into capitalist social relations of production."[262] Ironically, in Seabrook's hands, this social critique became the vehicle for the export of another kind of commodity, the hybridized specter of the "zombie," which over the next decade proved far more lucrative for American investors than most of the fly-by-night agricultural operations that came and went in rural Haiti during the occupation.[263]

The story of *zonbi* slaving at HASCO might suggest yet another way to think about the idea that the occupation "promoted" or "spread" prohibited ritual practices (or rumors thereof) even as marines applied the laws against *les sortilèges* with opportunistic force. In considering the logic of that accusation, I have stressed the role played by the severe campaign that U.S. military forces launched against popular ritual practices in Haiti after 1915 in materializing imperial images of "voodoo" and "zombies" that took on lives of their own in foreign imaginaries during and after the occupation.[264] These images both justified the repressive regime and incited ever greater fascination with the practices that were its object. Seabrook's report of the rumor in the Cul-de-Sac of *zonbi* forced into labor at HASCO also raises the question of whether the occupation's manifold disruptions of rural life intensified and redirected local discourses of supernatural corruption and aggression in Haiti. Such a question cannot be approached without consideration of the marines' enforcement of the penal regime against *les sortilèges* and of North American capitalist penetration in Haiti, both of which were more intense in some parts of the country than others. Of course, as we have seen, John Russell considered these imperial projects to be closely linked: in his view, without the repression of "voodoo" and the nefarious influence of the "papaloi" there could be no possibility of justice in the Haitian courts for American agro-industrial investors. The Cul-de-Sac plain was a particular focal point for both interventions because of the region's proximity to the capital, the extent of *kako* activity localized north of the plain during the insurgency, and the unusual potential for large-scale plantation agriculture thanks to the existence of estates that had already been consolidated. It was near the regional center of Croix-des-Bouquets that the *oungan* Leonard Placide or Destine Jean was arrested and executed the following year in the midst of the mounting popular rebellion.

Laënnec Hurbon has analyzed how episodes of repression against the popular practices defined legally as *sortilèges* and ecclesiastically as superstition or fetishism always seemed to incite further rumors of malicious magic."[265] This was partly because such campaigns were interpreted according to popular definitions of criminal sorcery and, through local pressures, ultimately directed toward those ends. Marine complaints about popular pressure to enforce the laws in ways that seemed antithetical to the occupation's purportedly rationalizing mission in Haiti are cases in point. With regard to the expansion of corporate agriculture during the occupation, Karen Richman has examined how in Léogâne in the first half of the twentieth century "the immorality of wage labor and [the] inhumane capitalist system that exploits it" came to be identified with magic and the utilization of *pwen*—in this context, spirits purchased from outside the community for the pursuit of individualistic gain.[266] She argues that if the widespread disruption of rural life in the Léogâne and the Cul-de-Sac plains during the occupation increased suspicions that *pwen* were being exploited for corrupt purposes (as opposed to those considered benign), this produced a countervailing expansion and augmentation of the power and prestige of Ginen as a social category and moral standard: "The discourse privileged peasant morality so that the peasants' increasing acclimation to alienated (wage) labor could be concealed."[267]

In a sense, then, the tale of *zonbi* toiling at HASCO can be understood as bringing together and commenting on the two principal ways in which, as I argued in the opening pages of this chapter, U.S. military officials and civil treaty officers in Haiti between 1915 and 1934 manipulated the Haitian legal corpus: on the one hand, through the revocation of existing laws that obstructed U.S. military and financial control in Haiti, and on the other, through the enforcement of penal laws in violation of customary norms. If stories of spiritual corruption and aggression focused on new agents and objects in the drastically reorganized rural conditions of places such as the Léogâne and Cul-de-Sac plains, so too did those conditions, and the regimes that produced them, become the objects of powerful social analysis and moral critique through such stories.

CHAPTER FOUR

Cultural Nationalist Policy and the Pursuit of "Superstition" in Post-Occupation Haiti

During a roundtable discussion focused on the early history of Haitian staged folklore performance that took place in Port-au-Prince in April 1997, one panelist noted that the so-called *mouvement folklorique* had "really begun" under the post-occupation presidency of Élie Lescot (1941–1946). Another then observed that "paradoxically, you also had under Lescot the *kanpay rejete*," the Catholic church's violent campaign against "superstition," which the state initially backed with military force.[1] This chapter focuses on the logic of that historical conjunction, examining official cultural nationalist policy in Haiti during the late 1930s and early 1940s in relation to the post-occupation legal regime against *les pratiques superstitieuses*. This was a new penal category, instituted by Lescot's predecessor, Sténio Vincent, a year after the departure of U.S. marines from Haiti in 1934. Abrogating the long-standing prohibition against *les sortilèges*, Vincent's government tightened the interdiction of ritual practices now defined as *pratiques superstitieuses*, while also affirming the right of peasants to organize "popular dances." This chapter explores the implications of that legal formulation through a close study of the Haitian state's initial civil and military support for the church's so-called *campagne anti-superstitieuse* (antisuperstition campaign), while it also annexed "folklore," and particularly choreographic constructions of ritual dance, as official national signs.

PART I

"Better Than the Laws Which Can Only Be Borrowed Finery"
Imperial myths of peasant ritualism had never been so highly charged as on the eve of the U.S. military's departure from Haiti in August 1934. However, neither had Haitian popular cultures ever been so forcefully

figured as the matrix for Haitian national identity. During the occupation, an intense nationalist concern for the ethnological study and literary
representation of the "folk" developed in Haiti among young urban intellectuals and writers. In 1927 Carl Brouard, a poet and one of the cofound-
ers of the short-lived landmark literary journal *La Revue indigène,* introduced the iconoclastic "new school" as a reaction against the "too servile
imitation" of European models that, he and others charged, had stunted
the development of Haitian arts and letters.[2] The proponents of what became known as *indigénisme* defined their break with the past by figuring
popular cultures as the proper source and subject for the building of a national literature. Pierre Buteau notes that although there had been earlier efforts to establish a national literary school based on popular themes,
including that advanced by Émile Nau in the 1830s, none of these initiatives exerted the political force that *indigénisme* would, particularly on
state policy: "Above all, '*indigénisme*' changed the terms of the debate."[3]

Catalyzed, in part, by the shock of imperial domination, the poetics of
what became known as *indigénisme* emerged in dialogue with a confluence
of other post–World War I literary and political currents. A number of
the self-identified *indigénistes*, most of whom were from elite families, had
recently returned from study in Europe.[4] Dada and surrealism, the poetry
of the Harlem Renaissance, Garveyism, Pan-Africanism, Marxist anti-
colonialism, Spengler's theory of Western decadence, the burgeoning *afrocubanismo* cultural movement in Havana, and *indigenismo* literary currents throughout Latin America—these are some of the broad strokes of
Haitian *indigénisme*'s international context in the later 1920s.[5]

No one was more influential in the project of "re-evaluating" (as he
put it) Haitian popular cultures for national ends than Jean Price-Mars—
medical doctor, teacher, statesman, and founder of what became the Haitian school of ethnology (see fig. 9).[6] Born in 1876 in Grande-Rivière-du-
Nord, Price-Mars was a generation older than most of the self-identified
indigénistes and was not a poet. But he galvanized the movement through
his persistent public critique of the elite's failure to unite the nation. In
1928 a number of his lectures were published as *Ainsi parla l'oncle* (So Spoke
the Uncle), his classic study of Haitian popular culture.[7] In this enormously influential work, which a group of his students later called "the
basic book of our folklore," Price-Mars attacked the Haitian elite's cultural identification with France and the West more generally at the expense of "all that is authentically indigenous—language, customs, sentiments, beliefs."[8] He charged that the persistence of this *bovarysme collectif*
precluded the possibility of national unity and had so weakened Haitian
society that the country was left vulnerable to takeover by the United

FIGURE 9. Jean Price-Mars. Courtesy of Archives CIDIHCA.

States in July 1915.[9] "Our only chance to be ourselves," he wrote, "is to not repudiate part of our ancestral heritage. And! as for this heritage, eight-tenths of it is a gift from Africa."[10]

Price-Mars called for the reevaluation of Haitian culture through the intensive study of folklore, a concept that he defined, after the French folklorist Paul Sébillot (author of *Le folk-lore* [1913]), as the "oral traditions of a people," encompassing the inventory of "legends, tales, songs, riddles, customs, observances, ceremonies, and beliefs which are its own, or which it has assimilated in a way that gives them a personal imprint."[11] Above all, it was "the religious sentiment of the rural masses"—glossed, not unproblematically in Price-Mars's view, as "Vaudou"—that should be recognized as the wellspring of Haitian folklore and the primary source of the nation's cultural particularity.[12] Marshaling French sociological theory (and particularly Émile Durkheim's *Les formes élémentaires de la vie religieuse*), Price-Mars set out in *Ainsi parla l'oncle* to refute the colonial construction of popular belief and ritual as sorcery and methodically argue for their status as a religion, albeit a "very primitive" one, "formed in part by beliefs in the almighty Power of spiritual beings—gods, demons, disembodied souls—in part by beliefs in sorcery and magic."[13]

In Price-Mars's view, the implications of this reclassification were not simply academic, given that such practices were then subject to criminalization under Haitian penal law, repression at the hands of the marines and U.S.-trained Garde d'Haïti, and demonization by Catholic and Protestant clergies in Haiti. Although Price-Mars justifies his focus on popular religious belief and practice in *Ainsi parla l'oncle* with reference to their primacy in peasant life and culture, he also points throughout his book to the way in which "Vaudou" functioned as a potent sign, encapsulating for many urban elites "the undesirable legacy of a shameful past."[14] Price-Mars's analysis of the ways in which the penal prohibition of *le vaudoux* contributed to the Haitian peasantry's continued subjugation shaped the political stakes of *Ainsi parla l'oncle* and much of his subsequent work.

It is striking to note that formalized ethnological studies of Haitian popular ritual did not have their beginnings in Lombrosian criminal anthropology, as they did in the early published works of Raimundo Nina Rodrigues in Brazil, and Fernando Ortiz in Cuba. Ortiz's *Los negros brujos* (1906), for example, diagnosed the moral and criminal threat of "racial atavisms" to the Cuban republican social body and prescribed measures of "social therapy" underwritten by metaphors of "sanitation" and "hygiene" to eliminate it.[15] By the later 1920s, however, Ortiz had reconsidered such theories and was at the forefront of the emerging *afrocubanista* literary and artistic movement in Cuba. A question that lies beyond the scope of this study but warrants greater attention is the extent to which his own reevaluation of Afro-Cuban culture was stimulated by and/or stimulating for that which the *indigéniste* writers and Jean Price-Mars were advocating at the same moment in Haiti.[16]

At one point in *Ainsi parla l'oncle*, Price-Mars makes explicit his call for a shift away from earlier elite-centered, European-identified nationalist models and toward the construction of popular tradition as a commonly held, uniquely Haitian cultural endowment and patrimony:

> Better than the stories of great battles, better than the relation of the great deeds of official history always stiff from the constraint of only expressing a part of the elusive Truth, better than the theatrical poses of statesmen in attitudes of command, better than the laws which can only be borrowed finery ill fitted to our social state, in which short-lived holders of power condense their hatred, their prejudices, their dreams or their hopes, better than all these things which are most often . . . adopted by only one part of the nation—tales, songs, legends, proverbs, beliefs are works or prod-

ucts spontaneously sprung up, at a given moment, from an inspired mind, adopted by all.[17]

It is, of course, not incidental that Price-Mars singles out law in this inventory for particular critique. Later on he would argue that Haiti's Code Pénal served ruling classes as a space for the repudiation of the "primitive" through the prohibition of *les pratiques superstitieuses*.[18] *Ainsi parla l'oncle* is an extended rebuke of the Haitian elite for having disavowed and repressed precisely what they ought to have claimed and constructed as the repository of Haitian national identity, or as Price-Mars, after Herder, terms it, the "national soul."

For Price-Mars, the reevaluation of popular culture as folklore held the promise of national unification. The political force of this argument stemmed from its basis in an anti-imperial assertion of difference. However, the premises of the project were also shaped by nineteenth-century European romantic nationalism, and the increasingly ubiquitous way in which folklore was being promoted internationally as the cultural basis for state nationalist claims. This was the legacy of *indigénisme* for official cultural politics in Haiti during the late 1930s and early 1940s. The post-occupation state constructed popular practices, and particularly ritual dance, as indices of official Haitian identity and modernity, but at times framed such performances internationally as revivals of a transcended cultural past.

Popular Dances versus Superstitious Practices

When the government of Sténio Vincent promulgated its new *décret-loi* against *les pratiques superstitieuses* in September 1935, just a little more than a year after the U.S. occupation of Haiti had ended, the popular practices legally classified as *sortilèges* had been officially prohibited by the Haitian Code Pénal for precisely a century.[19] As discussed in chapter 2, article 405 of the 1835 Code Pénal prohibited the making of "*ouangas, caprelatas, vaudoux, donpèdre, macandals,* and other *sortilèges.*" In 1864, under President Fabre Nicolas Geffrard, the law was revised, its penalties reinforced, and its scope expanded so that "all dances and any other practices of the nature to keep alive in the populations the spirit of fetishism and superstition will be considered *sortilèges* and punished by the same sentences."[20] It was the 1864 Code Pénal that had been in effect during the U.S. occupation, and article 405 that had been enforced by U.S. military officials with such severity particularly during the early years of the nineteen-year intervention, when it both served the ends of counterinsurgency and enabled U.S. officials to justify the occupation as a "civilizing" mission.

Shortly following the U.S. departure from Haiti, the Vincent government decided to abrogate article 405, a century-old fixture of the Code Pénal, and two months later passed a new *décret-loi* against the unprecedented legal category of *pratiques superstitieuses*. Throughout this study I have been interested in how the Haitian penal law against *les sortilèges* functioned as both a sign and, at times, an instrument of the nineteenth- and early twentieth-century Haitian state's determination to enforce "civilized" modernity within its borders. Here I shall consider the ways in which this project was politically redefined in the early post-occupation moment, and how the 1935 *décret-loi* both marked and enabled these shifts.

Sténio Vincent had been a member of the Haitian legislature dissolved by U.S. military officials in 1917, when the Assemblée Nationale refused to approve the constitutional revisions demanded by Washington; these included lifting the interdiction against foreign landholding. Thereafter he was at the forefront of organized elite opposition to U.S. military presence and policy in Haiti and presented testimony on behalf of the nationalist Union Patriotique group during the 1921–1922 Senate inquiry into the occupation's administration and tactics. Such positions paved the way for his election to the presidency by the reconstituted legislature in November 1930, as Washington began to prepare for the removal of troops from Haiti (the occupation having become, both domestically and internationally, a political liability).[21] Vincent, an elite *milat* according to Haitian class and color identifications, grew increasingly dictatorial during his eleven years in office. Yet he fashioned himself as a populist reformer, launching several high-profile social programs and public works projects for the peasantry and urban poor. Known as a skillful orator, he sometimes gave addresses in Kreyòl rather than French, Haiti's official language at this time even though only a minority of Haitians spoke it.[22]

Whatever his nationalist credentials and populist gestures, Vincent was no public celebrant or defender of the legitimacy of popular religious practices, and his government was hostile to and opposed by leading proponents of *indigénisme*.[23] A strong defender of the French cultural tradition and Roman Catholicism in Haiti, Vincent's populism was more on the order of economic and moral "uplift." This was a major theme of his *Efforts et résultats* (1938), a glowing account of his government's accomplishments since the end of the occupation that paid particular attention to the "laws, decree-laws, orders, circulars and presidential instructions which bear witness . . . to our will to effect, with desirable order and peace, the protection and uplift of rural classes too long misunderstood and exploited."[24] Among the legal initiatives summarized in this account were the revisions to the Code Pénal that the legislature and his administration had undertaken in the summer of 1935. Early that July, the series of prohibitions collected under the penal category of *sortilèges* was almost entirely revoked. Article 405, prohibiting the making of *"ouangas, vaudoux, donpèdre, macandals*, and other *sortilèges"* and "all dances and any other practices of the nature to keep alive in the populations the spirit of fetishism and superstition," was abrogated, as was article 407, entailing the seizure and destruction of "the instruments, utensils, and costumes used or destined to be used" in the accomplishment of such actions. Only article 406, banning the practices of fortune-telling, was left largely intact.[25]

It is perhaps a little-recognized fact of Haitian juridical history that for two months during the summer of 1935, Haiti was without a penal prohibition against most of the practices formerly classified as *sortilèges*. The circumstances around the abrogation of this law, a fixture of the Code Pénal since its promulgation under Boyer in 1835, are unclear, but minutes from legislative discussions leading up to the decision are illuminating. A proposal to abrogate articles 405–407 and to modify article 228, prohibiting vagrancy, was actually first advanced in the Chambre des Députés in 1931 on account of the abuses that had long marked the enforcement of these statutes.[26] Then, in April 1935, a revision of article 405 was discussed in the Senate on different grounds: the concern was now to "suppress . . . the words 'donpèdre and macandale [*sic*]'" out of "respect for the glorious memory of two precursors of our independence who bore these names," suggesting that the law itself had become a space for cultural nationalist reevaluation.[27] That proposal was well received in the Chambre des Députés and prompted discussion of the abrogation that had been considered in 1931. By June the Senate had returned to the original proposal to redefine the law against vagrancy and rescind most of the provisions of the law against *les sortilèges*, and on 5 July Vincent signed off on these changes to the Code Pénal.[28]

There seems to have been little, if any, publicity around the lifting of the penal regime against "spells," and the extent to which it was publicly announced or implemented by district and section authorities across the country is unclear. The major newspapers, for example, did not mention it. However, Louis Raymond, a justice ministry employee who published a manual on Haitian penal law for police officers and justices of the peace later that year, reported that "a renewed outbreak of *pratiques superstitieuses*" had followed the "inopportune abrogation of article 405 of the Code Pénal." In order to "provide for the repression of these spells," he wrote, the government was forced to promulgate the new *décret-loi* against *les pratiques superstitieuses* that went into effect early that September.[29]

What exactly Raymond meant by "a renewed outbreak of *pratiques su-*

perstitieuses" is unclear. I have found no legislative records to corroborate or counter his account, or to explain why the terms of the new law departed so significantly from those of its antecedent.[30] It was not just that the 1935 law considerably tightened the penal regime that had been in place against these practices, doubling the minimum prison sentences and more than quadrupling the minimum fines. Such an escalation of penalties had also accompanied the 1864 revision of articles 405–407 under Geffrard. The most significant change in the new law lay not in its severity against prohibited practices, but in how they were legally defined: the subsuming penal category was no longer *les sortilèges*, but rather *les pratiques superstitieuses*. What is more significant, the new law did not inventory banned practices by name (i.e., *ouangas, caprelatas, vaudoux, donpèdre,* and *macandals*), but instead made their identification a matter of legal definition. Article 1 of the 1935 law read:

> Are considered to be *pratiques superstitieuses*:
> 1. the ceremonies, rites, dances, and meetings in the course of which are practiced, in offering to so-called divinities, sacrifices of cattle or fowl;
> 2. the act of exploiting the public in making believe that, by occult means, it is possible to manage either to change the situation of fortune of an individual, or to heal him of any illness, by processes unknown to medical science;
> 3. the fact of having in one's residence cabalistic objects serving to exploit the credulity or the naïveté of the public.[31]

Perhaps the first question to ask about the new law is, what was to be gained by these shifts, from nomination to definition and from "spells" to the new penal category of "superstitious practices"? First and foremost, through those shifts, and through the logic of safeguarding the public against those who might exploit their "credulity or naïveté," the new law circumvented the trap of affirmation with which, as we have seen, its antecedents had been mined. By redefining the subsuming legal category as *les pratiques superstitieuses* and by not banning by name different forms of *sortilèges*, the law avoided appearing to endorse, in its enforcement, the reality of malicious magic. That meant it also avoided all of the evidentiary problems that accompanied trying such cases. Now, according to lines 2 and 3, the crime was not the "occult" act performed, but the deceit of claiming its magical efficacy.

The listing of prohibited *sortilèges* (*ouangas, caprelatas, vaudoux, donpèdre,* and *macandals*), an eruption of Kreyòl words in the midst of French legalese, had always been a problematic feature of the earlier law, raising two major questions. First, were these names, taken individually, adequately referential, and secondly, were they, taken together, adequately inclusive to cover an entire field of prohibited practices? Without a definition or description of each *sortilège*, could the law be confident of a secure relationship between the legal name and its intended referent? Were such correspondences between name and act constant in popular usage over time?[32] Did the law point directly and unambiguously toward what it sought to ban? Had it ever done so? If not, then the law suffered from a crisis of reference in which it created supplements of what it intended to prohibit.

Christopher Bracken has analyzed this problem of legal nomination in his study of the Canadian penal regime against "potlatch" or "potlach" among First Nation peoples during the late nineteenth and early twentieth centuries. He argues that the various spellings of this word in Canadian regulatory discourses highlighted a perennial uncertainty surrounding its meaning and its relation to an actual practice: "Without reference the legal system breaks down, for a law that does not define what it bans makes it impossible for police and judges to identify the practices that are forbidden." As Bracken notes, such ambiguities led the Canadian government in 1895 to issue a new statute replacing the word "potlatch" and its variants with "brief descriptions identifying the acts that are henceforth forbidden." Thus, as with Sténio Vincent's 1935 law, the acts prohibited were henceforth legally defined, rather than named.[33]

Whatever differences need to be acknowledged between these two penal regimes and the circumstances of their promulgation, it seems striking that both new laws figured animal sacrifice as a primary object of their prohibitions.[34] In Vincent's *décret-loi*, such sacrifices "performed in offering to so-called deities" became a definitive mark of the *pratiques superstitieuses* that the state contracted itself to combat, and in this sense, arguably, the law targeted popular religious *sèvis* for the spirits even more stringently than had its predecessor. That earlier law, after all, had focused on interdicting various forms of spell making, however problematically *le vaudoux* was included among them. The new law, on the other hand, made ritual animal offerings a legal litmus test of what was defined and prohibited as "superstitious practice," thus criminalizing a primary way in which families served the spirits and ensured their benevolent reciprocity. Rachel Beauvoir and Didier Dominique note that, effectively, "this decree made all Vodouizan become criminals before the law."[35]

The preamble to the new law explained that the state had the responsibility not only to "protect and uplift" the rural classes, but moreover, to protect the *renommée du pays* (good name of the country) from harmful associations with "superstitious beliefs." That justificatory rationale did not go unappreciated when Vincent signed this legislation into effect. Coming so soon on the heels of the restoration of Haitian sovereignty, the new *décret-loi* was hailed in certain quarters as a kind of signature legislation. Although only months before the daily *Le Matin* had been antagonistic to Vincent's government and its increasingly authoritarian tendencies, the newspaper characterized the new law as representing a "turning point in national life," and one that would heighten the nation's prestige, given that "the most frequent subject of [foreign] denigration of our country is . . . *our* superstitious practices."[36]

It seems circumstantially notable in this regard that the 1935 law was promulgated only a few days after notices of the latest imperial travelogue had appeared in Port-au-Prince newspapers. This was a book entitled *Voodoo Fire in Haiti*, written and illustrated with woodcuts by an Austrian artist named Richard Loederer, which circulated widely in translation across Europe and North America.[37] In the United States, the book was published as a selection of the Literary Guild of America, just as W. B. Seabrook's *Magic Island* had been six years earlier, assuring it, as *Haïti-Journal* correctly noted in one of several critical reviews, *une grande popularité*.[38] Purportedly an account of the author's travels in Haiti, *Voodoo Fire in Haiti* was so replete with hallucinatory scenes of, in Loederer's words, "wild dances" that an American reviewer who lived in Haiti, H. P. Davis, characterized it as "not simply another sensational book on Haiti," but rather, "we sincerely hope, the extreme limit of this genre." Once head of the American Chamber of Commerce in Haiti and the author of *Black Democracy: The Story of Haiti* (1928), Davis continued, "After a first quick read, I turned, completely bewildered, to page 99 and, after having re-read these sentences: 'The fetid air clogged my lungs. My breath came in thick, short gasps. A fit of vomiting seized me . . . ,' I was grateful to the author of the book for having found an adequate expression for translating the effect that this work will produce on readers who really know Haiti and Haitians."[39]

Voodoo Fire in Haiti reads like a compendium of tropes taken from previously published texts. It features a particularly frequent return to primitivized and sexualized images of "native dance," which inspires his most derivative prose. In *Ainsi parla l'oncle*, Jean Price-Mars described such passages as constituting a kind of imperial plagiarism, whereby "accounts . . . [can be] made of the cultic ceremonies of 'Vodou' by writers who have not even had the opportunity to observe them."[40] The extent of the fantasy in *Voodoo Fire in Haiti* led Davis, as well as other readers at the time, to doubt that Loederer had ever set foot in Haiti.[41]

I do not mean to suggest that the publication of Loederer's book, in itself, prompted the Haitian government to pass new legislation against *les pratiques superstitieuses* in September 1935. Rather, I see *Voodoo Fire in Haiti* as emblematic of an occupation-era literature that, in constructing "voodoo" or *vaudoux* as the sign of either a felicitous primitivism or an abiding barbarism on the part of Haitians, played a compelling role in the perpetuation and tightening of this penal regime after the restoration of Haitian sovereignty. The pressure that such representations exerted on the Haitian state at this time was reflected in the first line of the 1935 legislation, which established that "the State has the duty to prevent the accomplishment of all acts, practices, etc. liable to foster superstitious beliefs harmful to the good name of the country."[42]

Yet if this legislation was compelled in part by the force of imperial sensationalism around "voodoo" just after the occupation, it also reflected, I want to argue, the influence of cultural nationalist discourse and politics in Haiti at this time. After asserting the state's responsibility for eradicating practices that were potentially damaging to Haiti's reputation, the prologue to the 1935 law conceded that, in the past, there had been an "exaggerated application" of the former Code Pénal articles against *les sortilèges* and explained that this was why articles 405 and 407 had been abrogated two months earlier. In an apparent softening of the penal regime toward peasant communities, this prologue then affirmed "the right of citizens, particularly country-dwellers, to enjoy themselves and organize dances according to local customs," making such dances explicit exceptions to the category of *pratiques superstitieuses*.

One might assume that the acknowledgment that there had been excesses in the application of the law against *les sortilèges* referred to the rigor with which these articles of the Code Pénal had been enforced by marines and the Haitian gendarmes under their command during the occupation. However, there is also evidence to suggest that an "exaggerated application" of these laws had continued under Vincent's governance. Léon Laforestrie, a lawyer and author of a typewritten manual entitled *Cours de droit pénal à l'usage des agents de la police judiciaire* that appeared sometime between 1931 and June 1935, wrote in his brief chapter "Des sortilèges" that "*habitants* are even forbidden to meet to dance to the sound of the drum out of fear that this form of healthy diversion would degenerate into *Vaudoux*, repressed by the law."[43] In April 1935, three months prior to the abrogation of the laws against *les sortilèges*, the anthropologist Melville J. Herskovits, who had conducted fieldwork in central Haiti the summer before, wrote to a contact at the U.S. legation in Port-au-Prince on behalf of Katherine Dunham, then a young student of anthropology at the

University of Chicago, who was preparing, under his tutelage at Northwestern, to undertake research on dance in the Caribbean. "Knowing the charm with which the Haitians care for visitors," Herskovits wrote, "I had no hesitancy, two or three months ago when the plans were laid out, in indicating Haiti as the logical place for her to work. Recent reports of the political situation, however, especially as these bear on the prohibition of dancing—this I get from my friends at Mirebalais with whom I am in correspondence—lead me to wonder how much work she will be able to do in Haiti." A representative of the legation wrote back that Dunham "would probably have little difficulty in finding opportunities to study native dances, since they occur almost nightly throughout the island, and attendance at any one of them could probably be arranged. The much discussed religious ceremonies, or voodoo dances, are banned by law, however, as you probably know."[44]

Whether the reference was to the occupation or to a more recent episode of enforcement, the concession that there had been past "exaggerated applications" of the law against les sortilèges does not entirely explain the unprecedented legal affirmation of "popular dances" that follows. Given the centrality of dance to rituals of serving the lwa, Laënnec Hurbon has interpreted the preamble to the 1935 law as a kind of juridical wink signifying the tacit forbearance of the government toward the pratiques superstitieuses the law apparently forbids, "as if surreptitiously they must tolerate Vodou, but without saying so, or rather while stating its prohibition."[45] Hurbon's analysis is particularly persuasive in light of reports of the ways peasants in certain parts of Haiti were already negotiating the local regulation of their spiritual traditions. Indeed, there is some evidence to suggest that the law might have been, in the sense that Hurbon suggests, a kind of official endorsement of a customary or informal legal status quo then in practice in some parts of the country.

George Eaton Simpson, an American sociologist and anthropologist who spent 1937 in northern Haiti on a Social Science Research Council postdoctoral fellowship, wrote that, according to his informants, the "dance without sacrifices" had been popularly "invented" in the late occupation period "to circumvent the law." Of the several foreign ethnographers who visited Haiti from the United States during the 1930s, Simpson was one of the few to acknowledge in his published work that these practices were officially prohibited, and he was, to my knowledge, the only scholar to consider seriously how local regulation shaped the ways in which different communities served the spirits. The fallacy of anthropological displacement of such questions is that the legal status of these practices has been, at different historical moments, constitutive of how they were performed. In describing the regulatory regime in Plaisance and elsewhere following the promulgation of the 1935 law, Simpson wrote: "Sometimes members of a family held their ceremony in the privacy of a bedroom while a dance was in progress in the courtyard."[46]

Hurbon's interpretation of Vincent's décret-loi, against its apparent grain, as signaling the state's surreptitious tolerance for that which it seemed to prohibit suggests that perhaps the new law was meant to keep a kind of "public secret": "If the foreigner, in reading this text, does not discern all its implications, no one is fooled in the very interior of the country."[47] Michael Taussig has written of the "margin of fiction separating the laws of the state from their actual observance, in which not only the law but also the system of community values is largely honored in the breach."[48] Similarly, Joseph Roach has discussed how, in seeking to regulate Mardi Gras in New Orleans, Louisiana law "has deliberately created in its interstices a space for easily overlooked transgression."[49]

Such a reading of the 1935 law against les pratiques superstitieuses is persuasive in light of the paradoxical political situation discussed in the foregoing chapters, whereby, as Hurbon writes, "the tolerance of Vodou [was] necessary to the general functioning of society. But its penalization, no less so."[50] However, there might be another way to interpret the state's sudden defense of rural pastimes, and in particular the unprecedented insistence on the distinction between "popular dances" and "superstitious practices," notably set apart here by the performance of sacrifice. It seems to me that the penal revisions of July and September 1935 mark the moment when it became both politically desirable, given the force of post-occupation cultural nationalism in Haiti, and epistemologically possible, given the turn toward "national folklore," for the state to distinguish "popular dances" from "prohibited ritual."[51] The latter then became subject to greater penalization under the law as "superstitious practice," while this excised construct—"popular dance"—was figured in ensuing years as "national culture."

In his 1910 portrait of Haiti, La République d'Haïti: Telle qu'elle est, Sténio Vincent anticipated the terms and perhaps also the sanitizing aspirations of this legislation in quoting at length Léon Audain's view that, in the way that "each people has its own special genre of recreation," vaudou was already well on its way at the turn of the century to becoming a simple country diversion: "It is necessary to purify the dance of vaudou of all that which can carry the mind back to the barbarism of past times, to suppress the ceremony that precedes the sacrifice, to prohibit the public bloodshed of animals, to check the tafiatic passion of initiates, to reduce, in a word, vaudou to a simple popular dance, joyful and decent."[52] Vincent himself classified "le vaudou" with "le meringue" as Haiti's "two principal local popular dances," describing the former as resembling, both rhythmically and choreographically, a slow waltz.[53]

This selection from Vincent's earlier writings, published for a primarily European readership during his tenure as the Haitian government's commissioner at the International and Universal Exposition of Brussels, serves to spotlight that the representation of Vodou as simply a rural entertainment was already a trope among certain Haitian elite writers at the turn of the century. It is interesting to consider, then, how this earlier discourse finds new life in official nationalist and, I would argue, legal constructions in the early post-occupation period, when cultural particularity became a crucial basis of state nationalist claims. In interpreting the 1935 law's validation of the right of peasants to hold popular dances as a concession to *indigénisme*, I also want to propose that the logic of such a conception of folklore, separating a unified "national culture" into an inventory of discrete cultural traits and forms—tales, songs, dances, "superstitious" beliefs, proverbs, and so on—influenced the formulation of this law as well. As officially appropriated, the concept of national folklore seemed both to politically compel and to epistemologically enable the constitutive separation upon which the 1935 legislation was premised. In a sense, by legalizing that which had never before been expressly prohibited, the law annexed the figure of popular dance to the state and laid a juridical groundwork for the subsequent promotion of this construct as official national culture.

However, in redoubling the proscription against prohibited ritual, now defined in part by the act of animal sacrifice, the new law also prescribed the constitutive exclusions on which post-occupation state cultural nationalism was founded. In *The Cultural Life of Intellectual Properties*, the legal theorist Rosemary Coombes reminds us that "law generates positivities as well as prohibitions."[54] I want to argue that the affirmations and negations built into the 1935 law against *les pratiques superstitieuses* were also those on which official constructions of national culture were founded in the late 1930s and early 1940s. Legally split away from prohibited ritual, the official figure of Haitian popular dance could be serviceable to a tightened regime of popular control at home, as much as to a renovated image of Haitian national culture abroad. Thus, I am interested in studying the connection between how the Haitian state constructed and, in conjunction with the Catholic Church, policed "superstitious practices" during the early post-occupation years, and how it constructed—and policed— representations of Haitian national identity and culture through investment in the study and particularly performance of folklore during those years.

Force of Law

How strictly or consistently the Vincent government's *décret-loi* against *les pratiques superstitieuses* was enforced after it was passed in September 1935, and what its material effects were for local communities of Vodouizan, are not questions that can be easily or conclusively answered. As prescribed in the Code Rural, the Haitian countryside was divided into 551 rural sections at this time, each under the jurisdiction of a rural police officer, or *chèf seksyon*, appointed by officers of the Garde d'Haïti.[55] Intersecting this civil division was the network of Roman Catholic parishes established by Haiti's 1860 Concordat with the Vatican.[56] Overseen by the predominantly French Catholic hierarchy in Haiti and administered by local *curés* (parish priests), the majority of whom were also French, the parishes of the rural interior encompassed small chapels often run by non-ordained Haitian peasants who were responsible for the catechism of their neighbors. The degree to which the turnover of the law was immediately felt in different parts of the country depended on the variable dispositions and relations of these local civil, military, and religious authorities.[57]

Writing on research he conducted in central Haiti in the summer of 1934, during the final weeks of the occupation, a year before the law was revised, Melville Herskovits described the local regulation of popular ritual practices in the town of Mirebalais: "Permission for *vodun* dances and for *services* must be obtained from the officer commanding the local detachment of the Garde d'Haïti, and this is not always granted. Penalties for illicit dances and ceremonies are severe, and because gossip is ubiquitous and no man lacks enemies, apprehension is prompt. Thus in the instance of one *service*, a misunderstanding regarding the permit was sufficient to cause the detention for some hours of the one responsible for the rite."[58]

In 1937, two years after the new legislation was passed, George Eaton Simpson sensed more continuity than disruption in the ways that local *chèf seksyon* in the region of northern Haiti where he was working, near the town of Plaisance, informally policed the rituals now defined as *pratiques superstitieuses*: "Some local officers who were on friendly terms with *houngans* ignored the new law, and others were bribed to allow ceremonies with sacrifices to be held on permits issued for *bals*" (see fig. 10).[59] As noted above, Simpson's account of his research even suggests that the new law made official an arrangement that was already customary in different parts

FIGURE 10. Rural police officer, Plaisance, Haiti, 1937. Photo by George Eaton Simpson. National Anthropological Archives, Smithsonian Institution, neg. 93-14-885.

of the country, in which offerings were made privately while dances were performed more publicly.

Alphonse Jean, an *oungan* with whom I spoke about this question in June 1997 in Tabarre, on the outskirts of Port-au-Prince, likewise remembered the 1935 Code Pénal revision as having little immediate impact in itself on the customary ways in which ritual *sèvis* were regulated by local authorities. He suggested, in fact, that there had been a lightening rather than a tightening of this penal regime in the mid-1930s with the departure of the marines and the end of the occupation.[60] In general, Jean said, if an *oungan* or *manbo* was on good terms with the local *chèf seksyon*, a permit could be purchased, its price negotiated according to the nature of the *sèvis* and its projected length.[61] Thus the criminalization of popular ritual practices, first as *sortilèges* and then as *pratiques superstitieuses*, became the condition of possibility for their "informal" regulation by and for the benefit of local authorities in rural Haiti. This draws attention to the way in which these laws functioned as an everyday pretext for graft, just as, more episodically, they were the pretext for force. In his journal of travels in Haiti in 1941 during the church's *campagne anti-superstitieuse*, Alfred Métraux recounts a conversation about the practice of Vodou with a Haitian corporal and soldier who informed him that "a tax" had to be paid "for every meeting."[62] Perhaps beyond any other writer of his generation, Milo Rigaud documented and critically analyzed the political economy of Vodou's penalization in its customary forms, juxtaposing, at one point in his *La tradition voudoo et le voudoo haïtien* (1953), the requirement that *ounfò* purchase "official permits" from the police to mount *sèvis*, "while the State pays . . . the Catholic Church to exercise its priesthood in Haiti."[63] Among the examples he cites of this "officially lucrative traffic" is one "lived by us," in which rural police raided and suspended a *sèvis* for which "the police permit *had already been paid to the bureaux du fisc.*"[64]

In his essay "Force of Law: The 'Mystical Foundation of Authority,'" Jacques Derrida discusses the value of the idiomatic expression in English "to enforce the law," compared with the French "appliquer la loi," in noting that "law is always an authorized force, a force that justifies itself or is justified in applying itself." He writes: "The word 'enforceability' reminds us that there is no such thing as law (*droit*) that doesn't imply *in itself, a priori, in the analytic structure of its concept*, the possibility of being 'enforced,' applied by force. There are, to be sure, laws that are not enforced, but there is no law without enforceability, and no applicability or enforceability of the law without force. . . ."[65] If it is important to recognize that the penal laws against *les sortilèges* and *les pratiques superstitieuses* were not and, politically, could not be strictly or consistently applied against the Vodou religion by the Haitian state, it is equally important to understand that, as Derrida underscores, they still had the *potential* of being enforced, and at times were violently so.

Le mélange

Five years after the law against *les pratiques superstitieuses* was promulgated it became the authorizing basis for the *campagne anti-superstitieuse* waged by the predominantly French Catholic clergy against the "impurity" of popularly practiced Catholicism.[66] The church claimed the 1935 law a legitimating sanction for its 1940–1942 campaign, and it was Élie Lescot's authorization of civil and military support for this offensive in June 1941, one of his first presidential acts upon assuming the office, that ensured, to begin with, its enforcement across rural Haiti.

The question of why the Catholic hierarchy in Haiti chose this moment to mount a major assault to "purify" the popular practice of Catholicism has generated a good many theories—especially among those who publicly opposed the campaign at the time. Jacques Roumain, *indigéniste* writer, cofounder of the Parti Communiste Haïtien (PCH) and founding director of the Haitian Bureau d'Ethnologie, was the church's most forceful public critic during the campaign and charged its hierarchy with deliberately attempting to undermine Haitian national unity and weaken its alliance with other American republics against fascism.[67] Élie Lescot himself later wrote that he came to deplore the campaign and saw it as a political ploy on the part of the predominantly French church hierarchy to obstruct his efforts to install a mission of the American Oblates of Mary Immaculate in Haiti and ultimately to destabilize his government.[68]

The church advanced its own narrative of why it launched the campaign in manuals compiled in the summer of 1941 defining the course and method of the missions. According to a handbook entitled *Campagne anti-superstitieuse: Documentation*, it was the "discovery" of the widespread practice of what was termed *le mélange* (the mixture) among the faithful that led the church hierarchy in Haiti to take action in 1940. Numerous examples of this phenomenon are cited in the manuals, all figured as recent revelations: that holy water was pilfered for use in popular ritual practices; that the Catholic first communion ceremony was considered a necessary step in the initiation of *ounsi*; and that saints' days, Lent, Christmas, and other Catholic holidays were all *époques superstitieuses* (superstitious times). One episcopal declaration noted that "far from Christianizing their paganism we were furnishing them the means to paganize Christianity. This game simply made churches the annexes of *hounforts*."[69] Alfred Métraux, a witness to the campaign during his first trip to Haiti and one of its most thorough chroniclers in his *Le vaudou haïtien* (1958), wondered at the "tardiness" of this "discovery" given that "in the rural parishes, *curés* had daily opportunities to become acquainted with 'superstitious' beliefs and practices."[70] Certainly there were documented cases of earlier interventions to purify Catholic belief and practice among the faithful, not least of all the turn-of-the-century campaign of Monsignor François-Marie Kersuzan and the Ligue Contre le Vaudoux. In spite of that and other precedents, the antisuperstition texts produced by the church in 1941 maintained that the campaign was galvanized by the clergy's "providential" discovery of the extent of *le mélange* in 1939.

This occurred when, according to church accounts, the *curé* of Hinche (in central Haiti) learned that growing numbers of his parishioners were renouncing "superstition" and calling themselves *rejetés* (in Kreyòl, *rejete*, or rejectors).[71] The animator of this grassroots movement was identified as a former sacristan of the Trou d'Eau chapel, Saint-Gilles Saint-Pierre, who went by the name Ti-Jules. According to church accounts, Ti-Jules broke with "superstition" when the treatments prescribed by a *bòkò* failed to heal the illnesses of his son and grandson. Members of his family followed suit, and soon people were coming from elsewhere—Mirebalais, Lascahobas, the Artibonite and the North—entreating Ti-Jules to "deliver" them "from the obligations of superstition."[72] By 1937–1938 Ti-Jules had a partner based near Hinche by the name of Simon Césaire, better known as Père Simon, who himself had been treated ineffectively by ritual specialists before turning to Ti-Jules, and thus could speak from experience: "His simple, clear speech, his direct testimony, 'I did this too,' powerfully struck those who heard it, first in Hinche, then in St.-Michel, and made them understand that in order to be a true Catholic they must abandon all superstition, not only the practice but also the belief." Simon is also remembered for introducing an oath to the growing movement.[73]

According to church handbooks, what became popularly known as the *kanpay rejete* (rejectors' campaign) thus spread across the Plateau Central, inciting anger and opposition, anxiety and repentance, and revealing to local priests and eventually to Haiti's bishops and archbishop the extent to which "superstition" and Catholicism intermingled in popular belief and practice. Even the directors of the small chapels in each parish "charged with the catechism of others," as Ti-Jules had been, "were no exception."[74] Carl Edward Peters, a Haitian priest and later the bishop of Jérémie, notes in his *La croix contre l'asson* (1960) that it was the *curé* of Hinche who approached the bishop of Gonaïves, Monsignor Paul Robert, about this "discovery" and the growing movement of the self-identified *rejete*. On 21 June 1940, after what Peters describes as a year of "research" into "unknown territory," the church imposed the "antisuperstition oath" in Hinche, and in October 1940 Monsignor Robert led eight days of sermons on true Catholicism, culminating in his call to parishioners to rise and publicly proclaim the oath: "In a single movement, to the great astonishment of all, an enormous crowd rose."[75] Missions were then begun in Port-de-Paix, and in May 1941, at the First National Congress of the Eucharistic Crusade in Gonaïves, the apostolic nuncio Monsignor Silvani gave his formal endorsement to the national extension of the campaign.[76]

The church documents from which I have been drawing here raise many more questions than they answer about the nature of the *rejete* movement in the mid- to late 1930s and its relationship to the *campagne anti-superstitieuse* that the church launched thereafter. How large the popular movement was before the church effectively took it over and to what extent its ends and means coincided with those that the hierarchy instituted in 1941 are points that remain unclear. In this context, the abiding disjunction between the popular Kreyòl and the ecclesiastical French names for the movements seems striking, the divergence between the *kanpay rejete* and the *campagne anti-superstitieuse* perhaps marking tensions unacknowledged in the church's seamless account of popular leaders recruiting priests to lead their struggle against *le mélange*. The name *kanpay rejete* seems to asserts a claim of agency and ownership that disappears in the church's references to its own *campagne anti-superstiteuse*, raising the question of to what extent the Catholic hierarchy regarded the popular groundswell of the mid- to late 1930s and the independent leadership of figures such as Ti-Jules and Père Simon with ambivalence, if not outright concern, before it took over.

To whatever extent the *campagne anti-superstitieuse* had roots, as official church history insists, in a spontaneous popular renunciation of *le mélange* in central Haiti, by mid-1941 it was a highly organized, systematically administered series of missions directed by the Catholic hierarchy in Haiti with, as of June of that year, explicit backing from the government. In a directive of 23 June 1941, President Élie Lescot, Vincent's recently elected successor, endorsed the campaign and directed the Haitian "civil and military authorities to give their most complete assistance," to the church's "mission . . . to combat fetishism and superstition," specifying, however, that "no violence [should be] used against those who exercise superstitious and fetishistic practices."[77] Thereafter, priests were accompanied on their antisuperstition raids in the countryside not only by groups of *rejete*, who aided in the destruction of "superstitious" objects and sites, but also by members of the Haitian Garde and/or local *chèf seksyon*.

A system was set up in each parish to register those who voluntarily gave up the "superstitious" objects in their possession. On the basis of this *nettoyage* (cleaning), residents were eligible to pledge an antisuperstition oath. This was administered by a *curé* either individually in the presence of other parishioners, or as a group: "I, M——, swear before Bon Dieu who is present in the tabernacle, before the Priest who is God's minister, that I 'renounce,'" began one of several possible versions in Kreyòl. The public witnessing of the oath, church authorities hoped, would discourage deceptions, or, when they occurred, lead to the denunciation of the offender by other parishioners. After taking the oath, *rejete* were given a card, the presentation of which authorized them to receive the Catholic sacraments in any parish.[78] *Curés* were forbidden to administer communion, marriage and burial rites, or any other sacrament to parishioners over the age of fourteen who failed or refused to comply with the campaign or to any strangers who could not produce a card.[79] Those *rejete* who deceived their *curé* or his agents by not destroying all their "superstitious objects" or who were caught attending a "superstitious ceremony" were to be sanctioned by at least a year of penitence, involving the confiscation of their card, their exclusion from communion, and the loss of the right to be godparents.[80]

A Protestant Threat

What becomes clear in examining the collection of manuals made available to *curés* stationed across Haiti in the summer of 1941 is that the church's campaign was mounted not simply as an offensive against *le mélange*, but also against the growing size and influence of Protestant denominations in Haiti at this time.[81] At least one of the antisuperstition oaths, in fact, required Catholics to swear both that they were "completely finished with superstitions" and that they would never become Protestants.[82] Protestants were demonized alongside "bocors" in antisuperstition sermons and hymns, one of which, written in Kreyòl, began: "We do not see Satan but we see people who do Satan's work: *bocors* and Protestants," and goes on to compare the sacrileges of each in a kind of counterpoint, concluding that Protestants were "more terrible, more evil."[83] If the *campagne antisuperstitieuse* overwhelmingly targeted and impacted peasants who served the *lwa* and considered themselves to be good Catholics, the church's effort to purify itself of the taint of "superstition" cannot be understood outside of the growing prestige and influence of Protestantism in Haiti at this time.

Over the course of the U.S. occupation, the Roman Catholic church had grown increasingly alarmed both by what it saw as a systematic erosion of its traditional position and authority in Haiti, and by the simultaneous rise in Protestant missionary activity across the country. At the start of the occupation in 1915, Wesleyan Methodist, Baptist, Episcopal, and African Methodist Episcopal churches had been a presence (albeit at times a tenuous one) in the country for several decades, with Seventh-Day Adventist and Pentecostal congregations established more recently.[84] Several years into the occupation it came to the attention of the Catholic hierarchy that the U.S. secretary of the navy, Edwin Denby, struck by how few American Protestant missionaries he encountered during a tour of inspection in Haiti, had contacted the Federal Council of the Churches of Christ to encourage missionary travel to Haiti among its membership.[85] Denby's call was echoed by representatives of U.S.-based Protestant organizations, whose published reports of their visits to Haiti were full of self-recrimination about American Protestant neglect of this country.[86] W. F. Jordan, of the American Bible Society, reproached U.S. Protestant organizations for sending missionaries to "Africa, India, [and] China" while "overlooking a great opportunity and shirking a great responsibility" closer to home.[87] "Whatever the reason," he concluded, "the fact remains that the door to Protestant missions in Haiti has always been open, though the American church has never seen it. There have been and still are small groups of Christians throughout the Island praying God to send the help from America that never comes."[88]

In the context of the U.S. imperial takeover and rising nationalist feeling across Haiti, that last statement was not strictly true. In fact, Haitian Protestants tended to regard the overtures of representatives of U.S. churches with ambivalence and wariness at this time.[89] What is more, the secretary of the navy's efforts notwithstanding, Protestants widely believed that U.S. authorities in Haiti favored the Catholic church at their expense. The small subsidies that the state had provided for Protestant educational programs were cut back, and even funding requests for projects designed in conformity with U.S. priorities—such as proposals to build industrial schools submitted by the Reverend L. Ton Evans of the Lott Carey Mission Society and the Reverend S. E. Churchstone-Lord, pastor of the A.M.E. Église Saint-Paul in Port-au-Prince—were turned down.[90] Louis Borno, who became the client president of Haiti in 1922, was known for his anti-Protestantism and reportedly sought to discourage further missionary activity in the country, arguing, as John H. Russell, the U.S. high commissioner in Haiti, reported, that it would only worsen already harmful divisions in the country.[91]

Yet, if Protestants felt themselves obstructed and marginalized by the occupation regime, the Catholic church continued to be alarmed by the growth of missionary activity in Haiti during the 1920s and following the departure of U.S. marine troops in 1934. The church was also concerned about the size and strength of several congregations led by Haitian pastors on Haiti's southern peninsula, including Nosirel Lhérisson's Baptist missions in the Jacmel area; the Methodist church led by Pierre Nicolas in Petit-Goâve; and the Episcopal ministry of Alexandre Baptiste in Léogâne.[92] The Episcopalians were particularly known for their wide-ranging missionary work in rural areas and, like the Seventh-Day Adventists, for the indigenization of their ministry at a time when Haitians were protesting or at least questioning the makeup of their Roman Catholic clergy, most of whom were French.

Also disturbing to the Catholic hierarchy and priesthood in Haiti were the charges made by some missionaries, both Haitian and foreign, that Catholicism in Haiti was "contaminated" by its having been assimilated into Haitian popular religious beliefs and practices. Reverend

L. Ton Evans testified during the 1921–1922 U.S. Senate inquiry that "the Roman Catholic Church in Haiti is a bastard production of voodooism, witchcraft, and other African heathenish cults with a gloss of Roman Catholicism," and decried the occupation government's continued subsidy, on the basis of the 1860 Concordat, of "a semibarbarous institution more or less mixed with voodooism."[93] Even more significant, the Catholic hierarchy and clergy in Haiti were troubled that Protestant missionary claims about the imbrication of Catholicism and Vodou seemed to have become an effective strategy for winning conversions across the country. A church declaration from early in the campaign cited, as cause for alarm and action, a persistent rumor that had "aroused astonishment" when it came to the attention of church authorities: "It was repeated more and more frequently that one must become a Protestant in order to extricate oneself from the obligations of superstition."[94] Métraux reports that Protestantism was popularly seen as a "magic circle," a refuge from angry *lwa*, particularly on the part of the sick, who sought conversion as a last resort. "'If you want the *loa* to leave you in peace—become a Protestant,'" he reports hearing throughout his later work in the Marbial Valley, where the campaign had been particularly severe.[95] Whatever its roots in a popular movement of renunciation, the *campagne anti-superstitieuse* institutionalized by the church between 1940 and 1942 needs to be understood, at least in part, as an effort to combat the spread and influence of Protestantism in Haiti.

This might be borne out by reports that Protestant pastors and missionaries became targets of intimidation over the course of the campaign. The Episcopal bishop, Spencer Burton, wrote to President Lescot in late 1941 about several incidents in which members of Episcopal congregations had been harassed by Catholic clergy, or by local police at the instigation of the former. In one of these cases, which allegedly took place in the commune of Mirebalais in August–September 1941, a band of *rejete* led by a Catholic sacristan and backed by the local *chèf seksyon* "began a series of operations against members of the Episcopal church, whom they deliberately assimilated to practitioners of *Vaudou*." The group threatened that if the members of the church failed to attend mass at the local Catholic chapel, they would suffer the consequences. According to Burton's report, late that September, while celebrating a saint's day the local *curé* "sprayed holy water on whips and batons destined for the punishment of Protestants." That night bands of *rejete* reportedly took a number of members of the church hostage, who, the next day, "tied up like criminals, were led to the [Catholic] presbytery, where . . . they were obliged to take *cartes de 'rejetés.'*" A letter to the editor of the newspaper *Le Matin* sent by a prominent member of the large Baptist congregation in Jacmel reported that in December 1941 a local *curé* had attempted to incite a crowd of *rejete* to act against local Protestants, and particularly the Haitian pastor Nosirel Lhérisson, under whose direction the Baptist mission in the area had widely expanded.[96]

Given state support for the church's *campagne anti-superstitieuse* in its early stages, it seems notable as well that in early August 1941, less than two months after Lescot ordered civil and military authorities to enforce the ensuing antisuperstition raids across the country, the government banned the practice of Pentecostalism in Haiti.[97] Alfred Métraux suggests that Pentecostalism held a particular appeal for Vodouizan who found "in the gatherings of these groups an atmosphere that reminded them of that of *Vaudou* sanctuaries."[98] *Haïti-Journal* reported approvingly that the authorities were ordered to dissolve these congregations, close the chapels, and disperse any Pentecostal meetings, thus putting "an end to the[ir] noisy revels and aggressive practices."[99] A decree bracing these measures was issued a few weeks later to justify the constitutionality of the ban on the grounds that the activities of the Pentecostals were "contrary to good morals and of a nature to disturb public order."[100]

Purifying Catholicism, Codifying "Superstition"

In the course of his testimony during the 1921–1922 U.S. Senate hearings, the Baptist missionary L. Ton Evans remembered the "joy of burning tomtoms and the whole paraphernalia used by papa and mamalois after conversion" and praised the Baptist Lhérisson in Jacmel for publicly burning "donkey loads of demon-worshipped implements."[101] In his memoir, H. Ormonde McConnell, a Wesleyan Methodist minister sent to Haiti by the London Methodist Missionary Society in 1933, describes the dramatic scenes of destruction that marked the conversions he "won" in western Haiti during the mid- to late 1930s and early 1940s. In one such event, which took place in Croix-des-Bossales in March 1937, a husband and wife "smashed and burned a trunk full of Voodoo fetishes in the presence of a crowd of possibly a thousand people."[102] According to McConnell and other missionaries, the smashing and then burning of sacred objects was the performative climax of the conversion process; converts were also encouraged to engage in other forms of ritualized violence, such as the felling of *repozwa* (sacred trees believed to be resting places for particular *lwa*; from French *reposoirs*).

Such accounts are striking in light of the degree to which the 1941–1942 Catholic church missions were likewise fixated, perhaps above all, on destroying, as systematically and also, it seems, as dramatically as possible, the material cultures and physical landmarks of "superstition." The attacks reported during the *campagne anti-superstitieuse* tend to resemble closely those sketched by Evans and McConnell. An article in *Haïti-Journal* in late October 1941, for example, noted that in Arcahaie, where a mission was "in full swing," it had become a common sight to see the *curé* or his vicar, accompanied by many "zealous auxiliaries," leading off "several horses or donkeys loaded with relics, dishes, images, stones and other pieces making up the gear of '*houmforts*.'" These sacred objects would then be publicly burned.[103]

Roger Riou was a young Breton priest based in Port-de-Paix in 1941, one of the early sites of the campaign, and described these processions in his memoir: "The townspeople would usually come for me around eight or nine o'clock [in the morning]. We'd start out across the *habitations* and the jungle. It wouldn't be long before I'd come across a totem, the dwelling place of a *loa*. I'd have to take it down. The stuff was piled up all over the place. We had to send for mules to haul it away to the site of the pyre. At night, it was all burned and the people sang around the fires."[104] Riou discloses that he suffered a physical breakdown as a result of the missions ("I couldn't take any more after that campaign. I was spitting up blood") but does not describe the confrontations that, by other accounts, regularly took place in the course of these raids. Although he acknowledges that "the affair made a lot of commotion," he attributes the "frenzy of smashing and burning" that went on to "the distrust that the Haitians traditionally bear toward one another [which] really exploded at the time of our campaign."[105]

Métraux confirms that the *kanpay rejete* did become the occasion for the settling of local accounts, both when priests accompanied groups of *rejete* on these missions and when, at the height of the campaign, they sent these bands out on their own, armed with a warrant.[106] One of the church manuals suggested that these bands might prove to be more effective acting on their own than with the French priests given that, since they were made up of members of the local community, "it is very difficult to deceive them."[107] However, this literature also makes clear that the violence endemic to these raids was not just tolerated, but prescribed by church authorities. After emphasizing the "principle" that no one be allowed to take the antisuperstition oath who had not already destroyed "all the superstitious objects they possess," this handbook specifies that "the principle must be applied with the greatest exactitude and the greatest severity possible. It is necessary to truly destroy everything: to smash bottles, jugs, to tear up the pictures, to pull up and burn poles [*poteaux*] and crosses, to take away the stones, remove the necklaces, to crush the *cayes-loas* [literally, homes of the spirits], to cut down the *bois servis*, to profane all that which is 'served' superstitiously."[108] The destruction specified here, and reported by onlookers at the time, was clearly not simply a means of the campaign, but an end in itself. The manual goes on to insist, rather ambiguously, that although such tactics might seem painful to begin with, the people would "have no confidence"—presumably either in the priest's ability to rid them of their obligations to the *lwa* or in their own ability to practice an "undiluted" Catholicism—"if the severe method is not employed."[109]

The particular priority that the church gave to destroying the material cultures of superstition during these missions, however, produced several problems and striking paradoxes. First, foreign priests faced a dilemma of identification: how to recognize the sites, structures, and objects associated with *pratiques superstitieuses* among their parishioners? Certainly, priests relied heavily on the groups of *rejete* who traveled with them, serving both as informants and informers (that is, on their neighbors). However, church authorities were concerned, as the official literature reveals, with the possibility that *curés* could still be "tricked" or deceived by their parishioners and thus emphasized the importance of becoming closely acquainted with, as one manual put it, "very precise facts on superstition."[110] To this end, in a circular letter of 15 August 1941, the archbishop of Port-au-Prince counseled *curés* to begin preparations for the upcoming weeks of *missions anti-superstitieuses* (antisuperstition missions) in the Port-au-Prince diocese by compiling their own "documentation on this serious subject of *pratiques superstitieuses*."[111] He also announced that several priests, aided by the confessions of "repentant '*bocors*,'" had been engaged in research on the subject for several months and recommended that they purchase two booklets, both by Haitian clergy, which "contain the essentials on *pratiques superstitieuses* of Haiti": *Lumière sur le humfort* by Père Carl Edward Peters, who had achieved national recognition for the antisuperstition mission he launched in the diocese of Port-de-Paix; and *Notes sur le vaudou* by Père Rémy Augustin, then a vicar at the Cathedral of Port-au-Prince, and creator of a booklet of antisuperstition canticles in Kreyòl; he was later appointed the first Haitian bishop.[112]

Peters's and Augustin's texts reveal the extent to which the church's directive to "purify" the popular practice of Catholicism relied on an elaborate ethnographic codification of "superstition."[113] To my knowledge, this had not been the case during earlier campaigns. Peters's work drew on the two authoritative social-scientific works of the time: J. C. Dorsainvil's *Vodou et névrose* (Vodou and Neurosis, 1931), which he quotes at length, and Price-Mars's *Ainsi parla l'oncle*, which he cites more sparingly.

Augustin's text, which is a good deal shorter and typed rather than professionally printed and published, relies less conspicuously on attributed sources and is therefore the more idiosyncratic work. What is striking about Augustin's descriptive inventory of the "vaudouesque pantheon" is less his prejudicial descriptions of *lwa*, which might be expected of such a report, than the fact that the popular identifications of these spirits with Catholic saints go largely unmentioned. Peters's booklet does touch on these associations. However, neither he nor Augustin dwells extensively on the subject of *le mélange*.[114]

The potential utility of these documents to *curés* preparing for anti-superstition missions lay more, one might imagine, in their detailed cataloguing and descriptions of the material cultures and sacred sites of popular belief and ritual: the typical contents of an *ounfò*, and the form and function of ritual objects and instruments. In his memoir, Roger Riou refers to the confiscation of the material cultures of "superstition" as having been a process of "inventorying."[115] Yet here the evidence of *le mélange* would have been most striking, and, one would think, perplexing for *curés* faced with the imperative to destroy the signs of superstition. In demolishing popular altars to the *lwa*, they were confronted with the destruction of the Catholic iconography and religious objects that formed an integral part of these assemblages.

Campagne anti-superstitieuse: Documentation, published soon after Peters's and Augustin's handbooks, gives a detailed inventory of the forbidden objects that were subject to confiscation and burning before the antisuperstition oath could be proclaimed.[116] These included the chromolithographs of the saints with whom, in popular belief and ritual, the identities of the *lwa* were metonymically matched. In the same way and at the same time that such images were becoming the textbook case of anthropological "syncretism" in the Americas, they were figured by the church in Haiti as one of the most conspicuous signs and symptoms of *le mélange*. *Curés* were thus placed in the disconcerting position of being obliged, as official literatures specified, to burn portraits of the saints found during these raids. Any other Catholic materials or iconography discovered in their course were likewise deemed superstitious and either destroyed on the spot or carried back to the pyre at the presbytery.

This was not the only paradox produced by the church's fixation on destroying the physical sites and signs of *le mélange* during the campaign. Did not the church's exorcism and axing of *repozwa* and demolition of other sites believed to be inhabited by *lwa* serve more to instantiate the spirit's presence and powers than to refute them? This was a point made by critics of the church at the time and most prominently by Jacques Roumain, who wrote in his polemic *À propos de la campagne "anti-superstitieuse"/ Las supersticiones* (1942) that, far from discouraging faith in the spirits, "the Clergy has itself contributed to maintaining the belief in the presence of the *loas*." He argued further that "in combating them as a formidable reality, in knocking down, for example, certain trees under the pretext of chasing bad spirits from them," *curés* provided peasants with "the clear confirmation of their existence."[117]

Yet, based on its own literature about the missions, it seems unlikely that the church had any other intention. In fact, the most thorough of the manuals distributed in preparation for the campaign, the *Campagne anti-superstitieuse: Documentation*, specifically warned clergy against such demystification in their preaching against *le mélange*: "A big pitfall to avoid in these sermons is to want to show the ridiculousness and the silliness of these beliefs in the *loas*. . . . The great theme to preach here is that it is possible for the priest of Jesus to chase away the devil and the bad spirits; that the demon cannot make those who are faithful to their baptism suffer his wickedness; that sicknesses are the punishment of sin and that it is necessary to suffer them."[118] The aim, then, was not to demystify the *lwa*, but rather to demonize them more effectively; not to ridicule them, but to reinterpret them through Catholic doctrine and, in so doing, to augment the clergy's prestige in the eyes of the faithful.

Again, one might detect the specter of Haitian Protestantism casting its shadow over this directive, especially if, for those peasants who wished to be rid of obligations to the *lwa*, the Protestant pastor or missionary was rumored to possess greater protective powers against angry spirits. However, Alfred Métraux suggests, on the basis of his conversations with *curés* at the time, that their diabolization of the *lwa* was sometimes a matter of belief. He writes that the "only divergence of opinion between the pastors and their flock on this point turns on their opposing conceptions of the *loa*." One priest affirmed to him: "'Judging by what I have seen with my own eyes, it is impossible to deny that the *loa* are real beings. Is there not a devil? The people of this country are truly possessed by the demon, for we are able to deliver them by our prayers.'"[119]

Renunciation and Resistance

It is Métraux who discusses most extensively, in his *Le vaudou haïtien* (1958), how peasants experienced these raids and the staging of antisuperstition missions across rural Haiti from 1940 to 1942. His account, based partly on his own observations and partly on the memories of peasants in the Marbial Valley with whom he spoke some eight years later, underscores the complexity of popular responses, both resistant and seemingly compliant, to the church's imperative. The *campagne anti-superstitieuse* was not without its popular supporters, as evidenced by the entourage of *rejete* accompanying priests on raids or carrying out these expeditions in their stead. In interviewing Marbial Valley residents, Métraux notes that "all who witnessed these scenes were struck by the behavior of those who had made themselves the agents of the persecution. They attacked the emblems of *vaudou* as though these were dangerous enemies whom they wanted to trample and exterminate. While the *curé* was engaged in exorcising the *arbres-reposoirs* [*repozwa*], fanatics threw stones at them, cursed them, and blamed them for all the money they had spent in vain on offerings and sacrifices."[120] Métraux proposes that the desire to be done with costly obligations to the *lwa* or to escape from their wrath might have explained "the ease with which many of them abjured and the enthusiasm they showed—probably to conceal secret misgivings."[121]

As during the occupation, when marines were called upon to arrest those accused of being sorcerers or *lougawou*, so too during the *campagne anti-superstitieuse*, according to Métraux, "women accused of being 'child-eaters' were dragged in front of Father X," who questioned them and exorcised those he believed to be guilty.[122] Jean Kerboull, a French priest and sociologist who conducted oral histories on the *kanpay rejete* in the 1960s and, in so doing, seemed to become an agent of its continuation, writes of *rejete* in the north invading the home of a *bòkò* because they believed the hound tied to his porch was actually an ensorcelled person. He also reports stories circulating during the campaign that *zonbi* were being released by their keepers, who feared they would be targeted by the mobilization.[123] Such accounts suggest that support for the church's campaign stemmed in part from popular understanding of it as an attack on alleged practitioners of malicious magic. Métraux notes that in Marbial many "believed that the occasion had come to rid themselves of *loups-garous* or at least to destroy their occult power."[124]

Whatever the extent of popular investment in the campaign, Métraux emphasizes the trauma of the missions for those who considered themselves to be good Catholics as they served the *lwa*. "Imagine," Métraux writes, "the confusion of a peasant who has spent all his life fulfilling his 'obligations' to his family *loa*, suddenly finding himself called an idolater and servant of the Devil."[125] The antisuperstition raids he described were scenes of grief, fear, and anger, as Vodouizan either reluctantly complied with the demands of *curés* and their surrogates to relinquish sacred objects or, when they refused, saw "their *lakou* . . . invaded by a band of zealots led by the *curé* or the local police."[126] Sometimes those who witnessed the destruction that followed became embodied by *lwa* whose icons, emblems, or residences were being desecrated, and the priest, if present, would have them restrained and then attempt to exorcise the "demons" that possessed them by holding a crucifix to their foreheads. Kerboull also reports a case in which some forty people (ten men and thirty women) attending an antisuperstition mass were mounted by *lwa* just before they were to pledge the oath "that they would thence forward follow pure Christian teaching."[127]

Métraux argues that the invasions and pillaging would have met stronger opposition on the part of Vodouizan had the rural police not been mobilized to enforce the campaign.[128] As it was, resistance to the campaign on the part of Vodouizan took multiple forms—evasion, subterfuge, sabotage, and public protest. Alphonse Jean remembered the crusades of a *curé* in the area of Tabarre who traveled to his family's *lakou* on more than one occasion, surrounded by *rejete*. Yet, Jean noted that if this *curé* had informants, so had his family, and as the priest and his followers made their conspicuous way each time, the family hid drums and sacred objects that would have been pillaged.[129] In his history *La croix contre l'asson* (1960), Carl Edward Peters documents several cases of practitioners organizing themselves against the campaign; these included the formulation of counter-oaths. In October 1941, for example, several days before the beginning of a major "mission" in l'Arcahaie, Peters writes that "seven of the most famous *bocors* of this region met on the evening of the feast day for Saint Thérèse, for a fantastic *gombo*. There around a great fire, after having sacrificed animals reserved for the Loas, they pledged on this pyre never to take the antisuperstition oath." He also cites the case of a "very famous bocoresse" in Croix-des-Missions with supporters in the capital who, around the same time, made herself "the depository and guardian of all the objects that the *bocors* in the plain wanted to shield from the gaze of the 'cleaners.'" Finally, he writes that in the south, "*bocors* boasted of being able to 'de-oath' [*dessermenter*] those who by weakness or cowardice betrayed their given word"—in other words, those who regretted renouncing their spiritual inheritance and obligations.[130] Haiti's bishops published a joint assessment of the campaign in August 1942, several months after its suspension, which found "inexplicable" all the "sorts of ruses" to which many resorted "in order to be able to continue to commit the sacrileges" that were interdicted by their pledge of the oath.[131] In his *Lumière sur le humfort* (1941), Peters warned foreign priests about a popular belief that held that pressing one's big toe into the ground while uttering any oath would render it "null and void."[132]

By early 1942 there was growing opposition in the establishment press and at the state level to the tactics, if not the ends, of the church's missions.

In his firsthand history of the campaign, Peters charges that although it was Lescot who in June 1941 mobilized military and police enforcement of the campaign, it also proved to be "the government of M. Lescot which most hindered the antisuperstition struggle" as the missions spread throughout the country.[133] That latter observation is a rare point of agreement between Peters's and Lescot's retrospective writings on the campaign, both of which highlight the government's role in undermining a massive "Congrès des Rejetés" planned for 8 February 1942 in Saint-Michel-de-l'Atalaye in the Artibonite. According to Peters, "the *Congrès* was only . . . the shadow of what it should have been," thanks to the government's strategies of containment.[134]

It was a tactical decision on the part of church authorities that, as the archbishop of Port-au-Prince announced in his circular letter of 15 August 1941, the "weeks of antisuperstition missions" be given first in the provincial parishes, and only later in those of the capital, "where we might encounter more practical difficulties."[135] Although the archbishop did not elaborate on his specific concerns, the forecast of "difficulties" in Port-au-Prince was prescient in light of events that took place a few weeks after the congress in Saint-Michel-de-l'Atalaye. A shift in the urban elites' regard for the campaign was registered late that month in the establishment press. On 23 February *Haïti-Journal* ran a scathing editorial calling for an "end to these proceedings which are too reminiscent of the Inquisition."[136] The day before a disturbance had broken out as Rémy Augustin, the young Haitian vicar at the Cathedral of Port-au-Prince, was leading a mass at a Delmas chapel to inaugurate a week of antisuperstition missions in the capital and its environs. The Catholic daily *La Phalange* reported the next day that over two hundred shots were fired in the air both inside and outside of the chapel, terrorizing the congregation.[137] In a somewhat different account of the incident, *Haïti-Journal*, which was at this point much less well disposed toward the campaign than it had been a month earlier, reported that the disturbance had begun as a protest on the part of a group of "persons who had been robbed by some brigands who [said] they were charged with collecting cabalistic objects."[138] Rumors spread that the disturbance at Delmas was not a popular demonstration at all, but had been staged by the government, with police masquerading as angry peasants, in order to discredit the campaign and create a pretext for the withdrawal of state support.[139]

Popular protest against the church's raids had become increasingly common across the country in the days leading up to these missions in the capital. As Métraux writes, "The peasantry whose sanctuaries had been pillaged and who could no longer beat their drums to call the *loa* of Guinée finally began to express their resentment more or less openly, which took, in some regions, the form of religious strikes."[140] However, such grievances may not have been the only or even the most decisive factor in the public withdrawal of elite and government support for the campaign at that moment. As the article in *Haïti-Journal* highlighted, it was the fact that "the *campagne anti-superstitieuse* . . . left our countrysides in order to install itself in the cities" that seemed, on the part of ruling classes, most objectionable: "This unexpected extension, and the obligation of families who have absolutely nothing to [do] with *vaudouesque* practices to 'reject' without delay, under the penalty of seeing themselves deprived of sacraments and of Christian burial, are of the nature to cause serious troubles for the Church to which we belong, and for our Country."[141]

It was one thing, then, to insist that peasants pronounce the antisuperstition oath that would deliver them from "exploitation" at the hands of *oungan* and *bòkò*, the identities of whom, as noted earlier, were entirely collapsed in these discourses. However, Catholics of the urban bourgeoisie and petite bourgeoisie took offense at being asked to proclaim an oath that identified them with the peasantry, one that, moreover, by the logic of renunciation, implied that they were themselves practitioners of "superstition." It is instructive to mark the contrast between those peasants who took the oath at least in part, according to observers like Métraux, because the act of renunciation seemed to negate a stigma that stood in the way of their social advancement, and those members of the Catholic urban elite and middle classes who regarded the oath as imparting rather than lifting the taint of "superstition."[142] Métraux reports that the clergy attempted to assure the latter that "it was because they were good Catholics that they were being asked to separate themselves from those who practiced *le mélange*."[143] However, this did not mitigate the outrage felt by many that their continued access to the sacraments depended upon the recital of an oath that implicated them in visiting *bòkò*, giving offerings to the *lwa*, and keeping "fetishes" around the house.

Métraux suggests that the fact that this insinuating oath was being imposed largely by foreign clergy amplified the resentment of the bourgeoisie, who had already been angered by comments made by the papal nuncio Monsignor Silvani during a trip to the Dominican Republic earlier that month. In an interview with the Dominican newspaper *Listín Diario* two days after the incident at Delmas, Silvani portrayed Haiti as a country where "there still remains the superstition of African origin, with its rites and its special priests or 'Papa-Bocó,'" but where, thanks to the church's crusade, "little by little, this people is overthrowing superstition for the true religion of Christ." These remarks were posed against his portrait of Dominicans as a people "marching forward," having accomplished a "prodigious transformation . . . in so short a time. In all aspects of its life: in the cultural, economic, and religious."[144] They also came five years after the Dominican military massacred an estimated fifteen thousand ethnic Haitians living in the regions along the Dominican Republic's northern border with Haiti and in the Western Cibao by the order of President Rafael Leonidas Trujillo.[145] The Haitian press pronounced Silvani "the worst denigrator of the Haitian people," and Lescot's government, which foresaw conflict with the monsignor over its nomination of an American (of the Oblates of Mary Immaculate) to the bishopric of Cayes, successfully pressed the Vatican for his removal.[146]

The mainstream press opposed the imposition of the antisuperstition oath on the urban elite and middle classes not simply on the grounds that it was unjust and humiliating to those who already practiced a "pure" Catholicism. The aforementioned article in *Haïti-Journal* argued that the campaign was also furnishing "a rich material to those foreigners of bad faith who have so often denigrated our country. . . . We are simply in the process of building the sad and false reputation of being the most superstitious country of the world." The newspaper called for the church and state to put an end to the campaign "for the respect of the Haitian name and the prestige of our country so often denigrated abroad," and because it was exacerbating divisions in wartime between Catholics and Protestants, between *rejete* and everyone else, and between Haiti and the Dominican Republic.[147]

When concentrated in the countryside, then, the *campagne anti-superstitieuse* seemed to hold the promise of ridding Haiti, through the performative violence of the raid, the pyre, and the antisuperstition oath itself, of what, "for our detractors," as J. C. Dorsainvil had once put it, was "the indelible mark of our inferiority, of our original fall."[148] Yet, when administered in Port-au-Prince, across all the capital's social classes, these missions were accused of having precisely the opposite effect: that is, of potentially further subsuming the nation under a mark of primitivism. Rather than alleviating this stigma, the *campagne anti-superstitieuse* seemed liable to reinforce it. Ultimately the organized persecution of Vodouizan by church and state authorities served only to intensify these associations. A memorandum written by J. C. White, the American cultural attaché stationed in Port-au-Prince at this time, to U.S. Secretary of State Cordell Hull in September 1942 noted that "much attention was attracted to voodoo beliefs and ceremonies during the antisuperstition campaign launched by the Roman Catholic Church last year."[149] Élie Lescot, who in his 1974 memoir accused the Roman Catholic hierarchy of attempting to destabilize his government through the *campagne anti-superstitieuse*, lamented that "all this din in our poor country in 1941 and 1942, under the fallacious pretext of converting our rural masses, constituted, abroad, the most deplorable publicity for Haiti."[150]

Whether the Lescot government had any role in staging the disturbance in Delmas on 22 February, or that which took place on the afternoon of 8 March, when shots were fired at local churches as antisuperstition missions began simultaneously in the four parishes of the capital, these incidents became the pretext for withdrawal of state support for the church's campaign. However, the department of the interior simultaneously issued a communiqué prohibiting on Holy Thursday and Good Friday the processions of the Rara bands that fill city streets and country byways in Haiti between Carnival and Easter, performing songs and spiritual works along their way.[151]

PART II

"This Awakened in Me the Desire to Undertake Its Study Before It Was Too Late"

During the season of polemics that followed the inauguration and then the hasty cancellation of the antisuperstition missions in Port-au-Prince, no writer identified with the then-burgeoning ethnological movement took a more prominent stand against the church's campaign than Jacques Roumain, who in October 1941 had become director of a new state agency, the Bureau d'Ethnologie de la République d'Haïti. Roumain's aforementioned three-part article in *Le Nouvelliste*, later published as *À propos de la campagne "anti-superstitieuse"/Las Supersticiones*, provoked a response in the Catholic newspaper *La Phalange* by a French priest named Père Foisset. During the next four months, between 30 March and 31 July 1942, Roumain engaged in a wide-ranging debate with Foisset over the premises, ends, and means of the church's campaign, which by then had been suspended.[152] His side of this exchange in the pages of *Le Nouvelliste* (with Foisset writing in *La Phalange*) illuminates his stakes in founding the bureau the previous October, bearing out Alfred Métraux's contention that the church's campaign had been a catalyst for Roumain's institutionalization of Haitian ethnological studies.

Roumain had been convicted of communist conspiracy under Sténio Vincent's government and was imprisoned from August 1934 to June 1936. Upon his release he left Haiti for Europe with his wife, Nicole, and their young son. He spent the next five years in a peripatetic political exile, studying, writing, and organizing in Brussels, Paris, Fort-de-France, New York, and Havana.[153] Even when forced to move because of political pressures, Roumain seems to have planned his travels during these years around the pursuit of ethnological and anthropological training. Upon arriving in Paris in September 1937, he enrolled at the Institut d'Ethnologie de l'Université de Paris, receiving a diploma the following summer, and also studied at the Institut de Paléontologie Humaine and the Sorbonne.[154] In April 1938 Roumain was arrested and briefly imprisoned by French authorities at the insistence of Dominican diplomats for having attacked Trujillo in print following the 1937 massacre of ethnic Haitians in the border regions. Thereafter, as the political climate in France became increasingly inhospitable to his anti-fascist stands, Roumain sought passage to the United States, where he hoped to continue his studies.[155] Eventually he was granted entry to the United States, arriving in New York in August 1939. Once there, he enrolled at Columbia University to continue his anthropological studies, withdrawing in February of the next year because he could no longer afford the tuition.[156] He remained in New York until late 1940 and then traveled to Cuba, invited by the poet Nicolás Guillén. Roumain returned to Haiti in May 1941 upon the election of Élie Lescot, who had signaled during his campaign that exiled opponents of the former government would be welcomed home should he become president.[157]

Alfred and Rhoda Métraux arrived in Port-au-Prince later that summer for the first of what proved to be a series of trips to Haiti culminating in the UNESCO-sponsored report *Making a Living in the Marbial Valley, Haiti* (1951), Alfred's classic monograph *Le vaudou haïtien* (1958), numerous articles, and Rhoda's dissertation, "Kith and Kin: A Study of Creole Social Structure in Marbial, Haiti" (1951). However, this visit in 1941 was not meant to be a research trip. Then based at Yale's Institute of Human Relations, Métraux had himself written to Herskovits that June to solicit advice, given that "somewhat prompted by your excellent book 'In a Haitian Valley'" he and Rhoda had decided to spend July and part of August in Haiti: "This trip of mine is by no means anthropological, it is a deferred honeymoon and a well deserved vacation. But as I happen to be a man who loathes tourism, tourists, and everything smacking of sightseeing, please tell me where to go to have the illusion of doing fieldwork and to get the feel of real Haitian life."[158] Herskovits obliged with suggestions and a letter of introduction to Jean Price-Mars.

Alfred and Rhoda Métraux and Jacques Roumain, then, all arrived in Haiti at precisely the moment when the church's crusade against *le mélange* became a systematically administered series of "missions" across the provincial countrysides: that is, prescribed by the Roman Catholic hierarchy, carried out by local *curés* accompanied by groups of *rejete* and enforced by local *chèf seksyon* and members of the Garde d'Haïti. In *Le vaudou haïtien*, Métraux writes of witnessing firsthand the pillage and destruction that ensued and pleading with *curés* to allow the salvage of certain pieces, "which[,] for scientific or aesthetic reasons, deserved to be spared," from the piles of drums, vessels, images, and other objects deposited behind presbyteries and destined for burning.[159] A number of these he brought or had shipped back to the United States and deposited in the Smithsonian Institution's collection; others would come to form the core of the Bureau d'Ethnologie's collection.[160] In mid-July Alfred and Rhoda Métraux met up with Roumain, who accompanied them later that month on a trip to the Île de la Tortue, off Haiti's northern coast.[161] Métraux writes: "The scale of the offensive directed against *vaudou*, and the brutality of the measures taken against its adepts, appeared to me to bode its disappearance; this awakened in me the desire to undertake its study before it was too late. The Haitian writer Jacques Roumain . . . was himself also convinced of the necessity to save the memory of *vaudou*, so gravely threatened. From our conversations was born the idea to create in Haiti a 'Bureau d'Ethnologie' especially charged with this task."[162]

In a 1997 interview Michel Lamartinière Honorat, an early graduate of the Bureau d'Ethnologie, observed that during the *campagne antisuperstitieuse*, as *curés* proceeded to destroy "all the 'records'" (*tous les "dossiers"*) through which Vodou could be studied, Haitian and foreign ethnologists "began visiting *ounfò* as though they were museums."[163] Métraux was particularly convinced of the religion's imminent decline and, in citing this as the stimulus for his subsequent ethnographic studies in Haiti, observed, "I am not [Vodou's] apologist and I know that sooner or later it must disappear."[164] Roumain's published writings from this time do not describe his travels with Métraux or attribute the founding of the bureau to their conversations. However, his polemics against the church's missions reflect a similar ambivalence, in his case inflected by Marxism, toward the beliefs and practices for which peasants were being persecuted. Indeed, Roumain does not simply forecast decline in these articles, but rather actively calls for the peasantry to be freed "of their mystical shackles" through an "anti-misery" campaign, rather than a *campagne antisuperstitieuse*, which would enable them "to overcome religious survivals rooted in their misery, ignorance, [and] age-old exploitation."[165]

Thus, if propelled by the impulse of ethnographic salvage, as Métraux remembers, Roumain's founding of the Bureau d'Ethnologie was not marked by the kind of anticipatory nostalgia that often characterizes such projects. His stakes in organizing the bureau seem rather to have focused primarily on protecting and preserving Haiti's archaeological heritage, and particularly the pre-Columbian artifacts that had been the object of his ethnological studies abroad and that he saw as the national patrimony most gravely threatened by the church's campaign.[166] Indeed, the sculpted Taíno ax heads, called *pyè-tonnè* (*pierres-tonnerres*, or thunderstones), that formed part of the sacred relics in many *ounfò* were targeted for confiscation (although, interestingly, not for destruction) by the church as *pierres superstitieuses* (superstitious stones).[167] Perhaps to rebut charges that the church was stealing archaeological treasures, Carl Edward Peters, one of the Haitian priests who took part in those "missions," later credited the *campagne anti-superstitieuse* with making a "magnificent contribution" to the founding of the Bureau d'Ethnologie, noting that several hundred of the inaugural objects of the collection were confiscated during the church's raids.[168]

The threat that Roumain considered the *campagne anti-superstitieuse* to represent to such archaeological artifacts seems to have figured strongly in his efforts to organize the Haitian Bureau d'Ethnologie in September and October 1941. The Lescot government was itself highly invested in this project. Indeed, André-Marcel d'Ans has argued that the new president saw the founding of the bureau as a way to offset public criticism that he was "co-author of—or at least an accomplice to—the most deplorable excesses of the 'antisuperstition campaign,'" given that he had placed military and police forces at the clergy's disposal.[169] Correspondence from Métraux's efforts to ship the sacred objects he "rescued" from bonfires in the area of Croix-des-Bouquets to the Smithsonian's United States National Museum during and in the months following his trip to Haiti suggests that government officials may also have been concerned about the exportation of antiquities from Haiti.[170] The Smithsonian was keen to receive the objects Métraux offered, and Camille Lhérisson, who took possession of the collection once Métraux left Haiti, advised the museum in September that it would need to make a formal request to the Haitian assistant secretary of the interior, Gontran Rouzier, who also sought (seemingly as a condition of the release of the objects) sample archaeological preservation laws on which to base Haiti's own legislation in this area.[171] A 5 November 1941 *décret-loi* instituted the Bureau d'Ethnologie as a state agency and identified as its mission the conservation of "archaeological and ethnographic pieces found in Haitian territory." Although "ethnographic pieces" were not defined, archaeological ones were identified as any objects "fabricated by pre-Columbian populations of the Republic and having a scientific or artistic importance" and were interdicted from exportation "without the authorization of the Department of the Inte-

FIGURE 11. Dantès Bellegarde, Camille Lhérisson, and Jacques Roumain, Port-au-Prince, 1941. Photo by Alfred or Rhoda Métraux. Courtesy of Daniel A. Métraux.

rior, after the prior report of the Bureau d'Ethnologie." The law further specified that any archaeological object discovered by a private individual had to be evaluated by the bureau to determine if "the said objects ought to be made part of the National Collections."[172]

One of the tasks with which the new bureau was immediately charged was the development of ethnological instruction.[173] Only a week after the bureau's institutionalization by *décret-loi*, the Haitian daily newspapers announced that a group of scholars, headed by Jean Price-Mars, had created an Institut d'Ethnologie as a private higher-education faculty for ethnological training.[174] That first term, Jacques Roumain taught a course on pre-Columbian ethnology; Suzanne Comhaire Sylvain, a linguist and folklorist, offered one on phonetics and linguistics; Catts Pressoir, who later wrote a book on Haitian Protestantism, taught the history of world religions; and Louis Mars, Price-Mars's son and future author of the psychologically based study *La crise de possession*, offered a course entitled "psychology of primitives and paranoias." There was also a biology course taught by Camille Lhérisson, as well as offerings in "morphology and ethnology" and "genetics and biometrics" (see fig. 11).[175] Through public programs, frequent public lectures, publications, and performances, the Bureau and the Institut d'Ethnologie became the epicenter of ethnological and folklore studies in Haiti.[176] These institutions reflected, in their affiliates and membership, the wide ideological heterogeneity and internal tensions of what by this time had been collectively nominated the *mouvement folklorique*.

On the one hand, there was Jacques Roumain, who saw Haitian color politics as an idiom of the class struggle and took a dim view of those who, in his view, cynically privileged the problem of color in public discourse to obscure the economic basis of inequality in Haiti.[177] Roumain's critique implicated a number of his colleagues at the bureau and institute who were members of the Griots group.[178] Named after the traditional storyteller musicians of West Africa, the Groupe des Griots, was founded in 1932 by Louis Diaquoi, a journalist, and Lorimer Denis and François Duvalier, then students of law and medicine, respectively; the three had been in conversation about ethnology and politics since the late 1920s. Diaquoi died shortly after the group's formation, and Denis and Duvalier were thereafter joined by two poets, Carl Brouard (who had been, with Jacques Roumain, a founder of *La Revue indigène*) and Clément Magloire *fils* (later, Magloire Saint Aude). In 1938, with financial support from Brouard's father, then mayor of Port-au-Prince, the group founded the journal *Les Griots*, which became an early (1938–1940) mouthpiece of the post-occupation political mouvement of *noirisme*, positioning Denis and Duvalier as its foremost ideologues.[179] Ethnology, they maintained in articles throughout the late 1930s and 1940s, scientifically corroborated the central *noiriste* political doctrine that Haiti's social structure and political institutions should reflect what they identified as the biologically and psychologically African nature of its masses. State power, consolidated throughout Haitian history in the hands of the *milat* elite, ought instead, they argued, to be held by representatives of the black middle class, who shared the interests of the peasants and were uniquely capable of acting on their behalf.[180]

The coldness with which Roumain and the Griots affiliated with the bureau are said to have regarded one another during the former's directorship is not difficult to understand given their ideological differences, conditioned and compounded to whatever extent, as the ethnologist Michel Lamartinière Honorat noted in our 1997 conversation, by differences in social class and intellectual training.[181] Roumain was himself from the *milat* elite and had studied across Europe; most of the self-identified Griots came from the *nwa* (French *noir*, or black) middle and lower-middle classes and completed their education in Haiti. Roumain, as founder of the Haitian Communist Party, was at this time the country's best-known Marxist; affiliates of the Griots group, in playful but pointed contradistinction, sometimes called themselves "Marsistes," after the author of *Ainsi parla l'oncle*.[182]

As ideologically divergent as Roumain's politics were from those of the Griots, their mutual investment in the study of ethnology was linked to an expressed solidarity with the peasantry and an advocacy for the redistribution of economic and political power in Haiti.[183] Another prominent sector of the self-identified *mouvement folklorique* in the late 1930s and early 1940s consisted of elite folk-song collectors and arrangers and art-music composers, such as Werner A. Jaegerhuber, a pianist of German-Haitian descent, who, as Michael Largey argues, sought to "create a music tradition that simultaneously celebrated the uniqueness of the home culture and demonstrated that culture's universal aesthetic appeal."[184] One of his collaborators was a classical pianist and vocal teacher named Lina Fussman-Mathon, who worked closely with Jaegerhuber on arrangements in the late 1930s, and with him, presented concerts of folk songs performed by her young students, often attired in national costume (see fig. 12).[185]

Their efforts were encouraged by the international success and popularity during these years of what were known as American Negro spirituals, harmonized and arranged for piano or orchestra. Another collaborator, Valério Canez, a violinist, felt strongly, as he explained in a two-part 1942 article in *Haïti-Journal*, that in order for its national character to be realized, Haitian folklore, "with its beautiful melodies and its unique rhythms[,] must be known, executed in all parts of the world." To this end, Canez advocated that Haitian popular songs, including those that ritually called and honored *lwa*, be "harmonized, purified, and presented in a universal musical form, a classical musical form, rendering them accessible to all, and extricating from them all primitive form, while preserving their national character." He further recommended that they be arranged as "lieders" for the piano and noted that Jaegerhuber had already harmonized a cycle of twelve Haitian folk songs in this form. In response to those who argued that it was necessary to use drums "to give the really typical, local character to our folklore," Canez cited the position of Ludovic Lamothe, a pianist and one of Haiti's most distinguished composers, that conical Haitian drums were, categorically, "not musical instruments." Canez maintained that in Jaegerhuber's piano arrangements, "the rhythm of the drums is exactly reproduced by the bass," and that in orchestral performances, the kettledrum could be utilized "to better give the realism of the African style that characterizes Haitian folklore."[186]

I quote Canez's article at some length here not only to highlight the divergent political, intellectual, and artistic projects encompassed, by the early 1940s, under the heading of the *mouvement folklorique*, but also to point to the particular contestation that surrounded the representation of

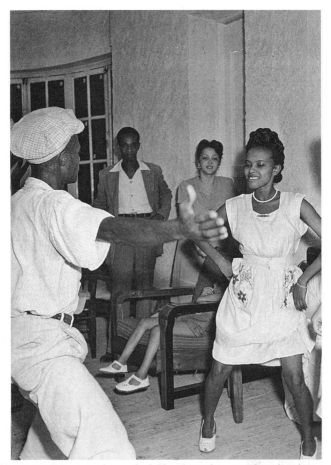

FIGURE 12. Lina Fussman-Mathon, in background, watching an informal performance at her home in the mid-1940s. Photo by Earl Leaf. Michael Ochs Archives, Getty Images.

performed genres of folklore as these were first being codified.[187] I suggested earlier that state investment in the representation of popular dance and music as national culture was presaged by the unprecedented penal exemption of such rural "entertainments" from the category of prohibited *pratiques superstitieuses* in the unusual formulation of Sténio Vincent's 1935 *décret-loi*. The negation of "superstition" through this tightened penal regime produced the positive category of "popular dance," constructed by the state during the early 1940s as a sign of official national particularity. It was under Lescot that the mutually constitutive negative and affirmative potentials of the 1935 law were realized, with his government's initial civil and military enforcement of the church's offensive against rural "superstition," on the one hand, and its simultaneous celebration of folklore performance as the embodiment of national culture, on the other. My concern in the remaining pages of this chapter, though, is not simply with how the Lescot government constructed popular performance, including codified versions of ritual dances, as national culture. It is also with how the state policed unofficial and even anti-official representations of folklore and ultimately banned the theatrical depiction of prohibited ritual practices onstage, with reference to the terms of the 1935 law against *les pratiques superstitieuses*. In the pages that follow, I want to think, in particular, about why the *performance* of folklore, as opposed to other genres of "folkloric" representation, was so politicized and contested in the early 1940s, and what this says about the complex relationship between prohibition and performance in the context of this history.

Performance and Prohibition

The theatrical staging of popular ritual practices has a shadow history in Haiti. During the occupation and thereafter, episodes of strict enforcement of the laws against *les sortilèges* and *les pratiques superstitieuses* often became the occasion for performative reenactments of the practices they prohibited. That is to say, the "performative" moment of these laws frequently led to the staging of performative supplements of the rituals they banned. Time and again during the occupation, the rigor with which marines enforced articles 405–407 proved inconvenient to the desire of North American travelers in Haiti who wished to see "voodoo ceremonies"— a desire no doubt heightened by the severity with which the prohibition was being applied.

Selden Rodman, a prolific writer on Haiti and, particularly, on the *naïf* visual arts movement of the 1940s and 1950s, reported that "when [W. B.] Seabrook pled with Dr. Price-Mars to show him a ceremony, the Haitian scholar had to get special permission from the Commandant to 'stage' one, engage a venerable *houngan* who couldn't find any drums, pay him $80— and finally be informed that it couldn't be managed!"[188] However, there were also occasions when marines and gendarmes themselves became the agents of such attempts at performative "surrogation."[189] Blair Niles, author of *Black Haiti: A Biography of Africa's Eldest Daughter* (1926), recounted her visit to a gendarmerie post in the Artibonite Valley, where she was entertained by the four lieutenants stationed there, three American and one Haitian. Niles reports that when she expressed her interest in attending a ceremony, one of the American lieutenants teased his Haitian colleague, "'Madame wants to see a Voodoo temple. . . . Haven't you one to show her?'" Niles explains to her reader that "Voodoo temples being against

FIGURE 13. "The prisoner who drummed." From Blair Niles, *Black Haiti: A Biography of Africa's Eldest Daughter*. Photo by Robert Niles, Jr. General Research and Reference Division, Schomburg Center for Research in Black Culture, The New York Public Library, Astor, Lenox, and Tilden Foundations.

the law, and it being the duty of every member of the gendarme force to raid and abolish them, [the Haitian lieutenant] had no idea where such a temple could be found." However, one of the prisoners then being held at the station was a drummer, arrested for stealing corn. So after their lunch, a confiscated drum was produced, and the man was summoned to play for the American visitor. The poignancy of that performance may be lost in the rhapsodic essentialism of Nile's description, but not in the accompanying photograph, captioned "The prisoner who drummed" (see fig. 13).[190] It is an image that documents how the prohibition and persecution of popular ritual practices during the occupation became the occasion for their displaced, and in this case forced, reenactment.

On the other hand, when Melville and Frances Herskovits arrived in the town of Mirebalais (at the suggestion of Jean Price-Mars) in the summer of 1934, three months before the official end of the occupation, local Vodouizan quickly ascertained that these foreign visitors could be effective advocates in lobbying authorities for the permits necessary to mount *sèvis*. Herskovits's early diary entries from this trip reflect the extent to which U.S. officials in Haiti sought to accommodate and facilitate his research and how, on at least one occasion, they intervened on his behalf against their own long-standing policy.[191] A few days after his arrival, Herskovits contacted the American legation in Port-au-Prince because one of his informants had told him "of an important ceremony for which there has been trouble in obtaining the necessary authorisation, this having been refused by Lieutenant Blaise, the commandant of this sub-district. Having in mind your offer to facilitate matters for us, I offered my good offices to help obtain the necessary permit from Port-au-Prince, without, of course, mentioning any names or making any promises."[192]

In his diary, Herskovits specifies that the Haitian lieutenant (stationed, incidentally, directly across the road from the house that the Herskovitses were renting) had "refused permission for an important 'cérémonie' which would entail 'feeding' the loas. I have offered my good offices to help them, and if they get their authorisation, we may see something interesting."[193] As it happened, Blaise was on his way to Port-au-Prince the next day to take examinations for a promotion, and Herskovits wondered in his note to Norman Armour, the American minister in Haiti, whether "his presence in the city might serve as an opportunity to pass on the word of which you spoke, and which might influence him in other instances of this nature." Armour wrote back a few days later saying that this was a matter in "which we have to 'watch our step' very carefully," but he had discussed it with Major General Clayton Vogel, the commander of the Garde d'Haïti, who "is going to see Lieutenant Blaise, probably today, and have a talk with him. I hope that, perhaps, this will have the general effect of helping matters along."[194] Thus, Herskovits advised the woman whose family had been denied the permission they sought to approach the lieutenant again, and this time, presumably on account of the intervention of the visiting researchers, authorization was granted. Herskovits describes attending this cycle of ceremonies in his diary in early July and notes that "since I had a hand in getting the authorisation, it seems as though we are very welcome."[195] Later that summer, he wrote back to Armour to let him know "how much I appreciate the word you put in about my work here, with special reference to the ceremony of which I wrote you shortly after my arrival. Whatever you did, it worked wonders. The ceremony for which permission was desired was quite an important one, lasting four days, and we were able to see everything; more than that, it established our position here as nothing else could have done. As a result, work has gone on in excellent fashion."[196]

The cycle of ceremonies on behalf of which Herskovits intervened seems to have been officially permitted by occupation and local authorities only because the visiting American researchers wished to attend them. In some sense, then, they were authorized because they had been officially reframed as ethnographic performances that were of scientific interest to these foreign visitors.[197] Although these ceremonies became the basis for the ninth chapter of his *Life in a Haitian Valley* (1937), "Vodun Worship: The Service," in his book Herskovits mentions neither the circumstances that prompted him to intervene, nor the fact of the intervention itself. His discussion of the regulation, penalization, and persecution of such rituals under the U.S. occupation in that monograph is limited to the paragraph in his penultimate chapter quoted above.[198] However, in his field diary Herskovits notes frequent complaints from informants both about the repression to which their religious practices had been subject earlier in the occupation and about the regime that was then in effect. In the context of securing permission for the above-mentioned *sèvis*, Herskovits reported a conversation between his principal informant and interpreter, Léonce Joachim, and another visitor about "how difficult it is to get to [ceremonies where sacrifices are offered] because of the fact that they imprison for them, unless one knows the officials and these are willing to turn their backs."[199] Even after receiving authorization for the *sèvis* through Herskovits's intercession, the woman who mounted them had been "summoned to the Chef de Section to explain why she had not obtained permission [from him] for her dance last Saturday. Apparently that sort of harassing the Vodu people goes on all the time."[200] It was Joachim's sense that authorities were actually stiffening the regulatory restrictions in advance of the imminent departure of the marines that August.

After the occupation ended, other ethnographic analogs to the theatrical staging of popular forms emerged. For George Eaton Simpson, the American sociologist who conducted research in northern Haiti in 1937, staging was a practical aspect of the research process.[201] In his 1940 article "The Vodun Service in Northern Haiti," Simpson acknowledges with characteristic candor that his composite description of a *sèvis* for the *lwa* was based on a ceremony he had attended in July 1937, the contributions of the novelist J. B. Cinéas (who served as his interpreter), conversations with *oungan* and other Vodouizan, and "parts of ceremonies staged in my house on a number of occasions by informants some of whose relatives were *houngans*, or *vodun* priests."[202] In his 1946 article "Four Vodun Ceremonies," he notes again that "the ceremonies given here were staged in my house near Plaisance on a number of occasions" and goes on to name several of those who took part in these performances (and perhaps were remunerated in some way for them). Simpson does not specify whether such staging was a matter of ethnographic necessity or convenience, writing only that "it would be impossible to obtain full accounts at actual ceremonies."[203] However, to a greater extent than those of his several North American colleagues working in Haiti during the mid-1930s, Simpson's published writings document how local regulation and penalization impacted both popular ritual practices and his own fieldwork. For example, he discusses the constraining effect that the occupation had on the duration of important annual *sèvis*: whereas, in an earlier generation, these could have lasted for nearly a month, since the occupation they had been abbreviated to less than a week.[204] In another article he notes that the number of public ceremonies was reduced at the time of his fieldwork because "in 1937 the government was enforcing the laws against vôdoun in an attempt to stamp it out."[205] In a later study he relates how one of the most distinguished *manbo* in northern Haiti, Madame Ti-Nomme, had made a point of assuring him during a June 1937 celebration in honor of the feast day for St. John (in Kreyòl, Sen Jan Batis) that there would be no animal sacrifices and that "there was nothing on her altar except the images of the Saints, that there was nothing to conceal, and that everything was in accordance with Haitian law" (see figs. 14 and 15).[206] Such a disclaimer highlights what must have been the ambiguous position of the several white male American researchers who worked in rural Haiti as the occupation was ending, and in the several years thereafter.[207] Her defensiveness might also serve to contextualize Simpson's disclosure that his research on religious ceremonies in Plaisance relied on enactments staged in the privacy of his house there.[208]

With the founding of the Bureau and Institut d'Ethnologie in 1941, the staging of ritual came to have a formalized place in Haitian ethnographic research and pedagogy. At a time when North American anthropologists often declined to study dance on the grounds that it resisted objectivist methodologies, the integration of such performances into the institute's curriculum is notable.[209] Jean-Léon Destiné (see fig. 16), who was a student at the institute in the early 1940s and later became one of Haiti's premier folklore performers, recalls that classes sometimes featured demonstrations of ritual dances and rhythms performed by practitioners: "That is how we learned. As they danced in front of us, we would analyze the steps, trying to see what they meant, trying to see the background, and

FIGURE 14. Madame Ti-Nomme, Plaisance, Haiti, 1937. Photo by George Eaton Simpson. National Anthropological Archives, Smithsonian Institution, neg. 2046.

the interpenetration of the songs and rhythms. Naturally we also learned from books, but we got to associate what we read with what we saw."

Staged representations of popular and ritual forms were also a featured aspect of the bureau's public programming, particularly after Jacques Roumain left its directorship in November 1942 to become Haiti's chargé d'affaires to Mexico.[210] Lorimer Denis, then head of the bureau's Section d'Ethnographie Afro-Haïtienne, exerted a greater influence over the institution's programming thereafter and was instrumental in establishing the performative orientation of a series of public lectures inaugurated that November. The first of these, René Victor's talk "Les voix des nos rues," was accompanied by popular songs sung by students from the École Normale d'Agriculture.[211] Shortly thereafter, the bureau formed its own in-house troupe of performers, "Mater Dolorosa" (see fig. 17). Billed as Haiti's first *choeur populaire folklorique*—signaling that the choir's members

FIGURE 15. Altar in Madame Ti-Nomme's home, Plaisance, Haiti, 1937. Photo by George Eaton Simpson. National Anthropological Archives, Smithsonian Institution, neg. 93-14-807.

came from the *pèp* (the people)—Mater Dolorosa was assembled and directed by Saint Erlonge Abraham, a Port-au-Prince *oungan* who was probably the bureau's most important informant in its early years.[212] It was on the basis of information provided by Abraham, for example, that Jacques Roumain wrote his classic monograph *Le Sacrifice du tambour-assoto(r)* (1943) on the construction, baptism, and ritual uses of these six-foot-tall drums.[213]

With the support of Denis, Abraham assembled a group of about a dozen performers, mostly women, drawn from his own religious family in the Port-au-Prince neighborhood of Fort Saint-Clair.[214] Mater Dolorosa performed ritual songs and dances for the bureau's second public lecture in early 1943, a presentation by Lorimer Denis entitled "De l'évolution stadiale du vodou," written in collaboration with François Duvalier; as well as for several subsequent talks and a bureau-sponsored *gala folklorique*. It is clear from the recollections of those who were affiliated with the bureau during the early 1940s, as well as from tributes and acknowledgments in later bureau publications, that members of Mater Dolorosa, as both performers and informants, played a key role in the ethnological

FIGURE 16. Jean-Léon Destiné in 1946. Courtesy of Jean-Léon Destiné.

interpretation and codification of ritual performance as "folklore" in the early and mid-1940s.[215]

Staging Folklore and bon voisinage

The degree to which performance was prioritized at these two ethnological centers reflected as it also augmented the growing popularity of theatrically staged folklore among middle-class and elite audiences in Port-au-Prince by the early 1940s. Outside of the Bureau d'Ethnologie, most folklore productions were mounted at the Rex Theatre, a concert hall that doubled as a cinema. The Rex had opened in October 1935, and it was there, according to the ethnologists who authored the monograph *Le mouvement folklorique en Haïti* (1952), "where one saw born a veritable *'théâtre folklorique.'*"[216] Six months after it opened, the Rex featured a short program by Katherine Dunham, billed as the "talented ballerina from the Chicago Grand Opera," who was a student of anthropology at the University of Chicago and the recipient of a Rosenwald Fund Fellowship to study popular dance cultures in Jamaica, Martinique, Trinidad, and par-

FIGURE 17. Members of the troupe Mater Dolorosa performing in Pétionville, 1945. Photo by Earl Leaf. Michael Ochs Archives, Getty Images.

ticularly Haiti (see fig. 18). Arriving in Port-au-Prince one year after the occupation had ended, Dunham entered into the intellectual and artistic milieu of *indigéniste* cultural reevaluation as she pursued her own ethnographic research at a *lakou* in the Cul-de-Sac plain.

Dunham's performance at the Rex in April 1936, on a shared program with a visiting opera singer from France and a Haitian pianist, may have been the first time that Haitian dance ritual was interpreted onstage in Port-au-Prince. Dunham wrote in her ethnographic memoir *Island Possessed* that she had proposed to the management of the Rex in advance of her concert that she be supported "by a corps de ballet of my friends from the Cul-de-Sac." She recalled, "I could see no reason why traditional material done by those most accomplished in its execution could not be presented at the Rex Theatre." That proposal being, as she put it,

FIGURE 18. Katherine Dunham with friends in Haiti, 1936. Special Collections Research Center, Morris Library, Southern Illinois University Carbondale.

"eloquently opposed" by the theater, Dunham presented a solo program, accompanied by the pianist Carmen Brouard, that featured, among other choreography (a work on pointe and flamenco- and Russian-themed dances), a new piece entitled *Danse rituel du feu* (Ritual Fire Dance), performed to Manuel de Falla's composition of the same name.[217] This performance took place shortly after she underwent a three-day ritual called a *lave tèt* (literally, head washing) at the *ounfò* in the Cul-de-Sac. The glowing review of her performance that appeared in *Haïti-Journal* two days later obliquely referenced her involvement with this community. The writer René Piquion suggested that Dunham had been "intoxicated by the rhythms in this wonderful plain of Cul-de-Sac" and inspired to create a new choreographic idiom. He hailed her work as part of "this irresistible black renaissance that we are seeing these days."[218]

During her long career, Dunham frequently acknowledged the extent to which her choreographic idiom and technique were shaped by Haitian ritual dance cultures. Jean Coulanges, a well-known performer and scholar of Haitian popular music in Port-au-Prince today, told me that he considered Dunham's work in Haiti in 1935–1936 to have been an important stimulus for the cultural and intellectual currents of that moment as well.[219] He suggested that it took precisely such affirmative international interest for many in the urban middle and elite classes to begin to recognize popular cultures as *yon bel bagay*—a beautiful thing.[220] One wonders, in particular, what impact Dunham's well-publicized research on ritual dance, the news of her *lave tèt* in the Cul-de-Sac, and her presentation at the Rex that April had on the emergence of staged folklore performance in the late 1930s.[221] Up until this point, the *indigéniste* turn in Haitian arts and letters was primarily literary, even though as early as 1928 Jean Price-Mars had called for the development of theatrical and musical works based on ritual themes and incorporating popular performance genres.[222]

There is near-universal consensus among those who followed or participated in the folklore performance movement of the 1940s that two pioneers, Lina Fussman-Mathon (later Mathon-Blanchet) and Clément Benoit, deserve the greatest credit for first taking up Price-Mars's call.[223] In 1939 Fussman-Mathon formed a small choir composed of secondary school students from middle-class and elite families, "with the end," as Jean-Léon Destiné, one of these students, wrote in a tribute upon her death in 1994, "of introducing us to our folkloric songs and dances harmonized by her."[224] The group gave musical performances in 1939–1940 at clubs such as the Cercle Port-au-Princien and Cercle Bellevue, at charity events, and, as Destiné remembers, "at the military club where Dr. Price-Mars . . . gave lectures illustrated by songs and dances."[225]

Benoit was one of the self-identified "new generation" of Haitian artists and intellectuals who had come of age during the occupation, been inspired by the *indigéniste* literary revolt and who saw the turn toward folklore in populist political terms. In a 1935 review of Maurice Casseus's novel *Viejo*, for example, Benoit praised the novelist for wielding "the pen as a sword" and for "hastening the advent of Justice and Truth" through his portrayal of the social realities of the popular milieu.[226] For him, such representations were a form of advocacy. Benoit saw the indigenization of Haitian letters as being connected, politically and aesthetically, to internationalist currents of the time and particularly, as he notes in the review of Casseus's novel, to the work of "New Negro" writers such as Langston Hughes and Claude McKay. In 1940 Benoit assembled a small troupe of singers, musicians, and performers and created a weekly radio series entitled *L'heure de l'art haïtien* (The Haitian Art Hour). First broadcast on station HH2S, it then jumped to station HH3W that September, where it ran every Wednesday night at 9 p.m.[227] Presenting performances of folk songs, poetry readings, *comédies de mœurs* (comic sketches of local manners), scores by Haitian composers such as Justin Elie and Occide Jeanty, as well as addresses by Benoit and his collaborators, *L'heure de l'art haïtien* was warmly received by both the establishment and opposition press.

If today Fussman-Mathon and Benoit are together recognized as the vanguard of what became the folklore performance movement in

Haiti, their differing approaches to the codification and representation of popular song in the late 1930s and early 1940s established distance between their projects. A decade later, as directors of the numerous folklore troupes that had multiplied in Port-au-Prince since the mid-1940s competed for the directorship of the new Troupe Folklorique Nationale, Benoit remembered his early differences with Fussman-Mathon in a review of a performance that had just taken place at the Rex Theatre. Regretting the fact that only one drummer was featured, rather than the traditional Rada battery of three, Benoit wrote: "I believe, as I made it understood, in 1938, to Mme Lina Mathon Fussman, the delicate pianist, now the great folkloric star, that never could the piano replace the great drum; I will add today that, alone, one great drum . . . cannot replace the set of three drums."[228] In recently examining this article, Jean-Léon Destiné, one of the students who began working with Fussman-Mathon in 1939, noted that, indeed, at first, the group rehearsed and performed to piano accompaniment without the use of drums. He understood Benoit's chiding of Fussman-Mathon on this point as symptomatic of a certain competitiveness between them, with her productions appealing more to elite audiences and Benoit's presentations, broadcast on the new medium of mass transmission, drawing listeners from the middle class.[229]

Yet whatever their early differences, Fussman-Mathon and Benoit were both congratulated by the Port-au-Prince establishment in the early 1940s for spotlighting the uniqueness of Haitian culture in the spirit of wartime pan-Americanism.[230] Indeed, both lent support to this U.S.-orchestrated campaign for inter-American solidarity, Fussman-Mathon's troupe performing on the occasion of "Pan-American Day" (14 April) in 1939 and 1940 and Benoit publishing an article in Haïti-Journal in August 1942 entitled "Haïti, champion du panaméricanisme."[231] The theme of pan-Americanism was promoted as part of the Good Neighbor Policy, through which Washington aimed to secure interhemispheric alliances in the years leading up to and during World War II while (or by) drawing southern economies more tightly into its own. Though first outlined under the Hoover administration, the Good Neighbor Policy is principally associated with the presidency of Franklin D. Roosevelt, beginning in 1933. Roosevelt's goodwill visit to Cap-Haïtien in July 1934 to announce that the last marines would depart from Haiti by 15 August was symbolically weighted to mark the end of an age of repeated American military aggressions in the Caribbean and Latin America and the beginning of an era of bon voisinage (good neighborliness).[232]

Of course, the withdrawal of U.S. troops did not alter the fundamentally neocolonial nature of U.S. involvement in Haitian affairs; in fact,

Haiti remained under American financial supervision for thirteen more years.[233] However, in keeping with the mandate of pan-Americanism, the U.S. legation in Port-au-Prince focused a spotlight on Haitian and American cultural relations, which it sought to promote among the elite and middle classes through a wide array of programs, sponsorships, collaborations, and exchanges. In April 1942 the Institut Haïtiano-Américain (Haitian-American Institute) was founded to facilitate opportunities for cultural interchange and encourage study of the English language, with Jean Price-Mars as its first president and the American cultural attaché, Horace Ashton, serving as an advisor. A year later Ashton inaugurated the institute's Comité d'Anthropologie, specifying that the group would aim "to reinforce the cultural ties between Haiti and the United States and highlight the elements of Haitian folklore, one of the richest, if not the richest and the most original of the world."[234]

"Folklore" was a crucial commodity in the context of the Good Neighbor Policy. U.S. efforts to foster a sense of pan-Americanism through cultural means converged with the efforts of Latin American and Caribbean states to construct popular cultures as the repository of national particularity. This was made official in 1943, when the Assembly of Ministers and Directors of Education of the American Republics, meeting in Panama, approved a "Resolution on Folklore," which recommended that each country intensify its efforts to study, collect, popularize, and preserve the "local tradition" in which "the spiritual expressions of a people perpetuate themselves deeply and spontaneously." The resolution also called on diplomatic representatives to "aid in the development of artistic programs in the state theaters where interpretive groups display the best folkloric expression of the country they represent." It proposed that this exploitation of the "rich American folkloric tradition" would "help to develop a feeling of solidarity and friendship" among the peoples of the American republics and "contribute notably to the formation of a continental consciousness."[235] Folklore performance had already become a particularly widespread vehicle of pan-Americanism. Whether packaged as tourist attractions on the national stage or exported abroad for displays of hemispheric unity, national ballets and folklore groups became a key currency of interhemispheric relations and diplomacy, to be circulated and exchanged much in the same spirit as reciprocal trade.[236]

"It's Just an Old Dance They Like to Break Out Occasionally"
One of the earliest high-profile occasions for such an exchange of inter-American folk performance was the Eighth Annual National Folk Festival, which took place in Washington, D.C., in early May 1941, sponsored

by the *Washington Post*'s Folk Festival Association. Up to that point this annual festival had been national in scope, with each featured group representing a particular state or territory. That year, however, as the festival's director, Sarah Gertrude Knott, explained in a letter she wrote to Melville Herskovits in early 1941, the organizers decided to explore the possibility of "inviting guest groups from Canada, Mexico, one South American country and some of the Islands." She went on: "We feel that there has never been a time when the need was so obvious for better understanding, more tolerance and a stronger National Unity. We believe the use and interchange of folk traditions will help to bring this about."[237]

Knott was writing to solicit Herskovits's advice about inviting folklore groups from Peru and Haiti to perform at the festival in May. She was clearly also hoping that he would authoritatively intervene in a dispute she was having with the Haitian minister to the United States over what sort of group should be presented. This minister was Élie Lescot, who would succeed Sténio Vincent as president of Haiti four months later. Knott explained the nature of their disagreement: "The Minister from Haiti is interested in sending a small group demonstrating the Voodoo. It seems to me that this is the thing that we would have to handle especially careful [*sic*], isn't it? He too, had an idea of bringing a group of the natives who had been sort of polished off. I feel that it would be much better to have the genuine thing or nothing. What do you think?. . . . We shall appreciate any information which might help us to secure the most genuine representation." Herskovits obliged with a strongly worded reply against the kind of group that Lescot had proposed. Stating that he would consider it "very unfortunate if anything but a group of peasants were brought to do this," he recommended that "singers and drummers be obtained from the southern peninsula of the island, particularly Miragoâne or Léogâne." He further specified: "This group should be headed by a *hungan*, or native priest, and the group should be brought with the idea of performing a *vodun bamboche*, which means that they would drum the *vodun* rhythm and sing the accepted songs without spirit possession ensuing, since this might be a little embarrassing. If it did happen, the *hungan* could take care of it."[238]

Two weeks before the festival was to begin, Knott again wrote to Herskovits, hoping that he would agree to vet the program notes prepared for the Haitian dances and announcing, rather apologetically, that these would be performed by the type of group that Lescot had originally recommended. She explained: "A number of people, including the Minister, told me that if we brought the type of group we were thinking of at first we could not depend on what would happen. In the first place, they might decide not to dance or if they got under the power we might not be able to stop them." The group that had been invited in the end was the student troupe of Lina Fussman-Mathon (see figs. 19 and 20). "Of course," she wrote, "the type of group in which we both were interested at first would be of more interest to Anthropologists, but in our Festival we are showing things as they are done today and I am absolutely convinced that this is a true group of its kind."[239]

If Lescot was already invested, as his initiative suggests here, in fashioning new images of Haitian national culture and identity through folklore performance, he seems to have recognized that such a project was not without risks. On the one hand, constructions of dance and music folklore had become a ubiquitous vehicle for representing modern nationhood. On the other hand, the Haitian popular forms on which these might be based had long been sensationally constructed abroad as evidence of Haiti's "primitivism." Lescot evidently had convinced Knott that it would be a mistake to invite a group of Vodouizan to perform at the festival who might "lose control" of themselves and, in their performances, exceed the domain of representation. The control actually at stake here, of course, was that which the state sought to exercise over the construction of ritual dance as an exemplary sign of Haitian national culture. The implication of the argument that Knott recounted to Herskovits in defense of the festival's decision to invite Fussman-Mathon's troupe was that a group of peasants who themselves served the spirits could not perform the nation's modernity.

In fact, the invitation to perform at the National Folk Festival required Fussman-Mathon to make certain overnight changes to her young troupe's repertory. Most significantly, although up to that point they had been performing popular songs she had collected and harmonized with her collaborator, Werner Jaegerhuber, Lescot specifically wanted to send a dance troupe. Jean-Léon Destiné, then a young member of the company, emphasized this point during a 1997 panel in Port-au-Prince: "We did not begin with the dance; we were singers. There was no dance. It was when we were going to Washington to do the show that we began to study seriously, with a young woman or a young man who came to the home of Mme Fussman-Mathon's to teach us a few steps. But Mme Mathon danced herself too. She taught us the *petwo*, the *juba*—a society woman dancing Vodou."[240]

For the most part, the troupe was coached in ritual dances such as the *kongo*, *yanvalou*, and *banda* in Fussman-Mathon's home by Vodouizan she had met through her own research. Destiné relates, however, that one Saturday, intending to "expose us to the very source of folklore," Fussman-Mathon took several members of the troupe, all young men, to attend a

FIGURE 19. The troupe of Lina Fussman-Mathon before their trip to Washington, D.C. to perform at the 1941 National Folk Festival. Jean-Léon Destiné is standing fourth from the right. Courtesy of Jean-Léon Destiné.

sèvis on the outskirts of the capital. Destiné recalls this experience vividly on account of the excitement and distress that it produced in him and his friends at the time. "What adventure! What anxiety!" he wrote in a 1994 tribute to his former teacher. "The mambo [Lorgina Delorge], highly respected in her community, graciously received us. Her assistant [Cicéron St. Aude] showed us the ritual forms to observe, which we would perform to the letter, but not without a certain fear." This was a fear, Destiné specifies, cultivated by clerical demonization of these practices, which had recently intensified with the launching of the church's campaign against *le mélange* elsewhere in the country: "Drums, dances, songs, all of this mounted in my head and, timidly, in movements hardly sketched, I imitated the participants. Conscious of the terror that the 'forbidden fruit' inspired in me, I already saw myself at the confessional of the 'bon père,' admitting my sin of having attended a *Vaudou* meeting." It may have been such a *bon père* who, hearing drums that day, dispatched the "gendarme" who broke up the *sèvis* Fussman-Mathon and her troupe members were attending and, as Destiné writes, "arrested us all and conducted us to the nearest police station." There, while Fussman-Mathon secured their release, her students were lectured by a sergeant who admonished them "that such 'diabolical ceremonies' were legally interdicted, and to no longer participate in them."[241]

FIGURE 20. Jean-Léon Destiné and Gladys Hyppolite rehearsing in preparation for their performances at the National Folk Festival in Washington, D.C. The drummers are, *left to right*: Jonas, Léandre Lunique, and André Janvier. Courtesy of Jean-Léon Destiné.

The other major change in the group's repertory that followed the invitation to perform in Washington was that from then on their performances would be accompanied by drums. In part, this was a function of the shift to performing dances in addition to harmonized arrangements of traditional songs. However, it also seems likely that the festival, which was invested in the presentation of indigenous forms of instrumentation, exerted some pressure on this decision. In soliciting Herskovits's intervention in another case in which a diplomat from Peru proposed that Peruvian songs be performed by "some white people . . . using the piano," for example, Knott specified, "We have never used the piano accompaniment."[242] At the same moment, then, that Vodouizan in some parts of the countryside were forced to conceal drums to preserve them from antisuperstition bonfires in the courtyards of presbyteries, three drummers were added to the twelve-member student troupe who were to represent Haiti in Washington.

These *ambassadeurs de l'art populaire haïtien*, as one article called them, left Port-au-Prince aboard the *America* on 18 April 1941, accompanied by Fussman-Mathon as well as Antoine Bervin, the Haitian commissioner of tourism, who served as the group's spokesperson, and Destiné recalls, master of ceremonies.[243] The official national status of the company had been magnified three days earlier with Lescot's election to the presidency by the Assemblée Nationale.[244] This identification intensified once they arrived in Washington, where Lescot was still stationed.

As part of the Folk Festival, the group gave six performances over a three-day engagement at Constitution Hall, breaking the color bar where two years earlier the Daughters of the American Revolution had refused to allow Marian Anderson to sing.[245] They also performed at Howard University, at Washington's International House, and at venues in Wilmington, Delaware, and in Boston. The Port-au-Prince dailies followed their travels closely, reporting the warm reception that the group received from audiences in Washington, as well as in the pages of the festival's sponsor, the *Washington Post*. *Le Nouvelliste* printed excerpts from a review that appeared in the 29 April edition of that newspaper praising the troupe's performance at a banquet that Lescot organized at the Hotel Carlton prior to the opening of the festival. Attended by Washington's political elite, including the U.S. undersecretary of state, Benjamin Sumner Welles, the Mexican ambassador to the United States, and representatives of the diplomatic corps from Latin America, the event reflected Lescot's deft ability, even at this earliest moment of his presidency, to exploit the nationalist opportunities of pan-Americanism. Illustrated by a photograph of Gladys Hyppolite and Jean-Léon Destiné performing choreography based on the ritual dance of *yanvalou*, the *Post* article described in particular detail the troupe's staging of a scene of "possession," one that Destiné recently noted was "the product of the author's own imagination." In closing, the article reported that at some point during the reception, "it was explained that the Haitians didn't believe in Voodooism. It's just an old dance they like to break out occasionally."[246]

We have no access to what was actually said, but one hears in this rendering of those remarks an echo of earlier elite disavowals, such as Léon Audain's portrait of *la danse du vaudou* in his book *Le mal d'Haïti* (1908) as a form of popular entertainment that could be "purified" of all that remained of the "barbarism of past times," and that was "today a true anachronism that the people do not understand."[247] "Folklore" had become, since Audain wrote, an international currency of official national self-representation and identity, a status that the cultural policies of pan-Americanism served only to reinforce in the Americas during the 1930s and 1940s. In Haiti, *indigéniste* writers had located the Haitian national "soul" in peasant culture, and particularly in popular religious practice. Lescot's presentation of Fussman-Mathon's student troupe at the banquet marked the first time that "folklore dance," based on ritual performance, was officially constructed as representative of Haitian cultural identity in an international setting. However, the remarks reported in the *Washing-*

ton Post seemed to suggest that these dances could be indexed as national only if they were simultaneously figured as transcended. In that case, it would seem that through these folkloric constructions Lescot sought to negate both the contemporary reality of the popular practices that served as their referents and also imperialist representations of an enduring, atavistic "voodoo" that held all of Haiti, including the state, in its thrall. The primitivizing optic of the *Washington Post* article itself suggests both the high stakes and risks of this project.

Destiné remembers that in the course of another reception Lescot held for the troupe at the Haitian embassy before they left Washington, the lead drummer, André Janvier, was moved to ask Fussman-Mathon's permission to address the gathering. Lescot had just finished praising the troupe's performances in "highly laudatory terms," and for these accolades Janvier thanked the president-elect. Then Janvier asked Lescot for a memento or souvenir to prove upon his return to Haiti that drummers and dancers who were "so unappreciated in our country" were "recognized as great artists abroad." With this intervention, Janvier effectively insisted that the new president acknowledge the contemporaneity of ritual practices in Haiti and their immediate relationship to the representations the troupe had staged as national folklore. What's more, in asking for a memento, Janvier forced the president-elect to confront the discrepancy between his acclaim for the troupe's theatrical staging of ritual performance abroad and the repression to which ritual ways of serving the *lwa* were then increasingly subject in Haiti. It was only a month later that Lescot issued his presidential letter directing the Haitian civil and military authorities "to give their most complete assistance" to the church's crusade "to combat fetishism and superstition."[248] That night, as Destiné recalls, "in the face of such aplomb," the president-elect offered Janvier "a medallion, under the sustained applause of the guests."[249]

Lescot had convinced Knott that it would be unwise to invite a group of Vodouizan to perform at the folk festival and risk the possibility that they might become spiritually embodied. I have already suggested that the control at stake here was that which the president-elect sought to exercise over the construction of ritual dance as an exemplary sign of Haitian national culture and identity. The disclaimer that Lescot or another governmental representative made at the first reception in Washington reflected the imperative for controlling these representations while at the same time casting doubt on how effective such efforts could be. On the one hand, as Janvier highlighted in his remarks, there was the mimetic relation of these "folkloric" choreographies to contemporary ritual practices; on the other hand, as the *Washington Post* article reflected, there was the likelihood that foreign audiences would mistake such representations for what they were meant to negate. One witnesses, for example, an unmistakable slippage in the *Washington Post* review of the students' performance at the reception, which first describes their entrance as performers "in native costume" but then goes on to depict one of the dancers as falling "on the floor palpably voodooed" and having to be revived onstage, prompting Destiné's observation about the reporter's fertile imagination.[250] Such willful misreadings, much like earlier misreadings of the law, could throw into question the modernity that the representation aimed to assert.

The clearly justified concern that such audiences would mistake folkloric constructions for actual ritual was shadowed by the doubt that such performances might not always be purely representational. There was, in a sense, a suspicion that the signified (the choreographed ritual dance) could overwhelm and seep into the signifier (the dancer), almost, as Rosalind Morris has analyzed, like spirit "possession" itself.[251] Destiné recalls that once he and the other members of Fussman-Mathon's group began learning and performing choreography based on ritual, as opposed to simply singing harmonized "folk songs," they began to be stigmatized by some of their peers from bourgeois families. During the panel in Port-au-Prince in 1997 he remembered:

> I didn't want to tell my friends that I was studying folklore. . . . Everyone knew that young men and women were dancing [folklore with Fussman-Mathon] and they began to speak badly about us. Once, there was a little dance and when I arrived no one wanted to dance with me. The young women of my generation said, oh-oh, he's a Vodou man—that was enough to discourage anyone to quit. What happened was, I had gone to . . . a little gathering where people were dancing, and it seemed that while the dance was going on someone was possessed. They always associate Vodou with orgies or black magic or something. When they heard that I went out to a Vodou ceremony they believed that I could contaminate them.[252]

If it was suspected that performers could be "contaminated" by their bodily mimesis of ritual forms, there also seemed to be official unease around the participation of practitioners in folklore representations, at first primarily as drummers but increasingly, in independent productions, as dancers and singers. Janvier's request for a souvenir from Lescot at the second reception was premised on his belief that there was a continuity between his ritual drumming in Haiti and his "folkloric" drumming in Washington, D.C., and a discrepancy in the Haitian state's reception in each case. However, the official disavowal reportedly made at the first reception in Washington asserted a temporal as well as spatial distance between the folkloric representation and its referent: these constructions of ritual dance had to signify "pastness" in that context if they were to signify modernity.

The following year the American cultural attaché to Haiti, J. C. White, sent a memorandum to the U.S. secretary of state, Cordell Hull, concerning what he perceived to be a changing attitude toward "voodoo" on the part of the elite, and suggesting that the "reported success" of Fussman-Mathon's group in Washington "may be partially responsible for the awakening of Haitian interest in their folklore." However, he noted that there appeared "to be two conflicting attitudes toward voodoo among the intellectuals of Haiti": "One group believes that the songs and dances of the voodoo ceremonies should be developed systematically as Haiti's folklore, and exhibited at home and abroad largely in order to interest and attract tourists; whereas the other group believes that they should be ignored or denied, if not actually stamped out, as an unfortunate and debasing heritage from the dark days of slavery in the French colony, declaring that it is not a part of the life of the independent nation of Haiti."[253] However, what is signaled by the disclaimer apparently made at the reception in Washington, no less than by Lescot's presidential letter a month later backing the church's crusade against "superstition" with military force, is that for the elite state there was not necessarily a conflict between exploiting "folklore . . . to interest and attract tourists" and ignoring, denying, even "stamping out" the practices on which such folkloric forms were based. This was consistent with the logic of the 1935 legislation against *les pratiques superstitieuses*, in which the figure of popular dance, once divorced from the category of superstition, lent itself to a tightened regime of popular control at home as much as to a renovated image of national culture abroad.[254]

"Without the Inclusion of One Ritual Note"

Perhaps all this begins to explain why, during the early 1940s, the independent staging of folklore was subject to greater state surveillance and censorship than other forms of "folkloric" representation. As folklore performance became an increasingly primary space for the official elaboration of national particularity, the stakes rose for controlling the ways in which ritual dance could be theatrically represented on the basis of the above concerns. Although there were numerous ethnographic accounts of *sèvis* in publications of the Bureau d'Ethnologie, frequent literary representations of ritual in the genre of the so-called peasant novel, and radio broadcasts of Vodou rhythms and songs, there was a greater imperative on the part of Lescot's state to police representations of ritual practice by independent dance and theater artists.

Interestingly, it was the radio producer Clément Benoit, creator of *L'heure de l'art haïtien*, who brought this issue to a head, when in September 1942 his company mounted its first theatrical performance on the stage of the Rex Theatre. By this point Benoit was a well-known producer whose broadcasts of popular songs, storytelling, and comedies of local manners (Languichatte Débordus, a much-loved character created by Théodore Beaubrun, debuted on the program) were widely acclaimed and even endorsed by President Lescot, under whose "high patronage" the program's first anniversary was celebrated in May 1941.[255] The following summer, in July 1942, Benoit published *Chants sauvages*, a collection of poems that he described, in *indigéniste* terms, as "eternal songs of the African ancestor," compressed "in the depths of the Haitian soul." In his preface to this volume, Benoit asked his reader to remember "the artistic inspiration that guided the author" if reviewers should denounce the work as scandalous for its depiction of popular religion.[256] Of course, although Benoit's poems depicted scenes from *sèvis* for the *lwa*, including the sacrificial preparation of ritual offerings prohibited by the Code Pénal, no such denunciations were forthcoming in the daily press. *Haïti-Journal*, to which Benoit was an occasional contributor, lauded the volume as a "landmark in the history of our letters" and a major contribution "to the indispensable nationalization of our letters."[257]

The reception that Benoit received for *L'heure de l'art haïtien*'s first theatrical venture at the Rex two months later was, however, another matter altogether. Well publicized in advance by the Port-au-Prince dailies, "Gabélus," as it was entitled, was advertised as being "a *gala folklorique* without precedent."[258] On the evening of the performance, before the curtain rose, Benoit addressed the capacity audience with a short "manifesto" that was published a few days later in *Haïti-Journal*.[259] He began by expressing his satisfaction with the flight of interest in folklore since the founding of *L'heure de l'art haïtien* and with what he sensed was a new openness in public discourse around the subjects of "*Vaudou, loas, houngans, etc.*" He attributed this candor to a growing recognition of "the value that the people have always had in the life of a nation, and therefore the value of their practices in the domain of Art." In a disclaimer not unlike that with which he prefaced his collection of poems, Benoit announced, "If we present today religious ceremonies of the peasant cult, it is without doubt because we are certain that Haitian art cannot be found elsewhere—and that in very large measure, the art of the people in Haiti can only be the most integral expression of a life truly Haitian and national . . . . Thus, we present for you, without great pretensions, some scenes of peasant life which deal with their religious customs."

The performance began with the company staging a piece that Benoit introduced in his remarks as dramatizing "the antagonism between peasants rooted to their land, to their customs and traditions" and those who leave for the cities. As discussed in chapter 3, such migrations had been under way for years and intensified during the occupation, with its manifold disruptions of peasant life and labor in different regions of the country. More recently, beginning in 1941, large tracts of farmland had been seized for U.S. wartime rubber production in a debacle known by the acronym SHADA (Société Haïtiano-Américaine de Développement Agricole).[260] Benoit may have had these displacements in mind in thematizing the piece, but its focus was not primarily on protesting such policies. Rather, in structuring the scenes around the staging of a ritual offering, Benoit and his collaborators aimed, according to his pre-curtain statement, to affirm the legitimacy of such rituals as both religion and subject of artistic representation.

The well-known singer Marthe Augustin, who performed as a soloist on *L'heure de l'art haïtien*'s radio broadcasts and, upon occasion, with Mater Dolorosa, played the figure of the *manbo*, supported by a cast of *ounsi* played by a group identified in newspaper reviews of the production only as "peasants." Jean-Léon Destiné remembers that Benoit worked with Vodouizan in this production, not as the usual behind-the-scenes choreographic consultants, but as performers themselves, who were also meant, in some sense, to perform themselves. Their participation in the production seems particularly notable given that six years earlier the management at the Rex had refused Katherine Dunham permission to work with her friends from the Cul-de-Sac as performers. In the course of this dramatization, the figure of the *manbo* sacrificed a *kòk*, or rooster, on the stage of the theater as an offering to the spirits. The reviewer in *Le Nouvelliste* gave an account of the scene: "It would be necessary to be an initiate, or a 'specialist,' in order to explain . . . the sense and meaning of these attitudes and movements, these abrupt and jerky gestures, these steps of the Mambo, . . . the entire sacrifice, in a word, moving given the sincerity of a rite older than a thousand years. . . . Abruptly. The sacrifice of the victim: a rooster. The public, breathless, stifled, followed the brief, quick and expert movements of the mambo, twisting, tearing off the neck of the victim and drinking its blood."[261] This offering was followed by a cycle of ritual dances—the *vaudou*, *kongo*, and *makaya*—and the production closed with a popular love song, the eponymous "Gabélus," around which, as *Le Nouvelliste* described, Benoit had "embroidered a little scenario" of peasant life and customs.[262]

The two major Port-au-Prince dailies highly praised Augustin's performance of "Gabélus," the final sketch. They were extremely critical, however, of Benoit's staging of the ritual offering on the program. Discounting his pre-curtain claim that this enactment of ritual held the status of art, both reviews argued that with this production Benoit had betrayed what he had in fact intended to honor. *Le Nouvelliste* contended that the performance had transformed what was "a pious and clearly religious ceremony" into a ridiculous spectacle, and that such a reconstruction, "with all the realism of its rites, but without the atmosphere which is indispensable to it, is very exactly the opposite of an artistic performance."[263] Two days following the performance, *Haïti-Journal* published a thinly veiled rebuke, without naming its contributor, of artists who, whether "intentionally or unconsciously, render popular art ridiculous," describing this as "a crime against . . . the masses" and a betrayal of the cause of revolutionary art.[264] The public debate incited by the performance in late September 1942 was such that it motivated the American cultural attaché, J. C. White, to send his memo to the U.S. secretary of state a few days later. Describing Benoit's production as "probably the most important of its kind yet given in Haiti," White read the contestation surrounding it as "evidence that opinion is divided as to whether Haitian folklore composed of voodoo ceremonies, songs and dances shall be recognized and presented to the world, or denied like an illegitimate child."[265]

Benoit's contemporaries, folklore performers, and ethnologists of his generation still discuss the September 1942 performance as a decisive marker in the history of the *mouvement folklorique* in Haiti. However, their interpretations of the controversy complicate that offered by White. On the subject of this performance during the 1997 conference in Port-au-Prince on the history of Haitian folklore dance, some participants remained critical, maintaining that Benoit had an artistic responsibility to further "translate" the rite for the stage: "We must remember," Destiné said in this context, "that there is a difference between what the peasant does under the *peristil* and that which is done in the theater. . . . The end of theater is not to reproduce but to communicate, and in our case, to adapt the raw material [*la matière brute*] in the best way possible, with taste, integrity, and the greatest artistic ability." In staging the ritual offering, Benoit had marked, in crossing, what his colleagues thereafter identified as the limit of folkloric representation. Pierre Desrameaux, a former folklore performer and well-known folklore dance teacher in Port-au-Prince, emphasized in discussing Benoit's performance and the protocols of staging ritual more generally, that in representing sacred acts and performances onstage, whether sacrificial offerings or spirit embodiments, *fok ou "mime" yo* (you must mime them), otherwise "you are not in the theater anymore."[266]

In discussing "Gabélus" in an interview that same year, the ethnologist Michel Lamartinière Honorat likewise noted, as others had, that Benoit was not a "person of the theater." However, he set aside the question of whether or not this staged reenactment of the ritual was art and emphasized the opprobrium that the performance generated among the bourgeois public. There are many questions that one might want to ask about this section of Benoit's production, which raises, of course, a host of ethical issues. What I would like to focus on here, taking Honorat's cue, is how socially and politically confrontational the performance was at that moment. It presented as "folklore" precisely the act by which *les pratiques superstitieuses* were defined and prohibited in the 1935 law, and it did so as the state claimed folklore performance as an official national sign.

The production was arguably a good deal more challenging to the 1935 legal redefinition and prohibition of *les pratiques superstitieuses* as, specifically, any dance, ceremony, or meeting involving animal sacrifice, than most foreign anthropological and Haitian ethnological writings at this time. I have already discussed the general inattention to the legal regime against Vodou in the published work of international scholars of the religion. In Haiti, the law was tightened at the same moment that ethnological studies were being inaugurated. Yet published calls for the decriminalization of popular ritual seem to have been few and far between, with several notable exceptions. Jean Price-Mars, in asserting the status of Vodou as a religion in *Ainsi parla l'oncle* (1928), had implicitly challenged the construction and interdiction of these practices as *sortilèges* in legal discourses.[267] That same year, the esotericist Arthur Holly had gone further in his *Dra-Po*, calling for the extension of "the constitutional provisions relating to the liberty of worship . . . to the practice of divine and orthodox Mysteries of the Voudo religion."[268] A decade later Kléber Georges-Jacob, a lawyer and an associate of the Griots, criticized the penalization of popular ritual as part of his more general *noiriste* argument against the liberal republican political institutions that Haiti had "borrowed" from Europe after independence, "with which," he wrote in his anthology *L'ethnie haïtienne* (1941), "we have nothing in common."[269] In this work Georges-Jacob made Price-Mars's reclassification the basis of a legal argument against Vodou's interdiction, with reference to the Haitian constitution's protection of religious freedom. He reasoned that if these were practices of a religious nature, as Price-Mars had proved, and if, constitutionally, each citizen had the right to profess his religion as long as it did not disturb the public order, then the prohibition should be lifted, because such family-based rites "constitute neither an immediate nor an indirect danger for society."[270]

Outside of Price-Mars's, Holly's, and Georges-Jacob's work, amidst the proliferation of close ethnographic studies of Vodou in the 1940s, most notably those published by Lorimer Denis and François Duvalier, strikingly little ethnological attention was paid to the question of law, either juridical or "customary." Later that decade Emmanuel C. Paul, a professor of ethnology with the Bureau d'Ethnologie, noted the paucity of ethnological legal studies in general and challenged his colleagues to develop this area, with a view to the reform of the Haitian legal system. He proposed that the publication of even "ten or so monographs on our juridical folklore would furnish our jurists with enough material for the first steps in elaborating [a] Haitian law."[271] The decriminalization of popular ritual would seem central to this project, although Paul does not make specific reference to it. In his *La tradition voudoo et le voudoo haïtien* (1953), Milo Rigaud forcefully critiqued the penalization of Vodou and argued that the religion could not be understood outside of its imbrication in "the national and even international economic, social, political, order." He continued: "To speak of the mysteries of voudoo without considering these questions . . . would be to make a very incomplete study of it."[272]

Beyond these important voices, outright calls for the lifting of the interdiction against *les pratiques superstitieuses* during the late 1930s and 1940s were rare in the burgeoning social scientific literature on popular religion. By contrast, Benoit's performance directly violated the 1935 law, defined in part by the act of animal sacrifice. Certainly he and his company members did not suffer what would have been at that time the official penalties for such a transgression—six months' imprisonment and fines equivalent to $80. Yet Benoit's contemporaries emphasize that his staged representation of a prohibited ritual had its own repercussions. Lamartinière Honorat associates the departure of Benoit's star performer, Marthe Augustin, from the group shortly thereafter with the negative publicity surrounding the production and remembers that other members left at that point as well.[273] Although *L'heure de l'art haïtien*'s radio broadcasts continued through the mid-1940s, Benoit seems not to have returned to the stage until the late 1940s, when he founded another folklore troupe called "Pierre Damballah."

What is interesting, however, is that in spite (or perhaps more likely because) of the scandal it generated, Benoit's *gala folklorique* in September 1942 seemed to catalyze a new trend in folklore performance and popular theater in Port-au-Prince. Whether motivated by political protest in solidarity with the peasantry, theatrical provocation in a surrealist vein, and/or the strong box-office receipts that burlesque comedies of popular manners frequently yielded, for nearly ten months thereafter performances of

prohibited ritual continued to take place on the stages of the city's concert halls. By early 1943 *Haïti-Journal* was denouncing, as Pierre Mayard, a
writer and notable figure in popular theater himself, put it in one article,
"the great vogue, these last months, of theatrical performances: I dare not
say of Haitian theater!! The theater is something honest and clean."[274] In
a favorable review of a lecture by the ethnologist Lorimer Denis a few
months later, the poet and journalist Roussan Camille wrote of the importance of distinguishing "between the serious work of a scholar [such
as Denis] and the grotesque exhibitions to which imbecilic parvenus have
attempted, as of late, to accustom a public too weak to boo and stone
them as it should."[275] A few days later another article warned the authors,
directors, and players of local *comédies de mœurs* that "the public . . . is beginning to complain of these grotesque comedies in which, in the guise of
theater, they are offered buffooneries of clearly bad taste, augmented by
licentious subjects which are no longer even amusing."[276]

Such protests did not deter the writer and director René Rosemond
from staging his three-act *comédie folklorique* called *Mambo-chérie* at the Rex
Theatre on 2 June 1943.[277] Taking the stage before the curtain rose, as Clément Benoit had done the previous September, Rosemond announced
that with this performance, what had formerly been a *mouvement folklorique* would henceforth become a *révolution folklorique*.[278] In the newspapers
the next day appeared categorical denunciations of Rosemond's production. *Le Nouvelliste* was particularly critical, rebuking Rosemond for his
failure to recognize "the necessity of showing the beauty of our folklore"
and for not bringing "a more refined sense, a more delicate taste to the
national theater."[279] Beyond such pronouncements, however, there was
little in the way of description to give a sense of what kind of "folkloric
revolution" *Mambo-chérie* had augured.

This might better be gauged by the official response to the show—
and, one senses, its genre—which came two days later. On 5 June 1943 a
new ordinance was issued by the office of the wartime government cen-
sor, the Bureau d'Information à la Presse, or B.I.P., forbidding the staged
representation of prohibited rituals. As printed in both *Haïti-Journal* and
Le Nouvelliste (in the latter under the headline "An Excellent Decision"), it
began: "For some time now, authors have been presenting to the public,
under the pretext of folkloric exhibitions, scenes that are instead only
imitations of prohibited ritual ceremonies. This practice, which has no
artistic character whatsoever, can only throw Haitian customs into disrepute. Consequently, these sorts of performance are henceforth formally
interdicted."[280] Up until that time the B.I.P had been charged in general
terms with censoring "theater plays and other publications judged to be

contrary to the foreign policy of the Government of the Republic, and harmful to national defense and domestic peace." Two months earlier, in the midst of this wave of objectionable folklore productions, the government had issued a warning to theaters that because the B.I.P. "only practices political censorship"; it was "up to them [the theaters themselves] to interdict the performance of plays likely to ridicule Haitian intellectualism."[281] The new B.I.P. ordinance, however, was specifically addressed to folklore performance. In banning the staging of prohibited rituals, it further specified that from then on, "folkloric performances must be limited to the presentation of popular dances and songs without, under any circumstances, the inclusion of one ritual note."[282] An editorial in *Le Nouvelliste* commended the government for putting a stop to the "trend of transporting prohibited practices to the stage," adding: "We have been vindicated in our call for the end of this genre of folklore."[283]

★   ★   ★

The B.I.P. ordinance was, in one sense, characteristic of what historians have characterized as President Lescot's inclination, whenever possible, to exploit the war as a pretext for further curtailing civil liberties in Haiti. Yet what seems most striking about this law is its reiteration of the split between prohibited ritual and popular dance that, I have argued, structured both the 1935 legislation against *les pratiques superstitieuses* and official cultural nationalist policy in early post-occupation Haiti. I have examined how these two categories were mutually constitutive, and particularly how the legal negation of prohibited ritual served as a kind of juridical groundwork for the state's annexation of popular dance as national folklore in the early 1940s. Whatever their diverse motives in staging interdicted rituals on the stage of the Rex Theatre, Clément Benoit and the popular theater artists who followed his lead could scarcely have chosen a more politically provocative object of "folkloric" representation in the early 1940s.

The official stakes for policing performed folklore were particularly high in the early post-occupation moment given Euro-American representation of "voodoo" as evidence of Haiti's premodernity, whether this was deemed cause for censure or celebration. Because it was in part state concern over the depiction of Haitian popular ritualism that propelled the passage of the law against *les pratiques superstitieuses* in 1935, folklore performers and popular theater artists who transgressed that prohibition in the early 1940s were subject to the same interdiction, if not the same potential penalties. As the government's censorship drove home, these

staged representations of ritual were at least as threatening to state authorities as the "real" they indexed, if not more so for being publicly performed.

However, to point to the representational stakes of the 1935 law against
les pratiques superstitieuses, promulgated at a moment when Euro-American
literary and cinematic sensationalism about Haiti had perhaps reached an
all-time high, is not to propose that this law had no or was of no material
consequence for communities of Vodouizan. Derrida's insight that there
is "no such thing as a law . . . that doesn't imply *in itself* . . . the possibility
of being 'enforced'" was borne out repeatedly in Haiti's juridical history,
beyond the customary ways in which officially interdicted practices were
locally regulated much of the time. Most notably, United States military
officials made the strict application of Haitian laws against "voodoo" both
a hallmark of official policy and a sometime justification for the continued
occupation of Haiti. After the departure of the marines from Haiti, the
full force of Sténio Vincent's new law against *les pratiques superstitieuses* was
realized in the Catholic church's *campagne anti-superstitieuse*, backed by the
Haitian military and police as of June 1941. Even outside of such episodes
of strict enforcement, in criminalizing a primary way in which Vodouizan ensured mutually beneficial relations with the spirits, the 1935 legislation served to perpetuate, as its antecedents had, the political marginalization, social stigmatization, and everyday economic exploitation of the
subaltern majority in Haiti. It joined the battery of laws regulating peasant life through which, as Laënnec Hurbon has written, the state maintained "a peasant society closed in on itself, based on its own traditions,
and effectively constituting another country in the interior of Haiti."[284]

Yet, in some sense, both the 1935 law against *les pratiques superstitieuses*
and the 1943 ordinance against its theatrical staging exposed their own
impossibility in attempting to legislate an absolute distinction between
prohibited ritual and popular dance. This is why Hurbon interprets the
1935 law's validation of rural dancing as a kind of juridical wink, surreptitiously acknowledging the impossibility of establishing such a strict separation between popular dance and ritual practice even while attempting
to legally set one. The 1943 ordinance against the staging of prohibited
rituals aspired to another impossible detachment in restricting folklore
performance to the presentation of popular dance and songs, "without,
under any circumstances, the inclusion of one ritual note." The embod-
iedness of these representations affiliated them with the ritual practices
that the official figure of popular dance, constructed in legal discourse as
well as in national culture formations, was meant to repudiate and supplant. This meant that even state-sponsored folklore bore witness to the

spiritual practices performed on the other side of official sanction. Was this not the drummer Janvier's point when, after listening to Lescot's accolades in Washington, D.C., he requested that the president-elect provide him with a tangible memento to mark the Haitian government's appreciation abroad for practices then subject to repression in Haiti?

Barbara Kirshenblatt-Gimblett has characterized "folkloricization" as a mode of cultural production through which "errors" are converted into "archaisms," a process transvaluing "the repudiated . . . as heritage."[285] It seems to me that this is a helpful way to think about the penal and performative processes that I have analyzed in early post-occupation Haiti.[286] Over the course of the chapter, I have been concerned with examining the interconnections between the post-occupation Haitian state's legal construction of fundamental ways of serving the spirits as "prohibited ritual," and its elevation and international presentation of "popular dance" as an official national sign. This has meant thinking about the relationship between state nationalist rhetoric that, at times, constructed folklore performance as reviving a transcended past, and the penal and ecclesiastical regimes that seemed designed to relegate forms of popular ritualism to the past. Yet, Janvier's confrontation of Lescot, and perhaps also the performances of those credited only as "peasants" in Benoit's theater production, suggest that folkloricization became itself the occasion for popular political challenges to the law's repressive regime.

In February 1941 a notice appeared in Haiti's official journal *Le Moniteur* announcing that a businessman named Elias Noustas, better remembered as founder of the Port-au-Prince department store La Belle Créole, had registered a new trademark, "Voodoo," to which he would own the rights for twenty years thenceforth. Noustas, according to the announcement, intended to apply the trademark to lines of handbags, sandals, perfumes, and "in a general way to cosmetics and beauty products."[1]

Whether or not Noustas produced any commodities under this brand, his trademarking of "voodoo" signals the complexity of how this word was signifying in international circulation, as well as among middle-class and elite consumers in Haiti at this time. In *Vodou et névrose* (1931), J. C. Dorsainvil assessed the historical and persistent force of colonial images of Haitian popular ritualism in observing that "for our denigrators . . . [Vodou is] the indelible mark of our inferiority, of our original fall."[2] Four years later, *Le Moniteur* published the law that tightened the penal regime against what were now legally constructed as *les pratiques supersti-tieuses* on the grounds, in part, that the state had a responsibility to protect the nation's reputation from such association with "superstition." When Noustas's registry of his trademark was made official in the same pages five and a half years later, the Roman Catholic church had already begun its anti-Vodou missions in Hinche and Port-de-Paix; four months afterward, President Lescot endorsed that campaign with police and military backing.

Yet Noustas's branding of "voodoo" is a sign of the powerful counter-vailing currents shaping how Haitian popular ritual practice was regarded among different sectors of the Haitian urban middle class and elite, as well as internationally. *Indigénisme*, Haitian ethnology studies, and the *mouve-ment folklorique* figured Vodou as the central locus and repository of Haitian national identity and culture. Beyond Haiti's borders, Vodou was the object of intense fascination and, for writers disenchanted with industrialized modernity, sometime celebration during and after the U.S. occupation. Haiti was also becoming the site of intensive foreign anthropological interest during these years, and Vodou was the primary ethnographic object of North American and Western European researchers who traveled there. As Dorsainvil acutely observed, since the mid-nineteenth century Haiti's defamers had concentrated their racial stigmatization of the "Black Republic" in the figure of *le vaudoux* and eventually of "voodoo," which they mobilized as evidence of the decline of colonial civilization in the country and the incapacity of people of African descent to be self-governing. However, by the end of the occupation, these were also powerfully attractive constructs, the erotics of which Cole Porter drew upon and further charged in his 1929 song "You Do Something to Me," with its refrain, "Do do that voodoo that you do so well."[3] Given the international artistic, intellectual, and popular cultural confluences and feedback loops of this period, as well as the promise of post-occupation tourist development in Haiti, Noustas's branding of "voodoo" to sell cosmetics and beauty products is not too surprising. In fact, the word had been trademarked in the United States by a cosmetics firm in 1939 and would thereafter name a popular scent marketed by the Dana company in a 1950 advertising campaign as "Voodoo: Perfume of the Night."[4]

In studying the social life of laws against popular ritual practices in Saint-Domingue and Haiti over the course of two centuries, this study has also necessarily focused on the history of *le vaudoux* and its cognates as signs. This has entailed, in part, examining the disjuncture between how these words were constructed by outsiders versus how the word "Vodou" was popularly understood, and what that divergence meant at different conjunctures for the penal regime to which practitioners were subject. To the extent that the Haitian laws against first *les sortilèges* and, a century later, *les pratiques superstitieuses* were motivated and shaped by colonial and imperial representations of *le vaudoux* and "voodoo," however ambivalent, this history stands as testimony to how denigration of African and African diasporic religious practices has materially impacted the lives of subaltern Haitian populations over generations.

Yet, I have also repeatedly stressed that beyond asserting Haiti's national modernity, such laws, in their promulgation and application, were also shaped by local stakes over the course of their cumulative 152-year history. Although they were seldom enforced rigorously against socially sanctioned family- or temple-based religious practices, they nevertheless always retained that potential, as the different campaigns and offensives discussed above document. Moreover, outside of episodes of violent enforcement, these laws were the pretext and condition of possibility for customary, everyday forms of exploitation of the peasantry and urban poor; they formed part of a battery of legislation that specifically targeted the Haitian majority and seemed designed to marginalize and contain those populations.

What was the nature and history of this penal regime in Haiti after the mid-1940s? When Alphonse Jean discussed this question with me in Tabarre, Haiti, in June 1997, he had been a practicing *oungan* for fifty-one years. He noted that outside of the persecutions suffered during the church's antisuperstition campaign between 1940 and 1942, there was little difference in how officially prohibited ritual practices were informally regulated in this locale (just outside of Port-au-Prince) under the post-occupation governments of Sténio Vincent, Élie Lescot, Dumarsais Estimé (1946–1950), and Paul Magloire (1950–1956).[5] As noted before, in order to mount a *sèvis*, a permit had to be purchased from the local *chèf seksyon* at a variable rate depending on the nature of the ceremony. However, Jean noted, this long-standing customary arrangement was significantly altered once François Duvalier came to power in 1957.

As an ethnologist publishing articles in *Les Griots* and the *Bulletin du Bureau d'ethnologie* during the late 1930s and 1940s, the elder Duvalier and his collaborator Lorimer Denis had focused their research on Vodou, analyzing the religion as "the crystallization of the origins and psychology of the Haitian people" and the "supreme factor of Haitian unity, in view of national independence."[6] As *président à vie* (president for life), Duvalier became internationally known for appropriating iconography from Vodou in the service of his own self-fashioning, as well as for exploiting the popular identification of political power with sorcery. Gérard Pierre-Charles notes that from the beginning of his regime Duvalier constructed himself as the *père spirituel* (spiritual father) of the nation and encouraged the sobriquet "Papa Doc," invoking the popular term of respect for *oungan* in addition to his own status as a medical doctor.[7] Most famously, he constructed his persona through visual motifs of the Gede *lwa*, associated, in part, with cemeteries and the dead, and theatricalized such associations by donning the characteristic dark vestments and hat of these spirits and their leader, Bawon Samdi.[8]

The elder Duvalier was also known for his attempts to co-opt and instrumentalize popular religious organizations across the country in the service of his regime. Laënnec Hurbon, Michel-Rolph Trouillot, and other analysts have examined how Duvalier *père* consolidated power by systematically neutralizing and "domesticating" or silencing any potentially autonomous institution or system within the country: the army, the Roman Catholic church, the legislature, the judiciary, the schools and universities, the press, and so on.[9] Although Haitian governments had long regarded Vodou as a potential parallel power, no president had attempted to co-opt this decentralized religion on the scale undertaken by Duvalier. In so doing, he pursued the most influential popular religious leaders across the country and exploited what Michel Laguerre has called the "inextricable lattice of intersecting networks" connecting temples with one another and with *sosyete sekrè*.[10] Just as Duvalier sought to install members of his secret police, the *tonton makout* (themselves named after a childhood bogeyman), in the hierarchies of governmental, military, and civil society institutions, so he recruited *oungan, manbo, bòkò,* and *sosyete sekrè* officers to join this force and, after 1962, to serve in his civil militia, the Volontaires de la Sécurité Nationale (VSN). Trouillot notes that this paramilitary organization drew its membership primarily from among the rural and urban poor, and furthermore, that it represented one of the very few official national organizations that had ever solicited their membership and, in so doing, recognized their citizenship. The denim uniforms and red kerchiefs of the VSN indexed the garb of the agricultural spirit Azaka and, at the same time, that of the *kako* armies who resisted U.S. invasion in 1915.[11]

Laguerre notes that the Duvalier regime's efforts to politicize Vodou congregations across the country stemmed from its recognition of their status as "a center of power in the local community," and of the Vodou "priest as a broker on behalf of his congregation."[12] Duvalier departed from the surreptitious patronage that defined the relationship of many earlier politicians with important popular religious organizations, and took no pains to conceal the access that politically loyal *oungan, manbo,* and *bòkò* had to the National Palace. Exploiting the popular linkage between political power and sorcery, his regime also encouraged rumors that the *président à vie* was himself a potent manipulator of supernatural forces.[13] However, as Hurbon has argued, that was actually a double-edged reputation. In fact, "the attribution of sorcery powers (or of evil magic) to Duvalier constituted an oblique mode of contestation of his regime" because, according to popular belief, their exploitation "returns sooner or later against its users."[14] Internationally, the publicity surrounding these iconographic appropriations and political co-optations further charged the sensationalism associated with "voodoo," with, as Gérard Pierre-Charles argues, some foreign commentators linking the "barbarism of the Duvalierist political regime" with "the 'diabolic' character of this 'black sect.'"[15]

Neither the conclusion that Vodou practically attained the status of an "official religion" in Haiti under Duvalier nor that his power "founded itself truly on the will to promote Vodou" is borne out by on-the-ground realities.[16] Hurbon notes that, "far from envisaging a promotion of Vodou or of popular culture, Duvalier worked—like other chiefs of State—to exercise the strictest control over Vodou."[17] To whatever extent he succeeded in insinuating his power into popular religious imaginaries and organizations, the fact remains that Duvalier maintained the official prohibition against *les pratiques superstitieuses* over the course of his dictatorship, as did his successor and son, Jean-Claude Duvalier (1971–1986). It was not repealed until the promulgation of the 1987 constitution following the latter's overthrow.

However, the preservation of that law did not mean that the regulatory regime to which Vodouizan were subject was entirely continuous with that enforced under previous governments. Jean Kerboull reported that in March 1963, upon the order of the president, the country's civil and military authorities announced in "public places that the populations of Haiti were henceforth free to take part in the *Vaudou* ceremonies of their choice."[18] The condition of that freedom, however, was increased taxation and state surveillance, with the potential for graft on the parts of *chèf seksyon* and other local officers undiminished. Commentators have stressed the burden of heavier taxation on Vodouizan during these years to the point that, according to Gérard Pierre-Charles, "certain temples were obliged to cease functioning."[19] Alphonse Jean noted that although Vodouizan could practice with greater openness and liberty under the Duvaliers, the official regulation of their ritual practices—through the requirement of purchased licenses—was more centralized than under previous governments.[20] Michel Laguerre documents that those ritual leaders and specialists who were themselves *tonton makout* or *milisyen* (members of the civil militia) could elude this regulatory regime and the harassment that the maintenance of official prohibition enabled.[21] That local authorities otherwise still exploited the official penal prohibition of *les pratiques superstitieuses* as a pretext for graft is well documented in British anthropologist Francis Huxley's 1966 ethnography *The Invisibles*, based on research in Haiti under the elder Duvalier. For example, in Jacmel, where most of Huxley's work was based, there were instances of police and soldiers interrupting properly licensed *sèvis* to exact additional fees, "small satisfactions," with the threat that they "could otherwise stop any ceremony at which blood was shed," based on the 1935 law. In another case, a soldier broke up a Saturday night "dance" on the grounds that it was departing from the "congo" authorized on the license.[22]

Even as the penal prohibition of *les pratiques superstitieuses* was maintained on the books, both Duvalier governments openly acknowledged in their regular statistical bulletins the significant contribution that popular religious leaders and ritual specialists were making to the gross domestic product of Haiti as part of the Haitian economy's *secteur des services personnels* (personal services sector). The *Guide économique de la République d'Haïti* of July 1964, for example, lists expenditures of some 2.52 million gourdes ($504,000 at the official exchange rate) in Haiti in 1961 for the services of *prêtres du voodu*, who were grouped with advertising agencies, automotive repair services, and morticians.[23] The December 1971 *Guide économique de la République d'Haïti*, published the year François Duvalier died and his son succeeded him to power, lists *prêtres du vodou* as generating 3.076 million gourdes ($615,200) for the gross domestic product, now classified under the interesting heading of "Juridical Services and Professional Associations," where they were in the company of an expanded range of professionals that encompassed, in addition to the previous cohort, lawyers, notaries, accountants, architects, and engineers.[24]

These reports, all produced by the Institut Haïtien de Statistique of the Département des Finances et des Affaires Économiques, are fascinating documents not only for what they reveal about the political economy of popular ritual practice in Haiti during the Duvalier years, but also for their inclusion of comparative statistics going back to at least 1950, which, to my knowledge, had not been published at the time.[25] Here we learn that, according to government statistics for this tumultuous year when Dumarsais Estimé was ousted from the presidency and Paul Magloire eventually took office, those encompassed by the designation *prêtres du voodu* provided services to clients totaling 2.030 million gourdes ($406,000).[26]

The publication of these figures is significant, whatever their accuracy, given that the stimulus of Vodou to the Haitian economy had almost never been recognized publicly in this way.[27] Indeed, denigrators of Vodou, clerical and otherwise, frequently condemned *oungan* and *manbo* for their negative economic impact in "swindling" credulous and impoverished peasants through their "charlatanry." Asks Ferdinand Delatour, "Is it not a paradoxical situation" when government publications "recognize the existence" and, indeed, the economic contribution of "services" that were officially prohibited under law?[28] That seeming contradiction reveals much about the nature of Duvalierist policies toward popular religious practice and organization between 1957 and 1986. The public incorporation of such data into economic reports is a marker of how official discourses concerning the religion shifted during these years, proclaiming greater freedom, openness, valuation, and legitimacy, even as the mechanisms of control and exploitation were maintained and, in insidious ways, intensified under both regimes.

Throughout this study, I have also emphasized the degree to which Vodouizan contested the enforcement of the laws prohibiting first *les sortilèges* and later *les pratiques superstitieuses* against socially sanctioned family- or temple-based ritual practices over the course of their cumulative 152-year history. Such popular pressure seems to have been a decisive factor, for example, in forcing President Geffrard's reversal in 1864, when he instructed local authorities to follow *la clameur publique* in enforcing the law against *les sortilèges*. It was also a source of confusion and consternation for some U.S. marines stationed in Haiti during the occupation, who complained that arresting *lougawou* and alleged "sorcerers" undermined their efforts to suppress such beliefs, which they consolidated under the gloss of "voodoo." In analyzing such cases, I have pointed to the political force of popular interpretations of the laws, which maintained that they ought to be applied against those suspected or accused of harnessing supernatural powers to malevolent ends, or, in some cases, of providing ineffective or harmful treatments.

However, as crucial as it is to recognize the influence of subaltern rural and urban communities in determining the proper object of these laws and in shaping the customary regime of their enforcement, it is also important to understand that the statutes remained, at all times, a repressive force. Upon their abrogation, they became a spectral one. A decade after the 1987 repeal of the penal law against *les pratiques superstitieuses* following the overthrow of Jean-Claude Duvalier, local authorities in Haiti were sometimes still arresting people on this charge—often, it seems, in response to communal pressure. In the late 1990s the United Nations' International Civilian Mission in Haiti (MICIVIH) reported illegal detentions for "sorcery" as symptomatic of the "human rights violations throughout the judicial system, which is supposed to be the principal guarantor of such rights."[29]

For decades, popular religious leaders and communities had vigorously and effectively protested the enforcement of the law prohibiting *les pratiques superstiteuses* against popularly sanctioned family- or temple-based religious practices. After the overthrow of Jean-Claude Duvalier, and in the context of the *dechoukaj* that followed, this activism intensified and gained supporters, particularly in response to the killing of *oungan* and *manbo* identified as collaborators with the deposed regime and/or as "sorcerers."[30] Yet, after the statute's abrogation by the 1987 constitution, local calls for the continued public prosecution of cases of sorcery suggest that accusers also saw the law as an indispensable recourse in the face of an ever-present, often proliferating threat. The demand for public adjudication of such cases seems all the more significant given the availability of clandestine means for protecting oneself from, diagnosing, and/or retaliating against malicious *maji*. Of course, such alternatives are not mutually exclusive, and those who believed themselves threatened or harmed by sorcery might take advantage of every possible social defense available against "its" practice. The detentions on the grounds of *sorcellerie* or *pratiques superstitieuses* after 1987 were, of course, themselves extrajuridical, having no basis in the Code Pénal, but rather, it seems, rationalized by local members of the police and judiciary as a lesser evil in the service of protecting public order and tranquility.[31]

The investment in these laws as weapons against supernatural harm connects to what I have analyzed throughout this study as their paradoxical tendency to affirm what they ban. This is why penal statutes that were intended, at least in part, by their original framers to serve as a sign and force of political modernity so frequently malfunctioned and were understood either to prove the existence or to instantiate the reality of what they interdicted. In fact, through the action of prohibition, the law that banned *les sortilèges* was itself implicated in the logic of the beliefs that it ostensibly sought to eliminate. It was not, then, that those who felt threatened or victimized by sorcery in their communities made a great interpretive leap in calling for the enforcement of the statutes against *les sortilèges*. These laws were always already complicit with popular discourses of sorcery. The calls for the continued enforcement of the law against *les pratiques superstitieuses* a decade after its repeal are a measure of the extent to which, historically, such laws had been assimilated into local defenses against malicious magic, which is also to say into local relations of power shot through with their own potentially oppressive dynamics. These cases also spotlight the law's productive capacity insofar as, over the course of their long histories, the prohibitions against *les sortilèges* and *les pratiques superstitieuses* generated legal rituals that ultimately seem to have exceeded the life of the statutes themselves. This raises the larger questions of how such local legal processes shifted once the category of *pratiques superstitieuses* had been stricken from the Code Pénal, and how popular responses to the fear of sorcery have evolved in the more than two decades since the law was repealed.

For some scholars and development officials such popular beliefs are symptomatic of a "superstitious" mentality that makes the Haitian poor cultural agents of their own impoverishment. Yet, in profoundly disrupting local life, top-down "modernizing" initiatives, prescribed, in part, as the antidote to peasant "backwardness"—from the 1915–1934 U.S. occupation to the present day—have themselves intensified sorcery rumors, which, in turn, have served as an idiom for popular critique of such policies. Long figured as modernity's constitutive outside, sorcery belief ought rather to be understood as its internal production. To recognize this is to break with assumptions about Haitian popular culture that rationalize disempowering development programs and perpetuate the conditions that, among other ills, give rise to such accusations.

NOTES TO INTRODUCTION

1 Her-Ra-Ma-El [Arthur Holly], *Dra-Po: Étude ésoterique de égrégore africain, traditionnel, social et national de Haïti* (Port-au-Prince: Imprimerie Nemours Telhomme, 1928), ii–iii. Unless otherwise noted, all translations are my own.

2 Hannibal Price, *De la réhabilitation de la race noire par la République d'Haïti* (Port-au-Prince: Imprimerie J. Verrollot, 1900), 163. The orthographies of the word now usually written "Vodou" are multiple. In quoting from other texts I preserve their spellings and capitalization. When used in a general way without reference to a specific source, French words such as *le vaudoux* or *le vaudou* are lowercased and italicized.

3 See, in particular, Jean Price-Mars, *Ainsi parla l'oncle* (1928; Ottawa: Éditions Leméac, 1973); Price-Mars, *Folklore et patriotisme: Conférence prononcée sous les auspices de l'Alliance Française, le 24 Novembre 1951* (Port-au-Prince: Imprimerie "Les Presses Libres," 1951); Laënnec Hurbon, *Le barbare imaginaire* (Port-au-Prince: Éditions Henri Deschamps, 1987); and Hurbon, *Comprendre Haïti: Essai sur l'état, la nation, la culture* (Port-au-Prince: Éditions Henri Deschamps, 1987). Duverneau Trouillot in the mid-1880s, Kléber Georges-Jacob in the early 1940s, Milo Rigaud in the early 1950s, Guérin Montilus and Ferdinand Delatour in the 1970s, and Léon-François Hoffmann more recently have likewise analyzed this legal regime, and I am indebted to their work as well.

4 See Michel-Rolph Trouillot, *Silencing the Past: Power and the Production of History* (Boston: Beacon Press, 1995). For an analysis of how the "disavowal" of Haitian modernity in nineteenth-century Dominican and Cuban letters was "productive in that it brings forth further stories, screens, and fantasies that hide from view what must not be seen," see Sibylle Fischer, *Modernity Disavowed: Haiti and the Cultures of Slavery in the Age of Revolution* (Kingston: University of West Indies Press, 2004), 38. See also

Ada Ferrer, "Talk about Haiti: The Archive and the Atlantic's Haitian Revolution," in *Tree of Liberty: Cultural Legacies of the Haitian Revolution in the Atlantic World*, ed. Doris L. Garraway (Charlottesville: University of Virginia Press, 2008), 21–40.

5 Jacques Derrida, "Force of Law: The 'Mystical Foundation of Authority,'" trans. Mary Quaintance, *Cardozo Law Review* 11, nos. 5–6 (July–August 1990): 925–927.

6 This is also why "the [Roman Catholic church's] major 'antisuperstition' campaigns of 1896 and of 1941 will be at least partly approved by the vodouisant," for the specter of sorcery threatens both "his life and his dignity as a 'civilized' person." Hurbon, *Le barbare imaginaire*, 219.

7 My thanks to Yanick Guiteau Dandin for discussing the meaning of this proverb with me. I examine it more closely in chapter 2.

8 In my discussions of "peasants" throughout this book, I follow Haitian Kreyòl usage, which refers to *peyizan* or *abitan*.

9 For an analysis of magic's "trickery," see Michael Taussig, "Viscerality, Faith, and Skepticism: Another Theory of Magic," in *Magic and Modernity: Interfaces of Revelation and Concealment*, ed. Birgit Meyer and Peter Pels (Stanford, CA: Stanford University Press, 2003), 272–273.

10 Theophus H. Smith, *Conjuring Culture: Biblical Formations of Black America* (New York: Oxford University Press, 1994), 82. See also Sharla Fett, *Working Cures: Healing, Health, and Power on Southern Slave Plantations* (Chapel Hill: University of North Carolina Press, 2002), 38–42.

11 A number of prominent scholars, such as Rachel Beauvoir-Dominique and Gerdès Fleurant, prefer the orthography "Vodoun" or "Vodun." See Rachel Beauvoir-Dominique, "Underground Realms of Being: Vodoun Magic," in *Sacred Arts of Haitian Vodou*, ed. Donald J. Cosentino (Los Angeles: Fowler Museum of Cultural History, 1995), 153; and Gerdès Fleurant, *Dancing Spirits: Rhythms and Rituals of Haitian Vodun, the Rada Rite* (Westport, CT: Greenwood Press, 1996).

12 In addition to *lwa*, the spirits are also referred to as *sen* (saints), *mistè* (mysteries), *zanj* (angels), and *envizib* (invisibles).

13 William W. Newell, "Myths of Voodoo Worship and Child Sacrifice in Hayti," *Journal of American Folk-Lore* 1, no. 1 (April–June 1888): 16–30.

14 *The Negro Church*, ed. W. E. Burghardt Du Bois (Atlanta: Atlanta University Press, 1903), 5–6.

15 Price-Mars, *Ainsi parla l'oncle*, 99. Suzanne Preston Blier elaborates: "[V]odun's cultural origins lie in the language family of the Ayizo. . . . Peoples speaking these languages reside in the lower areas of the West African countries of Benin (ex-Dahomey) and Togo, a region known to early [European] travelers in the area variously as the Guinea Coast, the Slave Coast, and the western reaches of the Bight of Benin"; Blier, "Vodun: West African Roots of Vodou," in *Sacred Arts of Haitian Vodou*, ed.

Donald J. Cosentino (Los Angeles: Fowler Museum of Cultural History, 1995), 61.

16 Even accepting this etymology of "Vodou" as authoritative, it still seems possible that Newell may not have been entirely on the wrong track. Dictionaries of sixteenth- and seventeenth-century French define *vaudoierie* and *vaudoiserie*, generically, as *sorcellerie* (sorcery), and *vaudois* and *vaudoyeur* as synonyms for *sorcier*, *magicien*, or *enchanteur*. See, for example, Edmond Huguet, ed., *Dictionnaire de la langue française du seizième siècle* (Paris: Librairie M. Didier, 1966), 7:408.

17 See Rachel Beauvoir and Didier Dominique's extended discussion of the complexities of this terminology in their *Savalou E* (Montréal: Les Éditions du CIDIHCA, 2003), 71–72. As they note, "Danhomen/Vodoun" is another name for the Rada rite (87).

18 Ginen is also the lost and mythical African homeland, as well as the watery site beneath the earth where the spirits live and where the dead go before being ritually called back by their families. See Karen McCarthy Brown, "Afro-Caribbean Spirituality: A Haitian Case Study," in *Vodou in Haitian Life and Culture*, ed. Claudine Michel and Patrick Bellegarde-Smith (New York: Palgrave Macmillan, 2006), 9. See also Beauvoir and Dominique's detailed analysis of the meaning of Ginen in *Savalou E*, 70–72.

19 On the association of the Rada spirits with Ginen, see Karen McCarthy Brown, "Systematic Remembering, Systematic Forgetting: Ogou in Haiti," in *Africa's Ogun: Old World and New*, ed. Sandra T. Barnes (Bloomington: Indiana University Press, 1989), 67; Guerin C. Montilus, "Africa in Diaspora: The Myth of Dahomey in Haiti," *Journal of Caribbean Studies* 2, no. 1 (Spring 1981): 82 nn. 42 and 44; and Jean Kerboull, *Le vaudou: Magie ou religion?* (N.p.: Éditions Robert Laffont, 1973), 255. On the more inclusive usage of the term "Ginen," see Andrew Apter, "On African Origins: Creolization and *Connaissance* in Haitian Vodou," *American Ethnologist* 29, no. 2 (2002): 249; Beauvoir-Dominique, "Underground Realms of Being," 167; and Beauvoir and Dominique, *Savalou E*, 72.

20 On the figure of Bondye or Gran Mèt in Vodou, see Laënnec Hurbon, *Dieu dans le vaudou haïtien* (Port-au-Prince: Éditions Deschamps, 1987), 121–125; and Beauvoir and Dominique, *Savalou E*, 73–88.

21 See Ira Paul Lowenthal, "'Marriage Is 20, Children Are 21': The Cultural Construction of Conjugality and the Family in Rural Haiti" (Ph.D. diss., John Hopkins University, 1987), 194–283; and Karen E. Richman, *Migration and Vodou* (Gainesville: University Press of Florida, 2005), 117–118.

22 See Richman, *Migration and Vodou*, 116–149; and Beauvoir and Dominique, *Savalou E*, 185–186.

23 Brown, "Afro-Caribbean Spirituality," 12.

24 See Andrew Apter's argument that "less a screen for maintaining African traditions than a form of collective appropriation, the saints were African-

ized by New World blacks as double agents in their religious sanctuaries and societies. If the public identity of a saint was European Catholic, then its secret, deeper, and more powerful African manifestation could be invoked and manipulated by initiates." Apter, "On African Origins," 238.

25 Lilas Desquiron writes: "Vodou permits the conceptualization of these forces, a dialogue with them, without denying them." Desquiron, *Racines du vodou* (Port-au-Prince: Éditions Henri Deschamps, 1990), 180.

26 Gerdès Fleurant, "Introduction," in *Vodou: Visions and Voices of Haiti*, by Phyllis Galembo (Berkeley, CA: Ten Speed Press, 2005), xxvii.

27 For example, of the *lwa* Ezili in her multiple emanations, Joan/Colin Dayan writes: "Ezili, known in written representations as 'the Black Venus,' 'the Tragic Mistress,' or 'The Goddess of Love,' remains a commentary on the harrowing reality of Saint-Domingue." Dayan, *Haiti, History, and the Gods* (Berkeley and Los Angeles: University of California Press, 1995), 58.

28 On the Kongo roots of the Petwo nation, see Desquiron, *Racines du vodou*, 120, 136, and 193–194; Robert Farris Thompson, "From the Isle beneath the Sea: Haiti's Africanizing Vodou Art," in *Sacred Arts of Haitian Vodou*, ed. Donald J. Cosentino (Los Angeles: Fowler Museum of Cultural History, 1995), 101–114; Elizabeth McAlister, *Rara! Vodou, Power, and Performance in Haiti and Its Diaspora* (Berkeley and Los Angeles: University of California Press, 2002), 87; and Gerdès Fleurant, "Vodun, Music, and Society in Haiti: Affirmation and Identity," in *Haitian Vodou: Spirit, Myth, and Reality*, ed. Patrick Bellegarde-Smith and Claudine Michel (Bloomington: Indiana University Press, 2006), 52–53. As discussed below, many enslaved Kongos were Christians before their arrival in Saint-Domingue.

29 Karen McCarthy Brown, "Serving the Spirits: The Ritual Economy of Haitian Vodou," in *Sacred Arts of Haitian Vodou*, ed. Donald J. Cosentino (Los Angeles: Fowler Museum of Cultural History, 1995), 423 n. 8. Note that Andrew Apter has argued for "locating the Petwo gods more firmly within a Dahomean-Yoruban cosmological schema," on the grounds that the structural opposition between the two principal *nanchon* of *lwa* closely reflects "the hot and cool valences of Yoruba pantheons and the dialectics of power and authority that they mediate." Apter, "On African Origins," 248 and 240. See also Joan/Colin Dayan on Vodou's rituals of history: "What those in power [in French colonial Saint-Domingue] called 'sorcery' became an alternative history, a questioning turn by those deemed unable to think." Dayan, "Querying the Spirit: The Rules of the Haitian *Lwa*," in *Colonial Saints: Discovering the Holy in the Americas, 1500–1800*, ed. Allan Greer and Jodi Bilinkoff (Routledge: New York, 2003), 32.

30 See Richman's analysis of the ritual process of *ranmase*, through which purchased spirits called *pwen* are "domesticated" into a type of Ginen spirit known as *lwa zandò*; these spirits then serve to "vitalize Guinea with Magic's illicit heat while at the same time preserving Guinea's morality." Richman, *Migration and Vodou*, 172.

31 This is not to suggest that the Ginen-*maji* dichotomy is itself timeless and unchanging. Karen Richman's research on its history in Léogâne suggests that the discourse of Ginen intensified, in fact, with the manifold disruptions of U.S. agro-industrial expansion in the region during the 1915–1934 occupation. Her argument that "the dialectic of Guinea and Magic is a peasantry's representation—and critique—of the encompassment of their moral economy by a system of capitalist production and their incorporation as producers of migrants for export" points to yet another aspect of how historical upheavals and relations of power are critically objectified, analyzed, and reinterpreted in Vodou belief and ritual practice. Richman, *Migration and Vodou*, 22.

32 See Serge Larose, "The Meaning of Africa in Haitian Vodu," in *Symbols and Sentiments: Cross-Cultural Studies in Symbolism*, ed. Ioan Lewis (London: Academic Press, 1977), 85–92.

33 Jerome S. Handler and Kenneth M. Bilby consider the extent to which "the written laws and regulations intended to suppress Obeah" across the late eighteenth- and early nineteenth-century British Caribbean in fact played a role in the diffusion of the term. See Handler and Bilby, "On the Early Use and Origin of the Term 'Obeah' in Barbados and the Anglophone Caribbean," *Slavery and Abolition* 22, no. 2 (August 2001): 99 n. 27.

34 Price-Mars, *Folklore et patriotisme*, 18.

35 Earl Lovelace, *The Wine of Astonishment* (1982; New York: Vintage Books, 1984), 34. For the text of the Shouters Prohibition Ordinance, see Melville J. Herskovits and Frances S. Herskovits, *Trinidad Village* (New York: Alfred A. Knopf, 1947), 340–345. See also Frances Henry, *Reclaiming African Religion in Trinidad: The Socio-Political Legitimation of the Orisha and Spiritual Baptist Faiths* (Barbados: University of the West Indies Press, 2003), 32–36. The ordinance was repealed in 1951.

36 Lovelace, *The Wine of Astonishment*, 47.

37 Ibid., 133.

38 See Hurbon, *Comprendre Haïti*, 153–156.

39 See Michel-Rolph Trouillot's discussion of the militia's respect for rural hierarchies "to the extent that it tended to recruit major Vodoun priests, village big men, rich peasants, or landowners as commanders." Michel-Rolph Trouillot, *Haiti, State against Nation: The Origins and Legacy of Duvalierism* (New York: Monthly Review Press, 1990), 191.

40 See Hurbon, *Comprendre Haïti*, 143–169.

41 See Beauvoir and Dominique, *Savalou E*, 17–63.

42 See, for example, the announcement of a series of "séances de réflexion" on Vodou and popular culture in early December 1986 organized by the Port-au-Prince chapter of Zantray in *Le Nouvelliste*, 2 December 1986.

43 This text is transcribed in its entirety in Beauvoir and Dominique, *Savalou E*, 101–102. Léon-François Hoffmann quotes from it in *Haïti: Couleurs, croyances, créole* (Montreal: CIDIHCA, 1990), 148. See also the article "De-

mande de reconnaissance du vodou comme religion nationale," *Le Nouvel-liste*, 4 February 1987.

44 "All laws, all decree laws, all decrees arbitrarily limiting the basic rights and liberties of citizens, in particular: a) The decree law of September 5, 1935 on superstitious beliefs . . . are and shall remain repealed." Final Provisions, Article 297, *Constitution of the Republic of Haiti*, 1987. http://www.haiti .org/images/stories/pdf/1987_Constitution.pdf (Embassy of the Republic of Haiti in Washington, D.C.; translation from the Web site). Accessed 28 May 2010.

45 "Arrêté relatif à la reconnaissance par l'État haïtien du vodou comme religion à part entière sur toute l'étendue du territoire national, donné au Palais National, à Port-au-Prince, le 4 avril 2003." http://www.haiti-refer ence.com/religion/vodou/vodou-decret.htm. Accessed 17 July 2009. This is not to suggest that a political calculus was entirely absent here. Even some supporters of the decree interpreted it as, in part, an effort to shore up Aristide's popular base at a moment of ongoing political strife, further socioeconomic decline, and increasing popular unrest.

46 Of course, at the same time, this new dispensation also potentially ties Vodou organizations more closely to the state.

47 Élie Duverger, quoted in Carol J. Williams, "Haitians Hail the 'President of Voodoo'," *Los Angeles Times*, 3 August 2003; newspaper's translation.

48 Brown, "Serving the Spirits," 205. Patrick Bellegarde-Smith analyzes this objectification as an "'invention' necessitated by the presence of other religions in the landscape" in his "Resisting Freedom: Cultural Factors in Democracy—The Case for Haiti," in *Vodou in Haitian Life and Culture: Invisible Powers*, ed. Claudine Michel and Patrick Bellegarde-Smith (New York: Palgrave Macmillan, 2006), 113 n. 13. His argument resonates with those of Wilfred Cantwell Smith in *The Meaning and End of Religion: A New Approach to the Religious Traditions of Mankind* (1962; Minneapolis, MN: Fortress Press, 1991).

49 On the invention of the concept of "religion" itself in early modern Europe see Smith, *The Meaning and End of Religion*; and David Scott, *Refashioning Futures: Criticism after Postcoloniality* (Princeton, NJ: Princeton University Press, 1999). See also Talal Asad, *Genealogies of Religion: Discipline and Reasons of Power in Christianity and Islam* (Baltimore, MD: Johns Hopkins University Press, 1993); and David Scott, *Formations of Ritual: Colonial and Anthropological Discourses on the Sinhala Yaktovil* (Minneapolis: University of Minnesota Press, 1994). These latter works call on anthropology and other disciplines to be more reflexive about the genealogical histories of the conceptual objects they deploy (such as "religion" and "ritual"). On the terms "religion and religions" as "products of the colonial situation," see David Chidester, *Savage Systems: Colonialism and Comparative Religion in Southern Africa* (Charlottesville: University of Virginia Press, 1996), 16.

50 I use the expression *gens de couleur* to refer to free people of African descent in Saint-Domingue, including those of "mixed" ancestry.

51 See Leslie G. Desmangles, *The Faces of the Gods: Vodou and Roman Catholicism in Haiti* (Chapel Hill: University of North Carolina Press, 1992), 3.

52 Price-Mars, *Ainsi parla l'oncle*, 84 and 86; and see Price-Mars, *Une étape de l'évolution haïtienne* (Port-au-Prince: Imprimerie "La Presse," 1929), 132–135. See also Kesner Castor, *Éthique vaudou: Herméneutique de la maîtrise* (Paris: L'Harmattan, 1998), 11–12; Jacquelin Montalvo-Despeignes, *Le droit informel haïtien: Approche socio-ethnographique* (Paris: Presses Universitaires de France, 1976), 24, 38–40, 56–59, and 62; Martial Celestin, "Vaudou et droit haïtien," *Revue juridique et politique, indépendance et coopération* 38, no. 2 (1984): 484; Beauvoir and Dominique, *Savalou E*, 70–72; and Erika Bourguignon, "Religion and Justice in Haitian Vodou," *Phylon* 46, no. 4 (1960): 292–295. Questions of land tenure and inheritance vis-à-vis Vodou have been a particularly productive focus of research in recent years. See Gerald Murray's analysis of the way in which serving the family spirits shapes land tenure practices on the Cul-de-Sac Plain; Martial Celestin's work on the articulation between the Code Civil and rural practices of inheritance; and Ira Lowenthal's analysis of the concept of *eritaj* as both a landed and a spiritual legacy inherited from a founding ancestor. See Gerald F. Murray, "Population Pressure, Land Tenure, and Voodoo: The Economics of Haitian Peasant Ritual," in *Beyond the Myths of Culture: Essays in Cultural Materialism*, ed. Eric B. Ross (New York: Academic Press, 1980), 295–321; and Lowenthal, "'Marriage Is 20, Children Are 21,'" 195. See also Jean Rosier Descardes, "Dynamique Vodou et état de droit en Haïti: Droits de l'homme et diversité culturelle" (Ph.D. diss., Université Paris I–Panthéon–Sorbonne, 2001), 195. Earlier works on these questions include Alfred Métraux, "Droit et coutume en matière successorale dans la paysannerie haïtienne," *Zaïre: Revue congolaise* (April 1951): 339–349; and J. B. Romain, *Quelques mœurs et coutumes des paysans haïtiens: Travaux pratiques d'ethnographie sur la région de Milot à l'usage des étudiants*, Revue de la Faculté d'ethnologie 2 (1959; Folcroft, PA: Folcroft Library Editions, 1974).

53 See, for example, *Paper Laws, Steel Bayonets: Breakdown of the Rule of Law in Haiti* (New York: Lawyers Committee for Human Rights, 1990); and, more recently, "Haïti: Réforme de la justice et crise de la sécurité," Briefing Amérique Latine/Caraïbes no. 14, International Crisis Group, Port-au-Prince/Brussels, 31 January 2007.

54 See Diana Paton's discussion of how, after emancipation, "Jamaicans from all walks of life tried to make use of the legal resources that were available to them, even while many of them perceived the formal legal structures of their society as fundamentally unjust." Paton, *No Bond but the Law: Punishment, Race, and Gender in Jamaican State Formation, 1780–1870* (Durham, NC: Duke University Press, 2004), 160.

55 Jennie M. Smith, *When the Hands Are Many: Community Organization and Social Change in Rural Haiti* (Ithaca, NY: Cornell University Press, 2001), 104.

56 See Beauvoir and Dominique, *Savalou E*, 139–181. See also Hurbon, *Le bar-bare imaginaire*, 173–191 and 259–296; Michel S. Laguerre, *Voodoo and Politics in Haiti* (New York: St. Martin's, 1989), 71–81; and Wade Davis, *Passage of Darkness: The Ethnobiology of the Haitian Zombie* (Chapel Hill: University of North Carolina Press, 1988), 213–284.

57 Hurbon, *Le barbare imaginaire*, 278.

58 Beauvoir and Dominique, *Savalou E*, 154.

59 Ibid., 169. Note here the strong role that women play in these organiza-tions. Based on their research on the Chanpwèl, Beauvoir and Dominique argue that women are the *potomitan* (or spiritual centerpost) of the *sosyete* and often their most active members (166). See chapter 2 for discussion of the restrictions on peasant movement written into Jean-Pierre Boyer's 1826 Code Rural. See the description of a Bizango passport, on stamped paper purchased from the Bureau des Contributions (tax office), in Laguerre, *Voo-doo and Politics in Haiti*, 76.

60 Diana Paton, *No Bond but the Law*, 161.

61 Ibid., 185.

62 For example, while conducting research in Haiti's Plateau Central in the early 1960s, and then again in the mid-1970s, Michel Laguerre was told by a "soldier-informant" that the majority of armed forces in the region had joined the Bizango *sosyete* in order to be ensured of safe passage during their nighttime patrols. Laguerre, "The Voodooization of Politics in Haiti," in *Blackness in Latin America and the Caribbean: Social Dynamics and Cultural Transformation*, ed. Arlene Torres and Norman E. Whitten, Jr. (Blooming-ton: Indiana University Press, 1998), 2:532.

63 "'The government cooperates with us. They have to. . . . The people in government in Port-au-Prince must cooperate with us. We were here be-fore them, and if we didn't want them, they wouldn't be where they are.'" Quoted in Davis, *Passage of Darkness*, 268. See Hurbon on how "the rural section chief is sometimes part of these bands, and in any case must give his authorization to their *sortie*, as he usually does for any Vodou ceremony." Hurbon, *Le barbare imaginaire*, 182.

64 See Hurbon's analysis of the Duvalier regime's "ideological use of the se-cret society. . . . Between the imaginary of sorcery and the political order, there is no longer any perceived distance." *Le barbare imaginaire*, 283.

65 The Kreyòl word *lalwa* also means "law" and can be used interchangeably with the word *lwa*, meaning the same. However, a class distinction nuances the usage of these words: *lwa* is more identified with *kreyòl lavil* (town or city Kreyòl), whereas *lalwa* is considered more characteristic of traditional rural Kreyòl. My thanks to Marvel Dandin for discussing these nuances with me.

66 Price-Mars writes: "Does not obeying the *laws* [*lois*] of the Church, bow-ing before the *Mystères* of Religion, making one's devotion *to the angels and saints* of Paradise, form part of the teaching of the Church?" He suggests

that the identification of the pantheon of popular spirits by such terminology "denotes one of the forms of influence exercised by Catholicism on the evolution of *Vaudou*." Price-Mars, *Ainsi parla l'oncle*, 182.

67 George Eaton Simpson, "The Belief System of Haitian Vodun," *American Anthropologist* 47, no. 1 (January–March 1945): 54.

68 Dayan, *Haiti, History, and the Gods*, 72. For an analysis of the significance of this homology, see Dayan, "Querying the Spirit," 42. See also André-Marcel d'Ans, *Haïti: Paysage et société* (Paris: Éditions Karthala, 1987), 290 n. 8.

69 The verb here was likely *assister à* and, if so, should have been translated as "attending" rather than "assisting."

70 Case of Cadeus Bellegarde, 6 April 1920, Record of Proceedings of a Military Commission convened at the Marine Barracks, Port-au-Prince, Republic of Haiti, By order of the Brigade Commander, First Provisional Brigade, United States Marine Corps, Port-au-Prince, Republic of Haiti. RG 80 (General Records of the Navy), Secretary of the Navy General Correspondence, 1916–1926, Folder 5526 (39:299), 16, U.S. National Archives.

71 On the Yoruba etymology of *lwa*, see Suzanne Comhaire-Sylvain and Jean Comhaire-Sylvain, "Survivances africaines dans le vocabulaire religieux d'Haïti," *Études dahoméennes*, no. 10 (1955): 13; and Pierre Anglade, *Inventaire étymologique des termes créoles des Caraïbes d'origine africaine* (Paris: L'Harmattan, 1998), 140–141.

72 C. L. R. James, *The Black Jacobins: Toussaint L'Ouverture and the San Domingo Revolution* (1938), 2nd ed. (New York: Vintage Books, 1963).

73 The total number of those who lost their lives in the earthquake is uncertain, and the Haitian government issued various figures in the weeks thereafter. These casualty statistics come from the Post-Disaster Needs Assessment prepared by the Haitian government in conjunction with the international community. See "Plan d'action pour le relèvement et le développement national d'Haïti," http://www.refondation.ht/resources/Plan_d'Action_12Avril.pdf (accessed 21 July 2010).

74 See, for example, Alex Dupuy, "Beyond the Earthquake: A Wake-Up Call for Haiti," and the essays of other contributors to the Social Science Research Council's online forum "Haiti, Now and Next," http://www.ssrc.org/features/pages/haiti-now-and-next/1338/1339/ (accessed 22 March 2010).

75 Harrison is the author of such works as *Underdevelopment Is a State of Mind: The Latin American Case* (Lanham, MD: Center for International Affairs, Harvard University, and University Press of America, 1985), and *The Central Liberal Truth: How Politics Can Change a Culture and Save It from Itself* (Oxford: Oxford University Press, 2006).

76 David Brooks, "The Underlying Tragedy," *New York Times*, 14 January 2010; and Lawrence Harrison, "Haiti and the Voodoo Curse: The Cultural Roots of the Country's Endless Misery," *Wall Street Journal*, 5 February 2010.

77 See chapter 1.

78 See chapter 2.

79 See chapter 3.

80 Palmié writes: "What I aim to demonstrate is that, far from designating even only typological opposites, the meanings associated with the terms *Western modernity* and *Afro-Cuban tradition* represent mere facets or perspectival refractions of a single encompassing historical formation of transcontinental scope. . . . It is only by disembedding Afro-Cuban religious knowledge from the historical context out of which it emerged that we can juxtapose it to what we have come to designate as Western *modernity*. Whatever else Afro-Cuban religion is, it is as modern as nuclear thermodynamics, or the suppositions about the nature of our world that underlie DNA sequencing, or structural adjustment policies, or on-line banking. For the same reason, I have found it useful to think of Western modernity as a configuration of thought and practices that might profitably be understood as a culturally specific—if nowadays globally diffused and locally multiply refracted—tradition in its own right." Stephan Palmié, *Wizards and Scientists: Explorations in Afro-Cuban Modernity and Tradition* (Durham, NC: Duke University Press, 2002), 15–16.

81 See Jennie Smith's analysis of such programs: "Experiences with aid undermining the interests of the aided are now familiar to Haitians. This has led many Haitians, particularly those involved in the popular movement, to see foreign-sponsored development and democratization initiatives as inherently exploitative strategies—as being aimed primarily at breeding dependency and undermining grassroots efforts directed at real change." Smith, *When the Hands Are Many*, 30–31.

82 Testimony of Paul Farmer before the U.S. Senate Committee on Foreign Relations, 27 January 2010. Full text at: http://standwithhaiti.org/haiti/news-entry/pih-co-founder-paul-farmer-testifies-at-senate-foreign-relations-committee/ (accessed 21 March 2010).

NOTES TO CHAPTER 1

1 Louis Sala-Molins, *Le Code noir, ou Le calvaire de Canaan* (Paris: Presses Universitaires de France, 1987), 9; and Dayan, *Haiti, History, and the Gods*, 202. Vernon V. Palmer argues that "developing a comprehensive slave ordinance was a natural extension" of the mercantilist policies for which Colbert is more famous. See Palmer, "The Origins and Authors of the Code Noir," in *An Uncommon Experience: Law and Judicial Institutions in Louisiana, 1803–2003* (Lafayette: Center For Louisiana Studies, University of Southwestern Louisiana, 1997), 337.

2 See Palmer, "The Origins and Authors of the Code Noir," 333–334.

3 Malick Walid Ghachem, "Sovereignty and Slavery in the Age of Revolution: Haitian Variations on a Metropolitan Theme" (Ph.D. diss, Stanford

University, 2001). See especially his second chapter, "'Two Governments':
The Critique of the Domestic Sphere." For a comparative analysis of Spanish, British, and French slave laws, see also Elsa Goveia, "The West Indian Slave Laws of the Eighteenth Century," in *Caribbean Slavery in the Atlantic World*, ed. Verene Shepherd and Hilary McD. Beckles (Kingston, Jamaica: Ian Randle, 2000), 590.

4 Sala-Molins, *Le Code noir*, 124; and Ghachem, "Sovereignty and Slavery," 45.

5 Sala-Molins, *Le Code noir*, 94. Doris Garraway argues that "a notion of reciprocity subtends the argument [justifying slavery on these grounds], implying that African bodies may be sacrificed to pay for the soul's redemption." Garraway, *The Libertine Colony: Creolization in the Early French Caribbean* (Durham, NC: Duke University Press, 2005), 158.

6 Chidester, *Savage Systems*, 13. On the history of the concept of the "fetish," especially as applied to West Africans by Portuguese and other European traders from the sixteenth century, see William Pietz, "The Problem of the Fetish, II: The Origin of the Fetish," *Res* 13 (Spring 1987): 23–45.

7 Trouillot, *Silencing the Past*, 82–83.

8 For a discussion of this ambivalence see Henock Trouillot, *Introduction à une histoire du vaudou* (1970; Port-au-Prince: Les Éditions Fardin, 1983), 97. See also Hurbon's argument that for those with political power, "Vodou could only be a place of unavowable consensus." Hurbon, *Le barbare imaginaire*, 92.

9 For overviews of Hispaniola's early colonial history see Jan Rogozinski, *A Brief History of the Caribbean: From the Arawak and Carib to the Present* (New York: Plume/Penguin, 1999), 34–55; Frank Moya Pons, *History of the Caribbean: Plantations, Trade, and War in the Atlantic World* (Princeton, NJ: Markus Wiener Publishers, 2007), 1–59; Richard Lee Turits, *Foundations of Despotism: Peasants, the Trujillo Regime, and Modernity in Dominican History* (Stanford, CA: Stanford University Press, 2003), 25–31; and Laurent Dubois, *Avengers of the New World: The Story of the Haitian Revolution* (Cambridge, MA: Belknap Press of the Harvard University Press, 2004), 13–19.

10 On piracy in the Caribbean in the seventeenth century, see Kris E. Lane, *Pillaging the Empire: Piracy in the Americas, 1500–1750* (Armonk, NY: M. E. Sharpe. 1998), 96–130.

11 See Carolyn E. Fick, *The Making of Haiti: The Saint Domingue Revolution from Below* (Knoxville: University of Tennessee Press, 1990), 15.

12 Peter Linebaugh and Marcus Rediker, *The Many-Headed Hydra: The Hidden History of the Revolutionary Atlantic* (London: Verso, 2000), 171–173.

13 According to one of the colony's early governors, cited by John Garrigus, at least half of the freebooters based in Saint-Domingue used their profits to purchase land. Garrigus's research documents that "such long-bearded sun-baked frontiersmen could still be found in Saint-Domingue in the late eighteenth century." John D. Garrigus, *Before Haiti: Race and Citizenship in French Saint-Domingue* (New York: Palgrave, 2006), 24–25.

14 See Dubois, *Avengers of the New World*, 26; and Georges Corvington, *Port-*

au-Prince au cours des ans: La ville coloniale, 1743–1789 (Port-au-Prince: Imprimerie Henri Deschamps, 1992), 28–29 and 241.

15 Dubois, *Avengers of the New World*, 24–28; and John D. Garrigus, "Blue and Brown: Contraband Indigo and the Rise of a Free Colored Planter Class in French Saint-Domingue," *Americas* 50 (October 1993): 244–245. Cacao was also grown in mountain valleys throughout the colony, although it was struck by blight in 1715. Garrigus, *Before Haiti*, 36.

16 David Geggus, "Sugar and Coffee Cultivation in Saint Domingue and the Shaping of the Slave Labor Force," in *Cultivation and Culture: Labor and the Shaping of Slave Life in the Americas*, ed. Ira Berlin and Philip D. Morgan (Charlottesville: University Press of Virginia, 1993), 73; and Garrigus, "Blue and Brown," 235.

17 See Ghachem, "Sovereignty and Slavery," 24–25; and Dubois, *Avengers of the New World*, 29–30.

18 On the composition and functions of the Conseils Supérieurs, see Ghachem, "Sovereignty and Slavery," 26–29.

19 See Goveia, "The West Indian Slave Laws," 588–589.

20 See Ghachem, "Sovereignty and Slavery," 28 and 83.

21 William B. Cohen, *The French Encounter with Africans: White Response to Blacks, 1530–1880* (Bloomington: Indiana University Press, 1980), 47; and Ghachem, "Sovereignty and Slavery," 32.

22 It has been frequently observed that sugar operations across the Caribbean and Brazil were proto-industrial in their labor regime, given the need for sugarcane to be processed partially on the plantation itself, and given the extreme time sensitivity and synchronization of these processes after harvesting (i.e., crushing, boiling, and crystallization). See Eric Williams, *Capitalism and Slavery* (1944; Chapel Hill: University of North Carolina Press, 1994), 24–27; and Sidney W. Mintz, *Sweetness and Power: The Place of Sugar in Modern History* (New York: Penguin, 1985), 46–52.

23 Dubois, *Avengers of the New World*, 39–40; Paul E. Lovejoy, "Ethnic Designations of the Slave Trade and the Reconstruction of the History of Trans-Atlantic Slavery," in *Trans-Atlantic Dimensions of Ethnicity in the African Diaspora*, ed. Lovejoy and David V. Trotman (London: Continuum, 2003), 22; and Fick, *The Making of Haiti*, 26.

24 Dubois, *Avengers of the New World*, 40; David Geggus, "Haitian Voodoo in the Eighteenth Century: Language, Culture, Resistance," *Jahrbuch für Geschichte von Staat, Wirtschaft und Gesellschaft Lateinamerikas* 28 (1991): 36. This paralleled larger patterns of the Atlantic slave trade, with the Bight of Benin surpassing West Central Africa and all other regions as the largest source of slaves during the decades the sugar economy in Saint-Domingue dramatically expanded; then, by the mid-eighteenth century, greater numbers of captives were leaving from West Central Africa than from any other region. See Paul E. Lovejoy, *Transformations in Slavery: A History of Slavery in Africa*, 2nd ed. (1983; Cambridge: Cambridge University Press, 2000), 53–

57; and Philip D. Curtin, *The Atlantic Slave Trade: A Census* (Madison: University of Wisconsin Press, 1969), 163–203.

25 Dubois, *Avengers of the New World*, 42, citing Médéric-Louis-Élie Moreau de Saint-Méry. Fick notes that figures for the enslaved population in Saint-Domingue vary widely from one source to another, but most official census reports in the last years of the regime give statistics averaging between 450,000 and 500,000, compared with around 30,000 whites and a similar number of free people of color. *The Making of Haiti*, 278 n. 14.

26 Fick, *The Making of Haiti*, 26.

27 See Ghachem's analysis of the controversies in eighteenth century Saint-Domingue over the "conflicting spheres of sovereignty" in chapter 2, "'Two Governments': The Critique of the Domestic Sphere," of his "Sovereignty and Slavery," 104–170.

28 Sala-Molins, *Le Code noir*, 174–176. Note, though, that Article 42 authorized those masters who believed that "their slaves merited it" to chain and to beat them, as if those punishments did not themselves constitute forms of torture and mutilation. As Elsa Goveia notes, "In the matter of punishments, the code prohibited the private infliction of torture and mutilation, but did not prevent their use by judicial authorities." Goveia, "The West Indian Slave Laws," 592.

29 Dayan, *Haiti, History and the Gods*, 216.

30 Ghachem, "Sovereignty and Slavery," 138–140.

31 Ibid., 158–163.

32 Quoted in Fick, *The Making of Haiti*, 37–38; translation Fick's. Le Jeune defended himself by arguing that "it is not the fear and equity of the law that forbids the negro from stabbing his master, it is the consciousness of absolute power that he has over his person." Dayan, *Haiti, History, and the Gods*, 217; translation Dayan's.

33 Article 16, Code Noir, in Sala-Molins, *Le Code noir*, 122. See Sala-Molins's commentary and also the discussion in Pierre Pluchon, *Vaudou, sorciers, empoisonneurs de Saint-Domingue à Haïti* (Paris: Éditions Karthala, 1987), 57–58.

34 Sala-Molins, *Le Code noir*, 124.

35 Ibid., 122.

36 See Pluchon, *Vaudou, sorciers, empoisonneurs*, 18–19.

37 "Ordonnance du Gouverneur, qui défend les assemblées et danses des Nègres Esclaves," 1 August 1704, in Médéric-Louis-Élie Moreau de Saint-Méry, *Loix et constitutions des colonies françoises de l'Amérique sous le vent* (Paris: Chez l'auteur, etc., n.d.), 2:12–13.

38 "Lettre du Ministre à MM. de la Rochalard et Duclos, sur plusieurs objets d'humanité et de religion," 30 September 1727, in Moreau de Saint-Méry, *Loix et constitutions*, 3:222. See also Pluchon, *Vaudou, sorciers, empoisonneurs*, 144.

39 Quoted in Howard Justin Sosis, "The Colonial Environment in Haiti: An Introduction to the Black Slave Cults in Eighteenth Century Saint-

Domingue" (Ph.D. diss, Columbia University, 1990), 185, from the Archives Coloniales in the Archives Nationales, Paris, F.3.245.297; translation Sosis's. Note that both women and men were persecuted as "sorcerers" in Saint-Domingue. See Gabriel Debien, "Assemblées nocturnes d'esclaves à Saint-Domingue (La Marmelade, 1786)," *Annales historiques de la Révolution française* 208 (1972): 282–283.

40 This was effected through the royal edict of 1682, which redefined magic and divination (notably avoiding reference to "sorcery" altogether) as crimes of charlatanism that could lead the ignorant and credulous from "vain curiosities" to superstitions, impieties, sacrileges, and even evil spells (*les maléfices*) and poisoning. Promulgated three years before the Code Noir and likewise overseen by Colbert, this lengthy edict became the precedent for the ordinances that proliferated in mid-eighteenth-century Saint-Domingue against black healers, diviners, and "sorcerers," associating them with crimes of profanation, poisoning, and subversion. See "Édit pour la punition de différens [*sic*] crimes, et notamment celui d'empoisonnement, du mois de juillet 1682," in Moreau de Saint-Méry, *Loix et constitutions*, 1:371–375. See also Robert Mandrou, *Magistrats et sorciers en France au XVIe siècle: Une analyse de psychologie historique* (Paris: Plon, 1968), 466–486.

41 Portuguese missions had been particularly sustained and successful there since Nzinga a Nkuwu's baptism as João I in 1491. See John K. Thornton, "Les racines du vaudou: Religion africaine et société haïtienne dans la Saint-Domingue prérévolutionnaire," *Anthropologie et sociétés* 22, no. 1 (1998): 85–103; and Thornton, "'I Am the Subject of the King of Congo': African Political Ideology and the Haitian Revolution," *Journal of World History* 4, no. 2 (1993): 188.

42 Note above the French minister's hedging in his missive of September 1727: "even if the crime of *sortilège* is as real as it appears imaginary." See Vincent Brown's discussion of how in Jamaica whites "both believed in and doubted the efficacy of black supernatural power." Brown, *The Reaper's Garden: Death and Power in the World of Atlantic Slavery* (Cambridge, MA: Harvard University Press, 2008), 149.

43 Jean Kerboull, *Voodoo and Magic Practices*, trans. John Shaw (London: Barrie & Jenkins, 1977), 7. See also Alfred Métraux's discussion of this legacy in Haiti in the 1950s, referring to the "vogue enjoyed in popular circles, if not among the petit bourgeoisie, by the *Grand* and the *Petit Albert* as well as *La poule noire*. It is from these books, imported from France, that the *houngan* draw a part of their magical knowledge." Métraux, *Le vaudou haïtien* (Paris: Éditions Gallimard, 1958), 239. See also Doris Garraway's analysis of what she terms "colonial demonology," centering on how earlier missionaries in the French Caribbean, and in particular Jean-Baptiste Labat, "adapted early modern discourses of witchcraft to describe the unfamiliar beliefs and spiritual practices of Caribs and Africans." Garraway, *The Libertine Colony*, 36.

44 See Pluchon, *Vaudou, sorciers, empoisonneurs*, 192. Also see Pluchon's argu-

ment that, from the beginning of colonization, "poisoners are . . . assimilated to sorcerers," 143.

45 Ibid., 169.

46 Ibid., 168–169. The governor and the intendant concluded that "les Nègres" were "driven only by the hope of promised liberties, by jealousy, resentment, and more often still by the sole wish to do harm." Quoted in Pluchon, *Vaudou, sorciers, empoisonneurs*, 168. Hein Vanhee suggests that Makandal was consulted for a range of problems, including protection against sorcery, and that he and those who worked with him may have "administered a kind of poison ordeal to detect witches." Vanhee, "Central African Popular Christianity and the Making of Haitian Vodou Religion," in *Central Africans and Cultural Transformations in the American Diaspora*, ed. Linda M. Heywood (Cambridge: Cambridge University Press, 2002), 251.

47 See Trouillot, *Silencing the Past*, 90–91.

48 Pluchon, *Vaudou, sorciers, empoisonneurs*, 169.

49 See David Patrick Geggus, "Marronage, Vodou, and the Slave Revolt of 1791," in *Haitian Revolutionary Studies* (Bloomington: Indiana University Press, 2002), 75; Franklin Midy, "Un document historique pour la généalogie du vaudou haïtien," *Chemins critiques* 1, no. 1 (March 1989): 137; Geggus, "Haitian Voodoo in the Eighteenth Century," 33; Vanhee, "Central African Popular Christianity," 251; and Comhaire-Sylvain and Comhaire-Sylvain, "Survivances africaines dans le vocabulaire religieux d'Haïti," 13.

50 "Arrêt de Réglement du Conseil du Cap, qui défend aux Nègres de garder des paquets appelés Macandals, ni de composer et vendre des drogues," 11 March 1758, in Moreau de Saint-Méry, *Loix et constitutions*, 4:222–223.

51 As Pluchon notes, in the view of the colonist, "only perversity" separated the black healer from the poisoner, "both experts in botany." Pluchon, *Vaudou, sorciers, empoisonneurs*, 15. This particular decree was also calculated to compel blacks to inform on the makers of such packets. In fact, citing the need for indulgence given the "great number of those who were drawn into this superstition by credulity," rather than criminal intent, the decree offered an amnesty for those who gave up their *makandal* to masters or local parish priests. This was offered, in part, so that such penitents could "speak with liberty on the subject of Poisoners, so-called Diviners, and Sorcerers and Creators of the said packets." "Arrêt de Règlement du Conseil du Cap, qui défend aux Nègres de garder des paquets appelés Macandals, ni de composer et vendre des drogues," 11 March 1758, in Moreau de Saint-Méry, *Loix et constitutions*, 4:222–223. On the pejorative sense of the term *nègre*, see Trouillot, *Silencing the Past*, 76.

52 "Arrêt en Règlement du Conseil du Cap, touchant la police des Esclaves, 7 avril 1758," in Moreau de Saint-Méry, *Loix et constitutions*, 4:225–227. Fick notes that by this time most planters were not permanent residents of the colony and were represented by their *procureurs*, who oversaw the administration of the plantations. Fick, *The Making of Haiti*, 16. Regarding the ban

on church gatherings, Dayan notes: "It seemed as if the more Christian you claimed to be, the more certainly you could be accused of conniving with the devil." Dayan, *Haiti, History, and the Gods*, 252.

53 Midy, "Un document historique," 136. See also Pluchon, *Vaudou, sorciers, empoisonneurs*, 208–219.

54 Note that the naturalist M. E. Descourtilz, who arrived in Saint-Domingue in 1799 and remained until May 1803, described the *calanda*, as he spelled it, as "a nocturnal funeral dance." Descourtilz, *Voyages d'un naturaliste, et ses observations*, vol. 3 (Paris: Dufart, Père, Libraire-Éditeur, 1809), 192. See also Médéric-Louis-Élie Moreau de Saint-Méry, *Description topographique, physique, civile, politique et historique de la partie française de l'isle Saint-Domingue*, vol. 1, ed. Blanche Maurel and Étienne Taillemite (1797; Paris: Société de l'Histoire des Colonies Françaises and Librairie Larose, 1958), 63.

55 For example, one responsibility of the colonial police force, the *maréchaussée*, which the governor reorganized under the name Première Légion de Saint-Domingue in 1765, was to "dissipate the Assemblies and Calendas of the Blacks." See "Ordonnance du Gouverneur Général, portant création d'un Corps de Troupes Légères, désigné sous le nom de Première Légion de Saint-Domingue, du 15 janvier 1765," in Moreau de Saint-Méry, *Loix et constitutions*, 4:825–831; see also Pluchon, *Vaudou, sorciers, empoisonneurs*, 64–66. The seeming impossibility of preventing such gatherings from taking place remained an official complaint and concern through the late colonial period.

56 Dayan, *Haiti, History, and the Gods*, 244.

57 See Sue Peabody, "'A Dangerous Zeal': Catholic Missions to Slaves in the French Antilles, 1635–1800," *French Historical Studies* 25, no. 1 (Winter 2002): 71–73.

58 "Arrêt de Règlement du Conseil du Cap, sur les abus, en matière de Religion, de la part des Gens de couleur," 18 February 1761, in Moreau de Saint-Méry, *Loix et constitutions*, 4:352–356.

59 "The Jesuits preached and gathered the blacks, thus forcing the planters to slow-down the rate of work. . . . It was to the Jesuits that the colonists attributed all the crimes which were so pernicious to the economy and the population around the Cap." Hilliard d'Auberteuil, *Considérations sur l'état présent de la colonie française de Saint-Domingue*, 2:68–69, quoted in Sosis, "The Colonial Environment in Haiti," 220; translation Sosis's.

60 Fick, *The Making of Haiti*, 65. Also see her translation of an extract from the transcript of Assam's interrogation, 251–258.

61 "Arrêt définitif du Conseil du Cap, qui prononce l'Extinction des Jésuites, et leur expulsion hors de la Colonie," 24 November 1763, in Moreau de Saint-Méry, *Loix et constitutions*, 4:626–628. The Jesuits had relied on enslaved labor to build their missions, tend their fields, and run their sugar mills and five sugar refineries. George Breathett, *The Catholic Church in Haiti, 1704–1785: Selected Letters, Memoirs and Documents* (Salisbury, NC: Documentary Publications, 1982), 15. In 1768, five years after the expulsion

of the Jesuits from Saint-Domingue, the Capuchin order took over the northern parishes. See Peabody, "'A Dangerous Zeal,'" 70 and 84.

62 See also the discussion of this trend in Rachel Beauvoir-Dominique, in collaboration with Eddy Lubin, "Investigations autour du site historique du Bois Caïman: Rapport," commissioned by the Ministère de la Culture, République d'Haïti, January 2000, 12. My thanks to Rachel Beauvoir-Dominique for sharing this study with me.

63 See Dubois, *Avengers of the New World*, 66, on the free-colored army units organized during the Seven Years' War.

64 Article 57, Code Noir, in Sala-Molins, *Le Code noir*, 196.

65 Garrigus, *Before Haiti*, 42; and Dubois, *Avengers of the New World*, 62. See also Ghachem's argument that planters regarded "manumission . . . as the exercise of an individual prerogative, a function of the master's domestic sovereignty," in his "Sovereignty and Slavery," 51.

66 See Doris Garraway's argument that "rather than viewing the coincidence of racially exclusionary law and interracial libertinage as a contradiction, I consider these phenomena to be mutually reinforcing and constitutive of the system of white supremacy and racial domination that shaped French slave societies." Garraway, *The Libertine Colony*, 30.

67 See Dubois, *Avengers of the New World*, 62; and Fick, *The Making of Haiti*, 20.

68 "Ordonnance du Roi, concernant la Chirurgie aux Colonies," 30 April 1764, in Moreau de Saint-Méry, *Loix et constitutions*, 4:724; and Paul Brodwin, *Medicine and Morality in Haiti: The Contest for Healing Power* (Cambridge: Cambridge University Press, 1996), 43. See the earlier royal law of December 1746 prohibiting "all slaves of either sex from composing and distributing any medicine, powdered or in some other form," and from "undertak[ing] the healing of any illness with the exception of snakebite." Gabriel Debien, "Assemblées nocturnes d'esclaves," 282.

69 "Ordonnance des Administrateurs, pour la Police de la Ville du Port-au-Prince," 23 May 1772, in Moreau de Saint-Méry, *Loix et constitutions*, 5:385. This was reinforced by a royal ordinance in March 1785 extending that interdiction to the entire colony but placing its enforcement under military rather than police purview. "Ordonnance du Roi touchant la Police des Bals des gens-de-couleur libres, et celle des spectacles," 11 March 1785, in Moreau de Saint-Méry, *Loix et constitutions*, 6:727.

70 "Arrêt du 16 mai 1786," cited in Pluchon, *Vaudou, sorciers, empoisonneurs*, 66–67.

71 Karol K. Weaver, *Medical Revolutionaries: The Enslaved Healers of Eighteenth-Century Saint Domingue* (Urbana: University of Illinois Press, 2006), 101–103. See also François Regourd, "Mesmerism in Saint Domingue: Occult Knowledge and Vodou on the Eve of the Haitian Revolution," in *Science and Empire in the Atlantic World*, ed. James Delbourgo and Nicholas Dew (New York: Routledge, 2008), 311–332.

72 Archives Nationales (Paris) 27 AP 12 (Papiers François de Neufchâteau), cited in Pluchon, *Vaudou, sorciers, empoisonneurs*, 68, and transcribed in Debien, "Assemblées nocturnes d'esclaves," 281–282.

73 Debien, "Assemblées nocturnes d'esclaves," 274–275. Geggus notes that in the 1780s, West Central Africans "accounted for almost sixty per cent of the African slaves in the North." Geggus, "Haitian Voodoo in the Eighteenth Century," 36.

74 Moreau de Saint-Méry, *Description*, 276. Debien also draws on "a declaration made by Gressier de la Jalousière, colonist of the district of Marmelade" on 26 May 1786; Debien, "Assemblées nocturnes d'esclaves," 279. John Thornton notes that, in their creation and use, these empowered and empowering objects resemble Kongo *min'kisi* (singular *n'kisi*), and that the use of the crucifix in some of these ritual preparations and assemblages likely stemmed from the long history of Christianity in West Central Africa. See Thornton, "Les racines du vaudou," 95. On Kongo *min'kisi*, see Wyatt MacGaffey, *Religion and Society in Central Africa: The BaKongo of Lower Zaire* (Chicago: University of Chicago Press, 1986), 135–160.

75 Debien, "Assemblées nocturnes d'esclaves," 276. See Anglade's listing of contemporary ritual meanings of the word *bila* in his *Inventaire étymologique des termes créoles*, 67–68. Also see Kerboull, *Le vaudou: Magie ou religion?*, 271.

76 Karen McCarthy Brown, *Mama Lola: A Vodou Priestess in Brooklyn* (Berkeley: University of California Press, 1991), 101. Moreau de Saint-Méry attributes a highly specific origin to what he called the "Danse à Dom Pèdre" in Saint-Domingue, writing in his *Description* that "un nègre" of Spanish descent, in Petit-Goâve on the southern peninsula, "abusing the credulity of the blacks by *pratiques superstitieuses*," began this "dance" in 1768, and that participants would mix "well-crushed" gunpowder in *tafia* (rum) to "produce still more effect" while they were dancing. He notes that colonial authorities attempted to repress these assemblies under "serious, and sometimes ineffective penalties," although no reference to "Dom Pèdre" appears in any of the statutes he codified through 1785. Moreau, *Description*, 69. See also Jean Price-Mars, "Lemba-Pétro: Un culte secret; Son histoire, sa localisation géographique, son symbolisme," *Revue de la Société haïtienne d'histoire et de géographie* 28 (1938), 12–31.

77 See Debien's discussion of this document in "Assemblées nocturnes d'esclaves," 275–276.

78 Quoted in ibid., 281.

79 Ibid., 282. Moreau de Saint-Méry, on the other hand, did not acknowledge Jérôme and Télémaque as fugitives, and reported that Jérôme was sentenced to life imprisonment and Télémaque to detention in an iron collar in one of the city's markets to prove "the impotence of his practices to escape the penalties that brazen charlatanism ought always pay to justice." Moreau de Saint-Méry, *Description*, 276.

80 Moreau de Saint-Méry, *Description*, 64–69.

81 David Geggus notes that it was in Saint-Domingue's western province "that Arada slaves were most numerous in the late eighteenth century." Also see his discussion of what seems to be "a very strong Kongo content in

what eighteenth century colonists called 'vaudou,' and which they linked specifically with the Aja-Fon of the Bight of Benin." Geggus, "Haitian Voodoo in the Eighteenth Century," 23 and 35.

82 He writes, for example: "It is not only as a dance that *le Vaudoux* merits consideration, or at least it is accompanied by circumstances that assign it a rank among the institutions where superstition and strange practices play a great part." Moreau de Saint-Méry, *Description*, 64.

83 There is fragmentary evidence beyond Moreau's account that by the late 1780s among the colonial and clerical establishment in Saint-Domingue, it was customary to refer to the "*Vaudoux* sect." For example, Jean Fouchard quotes an account by a nun of the Communauté des Filles de Notre-Dame du Cap-Français, ostensibly describing the August 1791 revolts, which refers to the "sect of *Gioux*, or *Vaudoux*, a sort of religious and dancing masonry introduced into Saint-Domingue by Arada blacks." However, this document seems to have been written in the 1880s based on correspondence from nuns of this order; it appeared in the 1889 *Lettre annuelle de l'Ordre de Notre-Dame*. Geggus points out that it also seems to draw a good deal on the accounts of Moreau de Saint-Méry and of Hérard Dumesle, *Voyage dans le nord d'Hayti, ou Révélations des lieux et des monuments historiques* (Aux Cayes: Imprimerie du Gouvernement, 1824). See Fouchard, *Les marrons du syllabaire: Quelques aspects du problème de l'instruction et de l'éducation des esclaves et affranchis de Saint-Domingue* (Port-au-Prince: Éditions Henri Deschamps, 1953), 39–40 and 151; Geggus, "Haitian Voodoo in the Eighteenth Century," 49; and Fick, *The Making of Haiti*, 104 and 265.

84 Price-Mars, "Lemba-Pétro," 15.

85 Pluchon notes, however, that in 1682 the Jesuit missionary R. P. Mongin referred to enslaved Aradas' belief in a being named "Boudou." Pluchon, *Vaudou, sorciers, empoisonneurs*, 20, 54, and 71.

86 Moreau de Saint-Méry, *Description*, 68. Note that attempts to evade colonial prohibitions sometimes created new forms of ritual. Charles Malenfant, a plantation manager in the western province, wrote that the "sect known under the name of *Vaudou*," was "very severely punished by the whites." Colonel Malenfant, *Des colonies, et particulièrement de celle de Saint-Domingue: Mémoire historique et politique* (Paris: Chez Audibert, 1814), 215. Malenfant himself, however, considered this "sect" to be wholly unthreatening and in fact provided twenty bottles of wine for the funeral of *le chef du Vaudou* when he was stationed on the Gourand plantation.

87 Pluchon, *Vaudou, sorciers, empoisonneurs*, 67.

88 Alfred Métraux notes that the word *calenda* was often used generically in colonial ordinances to refer to any illicit night gatherings of slaves and free people of color in the colony. The problem with his conclusion that "the word *calenda*, which is no longer used, must certainly have meant *Vaudou*" is that it ascribes a stable transhistorical identity to the latter, which practitioners have traditionally used in reference to specific rituals, and not in the

objectified, encompassing sense that became customary for outsiders since at least the mid-nineteenth century. See Métraux, *Le vaudou haïtien*, 26.

89 Moreau de Saint-Méry, *Description*, 68–69. For an analysis of these passages, see Garraway, *The Libertine Colony*, 252–255.

90 See Léon-François Hoffmann, "Histoire, mythe et idéologie: Le serment du Bois-Caïman," in *Haïti: Lettres et l'être* (Toronto: Éditions du GREF, 1992), 267–301; David Patrick Geggus, "The Bois Caïman Ceremony," in *Haitian Revolutionary Studies* (Bloomington: Indiana University Press, 2002), 81–92; Beauvoir-Dominique and Lubin, "Investigations"; Robin Law, "La cérémonie du Bois Caïman et le 'pacte de sang' dahoméen," trans. Maryse Villard, in *L'insurrection des esclaves de Saint-Domingue, 22–23 août 1791* (Paris: Éditions Karthala, 2000), 131–147; and Laurent Dubois, "The Citizen's Trance: The Haitian Revolution and the Motor of History," in *Magic and Modernity: Interfaces of Revelation and Concealment*, ed. Birgit Meyer and Peter Pels (Stanford, CA: Stanford University Press, 2003), 103–128.

91 See, for example, Dantès Bellegarde, *Histoire du peuple haïtien, 1492–1952* (Port-au-Prince: Collection du Tricinquantenaire de l'Indépendance d'Haïti, 1953), 63.

92 Dubois, "The Citizen's Trance," 111.

93 Hoffmann, "Histoire, mythe, et idéologie," 267; and Antoine Dalmas, *Histoire de la révolution de Saint-Domingue, depuis le commencement des troubles, jusqu'à la prise de Jérémie et du Môle S. Nicolas par les Anglais; Suivie d'un mémoire sur le rétablissement de cette colonie*, vol. 1 (Paris: Chez Mame Frères, 1814), 116–118.

94 Geggus notes, in particular, that Dalmas's account was based in part on interrogations of slaves after the first revolts, prematurely launched on the night of 21 August; that another version of the story, published by Hérard Dumesle, a Haitian senator from the south, in his 1824 *Voyage dans le nord d'Hayti*, seemed to be based in part on oral-historical testimony collected during a visit to the Le Cap region; and a third, by Céligny Ardouin (first published by his brother, Beaubrun Ardouin, in 1853), seemed to draw on an interview with an ex-soldier. See Geggus, "The Bois Caïman Ceremony," 82–83. See also Dumesle, *Voyage dans le nord d'Hayti*, 85–90.

95 Geggus, "The Bois Caïman Ceremony," 91.

96 See ibid., 85.

97 In the several years before their research and since, the battles over the history and legacy of Bwa Kayiman have not been simply or even primarily academic in Haiti. In 1995 the government of President René Préval declared thirty-two *carreaux* of land on the former Le Normand de Mézy plantation *utilité publique* and a *zone réservée* owing to its status as a "high place of our history" (see Annexe 4: "Arrêté," 12 August 1995, in Beauvoir-Dominique and Lubin, "Investigations," 92–93). In 1997–1998 groups of evangelical Christians made pilgrimages—which they called "holy invasions"—to "exorcise" the site where Boukman and his co-conspirators

took an oath, they claimed, "dedicating Haiti to serve the devil" (see Annexe 1: "Spiritual Victory in Haiti," by Joel Jeune, in ibid., 72–73). Popular organizations mobilized, including Zantray, which had been commemorating the Bwa Kayiman ceremony annually at the Bassin Caïman site, and the Haitian government intervened in 1998, first authorizing the *manifestations protestantes*, then censuring them, and then, under pressure from the American ambassador, granting "permission to all the churches and religions to hold prayers and crusades at Bois Caïman." See ibid., 65–66.

98 Ibid., 42. They ask "how to discuss modes of organization and religiosity of slaves without penetrating their encompassing cultural universe or while being unaware of the fundamental ideological and political imbrication that continues to span the Haitian social formation."

99 See ibid., 39 and 42. See also Rénald Clérismé, "Rapports actuels entre le vodou et le christianisme en Haïti," in *Le phénomène religieux dans la Caraïbe: Guadeloupe, Martinique, Guyane, Haïti*, ed. Laënnec Hurbon (Paris: Éditions Karthala, 2000), 226; Terry Rey, "The Politics of Patron Sainthood in Haiti: 500 Years of Iconic Struggle," *Catholic Historical Review* 88, no. 3 (July 2002): 524–525 and 542 n. 63; and Rey, "Kongolese Catholic Influences on Haitian Popular Catholicism: A Sociohistorical Exploration," in *Central Africans and Cultural Transformation in the American Diaspora*, ed. Linda M. Heywood (Cambridge: Cambridge University Press, 2002), 272.

100 Geggus, "Haitian Voodoo in the Eighteenth Century," 48; and Pluchon, *Vaudou, sorciers, empoisonneurs*, 138.

101 See Althéa de Puech Parham, trans. and ed., *My Odyssey: Experiences of a Young Refugee from Two Revolutions, by a Creole of Saint-Domingue* (Baton Rouge: Louisiana State University Press, 1959), 33–34. Also see the discussion in Fick, *The Making of Haiti*, 111. See also the analysis of this account in Jeremy Popkin, *Facing Racial Revolution: Eyewitness Accounts of the Haitian Insurrection* (Chicago: University of Chicago Press, 2007), 63–66.

102 Pierre Joinville-Gauban, *Voyage d'outre-mer et infortunes les plus accablantes de la vie de M. Joinville-Gauban . . .* (Bordeaux: Imprimerie de H. Haye fils, n.d.), 40. Quoted in Hoffmann, *Haïti: Couleurs, croyances, créole*, 123.

103 Malenfant, *Des colonies*, 217–219.

104 See Geggus, "The Bois Caïman Ceremony," 88–89. When Boukman was killed in November 1791, colonial witnesses were struck by the outpouring of grief among insurgents. See Jean Fouchard, *The Haitian Maroons: Liberty or Death*, trans. A. Faulkner Watts (New York: Edward W. Blyden, 1981), 342; and Thomas Madiou, *Histoire d'Haïti*, vol. 1, *1492–1799* (Port-au-Prince: Éditions Henri Deschamps, 1989), 97.

105 Madiou, *Histoire d'Haïti*, vol. 1, *1492–1799*, 96–97. The naturalist Descourtilz was told by former slaves that Dessalines offered the same reassurance to those fighting with "a supernatural fearlessness" under his leadership. Descourtilz, *Voyages d'un naturaliste*, quoted in Pluchon, *Vaudou, sorciers, empoisonneurs*, 134–135.

106 See Madiou, *Histoire d'Haïti*, vol. 1, *1492–1799*, 127–128. Why Romaine feminized his name by taking the moniker *la prophétesse* is uncertain. David Geggus notes that this seems to have been the case with other male religious and/or rebel leaders during the Revolution such as "Sainte Catherine" and "Mamzelle." Geggus, "Haitian Voodoo in the Eighteenth Century," 47 n. 127.

107 See Pluchon, *Vaudou, sorciers, empoisonneurs*, 138.

108 Fick, *The Making of Haiti*, 139.

109 Terry Rey, "The Virgin Mary and Revolution in Saint-Domingue: The Charisma of Romaine-la-Prophétesse," *Journal of Historical Sociology* 11, no. 3 (September 1998): 343 and 344.

110 "Decree of the National Assembly of May 15, 1791," in *Slave Revolution in the Caribbean, 1789–1804: A Brief History with Documents*, ed. Laurent Dubois and John D. Garrigus (Boston: Bedford/St. Martin's, 2006), 84; translation Dubois and Garrigus's. See also Dubois, *Avengers of the New World*, 125.

111 See David Patrick Geggus, *Slavery, War, and Revolution: The British Occupation of Saint Domingue, 1793–1798* (Oxford: Clarendon Press, 1982), 64–67. As Geggus writes, "Paradoxically . . . , Britain's efforts to save the slave regime in Saint Domingue may have been a major factor in bringing about its destruction," 102. Note that slavery was maintained or reinstituted in the parts of the colony under British occupation. Dubois, *Avengers of the New World*, 167.

112 James, *The Black Jacobins*, 143; Dubois, *Avengers of the New World*, 178–179 and 197; and Dubois and Garrigus, *Slave Revolution in the Caribbean*, 31.

113 Dubois, *Avengers of the New World*, 164.

114 See ibid., 184–193; and James, *The Black Jacobins*, 155–156.

115 "To enlighten this people and to make them moral," Sonthonax wrote in May 1797, "this is my goal and my duty." Sonthonax, quoted in Robert Louis Stein, *Léger Félicité Sonthonax: The Lost Sentinel of the Republic* (Rutherford, NJ: Farleigh Dickinson University Press, 1985), 123; translation Stein's.

116 The commission was a team of five agents charged with enforcing French law and overseeing the colony's post-emancipation economic recovery.

117 Reprinted in Jean Fouchard, *Les marrons de la liberté* (1972; Port-au-Prince: Éditions Henri Deschamps, 1988), 280–281. See also Hoffmann, *Haïti: Couleurs, croyances, créole*, 121–122. Note that according to Fouchard, this law was published in the *Bulletin officiel de Saint-Domingue*, 28 January 1797. Both Fouchard and Hoffmann transcribe the object of the law as having been spelled "Vaudou" rather than "Vaudoux."

118 Stein, *Léger Félicité Sonthonax*, 152. See Archives Nationales (Paris) Colonies CC9A 12.

119 Quoted in Stein, *Léger Félicité Sonthonax*, 152; translation Stein's. See Bibliothèque Nationale (Paris), manuscrits français 8987, 26 February 1797.

120 Stein, *Léger Félicité Sonthonax*, 168–170.

121 Geggus, "Haitian Voodoo in the Eighteenth Century," 47. Geggus cites three male religious leaders (two, again, with feminized names) who were arrested in this context: Sainte Jésus Maman Boudier, Sainte Catherine, and Saint Jean Père l'Eternité.

122 Cited in Beaubrun Ardouin, *Études sur l'histoire d'Haïti . . .* , vol. 4 (Paris: Dezobry & E. Magdeleine, 1853), 154–155. Also cited in Hoffman, *Haïti: Couleurs, croyances, créole*, 125–126, as reproduced from J. F. Thalès Manigat, *Conférence sur le vaudoux* (Cap-Haïtien: Imprimerie La Conscience, 1897).

123 Dubois, *Avengers of the New World*, 241; and Malick W. Ghachem, "Montesquieu in the Caribbean: The Colonial Enlightenment between Code Noir and Code Civil," *Historical Reflections/Réflexions historiques* 25, no. 2 (Summer 1999): 183–210.

124 From "Règlement de culture du 12 octobre 1800," reprinted in Claude Moïse, *Le projet national de Toussaint Louverture et la Constitution de 1801* (Port-au-Prince: Les Éditions Mémoire, 2001), 92.

125 Thomas Madiou, *Histoire d'Haïti*, vol. 2, *1799–1803* (Port-au-Prince: Éditions Henri Deschamps, 1989), 112. Note that Madiou figures *Vaudoux* here as an identity.

126 See Dayan, *Haiti, History, and the Gods*, 17 and 23–54; and Odette Mennesson-Rigaud, "Le rôle du vaudou dans l'indépendance d'Haïti," *Présence africaine* (February 1958): 65. See also Métraux, *Le vaudou haïtien*, 40–41.

127 See "Constitution de 1801," in Moïse, *Le projet national de Toussaint Louverture*, 72–85. For a thought-provoking analysis of the 1801 Constitution as the framework for the structuring of Haitian society after independence in 1804, a model which the author argues was founded in abolitionist thought and was fundamentally "neocolonial," see also Carlo A. Célius, "Le modèle social haïtien: Hypothèses, arguments et méthode," *Pouvoirs dans la Caraïbe: Revue du C.R.P.L.C.* (1998): 110–143.

128 Trouillot, *Silencing the Past*, 88. See also C. L. R. James's famous argument that this represented Louverture's "tragic flaw." James, *The Black Jacobins*, 291.

129 Dubois, *Avengers of the New World*, 251.

130 See Trouillot's discussion of these revolutionary leaders in "The Three Faces of Sans Souci: Glory and Silences in the Haitian Revolution," in *Silencing the Past*, 37–44.

131 Dubois, *Avengers of the New World*, 288–290.

132 Note, however, the refusal of some African-born leaders such as Sans Souci to recognize the authority of this alliance. See Trouillot, *Silencing the Past*, 43–44.

133 Leclerc to the First Consul, 26 September 1802 and 27 September 1802, quoted in James, *The Black Jacobins*, 350 and 352, translations James's. Bonaparte had ceded Louisiana to the United States in April of 1803. For an analysis of how "the Haitian Revolution was unthinkable in its time: it challenged the very framework within which proponents and opponents

had examined race, colonialism, and slavery in the Americas," see Trouillot, *Silencing the Past*, 82.

134 Trouillot, *Silencing the Past*, 94.

135 Dubois, *Avengers of the New World*, 299. See also David Patrick Geggus, "The Naming of Haiti," in *Haitian Revolutionary Studies* (Bloomington: Indiana University Press, 2002), 207–220; and Carlo A. Célius, "Neoclassicism and the Haitian Revolution," in *The World of the Haitian Revolution*, ed. David Patrick Geggus and Norman Fiering (Bloomington: Indiana University Press, 2009), 360.

136 See C. L. R. James's argument about the role that British agents played in the mounting of this massacre. James, *The Black Jacobins*, 370–374.

137 Price-Mars, *Ainsi parla l'oncle*, 231. See also Guérin Montilus, "Haïti: Un cas témoin de la vivacité des religions africaines en Amérique et pourquoi," in *Les religions africaines comme source de valeurs de civilisation: Colloque de Cotonou, 16–22 août 1970* (Paris: Présence Africaine, 1972), 298–299.

138 Unpublished letter from Christophe to Capoix, cited by Hénock Trouillot in his *Introduction à une histoire du vaudou*, 67. See also Hoffmann's discussion of this in his *Haïti: Couleurs, croyances, créole*, 126. On Dessalines's promotion of Christophe, see Vergniaud Leconte, *Henri Christophe dans l'histoire d'Haïti* (Paris: Éditions Berger-Levrault, 1931), 181; and Hubert Cole, *Christophe: King of Haiti* (New York: Viking Press, 1967), 148. See also Guy-Joseph Bonnet's claim that as king of the northern monarchy, "[Christophe] repressed by terror the superstitions of Africa and pursued to the utmost the sect of *Vaudous* and their frightful practices." Bonnet, *Souvenirs historiques . . . recueillis par Edmond Bonnet* (Paris: Librairie August Durand, 1864), 255, cited in Hoffmann, *Haïti: Couleurs, croyances, créole*, 126.

139 Beaubrun Ardouin, *Études sur l'histoire d'Haïti*, vol. 8 (Paris: Chez l'Auteur, 1856), 63–64.

140 Métraux, *Le vaudou haïtien*, 60; and Fleurant, introduction to Galembo, *Vodou: Visions and Voices of Haiti*, xxvii. See Thornton, "'I Am the Subject of the King of Congo,'" 200, for an analysis of how enslaved Africans recently arrived in the Americas "often looked to organizations formed by their 'nation'—a loose grouping of people from the same part of Africa or the same ethnolinguistic group—to provide leadership and perform mutual aid functions. One way of maintaining leadership of nations was through the election of kings and queens."

141 Beauvoir and Dominique, *Savalou E*, 169. See also Laguerre, "The Voodooization of Politics in Haiti," 527.

142 Elders in the communities in which she worked indicated that the leadership positions of king and queen were once more prominent than they are today. Note that the *sosyete* also function as "an informal judicial system." Smith, *When the Hands Are Many*, 104–108.

143 Hurbon, *Le barbare imaginaire*, 92.

144 See Henock Trouillot's argument that these were "religions of revolt," and

that once "in power, [the] former slaves who had more or less tolerated them for the needs of their cause, saw in them a danger for the established order." Trouillot, *Introduction à une histoire du vaudou*, 60.

NOTES TO CHAPTER 2

1 Edmond Huguet, *Dictionnaire de la langue française du XVIe siècle* (1925), quoted in Jean Starobinski, *Blessings in Disguise; or, The Morality of Evil*, trans. Arthur Goldhammer (1989; Cambridge, MA: Harvard University Press, 1993), 1.

2 Starobinski, *Blessings in Disguise*, 2.

3 Ibid., 12. *Policé*, in turn, is related etymologically to the verb *policer*, which contemporary French-English dictionaries define as "to civilize."

4 Ibid., 17.

5 Ibid., 19–20.

6 On the influence of republican thought on the Haitian Revolution and vice versa, see in particular James, *The Black Jacobins*; David Barry Gaspar and David Patrick Geggus, eds., *A Turbulent Time: The French Revolution and the Greater Caribbean* (Bloomington: Indiana University Press, 1997); and Dubois, *Avengers of the New World*.

7 Any person of African or Amerindian descent who sought residence in the republic would be recognized as Haitian and eligible for citizenship after one year. *Constitution de 1816*, Article 44, in *1801–1885: Le premier siècle de "Constitutions haïtiennes"; Textes complets de 14 constitutions dont sept amendements* (Port-au-Prince: Imprimerie Ateliers Fardin, 1985), 66. See also Mimi Sheller: "Many Afro-Caribbean people whether 'black' or 'brown,' rejected the white story line and built their own racial projects around a symbolic alliance with Haiti." Sheller, *Democracy after Slavery: Black Publics and Peasant Radicalism in Haiti and Jamaica* (Gainesville: University Press of Florida, 2000), 85.

8 Anténor Firmin, *The Equality of the Human Races*, trans. Asselin Charles, introd. Carolyn Fluehr-Lobban (Champaign: University of Illinois Press, 2002), 313 and 339. On the significance of Firmin's work to anthropology and pan-Africanist thought, see Carolyn Fluehr-Lobban, introduction to *The Equality of the Human Races*, xi–xlvi.

9 Louis-Joseph Janvier, *La République d'Haïti et ses visiteurs, 1840–1882*, vol. 1 (1883; Port-au-Prince: Les Éditions Fardin, 1979), 111.

10 Monsignor François-Marie Kersuzan, *Conférence populaire sur le vaudoux donnée par Monseigneur l'Évêque du Cap-Haïtien, le 2 août, 1896* (Port-au-Prince: Imprimerie H. Amblard, 1896), 17.

11 Alex Dupuy notes, "Pétion . . . sought legitimacy for his regime by giving it the appearance of a democratic government, when he in fact became its dictator." Dupuy, *Haiti in the World Economy: Class, Race, and Underdevelopment since 1700* (Boulder, CO: Westview Press, 1989), 89. Note too that the

strong peasant rebellion which Jean-Baptiste Perrier, also called Goman,
led in the southern Grand'Anse region between 1807 and 1820 meant that
the south was itself internally divided under Pétion. See Michel Hector,
Crises et mouvements populaires en Haïti, 2nd ed. (Port-au-Prince: Communication Plus . . . Livres, 2006), 112–123.

12 For a discussion of what the opposition termed *le gouvernement de famille*
under Boyer, see Leslie F. Manigat, *La révolution de 1843: Essai d'analyse historique d'une conjoncture de crise* (Port-au-Prince: Édition Le Normalien, 1959),
9. The *milat* (*mulâtre*) elite was fractured under Boyer by a liberal opposition, particularly strong in the southwestern region of the country, that
opposed many of his policies and led the ousting of his government in 1843.

13 Dispatch from President Boyer to the Grand Juge, 23 September 1822;
quoted in Thalès Jean-Jacques, *Histoire du droit haïtien* (Port-au-Prince: Imprimerie Nemours Telhomme, 1933), 271–272.

14 Clovis Kernisan, quoted in Crawford M. Bishop and Anyda Marchant, *A
Guide to the Law and Legal Literature of Cuba, the Dominican Republic, and Haiti*
(Washington, DC: Library of Congress, 1944), 224; Bishop and Marchant's
translation. See also Kernisan, *La vérité ou la mort* (Port-au-Prince: Imprimerie Modèle, 1933), 29–36. According to Jean-Jacques, "Some years after, the
imperfection of all our Codes promulgated in 1826 was recognized; and on
the observations of the courts, which demonstrated to the Grand-Juge the
gaps that they contained, he named in 1834 a commission of civil servants,
united under the presidency of Secretary-General M. B. Inginac, to the
end of effecting in our legislation all the modifications that it would judge
to be useful." Jean-Jacques, *Histoire du droit haïtien*, 789.

15 Jean-Jacques, *Histoire du droit haïtien*, 789. But note that, according to Clovis
Kernisan, the Code Rural, "in the beginning and in contrast to the others[,]
had been drawn up especially in accordance with the conditions and the
local customs emerging from the colonial regime." Bishop and Marchand,
A Guide to the Law and Legal Literature, 255.

16 See *Le Manifeste*, 19 December 1841, as paraphrased in David Nicholls, *From
Dessalines to Duvalier: Race, Colour and National Independence in Haiti* (1979;
New Brunswick, NJ: Rutgers University Press, 1996), 76.

17 Kernisan, quoted in Bishop and Marchant, *A Guide to the Law and Legal Literature*, 241; Bishop and Marchant's translation. See also Félix Magloire and
Félix Soray, "The Legal System of Haiti," trans. Carlos M. Sandoval, *Law
Notes* 48, no. 1 (February 1944): 4: "From 1805 special laws, purely Haitian,
were passed; but the influence so long exercised by the French Metropole
continued to make itself felt. In fact, the French Codes themselves were
adopted beginning with 1825."

18 The quote continues: "that the accused and the accuser, the innocent and
the guilty shall find equally in the sanctuary of the law, on the one hand,
the hand of justice that protects, and on the other, the sword that strikes."
Quoted in Jean-Jacques, *Histoire du droit haïtien*, 789. See also Bishop and
Marchant, *A Guide to the Law and Legal Literature*, 238.

19 Jean-Jacques, *Histoire du droit haïtien*, 789.

20 Ibid., 790.

21 Note that Félix Magloire and Félix Soray define the penal category of *contraventions* as "offenses involving negligence or dereliction of duty rather than active malice," and that of *délits* as "misdemeanors," and finally that of *crimes* as "felonies"; Magloire and Soray, "The Legal System of Haiti," 12. See also *Paper Laws, Steel Bayonets*, 22. On the Tribunaux de Paix, see Linstant Pradine, *Recueil général des lois et actes du gouvernement d'Haïti depuis la proclamation de son indépendance jusqu'à nos jours*, vol. 4, *1824–1826* (Paris: Auguste Durand, 1865), 304.

22 "Article 405: Tous faiseurs de ouangas, caprelatas, vaudoux, donpèdre, macandals et autres sortilèges, seront punis d'un mois à six mois d'emprisonnement, et d'une amende de seize gourdes à vingt-cinq gourdes; sans préjudice des peines plus fortes qu'ils encourraient à raison des délits ou crimes par eux commis pour préparer ou accomplir leurs maléfices. Article 406: Les gens qui font métier de dire la bonne aventure, ou de deviner, de pronostiquer les songes ou de tirer les cartes, seront punis de six jours à un mois d'emprisonnement, et de seize gourdes à vingt-cinq gourdes d'amende. Article 407: Les instruments, ustensiles et costumes servant ou destinés à servir aux faits prévus aux deux articles précédents, seront de plus saisis et confisqués." Reprinted in Linstant Pradine, annotator, *Code d'instruction criminelle et Code pénal* (Paris: A. Durand et Pedone-Lauriel, 1883), 186. See also "Anciens articles du Code pénal," in *Les codes haïtiens: Code d'instruction criminelle et Code pénal avec annexes*, ed. Léon Nau (Paris: Librairie Générale de Droit et de Jurisprudence, 1914), 338.

23 Six months of imprisonment and a fine of 25 gourdes, along with the confiscation of illicit objects, was the maximum penalty permitted for offenses classified as contraventions. The 1835 law against vagrancy specified one to three months of imprisonment (for recidivists, three to six months) employed in public works of the town or city, and those found guilty of larceny could receive a sentence of one to six months of labor for the commune. In neither case was a fine assigned in addition to a period of imprisonment, as it was in the case of the section defining *les sortilèges*.

24 Nau, *Les codes haïtiens* (1914), 322 n. 1. See also H. F. Rivière, ed., *Codes français* (Paris: Librairie A. Marescq Ainé, 1882), 101.

25 *Code pénal d'Haïti* (Port-au-Prince: L'Imprimerie du Gouvernement, 1826), 102–103. The punishments prescribed for infractions of the law against the *métier de Macandals* in the 1826 law were a fine of 11 to 15 gourdes and a maximum imprisonment of four days.

26 Kenneth M. Bilby and Jerome S. Handler, "Obeah: Healing and Protection in West Indian Slave Life," *Journal of Caribbean History* 38, no. 2 (2004): 167–168.

27 See Paton, *No Bond but the Law*, 140. See also Bilby and Handler, "Obeah," 169. In British colonial Jamaica, obeah was first prohibited in 1760 after Tacky's Rebellion. See Vincent Brown's analysis of this as "a ban on alter-

native authority and social power." *The Reaper's Garden,* 150. In contrast, in mid-to-late nineteenth-century Cuba, outside of the prohibition of the male *abakuá* secret society in 1876, no "legal grounds existed for the persecution of practitioners of other Afro-Cuban religions" under Spanish colonial rule. See Palmié, *Wizards and Scientists,* 225–226.

28 It should be noted that penalties for infractions of this section of minor offenses were significantly increased in the 1835 Code Pénal. Although, in 1826, the offenses listed under Articles 406–407 incurred a fine of 11 to 15 gourdes and a detention of at most four days, in the 1935 Code Pénal, Article 405, incriminating "all makers of *ouangas, caprelatas, vaudoux, don-pèdre, macandals,* and other *sortilèges,*" set a fine of 16 to 25 gourdes and an imprisonment of one to six months.

29 Etymologically derived from the Latin *sortilegium,* meaning "divination," *sortilège* is today translated as "spell." However, an early seventeenth-century French-English dictionary translates this word in a more general way to mean "witchcraft" as well as "divination by lots." See Randle Cotgrave, *A Dictionarie of the French and English Tongues* (1611; Menston, England: Scolar Press, 1968).

30 Sidney Mintz and Michel-Rolph Trouillot note that there is no generalized word for "sorcery" in Kreyòl, the closest being *fè mal,* a construction that literally means "to do bad" and is "not restricted to the use of supernatural forces." Mintz and Trouillot, "The Social History of Haitian Vodou," in *Sacred Arts of Haitian Vodou,* ed. Donald J. Cosentino (Los Angeles: Fowler Museum of Cultural History, 1995), 131.

31 In fact, the word is sometimes translated into French as *sortilège.* See, for example, Albert Valdman, Sarah Yoder, Craige Roberts, and Yves Joseph, eds., *Haitian-Creole-English-French Dictionary* (Bloomington: Indiana University, Creole Institute, 1981), 1:567. See also Karen McCarthy Brown, "Making Wanga: Reality Constructions and the Magical Manipulation of Power," in *Transparency and Conspiracy: Ethnographies of Suspicion in the New World Order,* ed. Harry G. West and Todd Sanders (Durham, NC: Duke University Press, 2003), 241–242.

32 See Drouin de Bercy, *De Saint-Domingue, de ses guerres, de ses révolutions, de ses ressources, et des moyens à prendre pour y rétablir la paix et l'industrie* (Paris: Chez Hocquet, 1814), 175; and Duverneau Trouillot, *Esquisse ethnographique: Le vaudoun; Aperçu historique et évolutions* (Port-au-Prince: Imprimerie R. Ethéart, 1885), 16. Hannibal Price, like Trouillot, suggests that competition often lay behind the use of the epithet *caplata* and gives the Kreyòl saying that Trouillot paraphrases: *Caplata pas vlé voué cammarade li poté gros macoute* (The Caplata does not want to see his comrade carrying a big sack [of herbs, medicines, etc]); Price, *De la réhabilitation de la race noire,* 415. In their important 1955 article "Survivances africaines dans le vocabulaire religieux d'Haïti," Suzanne and Jean Comhaire-Sylvain define *caplata* as an archaic word that in an earlier day meant both fortune-teller and *sortilège.* Comhaire-Sylvain and Comhaire-Sylvain, "Survivances africaines dans le

vocabulaire religieux d'Haïti," 9. See also the chapter entitled "The Transformative Power of the Kaperlata," in Weaver, *Medical Revolutionaries*.

33 See annotations by Moreau de Saint-Méry to "Arrêt du Conseil du Cap, touchant l'Empoisonneur Macandal et ses Complices. . . . Du 20 janvier 1758," in *Loix et constitutions*, 4:218. Hein Vanhee writes that "there is some evidence to suggest that Makandal was a Kongolese ritual specialist, composing and selling *nkisi* charms in the Kongolese tradition. His name may be a corruption of *Makenda*, being a title for the chief's executioner in early twentieth-century Mayombe, or of *makanda*, meaning a medicinal plant." Vanhee, "Central African Popular Christianity," 251. See also Lorimer Denis, "La religion populaire," *Bulletin du Bureau d'ethnologie* (December 1946): 39; and Richman, *Migration and Vodou*, 16–17.

34 Moreau de Saint-Méry, *Description*, 69. Beauvoir-Dominique characterizes the Petwo spirits today as "an overwhelmingly magical pantheon" in "Underground Realms of Being," 158. On the Kongo roots of Petwo ritual see also Thompson, "From the Isle beneath the Sea," 101–119.

35 Larose, "The Meaning of Africa in Haitian Vodu," 85 and 89.

36 Ibid., 86. He also writes: "There are many novelties which are accepted by society; however, as they are legitimated in terms of constancy to the Guinea traditions, they are not seen as innovations by the worshippers; if seen as such they are likely to be subsumed under the labels of magic and sorcery." Ibid., 89. Likewise: "The idea that a concrete group could embody a pure Guinea tradition has no foundation and no such group should be looked for in Haiti. God is always 'on our side,' and Guinea is a similar concept, a complex figure through which power is legitimated." Ibid., 92.

37 Building on Larose's work and also focusing on Léogâne, Karen Richman has analyzed the contemporary rituals of *ranmase* or "picking up," which "symbolically transformed pwen [concentrations of magical energy] into a class of lwa known as zandò," thus "vitaliz[ing] Guinea with Magic's illicit heat while at the same time preserving Guinea's morality." Richman, *Migration and Vodou*, 172. See also Rachel Beauvoir-Dominique's discussion of "Vodoun magic": "Born of necessity, Vodoun emerged with a fundamental vision in which magic and religion, though autonomous, nevertheless constitute a single body. . . . In Vodoun, each temple, even the most 'religious' in outlook, is set under the patronage of one or several *lwa travay*, divinities destined to work, render service, and even amass small fortunes for their possessors. During ceremony, these lwa are *summoned*, not 'worshiped.' The gesture in and of itself reveals the magic attitude." Beauvoir-Dominique, "Underground Realms of Being," 166.

38 See Apter, "On African Origins," 248.

39 Richman argues that "Guinea ritual discourse expanded while the local agricultural producers were being disrupted, undermined, and annexed as producers and feeders of mobile wage labor." Richman, *Migration and Vodou*, 150. See chapter 3 for a more detailed discussion of her argument.

40 Laënnec Hurbon argues similarly that "sorcery is . . . inscribed in the symbolic order of Vodou as a negative pole from which the faithful must unceasingly distance themselves." Hurbon, *Le barbare imaginaire*, 227.

41 Sidney Mintz once observed that in light of Haiti's treatment by colonial powers and many other postrevolutionary disabilities, "the wonder . . . is not that it fared badly, but that it has fared at all." Mintz, *Caribbean Transformations* (1974; New York: Columbia University Press, 1989), 263.

42 Louis Herns Marcelin, "Haiti," in *Encyclopedia of Anthropology*, ed. H. James Birx (Thousand Oaks, CA: Sage Publications, 2005), 3:1135.

43 In doing so, he posed the question, "Why . . . in spite of all [the] benefits that the colonials of the islands of our archipelago derive from their communications with us, do they not cease to hold in execration the Haitian name, and to insult our national character by unworthy acts?" Thomas Madiou, *Histoire d'Haïti*, vol. 6, *1819–26* (Port-au-Prince: Éditions Henri Deschamps, 1988), 366 and 522. See also Nicholls, *From Dessalines to Duvalier*, 62. In examining the provisions of the 1816 Constitution of Boyer's predecessor, Alexandre Pétion, Sibylle Fischer argues that "as Haiti was forced to respond to international pressure to provide assurances that it would not try to export its revolution . . . , it compensated by introducing constitutional clauses that would offer a right of residency to all people who had escaped slavery or genocide." Fischer, *Modernity Disavowed*, 239–240.

44 See Nicholls, *From Dessalines to Duvalier*, 63.

45 That sense of threat produced Haiti's "defensive militarization" during the first decades of the nineteenth century, overshadowing and weakening the development of civil institutions (including the justice system) and civil society. See Sheller, *Democracy after Slavery*, 59. See also Thalès Jean-Jacques's argument that "since the dawn of our independence, the critical state of the country did not permit [the founders] to establish an organization and a regular functioning of justice. Because they had their eyes turned unceasingly toward the shore." Jean-Jacques, *Histoire du droit haïtien*, 785.

46 David Nicholls notes that students at the national secondary school were instructed that Haiti's development should be pursued not simply for the material benefit of the nation but as a means of "destroy[ing] completely the prejudice which existed against their race." Nicholls, *From Dessalines to Duvalier*, 75.

47 Madiou, *Histoire d'Haïti*, vol. 6, *1819–1826*, 482. See "Loi qui déclare dette nationale, l'indemnité de 150,000,000 francs accordée à la France, pour la reconnaissance de l'indépendance d'Haïti," Port-au-Prince, 26 February 1826, in Pradine, *Recueil général*, 353. See also Dupuy, *Haiti in the World Economy*, 94.

48 Sheller, *Democracy after Slavery*, 50.

49 Madiou, *Histoire d'Haïti*, vol. 6, *1819–1826*, 461. The terms of the indemnity were renegotiated, and in 1838 an agreement was reached that, according to François Blancpain, required Haiti to pay France 90 million francs (not

60 million, as has often been written). See Blancpain, *La condition des paysans haïtiens: Du code noir aux codes ruraux* (Paris: Éditions Karthala, 2003), 143.

50 Madiou, *Histoire d'Haïti*, vol. 6, *1819–1826*, 477.

51 Ibid., 533.

52 Carlos Aguirre and Ricardo D. Salvatore, "Writing the History of Law, Crime, and Punishment in Latin America," in *Crime and Punishment in Latin America: Law and Society since Late Colonial Times*, ed. Ricardo D. Salvatore, Carlos Aguirre, and Gilbert M. Joseph (Durham, NC: Duke University Press, 2001), 4.

53 M. J. Isambert, quoted in Madiou, *Histoire d'Haïti*, vol. 6, *1819–1826*, 533. According to Madiou, Isambert was "avocat aux conseils du Roi et à la cour de Cassation."

54 See Mandrou, *Magistrats et sorciers*, 466–486; and Brian P. Levack, "The Decline and End of Witchcraft Prosecutions," in *Witchcraft and Magic in Europe: The Eighteenth and Nineteenth Centuries*, ed. Bengt Ankarloo and Stuart Clark (Philadelphia: University of Pennsylvania Press, 1999), 1–93.

55 Moreau de Saint-Méry, *Description*, 68–69; de Bercy, *De Saint-Domingue*, 176.

56 Alasdair Pettinger, "From Vaudoux to Voodoo," *Forum of Modern Language Studies* 40, no. 4 (2004): 416. Malenfant in fact wrote that "it is only fanatics, fools, or imbeciles who could worry about a sect that appeared to me rather like that of masonry." Malenfant, *Des colonies*, 215.

57 Ashli White's research on the reception of exiles from Saint-Domingue in U.S. cities in the late eighteenth and early nineteenth centuries provides further evidence that at that time the signifier *vaudoux* had little international recognition, much less notoriety. Although the refugees from the revolution were "othered" in multiple ways in their host cities, association with *vaudoux* seems not to have been a point of stigmatization. Personal communication. See White, *Encountering Revolution: Haiti and the Making of the Early Republic* (Baltimore, MD: Johns Hopkins University Press, 2010). I have not examined the frequency with which the signifier *vaudoux* appeared in Spanish-language writing during these years.

58 Victor Schoelcher, *Colonies étrangères et Haïti: Résultats de l'émancipation anglaise*, vol. 2 (Paris: Pagnerre, 1843), 295. See also Philippe Zacaïr, "Représentations d'Haïti dans la presse française du dix-neuvième siècle," *French Colonial History* 6 (2005): 103–112.

59 "I cannot avoid repeating, that Hayti must not be held up as an example of what can be accomplished by free labour; that it ought rather to be the beacon to warn the government of England against an experiment which may prove absolutely fatal to her colonial system." James Franklin, *The Present State of Hayti (Santo Domingo) with Remarks on Its Agriculture, Commerce, Laws, Religion, Finances, and Population* (1828; Westport, CT: Negro Universities Press, 1970), 364.

60 Indeed, Brown refers to "the African obi and the Catholic priest both com[ing] in for a share of their respect and homage," thus using terminol-

ogy ("obi") from the British Caribbean which, to my knowledge, had no currency in Haiti. Jonathan Brown, *The History and Present Condition of St. Domingo*, vol. 2 (Philadelphia: William Marshall, 1827), 273.

61 John Candler, *Brief Notices of Hayti with Its Condition, Resources, and Prospects* (London: Thomas Ward, 1842), 43.

62 Hurbon, *Le barbare imaginaire*, 115 and 92–93.

63 Joseph Balthazar Inginac, *Mémoires de Joseph Balthazar Inginac, Général de Division, Ex-Secrétaire-Général près S. E. l'ex-président d'Haïti, depuis 1797 jusqu'à 1843* (Kingston, Jamaica: Imprimé par J. R. De Cordova, 1843), 88.

64 Hurbon, *Comprendre Haïti*, 148.

65 Michel-Rolph Trouillot writes of the Haitian expression "*mounn andeyò* (literally, 'people outside') that urbanites use to describe the peasantry," seldom wondering "how a majority of the nation could be seen as being 'outside.'" Trouillot, *Haiti, State against Nation*, 81.

66 Article 190, sixth law of the 1826 Code Rural: "Sur la Police Rurale," in Roger Petit-Frère, *Code rural de Boyer, 1826* (Port-au-Prince: Archives Nationales d'Haïti/Maison H. Deschamps, 1992), 54.

67 See the analysis of this point in Célius, "Le modèle social haïtien," 129.

68 "Règlement de culture du 12 octobre 1800," reprinted in Moïse, *Le projet national de Toussaint Louverture*, 92.

69 See Dupuy, *Haiti in the World Economy*, 88–89.

70 Paul Moral, *Le paysan haïtien: Étude sur la vie rurale en Haïti* (Port-au-Prince: Les Éditions Fardin, 1978), 31. On Christophe's and Pétion's respective land policies, see also Dupuy, *Haiti in the World Economy*, 86–91.

71 See Trouillot, *Haiti, State against Nation*, 48; and Dantès Bellegarde, *La nation haïtienne* (Paris: J. de Gigord, 1938), 99.

72 Drexel G. Woodson, "Tout Mounn Se Mounn, Men Tout Mounn pa Menm: Microlevel Sociocultural Aspects of Land Tenure in a Northern Haitian Locality" (Ph.D. diss., University of Chicago, 1990), 388 and 393.

73 Rémy Bastien, *Le paysan haïtien et sa famille* (1951; Paris: Éditions Karthala, 1985), 151. See also Woodson, "Tout Mounn Se Mounn," 371–372. One legacy of such concessions has been, as Sidney Mintz notes, that "persons who own no land or who lack land to work are proportionally fewer in Haiti than in any other Caribbean country, and perhaps fewer than in any country in Latin America." Mintz, *Caribbean Transformations*, 272. Ira Lowenthal writes: "It is perhaps all too easy for the outsider to forget, in the face of today's poverty and problems, that this Afro-American peasantry indeed realized—quite early on and definitively—what remained the unfulfilled dream of generations of slaves throughout the New World. They gained their freedom and secured it from future encroachment through control over and ownership of agricultural land." Lowenthal, "'Marriage Is 20, Children Are 21,'" 254.

74 See Woodson, "Tout Mounn Se Mounn," 422; and Nicholls, *From Dessalines to Duvalier*, 68.

75 Dupuy, *Haiti in the World Economy*, 98.

76 Woodson, "Tout Mounn Se Mounn," 321. See his discussion of how the predecessor of the *demwatye* system, the "share system" or "quarter system," worked under Dessalines's government, 352–353. According to Woodson, it was under Pétion that the quarter system was abandoned in favor of the *demwatye* (half system), which doubled the portion of the harvest that cultivators received and ended the practice of granting unequal shares to cultivators who performed different forms of labor. Ibid., 382–383.

77 Jean Casimir, *The Caribbean: One and Divisible* (Santiago, Chile: United Nations Economic Commission for Latin America and the Caribbean, 1992), 79. See also Casimir, *La culture opprimée* (Delmas, Haiti: Imprimerie Lakay, 2001), especially chapter 4, "Haïti au XIXe siècle," 152–192.

78 Serge Larose, "The Haitian *Lakou*: Land, Family and Ritual," in *Family and Kinship in Middle America and the Caribbean*, ed. Arnaud F. Marks and René A. Rômer (Curaçao: Institute of Higher Studies and Leiden, Netherlands: Royal Institute of Linguistics and Anthropology, 1975), 482–512. See also Hurbon, *Le barbare imaginaire*, 219–221; Richman, *Migration and Vodou*, 117–119; and Smith, *When the Hands Are Many*, 80–81.

79 Ira Lowenthal defines *eritaj* as "perhaps the single most important socio-symbolic construct of Haitian peasant culture. Through it, individuals are brought into meaningful relationship not only with a discrete, yet extensive group of their contemporary consanguines, but with a sub-set of their consanguineal antecedents." Also note that "affiliation to an eritaj is not exclusive. That is membership in one does not preclude membership in others, available to ego in virtue of consanguineal connection to another apical ancestor." Lowenthal, "'Marriage Is 20, Children Are 21,'" 194 and 201.

80 See Bastien, *Le paysan haïtien et sa famille*, 168–171.

81 Bastien conducted ethnographic research in the Marbial valley in 1948 and noted that "according to the information furnished by the Marbialais whom we questioned, it does not seem that one can still find today in the valley descendants of the families who established themselves here before 1830." Ibid., 155. See his chapters 7–9 for an extended analysis of why the *lakou* declined so precipitously in Marbial after the third generation. See also Paul Moral, who argues that the *lakou* fared better "in the plains where . . . properties of a certain spaciousness could conserve themselves nearly intact." Moral, *Le paysan haïtien*, 170.

82 Larose, "The Haitian *Lakou*," 484.

83 For example, had they or their ancestors been enslaved or free in 1791? Were they African born or Creole? Were they or an ancestor part of the military?

84 See Franklin, *The Present State of Hayti*, 344; and Candler, *Brief Notices of Hayti*, 144. Here Candler notes that, "owing to the cheapness of good

land," a proprietor of a large estate, "if he wishes to secure the services of those who have long laboured for him on the moiety system, must be content to allow them even greater advantages that that system affords."

85 Woodson, "Tout Mounn Se Mounn," 426.

86 *Code rural de Boyer 1826, avec les commentaires de Roger Petit-Frère, Jean Vandal, Georges E. Werleigh* (Port-au-Prince: Archives Nationales d'Haïti/Maison H. Deschamps, 1992), 13–14. François Blancpain argues that the Code Rural seemed designed or destined "to create a sort of caste system in Haitian society in specifying that children of farmers would follow the condition of their parents." Blancpain, *La condition des paysans haïtiens*, 147.

87 *Code rural de Boyer*, 45. The section was established as the basic administrative unit of rural Haiti. See "Circulaire du Président d'Haïti, aux commandants d'arrondissement, concernant la nomination d'officiers de police rurale," Port-au-Prince, 6 March 1826, in Pradine, *Recueil général*, 358. See also Magloire and Soray, "The Legal System of Haiti," 12. As the sociologist Jean L. Comhaire noted in a 1955 study, these rural sections were not set up as "corporate bodies," but rather existed "only for police purposes." Comhaire, "The Haitian 'Chef de Section,'" *American Anthropologist* 57, no. 3 (June 1955): 621.

88 Comhaire, "The Haitian 'Chef de Section,'" 621. These officers were appointed by and reported to the *commandant d'arrondissement*, who, in turn, reported directly to the Haitian president. Between them in the hierarchy of rural governance were positioned the commandants of the commune. See the "Loi sur la police rurale," articles 123–125 and 127–129, in Petit-Frère, *Code rural de Boyer, 1826*, 41. Also see Pnina Lahav, "The Chef de Section: Structure and Functions of Haiti's Basic Administrative Institution," in *Working Papers in Haitian Society and Culture*, ed. Sidney W. Mintz (New Haven, CT: Antilles Research Program, Yale University, 1975), 51–83.

89 See Casimir's analysis of the inapplication of such laws in *La culture opprimée*, 181.

90 See the discussion of "tolerated illegalities" in Michel Foucault, *Discipline and Punish: The Birth of the Prison*, trans. Alan Sheridan (London: Penguin Books, 1977), 82.

91 In discussing the Haitian state's exploitation of the peasantry, Alex Dupuy notes that the government "did not pay the rural section chiefs and their agents who constituted the rural police. The latter earned their income by collecting various fees from the peasants which they divided among themselves and the state." Dupuy, *Haiti in the World Economy*, 104.

92 The evidence that such a system developed is fragmentary but suggestive. It is referenced, for example, in a pastoral letter circulated by Catholic bishops in 1913, following a presidential letter to arrondissement commanders: "No longer will one see, as in the past, military Commanders not only closing their eyes to *pratiques superstitieuses*, but encouraging them and

sometimes even making them a source of revenues in granting the authorization of holding 'a dance' or of 'celebrating a service' for a fee." "Lettre
pastorale de 1913," quoted in Carl Edward Peters, *La croix contre l'asson*
(Port-au-Prince: Imprimerie la Phalange, 1960), 48. For other references
see J. M. Jan, *Le Cap-Haïtien, 1860–1966: Documentation religieuse* (Port-au-
Prince: Éditions Henri Deschamps, 1972), 319, 323, and 326–327, which
suggest that the price of the permits depended on whether an animal was
to be sacrificed as an offering, and whether it was fowl, goat, sheep, pig,
and so on. See also Hurbon, *Le barbare imaginaire*, 182. An *oungan* named Alphonse Jean who shared his memories with me in Tabarre, Haiti, in June
1997 noted that under the post-occupation governments of Sténio Vincent,
Elie Lescot, Dumarsais Estimé, and Paul Magloire, in order to mount a *sèvis*
a permit had to be purchased from the local *chèf seksyon* (*chef de section*) at a
variable rate depending, in part, on the nature of the ceremony.

93 As will be discussed in chapter 3, this evidence is particularly strong during the U.S. occupation between 1915 and 1934, perhaps in part because
American military officials widely publicized that they would strictly enforce articles 405–407 of the Code Pénal and were taken at their word.

94 Hurbon, *Le barbare imaginaire*, 266 and 267.

95 See Jean-Jacques, *Histoire du droit haïtien*, on "Le décret du Gouvernement
provisoire du 22 mai 1843 sur la réforme du droit civil et criminel," 777 n. 2
and 841.

96 For an analysis of what the author argues were the three phases of the revolution, see Manigat, *La révolution de 1843*. See also H. Pauleus Sannon, *Essai
historique sur la revolution de 1843* (Cayes: Imprimerie Bonnefil, 1905); Sheller,
Democracy after Slavery; Bellegarde, *Histoire du peuple haïtien*, 142–146; and
Hector, *Crises et mouvements populaires*, 123–132 and 135–191.

97 See Sheller, *Democracy after Slavery*, 128: "The South had always been a
stronghold of affranchi power and landownership, even in colonial days,
and big coffee plantations had been maintained here after independence;
thus class solidarity of the ancien libres was probably stronger here than
elsewhere in the country."

98 Manigat, *La révolution de 1843*, 27; see also Sheller, *Democracy after Slavery*,
136; and Nicholls, *From Dessalines to Duvalier*, 78.

99 Leslie F. Manigat writes that "peasant bands of the southeast, from Saltrou
to Jacmel, were mixing religious claims with their sociopolitical demands
and expressing themselves in the form of a mystical and magical movement." Manigat, *La révolution de 1843*, 21.

100 Gustave d'Alaux, *L'Empereur Soulouque et son empire* (1856; Port-au-Prince:
Les Éditions Fardin, 1988), 111–112. See also Sheller, *Democracy after Slavery*,
139 and 136.

101 See d'Alaux, *L'Empereur Soulouque et son empire*, 112. This is how he wrote
the statement in Kreyòl: "Nègue riche qui connaît li et écri, cila mulâte;

mulâte pauve qui pas connaît li ni écri, cila nègue." For an analysis of this quotation in terms of her larger argument about popular civil agency in mid-nineteenth century Haiti, see Sheller, *Democracy after Slavery*, 135–136.

102 D'Alaux, *L'Empereur Soulouque et son empire*, 112–113.

103 Jean-Jacques, *Histoire du droit haïtien*, 841. See also Manigat, *La révolution de 1843*, 30.

104 D'Alaux, 64. This citation from Cabon is quoted in Bellegarde, *Histoire du peuple haïtien*, 150.

105 Thomas Madiou, *Histoire d'Haïti*, vol. 8, *1843–1846* (Port-au-Prince: Éditions Henri Deschamps, 1991), 318.

106 Pierre Adolphe Cabon, *Notes sur l'histoire religieuse d'Haïti: De la révolution au Concordat, 1789–1860* (Port-au-Prince: Petit Séminaire Collège Saint-Martial, 1933), 390–391. See also Bellegarde, *Histoire du peuple haïtien*, 150. According to d'Alaux, Frère Joseph later served in Faustin Soulouque's government (1847–1859). See d'Alaux, *L'Empereur Soulouque et son empire*, 197.

107 See Karen McCarthy Brown's discussion with Mama Lola about the meaning of *giyon* and treatments for it in Karen McCarthy Brown and Mama Lola, "The Altar Room: A Dialogue," in *Sacred Arts of Haitian Vodou*, ed. Donald J. Cosentino (Los Angeles: Fowler Museum of Cultural History, 1995), 237.

108 See Madiou, *Histoire d'Haïti*, vol. 8, *1843–1846*, 319.

109 Ibid, 318–320. These events seem to have taken place during the latter months of 1845.

110 Ibid.

111 Jean L. Comhaire, "The Haitian Schism, 1804–1860," *Anthropological Quarterly* 29, no. 1 (1956): 9. Étienne Charlier notes that his source for this information about Pierrot and Cécile Fatiman was their grandson, Général Pierrot Benoit Rameau, who authorized the writer to make it public for the first time. See Charlier, *Aperçu sur la formation historique de la nation haïtienne* (Port-au-Prince: Les Presses Libres, 1954), 49. On Cécile Fatiman see also Dayan, *Haiti, History and the Gods*, 47; and Fick, *The Making of Haiti*, 93–94, 242, and 265.

112 See Diana Paton's particularly insightful examination of these questions in *No Bond but the Law*, 156–190. See also Sherry B. Ortner, "Resistance and the Problem of Ethnographic Refusal," *Comparative Studies in Society and History* 37, no. 1 (January 1995): 173–193; Gayatri Chakravorty Spivak, "Subaltern Studies: Deconstructing Historiography," in Spivak, *In Other Worlds: Essays in Cultural Politics* (New York: Routledge, 1988), 197–221; Laura Lewis, *Hall of Mirrors: Power, Witchcraft, and Caste in Colonial Mexico* (Durham, NC: Duke University Press, 2003), 9–10; and Florencia Mallon, "The Promise and Dilemma of Subaltern Studies: Perspectives from Latin American History, *American Historical Review* 99, no. 5 (1994): 1491–1515.

113 See Edward Tylor, *Primitive Culture*, vol. 1 (London: John Murray, 1920),

113 ; Bronislaw Malinowski, *The Sexual Life of Savages in North Western Melanesia* (New York: Harcourt Brace, 1929), 199; and Michael Taussig, *Shamanism, Colonialism, and the Wild Man: A Study in Terror and Healing* (Chicago: University of Chicago Press, 1987), 215.

114 Hurbon, *Le barbare imaginaire*, 191.

115 Ibid, 219.

116 Smith, *When the Hands Are Many*, 79.

117 Trouillot, *Introduction à une histoire du vaudou*, 103.

118 "No. 2205.—Circulaire du Président d'Haïti, aux commandants d'arrondissement concernant l'Agriculture. Port-au-Prince, le 10 septembre 1846." Reprinted in Peters, *La croix contre l'asson*, 279–280.

119 "Circulaire du Secrétaire d'État de l'Intérieur—Aux Commandants d'Arrondissement, relative à la culture, aux tournées d'inspection, et à la police rurale." Reprinted in ibid., 280.

120 Ibid., 280–281. A month later, in late December 1846, Céligny Ardouin specified that this punishment only applied to recidivists. The particular significance of maritime prisons in the original law is unclear. The Haitian legal historian Thalès Jean-Jacques renders this law yet more mysterious by noting that, to his knowledge, no such prisons were ever built in Haiti. This law was carried over into the Code Pénal revisions of October 1864 under the presidency of Fabre Geffrard. Jean-Jacques, *Histoire du droit haïtien*, 843.

121 Justin Bouzon, *Études historiques sur la présidence de Faustin Soulouque, 1847–1849* (Port-au-Prince: Bibliothèque Haïtienne, 1894), 5–6.

122 Milo Rigaud, *La tradition voudoo et le voudoo haïtien: Son temple, ses mystères, sa magie* (Paris: Éditions Niclaus, 1953), is full of such accounts, unsourced and apparently taken from oral tradition; see especially 40–48. See also Patrick Bellegarde-Smith, "The Spirit of the Thing: Religious Thought and Social/Historical Memory," in *Fragments of Bone: Neo-African Religions in a New World*, ed. Patrick Bellegarde-Smith (Urbana: University of Illinois Press, 2005), 54.

123 Hurbon, *Comprendre Haïti*, 145.

124 *The Haitian Constitution, 1805*, in Dubois and Garrigus, *Slave Revolution in the Caribbean*, 194–195; Dubois and Garrigus's translation.

125 Cabon, *Notes sur l'histoire religieuse d'Haïti*, 94.

126 Ibid., 201–202.

127 Comhaire, "The Haitian Schism," 2; and Terry Rey, *Our Lady of Class Struggle: The Cult of the Virgin Mary in Haiti* (Trenton, NJ: Africa World Press, 1999), 46.

128 Cabon, *Notes sur l'histoire religieuse d'Haïti*, 149 and 202.

129 Ibid., 227. Cabon goes on: "It even seems that the more a priest proved himself unfaithful to his responsibilities as man and ecclesiastic, the better suited he was for Haiti, because he was opposed to Rome by all the antagonism created by his apostasy, his revolt, or his libertinage." Rachel

Beauvoir-Dominique notes that priests coming independently to the island—and seeking religious autonomy—were generally welcomed; however, priests sent to Haiti through official ecclesiastical channels were sometimes viewed with suspicion as agents of French imperialism. Beauvoir-Dominique, *L'ancienne cathédrale de Port-au-Prince: Perspectives d'un vestige de carrefours* (Port-au-Prince: Éditions Henri Deschamps, 1991), 70.

130 Anne Greene, *The Catholic Church in Haiti: Political and Social Change* (East Lansing: Michigan State University Press, 1993), 90–91. However, note that Catts Pressoir, a historian of Haitian Protestantism, characterizes Boyer as being more obstructive than supportive of the growth of Protestantism in Haiti. Pressoir, "Le protestantisme en Haïti," *Les Griots: La revue scientifique et littéraire d'Haïti* 3, no. 3 (January–March 1939), 389. See Comhaire, "The Haitian Schism," 6–8, for a succinct discussion of Protestantism in Haiti during the decades prior to the Concordat. On African American emigration to Haiti, see Chris Dixon, *African America and Haiti: Emigration and Black Nationalism in the Nineteenth Century* (Westport, CT: Greenwood Press, 2000). On freemasonry among Roman Catholics in nineteenth-century Haiti, see Beauvoir-Dominique, *L'ancienne cathédrale de Port-au-Prince*, 72–73; and see Sheller's analysis of freemasonry as "a kind of precursor to democratization" in *Democracy after Slavery*, 58.

131 Nicholls, *From Dessalines to Duvalier*, 70.

132 Hurbon, *Le barbare imaginaire*, 117.

133 Louis Napoléon became the object of frequent unflattering comparisons with Soulouque, most famously at the hands of Marx in *The Eighteenth Brumaire* (1851), who, as Joan/Colin Dayan writes, "compared what he called 'the best' of Louis Napoléon's 'bunch of blokes' to 'a noisy, disreputable, rapacious bohème that crawls into gallooned coats with the same grotesque dignity as the high dignitaries of Soulouque.'" Dayan, *Haiti, History, and the Gods*, 12.

134 D'Alaux, *L'Empereur Soulouque et son empire*, 14.

135 Ibid., 71. See also Murdo J. MacLeod, "The Soulouque Regime in Haiti, 1847–1859: A Reevaluation," *Caribbean Studies* 10, no. 3 (1971): 44–45.

136 D'Alaux refers to Frère Joseph as "the *vaudoux* prophet" of Acaau's band; D'Alaux, *L'Empereur Soulouque et son empire*, 71. See his discussions of Frère Joseph's role in Soulouque's government in chapters 8 and 11 in particular.

137 Ibid., 90–91.

138 See Philippe Zacaïr's analysis of representations of Haiti in two popular bourgeois French periodicals in the mid- to late nineteenth century, *L'Illustration* and *La Revue des deux-mondes*, which published d'Alaux's account in serial form. Zacaïr notes: "Haitian 'barbarism' became incarnated in *Vaudou* on the part of Alaux as in *L'Illustration* during this period." Interestingly, though, he writes that *Vaudou* "was never systematically associated with representations of Haiti" in these two publications. Zacaïr,

"Représentations d'Haïti," 112. I have not examined the frequency with which the word *vaudoux* (and its surrogates) appeared in Spanish-language publications during this period. However, see Sibylle Fischer's analysis of popular Dominican poet Juan Antonio Alix's "Diálogo cantado entre un guajiro y un Papá bocó haitiano en un fandango en Dajabón." Though it cannot be precisely dated, given that Alix was born in 1833, it must certainly have appeared during or following Soulouque's years in power. In Alix's verse, the *bòkò* character insists that the Dominican must *bailá vodú* (dance *vodú*); the latter refuses and finally stabs the Haitian "to rid himself of the impertinent suggestion that he, the good Christian, should submit to the Haitian vodun drums." Fischer, *Modernity Disavowed*, 172–173.

139 David Scott, *Conscripts of Modernity: The Tragedy of Colonial Enlightenment* (Durham, NC: Duke University Press, 2004), 81–82.

140 The English edition was published as *Soulouque and His Empire: From the French of Gustave d'Alaux*, trans. John H. Parkhill (Richmond, VA: J. W. Randolph, 1861); see p. xii. See also Paul Dhormoys, *Une visite chez Soulouque: Souvenirs d'un voyage dans l'île d'Haïti* (Paris: Librairie Nouvelle, 1859).

141 Cabon, *Notes sur l'histoire religieuse d'Haïti*, 478.

142 "Convention entre Sa Sainteté le Souverain Pontife Pie IX et Son Excellence Fabre Geffrard, Président de la République d'Haïti," 28 March 1860, in Cabon, *Notes sur l'histoire religieuse d'Haïti*, 511.

143 See Comhaire, "The Haitian Schism," 3; and Nicholls, *From Dessalines to Duvalier*, 84.

144 On the implications of the church's establishment of primary schools across Haiti, see Marc Péan, *L'illusion héroïque: 25 ans de vie capoise, 1890–1915*, vol. 1, *1890–1902* (Port-au-Prince: Imprimerie Henri Deschamps, 1977), 75; and Trouillot, *Haiti, State against Nation*, 51.

145 Joseph Le Gouaze, "Communication de Son Exc. Mgr l'Archevêque de Port-au-Prince, le 20 mars 1942." Held by the Bibliothèque Haïtienne des Pères du Saint Esprit, Port-au-Prince, Haiti.

146 Making a similar point, Elizabeth McAlister argues: "Institutional Catholicism depends on its opposition to Vodou, for it is its position against what is impure and illegitimate that strengthens Catholic virtue in Haiti." See McAlister, "'The Jew' in the Haitian Imagination: Pre-Modern Anti-Judaism in the Postmodern Caribbean," in *Black Zion: African American Religious Encounters with Judaism*, ed. Yvonne Chireau and Nathaniel Deutsch (New York: Oxford University Press, 2000), 215. See also Laënnec Hurbon, who writes that through the *campagne anti-superstitieuse* the church sought "to manifest its alterity with regard to *Vaudou*." Hurbon, *Dieu dans le Vaudou haïtien*, 19.

147 Quoted in Nicholls, *From Dessalines to Duvalier*, 84.

148 Hurbon, *Le barbare imaginaire*, 141.

149 The abolitionist Victor Schoelcher, who visited Haiti in 1832, under Boyer's rule, accused the clerics stationed there of being mercenaries, who, "far
from enlightening the people . . . [,] keep them fixed in the silliest superstitions." He went on: "One receives ten gourdes for prayers to bring rain
which a laborer needs, another accepts five good piasters for an exorcism
which is to bring peace of mind to an old woman accused of being a *loup-
garou*; and when you reproach this dealer for the masses, he imperturbably
replies: 'But monsieur, it is only faith that saves; this woman would still believe herself to be a *loup-garou* if I had not taken her money.'" Schoelcher,
Colonies étrangères et Haïti, vol. 2, 294.

150 Rey, "Kongolese Catholic Influences on Haitian Popular Catholicism,"
276–277.

151 Soulouque reportedly interpreted rumors of a series of apparitions of the
Virgin in 1849 as divine signs that he should be crowned emperor. One of
the sites of these apparitions was in the town of Ville Bonheur, near the
waterfall called Saut d'Eau, southwest of Mirebalais, which thereafter became the destination for an annual pilgrimage and festival every 16 July (the
day in 1849 when the Virgin was first rumored to have appeared), honoring
Our Lady of Mount Carmel and the *lwa* Ezili Dantò. See Laguerre, *Voodoo
and Politics in Haiti*, 87–88; and Cabon, *Notes sur l'histoire religieuse d'Haïti*,
406–407.

152 Vanhee, "Central African Popular Christianity," 262. See also Peters, *La
croix contre l'asson*, 43.

153 Peters, *La croix contre l'asson*, 44.

154 See, for example, "Statuts Synodaux Promulgués le 22 février 1872 par Mgr
Guilloux," printed in Peters, *La croix contre l'asson*, 250–251.

155 See Peters, *La croix contre l'asson*, 250. On *rad penitans* see Melville J. Herskovits, *Life in a Haitian Valley* (1937; Garden City, NY: Doubleday, 1971),
254–255.

156 Joseph Roach, *Cities of the Dead: Circum-Atlantic Performance* (New York:
Columbia University Press, 1996), 55.

157 See Joan/Colin Dayan's argument that "vodou, in responding over time to
the arbitrary power of mastery, literalized these moments of memory in
their gods and spirits. In short, like the law, vodou gives flesh to past narratives and life to the residue of old codes and penal sanctions," and "like law
itself, the spirits form the locus of embodied history." Dayan, "Querying
the Spirit," 41 and 42.

158 See Spenser St. John's report to the British Foreign Office of 23 June 1864
announcing that on 9 June "Monseigneur Testard Du Cosquer, Archbishop
of Port-au-Prince, arrived at this place to carry out the Concordat entered
into by Hayti with the Court of Rome; he was accompanied by about
thirty priests and several sisters of charity." Spenser St. John to the Right
Honorable Earl Russell K.G., 23 June 1864; Great Britain, Foreign Office,
General correspondence before 1906, Hayti, F.O. 35/61 (microfilm). My

thanks to Keith Manuel for his assistance with this research. See also J. M. Jan, *Collecta*, vol. 1 (Port-au-Prince, Haiti: Éditions Henri Deschamps, 1955), 204.

159 Métraux, *Le vaudou haïtien*, 43.

160 Price, *De la réhabilitation de la race noire*, 488. This work was published post-humously.

161 "Tribunal Criminel du Port-au-Prince," *Le Moniteur*, 20 February 1864.

162 Spenser St. John, *Hayti, or The Black Republic* (1889; London: Frank Cass, 1971), 215–216. This protest was not reflected in the official transcript of their collective trial.

163 A. Monfleury, "Le vaudoux en Haïti," *Le Moniteur*, 20 February 1864. This was also published in pamphlet form, a copy of which is held in the collection of the Bibliothèque Haïtienne des Frères de l'Instruction Chrétienne, Port-au-Prince.

164 Hoffmann, *Haïti: Couleurs, croyances, créole*, 133.

165 "Tribunal Criminel du Port-au-Prince," *Le Moniteur*, 27 February 1864. The aforementioned *commissaire du gouvernement* also noted in his statement that "*le vaudoux . . .* does not require human sacrifice."

166 A. Monfleury, "Le vaudoux en Haïti," *Le Moniteur*, 20 February 1864. For a summary of the *commissaire du gouvernement* M. Lavaud's remarks see "Tribunal Criminel du Port-au-Prince," *Le Moniteur*, 27 February 1864.

167 In his report of 23 February 1864 to the Foreign Office, Spenser St. John wrote that "the public mind is too excited by the incidents of the late trial to be careful as to the truth of the stories which are currently related; but it is stated that numerous children have lately disappeared, and that the police are making inquiries in various quarters." Spenser St. John to the Right Honorable Earl Russell K.G., 23 February 1864; Great Britain, Foreign Office, General correspondence before 1906, Hayti, F.O. 35/61 (microfilm). The parallels and correspondences between this case and the white Cuban panic around alleged cases of child sacrifice by black "brujos" in early republican Cuba warrant closer study. See Aline Helg, *Our Rightful Share: The Afro-Cuban Struggle for Equality, 1886–1912* (Chapel Hill: University of North Carolina Press, 1995); Palmié, *Wizards and Scientists*; Alejandra Bronfman, *Measures of Equality: Social Science, Citizenship, and Race in Cuba, 1902–1940* (Chapel Hill: University of North Carolina Press, 2004); Reinaldo L. Román, *Governing Spirits: Religion, Miracles, and Spectacles in Cuba and Puerto Rico, 1898–1956* (Chapel Hill: University of North Carolina Press, 2007; and Lara Putnam, "Rites of Power and Rumours of Race: The Circulation of Spernatural Knowledge in the Greater Caribbean, 1890–1940," paper presented at the conference "Obeah and Other Powers," 16 July 2008, Newcastle University, UK.

168 Hurbon, *Le barbare imaginaire*, 118.

169 Trouillot, *Introduction à une histoire du vaudou*, 99. He thus makes the crucial point that if, as this book maintains, these laws were at times enforced

under the pressure of foreign powers in Haiti, they were also at times enforced by Haitian authorities on account of the pressure of the *writings* of foreigners.

170 Spenser St. John to the Right Honorable Earl Russell K.G, 23 February 1864; Great Britain, Foreign Office, General correspondence before 1906, Hayti, F.O. 35/61 (microfilm).

171 Fabre Geffrard, "Circulaire aux Commandants d'Arrondissement, 5 mars 1864," *Le Moniteur*, 12 March 1864.

172 Ibid.

173 See Price, *De la réhabilitation de la race noire*, 409, for an argument similar to Geffrard's on the colonial origins of "sorcery." See also the discussion in Hoffmann, *Haïti: Couleurs, croyances, créole*, 134.

174 Price, *De la réhabilitation de la race noire*, 442.

175 V. Lizaire, "No. 4044—Circulaire du Secrétaire d'État de la Justice et des Cultes aux Commissaires du Gouvernement près les tribunaux civils de la République, relative au Vaudou," reprinted in Peters, *La croix contre l'asson*, 283. A handwritten copy of the original circular is held in the Kurt Fisher Haitian History Collection (General Correspondence, April–December 1864, Folder 2) at the Schomburg Center for Research in Black Culture, New York Public Library.

176 Foucault, *Discipline and Punish*, 82.

177 Lizaire, reprinted in Peters, *La croix contre l'asson*, 284.

178 Sherry Ortner critiques simplistic dichotomies of domination and resistance that see the latter as organized opposition to "a relatively fixed and institutionalized form of power" and thus run the risk of effacing structures of power internal to subaltern groups. See Ortner, "Resistance and the Problem of Ethnographic Refusal," 179.

179 See Diana Paton's discussions of such politics in the case of obeah and myalism in pre- and post-emancipation Jamaica: "There is plenty of . . . evidence that elites feared [obeah] because of its power to mobilize Afro-Jamaicans to political ends. Nevertheless, obeah and myalism were not inherently oppositional practices. In many cases, they were used against the same poor and marginal individuals who were also likely targets of court procedures." Paton, *No Bond but the Law*, 187–188. Mindie Lazarus-Black also notes obeah's "capacity to generate other forms of domination," in her *Legitimate Acts and Illegal Encounters: Law and Society in Antigua and Barbuda* (Washington, DC: Smithsonian Institution Press, 1994), 46.

180 Nau, *Les codes haïtiens* (1914), 265–266. This article will be discussed in chapter 3.

181 What, under article 405 in the 1835 Code Pénal, had been a minimum one-month sentence with a fine of 16–25 gourdes was increased to three months plus a fine of 60–150 gourdes. A provision for the punishment of recidivism was added, specifying "an imprisonment of six months to two years and a fine of 300 to 1000 gourdes," meaning that, on account of the higher class of potential penalties, such cases would henceforth fall under the jurisdic-

tion of the *tribunaux correctionnels*, rather than that of the local *tribunaux de paix*. There was considerable discussion in the meeting of the Chambre des Réprésentants on 7 October 1864 about whether or not an exception should be granted to allow *juges de paix* to try cases of recidivism themselves, in spite of the legal requirement that cases with penalties at that level be sent to the higher court; however, the Chambre decided against this in light of the potential for local corruption and what was hoped would be the deterrent effect of the threat of trial in a higher court. See "Chambre des Réprésentants, séance du 7 octobre 1864," in *Le Moniteur*, 22 October 1864.

182 "Chambre des Représentants, séance du 6 octobre 1864," *Le Moniteur*, 22 October 1864.

183 "Toutes danses et autres pratiques quelconques qui seront de nature à entretenir dans les populations l'esprit de fétichisme et de superstition seront considérées comme sortilèges et punies des mêmes peines." Nau, *Les codes haïtiens* (1914), 322.

184 Métraux, *Le vaudou haïtien*, 240.

185 The increase was from six days of imprisonment and 16 gourdes under the 1835 Code Pénal to two months and 100 gourdes in 1864. Its second paragraph prescribed that those convicted of *sortilèges* would "serve their sentence in maritime prisons and be employed in marine labor," following the terms of Jean-Baptiste Riché's aforementioned rural police law.

186 "Les instruments, ustensiles et costumes servant ou destinés à servir aux faits prévus aux deux articles précédents, seront de plus saisis et confisqués, pour être brûlés ou détruits." Nau, *Les codes haïtiens* (1914), 322.

187 Pierre Buteau, "Une problématique de l'identité," *Conjonction: Revue franco-haïtienne de l'Institut français d'Haïti* 198 (April–May–June 1993): 21.

188 Derrida, "Force of Law," 929.

189 Romain, *Quelques mœurs et coutumes*, 130. See also the discussion of a related proverb, *Avoka, notè, apantè: tout se vòlè tè* (Attorneys, notaries, surveyors: all practice land theft), in Karen Richman, "They Will Remember Me in the House: The *Pwen* of Haitian Transnational Migration" (Ph.D. diss., University of Virginia, 1992), 144.

190 Yanick Guiteau Dandin, e-mail correspondence, 21 January 2001.

191 Paul de Man, *Allegories of Reading: Figural Language in Rousseau, Nietzsche, Rilke, and Proust* (New Haven, CT: Yale University Press, 1979), 273.

192 As elaborated by J. L. Austin at the outset of his classic *How to Do Things with Words*, "constative" speech refers to statements that might be evaluated as true or false, in distinction to performatives, "in which to *say* something is to *do* something." This is a distinction that Austin actually goes on to undermine in a later lecture, when he acknowledges that every performative can also be read as a constative, just as every constative contains a degree of performativity in the sheer act of saying something. J. L. Austin, *How to Do Things with Words: The William James Lectures Delivered at Harvard University in 1955* (Cambridge, MA: Harvard University Press, 1962), 2–3 and 12.

193 De Man, *Allegories of Reading*, 273. For a discussion of de Man's essay with reference to Canadian laws banning potlatches among First Nations peoples in the late nineteenth century, see Christopher Bracken, *The Potlatch Papers: A Colonial Case History* (Chicago: University of Chicago Press, 1997), 121–127. My thanks to Jacqueline Shea Murphy for recommending Bracken's book.

194 In introducing the second edition of his book, St. John disclosed that he had "trustworthy testimony that in 1887 cannibalism was more rampant than ever," explaining: "A black Government dares not greatly interfere, as its power is founded on the goodwill of the masses, ignorant and deeply tainted with fetish-worship." Writing in the late 1880s as well, Froude attributed what he characterized as the Haitian state's recent disinclination to prosecute crimes of "Vaudoux" to fear of negative exposure: "A few years ago persons guilty of these infamies were tried and punished, now they are left alone, because to prosecute and convict them would be to acknowledge the truth of the indictment." St. John, *Hayti, or The Black Republic*, xii; and James Anthony Froude, *The English in the West Indies, or, The Bow of Ulysses* (1888; New York: Charles Scribner's Sons, 1900), 344.

195 Arthur de Gobineau, *Essai sur l'inégalité des races humaines* (Paris: Éditions Pierre Belfond, 1967), 76, 77.

196 As an example of this, see Stephen Bonsal, *The American Mediterranean* (New York: Moffat, Yard, 1913), 90.

197 See J. Michael Dash, *The Other America: Caribbean Literature in a New World Context* (Charlottesville: University Press of Virginia, 1998), 45.

198 Gobineau, *De l'inégalité des races humaines*; quoted in Firmin, *The Equality of the Human Races*, 220.

199 Firmin, *The Equality of the Human Races*, 339–340.

200 See as well, for example, Frederick Douglass's "The Claims of the Negro Ethnologically Considered: An Address Delivered in Hudson, Ohio, on 12 July 1854," in *The Frederick Douglass Papers*, ser. 1, ed. J. W. Blassingame (New Haven, CT: Yale University Press, 1982). Douglass served as minister resident and consul general to Haiti from 1889 to 1891.

201 Firmin, *The Equality of the Human Races*, 340.

202 "The cathedrals are slowly emptying. . . . Never has God's blessed flock suffered such a long crisis. Does not every sign seem to announce the coming of the last days? . . . The fact is, religious faith is dying." Ibid., 341.

203 Ibid., 341–343.

204 Ibid., 341. Gérarde Magloire-Danton makes the important point that Firmin "does not minimize the practice of Vodou in Haiti nor does he insist on its gradual disappearance as do his fellow Haitian thinkers, Hannibal Price, Louis Joseph Janvier, and Démesvar Delorme." Magloire-Danton, "Anténor Firmin and Jean Price-Mars: Revolution, Memory, Humanism," *Small Axe* 18 (September 2005): 161.

205 Firmin, *The Equality of the Human Races*, 361.

206 Price, *De la réhabilitation de la race noire*, 697.

207 Janvier, *La République d'Haïti et ses visiteurs*, 123. Janvier was the son of a
Protestant tailor and grandson of a peasant, who lived for many years in
Paris, studying medicine and political science there. He was an impassioned
advocate for the Haitian peasant in his published writings, and, as a leader
of the "ultranational" wing of the National party, called for land reforms
through the dissolution of large estates and extension of the system of
peasant smallholdings. See Nicholls, *From Dessalines to Duvalier*, 114.

208 Janvier, *La République d'Haïti et ses visiteurs*, ii.

209 Ibid., 84–107.

210 Ibid., 94.

211 Kersuzan, quoted in Peters, *La croix contre l'asson*, 248.

212 Price, *De la réhabilitation de la race noire*, 444.

213 Ibid., 492.

214 Ibid., 413.

215 Ibid., 419.

216 Ibid., 418–419.

217 Ibid., 442. Price spells this word variously as *vaudoux*, *vaudou*, and *voudou*.

218 Ibid., 442–443. Note Ira Lowenthal's observation, based on his ethnographic research in southern Haiti, that "the Haitian Creole term
vodoû . . . refers simply to a type of dance often held in the Haitian countryside, which does not necessarily occur in conjunction with religious ceremonial." Lowenthal, "Ritual Performance and Religious Experience: A
Service for the Gods in Southern Haiti," *Journal of Anthropological Research*
34, no. 3 (Autumn 1978): 393. My thanks to Terry Rey for drawing my attention to this article.

219 Price, *De la réhabilitation de la race noire*, 415.

220 Citing St. John's challenge to the incredulous to spend only twenty-four
hours in a Haitian town to be convinced of his charges, Price renewed the
proposition and offered a preview, again explicitly gendered, of what the
observer would witness: "two women, three at the most, poorly clothed,
barefoot, miserable scarves on their heads, flinging themselves about with
all their force, rather than dancing, shouting themselves hoarse under the
pretext of singing, for a day, an entire night, but in vain, neither attaining
the *monter-loi* themselves, nor transmitting around them the least nervous
contagion to whomever, male or female." Ibid., 443.

221 Emmanuel C. Paul writes: "We must wait until 1885 to count a first ethnographer, who is almost unknown [today]: we are referring to D. Trouillot who, on this date, published an ethnographic sketch entitled, 'Le Vodou
haïtien.'" Paul, *L'ethnographie en Haïti: Ses initiateurs, son état actuel, ses tâches,
et son avenir* (Port-au-Prince: Imprimerie de l'État, 1949), 12. Likewise,
Jacques Oriol, Léonce Viaud, and Michel Aubourg write that Trouillot
was "considered by all the first Haitian ethnographer." Oriol, Viaud, and
Aubourg, *Le mouvement folklorique en Haïti* (Port-au-Prince: Imprimerie de

l'État, 1952), 17. I located a copy of Trouillot's short book at the Biblio-thèque Haïtienne des Frères de l'Instruction Chrétienne in Port-au-Prince; the title page is handwritten, and it is only here that the spelling *le Vaudoun* appears; elsewhere in the book it is *le Vaudoux*.

222 Personal communication with Peter Frisch, 8 November 2002. I am in-debted to Mr. Frisch for sharing his research with me. Thanks as well to Maxime Dehoux, president of the Association de Généalogie d'Haïti, for referring me to Mr. Frisch.

223 Trouillot, *Esquisse ethnographique*, 10.

224 Ibid., 11.

225 Ibid., 9 and 10–11.

226 Ibid., 15.

227 Serge Larose, in fact, notes the parallel between ethnographic discourses of the inevitable and inexorable decline of these practices and those that prac-titioners rehearse themselves, citing both Trouillot's 1885 monograph and a 1955 article by Alfred Métraux entitled "La comédie rituelle dans la posses-sion." Larose, "The Meaning of Africa in Haitian Vodu," 87.

228 Trouillot, *Esquisse ethnographique*, 20.

229 Ibid., 28.

230 Ibid., 20.

231 Ibid., 22–23.

232 Ibid., 26.

233 Ibid., 17.

234 Philippe Delisle, *Le catholicisme en Haïti au XIXe siècle: Le rêve d'une "Bretagne noire," 1860–1915* (Paris: Éditions Karthala, 2003), 91.

235 On Kersuzan's appointment, see J. M. Jan, *Histoire religieuse du Cap: "Notes et documents"* (Port-au-Prince: Éditions Henri Deschamps, 1949), 128.

236 "Pastoral letter of Monseigneur François-Marie Kersuzan, bishop of Cap-Haïtien, 6 janvier 1896," reprinted in Peters, *La croix contre l'asson*, 241–242. See also J. M. Jan, *Collecta III: Pour l'histoire religieuse du diocèse du Cap-Haïtien* (Port-au-Prince: Éditions Henri Deschamps, 1958), 49–50.

237 Kersuzan, *Conférence populaire sur le vaudoux*, 3.

238 Péan, *L'illusion héroïque*, 123. In his first "Conférence populaire sur le vau-doux" on 2 August 1896, Kersuzan explained his insistence that the cam-paign be called a "crusade": "The valiant newspaper *La Croix* summoned us to the crusade and is not afraid to propose to you as a rallying cry that which Christian Europe repeated in the past, in arming itself against the Turk, enemy of civilization: *God wants it!* Let's take hold of this gloriously historic word. God wants us to free ourselves from any yoke foreign to his law, because he has intentions of mercy and love for Haiti." Kersuzan, *Conférence populaire sur le vaudoux*, 21.

239 For biographical information on Auguste, see Péan, *L'illusion héroïque*, as well as Charles Dupuy, *Le coin de l'histoire*, vol. 2 (Port-au-Prince: Presses de l'Imprimeur, 2002), 55–59; and Daniel Supplice, *Dictionnaire biographique*

des personnalités politiques de la République d'Haïti, 1804–2001 (Belgium: Lannoo Imprimerie, 2001), 63–64. Dupuy describes Auguste as having been, for much of his life, the *premier citoyen* of Cap-Haïtien. A strong supporter of Firmin's candidacy for the presidency in 1902, he later served as mayor of Cap-Haïtien. See Dupuy, *Le coin de l'histoire*, 55–59.

240 Dain Borges, "Healing and Mischief: Witchcraft in Brazilian Law and Literature, 1890–1922," in *Crime and Punishment in Latin America: Law and Society since Colonial Times*, ed. Ricardo D. Salvatore, Carlos Aguirre, and Gilbert M. Joseph (Durham, NC: Duke University Press, 2001), 185.

241 See, for example, ibid.; and Palmié, *Wizards and Scientists*. Although Cuban and Brazilian ethnographic traditions had roots in criminal anthropology, this was not the case in Haiti. This will be discussed in chapter 4.

242 See Élie Lhérisson, "Du vaudou: Étude de quelques manifestations psychiques et somatiques observées chez les danseuses," *La Lanterne médicale* 2, no. 3 (20 March 1899): 19–23. Lhérisson's theories were elaborated upon (and critiqued) by another medical doctor, J. C. Dorsainvil, who in 1913 published research on Vodou in the journal *Haïti médicale* that became the basis for his book *Vodou et névrose*, in which he defined the religion as "a hereditary, racial, religious psycho-neurosis." Dorsainvil, *Vodou et névrose* (1931; Port-au-Prince: Éditions Fardin, 1975), 58. Catts Pressoir also discusses the strong interest of J. B. Dehoux—who played a major role in the institutionalization of Haitian medicine and especially medical education in the 1870s and 1880s—late in his life (he died in 1893) in "our medical folklore and superstitions of our countryside." Although the agenda of Dehoux's research in these areas is unclear from this brief mention, elsewhere in his book Pressoir also notes the physician's abiding interest in botanical research. Pressoir, *La médecine en Haïti* (Port-au-Prince: Imprimerie Modèle, 1927), 85, 82–83. On Dehoux's career, see Monsieur le Juge Bourjolly, *À la mémoire honorée du Docteur J.-B. Dehoux* (Port-au-Prince: Imprimerie J. Verrollot, 1900). On the early history of Haitian medicine, in addition to Pressoir, see Ary Bordes, *Évolution des sciences de la santé et de l'hygiène publique en Haïti*, vol. 1 (Port-au-Prince: Imprimerie Deschamps, 1980); and Brodwin, *Medicine and Morality in Haiti*, 23–55.

243 See Borges, "Healing and Mischief"; Palmié, *Wizards and Scientists*; and Bronfman, *Measures of Equality*, on the influence of the theories of the Italian criminologist Cesare Lombroso on these burgeoning fields in Brazil and Cuba.

244 I was able to examine issues of this journal dating from April 1892 to April 1895, and from December 1899 to June 1912. Unfortunately, I have not been able to access volumes from the intervening years.

245 "Séance publique du 10 Avril 1904: Réception du Docteur Léon Audain," in *Revue de la Société de législation* 11: 112. See also Léon Audain, *Le mal d'Haïti: Ses causes et son traitement* (Port-au-Prince: Imprimerie J. Verrollot, 1908), 56–57. For a detailed discussion of Audain's career, see Pressoir, *La*

médecine en Haïti. See also Brenda Gayle Plummer's discussion of his work in *Haiti and the Great Powers, 1902–1915* (Baton Rouge: Louisiana State University Press, 1988), 30–31.

246 Palmié, *Wizards and Scientists*, 246.

247 Msgr. J. M. Jan attributes the founding of *La Croix* to Kersuzan. See Jan, *Collecta III*, 2 and 58; and Jan, *Le Cap-Haïtien*, 309–10. *La Croix* figured *vaudoux* and Protestantism as "two enemies of religion and of the country." Jan notes that "at the same time as its campaign against superstition, the newspaper led the struggle against Protestants. The sect, very few in number, came to hold important posts in all the administrations and schools. The journal . . . pointed out its combative spirit, its intolerance, and the pernicious influence that it exercised." Jan, *Collecta III*, 60.

248 The latter were growing in the north in the mid-1890s through the efforts, in part, of a French-born, American-educated pastor named Elie Marc who arrived in Cap-Haïtien in 1894, pastored the Église Baptiste du Trou du Nord, and with local collaborators, proceeded to organize congregations across the department. See Pressoir, "Le protestantisme en Haïti," 395. On the history of Haitian Protestantism, see also Catts Pressoir, *Le protestantisme haïtien*, vol. 1, pt. 1 (Port-au-Prince: Imprimerie de la Société Biblique et des Livres Religieux d'Haïti, 1945); Pressoir, *Le protestantisme haïtien*, vol. 1, pt. 2 (Port-au-Prince: Imprimerie de la Société Biblique et des Livres Religieux d'Haïti, 1946); and Pressoir, *Le protestantisme haïtien*, vol. 2 (Port-au-Prince: Imprimerie de Séminaire Adventiste, 1976).

249 Micial M. Nérestant argues that Kersuzan's campaign must also be understood in light of the dictates set forth by the First Vatican Council and religious politics in fin-de-siècle France: "It is known, in effect, that at the end of the 19th century and beginning of the 20th century, a true anti-Protestant campaign developed in France. Protestantism was attacked as a baleful religious system, engendering condemnable socio-political ideologies and behaviors, detrimental to the homeland." Nérestant, *Religions et politique en Haïti* (Paris: Karthala, 1994), 131.

250 "Lettre de l'archevêque du Cap-Haïtien au supérieur général, 14 septembre 1892"; quoted in Delisle, *Le catholicisme en Haïti au XIXe siècle*, 76.

251 Both Auguste and Manigat were affiliated with the National Party. See Péan, *L'illusion héroïque*, 85; and David Nicholls, "The Wisdom of Salomon: Myth or Reality," *Journal of Interamerican Studies and World Affairs* 20, no. 4 (November 1978): 382. See also Manigat, *Conférence sur le vaudoux*.

252 Editorial, *La Croix*, 16 May 1896; quoted in Péan, *L'illusion héroïque*, 124. Péan has changed the spelling to "vodou" throughout his study.

253 Ibid., 126. Note that church literatures against *vaudoux* and "superstition" usually collapsed popular distinctions between the identities of *oungan* and *bòkò*, referring to all male religious elders as *bòkò*.

254 Alexis, "Bocors à la campagne," *La Croix*, 19 September 1896. I was able to examine all of the issues of *La Croix* which appeared between 25 July 1896

and 16 January 1897. For the issues of the newspaper that fall outside of these dates, I rely on Péan's work.

255 Delisle, *Le catholicisme en Haïti au XIX siècle*, 95.

256 Péan notes that the bishop of Cayes, Monseigneur Morice, had made remarks about the former president's affiliations shortly after the latter's death. See Péan, *L'illusion héroïque*, 128. However, Laënnec Hurbon quotes from a Port-au-Prince police circular issued to arrondissement commanders in May 1896, under Hyppolite's presidency, about a recent "recrudescence" of "la danse du vodou," which ordered local authorities to see that "delinquents" were "delivered to justice and punished in conformity with the law." Hurbon, *Comprendre Haïti*, 147.

257 Alexis, "Vaudoux: La mecque," *La Croix*, 25 July 1896; and Alexis, "Bocors à la campagne," *La Croix*, 19 September 1896. The Hyppolite government is also remembered for its infrastructural modernizations.

258 See "Obeahmen Working against Hippolite [*sic*]: But Haiti's President Is a Voodoo Himself and Jamaica's Laws Are Rigid," *New York Times*, 3 December 1895; and "Haiti's President Dead: Florville Gelan Hippolyte [*sic*] as Soldier and Politician," *New York Times*, 26 March 1896. Note that a popular song collected in the mid-twentieth century by Harold Courlander attributes Hyppolite's sudden death to the supernatural intervention of a political rival and *oungan* in Jacmel, Mérisier Jeannis, who was leading a rebellion against Hyppolite that the president was on his way to put down when he suffered his fatal heart attack. For an analysis of this song and its history, see Michael Largey, *Vodou Nation: Haitian Art Music and Cultural Nationalism* (Chicago: University of Chicago Press, 2006), 64–69. See also Harold Courlander, "Haiti's Political Folksongs," *Opportunity* 19, no. 4 (1941): 114–118.

259 Quoted in Peters, *La croix contre l'asson*, 246.

260 Jan, *Collecta III*, 60.

261 See the report in *La Croix*, 8 August 1896.

262 Kersuzan, *Conférence populaire sur le vaudoux*, 3.

263 Ibid., 13.

264 Ibid., 10.

265 Ibid., 8.

266 Ibid., 17.

267 Nicholls, *From Dessalines to Duvalier*, 117. He is paraphrasing an article entitled "Les dernier mots de Salnave," *L'Avant-Garde*, 27 April 1882.

268 Janvier, *La République d'Haïti et ses visiteurs*, 372 and 373.

269 For example, that Catholicism was itself a form of primitive fetishism, that priests made slaves of their congregants, that the church was a source of social division and discord, and that it robbed those who were already impoverished.

270 His consistent use of the pronoun "we" throughout the address reinforces that identification.

271 Kersuzan, "Allocution prononcée contre le vaudoux à l'Hospice Justinien, le 13 février 1898," reprinted in Peters, *La croix contre l'asson*, 249. See also Jan, *Collecta III*, 56.

272 Interestingly, Firmin's letter and Kersuzan's response were published as an appendix to the latter's address in 1896; see n. 273 below.

273 Kersuzan, *Conférence populaire sur le vaudoux*, 16 and 17.

274 Anténor Firmin, "Anténor Firmin à Monseigneur Kersuzan, 3 août 1896," appendix to *Conférence populaire sur le vaudoux donnée par Monseigneur l'Évêque du Cap-Haïtien, le 2 août 1896* (Port-au-Prince: Imprimerie H. Amblard, 1896).

275 Kersuzan, *Conférence populaire sur le vaudoux*, 22.

276 Max Manigat notes that *gombo* (or *gonbo*) refers in northern Haiti to a "meal in honor of the spirits." See Max Manigat, *Mots créoles du nord d'Haïti: Origines, histoire, souvenirs* (Coconut Creek, FL: Educa Vision, 2007), 135–136.

277 See "Correspondance, Saint-Marc, le 5 août 1896," *La Croix*, 14 August 1896. See also "Lutte pratique contre le vaudoux," *La Croix*, 24 October 1896.

278 "Correspondance des Cayes," *La Croix*, 8 August 1896. For inventories of objects confiscated in high-profile raids, see "Correspondance des Gonaïves: Le grand vaudoux de Hinche," *La Croix*, 10 October 1896; and "Chasse aux bocors—Terrier-rouge," *La Croix*, 12 December 1896.

279 Alexis, "Le vaudoux: Vainqueur ou vaincu," *La Croix*, 17 October 1896.

280 "On nous rapporte le fait suivant comme s'étant passé à Quartier-Morin," *La Croix*, 1 August 1896.

281 "Le vaudoux et l'honneur national," *La Croix*, 24 October 1896.

282 Emmanuel Oreste Zamor was born in Hinche in 1861. After entering the army he served as *commandant de la place* of Saint-Michel and then of Hinche. See Supplice, *Dictionnaire biographique*, 697.

283 The presiding *oungan* was eventually arrested; however, Zamor himself seems not to have been. See "Un grand vaudoux à Hinche," *La Croix*, 26 September 1896; and "Correspondance des Gonaïves: Le grand vaudoux de Hinche," *La Croix*, 10 October 1896.

284 Olivine Pierre and her group were tried, convicted, and sentenced to three months imprisonment, plus a fine of 30 gourdes for Pierre and 15 gourdes for the others. Their drums were to be burned publicly at the local marketplace. See "Chasse aux vaudoux: Cap-Haïtien et Plaine-du-Nord," *La Croix*, 9 January 1897; and "Chasse au vaudoux: Olivine condamnée," *La Croix*, 16 January 1897.

285 "Chasse aux vaudoux," *La Croix*, 9 January 1897. For another reference to public celebrations of Haitian Independence Day on the parts of Vodouizan, this time from Dondon in 1912, see Jan, *Le Cap-Haïtien*, 320.

286 Jan, *Collecta III*, 59; and Péan, *L'illusion héroïque*, 133.

287 Péan, *L'illusion héroïque*, 133.

288 Jan, *Collecta III*, 55.

289 Péan, *L'illusion héroïque*, 133.

290 Jan, *Collecta III*, 55.

291 Quoted in Peters, *La croix contre l'asson*, 249. Peters spells this word in multiple ways in compiling church documents.

292 Ibid., 250. See also Jan, *Collecta III*, 56.

293 Péan, *L'illusion héroïque*, 134.

294 Ibid., 135, especially n. 1. See also Jan, *Collecta III*, 61.

295 Péan, *L'illusion héroïque*, 135.

296 See Jan, *Collecta III*, 60.

297 Ibid., 58.

298 Ibid., 60.

299 Ibid., 62.

300 Cited in Péan, *L'illusion héroïque*, 137. This was taken from *Le Bulletin de Notre dame du perpétuel secours*, founded by Msgr. Kersuzan.

301 See also Jan, *Collecta III*, 63.

302 Notably, the name of another member of this spirit family, Ogou Panama, came from a story about this former president. As the legend goes, Hyppolite was embarking on a mission to suppress political opposition in the southern town of Jacmel when his hallmark panama hat tumbled to the ground. His son took this as a bad omen and begged his father not to go, but to no avail. Hyppolite fell unconscious from his horse before even reaching the outskirts of Port-au-Prince and died not long thereafter. For a transcription of a song narrating these events, see Harold Courlander, *The Drum and the Hoe: Life and Lore of the Haitian People* (Berkeley: University of California Press, 1960), 151–152; and see also the analysis of this story in Brown, "Systematic Remembering, Systematic Forgetting," 78.

303 Péan, *L'illusion héroïque*, 137–138.

304 J. M. Jan, *Monographie religieuse des paroisses du Cap-Haïtien* (Port-au-Prince: Éditions Henri Deschamps, 1950), 47. See also Péan, *L'illusion héroïque*, 138.

305 Today, the town is the destination of pilgrims from across the country in honor of Ogou/Sen Jak, who come to bathe in Trou Sen Jak, a small pond that fills with mud during the summer rainy season. For more on the annual July pilgrimage to Plaine-du-Nord in honor of Ogou/Saint-Jacques, see Donald J. Cosentino, "It's All for You, Sen Jak!," in *Sacred Arts of Haitian Vodou*, ed. Donald J. Cosentino (Los Angeles: Fowler Museum of Cultural History, 1995), 243–265.

306 Jan, *Monographie religieuse des paroisses du Cap-Haïtien*, 49.

307 Ibid., 52.

308 Péan, *L'illusion héroïque*, 143. See the discussion of this episode in Léon Descos [French minister to Haiti, writing under the pseudonym Eugène Aubin], *En Haïti: Planteurs d'autrefois, négres d'aujourd'hui* (Paris: Armand Colin, 1910), 335–336.

309 Hurbon, *Le barbare imaginaire*, 129–130.

NOTES TO CHAPTER 3

1 Theodore Roosevelt, "Annual Message to Congress, 6 December, 1904," in *Encyclopedia of American Foreign Policy*, vol. 1, ed. Alexander DeConde, Richard Dean Burns, and Fredrik Logevall (New York: Charles Scribner, 1978), 221.

2 Hans Schmidt notes that on "the eve of the American intervention, 80 percent of government revenues were pledged to debt service." Schmidt, *The United States Occupation of Haiti, 1915–1934* (1971; New Brunswick, NJ: Rutgers University Press, 1995), 43.

3 Ibid., 38–41; and Mary A. Renda, *Taking Haiti: Military Occupation and the Culture of U.S. Imperialism* (Chapel Hill: University of North Carolina Press, 2001), 81–82.

4 See Schmidt, *The United States Occupation of Haiti*, 96–100; Suzy Castor, *L'occupation américaine d'Haïti* (Port-au-Prince: Imprimerie Henri Deschamps, 1988), 64–67; and Roger Gaillard, *Les blancs débarquent: 1917–1918; Hinche mise en croix* (Port-au-Prince: Imprimerie Le Natal, 1982), 130–133.

5 The question of whether the Haitian constitution ought to be revised to permit foreign landholding had been vigorously debated in Haiti since the nineteenth century.

6 See Castor, *L'occupation américaine d'Haïti*, 91, for a summary of these, including the law of 22 December 1922 authorizing the long-term lease of state lands to foreign investors; and the law of 20 February 1924 authorizing the lease of unoccupied lands and the sale of state properties to such parties. On the eve of the occupation, Haiti's major exports were coffee, logwood, sugar, and cacao; ibid., 20.

7 Paul Moral argued, as others have since, that "in the evolution of the Haitian rural world, the American occupation did not constitute, in effect, a chance or 'aberrant' event. To the contrary, the foreign intervention is the logical outcome of a terrible decade that threw alarm into the heart of the peasantry." He situates the effects of the occupation on the peasantry in the context of longer-standing demographic pressures that resulted in an increasing scarcity of arable land, and in the extension of foreign capital into Haitian agricultural and other enterprises. Moral, *Le paysan haïtien*, 60. See also Karen Richman's documentation of the systematic dispossession of Haitian peasant landholders in Léogâne by a member of the Haitian elite named Joseph Lacombe at the turn of the twentieth century as a form of debt collection. Amassing extensive holdings of coffee-producing lands in the hills, Lacombe likewise consolidated peasant smallholdings on the plains into vast sugarcane plantations, which he leased to the Haytian American Sugar Company (HASCO) in 1920. Richman, *Migration and Vodou*, 90–109.

8 Kethly Millet, *Les paysans haïtiens et l'occupation américaine d'Haïti, 1915–1930* (La Salle, Quebec: Collectif Paroles, 1978), 39.

9 See, for example, Michel-Rolph Trouillot's analysis: "The occupation . . . accelerated Haiti's economic, military, and political centralization, leaving the rest of the country unable to restrain the hegemonic tendencies of the 'Republic of Port-au-Prince.' It signalled the beginning of the end for the regional economies." Trouillot, *Haiti, State against Nation*, 104.

10 Haiti, of course, was by no means alone in this regard. Lauren Derby notes that during the U.S. occupation of the Dominican Republic (1916–1924), "a barrage of new legislation seeking to regulate daily life apparently took a heavy toll on a population traditionally accustomed to a maximum degree of independence. . . . During the U.S. occupation, cockfights were confined to Sundays and holidays, the use of 'witchcraft. . . . hoodooism, or other superstitious or deceitful methods' in popular medicine were banned, and forced labor on public works was instituted." Derby, "Haitians, Magic, and Money: *Raza* and Society in the Haitian-Dominican Borderlands, 1900 to 1937," *Comparative Studies in Society and History* 36, no. 3 (July 1994): 505.

11 The Inquiry into the Occupation and Administration of Haiti and Santo Domingo was convened to investigate persistent reports of marine misconduct in both places. The charges included summary executions of prisoners without trial, the torture of prisoners, a "take no prisoners" policy, the indiscriminate killing of peasants in the pursuit of insurgents, the burning and pillaging of remote villages to the same end, and forced-labor abuses.

12 See "Treaty between the United States and the Republic of Haiti," in James H. McCrocklin, *Garde d'Haïti, 1915–1934* (Annapolis, MD: United States Naval Institute, 1956), 241.

13 See H. P. Davis, *Black Democracy: The Story of Haiti* (New York: Lincoln MacVeagh/Dial Press, 1928), 194–195. By December 1916 the gendarmerie had grown to 2,533 enlisted men. McCrocklin, *Garde d'Haïti*, 82.

14 She also wondered "what the effect of such a force would be after American withdrawal," speculating that one possible result could be the "self-maintenance in power of whomsoever has control of this force." Emily Greene Balch, "Public Order," in *Occupied Haiti: Being the Report of a Committee of Six Disinterested Americans Representing Organizations Exclusively American, Who, Having Personally Studied Conditions in Haiti in 1926, Favor the Restoration of the Independence of the Negro Republic*, ed. Emily Greene Balch (New York: Writers, 1927), 131.

15 McCrocklin attributes what he characterizes as the original misnomer of the force to a translation error in the French version of the 1915 Haitian-American treaty, in which the English term "constabulary" was rendered as *gendarmerie*, connoting "a unit engaged purely in police activities." McCrocklin, *Garde d'Haïti*, 177. See Michel-Rolph Trouillot's discussion of the post-occupation legacy of the civil/military ambiguity of this force in *Haiti, State against Nation*, 106–107.

16 McCrocklin, *Garde d'Haïti*, 147.

17 Ibid., 82.

18 Blair Niles, *Black Haiti: A Biography of Africa's Eldest Daughter* (New York: Grosset & Dunlap, 1926), 178. See also Trouillot, *Haiti, State against Nation*, 105.

19 McCrocklin, *Garde d'Haïti*, 61.

20 Ibid., 187.

21 Arthur C. Millspaugh, *Haiti under American Control, 1915–1930* (Boston: World Peace Foundation, 1931), 104.

22 McCrocklin, *Garde d'Haïti*, 129. See also Balch, *Occupied Haiti*, 132.

23 Frederic May Wise and Meigs O. Frost, *A Marine Tells It to You* (New York: J. H. Sears., 1929), 134–135.

24 See Renda, *Taking Haiti*, 128.

25 Wise and Frost, *A Marine Tells It to You,* 310.

26 See Balch, "Public Order," in Balch, *Occupied Haiti*, 133. One of Balch's collaborators noted that the Marine Corps already had the reputation at this point of being the most discriminatory division of the U.S. military forces, "'prid[ing] itself on absolute exclusion of the black American'"; quoted in Addie Hunton and Balch, "Racial Relations," in Balch, *Occupied Haiti*, 116. The marines were the last of the military services to permit African Americans to enlist, creating segregated units only in 1942. Until then, blacks were not even allowed to serve as messengers at marine headquarters in Washington, D.C. See Garry Donaldson, *The History of African-Americans in the Military* (Malaba, FL: Krieger, 1991), 106; and Martin Binkin and Mark J. Eitelberg with Alvin J. Schexnider and Marvin M. Smith, *Blacks and the Military* (Washington, DC: Brookings Institution, 1982), 18.

27 James Weldon Johnson, "Self-Determining Haiti, Part 2: What the United States Has Accomplished," *Nation,* 4 September 1920, 266.

28 Millet, *Les paysans haïtiens et l'occupation américaine*, 68.

29 See Trouillot, *Haiti, State against Nation*, 103; and Dupuy, *Haiti in the World Economy*, 134.

30 Millet, *Les paysans haïtiens et l'occupation américaine*, 68.

31 Ibid., 68–69.

32 Report of Major Franklin A. Hart on the Haitian Garde to the United States Marine Corps Commandant, 31 July 1934, quoted in McCrocklin, *Garde d'Haïti*, 17.

33 Dantès Bellegarde, *L'occupation américaine d'Haïti: Ses conséquences morales et économiques* (Port-au-Prince: Chéraquit, 1929), 12 n.

34 Assembled by the local rural police and overseen by the commune's *commandant de place*, those recruited were required to report at 6 a.m. on a Monday and work until 6 p.m. on Thursday, or until the repairs were finished. Through an innovation in the 1864 Code Rural, peasants of means could escape the labor requirement by paying four gourdes a day to replace themselves on the workforce. Interestingly, Jennie Smith notes that today in the Grand'Anse, on the southwestern peninsula, the word *kòve* refers to a popular collective work arrangement that "involves both labor exchange

and monetary payment." However in Kalfounò, in Haiti's northeastern mountains, "the meaning of *kòve* resembled that of the French term *corvée*, which connotes forced labor and drudgery." She further notes: "I was told by residents there that *kòve* elicited powerfully negative collective memories of chain gangs—namely, those instituted as part of the conscripted-labor projects conducted by U.S. troops during the 1915–1934 occupation in order to build roads, military headquarters, and other public structures." Smith, *When the Hands Are Many*, 86 and 87.

35 On the subject of these articles, J. Saint-Armand, editor of a 1903 edition of the 1864 Code Rural, noted that "this mode of upkeep and repair of public ways, consecrated by old customs . . . gives rise to abuses." Characterizing this section of the Code Rural as fundamentally at odds with Haitian republicanism, he hoped that it would "soon be replaced by a legislation more consistent with our institutions." J. Saint-Armand, *Le Code rural d'Haïti, publié avec commentaires et formulaire, notes et annexes à l'usage des fonctionnaires, officiers et agents de la police rurale* (Port-au-Prince: Imprimerie Vve J. Chenet, 1903), 37–38 and 43.

36 See the citation from *L'ABC*, 22 May 1897; quoted in Gaillard, *Les blancs débarquent: 1916–1917; La république autoritaire* (Port-au-Prince: Imprimerie Le Natal, 1981), 122.

37 See Hurbon on how, during the occupation, the Americans found an "ideological *prêt-à-porter*" in the decrees and circulars against Vodou. Hurbon, *Le barbare imaginaire*, 121.

38 Gaillard, *Hinche mise en croix*, 83; and McCrocklin, *Garde d'Haïti*, 95.

39 Quoted in Schmidt, *The United States Occupation of Haiti*, 100.

40 See Gaillard, *Hinche mise en croix*, 43.

41 Ibid., 43. Gaillard argues that the *kòve* must be considered a significant factor, among a complex of others, in the exodus of Haitian workers in unprecedented numbers from affected regions to work on plantations in Cuba and the Dominican Republic. He quotes Brigadier General Eli K. Cole as discounting a report in October 1917 of increased emigration from the region of the Cul-de-Sac plain to the Dominican Republic on account of the *kòve*. Ibid., 46.

42 In mid-October 1917, for example, *L'Essor* protested the double standard whereby peasants cultivating properties owned by Haitians were targeted for the *kòve*, while those working in fields owned by foreigners were left alone. See Gaillard, *Hinche mise en croix*, 44 and 43. Further protests appeared in the press as marines invoked paragraphs 61–63 of the Code Rural in borrowing oxcarts and livestock from peasants in order to transport materials for road-building purposes. Although article 63 provided that such requisitions were limited to one day per week, this specification was rarely followed, and complaints that equipment and mules were not being returned promptly or at all were published in several newspapers as the road construction got under way. See ibid., 43.

43 *Inquiry into Occupation and Administration of Haiti and Santo Domingo; Hearings before a Select Committee on Haiti and Santo Domingo, United States Senate, Sixty-Seventh Congress, First and Second Sessions . . .* (Washington, DC: Government Printing Office, 1922), 1:560. Hereafter cited as *Senate Hearings.*

44 Gaillard writes: "Our rider was wearing a helmet to shield from the sun, leggings for crossing the thickets, and, obviously, black skin." See Gaillard, *Hinche mise en croix,* 152–153.

45 *Senate Hearings,* 479–480: "Maj. Turner: 'I have no doubt there were many killed in the corvee.' The Chairman: 'You mean that many were killed in attempting to escape from work under the corvee?' Maj. Turner: 'Yes.' The Chairman: 'When they would jump and run they would be shot?' Maj. Turner: 'They were shot.'"

46 Millet, *Les paysans haïtiens et l'occupation américaine,* 67.

47 Johnson, "Self-Determining Haiti, Part 2," 265.

48 Gaillard, *Hinche mise en croix,* 224.

49 This was followed in October 1918 by a second and final order terminating the *kòve.*

50 See "The Brigade Commander to the Major General Commandant, Report of Investigation of Certain Irregularities Alleged to Have Been Committed by Officers and Enlisted Men in the Republic of Haiti," 13 March 1920, held in Reference Section Geographical Files, Marine Corps History and Museums Division, Washington, DC.

51 Often originating in the north of the country, *kako* armies would first take the major towns and cities of their department, then travel to Port-au-Prince and attempt to occupy the capital and oversee the legislative election of their candidate. See Plummer, *Haiti and the Great Powers,* 36–37. See also Jean Casimir's discussion of the identity and significance of *kako* in his *La culture opprimée* (Delmas, Haiti: Imprimerie Lakay, 2001), 176–179. Harold Courlander notes that "in some popular songs the Marines were referred to by the peaceful peasantry as 'cacos in khaki.'" Courlander, *The Drum and the Hoe,* 159.

52 *Senate Hearings,* 244. This view was shared by certain marines who had been stationed in these regions during the enforcement of the *kòve.* A former marine, Frederick C. Baker, interviewed about the illegal prolongation of the *kòve* and reports of atrocities in the north, testified: "It is my opinion that the *corvée* illegally formed after October 1, 1918, and after the Haitian public generally knew and well understood that all *corvée* and forced labor had been ordered suspended constituted the chiefest factor in the dissatisfaction which led to revolution and it is well understood that the first caco forces were largely recruited from this last formed *corvée.*" *Senate Hearings,* 466.

53 James Weldon Johnson, "Self-Determining Haiti, Part 1: The American Occupation," *Nation,* 28 August 1920, 237. The anthropologist Elsie Clews Parsons reinforced Johnson's view of the occupation as being self-

perpetuating in a letter to the *New York Times* in the fall of 1920. Having spent time in Haiti eight years earlier "on a riding trip in the interior of the island," she was interested "to learn why so many bandits have developed in Haiti since the American occupation," wondering: "Is it possible that the term bandit has become confused with the term nationalist?" Elsie Clews Parsons, letter to the editor, *New York Times*, 15 October 1920; quoted in *Senate Hearings*, 245.

54 McCrocklin, *Garde d'Haïti*, 149.

55 The lack of coherent policy direction from Washington became a complaint for marine officers posted in Haiti, who, when U.S. public sentiment turned against the occupation, felt that they were being scapegoated.

56 Alex Lichtenstein argues that far from representing an aberration or anomaly in the "New South's" modernization efforts, convict labor, or "penal slavery," must be understood as internal and critical to those processes: "The convict lease was not the persistence of a 'precapitalist' form of labor coercion, but the extension and elaboration of a new forced-labor system wholly compatible with regional industrial development and the continuation of racial domination." Lichtenstein, *Twice the Work of Free Labor: The Political Economy of Convict Labor in the New South* (London: Verso, 1996), 13.

57 As will be discussed later in the chapter, during his post on the island Wirkus was apparently inducted into La Gonâve's *sosyete kongo*, a cooperative labor and mutual benefit organization. He attributed this honor in part to the fact that he shared a name with one of Haiti's most legendary heads of state, Faustin Soulouque, who installed himself as emperor (Faustin I) in 1849.

58 Faustin Wirkus and Taney Dudley, *The White King of La Gonave* (Garden City, NY: Doubleday, Doran, 1931), 205–206.

59 *Rural Code of Haiti, Gendarmerie d'Haïti*, trans. R. S. Hooker (Port-au-Prince: Imprimerie Edm. Chenet, 1916), 69–70.

60 Interview with Étienne Germain, Tabarre, Haiti, 15 June 1997. My thanks to Yanick Guiteau Dandin for introducing me to Germain.

61 Of this magistrate, Wirkus noted: "Justice Camelo was a useful if not exactly an admirable citizen. He would have been less useful to me had he been more admirable. His findings were always, after I had been in Petite Rivière a short time, in accordance with my wishes." Wirkus and Dudley, *The White King of La Gonave*, 186.

62 Ibid., 187.

63 *Senate Hearings*, 673.

64 The language of "clean-up" was frequently used with regard to occupation campaigns against "voodoo," as, for example, when Major Philip T. Case reported to the *New York Times* that "there is still a great deal of voodoo worship down there, and we ran into more or less of that, and we had to clean up and disarm one voodoo stronghold up in the mountains." N. A., "Marine Officer on Haiti," *New York Times*, 31 October 1920.

65 *Senate Hearings*, 692.

66 Ibid., 630. As in the past, U.S. military-official and other imperial commentators attributed this apparent tolerance or indifference on the part of former Haitian governments and ruling classes to their implication in such practices. See, for example, *National Geographic Magazine*, December 1920, 503.

67 *Senate Hearings*, 630–631.

68 Wirkus and Dudley, *The White King of La Gonave*, 167.

69 As Blair Niles wrote of such stories in her 1926 travelogue: "It is so easy to believe what has been countless times said; to believe what many before you have credited, for repetition greases the ways of belief." Niles, *Black Haiti*, 5.

70 Peter Hulme, *Colonial Encounters: Europe and the Native Caribbean, 1492–1797* (London and New York: Methuen, 1986), 84–87. As Hulme notes, "'cannibalism' is a term that has no application outside the discourse of European colonialism: it is never available as a 'neutral' word," that is, as a non-ideological one. It has always been the mark of the absolute other, who has to be bordered off from the conquering society even while being forcibly incorporated into—or, as Hulme might say, consumed by—it.

71 See, for example, Millet, *Les paysans haïtiens et l'occupation américaine*, and Castor, *L'occupation américaine d'Haïti*; both cite marine sources as references on this point.

72 Valéra Michaud, who had served as a *gendarme* in the Garde d'Haïti from 1917 to 1926, told Roger Gaillard in a 1970 interview that Batraville possessed *pwen* that could make him and his horse instantly invisible at will. See Roger Gaillard, *Les blancs débarquent: 1919–1934; La guérilla de Batraville* (Port-au-Prince: Imprimerie Le Natal, 1983), 62–63. See Gaillard's consideration (61–62) of whether or not Batraville was an *oungan*, there not being a consensus on this question among his informants. One of Batraville's secretaries, Claudius Chevry, emphasized that the rebel leader was considered a great healer by his troops: "There were several '*docteurs-feuilles*' in the army, for tending the wounded. But Benoît was the strongest of all. When the wound was serious, the preference was to go see Benoît" (66).

73 Wirkus and Dudley, *The White King of La Gonave*, 99.

74 John Houston Craige, *Black Bagdad* (New York: Minton, Balch, 1933), 28–29.

75 Letter from Barnett to Russell, 2 October 1919, printed in *Senate Hearings*, 1722.

76 Quoted in *Senate Hearings*, 427. Second quote from Report, Inquiry into Occupation and Administration of Haiti and the Dominican Republic, 67th Congress, 2nd Session, Report no. 794, 18.

77 The last paragraph of Barnett's letter to Russell read: "I want personal instructions sent to every officer and noncommissioned officer, both with the marines and the gendarmerie, that conditions as shown by the evidence in

the trial of the private above referred to must be corrected, and such action can not be tolerated for a moment; and I want every case thoroughly sifted and the guilty parties brought to justice. I think this is the most startling thing of its kind that has ever taken place in the Marine Corps, and I don't want anything of the kind to happen again. I think, judging by the knowledge gained only from the cases that have been brought before me, that the Marine Corps has been sadly lacking in right and justice, and I look to you to see that this is corrected and corrected at once." Printed in *Senate Hearings*, 1722–1723.

78 See John W. Blassingame, "The Press and American Intervention in Haiti and the Dominican Republic, 1904–1920," *Caribbean Studies* 9, no. 2 (July 1969): 27–43.

79 Editorial, *Nation*, 25 September 1920, 337–338.

80 "Natives in Haiti Ate Marine Officer; Naval Inquiry Court Testimony Cites Cases of Other Americans Slain and Mutilated; Gruesome Details Given; Lieut. Col. Hooker Tells of Practices of Bandits against Marines and Natives," *New York Times*, 4 January 1921.

81 "Record of Proceedings of a Court of Inquiry Convened at the Navy Department, Washington, October 19, 1920, by Order of the Secretary of the Navy, to Inquire Into the Conduct of the Personnel of the Naval Service That Has Served in Haiti since July 28, 1915," in *Senate Hearings*, 1667 and 1668.

82 These were Lieutenant Colonel Alexander S. Williams, Major Clarke H. Wells, Sergeant Dorcas L. Williams, former Private Ernest Lavoie, and former Sergeant Freeman Lang. Indeed, a report submitted by Barnett's successor, Marine Corps Major General Commandant John A. Lejeune, and Brigadier General Smedley D. Butler to the Secretary of the Navy just prior to the Mayo Inquiry, "Investigation of Offenses Alleged to Have Been Committed by Certain Officers of the Gendarmerie of Haiti at Hinche and Massade [*sic*], during the Winter of 1918–19," contains extensive incriminating evidence against these individuals, presented as positive fact. See *Senate Hearings*, 1753–1766.

83 The Mayo Naval Court of Inquiry regarded those charges as "ill considered, regrettable, and thoroughly unwarranted reflections on a portion of the United States Marine Corps which has performed difficult, dangerous, and delicate duty in Haiti in a manner which, instead of calling for adverse criticism, is entitled to the highest commendation." Printed in *Senate Hearings*, 1668.

84 *Senate Hearings*, 453.

85 *Senate Hearings*, 453–454. An interesting line of research would examine how the U.S. regime against "voodoo" in Haiti may have been conditioned by that against "brujería" in early republican Cuba, when rumors of black "brujos" ritually sacrificing white children produced panic among Havana elites and intensified the surveillance and persecution of Afro-Cubans.

86 See Millspaugh, *Haiti under American Control*, 175. See also Schmidt, *The United States Occupation of Haiti*, 134.

87 This was, in fact, a ploy surreptitiously rigged by the U.S. financial adviser in Haiti at that time, W. W. Cumberland, to demonstrate the independence of the Haitian client government from U.S. control. John Russell, who had been appointed American high commissioner in Haiti with the 1922 reorganization of the occupation that followed the Senate hearings, along with the State Department publicly averred that they had encouraged Borno not to exclude King but were powerless to intervene in his decision. See Schmidt, *The United States Occupation of Haiti*, 190.

88 The courts-martial ordered for the alleged perpetrators of these atrocities were among those canceled after the release of the Mayo report. Lejeune and Butler's report is printed in the *Senate Hearings*, 1753–1766.

89 See the discussion of the cases of Mike Morris and Lawrence Muth in Renda, *Taking Haiti*, 166–175. In particular, see her argument that "the stories of Muth and Morris suggest that the salience of cannibalism for marines had something to do with the fragility of national and racial identity in a paternalist occupation." Renda, *Taking Haiti*, 175.

90 One of the earlier witnesses to testify before the Senate committee was Reverend L. Ton Evans, a Baptist field secretary and missionary in Haiti, who had himself publicly decried marine abuses and lobbied for an investigative commission. Evans attempted to inject a dose of righteous outrage at several points during his testimony, referring to the "immoral and barbaric conduct" of military personnel in Haiti, who had grown progressively "more daring and defiant in their brutality and savagery" over the course of six years of occupation. *Senate Hearings*, 145–146.

91 Ibid., 578.

92 Ibid., 425.

93 Ibid., 578.

94 Wise and Frost, *A Marine Tells It to You*, 304.

95 *Senate Hearings*, 578–579.

96 Ibid., 433.

97 Testimony from the courts-martial cited elsewhere revealed "that these same men had been present at the execution of still one more Haitian prisoner five days earlier, also under the orders of the same lieutenant. There is no doubt but that those who were executed had already been taken prisoner and were shot without trial." Report, Inquiry into Occupation and Administration of Haiti and the Dominican Republic, 67th Congress, 2nd Session, Report no. 794, 18.

98 These court-martial files should be located in Record Group 125, Records of the Judge Advocate General (Navy), Entry 27, Proceedings of General Courts-Martial (unbound), 1866–1942. The Archives and Special Collections Branch of the Library of the Marine Corps likewise reported that it does not hold the transcripts of these courts-martial.

99 Colonel L. McCarty Little was the convening authority in the Johnson court-martial. His comments on the findings and sentence of that court-martial were read aloud during Frederick Spear's Senate hearing testimony: "'The proceedings of the general court-martial, in revision, in the foregoing case of Walter E. Johnson, private, United States Marine Corps, are approved; the findings on the first charge and specification thereunder are approved; and the findings on the second and third charges and specifications thereunder and acquittal, are disapproved. The reviewing authority, after careful consideration, is at a loss to understand how officers of the service and experience of some of those who constituted this court could so disregard their oaths and obligations to enforce the laws and regulations of the military service of their country, as to find the accused not guilty of the third charge and specifications thereunder, after the testimony which was presented. The plea of the defense that it was in obedience to the order of a superior officer is untenable. All regulations state that the order must be lawful. The fact that the accused claimed he did not aim at the executed man, does not relieve him from responsibility in the man's death. He made no protest. The very fact that he aimed and fired led the other members of the firing squad to believe he was shooting at the man, and the example thus set by him certainly makes him a party to the execution. Subject to the foregoing remarks the sentence is approved.'" *Senate Hearings*, 587–588.

100 J. Dryden Kuser, *Haiti: Its Dawn of Progress after Years in a Night of Revolution* (1921; Westport, CT: Negro Universities Press, 1970), 57–58. Kuser was married to Brigade Commander John Russell's daughter Brooke, who went on in life and marriage to become the socialite and philanthropist Brooke Astor. See Frances Kiernan's biography of Astor, *The Last Mrs. Astor: A New York Story* (New York: W. W. Norton, 2007), 52–68, for a discussion of her unhappy marriage to Kuser.

101 Take the cases in early 1917 reported by Msgr. J. M. Jan: "The famous *bocor* Massillon Noires, oracle so often consulted even by the people of Cap, just arrested Thursday 15 February and conducted, with his wife and his daughter, to the prison of Grand-Rivière. . . . This houmfort so well-known was committed to flames and the proprietor to justice as a common-law criminal. Today, one can see him in the dress of a worker in the streets of Grande-Rivière under the protective eye of the police. What shame for him!" Two days later the authorities arrested a "maman-loa" named Gemésine in the middle of a *gombo* ceremony between Saint-Michel and Saint-Raphaël. Jan, *Collecta III*, 136.

102 Report, Inquiry into Occupation and Administration of Haiti and the Dominican Republic, 67th Congress, 2nd Session, Report No. 794, 17.

103 *Senate Hearings*, 589.

104 Taussig, *Shamanism, Colonialism, and the Wild Man*, 134.

105 Ibid., 121.

106 Lowell Thomas, *Old Gimlet Eye: The Adventures of Smedley D. Butler* (New York: Farrar & Rinehart, 1933), 195.

107 Renda, *Taking Haiti*, 138.

108 McCrocklin, *Garde d'Haïti*, 104. Working from military records, McCrocklin reports that "in the last ten months of bandit activities, 11,656 cacos and 165 caco chiefs surrendered to Marine and Gendarmerie posts and patrols," a figure that, if considered reliable, gives some indication of the scale of the insurgency. Ibid., 125.

109 A former Haitian army officer and a member of an influential Plateau Central family, Péralte was the most prominent of several rebel leaders who led guerrilla attacks on marine bases and gendarmerie patrols in central and northern Haiti between late 1917 and 1920. Arrested with his brothers Saül and Saint-Rémy in connection with an attack on the home of Captain John L. Doxey, the marine commander of the gendarmerie district of Hinche, Péralte was sentenced in January 1918 to five years of hard labor in Cap-Haïtien. He escaped the next September, having convinced the sentry in charge of his work party to desert the gendarmerie and join the resistance. Péralte established a revolutionary government and military network in the north, making alliances with other insurgent leaders across that region and central Haiti. The most important among them was Benoît Batraville. Péralte was assassinated by marines on 1 November 1919, and Batraville took over. He led the insurgency until he was killed by marines in May 1920. See Millet, *Les paysans haïtiens et l'occupation américaine*, 11; and McCrocklin, *Garde d'Haïti*, 115. Suzy Castor writes that as the insurgency grew, "little by little each locality had its own leaders, in charge of the war in the area under its jurisdiction." Castor, *L'occupation américaine d'Haïti*, 138.

110 Castor, *L'occupation américaine d'Haïti*, 139.

111 Wise and Frost, *A Marine Tells It to You*, 315.

112 Millet, *Les paysans haïtiens et l'occupation américaine*, 76.

113 *Senate Hearings*, 451. Barnett reported that 2,250 Haitians were killed during the first five years of the occupation, as compared to 14 or 16 marines. However, Hans Schmidt notes that according to casualty statistics, a total of 3,071 Haitians were killed in the period between March 1919 and November 1920 alone. See Schmidt, *The United States Occupation of Haiti*, 103.

114 This was precisely what W. B. Seabrook asserted: "The Haitian peasants are . . . double-natured in reality—sometimes moved by savage, atavistic forces whose dark depths no white psychology can ever plumb—but often, even in their weirdest customs, naïve, simple, harmless children." Seabrook, *The Magic Island* (New York: Harcourt, Brace, 1920), 91.

115 Marine and other officials testifying during the Senate hearings drew on comparative U.S. imperial experience in the Caribbean, Latin America, and the Pacific to assure the committee that such claims were not exaggerated.

116 Concerning U.S. official claims for the necessity of continued "democratic

tutelage" in Haiti and the Dominican Republic, the *Nation* noted that "martial law in both countries is not the best means of educating the citizens of either to the responsibilities of representative government." "America's Ireland: Haiti—Santo Domingo," *Nation*, 21 February 1920, 234.

117 *Senate Hearings*, 443.

118 Ibid., 291.

119 Bellegarde, *L'occupation américaine d'Haïti*, 6 and 7.

120 "As for the theme of despotism, it does not stop moving between two contradictory positions: sometimes the excess of power (the hubris peculiar to the Barbarians), sometimes the incapacity to govern." Hurbon, *Le barbare imaginaire*, 10.

121 This was the testimony of the occupation apologist Carl Kelsey, professor of sociology at the University of Pennsylvania, who traveled to Haiti and the Dominican Republic in 1921 to make a study of the American interventions at the behest of the chief of the Latin American Division of the State Department. His published report and oral testimony during the hearings were believed to have strongly influenced the Senate committee. Asked if revolution was likely to follow the American pull-out in Haiti, he replied: "Oh absolutely. I do not see any present possibility of permanent government on the part of the Haitians." *Senate Hearings*, 1252.

122 Ibid., 124. On Farnham, see also Johnson, "Self-Determining Haiti, Part 3: Government Of, By, and For the National City Bank," *Nation*, 11 September 1920, 295; Schmidt, *The United States Occupation of Haiti*, 48–49; and Renda, *Taking Haiti*, 98–99.

123 Wise and Frost, *A Marine Tells It to You*, 310. Faustin Wirkus described the surrender of a group of 450 insurgents in early 1920, who then "came down to Port-au-Prince and became good Haitians at twenty cents . . . a day." Wirkus and Dudley, *The White King of La Gonave*, 113.

124 Memorandum from the Brigade Commander to the Major General Commandant, USMC, 15 August 1920; published in *Senate Hearings*, 1730.

125 Ibid., 517.

126 Ibid., 517–518.

127 Ibid., 517.

128 In public statements and in his writings, Butler divided Haitians into two classes: those who wore shoes and those who did not. "Those that wear shoes I took as a joke. Without a sense of humor, you could not live in Haiti among those people, among the shoe class." *Senate Hearings*, 517. For a discussion of the logic and force of such images in the works of occupation apologists, see J. Michael Dash, *Haiti and the United States: National Stereotypes and the Literary Imagination* (1988), 2nd ed. (New York: St. Martin's, 1997), 27.

129 Kuser, *Haiti: Its Dawn of Progress*, 57.

130 See Ranajit Guha, "The Prose of Counter-Insurgency," in *Selected Subal-*

tern Studies, ed. Ranajit Guha and Gayatri Chakravorty Spivak (New York: Oxford University Press, 1988), 45–47. See also Michel-Rolph Trouillot, *Silencing the Past: Power and the Production of History* (Boston: Beacon Press, 1995), 90–95.

131 Colonel John H. Russell, "Memorandum on the Judicial System of Haiti," 16 March 1920, RG 80 (Secretary of the Navy files), 5526-254-1, U.S. National Archives.

132 Letter from Rear Admiral H. S. Knapp, U.S. Navy to the Secretary of State, 4 December 1920, dec. file 838.00/1733, U.S. National Archives.

133 Colonel John H. Russell, "Memorandum on the Judicial System of Haiti," 16 March 1920, RG 80 (Secretary of the Navy files), 5526-254-1, U.S. National Archives.

134 See also Merwin Silverthorn's emphasis on this in an oral historical interview: "They had male and female priests. They called them Papa Loi and Mama Loi—meaning law." Lieutenant General Merwin H. Silverthorn, Oral History Transcript, 160–161, USMC Archives, Library of the Marine Corps, Quantico.

135 See Hurbon, *Le barbare imaginaire,* 98–102.

136 Memo from the Brigade Commander to Captain Bruce B. MacArthur. USMC, Judge Advocate, Military Commission, Port-au-Prince, Republic of Haiti, 1 April 1920, RG 80 (General Records of the Navy) Secretary of the Navy General Correspondence, 1916–26, 5526-39:299: Cadeus Bellegarde, "B-1," U.S. National Archives.

137 John H. Russell, Daily Diary Report, 31 March 1920, dec. file 838.00/1634, U.S. National Archives.

138 Opening Argument of the Judge Advocate, n.d., RG 80 (General Records of the Navy) Secretary of the Navy General Correspondence, 1916–26, 5526-39:299: Cadeus Bellegarde, U.S. National Archives.

139 In fact, in response to an inquiry by the U.S. Secretary of State about the "validity of the proclamation of Military Occupation, issued by Admiral Caperton in Haiti, in September, 1915," the Secretary of the Navy, Josephus Daniels, referred him to the judge advocate general's opinion in the case of Cadeus Bellegarde. Josephus Daniels to the Secretary of State, 13 December 1920, dec. file 838.00/1728, U.S. National Archives.

140 Report of the Office of the Judge Advocate General, Department of the Navy, submitted to the Secretary of the Navy, 22 September 1920. In RG 80 (General Records of the Navy) Secretary of the Navy General Correspondence, 1916–26, 5526-39:299: Cadeus Bellegarde, U.S. National Archives.

141 According to Hans Schmidt, 911 Haitians were tried in military provost courts in 1920. See Schmidt, *The United States Occupation of Haiti,* 190.

142 Russell, Daily Diary Report, 1 December, 1920, dec. file 838.00/1734, U.S. National Archives.

143 H. S. Knapp to the Secretary of State, 4 December 1920, dec. file 838.00/

1733, U.S. National Archives. For a brief discussion of this case, see Georges Corvington, *Port-au-Prince au cours des ans: La capitale d' Haïti sous l'occupation, 1915–1922* (Port-au-Prince: Imprimerie Henri Deschamps, 1984), 117.

144 Combating "superstition" was also the priority of the Service d'Hygiène Nationale (National Public Health Service), organized by U.S. naval medical officers in 1917. Space does not allow for an extended analysis of this institution, which was in charge of sanitation, hospitals, and quarantine and eventually took over direction of the school of medicine. The triumph of the medical scientist over the "voodoo" doctor was a frequent theme of the publicity for the Service d'Hygiène's successes. The headline of a *New York Times* article from March 1928 noted both that a quarter of the population of Haiti was being treated at rural clinics established by the public health service and also that the "Voodoo Doctor Is Ousted." The article went on to explain that although "superstition made the peasants fearful, and the voodoo doctors did their utmost to exploit this fear and maintain their ascendancy," the U.S. doctors won over the population "by performing 'miracles' more astounding than the voodoo doctors said they themselves performed." The director of the Service d'Hygiène, Kent Melhorn, was quoted as saying, "A few [cataract] operations here and there, a few shots of bismuth or salvarsan [used to cure yaws], and the voodoo smoke clears away." See Clarence K. Streit, "Fourth of Haitians Patients at Clinics," *New York Times*, 25 March 1928. See also Robert P. Parsons, *History of Haitian Medicine* (New York: Paul B. Hoeber, 1930).

145 See Corvington, *Port-au-Prince au cours des ans: La capitale d' Haïti sous l'occupation, 1915–1922*, 259. In the first instance, he quotes from a report in *Le Matin*, 13 December 1915. Dornéval's circular is also reported in Jan, *Collecta III*, 130.

146 This is reported in Jan, *Collecta III*, 130.

147 Cincinnatus Leconte, "Circulaire aux commandants des arrondissements de la république," in *Le Moniteur*, 23 March 1912. Likewise, see Philippe Delisle's discussion of the Catholic church's campaign against Vodou in 1912, when the national political context seemed "favorable" in light of public statements by Leconte and his successor, Tancrède Auguste. Delisle, *Le catholicisme en Haïti au XIXe siècle*, 97.

148 Homer L. Overley, "A Marine Patrol," 11, in Homer L. Overley Papers, Personal Papers Collection, USMC Archives, Library of the Marine Corps, Quantico. See the discussion of this encounter in Renda, *Taking Haiti*, 41.

149 Faustin E. Wirkus, "The Black Pope of Voodoo, Part 1," *Harper's*, December 1933, 41.

150 See Alfred Métraux's detailed description of the cycle of ceremonies in which he took part in December 1947, culminating with Christmas night. These had as their primary aim to "bring luck to the faithful of *Vaudou* through 'baths' and to permit priests to prepare, with all the solemnity re-

quired, the magical powders used in their 'treatments.'" Alfred Métraux, *Le vaudou haïtien* (Paris: Éditions Gallimard, 1958), 216.

151 Wirkus and Dudley, *The White King of La Gonave*, 177–180.

152 Ibid., 180–182.

153 Faustin Wirkus, "The Black Pope of Voodoo, Part I," *Harper's*, December 1933, 41.

154 One wonders if this was the case in December 1924 when the subdistrict commander for Jacmel, in southern Haiti, reported that "two patrols made by gendarmes in an attempt to raid vaudoo dances" were unsuccessful. "The police rurale had information that these dances were to be held on a certain date but they were not found." Subdistrict commander to department commander, department of the south, Report on Activities of Police Rurale, December 1924, in Intelligence Reports Folder, RG 127 (Records of the USMC), Report of Conditions, Strength and Distribution, Intelligence Reports from Districts 1921–1934, Monthly Reports Dec. 1924 to Monthly Reports Jan. 1926, Box 5, U.S. National Archives.

155 Wirkus and Dudley, *The White King of La Gonave*, 169. Wirkus had originally learned of this strategy from Haitian guides while pursuing insurgents near Perodin during the peasant uprising: "All evening we had heard a dull booming from the camp faint as an echo. The guides said the drums were stuffed with cotton to muffle the sound" (103).

156 Ibid., 287. See also Jacques Roumain, *Le sacrifice du tambour-assoto(r)* (Port-au-Prince: Imprimerie de l'État, 1943).

157 Seabrook, *The Magic Island*, 301 n. 3.

158 Courlander, *The Drum and the Hoe*, 196–197. Gerrit S. Miller Jr., curator of mammals at the former U.S. National Museum of the Smithsonian Institution, was one of several researchers affiliated with that museum who worked in Haiti during the occupation. He returned from a 1925 trip not only with animal specimens from Hispaniola, but also with "two primitive voodoo drums" that sound much like the percussion instruments Courlander describes. Miller found them while exploring a cave near Saint-Michel-de-l'Atalaye in the Artibonite and learned from an informant that they were not only hidden but also played there in religious ceremonies. Accession number 87443, Department of Anthropology, National Museum of Natural History, Smithsonian Institution.

159 Lieutenant General Merwin H. Silverthorn, Oral History Transcript, 160 and 162, USMC Archives, Library of the Marine Corps, Quantico.

160 Simpson, "The Belief System of Haitian Vodun," in *Religious Cults of the Caribbean: Trinidad, Jamaica, and Haiti* (Rio Piedras, Puerto Rico: Institute of Caribbean Studies, 1970), 255.

161 W. B. McCormick, "Voodooism in Haiti: Ritualistic Dance and Pig with Ruffled Collar Part of One Ceremony," *New York Times*, 12 February 1922.

162 Wirkus, "The Black Pope of Voodoo, Part 1," 41.

163 Gaillard, *Hinche mise en croix*, 220.

164 McCrocklin, *Garde d'Haïti*, 160–161.

165 Although Jean L. Comhaire, in his brief "The Haitian 'Chef de Section,'" agrees that, from this point on, "things slowly but surely proceeded to revert to the past," he also notes that "The U.S. Marine Corps captains in charge after 1915, and the Haitian officers of same rank who succeeded them, were anxious to curb the power of the 'commandant' down to the limits set in the law. Men without prestige or without wealth often were appointed, some even foreign to the section they had to keep under their control." See Comhaire, "The Haitian 'Chef de Section,'" 621 and 622.

166 Seabrook, *The Magic Island*, 22. See also Price-Mars, *Une étape de l'évolution haïtienne*, 156.

167 Wirkus, "The Black Pope of Voodoo, Part 1," 45–46.

168 McCrocklin, *Garde d'Haïti*, 143.

169 Craige, *Black Bagdad*, 272. Craige uses the terms *houngan* and *bocour* interchangeably, obscuring their popular meanings. Michel Laguerre notes that it was "during the US occupation of 1915–1934 that networks of voodoo priests became an institutional feature of the Haitian military intelligence system" and suggests that this role continued after the end of the U.S. occupation. See Laguerre, *The Military and Society in Haiti* (Knoxville: University of Tennessee Press, 1993), 138.

170 Letter to the director, *La Presse*, 20 February 1930; and "Les danses dites 'Vaudou,'" in *Le Nouvelliste*, 21 February 1930, in Frank R. Crumbie Papers, Scrapbook 6, Box 1, MS Group 14, 5, Special Collections, George A. Smathers Libraries, University of Florida, Gainesville.

171 Confidential memorandum from the chief of the Gendarmerie d'Haïti to the department commanders of the north, south, and central departments, and to the chief of police of Port-au-Prince, 13 November 1924, in Garde d'Haïti (Misc. Corres. 1924–32), RG 127 (Records of the USMC), Gendarmerie d'Haïti 1915–26, General Correspondence, Box 4, U.S. National Archives.

172 These rosters listed names, titles, addresses, and in some cases physical descriptions such as height and color. The titular identifications included *houngan, mambo, bocor, loup garou, mama loi, papa loi, manger loi, voudoo,* and *wanga,* among others.

173 All of these reports are contained in Folder 18, 4th Drawer—G2, 1925, "Voodooism," RG 127 (Records of the USMC), General Correspondence (1923–25), chief of the Gendarmerie d'Haïti, Box 1, U.S. National Archives. In the late 1920s W. B. Seabrook claimed that "the Americans no longer persecute actively or seek to stamp out the mysterious, immemorial religious tradition which is the real soul of this black peasantry," arguing further that "in actual practice . . . the application of this law is comparable to that of the Volstead law in the United States. Great piles of drums and other sacred objects were confiscated and either burned or sent home as souvenirs by the Marine Corps during the early years of the occupation, and a num-

ber of temples were burned. But today Voodoo temples stand unmolested by the main public motor highways, and on any quiet night, even from the stairway of the national palace in Port-au-Prince, one may hear Rada drums booming in the hills." Seabrook, *The Magic Island*, 167 and 295.

174 District commander to the department commander, department of the south, Report on Activities of Police Rurale for November 1924, in Intelligence Reports Folder, November 1924, RG 127 (Records of the USMC), Report of Conditions, Strength and Distribution, Intelligence Reports from Districts 1921–1934, Monthly Reports December 1923 to Monthly Reports November 1924, Box 4, U.S. National Archives.

175 District commander to the chief of the Gendarmerie d'Haïti, Intelligence Report for the month of November 1924, in Intelligence Reports Folder, November 1924, RG 127 (Records of the USMC), Report of Conditions, Strength and Distribution, Intelligence Reports from Districts 1921–1934, Monthly Reports December 1923 to Monthly Reports November 1924, Box 4, U.S. National Archives.

176 District commander to the chief of the Gendarmerie d'Haïti, Report of Police Rurale for January 1925, in Intelligence Reports Folder 68-34, January 1925, RG 127 (Records of the USMC), Report of Conditions, Strength, and Distribution, Intelligence Reports from Districts, 1921–1934, Monthly Reports December 1924 to Monthly Reports January 1926, Box 5, U.S. National Archives.

177 A more global picture of the penal regime against Vodouizan in its regional variation emerges from the data generated by the order of the chief of the gendarmerie to all department commanders to submit reports on the activities of civil courts across the country from 1 January to 1 December 1926. These reports reveal that the rates of conviction varied regionally. In the department of the north, 34 percent of those arrested were found guilty in 1926, whereas in the central department 86 percent were. Were there different evidentiary regimes and standards of proof at play here? Were these "typical" post-insurgency rates of arrest and conviction? I have not been able to find comparative data from earlier or later years. See Report of Activities of Civil Courts of the Republic of Haiti During the Year of 1926 (to 1 December), in Civil Court Activities (1927) Folder, RG 127 (Records of the USMC), Gendarmerie d'Haïti, 1915–1926, Entry 165, Box 5, U.S. National Archives.

178 Price-Mars, *Ainsi parla l'oncle*, 237.

179 Herskovits, *Life in a Haitian Valley*, 286–287. See also Laguerre, *Voodoo and Politics in Haiti*, 97. Cadeus Bellegarde was blamed for the burning of Father François Colib's house at Saut d'Eau on 4 July 1919. See RG 80 (General Records of the Navy), Secretary of the Navy General Correspondence, 1916–26, 5526-39:299: Cadeus Bellegarde, "Exhibit A," U.S. National Archives.

180 Métraux, *Le vaudou haïtien*, 74, and Alfred Métraux, *Itinéraires 1, 1935–1953: Carnets de notes et journaux de voyage* (Paris: Payot, 1978), 150. See also

Rigaud, *La tradition voudoo et le voudoo haïtien*, 56–57. As Rigaud notes, the best-known case of an American posted to Haiti during the occupation who was initiated and became, by several accounts, an *oungan* himself was that of Stanley ("Doc") Reser. A native of Utah, Reser was sent to Haiti in 1927 as a U.S. Navy pharmacist's mate, first class, serving as an assistant to the public health officer (a U.S. naval medical officer) in Port-de-Paix in northern Haiti. He was later appointed superintendent of an asylum for the mentally ill at Pont Beudet in the Cul-de-Sac plain, a position that he held for twelve years. Reser returned to the United States in 1941 to reenlist during World War II but went back to Haiti after the end of the war. He assisted numerous foreign researchers and writers with their work there from the 1930s to the 1950s, including Katherine Dunham, Zora Neale Hurston, Alan Lomax, and Marcus Bach. For a profile of Reser, see Bernard Diederich, *Bon Papa: Haiti's Golden Years* (n.p.: Xlibris, 2007), 56–59. See also Katherine Dunham, *Island Possessed* (1969; Chicago: University of Chicago Press, 1994), 18–20; and Zora Neale Hurston, *Tell My Horse: Voodoo and Life in Haiti and Jamaica* (1938; New York: Harper & Row, 1990), 245–257. Reser's obituary appeared in the *New York Times* on 27 January 1959.

181 Niles, *Black Haiti*, 140.

182 Léon-François Hoffmann quotes a report from the Port-au-Prince daily *Le Nouvelliste* on 17 October 1917, a little over two years into the occupation, about the arrest of a "woman . . . accused of having 'taken the soul' of a child," but who was then able to perform a resuscitation at the police station. She was subsequently convicted and given a six-month prison sentence for *maléfices*. Hoffmann, *Haïti: Couleurs, croyances, créole*, 137.

183 Faustin Wirkus, "The Black Pope of Voodoo, Part 2," *Harper's*, January 1934, 190.

184 See Karen Fields, *Revival and Rebellion in Colonial Central Africa* (Portsmouth, NH: Heinemann, 1997), 72–73.

185 Hans Schmidt notes that when General John H. Russell was appointed high commissioner in Haiti in February 1922, he was intrigued by parallels between the two occupations, and between his position and that of the British high commissioners. He had "read Lord Cromer's 'interesting and instructive' book on Egypt, but when he requested special reports on Egypt the State Department demurred, replying: '. . . . You will doubtless realize that critics of this Government's policy toward Haiti have sometimes made this same comparison a basis for attacks upon the Department.'" Schmidt, *The United States Occupation of Haiti*, 126.

186 Fields, *Revival and Rebellion in Colonial Central Africa*, 76.

187 Ibid.

188 Ibid., 73.

189 See also Martin Chanock, *Law, Custom and Social Order: The Colonial Experience in Malawi and Zambia* (Cambridge: Cambridge University Press, 1985), 97–98.

190 Hoffmann, *Haïti: Couleurs, croyances, créole*, 134–135.

191 The paper was founded by Joseph Jolibois, Jr., and its first directors were Constant Vieux and Joseph Lanoue, whom Dartiguenave allegedly referred to as *kako*. Jolibois and Lanoue (Vieux having by then left the paper) were convicted of sedition by a military court in June 1921 and sentenced to six months' hard labor and a fine. Letter in English from *Le Courrier haïtien* addressed "Dear colleague," 20 March 1922, dec. file 838.00/1857, U.S. National Archives. For a discussion of *Le Courrier haïtien* see Corvington, *Port-au-Prince au cours des ans: La capitale d'Haiti sous l'occupation, 1915–1922*, 249–250.

192 See "Need Asserted of Marines in Haiti," *Christian Science Monitor*, 14 February 1921, 7; and "Knapp Report on Haiti Challenged," *Christian Science Monitor*, 15 February 1921, 9. I was unable to locate this image in the newspaper.

193 Several months after the Mayo Naval Court of Inquiry issued its report and a few months before the *Courrier haïtien* articles, the Department of the Navy strategically selected and released excerpts from testimony given to the court by Lieutenant Colonel Richard S. Hooker, record keeper of the gendarmerie, alleging multiple cases of *kako* killing and mutilation of marines and gendarmes. An article in the *New York Times* notes that while no connection with "voodoo" was made in the testimony itself, "the report of the Court of Inquiry states that the Haitian bandits practiced voodooism" and goes on to explain the ritual "function" of the said mutilations. See "Natives in Haiti Ate Marine Officer," *New York Times*, 4 January 1921.

194 "Contre le Rapport Knapp," *Le Courrier haïtien*, 23 March 1921.

195 "La Gendarmerie d'Haïti et le Vaudou," *Le Courrier haïtien*, 12 March 1921.

196 It is important to note that such charges against the occupation were not restricted to this newspaper, but were a dimension of elite and ecclesiastical protest against the occupation more broadly. See, for example, the series of articles that appeared in *Le Nouvelliste* between January and February 1929. One of these suggests that Seabrook's recently published book *The Magic Island*, with its particular focus on "voodoo," reflected most poorly not on Haitians, but on the effectiveness of the U.S. occupation's purported "civilizing mission" in Haiti. "Mr. Seabrook et l'intervention américaine," *Le Nouvelliste*, 14 February 1929. See also Jan, *Collecta III*, 342.

197 Seabrook, *The Magic Island*, 103. He renders this incorrectly as "article 249." See Jean Price-Mars's scathing critique of Seabrook's book, and particularly his representations of Vodou ritual, in his *Une étape de l'évolution haïtienne*, 153–188.

198 Plate featured in Bryan Senn, *Golden Horrors: An Illustrated Critical Filmography of Terror Cinema, 1931–1939* (Jefferson, NC: McFarland, 1996), 86.

199 In a 1929 letter to Melville Herskovits, John Houston Craige noted that there was "a red-hot official inquiry going on under cover at the present moment" to discover how Seabrook had come into "possession of consid-

erable information supposed to be of a confidential character." Craige implicated H. P. Davis, a longtime resident of Port-au-Prince, as Seabrook's source. Letter from Craige to Herskovits, 19 January 1929, in Melville J. Herskovits Papers, Box 6, Northwestern University Library.

200 Seabrook, *The Magic Island*, 88.

201 Ibid., 35 n. However, see Leslie Desmangles's argument that "although crucifixes appear on every *pé*, their uses in the Vodou rituals have little to do with Christian iconology, but are interpreted in terms of Dahomean mythology." Leslie G. Desmangles, "African Interpretations of the Christian Cross in Vodou," in *Vodou in Haitian Life and Culture: Invisible Powers*, ed. Claudine Michel and Patrick Bellegarde-Smith (New York: Palgrave Macmillan, 2006), 42.

202 Seabrook, *The Magic Island*, 302 n. 1.

203 See Stephan Palmié's discussion of the collaborations of criminal anthropology and law enforcement against Afro-Cuban religious practitioners in early twentieth century Cuba and the way in which such inventories of confiscated objects "came to perform multiple functions in the making of brujería." These "sadly jumbled remains of sacred objects and ensembles. . . . not only objectified the presumed existence of the referent of brujería but served as palpable signs of the effectiveness of the reconnaissance strategies with which law-enforcement and scholarly agencies pursued what otherwise seemed to elude them." Palmié, *Wizards and Scientists*, 247. See also the discussion of the circulation of such confiscated objects between legal and scientific institutions in early Republican Cuba in Bronfman, *Measures of Equality*, 17–35.

204 Wirkus and Dudley, *The White King of La Gonave*, 167.

205 Craige, *Black Bagdad*, 72.

206 Silverthorn, Oral History Transcript, 161–162, USMC Archives, Library of the Marine Corps, Quantico.

207 I have identified occupation-era Haitian drums, apparently confiscated in the course of raids, at the Smithsonian Institution, Department of Anthropology, National Museum of Natural History; and the University of Pennsylvania Museum of Archaeology and Anthropology, Philadelphia, PA. There are also, apparently, a number of drums held at the National Museum of the Marine Corps, Triangle, VA, some of which are presumed to be Haitian; however, their provenience has not been established. Phone conversation with Stefan Rohal, National Museum of the Marine Corps, 25 July 2007.

208 Arthur C. Holly, *Les daïmons du culte voudu* (Port-au-Prince: Edmond Chenet, 1918), iv; emphasis in original.

209 Wise and Frost, *A Marine Tells It to You*, 135–136.

210 Adolph B. Miller, "Personal Log," 16–17 October 1915, in Adolph Miller Papers, Personal Papers Collection, USMC Archives, Library of the Marine Corps, Quantico. Lieutenant General Merwin H. Silverthorn, Oral

History Transcript, 160, USMC Archives, Library of the Marine Corps, Quantico. I am grateful to Mary A. Renda's *Taking Haiti* for alerting me to the existence of these and other oral histories and unpublished personal papers held at the Library of the Marine Corps.

211 Accession number 60237, Department of Anthropology, National Museum of Natural History, Smithsonian Institution.

212 For example, Captain Thomas A. Tighe donated a "collection of six wooden drums used in Voodoo rites, collected by the donor near Hinche, Haiti in 1921" (accession no. 153259); and an ex-marine named F. C. Baker, who testified against his superiors during the Senate hearings, sold a carved *celt* (a Taíno tool) "collected" from a "Voodoo houmfort, near Maïssade" (accession no. 157847). Department of Anthropology, National Museum of Natural History, Smithsonian Institution.

213 Craige, *Black Bagdad*, 275. After leaving Haiti in 1928, Craige was placed in charge of the Marine Corps Recruiting Bureau in Philadelphia. Letter from Craige to Melville Herskovits, 10 September 1928, in Melville J. Herskovits Papers, Box 6, Northwestern University Library. The tall drum Craige mentions was an *asòtò*. See the extraordinary photograph of Craige, in uniform, "playing" these drums with two drumsticks in Renda, *Taking Haiti*, 214.

214 Accession cards 51-2-1 to 51-2-4, catalogued 13 January 1951, University of Pennsylvania Museum of Archaeology and Anthropology, Philadelphia, PA.

215 Bruce W. Merwin, "A Voodoo Drum from Hayti," *Museum Journal* 8, no. 2 (June 1917): 123 and 125.

216 There is little information on this particular object, save for it being part of a large donation by the estate of John Oliver La Gorce (one-time editor of *National Geographic*) and part of "a complex accession originating in the division of military history." This latter information and the fact that *National Geographic* published several praising reports on the occupation in the 1920s might suggest that this drum was likewise confiscated by marines. Accession no. 229198, Department of Anthropology, National Museum of Natural History, Smithsonian Institution.

217 These powers included the potentially maddening effect of drumming on white foreigners. Craige was particularly attached to this colonial trope. See his account of the gradual deterioration of a Lieutenant South's mental state while posted in a village of the Haitian interior. Craige, *Black Bagdad*, 88–90. In their published and unpublished writings on the occupation, marines also frequently mentioned listening to, as Adolph Miller wrote in his personal log, "the beating of tom-toms and yelling all night long up at the Caco village" in the hours before an attack. Adolph B. Miller, "Personal Log," 16–17 October 1915, in Adolph Miller Papers, Personal Papers Collection, USMC Archives, Library of the Marine Corps, Quantico.

218 Palmié, *Wizards and Scientists*, 254.

219 Métraux, *Le vaudou haïtien*, 163.

220 I am contextualizing this discussion in the writings of mid-twentieth-century ethnographers because according to more recent ethnographic accounts, the elaborate rituals that Herskovits, Roumain, Courlander, and Métraux describe have, over time, become attenuated in Haiti and, especially, in the diaspora. For discussion of the sacred status of drums, see Fleurant, *Dancing Spirits*; and Lois Wilcken, *The Drums of Vodou* (Tempe: White Cliffs Media, 1992). Note that Fleurant specifies that the *ountò* "is both an instrument—the lead drum, as well as the person who plays it, the master drummer." Fleurant, *Dancing Spirits*, 108.

221 Quoted in Fleurant, *Dancing Spirits*, 38.

222 Ibid., 38. See Rigaud, *La tradition voudoo et le voudoo haïtien*, 56.

223 Courlander, *The Drum and the Hoe*, 190.

224 This question will be taken up in a preliminary way in the next chapter. For reflections on these relations with respect to Seabrook's *The Magic Island*, see Steven Gregory, "Voodoo, Ethnography, and the American Occupation of Haiti: William B. Seabrook's *The Magic Island*," in *Dialectical Anthropology: Essays in Honor of Stanley Diamond*, vol. 2, *The Politics of Culture and Creativity: A Critique of Civilization*, ed. Christine Ward Gailey (Gainesville: University Press of Florida, 1992), 169. There seem to have been few anthropologists among the Americans who traveled to Haiti during the occupation and wrote about their experiences. Robert Burnett Hall, of the University of Michigan, visited La Gonâve to study the island's "Société Congo" (*sosyete kongo*) cooperative labor and mutual benefit associations in 1926, and Elsie Clews Parsons, a public critic of the occupation, conducted fieldwork in Haiti in 1927. See Robert Burnett Hall, "The Société Congo of the Île à Gonave," *American Anthropologist* 31, no. 4 (October–December 1929): 685–700. Herskovits and his wife, Frances, passed through Haiti in 1928 on their way to Dutch Guiana before returning in the summer of 1934, just as the occupation was ending. The Smithsonian Institution sponsored research investigations in Haiti that had ethnological and archaeological dimensions during the occupation, including that undertaken in 1925 by Gerrit S. Miller, Jr., curator of mammals at the former U.S. National Museum of the Smithsonian, and that carried out in 1931 by Herbert W. Krieger, archaeologist and curator of the division of ethnology at the same institution. See, respectively, accession nos. 87443 (19 May 1925) and 113146 (13 August 1931), Department of Anthropology, United States National Museum, Smithsonian Institution.

225 Letter from Craige to Herskovits, 10 September 1928, in Melville J. Herskovits Papers, Box 6, Northwestern University Library. Note that Zora Neale Hurston, in New York, had also been recruited by Herskovits to collect measurements and samples for his study.

226 Letter from Craige to Herskovits, 13 February 1932, in Melville J. Herskovits Papers, Box 6, Northwestern University Library. Herskovits regretted this refocusing in his next letter: "Having heard a few of the stories

which I presume you had intended to incorporate in it had you not decided to change the book a bit, I must confess I am very sorry they are not to be made generally available." Letter from Herskovits to Craige, 19 February 1932, in Melville J. Herskovits Papers, Box 6, Northwestern University Library. Craige wrote again to Herskovits just before the 1933 publication of his *Black Bagdad*, "As you know I was originally much interested in the political aspects of the Occupation of Haiti. However, I didn't want to join the Army of the Unemployed, especially under the present conditions [referring to the Depression]. . . . Eventually I eliminated all references to political actions and personages." Letter from Craige to Herskovits, 6 March 1933, in Melville J. Herskovits Papers, Box 6, Northwestern University Library.

227 See Melville J. Herskovits, "Lo, the Poor Haitian," *Nation*, 13 February 1929, 198–200.

228 Of the first, Herskovits wrote to Craige upon its publication that he thought it was "one of the most exciting books I have read in many a long day," while adding, "I realise that you have your point of view and I respect you for being honest about it but I very frankly don't think that your theory about racial differences has a scientific leg to stand on." Letter from Herskovits to Craige, 20 March 1933, in Melville J. Herskovits Papers, Box 6, Northwestern University Library.

229 Letter from Craige to Herskovits, 22 April 1933, in Melville J. Herskovits Papers, Box 6, Northwestern University Library. Perhaps Craige remembered the extensive coverage that the publication of Seabrook's *The Magic Island* had received in the Haitian press upon its publication a few years earlier.

230 Letter from Craige to Herskovits, 24 December 1929, in Melville J. Herskovits Papers, Box 6, Northwestern University Library.

231 William B. Seabrook, introduction to Faustin Wirkus and Taney Dudley, *The White King of La Gonave* (Garden City, NY: Doubleday, Doran), xii–xiii.

232 Eugene O'Neill, *The Emperor Jones, Anna Christie, The Hairy Ape* (New York: Modern Library, 1937), 13.

233 But see Mary Renda's analysis of *The Emperor Jones* in the context of the occupation in her *Taking Haiti*, 198–212.

234 See the chapter entitled "The *Sosyete*," in Smith, *When the Hands Are Many*, 104–140.

235 Gruening wrote, for example: "As a straight adventure story of a unique experience, the tale stands up well. A tropical island, especially one as virgin as La Gonave, makes an ideal setting. But as a document in an obscure and complex chapter of history, imperialism, interracial and intercultural relations, the book contains much of greater value." Ernest Gruening, "White Majesty," *Nation*, 15 July 1931, 70.

236 Returning to active duty in 1942, Wirkus recalled the days when he "used

to get $125 and expenses for a lecture on Haiti." "Emporer [*sic*] Faustin II Back in United States Marines," *The Wilkes-Barre (Pennsylvania) Record*, 12 May 1942. My thanks to Bob Aquilina at the Marine Corps Historical Center in Washington, D.C., for bringing this clipping to my attention.

237 I am indebted to John Szwed for first alerting me to the existence of this film. I am also grateful to George E. Turner for directing me in a February 1998 phone conversation to Esselle Parichy, "Marine Sergeant Turns Adventurer: Faustin Wirkus Only White Ever Crowned King of Haitian Blacks by Popular Consent—Films Will Illustrate Lecture," *International Photographer* (November 1931): 4–5.

238 Gary D. Rhodes writes that "the film immediately found problems in obtaining bookings; at 36 minutes, it was too long to be considered a short and not long enough to stand alone as a feature." See Rhodes, *White Zombie: Anatomy of a Horror Film* (Jefferson, NC: McFarland, 2001), 177. Although copyrighted, *Voodoo* is not held by the Library of Congress nor by the Smithsonian, the George Eastman House, the Museum of Modern Art, or UCLA. Nor was a copy deposited at the Marine Historical Center in Washington, D.C. Sol Lesser's son Julian regretted in our March 1998 correspondence that *Voodoo* was not preserved in the archive of films that his father financed and presented. See also "Reminiscences of Sol Lesser: Oral History, 1970," in the Columbia University Oral History Collection, Columbia University Library, particularly for information on the production, distribution, and presentation of independent films in the early 1930s.

239 Clipping of review by Lucius Beebe, "Voodoo—Cameo," n. p., 25 March 1933, in Frank R. Crumbie Papers, Scrapbook 10, Box 6, MS Group 14, Special Collections, George A. Smathers Libraries, University of Florida, Gainesville.

240 Phone conversation with George Turner, 15 February 1998. See George E. Turner and Michael H. Price, *Forgotten Horrors: Early Talkie Chillers from Poverty Row* (South Brunswick, NJ: A. S. Barnes, 1979), 84. Note that Turner and Price spell the title of the film "Voodo." However, the Library of Congress's directory, *Motion Pictures, 1912–1939*, refers to the film as "Voodoo." An unrelated film called "Drums o' Voodo" was released in 1934. My thanks to my father for tracking down these references for me.

241 Clipping of review by Lucius Beebe, "Voodoo—Cameo," n. p., 25 March 1933, in Frank R. Crumbie Papers, Scrapbook 10, Box 6, MS Group 14, Special Collections, George A. Smathers Libraries, University of Florida, Gainesville. Gary D. Rhodes quotes *Motion Picture Daily*'s review from 25 March 1933 as noting that "the picture would have been considerably more effective if [Wirkus] had eliminated the fake dramatics for a straight recounting of life among the voodoo believers," and the *Motion Picture Herald*'s review from 13 May 1933 as observing: "Interesting is the pictorial record of the frenzied ritual of the blacks, but when the planned sacrifice of a girl is frustrated by the efforts of Wirkus, the picture smacks too much of

the posed melodramatic to be highly effective." See Rhodes, *White Zombie*, 177.

242 See Fatimah Tobing Rony, *The Third Eye: Race, Cinema, and Ethnographic Spectacle* (Durham, NC: Duke University Press, 1996), 131 and 160–166.

243 Unidentified and undated newspaper clipping, in Frank R. Crumbie Papers, Scrapbook 10, Box 6, MS Group 14, Special Collections, George A. Smathers Libraries, University of Florida, Gainesville.

244 Senn, *Golden Horrors*, 83.

245 "The figure of the zombie generally became less threatening and more amusing over the course of the decade. Moreover, as white discourses began to merge diverse racial 'others' into a single, fluid and generic, exotic object, they tended to emphasize less the specific horrors that had been attributed to Haiti since the early years of the occupation." Renda, *Taking Haiti*, 225–226. See also Markman Ellis, *The History of Gothic Fiction* (Edinburgh: Edinburgh University Press, 2000), 233–235.

246 For helpful production notes on the film, see Senn, *Golden Horrors*, 88–91.

247 See Rhodes, *White Zombie*, 85–87.

248 In his article "White Zombie: Haitian Horror," Tony Williams argues that the servitude of Legendre's "zombies" in the film "represents a macabre version of the forced labor system which the U.S. inflicted on the Haitian population in 1918." Tony Williams, "White Zombie: Haitian Horror," *Jump Cut* 28 (Spring 1983): 19.

249 See the profile of Constant Polynice in René J. Rosemond, *L'énergie nationale: "Les précurseurs"* (Port-au-Prince: Imprimerie du College Vertières, 1942), 139.

250 Georges Corvington notes that the construction of the factory began at the end of 1916 and was finished two years later. See Corvington, *Port-au-Prince au cours des ans: La capitale d'Haïti*, 236. Candelon Rigaud notes that "the Company is fed in cane by 8,000 *carreaux* of land," breaking down to 6,200 *carreaux* in the Plaine du Cul-de-Sac and 1,800 *carreaux* on the Plaine de Léogâne. See Candelon Rigaud, *Promenades dans les campagnes d'Haïti: La plaine de la Croix des Bouquets (Cul-de-Sac), 1789–1928* (Paris: L'Édition Française Universelle, 193?), 189–190.

251 Seabrook, *The Magic Island*, 95. Candelon Rigaud writes of the scale and automation of HASCO's great factories: "We are in the presence of six furnaces representing 750 horsepower. The immense mill swallows 200 tons of cane every 24 hours. The cane is brought under the pressure of rolls by an endless chain, which is going, without interruption, to take them into the hole where the wagons throw them automatically. This mill runs and runs, pulverizing all the cane that the endless chain brings to its gluttony." Rigaud, *Promenades dans les campagnes d'Haïti*, 198.

252 Brenda Gayle Plummer, *Haiti and the United States: The Psychological Moment* (Athens: University of Georgia Press, 1992), 102.

253 Richman, *Migration and Vodou*, 103.

254 Ibid., 100–101. Arthur Millspaugh writes that "compensation of unskilled labor [in Haiti] in 1923 was about 30 cents per day," whereas in Cuba "the wage scale was about five times as high." Millspaugh, *Haiti under American Control*, 143. However, most other sources say that the standard wage for day labor in Haiti at this time was twenty cents, and Castor notes that this was only for men—women and children were paid ten cents a day. See Castor, *L'occupation américaine d'Haïti*, 96. Paul Moral makes the point that HASCO was a "relatively modest enterprise" by the standard of the vast American-financed *ingenios* in Cuba. Moral, *Le paysan haïtien*, 64–65.

255 Rigaud, *Promenades dans les campagnes d'Haïti*, 125.

256 Schmidt, *The United States Occupation of Haiti*, 178; and Rigaud, *Promenades dans les campagnes d'Haïti*, 200. Richman notes that the role of these overseers in the early HASCO operations was the object of strong resentment in Léogâne on the part of some of her informants even decades later. Richman, *Migration and Vodou*, 104. Unlike most American agribusiness ventures in Haiti, which were short-lived, HASCO operated for sixty years. Paul Moral attributes the failure of the majority of these foreign operations to the agrarian structure of the country and, principally, to "the absence of vast estates in a single block." Moral, *Le Paysan haïtien*, 64. On this, see also Castor, *L'occupation américaine d'Haïti*, 105–106. Part of the logic of HASCO's basing its operations in the Cul-de-Sac plain was that such consolidated estates were available, if not for purchase, then for leasing. As Gerald F. Murray writes: "HASCO has been able to rent great blocs of land to cultivate the cane itself, or has been able to make contracts with landowners who themselves would plant their extensive holdings in cane and subsequently sell the cane to HASCO." Murray, "The Evolution of Haitian Peasant Land Tenure: A Case Study in Agrarian Adaptation to Population Growth" (Ph.D. diss., Columbia University, 1977), 123.

257 Richman, *Migration and Vodou*, 111.

258 Michael Taussig, *The Devil and Commodity Fetishism in South America* (Chapel Hill: University of North Carolina Press, 1980), xi. He writes: "It would be a shocking oversight not to realize that these beliefs occur in a historical context in which one mode of production and life is being supplanted by another and that the devil dramatically represents this process of alienation" (17). See also Hurbon's extensive discussion of *zonbi*: "The rumors of zombis, but also the accounts of zombis who claim to have been ensorcelled, are only the very pale metaphor of a general situation of crisis in Haiti with its thousands of wandering beggars, without identity, without shelter, without hospitals where to die, and without cemeteries to receive them." *Le barbare imaginaire*, 296. See also Jean and John Comaroff's analysis of the association of zombies with "rapidly changing conditions of work under capitalism in its various guises; conditions that rupture not just established relations of production and reproduction, but also received connections of persons to place, the material to the moral, private to public,

the individual to the communal, past to future." Jean Comaroff and John Comaroff, "Alien-Nation: Zombies, Immigrants, and Millennial Capitalism," *South Atlantic Quarterly* 101, no. 4 (Fall 2002): 795–796. For an analysis of the figure of the zombie in relation to the social history and memory of colonial slavery, see Franck Degoul, "Du passé faisons table d'hôte: Le mode d'entretien des zombi dans l'imaginaire haïtien et ses filiations historiques," *Haïti: Face au passé/Confronting the Past*, special issue, *Ethnologies* 28, no. 1 (2006): 241–248.

259 Gaillard, *Hinche mise en croix*, 72–73. The letter was published in *Le Matin*, 5 December 1917.

260 Métraux, *Le vaudou haïtien*, 238.

261 Taussig has written: "In a myriad of improbable ways, magic and rite can strengthen the critical consciousness that a devastatingly hostile reality forces on the people laboring in the plantations and mines. Without the legacy of culture and without its rhetorical figures, images, fables, metaphors, and other imaginative creations, this consciousness cannot function." *The Devil and Commodity Fetishism*, 232.

262 Palmié, *Wizards and Scientists*, 66.

263 See Mary Renda's larger argument along these lines: "Relations of power at work in the occupation gave marines access to Haitians—their bodies and their services—as well as to Haitian cultural objects and lore. Ironically, this turned out to be more profitable, at least in the short run, than the development of Haitian agricultural or manufacturing pursuits." Renda, *Taking Haiti*, 212. Gary Rhodes notes that the $1.75 million *White Zombie* had grossed by 1936 was "almost astonishing for an independently made production." See Rhodes, *White Zombie*, 162.

264 The countervailing Haitian ethnological and American anthropological construction of Vodou during the 1920s–1940s in relation to both occupation and post-occupation legal regimes is a focus of the next chapter.

265 Hurbon, *Le barbare imaginaire*, 129.

266 Richman, *Migration and Vodou*, 164. Richman draws on Karen McCarthy Brown's work in defining *pwen* more generally as a kind of mimetic capturing, condensation, or crystallization of truths about the complexities of relationships, conditions, or situations. See Richman, *Migration and Vodou*, 163 and 165; and Brown, *Mama Lola*, 94.

267 Richman, *Migration and Vodou*, 147–149 and 150.

NOTES TO CHAPTER 4

1 Remarks made by Maritou Chenêt Moscoso and Déita (Mercédes Foucard Guignard) during the panel "Les débuts des danses folkloriques haïtiennes sur scène théâtrale," at the conference "La danse haïtienne: Histoire et traditions," 3 April 1997, Port-au-Prince, Haiti. Videotape footage of this conference is held in the Performing Arts Research Collections, New York Public Library.

2 Carl Brouard, "Doctrine de la Nouvelle École," *Conjonction: Revue franco-haïtien de l'Institut français d'Haïti* 198 (April–May–June 1993): 39. See J. Michael Dash, "The Indigenous Movement," in Dash, *Literature and Ideology in Haiti, 1915–1961* (London: Macmillan, 1981), 65–97.

3 Buteau, "Une problématique de l'identité," 25.

4 See Valerie Kaussen's analysis of *indigénisme* as "a form of cosmopolitan modernism that, like many international modernisms, appropriated and engaged a range of aesthetic, cultural and philosophical trends," but also "drew inspiration from yet another phenomenon: the massive migration of Haiti's peasantry both into the city and over the borders separating Haiti from Cuba, the Dominican Republic, and other locations in the burgeoning U.S./Caribbean empire." Kaussen, *Migrant Revolutions: Haitian Literature, Globalization, and U.S. Imperialism* (Lanham, MD: Lexington Books, 2008), 27.

5 See Dash, *Literature and Ideology in Haiti*, 65–73; and Dash, *Haiti and the United States*, 45–72. For an analysis of transnational black culture in the 1920s and 1930s, see also Brent Hayes Edwards, *The Practice of Diaspora: Literature, Translation, and the Rise of Black Internationalism* (Cambridge, MA: Harvard University Press, 2003). The interconnections between *indigénisme*, *afrocubanismo*, and Latin American *indigenismo* warrant further study. Note that the revolutionary forces that overthrew French colonialism in the former Saint-Domingue ultimately called themselves the "indigenous army."

6 Price-Mars was the most influential pioneer of the ethnology movement in Haiti, but this should not minimize the significance of the work of two of his contemporaries, J. C. Dorsainvil and Arthur Holly. In research first published in the journal *Haïti médicale* in 1913, which later became the basis for his 1931 book *Vodou et névrose*, Dorsainvil focused on spirit embodiment in Vodou as a psychological phenomenon, arguing that "true, authentic, vôdouisme, not simulated towards a mercantile end, is a hereditary, racial, religious psycho-neurosis, characterized by a splitting of the personality with functional alterations of sensibility, motility, and a predominance of pythiatic symptoms." Dorsainvil, *Vodou et névrose*, 58. Dorsainvil's book pathologized "possession," but it also insisted that Haitian popular religion was a worthy object of serious scientific inquiry and was frequently ambivalent in its conclusions, suggesting at one point, for example, that the "state of nervous disequilibrium which seems to be . . . the lot of our little society" could be "the secret of our ideological intelligence," as exemplified first and foremost by heroes of the Haitian Revolution. Ibid., 60–61. See the discussion of Dorsainvil's work in Carlo A. Célius, "Cheminement anthropologique en Haïti," *Gradhiva* 1, n.s. (2005): 50–51. Arthur Holly was a medical doctor and the son of James Theodore Holly, the African American founder and first bishop of the Église Episcopale d'Haïti, who emigrated to Haiti in 1861. Arthur Holly identified himself as an esotericist, and in two works published during the occupation, *Les daïmons du culte*

voudo and Her-ra-ma-el [Arthur Holly], *Dra-Po* he refuted the "the accusations according to which our African Fathers bequeathed to us a "diabolical cult," by making the case that "Voudo, in principle and doctrine, is the religion of Christian Humanity." Holly, *Dra-Po*, ii; and *Les daïmons du culte voudo*, 522. Holly drew a strong connection between the elite's "abandonment of this truly Christian Tradition" and the occupation's conditions of possibility: "our hands became weak, incapable of supporting the weight and responsibilities of our sovereignty" (*Dra-Po*, 360).

7   Price-Mars, *Ainsi parla l'oncle*. A series of his earlier lectures on the responsibilities and failures of the elite were published in 1919 as *La vocation de l'élite* (1919; Éditions des Presses Nationales d'Haïti, 2001).

8   Oriol, Viaud, and Aubourg, *Le mouvement folklorique en Haïti*, 20; and Price-Mars, *Ainsi parla l'oncle*, 45.

9   Price-Mars, *Ainsi parla l'oncle*, 44. See Michel-Rolph Trouillot's analysis of Price-Mars's project as one of "civil ethics, profoundly Durkheimian in its social beliefs." Trouillot, "Jeux de mots, jeux de classe: Les mouvances de l'indigénisme," *Conjonction* 197 (1993): 39.

10   Price-Mars, *Ainsi parla l'oncle*, 290.

11   Ibid., 51. Price-Mars notes that Sébillot derives the definition of "folklore" in his *Le folk-lore: Littérature orale et ethnographique traditionnelle* (Paris: O. Doin et fils, 1913) from the work of the English antiquarian William J. Thoms (1803–1885). Price-Mars quotes Thoms (from Sébillot) as proposing that folklore "'holds a position in the history of a people corresponding exactly to that which the famous unwritten law occupies in regard to codified law.'" Price-Mars, *Ainsi parla l'oncle*, 49.

12   Ibid., 170. Price-Mars problematizes the word "Vaudou" in discussing its African roots: "In our view the term *Vaudou* carries an ambiguity that should be cleared up forthwith. Nowhere have we found it to signify a set of beliefs codified in formulas and dogmas." Ibid., 90–91.

13   Ibid., 88–89. See also Price-Mars's elaboration of this argument in his 1929 *Une étape de l'évolution haïtienne*, in discussing "le sentiment et le phénomène religieux chez les nègres de St-Domingue," 115–152. See also Gérarde Magloire-Danton's analysis: "The observation that Vodou is at the heart of discursive formations about Haiti—scientific or literary—led Price-Mars to make it the central subject of his inquiry in *Ainsi parla l'Oncle*." Magloire-Danton, "Anténor Firmin and Jean Price-Mars," 168.

14   Price-Mars, *Ainsi parla l'oncle*, 232.

15   See Palmié, *Wizards and Scientists*, 233–241; and Borges, "Healing and Mischief," 192–194. Ortiz later wrote, "It is certain that I, like Dr. Nina Rodrigues somewhat earlier in Brazil, came to the ethnographic study of Cuba from the field of criminal anthropology, to which I had dedicated my most fervent zeal"; quoted in Palmié, *Wizards and Scientists*, 233; Palmié's translation.

16   Price-Mars does not cite Ortiz's work in *Ainsi parla l'oncle*. Jacques Car-

meleau Antoine notes that the two met in Washington in 1943, when the former was invited by the State Department to make a tour of the United States. Antoine, *Jean Price-Mars and Haiti* (Washington, DC: Three Continents Press, 1981), 178. On Ortiz and *afrocubanismo*, see Robin Moore, *Nationalizing Blackness: Afrocubanismo and Artistic Revolution in Havana, 1920–1940* (Pittsburgh: University of Pittsburgh Press, 1997), 125; Alejandro de la Fuente, *A Nation for All: Race, Inequality, and Politics in Twentieth-Century Cuba* (Chapel Hill: University of North Carolina Press, 2001), 182–183; Palmié, *Wizards and Scientists*, 232; and Bronfman, *Measures of Equality*, 148.

17 Price-Mars, *Ainsi parla l'oncle*, 253–254.

18 Price-Mars, *Folklore et patriotisme*, 18. In a 1917 lecture, "La domination économique et politique de l'élite," which was later compiled in his 1919 *La vocation de l'élite*, Price-Mars critiques the Haitian Code Rural for establishing "a category of individuals whose social and economic role merited being defined by special laws in order to demonstrate more accurately that they do not resemble us and that we are able to dispose of their goods, of their liberty and even of their life at will!" Quoted in and translated by Magdaline Shannon, *Jean Price-Mars, the Haitian Elite and the American Occupation, 1915–1935* (New York: St. Martin's, 1996), 42.

19 This legislation would remain in effect thereafter, although not consistently enforced, until it was repealed by the 1987 Haitian Constitution following the overthrow of the Duvalier dictatorship.

20 Nau, *Les codes haïtiens* (1914), 321–322 and 338.

21 Vincent founded the daily newspaper *Haïti-Journal* in 1930 and was thus in a position during the campaign to keep his nationalist record before the literate public. Elections held on 14 October 1930 reconstituted the Chamber of Deputies and the Senate, which had been replaced for most of the occupation by a Conseil d'État. One of the primary contenders for the presidency in 1930 was Jean Price-Mars, then a senator representing the department of the north. René Piquion, a *noiriste* ideologue, would later charge that Price-Mars lost this election because he refused to campaign on a politics of color. Price-Mars himself denied that this was the case, attributing his loss to having been outspent and outmaneuvered politically by Vincent. See Shannon, *Jean Price-Mars, the Haitian Elite and the American Occupation*, 98. See also René Piquion, *Manuel de négritude* (Port-au-Prince: Éditions Henri Deschamps, 1966), 168; and Price-Mars, *Lettre ouverte, au Dr. René Piquion: Le préjugé de couleur, est-il la question sociale?* (Port-au-Prince: Éditions des Antilles, 1967), 22–25.

22 On Vincent's pseudo-populism, see Antoine, *Jean Price-Mars and Haiti*, 170; Trouillot, *Haiti, State against Nation*, 107; and Shannon, *Jean Price-Mars, the Haitian Elite and the American Occupation*, 140.

23 The poet and novelist Jacques Roumain, for example, who co-founded *La Revue indigène* in 1927 and the Haitian Communist Party in 1934, was convicted as a communist conspirator in late 1934. Jean Price-Mars was one

of eleven senators ousted from the National Assembly by Vincent in 1935 for opposing his intended revisions to the 1932 Constitution strengthening executive power and extending his term by an additional five years. Thereafter, Price-Mars was one of the foremost critics and opponents of the Vincent regime. See Shannon, *Jean Price-Mars, the Haitian Elite and the American Occupation*, 150–151.

24 Sténio Vincent, *Efforts et résultats* (Port-au-Prince: Imprimerie de l'État, 1938), 55.

25 With the July 1935 abrogations, only the second line of Article 406, specifying that the sentences for the crimes listed in Articles 405 and 406 were to be served in labor camps at maritime prisons, was deleted.

26 "Chambre des Députés, 4 août 1931," *Le Moniteur*, 13 March 1933. One might recall the exploitation of the laws against vagrancy and *les sortilèges* during the occupation (ongoing at this time) to exact peasant labor.

27 "Sénat, Séance du 12 avril 1935," *Le Moniteur*, 7 March 1940.

28 "Loi complétant les articles 229 et 230 du Code Pénal et abrogeant les articles 405, 407, etc. du même code," *Le Moniteur*, 25 July 1935.

29 Louis Raymond, *Manuel des officiers de police judiciaire et des juges de paix* (Port-au-Prince: Imprimerie de l'État, 1935), 78. See also Carl Edward Peters, who makes a thinly veiled reference to a "certain government" abrogating these articles, "under the fallacious pretext of permitting people to enjoy themselves without restriction." He goes on: "This same government, appalled at the outburst of iniquities to which it thus gave rise, was forced to reconsider this decision. President Vincent, by the *décret-loi* of 5 September 1935, thus set right the boat placed in peril." See Peters, *La croix contre l'asson*, 49.

30 "Vu les articles 21 et 30 de la Constitution; Considérant que l'État a pour devoir de prévenir l'accomplissement de tous actes, pratiques ou autres susceptibles d'entretenir les croyances superstitieuses nuisibles à la renommée du pays; Considérant en outre que les articles 405, 406, 2ème alinéa et 407 du Code pénal ont été abrogés en raison d'une application exagérée de ces textes, au préjudice du droit qu'ont les citoyens, particulièrement les ruraux de s'amuser et d'organiser des danses, selon les coutumes locales; Considérant qu'il convient de trouver les moyens d'enrayer les pratiques superstitieuses tout en ne mettant pas obstacle au droit légitime des paysans de s'amuser d'une manière honnête et décente; Sur le rapport du Secrétaire d'État de la Justice; Et de l'avis du Conseil des Secrétaires d'État; Et après approbation du Comité Permanent de l'Assemblée Nationale, DECRETE: Art. 1er.—Sont considérées comme pratiques superstitieuses: (1) les cérémonies, rites, danses et réunions au cours desquels se pratiquent, en offrande à des prétendues divinités, des sacrifices de bétail ou de volaille; (2) le fait d'exploiter le public en faisant accroire que, par des moyens occultes, il est possible d'arriver soit à changer la situation de fortune d'un individu, soit à le guérir d'un mal quelconque, par des procédés ignorés par la science médicale; (3) le fait d'avoir en sa demeure des objets cabalistiques servant

à exploiter la crédulité ou la naïveté du public. Art. 2.—Tout individu convaincu des dites pratiques superstitieuses sera condamné à un emprisonnement de six mois et à une amende de quatre cents gourdes, le tout à prononcer par le Tribunal de simple police. Art. 3.—Dans les cas ci-dessus prévus, le jugement rendu sera exécutoire, nonobstant appel ou pourvoi en cassation. Art. 4.—Les objets ayant servi à la perpétration de l'infraction prévue dans l'article 3 seront confisqués. . . . " In *Bulletin des lois et actes, 1934–35* (Port-au-Prince: Imprimerie Nationale, 1935), 351–352.

31 "Décret-loi sur les pratiques superstitieuses," in *Bulletin des lois et actes, 1934–35* (Port-au-Prince: Imprimerie de l'État, 1935), 351.

32 These questions are particularly interesting in light of a typed manual compiled by a lawyer named Léon Laforestrie in the early or mid-1930s (prior to the abrogation of these articles), which attempts to define the names listed in the 1864 interdiction. See Laforestrie, *Cours de droit pénal à l'usage des agents de la police judiciaire* (Port-au-Prince: N.p., n.d.), 64. Collected in the file "Superstitions en Haïti," at the Bibliothèque Haïtienne des Pères du Saint Esprit, Port-au-Prince.

33 Bracken, *The Potlatch Papers*, 113 and 118.

34 Bracken writes: "The acts that were formerly gathered under the name 'tamanawas' are called into the open and catalogued: 'and every Indian or other person who engages or assists in any celebration or dance of which the wounding or mutilation of the dead or living body of any human being or animal forms a part or is a feature, is guilty of an indictable offense and is liable to imprisonment for a term not exceeding six months and not less than two months.' . . . This part of the statute bans cannibalism and animal sacrifice. In effect, the law that aimed to put the First Nations of British Columbia to death by helping white Canadian society swallow them alive is a law against eating others." Ibid., 119.

35 Beauvoir and Dominique, *Savalou E*, 37.

36 The article went on to affirm that this "Presidential Act will have considerable repercussions for the prestige of the nation," because Vincent "included in his reform of the state this reform of our customs, this reform of our mentality, banishing from our habits these shameful vestiges of Africa which have always made us considered a strange people, backward, withdrawn from the great lights of civilization and presenting the paradoxical characteristic of appropriating the most refined elements of civilization while preserving in secret beliefs and practices of barbarous peoples." "La réforme de l'état, les décrets-loi," *Le Matin*, 9 October 1935.

37 Richard A. Loederer, *Voodoo Fire in Haiti*, trans. Desmond Ivo Vesey (New York: Literary Guild, 1935).

38 Richard Pattée, "Vaudou, Haïti et un livre malicieux," reprinted from *El Mundo de Puerto-Rico, Haïti-Journal*, 26 September 1935.

39 H. P. Davis, "La fumée s'élève des feux du vaudou," *Haïti-Journal*, 6 November 1935.

40 Price-Mars, *Ainsi parla l'oncle*, 173. A similar point is made in Stephan Palmié, "Conventionalization, Distortion, and Plagiarism in the Historiography of Afro-Caribbean Religion in New Orleans," in *Creoles and Cajuns: French Louisiana—La Louisiane Française*, ed. Wolfgang Binder (Frankfurt: Peter Lang), 315.

41 "It was only after having verified everything scrupulously that I concluded that the author of this tale had never set foot in Haiti." Davis, "La fumée s'élève des feux du vaudou."

42 In summarizing the necessity of this law, Vincent again asserted the "moral duty of the State to repress all acts or practices liable to foster superstitious beliefs or to be harmful to the good name of the country." Vincent, *Efforts et résultats*, 58.

43 Laforestrie, *Cours de droit pénal*, 64.

44 Letter from Melville J. Herskovits to Norman Armour, American Legation, Port-au-Prince, 12 April 1935, and letter from Selden Chapin to Melville J. Herskovits, 28 May 1935; Haiti Field Trip file, Box 8, Folder 22, Melville J. Herskovits Papers, Northwestern University Library.

45 Hurbon, *Le barbare imaginaire*, 124. See also Hoffmann, *Haïti: Couleurs, croyances, créole*, 139.

46 George Eaton Simpson, *Religious Cults of the Caribbean: Trinidad, Jamaica, and Haiti* (Rio Piedras, Puerto Rico: Institute of Caribbean Studies, 1970), 255. In his 1941 handbook for the church's antisuperstition campaign, Père Rémy Augustin discussed this practice: "In order not to be disturbed, one usually asks the magistrate for the authorization to organize a *vaudou* dance. But most often, when this precaution is taken, it is with the intention to celebrate a true 'service.'" Augustin, *Notes sur le vaudou* (Port-au-Prince: N.p., 1941), 12, held by the Bibliothèque Haïtienne des Pères du Saint Esprit, Port-au-Prince.

47 Hurbon, *Le barbare imaginaire*, 124–125.

48 Michael Taussig, *Defacement: Public Secrecy and the Labor of the Negative* (Stanford, CA: Stanford University Press, 1999), 61.

49 Roach, *Cities of the Dead*, 243.

50 Hurbon, *Le barbare imaginaire*, 92.

51 In discussing Vincent's *décret-loi*, Léon-François Hoffmann makes a similar point. He also sees "the influence of Jean Price-Mars and his disciples, who pleaded for the conservation and study of national folklore," but detects this in the new law's provision for the confiscation of *objets cabalistiques*, rather than their destruction, as article 407 of the 1864 Code Pénal had prescribed. Hoffmann, *Haïti: Couleurs, croyances, créole*, 138.

52 Audain, *Le mal d'Haïti*; quoted in Sténio Vincent, *La République d'Haïti: Telle qu'elle est* (Brusells: Société Anonyme Belge d'Imprimerie, 1910), 283–284.

53 Vincent, *La République d'Haïti*, 285 and 368.

54 Rosemary J. Coombe, *The Cultural Life of Intellectual Properties: Authorship, Appropriation, and the Law* (Durham, NC: Duke University Press, 1998), 25.

55 A 1934 state publication detailed Haiti's political division at this time: "The
Republic of Haiti is comprised of five Departments: the North, the Northwest, the Artibonite, the West, and the South. The Departments are subdivided into Arrondissements, administered by civil servants who are called
Prefects; Arrondissements into Communes, administered by a Communal
Council [*Conseil Communal*]; and communes into rural sections controlled
by Conseillers d'Agriculture." On the subject of the Police Rurale, it notes
that "Order is assured in rural sections by the Rural Police which is one
branch of the Garde d'Haïti. . . . These agents are under the control of the
Garde, and report regularly to their *chefs*, who inspect the rural sections fre-
quently." See *Port-au-Prince et quelques autres villes d'Haïti* (Port-au-Prince:
Imprimerie de l'État, 1934), 10 and 23. See also Comhaire, "The Haitian
'Chef de Section,'" 621.

56 For a short summary of the terms of the Concordat, see *Port-au-Prince et
quelques autres villes*, 47. In 1934 the church hierarchy was headed by the archbishop based in Port-au-Prince, Msgr. Le Gouaze, and four bishops based in
Cap-Haïtien, Les Cayes, Port-de-Paix, and Gonaïves. There were 103 urban
churches and 350 rural chapels. See *Port-au-Prince et quelques autres villes*, 50.

57 Melville Herskovits reported of his research in Haiti in the summer of
1934: "One of the sentiments about the Church most frequently heard during this field-work, coming as it did just at the end of the American occupation, was: 'The *Garde* has finally been Haitianized. Now it is the turn of
the Church.'" Herskovits, *Life in a Haitian Valley*, 292.

58 Ibid., 293. As will be examined further below, local Vodouizan quickly ascertained that the Herskovitses could be effective advocates in their efforts
to secure these permits.

59 Simpson, "The Belief System of Haitian Vodun," *American Anthropologist*
47, no. 1 (January–March 1945): 58.

60 Interview with the author, Tabarre, Haiti, 15 June 1997. My thanks to
Yanick Guiteau Dandin and Etienne Germain for arranging this meeting.

61 The broad powers conferred on this rural police officer by the Code
Rural, and the abuses to which they were frequently subjected, had long
been a subject of political and public debate in Haiti, and calls for the reform of this office stepped up in the early post-occupation years. In a 1941
article in *Le Nouvelliste*, for example, Emmanuel Paul, who became one of
Haiti's foremost ethnologists, denounced the numbers of *chèf seksyon* who
"use their charge to their personal ends," and who, "full of their authority, . . . pride themselves on exercising it by acts of brutality." In September 1942 the major newspapers reported that the government of Élie Lescot
was planning to "open a school for the training of Chefs de Section." See
Emmanuel Paul, "Le chef de section et la classe paysanne," *Le Nouvelliste*,
10 February 1941; and Louis Mercier, "*Le Nouvelliste* nous a appris que l'on
va bientôt ouvrir une école pour la formation de chefs de section," *Haïti-
Journal*, 9 September 1942.

62 Métraux, *Itinéraires*, 140 (text was written in English).

63 Rigaud, *La tradition voudoo et le voudoo haïtien*, 51; emphasis Rigaud's.

64 Ibid., 51–52; emphasis Rigaud's. In another case, he spotlights how a Catholic priest "changed into a police officer to interrupt a Voudoo service" that had been authorized by local authorities for 150 gourdes. Ibid., 57–59.

65 The last sentence continues, "whether this force be direct or indirect, physical or symbolic, exterior or interior, brutal or subtly discursive and hermeneutic, coercive or regulative, and so forth." Derrida, "Force of Law," 925–927.

66 Jean Price-Mars argued in *Ainsi parla l'oncle* that the so-called *mélange* should be understood itself as the historical consequence of that penal regime, "the phenomenon [being] especially evident wherever . . . the State interferes to protect one religion at the expense of others." Price-Mars, *Ainsi parla l'oncle*, 245.

67 Jacques Roumain, *À Propos de la campagne "anti-superstitieuse"/Las supersticiones* (Port-au-Prince: Imprimerie de l'État, 1942), 12–13.

68 See Lescot, *Avant l'oubli: Christianisme et paganisme en Haïti et autres lieux* (Port-au-Prince: Imprimerie H. Deschamps, 1974), 138–151; see also Beauvoir-Dominique, *L'ancienne cathédrale de Port-au-Prince*, 133–136; and Georges Corvington, *Port-au-Prince au cours des ans: La ville contemporaine, 1934–1950* (Port-au-Prince: Imprimerie Henri Deschamps), 247.

69 Quoted in *Campagne anti-superstitieuse: Documentation* (Port-au-Prince: N.p., 1941), 5, held by the Bibliothèque Haïtienne des Pères du Saint Esprit, Port-au-Prince.

70 Métraux, *Le vaudou haïtien*, 300.

71 This official account of the origins of the antisuperstition campaign is taken from *Campagne anti-superstitieuse: Documentation*, 7–12. See also Métraux, *Le vaudou haïtien*, 300–301, for a similar account.

72 What exactly this meant is unclear. A handbook published at the outset of the church's campaign noted that he recited an exorcism formula that he had seen a priest perform; interviews conducted in the 1960s by the French priest and sociologist Jean Kerboull with those who had sought out Ti-Jules and his "students" three decades earlier suggest that people paid a small fee for their "deliverance." See *Campagne anti-superstitieuse: Documentation*, 8; and Kerboull, *Le vaudou: Magie ou religion?*, 338.

73 *Campagne anti-superstitieuse: Documentation*, 9; and Peters, *La croix contre l'asson*, 60. It should be noted that the popular roles and identities of *oungan*, priests of Vodou, and *bòkò*, who "worked with both hands," for good and ill, were entirely conflated in the literature the church produced for the campaign. For the most part, these texts referred solely to *bòkò* but often seem to mean *oungan*.

74 *Campagne anti-superstitieuse: Documentation*, 9.

75 Ibid., 11; and Peters, *La croix contre l'asson*, 60. Peters notes that of the five dioceses of Haiti, only Les Cayes did not enter into "the struggle" at this

point because of the retirement of the bishop and death of his successor; Peters, *La croix contre l'asson*, 71. See also Nicholls, *From Dessalines to Duvalier*, 182.

76 Peters, *La croix contre l'asson*, 66–67.

77 *Campagne anti-superstitieuse: Documentation*, 112. Matthew Smith speculates that this may have "been a shrewdly calculated maneuver to give apparent support to the French clergy" while also seeking to Americanize the church hierarchy; Smith, *Red and Black in Haiti* (Chapel Hill: University of North Carolina Press, 2009), 50. Lescot had served as the minister of justice, the minister of the interior, and the minister to the United States under Vincent. See preface, in *Elie Lescot: Le diplomate et l'animateur* (N.p.: International Business Machines, 1944).

78 Joseph Le Gouaze, Archbishop of Port-au-Prince, "Lettre circulaire sur les pratiques de superstition et les 'semaines de mission anti-superstitieuse,'" 15 August 1941, 4. Bibliothèque Haïtienne des Pères du Saint Esprit, Port-au-Prince.

79 Alphonse Jean noted that in spite of the fact that his father, who had also been a well-known *oungan*, considered himself to be a lifelong Catholic, when he died the local clergy refused to perform a Catholic burial. Interview with Alphonse Jean ("Kazo"), Tabarre, Haiti, 15 June 1997.

80 *Campagne anti-superstitieuse: Documentation*, 90–91 and 106–10.

81 This charge was made in an article that appeared in the Port-au-Prince newspaper *Le Matin* on 21 March 1942 entitled "Lutte religieuse sous le couvert de l'anti-superstition" (Religious Struggle under the Cover of Antisuperstition). See also Peters, *La croix contre l'asson*, 195–99, for the church's response.

82 *Campagne anti-superstitieuse: Documentation*, 91.

83 A rosary published in the same manual and dedicated to "Les Protestants" explained that Satan conscripted Luther in his ambition to "spoil the work of the church by preventing it from saving people," and that "after Luther, the Protestants made more than 300 kinds of Protestants, . . . but all they say is, in truth, a tower of Babel." *Campagne anti-superstitieuse: Documentation*, 31–32 and 66–67.

84 The first Methodist missionaries, John Brown and James Catts, arrived in Haiti under the auspices of the London-based Wesleyan Methodist Missionary Society in 1817. The first Baptist mission was sent to Haiti in 1823 by the Baptist Missionary Society of Massachusetts. The first Episcopal congregation was founded by the African American missionary James Theodore Holly in 1861. The A.M.E. church began sending missionaries to Haiti beginning in the 1840s and established an ongoing mission in Port-au-Prince in 1884. See Pressoir, "Le protestantisme en Haïti," and Pressoir, *Le protestantisme haïtien*, vol. 1, pt. 1, 48–49.

85 Léon Denius Pamphile, *La croix et le glaive: L'église catholique et l'occupation américaine d'Haiti, 1915–1934* (Port-au-Prince: Éditions des Antilles, 1991), 68.

86 Samuel Guy Inman of the Disciples of Christ fellowship wrote of Haiti as a new frontier for American Protestant workers: "We may consider the Republic as practically a virgin field." Inman, *Through Santo Domingo and Haiti: A Cruise with the Marines* (New York: Committee on Co-operation in Latin America, 1920), 90. It is important to note that a number of the occupation's most vocal critics were emissaries of U.S. Protestant organizations. For example, the Reverend L. Ton Evans of the Lott Carey Mission Society testified forcefully during the 1921–1922 U.S. Senate committee investigation of the occupation against what he characterized as marine "barbarism" towards Haitian peasants. The Reverend S. E. Churchstone-Lord, pastor of the A.M.E. church in Haiti, accused the military hierarchy in Haiti of tolerating rapes of Haitian girls and women committed by some U.S. marines.

87 W. F. Jordan, *Crusading in the West Indies* (New York: Fleming H. Revell, 1922), 132 and 133.

88 Ibid., 136.

89 For example, see Pressoir, *Le protestantisme haïtien*, vol. 1, pt. 2, 364.

90 Pamphile, *La croix et le glaive*, 49. Catts Pressoir notes that the prefect of the town Les Cayes, Malherbe Pressoir, early on in the occupation asked an American officer, "'How is it that the American occupation, which is rather Protestant, so conspicuously favors the Catholic clergy, and grants nothing to the Protestant churches?'" The officer replied that it was a matter of security: "'When we arrive in one of your towns, we always seek to know the life and feelings of those who live there, and no one better than the priest can inform us in this regard.'" See Pressoir, *Le protestantisme haïtien*, vol. 2, 99.

91 Pamphile, *La croix et le glaive*, 84. Although Borno was all but impotent in directing the course of government policy, his advocacy on behalf of the church's concerns seems to have empowered Catholic protest against new Protestant missionary projects around the country. There were reports of local governmental authorities shutting down Protestant schools and preventing missionaries from evangelizing in particular communities. Ibid., 130.

92 Writing in the early 1920s, W. F. Jordan noted that "Jacmel has the largest and most active Protestant community in Haiti" and later described the Baptist church under Lhérisson's leadership as "the largest and most successful missionary church in the West Indies." Jordan, *Crusading in the West Indies*, 104–105 and 112. Catts Pressoir called Lhérisson's work "the great missionary success of Haitian Protestantism," in Pressoir, "Le protestantisme en Haïti," 394. On Pierre Nicolas's work, see Pressoir, *Le protestantisme haïtien*, vol. 1, pt. 2, 380; and on Alexandre Baptiste and Ledoux Paraison's work see Jordan, *Crusading in the West Indies*, 131; and Pressoir, "Le protestantisme en Haïti," 395.

93 Testimony of Reverend L. Ton Evans, *Senate Hearings*, 233–234. See also Jordan, *Crusading in the West Indies*, 134–135.

94 *Campagne anti-superstitieuse: Documentation*, 7.

95 Métraux, *Le vaudou haïtien*, 312. See also Métraux, "Réactions psychologiques à la christianisation de la vallée de Marbial (Haïti)," *Revue de psychologie des peuples* 3 (1953): 251–252; Métraux, *Making a Living in the Marbial Valley (Haiti)* (Paris: UNESCO, 1951), 111; and Christine Laurière, "D'une île à l'autre: Alfred Métraux en Haïti," *Gradhiva* 1, n.s. (2005): 193.

96 Bishop Burton to the president of the republic, 12 December 1941; and "La campagne anti-superstitieuse donne encore lieu à des abus." Letter from Dr. Nerva Gousse to the director of *Le Matin*, 30 January 1942; enclosures with memo from J. C. White, U.S. Legation in Haiti, to the U.S. Secretary of State, 2 February 1942, dec. file 838.404/48, U.S. National Archives.

97 The Église de Dieu en Christ had been growing rapidly since the late 1930s, with a church in the capital and missionary work in the provinces and featuring, as the historian Georges Corvington notes, "religious music, a girls choir, prayers out loud, singing of tuneful canticles, hand-clapping, and arm movements." Corvington, *Port-au-Prince au cours des ans: La ville contemporaine*, 257–58.

98 Métraux, *Le vaudou haïtien*, 316.

99 See Corvington, *Port-au-Prince au cours des ans: La ville contemporaine*, 258–259. Corvington reports that the ban lasted for two and a half years and was lifted as a result of the intervention of a U.S. senator whose support President Lescot wished to have in the U.S. Congress.

100 "Les activités de la Secte dite 'Les Pentecôtistes et Trembleurs' étant contraires aux bonnes mœurs, et de nature à troubler l'ordre public, sont interdites." *Bulletin des lois et actes: 15 mai 1941–15 septembre 1942* (Port-au-Prince: Imprimerie de l'État, n.d.), 130. See also *Le Moniteur*, 8 September 1941.

101 Testimony of Reverend L. Ton Evans, *Senate Hearings*, 200.

102 H. Ormonde McConnell, *Haiti Diary, 1933–1970: Mission Extraordinary* (n.p.: United Methodist Committee on Relief, n.d.), 21.

103 "À l'Arcahaie: La campagne contre la superstition bat son plein," *Haïti-Journal*, 28 October 1941. These scenes sound very similar to stories Melville Herskovits reported hearing from informants in Mirebalais about the collaboration between the church and the marines in repressing Vodou earlier in the occupation: "In the *place* huge bonfires were made of *vodun* drums painted and 'dressed' in elaborate manner. Everything found in the *humforts* and the private houses of worship was confiscated, and the 'thunder stones,' necklaces of the devotees, and other sacred objects that would not burn were thrown into the Artibonite River." Herskovits, *Life in a Haitian Valley*, 293.

104 Roger Riou, *The Island of My Life: From Petty Crime to Priestly Mission*, trans. Martin Sokolinsky (New York: Delacorte Press, 1975), 154.

105 Ibid., 154.

106 Peasants in the Marbial Valley later told Métraux that "headed by the Chef de Section . . . these voluntary inquisitors took the opportunity of settling

private scores or even of committing small thefts." Métraux, *Le vaudou haï-tien*, 307.

107 See *Campagne anti-superstitieuse: Documentation*, 18: "At first, it must be the Priest himself who goes to carry out this task. The people would not do it because they are afraid. But quickly, one finds men who triumph over this fear and who thus agree to go destroy the objects of superstition."

108 Ibid., 18.

109 Ibid., 18. This ecclesiastical mandate to destroy the material signs and sites of "superstition" exceeded the terms of the 1935 law against *les pratiques su-perstitieuses* that served as an authorizing legal basis for the campaign. While the 1864 law against *les sortilèges* braced its 1835 precedent by specifying that the "instruments, utensils, and costumes" associated with such practices would be seized in order "to be burnt and destroyed," the law passed under Vincent in 1935 states only that these objects should be confiscated.

110 Ibid., 14.

111 Joseph Le Gouaze, Archbishop of Port-au-Prince, "Lettre circulaire sur les pratiques de superstition et les 'semaines de mission anti-superstitieuse,'" 15 August 1941, 3, held by the Bibliothèque Haïtienne des Pères du Saint Esprit, Port-au-Prince.

112 See Augustin, "Cantiques pour la campagne anti-superstitieuse (1ère série)," held by the Bibliothèque Haïtienne des Pères du Saint Esprit, Port-au-Prince. Several of the canticles are anti-Protestant. On Augustin's ap-pointment as bishop under the presidency of Paul Magloire, see Diederich, *Bon Papa*, 97. On the history of the church's delayed formation of a Haitian clergy, see Beauvoir-Dominique, *L'ancienne cathédrale de Port-au-Prince*, 133–139.

113 See Steven Mullaney's discussion of the historiographical paradoxes pre-sented by such literatures: "It is customarily regarded as one of the ironies of history that works such as Phillip Stubbes' *Anatomie of Abuses* (1583) pro-vide us with our fullest account of the country, alien, heathen, or other-wise strange ways they would see repressed but must first review or re-hearse at some length." Mullaney, *The Place of the Stage: License, Play, and Power in Renaissance England* (Chicago: University of Chicago Press, 1988), 72.

114 Carl Edward Peters, *Lumière sur le humfort* (Port-au-Prince: Chéraquit, Imprimeur-Éditeur, 1941); and Augustin, *Notes sur le vaudou*, held by the Bibliothèque Haïtienne des Pères du Saint Esprit, Port-au-Prince.

115 "For a whole year, we inventoried the *caille-loas*, thatched huts built for voodoo spirits." Riou, *The Island of My Life*, 155.

116 Peters identifies the author of this booklet as Monsignor Jan of Cap-Haïtien. Peters, *La croix contre l'asson*, 61.

117 Roumain, *À propos de la campagne "anti-superstitieuse,"* 11. In singling out this example, Roumain may have been thinking about the reportedly centuries-old mapou tree—the "Mapou Dampus," a nationally known and

beloved *repozwa* that stood at the entrance to Léogâne and was axed during the mission in that region in late 1941. Elie Lescot writes of his private outrage over the felling of this tree and denies Carl Edward Peters's account that he was informed in advance that it was planned. Peters writes that it was "the pressure of the people" that led to its being chopped down; Lescot writes that it was ordered by Msgr. Le Gouaze, archbishop of Port-au-Prince. Note Peters's account of the party that was assembled for the felling, including "the communal magistrate, lieutenant, team of prisoners, missionaries, armed with hatchets, shovels, and picks." See Lescot, *Avant l'oubli*, 363–364; and Peters, *La croix contre l'asson*, 80–81.

118 *Campagne anti-superstitieuse: Documentation*, 15.

119 Métraux, *Le vaudou haïtien*, 298–299.

120 Ibid., 307.

121 Ibid., 303.

122 Ibid., 308. See also Hurbon, *Le barbare imaginaire*, 129, on the "two great campaigns against Vodou, that of 1896 and that of 1941." He writes: "Everyone agreed on the object of the campaigns: the uprooting of sorcery. On the one hand, the missionaries, as we have seen, assimilated Vodou to sorcery, on the other, the people accepted the denunciation of 'makers of wanga,' that is to say evil-doers, because, for them, Vodou is supposed to reject sorcery."

123 Kerboull, *Voodoo and Magic Practices*, 75 and 185.

124 Métraux, "Réactions psychologiques," 256. See also "La campagne anti-superstitieuse: Un bôcor renommé est arrêté à Milot," *Haïti-Journal*, 16 January 1942, which reported that "thousands" crowded the street to witness the arrival in custody of a "bôcor" named Casséus from Maïssade, accused of "cabalistic crimes" and long sought after by the police.

125 Métraux, *Le vaudou haïtien*, 306.

126 Ibid., 306.

127 Kerboull, *Voodoo and Magic Practices*, 172. Métraux writes that the campaign "provoked veritable epidemics of trance." "Réactions psychologiques," 252.

128 Ibid, 253.

129 Interview with Alphonse Jean ("Kazo"), Tabarre, Haiti, 15 June 1997.

130 Peters, *La croix contre l'asson*, 123. Note as well that a church report from Port-de-Paix in 1948 regretted that the cards distributed since the campaign "prove absolutely nothing, since a very great number of those who have cards live in superstition . . . as if they did not 'take the oath,'" and had also become the object of "a shameful traffic." "Mesures établies dans le diocèse de Port-de-Paix pour maintenir la vérité catholique contre la superstition et le 'mélange,'" 29 September 1948. File "Superstitions en Haïti," Bibliothèque Haïtienne des Pères du Saint Esprit, Port-au-Prince. See also Bernard Diederich and Al Burt, *Papa Doc and the Tonton Macoutes* (Port-au-Prince: Éditions Henri Deschamps, 1986), 351.

131 Joseph Le Gouaze, Jean-Marie Jan, Paul Robert, and Albert Guiot, *Apostolat de quatre vingts ans* (Cap-Haïtien: Presse Almonacy, 1942), 21.

132 Peters, *Lumière sur le humfort*, 38.

133 Ibid., 49. See also the report by the bishop of Gonaïves, Paul Robert, in July 1947 that "the police received the order to close their eyes to all the affairs of *Vaudou*." Robert, "Texte du rapport sur la superstition," July 1947, held by the Bibliothèque Haïtienne des Frères de l'Instruction Chrétienne, Port-au-Prince, Haiti.

134 See Peters, *La croix contre l'asson*, 84–86; and Lescot, *Avant l'oubli*, 358–360.

135 Joseph Le Gouaze, archbishop of Port-au-Prince, "Lettre circulaire sur les pratiques de superstition et les 'semaines de mission anti-superstitieuse,'" 15 August 1941, 4. Bibliothèque Haïtienne des Pères du Saint Esprit, Port-au-Prince.

136 "La campagne anti-superstitieuse dégénère en manifestations de haine et de discorde," *Haïti-Journal*, 23 February 1942.

137 "Grave incident à Delmas," *La Phalange*, 23 February 1942.

138 "La campagne anti-superstitieuse dégénère en manifestations de haine et de discorde," *Haïti-Journal*, 23 February 1942.

139 Corvington, *Port-au-Prince au cours des ans: La ville contemporaine*, 246–247. See also Smith, *Red and Black in Haiti*, 49.

140 Métraux, *Le vaudou haïtien*, 304.

141 "La campagne anti-superstitieuse dégénère en manifestations de haine et de discorde," *Haïti-Journal*, 23 February 1942.

142 See Métraux, *Le vaudou haïtien*, 309, and Kerboull, *Le vaudou: Magie ou religion?*, 42.

143 Métraux, *Le vaudou haïtien*, 303.

144 "The Peace of the World Has to Be Based on the Rights of Man and the Liberty of All Nations: Important Statements Made by the Envoy of His Holiness the Pope to One of Our Reporters," *Listin Diario*, 24 February 1942. Enclosure in dispatch number S45 from the American Legation at Ciudad Trujillo, D.R., to U.S. Secretary of State, 11 March 1942, dec. file 838.404/66, U.S. National Archives; translation by the American Legation. For an analysis of the Trujillo regime's "extensive financial support of the Catholic Church" and the "church's constant, often effusive praise of Trujillo and the progress of his era," see Richard Lee Turits, *Foundations of Despotism: Peasants, the Trujillo Regime, and Modernity in Dominican History* (Stanford, CA: Stanford University Press, 2003), 19.

145 Trujillo ordered this massacre at the beginning of October 1937, instructing his armed forces to use machetes rather than guns in order to be able to claim that the killings were a spontaneous popular Dominican uprising against poaching by Haitian migrants. In 1938 Trujillo ordered another campaign against ethnic Haitians in the southern frontier region. In both cases, many if not most of those targeted had been living in these regions

for generations. See Turits, *Foundations of Despotism*, 144–180. See also Matthew Smith's analysis of the Vincent government's muted response to the massacre in *Red and Black in Haiti*, 32.

146 See Corvington, *Port-au-Prince au cours des ans: La ville contemporaine*, 247. See also the report from the U.S. Legation in Haiti on 7 March 1942 that Lescot had "telegraphed the Vatican requesting the recall of the Papal Nuncio in Haiti, as a result of statements made by the Nuncio to the press in [*sic*] Dominican Republic which were interpreted as reflecting unfavorably upon the Haitian people." Dec. file 838.404/62, U.S. National Archives. See as well the U.S. military intelligence report of 26 May 1943, which provides a translation into English of the Lescot government's agreement with the American branch of the Oblates of Mary Immaculate and suggests that Lescot's "most cherished ambition is to replace the influence of the French Catholic clergy in Haiti by an American Catholic clergy." "Agreement between the Congregation of the Oblate Missionaries and the Haitian Government," 26 May 1943, dec. file 838.404/127, U.S. National Archives.

147 "La campagne anti-superstitieuse dégénère en manifestations de haine et de discorde," *Haïti-Journal*, 23 February 1942. Such tensions and divisions were unquestionably heightened by the campaign, which required *rejete* to break ties (*désolidariser*) with those who, for whatever reason, refused to take the antisuperstition oath.

148 See Dorsainvil, *Vodou et névrose*, 139.

149 In his memorandum White sought to document and account for what he perceived to be an increase in public discourse about "voodoo" in Port-au-Prince that year. J. C. White to the Secretary of State, "Change in Attitude towards Voodoo on the Part of the Intellectual Classes in Haiti as Evidenced by Development of Expressions of Interest in Folklore," 24 September 1942, dec. file 838.404/85, U.S. National Archives.

150 Lescot, *Avant l'oubli*, 360.

151 Corvington, *Port-au-Prince au cours des ans: La ville contemporaine*, 248. On Rara, see McAlister, *Rara! Vodou, Power, and Performance*. Alphonse Jean, the elderly *oungan* with whom I spoke in 1997, made a point of mentioning, during a conversation about the *kanpay rejete*, that Lescot had banned Rara bands. In the course of my research, I frequently heard this interdiction cited as a factor in the fall of Lescot's government in 1946. The municipal authorities of Port-au-Prince, in conjunction with the government, also canceled the organization of a street carnival that year, as they had a year before under Vincent, on account of the war. See "Autour de la saison carnavalesque," *Le Nouvelliste*, 23 January 1941.

152 Joseph Le Gouaze, Archbishop of Port-au-Prince, announced in a confidential letter dated 20 March 1942 that the antisuperstition missions were to be indefinitely postponed, even while assuring that the "antisuperstition crusade" would continue and that it couldn't *not* continue, because it

was "the *raison d'être* of the Church." "Communication de Son Exc. Mgr l'Archevêque de Port-au-Prince," 20 March 1942, held by the Bibliothèque Haïtienne des Pères du Saint Esprit, Port-au-Prince.

153 See Carolyn Fowler, *A Knot in the Thread: The Life and Work of Jacques Roumain* (Washington, DC: Howard University Press, 1980), 175–211.

154 Letter from Jacques Roumain to Melville J. Herskovits, 6 June 1939; Jacques Roumain file, Box 20, Folder 25, Melville J. Herskovits Papers, Northwestern University Library.

155 Fowler, *A Knot in the Thread*, 183–184 and 205–206.

156 See Fowler, *A Knot in the Thread*, 209–210; and André-Marcel d'Ans, "Jacques Roumain et la fascination de l'ethnologie," in *Jacques Roumain: Oeuvres complètes*, ed. Léon-François Hoffmann (Madrid: Collection Archivos, 2003), 1389–1391. My thanks to Gérarde Magloire-Danton for sending me a copy of this article.

157 Fowler, *A Knot in the Thread*, 206. Also see letters from Jacques Roumain to Melville J. Herskovits, 6 June 1939 and 4 August 1939; Jacques Roumain file, Box 20, Melville J. Herskovits Papers, Northwestern University Library. See also Léon-François Hoffmann, "Biographie de Jacques Roumain," Île en Île, http://www.lehman.cuny.edu/ile.en.ile/paroles/roumain_bio.html, accessed 1 June 2010.

158 Letter from Alfred Métraux to Melville J. Herskovits, 3 June 1941; Alfred Métraux 1936–1941 file, Box 13, Folder 25, Melville J. Herskovits Papers, Northwestern University Library.

159 Métraux, *Le vaudou haïtien*, 13.

160 André-Marcel d'Ans quotes from the first *Bulletin du Bureau d'ethnologie* (1942): "'In the presbyteries of Pétionville, Léogane, Cabaret, Arcahaie, Croix-des-Bouquets, Thomazeau, Gressier, following the *campagne anti-superstitieuse*, 493 objects have been collected, in particular by M. Kurt Fischer [*sic*]. It is deplorable that a considerable number of objects have been destroyed.'" D'Ans, "Jacques Roumain et la fascination de l'ethnologie," 1400. Kurt Fisher was an Austrian who had studied archaeology at the University of Vienna and became affiliated with the Bureau d'Ethnologie as a "Specialist of Archaeology." He donated Haitian archaeological objects to the Smithsonian in the fall of 1941, as Métraux was in the process of arranging the transfer of those he had collected. See accession nos. 158029, 160156, and 160547, Haiti Collection, Department of Anthropology, National Museum of Natural History, Smithsonian Institution.

161 Métraux's journal entries from this trip reveal the extent to which his and Rhoda's travels with Roumain were focused on the collection of pre-Columbian pottery fragments, ax heads, and pestles, which they purchased from locals and searched for themselves in caves identified as "trou-zind" (*trous des Indiens*). See Métraux, *Itinéraires*, 133–142.

162 Métraux, *Le vaudou haïtien*, 13. See as well Métraux's account of his discussions with Roumain in his tribute "Jacques Roumain, archéologue et eth-

nographe," *Cahiers d'Haïti* (November 1944): 23–24. Interestingly, Métraux does not mention discussing the creation of such an institution with Roumain in his journal from this trip. However in the midst of their travels together, on 1 August 1941, Métraux recorded an entry that may shed light on why he later claimed to have been an influence on Roumain's founding of the Bureau: "Quarrel with Roumain who expresses the most derogatory views on museums. I feel irritated beyond control and reason." *Itinéraires 1 (1935–1953)*, 139 (text written in English).

163 Interview with Michel Lamartinière Honorat, Pétionville, Haiti, 4 June 1997.

164 Métraux, *Le vaudou haïtien*, 17. George Eaton Simpson reported in 1945 that "Dr. Alfred Métraux, of the Smithsonian Institution, stated in October, 1941, that *vodun* shrines were being abandoned so rapidly that within a few months it would be difficult to find any trace of the cult except in the most remote sections of the interior." Simpson, "The Belief System of Haitian Vodun," 59.

165 Roumain, *À propos de la campagne "anti-superstitieuse,"* 12.

166 In one of his 1939 letters to Herskovits, in fact, Roumain wrote that in continuing his anthropological studies in the United States, he hoped to be able "to bring forth my book on the pre-Columbian ethnology of Haiti." Letter from Jacques Roumain to Melville J. Herskovits, 6 June 1939; Melville J. Herskovits Papers, Jacques Roumain File, Box 20, Northwestern University Library; see also Fowler, *A Knot in the Thread*, 175–176. Note the wider interest in pre-Columbian archaeology in Haiti at this time, as evidenced by Edmond Mangones and Louis Maximilien's organization of the exposition documented in their *L'art précolombien d'Haïti: Catalogue de l'exposition précolombienne organisée à l'occasion du IIIe Congrès des Caraïbes sous le haut patronage de Son Excellence M. Stenio Vincent* (1941).

167 Although large rocks believed to be inhabited by spirits were to be "crushed," one antisuperstition handbook for priests specified that *pierres superstitieuses* were to be "carried away" rather than destroyed. See *Campagne anti-superstitieuse: Documentation*, 30. See also Augustin, *Notes sur le vaudou*, 6. In an article-length memoir on his research in Haiti during the 1930s and 1940s, Harold Courlander provides an anecdote that suggests that individual members of the French Catholic Hierarchy in Haiti had been engaged in such collecting for some time. See Courlander, "Recollections of Haiti in the 1930s and '40s," *African Arts* 23, no. 2 (April 1990): 63.

168 Peters, *La croix contre l'asson*, 220–221. He notes that in mid-October 1941, at the height of the campaign, the archbishop of Port-au-Prince, Monsignor Le Gouaze, had published an invitation to researchers in *La Phalange* "to see the spoils coming from the hounforts and piling up in the courtyards of the presbyteries." Such "thunderstones" had been prized by some marine collectors during the occupation as well. It is worth pausing here to reflect on the significance of the *campagne anti-superstitieuse* for the building up of

collections of Haitian ethnographic artifacts—not only in Haiti, where, after its founding, the bureau became a repository for objects salvaged from the church's pyres, but also at major institutions in the United States and France. Alfred Métraux donated to the Smithsonian Institution pre-Columbian artifacts that he had found and purchased during his travels in Haiti in the summer of 1941, as well as a large collection of religious objects confiscated in the area of Croix-des-Bouquets—including five drums—that he had preserved from clerical destruction. These pieces joined those donated to the Smithsonian by U.S. military officials that had been confiscated in marine raids on *sèvis* during the occupation. See accession nos. 161294 and 163278, Haiti Collection, Department of Anthropology, National Museum of Natural History, Smithsonian Institution. Roger Riou, the French priest who wrote of the campaign in his memoir, recalls that he "sent the most interesting *ouangas* that we had taken down to the Musée de l'Homme in Paris. There were stones carved by the Arawak Indians, real hatchets and knives made out of solid granite, often bearing the form of men or animals" (Riou, *The Island of My Life*, 154–155). The Haitian ethnologist Emmanuel C. Paul's observation that most of the objects held by the Bureau d'Ethnologie's museum "relate to popular religion" might reflect both the research interests of many of its scholars, and the extent to which the collection originally was built on objects salvaged in 1941 from the church pyres. See Paul, *L'ethnographie en Haïti*, 23.

169 See d'Ans, "Jacques Roumain et la fascination de l'ethnologie," 1403. See also Élie Lescot Jr., "Une page d'histoire mise à l'endroit ou les dessous de la campagne anti-superstitieuse de 1941–1942," *Pour Haïti* 45 (3rd trimester 2003): 16–17. My thanks to Gérarde Magloire-Danton for sending me this article.

170 See Métraux to Julian Steward, 18 August 1941: "I must consult you on a point concerning the Smithsonian. From the first of July of this year the Catholic clergy has started a systematic persecution of the Voodoo cult; thousands of objects have been confiscated and piled up in the local presbyteries where they will be burned very soon. A great many of the specimens are of great anthropological interest and I made a plea to save them, asking the priests to give them to me for the National Museum in Washington. In spite of their distrust and unreliability, I have good hope of securing this material before the end of the week. In this case what shall I do to ship it to Washington?" Accession no. 163278, Haiti Collection, Department of Anthropology, National Museum of Natural History, Smithsonian Institution.

171 It appears that the Smithsonian sent a copy of the Mexican law on cultural patrimony. See Camille Lhérisson to Alexander Wetmore, 11 September 1941, accession no. 163278, Haiti Collection, Department of Anthropology, National Museum of Natural History, Smithsonian Institution.

172 Quoted in "Création d'un Bureau d'Ethnologie: Un important décret-loi

instituant ce bureau vient d'être promulgué," *Haïti-Journal*, 11 November 1941. For the law itself, see *Le Moniteur*, 10 November 1941. This law was preceded by that of 20 April 1940, which, as Félix Magloire and Félix Soray wrote in 1944, "protects archaeological, historical, or artistic treasures against depredations and unauthorized excavations." Magloire and Soray, "The Legal System of Haiti," 6. See also Célius, "Cheminement anthropologique en Haïti," 53.

173   Although not mentioned as one of the bureau's original mandates in the *décret-loi* that founded it, "Le développement de l'enseignement de l'ethnologie" was listed among the other responsibilities of the bureau in the front pages of the *Bulletin du Bureau d'ethnologie* and its other publications.

174   "L'Institut d'Ethnologie: L'inauguration a eu lieu hier," *Haïti-Journal*, 18 November 1941.

175   Ibid. Price-Mars himself taught a range of courses at the Institut and later described the model he used there for teaching the theory and method of folklore study. After defining for students "the beliefs, traditions, customs, and habits of the Haitian people that are the constitutive elements of their folklore," he instructed them in the principles of collection, and "to illuminate the recommended methodology, . . . proceeded with students to rural and popular investigations." At the close of "each school cycle, my companions condensed the results of our investigations, with their own observations and personal remarks, into theses. I thereby transmitted to my young friends the principles that I learned in foreign universities." Price-Mars, *Folklore et patriotisme*, 15.

176   See Carlo Avierl Célius, "La création plastique et le tournant ethnologique en Haïti," *Gradhiva* 1, n.s. (2005): 71–94, for an analysis of the relative lack of attention to visual art at the Institut d'Ethnologie and, later, at the Bureau d'Ethnologie under the direction of Jacques Roumain's successors. This is particularly striking given that the so-called *art naïf* movement in painting, centered around the Port-au-Prince Centre d'Art founded by American Dewitt Peters in 1944, was strongly focused on popular religious themes.

177   See Nicholls, *From Dessalines to Duvalier*, 173; and Smith, *Red and Black in Haiti*, 20. See also Kaussen, *Migrant Revolutions*, 67, for an analysis of the political rifts in the indigenist movement toward the end of the occupation.

178   Denis became director of the Bureau d'Ethnologie in 1946 and served in this capacity until his death in 1957, the same year that his collaborator, François Duvalier, became president.

179   Nicholls, *From Dessalines to Duvalier*, 168–169.

180   See Lorimer Denis and François Duvalier, "Question d'anthroposociologie: Le determinisme racial," *Les Griots* (January–March 1939): 303–309; François Duvalier and Lorimer Denis, "Considérations sur nos origines historiques," *Les Griots* (October–December 1939): 621; Denis and

Duvalier, "Pour un humanisme totalitaire," *Les Griots* (April–September 1939): 468–472; Nicholls, *From Dessalines to Duvalier*, 168–172; and Smith, *Red and Black in Haiti*, 24–26.

181 Honorat, interview with the author, 4 June 1997, Pétionville, Haïti. See also Rachelle Charlier-Doucet: "The first team of *responsables* of the bureau brought together men of different social origin (*mulâtre* high bourgeoisie, black petite-bourgeoisie and middle class), all claiming the leftist tendencies of the period." Charlier-Doucet, "Anthropologie, politique et engagement social: L'expérience du Bureau d'Ethnologie d'Haïti," *Gradhiva* 1, n.s. (2005): 118.

182 Oriol, Viaud, and Aubourg, *Le mouvement folklorique en Haïti*, 20.

183 David Nicholls argues that the romantic populism of the Griots group was "to some extent shared by Roumain." See Nicholls, *From Dessalines to Duvalier*, 176.

184 Largey, *Vodou Nation*, 214; and Valério Canez, "Notre folklore musical," *Haïti-Journal*, 26 November 1942. See also Jean Coulanges, untitled essay, *Conjonction* 198 (April–May–June 1993): 85. Coulanges discusses the work of Jaegerhuber, Justin Elie, Ludovic Lamothe, Lina Mathon, and Frantz Casséus, among others: "Certain Haitian and foreign artists (living in Haiti), following the example of a Béla Bartók, for Hungary, of a Heitor Villa Lobos for Brazil, of a Manuel de Falla for Spain, utilized their technique and talent to make classical, concert, recital, salon, chamber work, from Haitian popular themes."

185 Corvington, *Port-au-Prince au cours des ans: La ville contemporaine*, 191–192 and 296–297. See the discussion of Jaegerhuber's ethnomusicological collaborations with Louis Maximilien, author of the 1945 study *Le vodou haïtien: Rites radas-canzo*, in Largey, *Vodou Nation*, 209–211 and 229. See also Harold Courlander's memories of Jaegerhuber in his "Recollections of Haiti in the 1930s and '40s," 65. Largey notes that Courlander and Jaegerhuber worked with the same informant, Libera Bordereaux, who brought rural singers to them to perform in "studio sessions." *Vodou Nation*, 207 and 218.

186 See Valério Canez, "Notre folklore musical: De même que les negro spirituals harmonisés et arrangés ont pu faire le tour du monde, le folklore haïtien, avec ses belles mélodies et ses rythmes uniques doit être connu dans tous les pays de monde," in *Haïti-Journal*, 26 November 1942; and Canez, "À propos de notre folk-lore musical," *Haïti-Journal*, 23 December 1942. See Michael Largey's discussion of Ludovic Lamothe's work, and particularly his compositions for piano, such as "Sous la Tonnelle" and "Loco," which took the ceremonial music of Vodou for their inspiration: "For Lamothe, 'national' artists were in a perpetual search for musical materials that would give their works cross-class appeal within their nation state and would appeal to audiences outside the nation as examples of a universal art music repertoire." *Vodou Nation*, 113.

187 Largey discusses another point of contestation in Haitian art music circles:

how to represent the meter of Haitian religious songs in presentational compositions: "[Jaegerhuber] believed that Haitian musicians should not sacrifice their 'rhythmic' connections to their African ancestry—especially the use of 5/8 meter—in order to make folk music–based Haitian classical music legible to foreign audiences." *Vodou Nation*, 218.

188   Selden Rodman, *Haiti: The Black Republic* (1954; New York: Devin-Adair, 1961), 68. Price-Mars writes that his efforts to enable Seabrook to see a ceremony failed at every turn, "because I met a stubborn mistrust on the part of all the peasants to whom I addressed myself in spite of my long-standing and cordial relations with them"; *Une étape de l'évolution haïtienne*, 161. For other examples of such staged performances of ritual dance during the occupation, see Largey, *Vodou Nation*, 157; and Samuel Guy Inman, *Trailing the Conquistadores* (New York: Friendship Press, 1930), 122.

189   "Performance . . . stands in for an elusive entity that it is not but that it must vainly aspire both to embody and to replace." See Roach, *Cities of the Dead*, 3.

190   Niles, *Black Haiti*, 185–189.

191   "I phoned Mr. Armour, the American minister, shortly before noon, and we went over at once. . . . We are assured of all cooperation from him, and this promise he has made good in excellent fashion. . . . The Legation people had arranged for me to meet General Vogel, the Commander of the Garde d'Haiti, and I had to go to see him and get a letter to the young Lieutenant at Mirebalais which would permit us to work undisturbed. His office is also arranging for the permit to take pictures from the Secretary of the Interior. Armour came to the home . . . to offer all aid once again." Melville J. Herskovits, "Haiti Diary," 22 June 1934, 1 and 4; Melville J. and Frances S. Herskovits Papers, MG 261, Schomburg Center for Research in Black Culture, Box 13, Folder 68.

192   Letter from Melville J. Herskovits to Norman Armour, 22 June 1934; Haiti Field Trip file, Box 8, Folder 22, Melville J. Herskovits Papers, Northwestern University Library.

193   Herskovits, "Haiti Diary," 22 June 1934, 8; Melville J. and Frances S. Herskovits Papers, MG 261, Schomburg Center for Research in Black Culture, Box 13, Folder 68. Herskovits was interested in studying dance and "motor behavior" more generally during his and Frances's fieldwork in Haiti. This is reflected in his film footage of their stay in Mirebalais, which at one point features an informant demonstrating the footwork for a dance, repeating these steps over and over with little upper-body movement. See Melville J. Herskovits, *Life In a Haitian Valley Film Study, 1934*, 77.1.2 1934; Human Studies Film Archives, Department of Anthropology, National Museum of Natural History, Smithsonian Institution.

194   Letter from Norman Armour to Melville J. Herskovits, 27 June 1934; Haiti Field Trip file, Box 8, Folder 22, Melville J. Herskovits Papers, Northwestern University Library.

195 Herskovits, "Haiti Diary," 6 July 1934, 24; Melville J. and Frances S. Herskovits Papers, MG 261, Schomburg Center for Research in Black Culture, Box 13, Folder 68.

196 Letter from Melville J. Herskovits to Norman Armour, 7 August 1934; Haiti Field Trip file, Box 8, Folder 22, Melville J. Herskovits Papers, Northwestern University Library.

197 This episode underscores that such events were framed in multiple ways depending on the subject positions and perspectives of those involved. Here, the family on whose behalf Herskovits intervened was not only aware of this reframing, but also tactically involved in engineering it; yet this did not mean that they would have regarded the *sèvis* that took place as diminished or altered in spiritual meaning and efficacy on that account.

198 Herskovits, *Life in a Haitian Valley*, 293.

199 Herskovits, "Haiti Diary," 2 July 1934, 22; Melville J. and Frances S. Herskovits Papers, MG 261, Schomburg Center for Research in Black Culture, Box 13, Folder 68. See Gérarde Magloire and Kevin A. Yelvington's discussion of Herskovits's near erasure of "all mention of the American occupation and the neocolonial context of his fieldwork" from his *Life in a Haitian Valley*; Magloire and Yelvington, "Haiti and the Anthropological Imagination," *Gradhiva* 1, n.s. (2005): 139.

200 Herskovits, "Haiti Diary," 24 July 1934, 50; Melville J. and Frances S. Herskovits Papers, MG 261, Schomburg Center for Research in Black Culture, Box 13, Folder 68. Herskovits notes, "We will go to the new Lieutenant concerning the matter if it isn't settled." The problem in this case, as explained to Herskovits, was that "new regulations from Port-au-Prince make it necessary to obtain authorization from the head of the guards in a given district, not from a chef de section." However, given the force of customary practice, this woman found herself on the wrong side of the local *chèf seksyon* in not seeking his permission—and likely paying him the fee which this usually entailed. Thus, as noted before, even when the law was not being enforced strictly or violently, the criminalization of Vodou became the pretext for informal regulation and graft on the part of local authorities.

201 The end of the occupation in August 1934 ushered in a moment of intense ethnographic interest in Haiti on the part of American anthropologists and folklorists. Elsie Clews Parsons had visited in 1926, Harold Courlander made his first trip in 1932, and Melville and Frances Herskovits arrived for a three-month stay in the summer of 1934 as U.S. military forces were preparing to leave. Under Herskovits's direction, Katherine Dunham, then a student of anthropology at the University of Chicago, researched social and ritual dances in Haiti in 1935–1936. Remarkably, in the early months of 1937, Harold Courlander, Alan Lomax, Zora Neale Hurston, Lydia Parrish, and George Eaton Simpson were all simultaneously conducting research in Haiti.

202 George Eaton Simpson, "The Vodun Service in Northern Haiti," *American Anthropologist* 42, no. 2 (April–June 1940): 236.

203 George Eaton Simpson, "Four Vodun Ceremonies," *Journal of American Folklore* 59, no. 232 (April–June 1946): 154.

204 Simpson, "The Vodun Service in Northern Haiti," 236–237. Elsewhere Simpson also discusses how "the poverty of peasants during the middle and late thirties prevented them from staging elaborate ceremonies." See Simpson, "The Belief System of Haitian Vodun," 58–59.

205 George Eaton Simpson, "Haitian Magic," *Social Forces* 19, no. 1 (1940): 100.

206 George Eaton Simpson, "Two Vodun-Related Ceremonies," *Journal of American Folklore* 61, no. 239 (January–March 1948): 49–50.

207 Michel Lamartinière Honorat, one of the young Haitian ethnologists who took part in the UNESCO-funded sociological survey of the Marbial Valley that Alfred Métraux led from 1948 to 1950, told me that some Vodouizan perceived this investigation as the *campagne anti-superstitieuse* all over again and did not want to tell the researchers anything. Métraux reported in *Le vaudou haïtien* that the church's crusade had been particularly violent in this region.

208 See also Simpson's film footage from his research in Plaisance, which is largely focused on dance demonstrations by several men. George Eaton Simpson, *Film Study of Plaisance, Haiti, 1937*, 92.12.1; Human Studies Film Archives, Department of Anthropology, National Museum of Natural History, Smithsonian Institution.

209 See, for example, Melville J. Herskovits's regret that "no method has as yet been evolved to permit objective study of the dance," in *The Myth of the Negro Past* (1941; Boston: Beacon Hill, 1958), 269.

210 Why Roumain accepted a diplomatic post from a conservative government that was consistently exploiting the wartime situation as an excuse to assume extraordinary powers is a perplexing question. One of Roumain's biographers, Carolyn Fowler, surveys ways in which this has been understood, based on interviews she conducted with those who know him. See Fowler, *A Knot in the Thread*, 223–224. Roumain died two years after assuming this post at the age of thirty-seven.

211 "La conférence de R. Victor: Elle fut prononcée samedi à l'Hôtel de Ville, en présence d'un audiotoire de choix," *Haïti-Journal*, 23 November 1942.

212 Oriol, Viaud, and Aubourg, *Le mouvement folklorique en Haïti*, 40.

213 See Roumain, *Le sacrifice du tambour-assoto(r)*. This study, incidentally, depended on and performed a kind of surrogacy itself: the antisuperstition campaign then under way made the elaborate cycle of ceremonies associated with the sacrifice of the *asòtò* drum impossible. Métraux writes that Roumain's text, "so rich in details on *Vaudou* ritual, was, unfortunately, not based on personal observations, but on the description of a ceremony which the *houngan* Abraham would have wished to celebrate." Métraux, *Le vaudou haïtien*, 164–165.

214 Michel Lamartinière Honorat recalled that Lorimer Denis was instrumental in forming Mater Dolorosa and gave the troupe its name. Interview with the author, 4 June 1997, Pétionville, Haiti. The folklore performer and choreographer Louines Louinis clarified that Abraham was from this neighborhood in Port-au-Prince and remembered that the members of Mater Dolorosa were drawn from Abraham's religious family. Interview with the author, 19 July 1998, Brooklyn, NY. One of Mater Dolorosa's most celebrated performers, Marie-Noël, was, as Métraux states at one point, the *renn chantrèl* (French *reine-chanterelle*, or choir leader) of Abraham's religious *sosyete*. Métraux, *Le vaudou haïtien*, 224.

215 Marie Noël was memorialized upon her death in a 1947 issue of the *Bulletin du Bureau d'ethnologie*: "The Afro-Haitian Ethnography Section to which Marie-Noël was attached as a Hougenicon owes to her the greatest part of its documentation on popular culture." The tribute goes on: "At the head of the choir 'Mater Dolorosa,' supervised by M. Saint Erlonge Abraham, she interpreted sacred hymns and popular songs. . . . Marie Noël participated, in a way, in the very life of the bureau: illustrating its lectures on the subject of the culture of the Haitian masses, collaborating with it in the collection of proverbs, tales and legends." See Regnor C. Bernard, "Hommage à Marie-Noel," *Bulletin du Bureau d'ethnologie* (March 1947): 27.

216 Oriol, Viaud, and Aubourg, *Le mouvement folklorique en Haïti*, 78. *Haïti-Journal* announced the inauguration of the "Cinéma-Théâtre 'Rex'" on 3 October 1935.

217 Publicity for the engagement noted that this was a dance performed "to chase away a malicious spirit." Advertisement which appeared in *Haïti-Journal*, 2 April 1936, under the heading "'Danses, Chant, Musique' / ce soir / soirée de grand gala." See also Dunham, *Island Possessed*, 146.

218 René Piquion, "Katherine Dunham, artiste et ethnographe," *Haïti-Journal*, 4 April 1936. Dunham remembered her excitement about the *Haïti-Journal* review: "That morning someone knocked and knocked at my door. And there was René Piquion, a young reporter, with some copies of the newspaper. I was so happy. I don't know if I had ever had a review before." Katherine Dunham, interview with the author, 9 April 1997, Habitation Leclerc, Haiti.

219 See also Oriol, Viaud, and Aubourg, who describe Dunham in 1952 as an "international star who collected an enormous body of documentation on folklore and particularly popular dances during her stay in our country and who also formed a troupe, the successful performances of which are benefiting the country." Oriol, Viaud, and Aubourg, *Le mouvement folklorique en Haïti*, 84.

220 Jean Coulanges, interview with the author, 13 May 1997, Port-au-Prince. This foreign interest was, of course, by no means limited to Dunham, although she was part of its vanguard. Other notable visitors during the 1930s and early 1940s included Langston Hughes, Melville J. Herskovits,

Zora Neale Hurston, Alain Locke, and W. E. B. Du Bois; Aimé Césaire from Martinique; and, from Cuba, the novelist Alejo Carpentier and the poet Nicolás Guillén. Corvington, *Port-au-Prince au cours des ans: La ville contemporaine*, 235–236. Given Dunham's choreographic success in the early 1940s and the extent to which her productions were publicized in terms of her Haitian research and experience, it seems highly likely that her work stimulated further North American and, once her company began touring abroad, international interest in Haitian popular culture.

221 The future folklore choreographer and performer Jean-Léon Destiné was only a young boy when Dunham was researching in Haiti, but in a tribute to her, held in New York in August 2000, he remembered being very aware of her visit and had in fact clipped her photograph out of one of the newspapers that featured an article on her. Within a decade Destiné was performing with the Dunham company on Broadway. He also noted that the *manbo* who conducted Dunham's initiation in the Cul-de-Sac was well-known in the capital.

222 "It seems to us that there would be reason to study these themes and draw from them poems, dramatic pieces that are of an original and new vein." Price-Mars, *Ainsi parla l'oncle*, 264.

223 Oriol, Viaud, and Aubourg describe Clément Benoit as having been one of the "courageous pioneers" of folklore performance, along with Lina Fussman-Mathon, and the Bureau d'Ethnologie's popular choir, Mater Dolorosa. Oriol, Viaud, and Aubourg, *Le mouvement folklorique en Haïti*, 79. Michel Aubourg writes: "It is infinitely pleasurable for us to recognize the great merit of M. Clément Benoit who used to play our popular songs on the radio in the rich programs of l'Heure de l'Art Haïtien. The Troupe of Mme Fusman [*sic*] Mathon also deserves our praise because its performances were inspired by our folkloric themes." See Aubourg, "Le mouvement folklorique d'aujourd'hui," *Haïti-Journal*, 8 August 1947. Likewise, for Michel Lamartinière Honorat, Benoit and Fussman-Mathon represented the vanguard of folklore performance in Haiti. Interview with author, 4 June 1997, Pétionville, Haïti.

224 Jean-Léon Destiné, "Hommage à Lina Mathon-Blanchet," *Haïti-Observateur*, 18–25 May 1994. Both Destiné and Gerard Résil, a professor of theater, emphasized during a roundtable discussion on the beginnings of folklore performance held in Port-au-Prince in 1997 how stigmatized the theater was for women of elite families, and how doubly stigmatized the performance of "folklore" was for both men and women, or in this case, young people of such families at that time. The fact that Fussman-Mathon was well regarded in Port-au-Prince elite society as a classical pianist may have mitigated parental objections.

225 Ibid. See also the tribute to Fussman-Mathon's work in Rosemond, *L'énergie nationale*, 146–147.

226 Clément Benoit, "En marge de 'Viejo,'" *Le Nouvelliste*, 2 September 1935.

227 "L'heure de l'art haïtien à la H.H.3 W," *Le Réveil*, 10 September 1940, and "L'heure de l'art haïtien," *Haïti-Journal*, 26 April 1941. On "La Station HH2S," see Rosemond, *L'énergie nationale*, 150.

228 Clément Benoit, "Autour du folklore national," *Haïti-Journal*, 26 July 1949.

229 Haiti's first radio station, Radio HHK, began broadcasting in 1926 under the control of U.S. marines. See Gage Averill, *A Day for the Hunter, a Day for the Prey: Popular Music and Power in Haiti* (Chicago: University of Chicago Press, 1997), 40–41.

230 Jean-Léon Destiné, remarks during the panel "Les débuts des danses folkloriques haïtiennes sur scène théâtrale," at the conference "La danse haïtienne: Histoire et traditions," 3 April 1997, Port-au-Prince, Haiti. Videotape footage of this conference is held in the Performing Arts Research Collections, New York Public Library.

231 Clément Benoit, "Haïti, champion du panaméricanisme," *Haïti-Journal*, 1 August 1942.

232 Reporting on talks held between Vincent and Roosevelt in Washington in April 1934 to work out the terms of an early departure of American troops from Haiti, H. P. Davis commented that "the complete restoration of Haitian sovereignty . . . , coincident with the withdrawal of the armed forces of the United States, unquestionably would be accepted throughout Latin America as a proof of the sincerity of Mr. Roosevelt's new 'good neighbor' policy." H. P. Davis, "Haiti and the 'Good Neighbor' Policy," *Literary Digest* 117, no. 17 (28 April 1934), 8.

233 See Schmidt, *The United States Occupation of Haiti*, 232; and Smith, *Red and Black in Haiti*, 114.

234 "À l'Institut Haïtiano-Américain—séance inaugurale du comité d'anthropologie," *Haïti-Journal*, 8 May 1943.

235 "Resolution sur le folklore, approuvée à l'assemblée des ministres et directeurs d'éducation des républiques américaines réunie à Panama du 27 septembre au 4 octobre 1943." Reprinted in *Bulletin du Bureau d'ethnologie* (March 1947): 39–40.

236 In Haiti's case, the development of a national tourist industry was a particular priority of the post-occupation state, and one in which the U.S. officials who still supervised the country's economy at that time played a key role. The American custodians of Haiti's finances took a keen interest in tourist development, both as a potential source of foreign exchange for the indebted nation (which had regained sovereignty in the midst of the global depression) and as a way to tie the Haitian economy yet more tightly to U.S. markets. A National Tourist Bureau was established by the Vincent administration in 1939, the immediate task of which became the identification of Haitian "attractions" that might appeal to, and draw, foreign visitors. "Tourist Bureau in Haiti," *Pan American Union Bulletin* 73, no. 9 (September 1939): 547.

237 Letter from Sarah Gertrude Knott to Melville Herskovits, 28 January 1941; National Folk Festival file, Box 14, Folder 11, Melville J. Herskovits Papers, Northwestern University Library.

238 Herskovits also asked Knott to "transmit to the Minister from Haiti my considered opinion that the music and dances of these people, as they perform these in their vodun rites, is artistically the equivalent of any folk music and many music art forms. The drumming is magnificent; I know of no Negro society where drumming has been perfected to a higher degree, and I would not exclude West Africa itself in this." Letter from Melville Herskovits to Sarah Gertrude Knott, 31 January 1941; National Folk Festival file, Box 14, Folder 11, Melville J. Herskovits Papers, Northwestern University Library.

239 Letter from Sarah Gertrude Knott to Melville Herskovits, 17 April 1941; National Folk Festival File, Box 14, Folder 11, Melville J. Herskovits Papers, Northwestern University Library.

240 Jean-Léon Destiné, remarks during the panel "Les débuts des danses folkloriques haïtiennes sur scène théâtrale," at the conference "La danse haïtienne: Histoire et traditions," 3 April 1997, Port-au-Prince, Haiti. According to another member of this panel, Maritou Chenêt Moscoso, Fussman-Mathon "often frequented the *peristil*" and in Port-au-Prince consulted with the well-known *manbo* Lorgina Delorge and her assistant Cicéron St. Aude, who was widely recognized as an extraordinary dancer. Alfred Métraux dedicated his 1958 book *Le vaudou haïtien* to Lorgina and to Odette Mennesson-Rigaud. Lorgina also had close ties to members of the Troupe Folklorique Nationale, founded in 1949. When I asked if he had known her, Louines Louinis laughed and replied, "You could not be part of the national troupe and not know Lorgina." Interview with the author, 19 July 1998, Brooklyn, NY.

241 Jean-Léon Destiné, "Hommage à Lina Mathon-Blanchet," *Haïti-Observateur*, 18–25 May 1994.

242 Letter from Sarah Gertrude Knott to Melville J. Herskovits, 28 January 1941; National Folk Festival File, Box 14, Folder 11, Melville J. Herskovits Papers, Northwestern University Library.

243 According to Jean-Léon Destiné, the young members of this troupe were Max, Denise, and Marie-Thérèse Roy; Carline Duré; Léon Walker; Carmen Dalencourt; Martial Day; Jacqueline Déjean; Gladys Hyppolite; Chaton Duplessis; and Léon Destiné. An article in *Le Nouvelliste* on the eve of their departure lists the drummers as André Janvier and Léandre Lunique; Destiné remembers a third drummer named Jonas. See Destiné, remarks during the panel "Les débuts des danses folkloriques haïtiennes sur scène théâtrale," at the conference "La danse haïtienne: Histoire et traditions," 3 April 1997, Port-au-Prince, Haiti. Videotape footage of this conference is held in the Performing Arts Research Collections, New York Public Library. Also see "Départ du groupe folklorique de Madame Fussman Mathon," *Le Nouvelliste*, 17 April 1941.

244 "L'Assemblée Nationale en sa séance de ce matin a élu le Citoyen Elie Lescot Président de la République," *Haïti-Journal*, 15 April 1941.

245 Lina Mathon-Blanchet, interview with the author, 25 June 1991, Port-au-

Prince, Haiti. Jean-Léon Destiné writes that the members of her group were "the first blacks to be admitted there." Destiné, "Hommage à Lina Mathon-Blanchet," *Haïti-Observateur*, 18–25 May 1994.

246 Jean Léon-Destiné, e-mail correspondence, 19 September 2009. "Haitians Sing to Voodoo Gods As Jungle Drums Beat at Party," *Washington Post*, 29 April 1941. This article was quoted in "Le groupe folklorique haïtien aux États-Unis," *Le Nouvelliste*, 8 May 1941. The paragraph in *Le Nouvelliste* that introduces the excerpts from the *Washington Post* article makes a point of describing the "janvalou" (*yanvalou*), which Destiné and Gladys Hyppolite were performing in the photograph that accompanied the article, as a "vaudouesque dance that is currently practiced in our countrysides."

247 Audain, *Le mal d'Haïti*, 56.

248 *Campagne anti-superstitieuse: Documentation*, 112.

249 See Destiné, remarks during the panel "Les débuts des danses folkloriques haïtiennes sur scène théâtrale," at the conference "La danse haïtienne: Histoire et traditions," 3 April 1997, Port-au-Prince, Haiti. See also Destiné's paraphrasing of Janvier's intervention in Millery Polyné, "'To Carry the Dance of the People Beyond': Jean-Léon Destiné, Lavinia Williams and Danse Folklorique Haïtienne," *Journal of Haitian Studies* 10, no. 2 (2004): 38.

250 "Haitians Sing to Voodoo Gods as Jungle Drums Beat at Party," *Washington Post*, 29 April 1941.

251 See Rosalind Morris's discussion of this: "Spirit mediums [in northern Thailand] . . . claim no responsibility for the words spoken through them. Indeed, mediumship is a mode of effacement, perhaps the ultimate aspiration of the signifier for subsumption by its signified." Morris, *In the Place of Origins: Modernity and Its Mediums in Northern Thailand* (Durham, NC: Duke University Press, 2000), 84.

252 See Jean-Léon Destiné, remarks during the panel "Les débuts des danses folkloriques haïtiennes sur scène théâtrale," at the conference "La danse haïtienne: Histoire et traditions," 3 April 1997, Port-au-Prince, Haiti.

253 J. C. White to the Secretary of State, "Change in Attitude towards Voodoo on the Part of the Intellectual Classes in Haiti as Evidenced by Development of Expressions of Interest in Folklore," 24 September 1942, dec. file 838.404/85, U.S. National Archives.

254 Recent scholarship on *afrocubanismo* suggests parallels with this analysis. Robin Moore writes that "African-derived culture in an abstract sense may have been essential to dominant conceptions of *cubanidad* beginning in the 1930s, but in many of its traditional forms it continued to be condemned as backward, lewd, or primitive." *Nationalizing Blackness*, 5. Kristina Wirtz argues that *afrocubanista* representations of Afro-Cuban religion likewise relied on a rhetoric of anachronism: "Living religious practices and practitioners were transformed into icons of the past that could be comfortably encountered through folkloric performances, such as those first organized by Fernando Ortiz himself, or by reading works like folklorist Lydia Ca-

brera's *El Monte*. . . . . Santería practitioners continued to experience police harassment and to keep their practices underground throughout the republic era." Wirtz, *Ritual, Discourse, and Community in Cuban Santería: Speaking a Sacred World* (Gainesville: University Press of Florida, 2007), 64 and 68. See also Reinaldo Román's argument that "the revaluation of objectionable practices and cultures—by means of a process that some scholars call 'folklorization'—has not resulted in the abandonment of efforts to manage superstition and control its meanings." Román, *Governing Spirits*, 20.

255 *Haïti-Journal* had announced this event several weeks earlier: "This will be the occasion of a great artistic and society event under the high patronage of the new chief of state, S.E. M. Elie Lescot." *Haïti-Journal*, 21 April 1941. This was, of course, soon after Lescot presented Fussman-Mathon's troupe at the Folk Festival in Washington, D.C. For more on Théodore Beaubrun's Languichatte, see Corvington, *Port-au-Prince au cours des ans: La ville contemporaine*, 315.

256 Clément Benoit, *Chants sauvages* (Port-au-Prince: Imprimerie du Collège Vertières, 1942), unpaginated.

257 "*Chants sauvages*: Le recueil de poèmes de Clément Benoit a été livré hier," *Haïti-Journal*, 2 July 1942.

258 "Ce soir au Rex Marthe Augustin Dans 'Gabélus': Un gala folk-lorique sans précédent." Advertisement in *Haïti-Journal*, 21 September 1942.

259 "Au gala folk-lorique au Rex, l'allocution du directeur de 'L'heure de l'art haïtien,' notre collaborateur Clément Benoit," *Haïti-Journal*, 24 September 1942.

260 SHADA took over massive tracts of peasant land to cultivate a latex-producing plant called cryptostegia. When the U.S. government abandoned the project in 1944, it provided no financial or other assistance for the resettlement of peasants on the confiscated land. See Plummer, *Haiti and the United States: The Psychological Moment*, 145–146; and Smith, *Red and Black in Haiti*, 43–46.

261 "Le gala folklorique de l'heure de l'art haïtien," *Le Nouvelliste*, 22 September 1942.

262 Georges Corvington reports that this song was "put out and popularized on the radio by Marthe Augustin. . . . Orchestrated by Luc Jean-Baptiste, it made the crowd dance at Sunday concerts on the Champ-de-Mars. The girls swooned from its throbbing melody and fell in love with Gabélus, this 'handsome boy' in 'green trousers' who did not appear very receptive to their advances." Corvington, *Port-au-Prince au cours des ans: La ville contemporaine*, 320.

263 "Le gala folklorique de 'L'heure de l'art haïtien,'" *Le Nouvelliste*, 22 September 1942.

264 Roussan Camille, "Regards," *Haïti-Journal*, 23 September 1942.

265 J. C. White to the Secretary of State, "Change in Attitude towards Voodoo on the Part of the Intellectual Classes in Haiti as Evidenced by Develop-

ment of Expressions of Interest in Folklore," 24 September 1942, dec. file 838.404/85, U.S. Department of State, U. S. National Archives.

266 "Under the *peristil*, they can dance freely, no matter which way," Desrameaux said. "One bumps into another, things like that." He described the codification of such dances for the stage as a process of choreographing them to counts, in arranged patterns, to set drum rhythms. Interview with the author, Port-au-Prince, Haiti, 27 May 1997.

267 In his 1951 lecture "Folklore et patriotisme," probably his strongest published statement against the legal prohibition of Vodou, Price-Mars built on this earlier redefinition in arguing against the injustice of the law's failure "to disassociate archaic and old-fashioned religious practices from crimes of sorcery and magic." Price-Mars, *Folklore et patriotisme*, 17–18.

268 Holly distinguishes such practices from the "drunken disorders that are wrongly confused with the Mysteries of Voudo," and that he saw as rightly prohibited under civil law. Her-Ra-Ma-El [Arthur Holly], *Dra-Po*, 359.

269 Kléber Georges-Jacob, *L'éthnie haïtienne* (Port-au-Prince: Imprimerie de l'État, 1941), 65.

270 Ibid., 74.

271 Emmanuel C. Paul, *L'ethnographie en Haïti: Ses initiateurs, son état actuel, ses taches, et son avenir* (Port-au-Prince: Imprimerie de l'État, 1949), 35. Henri Terlonge, former professor at the École de Droit in Port-au-Prince and an associate of the Griots group, published an article in *Les Griots* in 1938 critiquing, as Georges-Jacob would as well a few years later, the "pile of laws, pale imitations of similar ones borrowed in most cases from our former masters," to which Haitians were forced to "succumb." He does not make specific reference, however, to the new law against *les pratiques superstitieuses* promulgated three years earlier. See Terlonge, "Sociologie juridique: Institutions et lois haïtiennes," *Les Griots* 2, no. 2 (October–December 1938): 177–180.

272 Rigaud, *La tradition voudoo et le voudoo haïtien*, 53.

273 It seems that Augustin may have soon thereafter formed her own company of performers. In May 1943 an advertisement in *Haïti-Journal* read: "This evening, at the Rex, the Great National Star Marthe Augustin and her troupe in a Great Folkloric Gala." *Haïti-Journal*, 12 May 1943. By the late 1940s, as folklore performance was reaching its peak under the cultural policies of President Dumarsais Estimé and the boom in tourism to Haiti, Marthe Augustin seems not to have been involved.

274 Pierre Mayard, "Raccourcis," *Haïti-Journal*, 17 February 1943. The year before, Mayard had adapted Justin Lhérisson's novel *La famille des Pitite-Caille* for the stage. Emerante de Pradines, another luminary of the *mouvement folklorique*, was a featured performer in this production. See "Les Pitite Caille," *Haïti-Journal*, 24 November 1942.

275 Roussan Camille, "Lorimer Denis et le folklore haïtien," *Haïti-Journal*, 3 May 1943.

276 "Dans le théâtre: Nos auteurs chôment . . . faute de public," *Haïti-Journal*, 7 May 1943.

277 Rosemond's earlier productions for the theater included four collaborations with Antoine Lubin and a "folkloric comedy" in Kreyòl entitled *Déclaration paysanne*. See the opening pages of Rosemond's *L'énergie nationale: "Les précurseurs."*

278 Quoted in "'Mambo-chérie' est 'malade,'" *Le Nouvelliste*, 3–4 June 1943.

279 "'Mambo-chérie' est 'malade,'" *Le Nouvelliste*, 3–4 June 1943.

280 "Une excellente décision," *Le Nouvelliste*, 5 June 1943; and "Au théâtre: Les imitations des cérémonies rituelles sont désormais interdites," *Haïti-Journal*, 5 June 1943.

281 "Le B.I.P. ne pratique que la censure politique," *Haïti-Journal*, 16 April 1943.

282 Authors and directors of this genre of folklore who had already had their works approved by the B.I.P. were required to present them again to the Under-Secretary of State for Information and the General Police to be re-examined in light of this new ordinance. In order to be mounted onstage, productions would require an official "visa" issued once a government representative had attended, and approved, a dress rehearsal. "Une excellente décision," *Le Nouvelliste*, 5 June 1943.

283 "L'incident est clos: Clos est le folklore . . . ," *Le Nouvelliste*, 7 June 1943.

284 Hurbon continues: "The specific task of the State—and . . . the service expected from the penalization of Vodou—consists first of all in producing the marginalization of the peasantry." Hurbon, *Le barbare imaginaire*, 143.

285 She writes: "The very term 'folklore' marks a transformation of errors into archaisms and their transvaluation once they are safe for collection, preservation, exhibition, study, and even nostalgia and revival." Barbara Kirshenblatt-Gimblett, *Destination Culture: Tourism, Museums, and Heritage* (Berkeley and Los Angeles: University of California Press, 1998), 161.

286 Perhaps this analysis points to a series of larger questions about the relationship between prohibition and performance in the staging of official national and postcolonial modernities: Given the persistent and global force of colonial ascriptions of backwardness and barbarism, have not the stakes for transvaluing "error into archaism" been particularly high for modernizing postcolonial and post-occupation states? What roles have law and theater played in such conversions in other postcolonial contexts? Finally, when governments have claimed the legitimacy of the "folk" by nationalizing popular performance cultures, what have been the consequences for populations who have regarded such cultures neither as errors nor as archaisms, nor as in need of such transvaluation?

NOTES TO EPILOGUE

1 *Le Moniteur*, 17 February 1941. Noustas also opened a bar and restaurant called Le Perchoir, with an adjacent tourist shop, overlooking the capital in

the mountains of Boutilier. Carl Fombrun, e-mail correspondence, 12 July 2009.

2 Dorsainvil, *Vodou et névrose*, 139.

3 Arguably, the force of such an attraction was always already there, even in the first published description of "le Vaudoux," by Moreau de Saint-Méry, who marveled over the "magnetism" of the "Vaudoux" rites. He wrote that "whites found spying on the mysteries of this sect" and touched by one of its members would abandon themselves to the dance, having to promise to pay the "Vaudoux Queen" in order to stop. Moreau de Saint-Méry, *Description*, 68.

4 The trademark was issued in January 1939 to Consolidated Cosmetics, and then transferred to the Dana Company who claimed at the time of a lawsuit it brought for infringement on that brand in the early 1950s that its sales of "Voodoo" products "had reached a quarter of a million dollars." See Rolley, Inc. *v.* Younghusband et al., No. 13389, United States Court of Appeals Ninth Circuit, 29 April 1953.

5 Interview with Alphonse Jean, Tabarre, 15 June 1997. My thanks to Yanick Guiteau Dandin and Étienne Germain for introducing me to Jean.

6 Lorimer Denis and François Duvalier, "L'évolution stadiale du Vodou," *Bulletin du Bureau d'ethnologie* 3 (February 1944): 23.

7 Gérard Pierre-Charles, *Radiographie d'une dictature* (Montréal: Éditions Nouvelle Optique, 1973), 84, 86, and 87.

8 Rachelle Charlier-Doucet notes that "Duvalier neglected the Bureau [d'Ethnologie] even while he exploited his knowledge of popular culture and particularly Vodou in order to maintain himself in power." Charlier-Doucet, "Anthropologie, politique et engagement social," 121.

9 Trouillot, *Haiti, State against Nation*, 159 and 171; and Hurbon, *Culture et dictature en Haïti*, 85.

10 Michel S. Laguerre, *Urban Life in the Caribbean: A Study of a Haitian Urban Community* (Cambridge, MA: Schenkman, 1983), 171 n. 12.

11 Trouillot, *Haiti, State against Nation*, 190–191. See Richard Lee Turits's similar point about Rafael Leonidas Trujillo calling upon Dominican peasants to be "active participants in the national state through devotion to agriculture as well as loyalty to his regime." Turits, *Foundations of Despotism*, 1.

12 Laguerre, "The Voodooization of Politics in Haiti," 522.

13 See Diederich and Burt, *Papa Doc and the Tonton Macoutes*, 347; Hurbon, *Culture et dictature en Haïti*, 98–99; and Pierre-Charles, *Radiographie d'une dictature*, 87.

14 Hurbon, *Comprendre Haïti*, 154.

15 Pierre-Charles, *Radiographie d'une dictature*, 88.

16 See Kerboull, *Le vaudou: Magie ou religion?*, 204; and see the critique in Hurbon, *Comprendre Haïti*, 151.

17 Hurbon, *Comprendre Haiti*, 151. See also Rémy Bastien, "Vodoun and Politics in Haiti," in *Religion and Politics in Haiti: Two Essays by Harold Courlander*

and Rémy Bastien (Washington, DC: Institute for Cross-Cultural Research, 1966), 61; and Pierre-Charles, *Radiographie d'une dictature*, 87.

18 Kerboull, *Le vaudou: Magie ou religion?*, 204. Kerboull provides no documentation for this announcement but implies that he was in Haiti at the time and was thus privy to it. There is also no record of such a proclamation in the Port-au-Prince newspapers that I have consulted; however this is unsurprising given press censorship under the dictatorship and also how rarely publications such as the *Le Nouvelliste* published articles on topics that were of primary concern to the Haitian majority. Kerboull notes that upon the payment of a "high tax (30 gourdes for example)," ceremonies were authorized "under the cover of '*spectacles publics*,'" or "'*prières avec abattage*'" (Kerboull, *Le vaudou: Magie ou religion?*, 204). See, too, David Yih's reference to the *spectacle publique* card authorizing *menwat* dances in Aquin and other towns on the southwest peninsula. Yuen-Ming David Yih, "Music and Dance of Haitian Vodou: Diversity and Unity in Regional Repertoires" (Ph.D. diss, Wesleyan University, 1995), 445.

19 Pierre-Charles, *Radiographie d'une dictature*, 88. Diederich and Burt note that "voudou, like every Haitian business, has been heavily taxed." Diederich and Burt, *Papa Doc and the Tonton Macoutes*, 348.

20 Interview with Alphonse Jean ("Kazo"), Tabarre, Haiti, 15 June 1997.

21 Based on his research in the Port-au-Prince neighborhood of Upper Belair in the mid-1970s, Laguerre notes that Vodou priests "may obtain 'permission-for-life' by accepting the role of tonton macoute as servant to the 'president-for-life.'" See Laguerre, *Urban Life in the Caribbean*, 119.

22 Francis Huxley, *The Invisibles* (London: Rupert Hart-Davis, 1966), 49, 147, and 163.

23 *Guide économique de la République d'Haïti* (Port-au-Prince: Institut Haïtien de Statistique, Département des Finances et des Affaires Économiques, July 1964), 118. The category of "*prêtres du voodu*" presumably included *oungan*, *manbo*, and *bòkò*, and possibly other healers such as *doktè fèy*, not otherwise represented on these charts. The official rate of exchange was fixed at five gourdes to one U.S. dollar.

24 *Guide économique de la République d'Haïti* (Port-au-Prince: Institut Haïtien de Statistique, Département des Finances et des Affaires Économiques, December 1971), 296–300. See also *Comptes nationaux, 1954–55 à 1971–72, et projections macro-économiques 1972–73 à 1980–81* (Port-au-Prince: Institut Haïtien de Statistique, Département des Finances et des Affaires Économiques, December 1974), 105–111; and *Guide économique de la République d'Haïti* (Port-au-Prince: Institut Haïtien de Statistique, Département des Finances et des Affaires Économiques, April 1977), 361–363.

25 The Institut Haïtien de Statistique was created in September 1951, during Paul Magloire's presidency, with the mission, in part, to "collect and, eventually, to publish all statistical information of a physical, demographic, economic, financial, social, and cultural character, and more generally all

statistical documentation." *Bulletin trimestriel de statistique* 2 (October 1951): 7. I examined issues of the Institut's *Bulletin trimestriel de statistique* published between October 1951 and December 1954 and found no data published on *prêtres du vodou* save in a census of two Port-au-Prince neighborhoods, La Saline and Trou Cochon, released in September 1952, which listed *guérisseurs* (healers) and *houngan* (singular because only one was counted) under the heading "Specialized Workers." Interestingly, these bulletins do list the numbers of arrests for the crime of *sortilèges* in each department of the country during a given three-month period, even though in 1935 the legal category of prohibition was switched to *les pratiques superstitieuses*.

26 *Guide économique de la République d'Haïti* (Port-au-Prince: Institut Haïtien de Statistique, Département des Finances et des Affaires Économiques, July 1964), 118.

27 One important exception is the discussion of the economic significance of Vodou in Rigaud's *La tradition voudoo et le voudoo haïtien*, 43–44.

28 Ferdinand Delatour, *Les 150 ans du régime du code civil dans le contexte social haïtien (1826–1976)* (Port-au-Prince: Éditions Fardin, 1978), 110. I am indebted to Delatour's reference to this feature of the December 1971 *Guide économique de la République d'Haïti*, which alerted me to the existence and publication of these statistics more generally.

29 "Situation of Human Rights in Haiti," report prepared by Adama Dieng, independent expert, 20 September 1999, United Nations General Assembly, Fifty-fourth session, Agenda item 116 (c). MICIVIH was created in 1993 at the request of then president-in-exile Jean-Bertrand Aristide to monitor the human rights situation in Haiti after the September 1991 coup. It was a joint mission between the U.N. and the Organization of American States. After the U.S.-led restoration of Aristide to office in 1994, MICIVIH broadened its mandate "to include the promotion of human rights and institution building." See the MICIVIH website: http://www.un.org/rights/micivih/first.htm.

30 See the introduction to this book for a more detailed discussion of this movement.

31 This conclusion is based, in part, on the 1997–1998 investigation by Sara Lechtenberg, a U.S. lawyer working with MICIVIH, whose research focused on illegal detentions for *pratiques superstitieuses* in towns in the Artibonite. Members of the judicial and law enforcement communities with whom Lechtenberg spoke consistently emphasized their role as conciliators in cases involving an accusation of sorcery. To what extent such mediation efforts on their parts predated or were a response to the abrogation of the law against *les pratiques superstitieuses* is a question that warrants further research. My thanks to Lechtenberg for sharing her research with me.

BIBLIOGRAPHY

ARCHIVAL SOURCES

HAITI
Port-au-Prince
Bibliothèque Haïtienne des Frères de l'Instruction Chrétienne
Bibliothèque Haïtienne des Pères du Saint Esprit
Bibliothèque Nationale d'Haïti
Institut Haïtiano-Américain

UNITED STATES
Carbondale, IL
Katherine Mary Dunham Papers, Special Collections, Morris Library, Southern
    Illinois University

College Park, MD
Records of the Department of State Relating to Internal Affairs of Haiti,
    Decimal Files 838.00 (political affairs) and 838.404 (religion), U.S. National
    Archives

Evanston, IL
Melville J. Herskovits Papers, University Archives, Northwestern University
    Library

Gainesville, FL
Frank R. Crumbie Papers, Special Collections, George A. Smathers Libraries,
    University of Florida
Great Britain Foreign Office, General Correspondence before 1906, Hayti, Latin
    America microfilm, George A. Smathers Libraries, University of Florida

New York, NY

Columbia University Libraries
   Butler Library
   Arthur W. Diamond Law Library
   Sol Lesser Collection, Oral History Research Office
New York Public Libraries
   General Research Division, Stephen A. Schwarzman Building
   New York Public Library for the Performing Arts
   Schomburg Center for Research in Black Culture
      Kurt Fisher Haitian History Collection
      Melville J. and Frances S. Herskovits Papers
      Photographs and Prints Division

Miami, FL

Florida International University Green Library Special Collections
University of Miami Libraries Special Collections

Philadelphia, PA

University of Pennsylvania Museum of Archaeology and Anthropology

Quantico, VA

United States Marine Corps Archives, Library of the Marine Corps
   Personal Papers Collection
      Adolph B. Miller Papers
      Homer L. Overley Papers
   Oral History Collection
      Merwin H. Silverthorn Oral History
United States Marine Corps History Division
   Reference Branch
      Geographical Files

Suitland, MD

Department of Anthropology, National Museum of Natural History, Smithsonian Institution
   Haiti Object Collections, Collections Unit
   Melville J. Herskovits Films, Haiti, 1934, Human Studies Film Archives
   George Eaton Simpson Papers, National Anthropological Archives
   George Eaton Simpson, Film Study of Plaisance, Haiti, 1937, Human Studies Film Archives

Washington, D.C.

Library of Congress
   Rhoda Bubendey Métraux Papers, Manuscript Division

National Archives
>   Record Group 80, General Records of the U.S. Navy
>   Record Group 125, Records of the Judge Advocate General (Navy)
>   Record Group 127, Records of the U.S. Marine Corps
National Museum of African Art, Smithsonian Institution
>   Melville Herskovits Photographs, 1928–1934, Eliot Elisofon Photographic
>   Archives

PERSONAL INTERVIEWS AND COMMUNICATIONS

Blot, Jean-Yves, interview with the author, Port-au-Prince, Haiti, 26 March 1997.

Corvington, Georges, interview with the author, Port-au-Prince, Haiti, 8 June 1997.

Coulanges, Jean, interviews with the author, Port-au-Prince, Haiti, 22 April and 13 May 1997.

Dandin, Yanick Guiteau, interview with the author, Port-au-Prince, Haiti, 23 April 1997.

Desrameaux, Pierre, interview with the author, Port-au-Prince, Haiti, 27 May 1997.

Destiné, Jean-Léon, multiple interviews with the author, New York, NY, 1991–2001.

Dunham, Katherine, interview with the author, Habitation Leclerc, Haiti, 9 April 1997.

Germain, Etienne, interview with the author, Tabarre, Haiti, 15 June 1997.

Honorat, Michel Lamartinière, interview with the author, Pétionville, Haiti, 4 June 1997.

Jean, Alphonse ("Kazo"), interview with the author, Yanick Guiteau Dandin, and Etienne Germain, Tabarre, Haiti, 15 June 1997.

Louinis, Louines, interview with the author, Brooklyn, NY, 19 July 1998.

Mathon-Blanchet, Lina, interview with the author, Port-au-Prince, Haiti, 25 June 1991.

Morse, Emerante de Pradines, interviews with the author, Port-au-Prince, Haiti, 25 June 1991, and Pélérin, Haiti, 14 February 1997.

Pierre, Florencia, interview with the author, Pétionville, Haiti, 16 June 1997.

Turner, George E., phone conversation with the author, 15 February 1998.

Wiener, Odette Latour, interviews with the author, Pétionville, Haiti, 13 November 1996 and 25 June 1997.

Williams, Lavinia, interview with the author, Port-au-Prince, Haiti, 23 June 1991.

NEWSPAPERS, JOURNALS, MAGAZINES, AND GOVERNMENT GAZETTES

Bulletin des lois et actes
Bulletin du Bureau d'ethnologie

Bulletin trimestriel de statistique (Institut haïtien de statistique)
Cahiers d'Haïti
Christian Science Monitor
Le Courrier haïtien
La Croix
Les Griots
Guide économique de la République d'Haïti
Haïti-Journal
Haïti médicale
Haïti-Observateur
Haïti Progrès
Harper's
La Lanterne médicale
Le Manifeste
Le Matin
Le Moniteur: Journal officiel de la République d'Haïti
Nation
National Geographic Magazine
New York Times
Le Nouvelliste
Pan American Union Bulletin
La Phalange
La Presse
Le Réveil
Revue de la Société de législation
Revue de la Société haïtienne d'histoire et de géographie
La Revue indigène
La Semaine médicale
Washington Post

PUBLISHED WORKS

1801–1885: Le premier siècle de "Constitutions haïtiennes"; Textes complets de 14 constitutions dont sept amendements. Port-au-Prince: Imprimerie Ateliers Fardin, 1985.

Abrahams, Roger D., and John F. Szwed, assisted by Leslie Baker and Adrian Stackhouse. *After Africa: Extracts from British Travel Accounts and Journals of the Seventeenth, Eighteenth, and Nineteenth Centuries concerning the Slaves, their Manners, and Customs in the British West Indies*. New Haven: Yale University Press, 1983.

Aguirre, Carlos, and Ricardo D. Salvatore. "Writing the History of Law, Crime, and Punishment in Latin America." In *Crime and Punishment in Latin America: Law and Society since Late Colonial Times*, edited by Ricardo D. Salvatore, Carlos Aguirre, and Gilbert M. Joseph, 1–32. Durham, NC: Duke University Press, 2001.

Alexis, Jacques Stephen. *Les arbres musiciens*. 1957. Port-au-Prince: Les Éditions Fardin, 1986.

————. "Contribution à la table ronde sur le folklore et le nationalisme." *Optique* no. 23 (January 1956): 25–34.

Anglade, Pierre. *Inventaire étymologique des termes créoles des Caraïbes d'origine africaine*. Paris: L'Harmattan, 1998.

Antoine, Jacques Carmeleau. *Jean Price-Mars and Haiti*. Washington, DC: Three Continents Press, 1981.

Apter, Andrew. "On African Origins: Creolization and *Connaissance* in Haitian Vodou." *American Ethnologist* 29, no. 2 (2002): 233–260.

Ardouin, Beaubrun. *Études sur l'histoire d'Haïti*. Vol. 4. Paris: Dezobry & E. Magdeleine, 1853.

————. *Études sur l'histoire d'Haïti*. Vol. 8. Paris: Chez l'Auteur, 1856.

Asad, Talal. *Genealogies of Religion: Discipline and Reasons of Power in Christianity and Islam*. Baltimore, MD: Johns Hopkins University Press, 1993.

Aubin, Eugène [Descos, Léon]. *En Haïti: Planteurs d'autrefois, négres d'aujourd'hui*. Paris: Armand Colin, 1910.

Audain, Léon. *Le mal d'Haïti: Ses causes et son traitement*. Port-au-Prince: Imprimerie J. Verrollot, 1908.

Augustin, Rémy. *Notes sur le vaudou*. Port-au-Prince: N.p., 1941.

Austin, J. L. *How to Do Things with Words: The William James Lectures Delivered at Harvard University in 1955*. Cambridge, MA: Harvard University Press, 1962.

Averill, Gage. *A Day for the Hunter, a Day for the Prey: Popular Music and Power in Haiti*. Chicago: University of Chicago Press, 1997.

————. "Ballad Hunting in the Black Republic: Alan Lomax in Haiti, 1936–37." *Caribbean Studies* 36, no. 2 (July–December 2008): 3–22.

Bailey, Michael D. "The Disenchantment of Magic: Spells, Charms, and Superstition in Early European Witchcraft Literature." *American Historical Review* 111, no. 2 (April 2006): 383–404.

Balch, Emily Greene, ed. *Occupied Haiti: Being the Report of a Committee of Six Disinterested Americans Representing Organizations Exclusively American, Who, Having Personally Studied Conditions in Haiti in 1926, Favor the Restoration of the Independence of the Negro Republic*. New York: Writers, 1927.

Balkin, J. M. "Deconstructive Practice and Legal Theory." *Yale Law Journal* 96 (1987): 743–786.

Bastien, Rémy. "Rapport annuel du Bureau d'Ethnologie de la République d'Haïti (1942–43)." *Bulletin du Bureau d'ethnologie* 3 (1944): 1–15.

————. "Vodoun and Politics in Haiti." In *Religion and Politics in Haiti: Two Essays by Harold Courlander and Rémy Bastien*, 39–68. Washington, DC: Institute for Cross-Cultural Research, 1966.

————. *Le paysan haïtien et sa famille*. 1951. Paris: Éditions Karthala, 1985.

Beauvoir-Dominique, Rachel. *L'ancienne cathédrale de Port-au-Prince: Perspectives d'un vestige de carrefours*. Port-au-Prince: Éditions Henri Deschamps, 1991.

―――. "Underground Realms of Being: Vodoun Magic." In *Sacred Arts of Haitian Vodou*, edited by Donald J. Cosentino, 153–177. Los Angeles: Fowler Museum of Cultural History, 1995.

―――. "Libérer le double, la beauté sera convulsive: À propos d'une collection d'art vodou." *Gradhiva* 1, n.s. (2005): 57–69.

Beauvoir, Rachel, and Didier Dominique. *Savalou E*. Montréal: Les Éditions du CIDIHCA, 2003.

Beauvoir-Dominique, Rachel, in collaboration with Eddy Lubin. "Investigations autour du site historique du Bois Caïman: Rapport." Commissioned by the Ministère de la Culture, République d'Haïti, January 2000.

Beckett, Greg. "Master of the Wood: Moral Authority and Political Imaginaries in Haiti." *Political and Legal Anthropology Review* 27, no. 2 (2004): 1–19.

Bell, Madison Smartt. *Toussaint Louverture: A Biography*. New York: Pantheon Books, 2007.

Bellegarde, Dantès. *L'occupation américaine d'Haïti: Ses conséquences morales et économiques*. Port-au-Prince: Chéraquit, 1929.

―――. *La nation haïtienne*. Paris: J. de Gigord, 1938.

―――. *Histoire du peuple haïtien, 1492–1952*. Port-au-Prince: Collection du Tricinquantenaire de l'Indépendance d'Haïti, 1953.

Bellegarde-Smith, Patrick. "Haitian Social Thought in the Nineteenth Century: Class Formation and Westernization." *Caribbean Studies* 20, no. 1 (March 1980): 5–33.

―――. *In the Shadow of Powers: Dantès Bellegarde in Haitian Social Thought*. Atlantic Highlands, NJ: Humanities Press International, 1985.

―――. *Haiti: The Breached Citadel*. Toronto: Canadian Scholars' Press, 2004.

―――. "The Spirit of the Thing: Religious Thought and Social/Historical Memory," in *Fragments of Bone: Neo-African Religions in a New World*, ed. Patrick Bellegarde-Smith, 52–69. Urbana: University of Illinois Press, 2005.

―――. "Resisting Freedom: Cultural Factors in Democracy; The Case for Haiti." In *Vodou in Haitian Life and Culture: Invisible Powers*, edited by Claudine Michel and Patrick Bellegarde-Smith, 101–115. New York: Palgrave Macmillan, 2006.

Bellegarde-Smith, Patrick, and Claudine Michel. "Introduction." In *Haitian Vodou: Spirit, Myth, and Reality*, edited by Patrick Bellegarde-Smith and Claudine Michel, xvii–xxvii. Bloomington: Indiana University Press, 2006.

Benoit, Clément. *Chants sauvages*. Port-au-Prince, Haïti: Imprimerie du Collège Vertières, 1942.

Benson, LeGrace. "How *Houngans* Use the Light from Distant Stars." In *Vodou in Haitian Life and Culture: Invisible Powers*, edited by Claudine Michel and Patrick Bellegarde-Smith, 155–179. New York: Palgrave Macmillan, 2006.

Bernard, Regnor C. "Hommage à Marie-Noel." *Bulletin du Bureau d'ethnologie* (March 1947): 27–28.

Bilby, Kenneth M., and Jerome S. Handler, "Obeah: Healing and Protection in West Indian Slave Life." *Journal of Caribbean History* 38, no. 2 (2004): 153–183.

Binkin, Martin, and Mark J. Eitelberg, with Alvin J. Schexnider and Marvin M. Smith. *Blacks and the Military*. Washington: Brookings Institution, 1982.

Bishop, Crawford M., and Anyda Marchant. *A Guide to the Law and Legal Literature of Cuba, the Dominican Republic, and Haiti*. Washington, DC: Library of Congress, 1944.

Blancpain, François. *La condition des paysans haïtiens: Du code noir aux codes ruraux*. Paris: Éditions Karthala, 2003.

Blassingame, John W. "The Press and American Intervention in Haiti and the Dominican Republic, 1904–1920." *Caribbean Studies* 9, no. 2 (July 1969): 27–43.

Blier, Suzanne Preston. "Vodun: West African Roots of Vodou." In *Sacred Arts of Haitian Vodou*, edited by Donald J. Cosentino, 61–87. Los Angeles: Fowler Museum of Cultural History, 1995.

Bonnet, Guy-Joseph. *Souvenirs historiques . . . recueillis par Edmond Bonnet*. Paris: Librairie August Durand, 1864.

Bonsal, Stephen. *The American Mediterranean*. New York: Moffat, Yard, 1913.

Bordes, Ary. *Évolution des sciences de la santé et de l'hygiène publique en Haïti*. Vol. 1. Port-au-Prince: Imprimerie Deschamps, 1980.

Borges, Dain. "Healing and Mischief: Witchcraft in Brazilian Law and Literature, 1890–1922." In *Crime and Punishment in Latin America: Law and Society since Colonial Times*, edited by Ricardo D. Salvatore, Carlos Aguirre, and Gilbert M. Joseph, 181–210. Durham, NC: Duke University Press, 2001.

Bourguignon, Erika. "Religion and Justice in Haitian Vodou." *Phylon* 46, no. 4 (1960): 292–295.

Bourjolly, Monsieur le Juge. *À la mémoire honorée du Docteur J.-B. Dehoux*. Port-au-Prince: Imprimerie J. Verrollot, 1900.

Bouzon, Justin. *Études historiques sur la présidence de Faustin Soulouque, 1847–1849*. Port-au-Prince: Bibliothèque Haïtienne, 1894.

Bracken, Christopher. *The Potlatch Papers: A Colonial Case History*. Chicago: University of Chicago Press, 1997.

Breathett, George. *The Catholic Church in Colonial Haiti, 1704–1785: Selected Letters, Memoirs and Documents*. Salisbury, NC: Documentary Publications, 1982.

———. "Catholicism and the *Code Noir* in Haiti." *Journal of Negro History* 73, nos. 1–4 (1988): 1–11.

Brodwin, Paul. *Medicine and Morality in Haiti: The Contest for Healing Power*. Cambridge: Cambridge University Press, 1996.

Bronfman, Alejandra. *Measures of Equality: Social Science, Citizenship, and Race in Cuba, 1902–1940*. Chapel Hill: University of North Carolina Press, 2004.

Brouard, Carl. "Doctrine de la Nouvelle École." *Conjonction: Revue franco-haïtienne de l'Institut français d'Haïti* 198 (April–May–June 1993): 39.

Brown, Jonathan. *The History and Present Condition of St. Domingo*. Vol. 2. Philadelphia: William Marshall, 1827.

Brown, Karen McCarthy. "Voodoo." In *The Encyclopedia of Religion*, edited by
Mircea Eliade, 16 vols., 15:296–301. New York: Macmillan, 1987.

———. "Systematic Remembering, Systematic Forgetting: Ogou in Haiti." In
Africa's Ogun: Old World and New, edited by Sandra T. Barnes, 65–89. Bloomington: Indiana University Press, 1989.

———. *Mama Lola: A Vodou Priestess in Brooklyn*. Berkeley and Los Angeles:
University of California Press, 1991.

———. "Serving the Spirits: The Ritual Economy of Haitian Vodou." In
Sacred Arts of Haitian Vodou, edited by Donald J. Cosentino, 205–223. Los
Angeles: Fowler Museum of Cultural History, 1995.

———. "Making Wanga: Reality Constructions and the Magical Manipulation
of Power." In *Transparency and Conspiracy: Ethnographies of Suspicion in the New
World Order*, edited by Harry G. West and Todd Sanders, 233–257. Durham,
NC: Duke University Press, 2003.

———. "Afro-Caribbean Spirituality: A Haitian Case Study." In *Vodou in
Haitian Life and Culture*, edited by Claudine Michel and Patrick Bellegarde-
Smith, 1–26. New York: Palgrave Macmillan, 2006.

Brown, Karen McCarthy, and Mama Lola. "The Altar Room: A Dialogue."
In *Sacred Arts of Haitian Vodou*, edited by Donald J. Cosentino, 227–239. Los
Angeles: Fowler Museum of Cultural History, 1995.

Brown, Vincent. "Spiritual Terror and Sacred Authority in Jamaican Slave Society." *Slavery and Abolition* 24, no. 1 (April 2003): 24–53.

———. *The Reaper's Garden: Death and Power in the World of Atlantic Slavery*.
Cambridge, MA: Harvard University Press, 2008.

Browning, Barbara. *Infectious Rhythm: Metaphors of Contagion and the Spread of
African Culture*. New Brunswick, NJ: Routledge, 1998.

Buck-Morss, Susan. *Hegel, Haiti, and Universal History*. Pittsburgh, PA: University of Pittsburgh Press, 2009.

Buteau, Pierre. "Une problématique de l'identité." *Conjonction: Revue franco-
haïtienne de l'Institut français d'Haïti* 198 (April–May–June 1993): 11–35.

Butler, Judith. *Bodies That Matter: On the Discursive Limits of "Sex."* New York:
Routledge, 1993.

Cabon, Pierre Adolphe. *Notes sur l'histoire religieuse d'Haïti de la Révolution au Concordat, 1789–1860*. Port-au-Prince: Petit Séminaire Collège Saint-Martial,
1933.

Campagne anti-superstitieuse: Documentation. Port-au-Prince: N.p., 1941.

Candler, John. *Brief Notices of Hayti with Its Condition, Resources, and Prospects*.
London: Thomas Ward, 1842.

Casimir, Jean. "A Case Study: The Problems of Slavery and the Colonization of
Haiti." In *Africa in Latin America: Essays on History, Culture, and Socialization*,
edited by Manuel Moreno Fraginals and translated by Leonor Blum, 306–
327. New York: Holmes and Meier, 1984.

———. *The Caribbean: One and Divisible*. Santiago, Chile: United Nations Economic Commission for Latin America and the Caribbean, 1992.

————. *La culture opprimée*. Delmas, Haiti: Imprimerie Lakay, 2001.

Castor, Kesner. *Éthique vaudou: Herméneutique de la maîtrise*. Paris: L'Harmattan, 1998.

Castor, Suzy. *L'occupation américaine d'Haïti*. Port-au-Prince: Imprimerie Henri Deschamps, 1988.

Celestin, Martial. "Vaudou et droit haïtien." *Revue juridique et politique, indépendance et coopération* 38, no. 2 (1984): 483–489.

Célius, Carlo A. "Le contrat social haïtien." *Pouvoirs dans la Caraïbe: Revue du C.R.P.L.C.*, 10 (1998): 27–70.

————. "Le modèle social haïtien: Hypothèses, arguments et méthode." *Pouvoirs dans la Caraïbe: Revue du C.R.P.L.C.*, special issue (1998): 110–143.

————. "Cheminement anthropologique en Haïti." *Gradhiva* 1, n.s. (2005): 47–56.

————. "La création plastique et le tournant ethnologique en Haïti." *Gradhiva* 1, n.s. (2005): 71–94.

————. *Langage plastique et énonciation identitaire: L'invention de l'art haïtien*. Québec: Les Presses de l'Université Laval, 2007.

————. "Neoclassicism and the Haitian Revolution." In *The World of the Haitian Revolution*, edited by David Patrick Geggus and Norman Fiering, 352–392. Bloomington: Indiana University Press, 2009.

Chanock, Martin. *Law, Custom and Social Order: The Colonial Experience in Malawi and Zambia*. Cambridge: Cambridge University Press, 1985.

Charles, Carolle. "Gender and Politics in Contemporary Haiti: The Duvalierist State, Transnationalism, and the Emergence of a New Feminism (1980–1990)." *Feminist Studies* 21, no.1 (1995): 135–164.

Charlier, Étienne. *Aperçu sur la formation historique de la nation haïtienne*. Port-au-Prince: Les Presses Libres, 1954.

Charlier-Doucet, Rachelle. "Anthropologie, politique et engagement social: L'expérience du Bureau d'Ethnologie d'Haïti." *Gradhiva* 1, n.s. (2005): 109–124.

Chasteen, John Charles. *National Rhythms, African Roots: The Deep History of Latin American Popular Dance*. Albuquerque: University of New Mexico Press, 2004.

Chidester, David. *Savage Systems: Colonialism and Comparative Religion in Southern Africa*. Charlottesville: University of Virginia Press, 1996.

Clark, Vèvè. "Fieldhands to Stagehands in Haiti: The Measure of Tradition in Haitian Popular Theatre." Ph.D. diss., University of California, Berkeley, 1983.

Clérismé, Rénald. "Rapports actuels entre le vodou et le christianisme en Haïti." In *Le phénomène religieux dans la Caraïbe: Guadeloupe, Martinique, Guyane, Haïti*, edited by Laënnec Hurbon, 221–226. Paris: Éditions Karthala, 2000.

Clifford, James. *The Predicament of Culture: Twentieth-Century Ethnography, Literature, and Art*. Cambridge, MA: Harvard University Press, 1988.

Code pénal d'Haïti. Port-au-Prince: L'Imprimerie du Gouvernement, 1826.

Code rural de Boyer 1826, avec les commentaires de Roger Petit-Frère, Jean Vandal, Georges E. Werleigh. Port-au-Prince: Archives Nationales d'Haïti/Maison H. Deschamps, 1992.

Cohen, William B. *The French Encounter with Africans: White Response to Blacks, 1530–1880.* Bloomington: Indiana University Press, 1980.

Cole, Hubert. *Christophe: King of Haiti.* New York: Viking Press, 1967.

Comaroff, Jean, and John Comaroff. "Alien-Nation: Zombies, Immigrants, and Millennial Capitalism." *South Atlantic Quarterly* 101, no. 4 (Fall 2002): 779–805.

Comhaire, Jean L. "The Haitian 'Chef de Section.'" *American Anthropologist* 57, no. 3 (June 1955): 620–623.

———. "The Haitian Schism, 1804–1860." *Anthropological Quarterly* 29, no. 1 (1956): 1–10.

Comhaire-Sylvain, Suzanne. "Influences indiennes dans le folklore haïtien." *La Relève* 7 (1938): 6–13.

———. *À Propos du vocabulaire des croyances paysannes.* Port-au-Prince: N.p., 1938.

Comhaire-Sylvain, Suzanne, and Jean Comhaire-Sylvain. "Survivances africaines dans le vocabulaire religieux d'Haïti." *Études dahoméennes*, no. 10 (1955): 5–20.

Coombe, Rosemary J. *The Cultural Life of Intellectual Properties: Authorship, Appropriation, and the Law.* Durham, NC: Duke University Press, 1998.

Corten, André. *Misère, religion et politique en Haïti: Diabolisation et mal politique.* Paris: Éditions Karthala, 2001.

Corvington, Georges. *Port-au-Prince au cours des ans: La capitale d'Haïti sous l'occupation, 1915–1922.* Port-au-Prince: Imprimerie Henri Deschamps, 1984.

———. *Port-au-Prince au cours des ans: La ville contemporaine, 1934–1950.* Port-au-Prince: Imprimerie Henri Deschamps, 1991.

———. *Port-au-Prince au cours des ans: La ville coloniale, 1743–1789.* Port-au-Prince: Imprimerie Henri Deschamps, 1992.

Cosentino, Donald J. "Vodou Vatican: A Prolegomenon For Understanding Authority in a Synthetic Religion." *Caribbean Quarterly* 9, nos. 3–4 (September–December 1993): 100–107.

———. "It's All for You, Sen Jak!" In *Sacred Arts of Haitian Vodou*, edited by Donald J. Cosentino, 243–265. Los Angeles: Fowler Museum of Cultural History, 1995.

Cotgrave, Randle. *A Dictionarie of the French and English Tongues.* 1611. Menston, England: Scolar Press, 1968.

Coulanges, Jean. "Indigénisme et musique en Haïti." *Conjonction*, no. 198 (April–May–June 1993): 59–75.

———. Untitled essay. *Conjonction*, no. 198 (April–May–June 1993): 85.

Coupeau, Steeve. *The History of Haiti.* Westport, CT: Greenwood Press, 2007.

Courlander, Harold. "Haiti's Political Folksongs." *Opportunity* 19, no. 4 (1941): 114–118.

————. *The Drum and the Hoe: Life and Lore of the Haitian People*. Berkeley: University of California Press, 1960.

————. "Recollections of Haiti in the 1930s and '40s." *African Arts* 23, no. 2 (April 1990): 60–70.

Courlander, Harold, and Rémy Bastien. *Religion and Politics in Haiti*. Washington, DC: Institute for Cross-Cultural Research, 1966.

Craige, John Houston. *Black Bagdad*. New York: Minton, Balch, 1933.

Curtin, Philip D. *The Atlantic Slave Trade: A Census*. Madison: University of Wisconsin Press, 1969.

d'Alaux, Gustave. *L'Empereur Soulouque et son empire*. 1856. Port-au-Prince: Les Éditions Fardin, 1988.

————. *Soulouque and His Empire: From the French of Gustave d'Alaux*. Translated by John H. Parkhill. Richmond, VA: J. W. Randolph, 1861.

Dalencour, François. *Précis méthodique d'histoire d'Haïti: Cinq siècles d'histoire, 1492–1935*. Port-au-Prince: N.p., 1935.

Dalmas, Antoine. *Histoire de la révolution de Saint-Domingue, depuis le commencement des troubles, jusqu'à la prise de Jérémie et du Môle S. Nicolas par les Anglais: Suivie d'un mémoire sur le rétablissement de cette colonie*. Vol. 1. Paris: Chez Mame Frères, 1814.

d'Ans, André-Marcel. *Haïti: Paysage et société*. Paris: Éditions Karthala, 1987.

————. "Jacques Roumain et la fascination de l'ethnologie." In *Jacques Roumain: Œuvres complètes*, edited by Léon-François Hoffmann, 1389–1391. Madrid: Collection Archivos, 2003.

Danticat, Edwidge. *Brother, I'm Dying*. New York: Alfred A. Knopf, 2007.

Dash, J. Michael. *Literature and Ideology in Haiti, 1915–1961*. London: Macmillan, 1981.

————. *Haiti and the United States: National Stereotypes and the Literary Imagination*. 1988. 2nd ed. New York: St. Martin's, 1997.

————. *The Other America: Caribbean Literature in a New World Context*. Charlottesville: University Press of Virginia, 1998.

————. "The Theater of the Haitian Revolution/The Haitian Revolution as Theater." *Small Axe* 18 (September 2005): 16–23.

Daut, Marlene L. "Un-Silencing the Past: Boisrond-Tonnerre, Vastey, and the Re-Writing of the Haitian Revolution, 1805–1817." *South Atlantic Review* 74, no. 1 (Winter 2009): 35–64.

Davis, H. P. *Black Democracy: The Story of Haiti*. New York: Lincoln MacVeagh/Dial Press, 1928.

————. "Haiti and the 'Good Neighbor' Policy." *Literary Digest* 117, no. 17 (28 April 1934): 8.

Davis, Wade. *Passage of Darkness: The Ethnobiology of the Haitian Zombie*. Chapel Hill: University of North Carolina Press, 1988.

Dayan, Joan/Colin. "Vodoun, or the Voice of the Gods." *Raritan* 10, no. 3 (Winter 1991): 32–57.

————. *Haiti, History, and the Gods*. Berkeley and Los Angeles: University of California Press, 1995.

————. "Querying the Spirit: The Rules of the Haitian *Lwa.*" In *Colonial Saints: Discovering the Holy in the Americas, 1500–1800,* edited by Allan Greer and Jodi Bilinkoff, 31–50. Routledge: New York, 2003.

De Barros, Juanita. "'Setting Things Right': Medicine and Magic in British Guiana, 1803–38." *Slavery and Abolition* 25, no. 1 (April 2004): 28–50.

de Bercy, Drouin. *De Saint-Domingue, de ses guerres, de ses révolutions, de ses ressources, et des moyens à prendre pour y rétablir la paix et l'industrie.* Paris: Chez Hocquet, 1814.

Debien, Gabriel. "Assemblées nocturnes d'esclaves à Saint-Domingue (La Marmelade, 1786)." *Annales historiques de la Révolution française* 208 (1972): 273–284.

————. *Les esclaves aux Antilles françaises (XVIIe–XVIIIe siècles).* Basse-Terre: Société d'Histoire de la Guadeloupe, 1974.

DeConde, Alexander, Richard Dean Burns, and Fredrik Logevall, eds. *Encyclopedia of American Foreign Policy.* Vol. 1. New York: Charles Scribner, 1978.

Degoul, Franck. "Du passé faisons table d'hôte: Le mode d'entretien des zombi dans l'imaginaire haïtien et ses filiations historiques." *Haïti: Face au Passé/ Confronting the Past,* special issue, *Ethnologies* 28, no. 1 (2006): 241–248.

de la Fuente, Alejandro. *A Nation for All: Race, Inequality, and Politics in Twentieth-Century Cuba.* Chapel Hill: University of North Carolina Press, 2001.

Delatour, Ferdinand. *Les 150 ans du régime du Code civil dans le contexte social haïtien, 1826–1976.* Port-au-Prince: Les Éditions Fardin, 1978.

Delince, Kern. *L'insuffisance de développement en Haïti.* Plantation, FL: Pegasus Books, 2000.

Delisle, Philippe. *Le catholicisme en Haïti au XIXe siècle: Le rêve d'une "Bretagne noire," 1860–1915.* Paris: Éditions Karthala, 2003.

de Man, Paul. *Allegories of Reading: Figural Language in Rousseau, Nietzsche, Rilke, and Proust.* New Haven, CT: Yale University Press, 1979.

Denis, Lorimer. "La religion populaire." *Bulletin du Bureau d'ethnologie* (December 1946): 16–40.

Denis, Lorimer, and François Duvalier. "Une cérémonie d'initiation." *Les Griots* 2–3, nos. 2–3 (October–December 1938 and January–March 1940): 657–659.

————. "L'évolution stadiale du Vodou." *Bulletin du Bureau d'ethnologie* 3 (February 1944): 9–32.

Derby, Lauren. "Haitians, Magic, and Money: *Raza* and Society in the Haitian-Dominican Borderlands, 1900 to 1937." *Comparative Studies in Society and History* 36, no. 3 (July 1994): 488–526.

————. *The Dictator's Seduction: Politics and the Popular Imagination in the Era of Trujillo.* Durham, NC: Duke University Press, 2009.

Deren, Maya. *Divine Horsemen: The Living Gods of Haiti.* 1953. New Paltz, NY: McPherson & Co., 1970.

Derrida, Jacques. "Signature Event Context." Translated by Samuel Weber and Jeffrey Mehlman. In *Limited Inc.,* edited by Gerald Graff, 1–23. Evanston, IL: Northwestern University Press, 1988.

———. "Force of Law: The 'Mystical Foundation of Authority.'" Translated by Mary Quaintance. *Cardozo Law Review* 11, nos. 5–6 (July–August 1990): 921–1045.

Descardes, Jean Rosier. "Dynamique Vodou et état de droit en Haïti: Droits de l'homme et diversité culturelle." Ph.D. diss., Université de Paris I–Panthéon–Sorbonne, 2001.

Descourtilz, Michel Étienne. *Histoire des désastres de Saint-Domingue.* Paris: Garnery, 1795.

———. *Voyages d'un naturaliste, et ses observations.* Vol. 3. Paris: Dufart, père, Librairie-Éditeur, 1809.

Desmangles, Leslie G. *The Faces of the Gods: Vodou and Roman Catholicism in Haiti.* Chapel Hill: University of North Carolina Press, 1992.

———. "African Interpretations of the Christian Cross in Vodou." In *Vodou in Haitian Life and Culture: Invisible Powers,* edited by Claudine Michel and Patrick Bellegarde-Smith, 39–50. New York: Palgrave Macmillan, 2006.

Desquiron, Lilas. *Racines du vodou.* Port-au-Prince: Éditions Henri Deschamps, 1990.

Dhormoys, Paul. *Une visite chez Soulouque: Souvenirs d'un voyage dans l'île d'Haïti.* Paris: Librairie Nouvelle, 1859.

Diederich, Bernard. *Bon Papa: Haiti's Golden Years.* N.p.: Xlibris, 2007.

Diederich, Bernard, and Al Burt. *Papa Doc and the Tonton Macoutes.* Port-au-Prince: Éditions Henri Deschamps, 1986.

Dixon, Chris. *African America and Haiti: Emigration and Black Nationalism in the Nineteenth Century.* Westport, CT: Greenwood Press, 2000.

Donaldson, Garry. *The History of African-Americans in the Military.* Malaba, FL: Krieger, 1991.

Dorsainvil, J.C. *Vodou et névrose.* 1931. Port-au-Prince: Éditions Fardin, 1975.

Douglas, Mary. "Techniques of Sorcery Control in Central Africa." In *Witchcraft and Sorcery in East Africa,* edited by John Middleton and E. H. Winter, 123–142. London: Routledge, 1963.

Douglass, Frederick. "The Claims of the Negro Ethnologically Considered: An Address Delivered in Hudson, Ohio, on 12 July 1854." In *The Frederick Douglass Papers,* ser. 1, edited by J. W. Blassingame. New Haven, CT: Yale University Press, 1982.

Dubois, Laurent. "Vodou and History." *Comparative Studies in Society and History* 43, no. 1 (2001): 92–100.

———. "The Citizen's Trance: The Haitian Revolution and the Motor of History." In *Magic and Modernity: Interfaces of Revelation and Concealment,* edited by Birgit Meyer and Peter Pels, 103–128. Stanford, CA: Stanford University Press, 2003.

———. *Avengers of the New World: The Story of the Haitian Revolution.* Cambridge, MA: Belknap Press of the Harvard University Press, 2004.

———. *A Colony of Citizens: Revolution and Slave Emancipation in the French Caribbean, 1787–1804.* Chapel Hill: University of North Carolina Press, 2004.

Dubois, Laurent, and John D. Garrigus, eds. *Slave Revolution in the Caribbean, 1789–1804: A Brief History with Documents.* Boston: Bedford/St. Martin's, 2006.

Du Bois, W. E. Burghardt, ed. *The Negro Church.* Atlanta, GA: Atlanta University Press, 1903.

Dumesle, Hérard. *Voyage dans le Nord d'Hayti, ou Révélation des lieux et des monuments historiques.* Aux Cayes: Imprimerie du Gouvernement, 1824.

Dunham, Katherine. *Dances of Haiti.* Los Angeles: Center for Afro-American Studies, University of California, Los Angeles, 1983.

———. *Island Possessed.* 1969. Chicago: University of Chicago Press, 1994.

Dupuy, Alex. *Haiti in the World Economy: Class, Race, and Underdevelopment since 1700.* Boulder, CO: Westview Press, 1989.

———. *The Prophet and Power: Jean-Bertrand Aristide, the International Community, and Haiti.* Lanham, MD: Rowman & Littlefield, 2007.

Dupuy, Charles. *Le coin de l'histoire.* Vol. 2. Port-au-Prince: Presses de l'Imprimeur, 2002.

Edwards, Brent Hayes. *The Practice of Diaspora: Literature, Translation, and the Rise of Black Internationalism.* Cambridge, MA: Harvard University Press, 2003.

Elie Lescot: Le diplomate et l'animateur. N.p.: International Business Machines, 1944.

Ellis, Markman. *The History of Gothic Fiction.* Edinburgh: Edinburgh University Press, 2000.

Fandrich, Ina Johanna. "Defiant African Sisterhoods: The Voodoo Arrests of the 1850s and 1860s in New Orleans." In *Fragments of Bone: Neo-African Religions in a New World*, edited by Patrick Bellegarde-Smith, 187–207. Urbana: University of Illinois Press, 2005.

Farmer, Paul. *The Uses of Haiti.* Monroe, ME: Common Courage Press, 1994.

Fernández Olmos, Margarite, and Lizabeth Paravisini-Gebert, eds. *Sacred Possessions: Vodou, Santería, Obeah, and the Caribbean.* New Brunswick, NJ: Rutgers University Press, 1997.

———. *Creole Religions of the Caribbean: An Introduction from Vodou and Santería to Obeah and Espiritismo.* New York: New York University Press, 2003.

Ferrer, Ada. "Talk about Haiti: The Archive and the Atlantic's Haitian Revolution." In *Tree of Liberty: Cultural Legacies of the Haitian Revolution in the Atlantic World*, edited by Doris L. Garraway, 21–40. Charlottesville: University of Virginia Press, 2008.

Fett, Sharla. *Working Cures: Healing, Health, and Power on Southern Slave Plantations.* Chapel Hill: University of North Carolina Press, 2002.

Fick, Carolyn E. *The Making of Haiti: The Saint Domingue Revolution from Below.* Knoxville: University of Tennessee Press, 1990.

Fields, Karen E. *Revival and Rebellion in Colonial Central Africa.* Portsmouth, NH: Heinemann, 1997.

Firmin, Anténor. "Anténor Firmin à Monseigneur Kersuzan, 3 août, 1896." Appendix to *Conférence populaire sur le vaudoux donnée par Monseigneur l'Évêque du Cap-Haïtien, le 2 août, 1896.* Port-au-Prince: Imprimerie H. Amblard, 1896.

———. *The Equality of the Human Races.* Translated by Asselin Charles. Introduction by Carolyn Fluehr-Lobban. Champaign: University of Illinois Press, 2002.

Fischer, Sibylle. *Modernity Disavowed: Haiti and the Cultures of Slavery in the Age of Revolution*. Kingston: University of West Indies Press, 2004.

Fleuhr-Lobban, Carolyn. "Anténor Firmin: Haitian Pioneer of Anthropology." *American Anthropologist* 102, no. 3 (December 2000): 449–466.

———. "Anténor Firmin and Haiti's Contribution to Anthropology." *Gradhiva* 1, n.s. (2005): 95–108.

Fleurant, Gerdès. *Dancing Spirits: Rhythms and Rituals of Haitian Vodun, the Rada Rite*. Westport, CT: Greenwood Press, 1996.

———. Introduction to Phyllis Galembo, *Vodou: Visions and Voices of Haiti*, xv–xxix. Berkeley, CA: Ten Speed Press, 2005.

———. "Vodun, Music, and Society in Haiti: Affirmation and Identity." In *Haitian Vodou: Spirit, Myth, and Reality*, edited by Patrick Bellegarde-Smith and Claudine Michel, 46–57. Bloomington: Indiana University Press, 2006.

Foucault, Michel. *Discipline and Punish: The Birth of the Prison*. Translated by Alan Sheridan. London: Penguin Books, 1977.

———. *The Foucault Effect: Studies in Governmentality: With Two Lectures by and an Interview with Michel Foucault*. Edited by Graham Burchell, Colin Gordon, and Peter Miller. Chicago: University of Chicago Press, 1991.

Fouchard, Jean. *Les marrons du syllabaire: Quelques aspects du problème de l'instruction et de l'éducation des esclaves et affranchis de Saint-Domingue*. Port-au-Prince: Henri Deschamps, 1953.

———. *Les marrons de la liberté*. 1972. Port-au-Prince: Éditions Henri Deschamps, 1988.

———. *The Haitian Maroons: Liberty or Death*. Translated by A. Faulkner Watts. New York: Edward W Blyden, 1981.

Fowler, Carolyn. *A Knot in the Thread: The Life and Work of Jacques Roumain*. Washington, DC: Howard University Press, 1980.

Franklin, James. *The Present State of Hayti (Santo Domingo) with Remarks on Its Agriculture, Commerce, Laws, Religion, Finances, and Population*. 1828. Westport, CT: Negro Universities Press, 1970.

Freidel, Franck. *Franklin Delano Roosevelt: The Apprenticeship*. Boston: Little, Brown, 1952.

Froude, James Anthony. *The English in the West Indies, or, The Bow of Ulysses*. 1888. New York: Charles Scribner's Sons, 1900.

Gaillard, Roger. *Les blancs débarquent: 1916–1917; La république autoritaire*. Port-au-Prince: Imprimerie Le Natal, 1981.

———. *Les blancs débarquent: 1917–1918; Hinche mise en croix*. Port-au-Prince: Imprimerie Le Natal, 1982.

———. *Les blancs débarquent: 1919–1934; La guérilla de Batraville*. Port-au-Prince: Imprimerie Le Natal, 1983.

———. "L'indigénisme haïtien et ses avatars." *Conjonction* 197 (1993): 9–26.

Garraway, Doris. *The Libertine Colony: Creolization in the Early French Caribbean.* Durham, NC: Duke University Press, 2005.

Garrigus, John D. "Blue and Brown: Contraband Indigo and the Rise of a Free Colored Planter Class in French Saint-Domingue." *Americas* 50 (October 1993): 233–263.

———. *Before Haiti: Race and Citizenship in French Saint-Domingue.* New York: Palgrave, 2006.

Gaspar, David Barry, and David Patrick Geggus, eds. *A Turbulent Time: The French Revolution and the Greater Caribbean.* Bloomington: Indiana University Press, 1997.

Geggus, David Patrick. *Slavery, War, and Revolution: The British Occupation of Saint Domingue, 1793–1798.* New York: Oxford University Press, 1982.

———. "Slave Resistance Studies and the Saint-Domingue Slave Revolt: Some Preliminary Considerations." Occasional Papers Series, Latin American and Caribbean Center, Florida International University, Miami, no. 4 (1983).

———. "Haitian Voodoo in the Eighteenth Century: Language, Culture, Resistance." *Jahrbuch für Geschichte von Staat, Wirtschaft und Gesellschaft Lateinamerikas* 28 (1991): 21–49.

———. "Sugar and Coffee Cultivation in Saint Domingue and the Shaping of the Slave Labor Force." In *Cultivation and Culture: Labor and the Shaping of Slave Life in the Americas,* edited by Ira Berlin and Philip D. Morgan, 73–98. Charlottesville: University Press of Virginia, 1993.

———. *Haitian Revolutionary Studies.* Bloomington: Indiana University Press, 2002.

Georges-Jacob, Kléber. *L'ethnie haïtienne.* Port-au-Prince: Imprimerie de l'État, 1941.

Geschiere, Peter. *The Modernity of Witchcraft: Politics and the Occult in Postcolonial Africa.* Translated by Peter Geschiere and Janet Roitman. Charlottesville, VA: University Press of Virginia, 1997.

Ghachem, Malick Walid. "Montesquieu in the Caribbean: The Colonial Enlightenment between Code Noir and Code Civil." *Historical Reflections/Reflexions historiques* 25, no. 2 (Summer 1999): 183–210.

———. "Sovereignty and Slavery in the Age of Revolution: Haitian Variations on a Metropolitan Theme." Ph.D. diss., Stanford University, 2001.

Gobineau, Arthur de. *Essai sur l'inégalité des races humaines.* Paris: Éditions Pierre Belfond, 1967.

Godbeer, Richard. *The Devil's Dominion: Magic and Religion in Early New England.* New York: Cambridge University Press, 1992.

Goveia, Elsa. "The West Indian Slave Laws of the Eighteenth Century." In *Caribbean Slavery in the Atlantic World,* edited by Verene Shepherd and Hilary McD. Beckles, 580–596. Kingston, Jamaica: Ian Randle, 2000.

Greene, Anne. *The Catholic Church in Haiti: Political and Social Change.* East Lansing: Michigan State University Press, 1993.

Gregory, Steven. "Voodoo, Ethnography, and the American Occupation of

Haiti: William B. Seabrook's *The Magic Island*." In *Dialectical Anthropology: Essays in Honor of Stanley Diamond*, vol. 2, *The Politics of Culture and Creativity: A Critique of Civilization*, edited by Christine Ward Gailey, 169–207. Gainesville: University Press of Florida, 1992.

Grenier, Robert. "La Mélodie Vaudoo—Voodoo Art Songs: The Genesis of a Nationalist Music in the Republic of Haiti." *Black Music Research Journal* 21, no. 1 (2001): 29–74.

Guha, Ranajit. "The Prose of Counter-Insurgency." In *Selected Subaltern Studies*, edited by Ranajit Guha and Gayatri Chakravorty Spivak, 45–84. New York: Oxford University Press, 1988.

Hainard, Jacques, Philippe Mathez, and Olivier Schinz, eds. *Vodou*. Geneva: Musée Ethnographie de Genève, 2008.

"Haïti: Réforme de la justice et crise de la sécurité." International Crisis Group, Briefing Amérique Latine/Caraïbes no. 14, Port-au-Prince/Brussels (31 January 2007).

Hall, Robert Burnett. "The Société Congo of the Île à Gonave." *American Anthropologist* 31, no. 4 (October–December 1929): 685–700.

Handler, Jerome S., and Kenneth M. Bilby. "On the Early Use and Origin of the Term 'Obeah' in Barbados and the Anglophone Caribbean." *Slavery and Abolition* 22, no. 2 (August 2001): 87–100.

Hatzfeld, Adolphe, Arsène Darmesteter, and Antoine Thomas, eds. *Dictionnaire général de la langue française du commencement du XVIIe siècle jusqu'à nos jours*. Paris: Librairie, Ch. Delgrave, 1900.

Hector, Michel. *Crises et mouvements populaires en Haïti*. 2nd ed. Port-au-Prince: Communication Plus . . . Livres, 2006.

Hector, Michel, and Claude Moïse. *Colonisation et esclavage en Haïti: Le régime colonial français à Saint-Domingue, 1625–1789*. Port-au-Prince: Éditions Henri Deschamps, 1990.

Helg, Aline. *Our Rightful Share: The Afro-Cuban Struggle for Equality, 1886–1912*. Chapel Hill: University of North Carolina Press, 1995.

Henry, Frances. *Reclaiming African Religion in Trinidad: The Socio-Political Legitimation of the Orisha and Spiritual Baptist Faiths*. Barbados: University of the West Indies Press, 2003.

Her-Ra-Ma-El [Arthur Holly]. *Dra-Po: Étude ésotérique de égrégore africain, traditionnel, social et national de Haiti*. Port-au-Prince: Imprimerie Nemours Telhomme, 1928.

Herskovits, Melville J. "Lo, the Poor Haitian." *Nation*, 13 February 1929, 198–200.

———. *Life in a Haitian Valley*. 1937. Garden City, NY: Doubleday, 1971.

———. *The Myth of the Negro Past*. 1941. Boston: Beacon Hill, 1958.

Herskovits, Melville J., and Frances S. Herskovits. *Trinidad Village*. New York: Alfred A. Knopf, 1947.

Hilliard d'Auberteuil, Michel-René. *Considérations sur l'état présent de la colonie française de Saint-Domingue*. 2 vols. Paris: Grangé, 1776–1777.

Hoffmann, Léon-François. *Haïti: Couleurs, croyances, créole*. Montreal: CIDI-HCA, 1990.

———. "Histoire, mythe et idéologie: Le serment du Bois-Caïman." In Hoffmann, *Haïti: Lettres et l'être*, 267–301. Toronto: Éditions du GREF, 1992.

———. "Biographie de Jacques Roumain." Île en Île, http://www.lehman.cuny.edu/ile.en.ile/paroles/roumain_bio.html.

Holly, Arthur C. *Les daïmons du culte voudu*. Port-au-Prince: Edmond Chenet, 1918.

Holly, James Theodore. "A Vindication of the Capacity of the Negro Race for Self Government and Civilized Progress." In *Black Separatism in the Caribbean, 1860: James Theodore Holly and J. Dennis Harris*, edited by Howard H. Bell. Ann Arbor: University of Michigan Press, 1970.

Honorat, Michel Lamartinière. *Les danses folkloriques haïtiennes*. Port-au-Prince: Imprimerie de l'Etat, 1955.

Huguet, Edmond, ed. *Dictionnaire de la langue française du seizième siècle*. 7 vols. Paris: Librairie M. Didier, 1966.

Hulme, Peter. *Colonial Encounters: Europe and the Native Caribbean, 1492–1797*. London and New York: Methuen, 1986.

———. "Introduction: The Cannibal Scene." In *Cannibalism and the Colonial World*, edited by Francis Barker, Peter Hulme, and Margaret Iverson, 1–38. Cambridge: Cambridge University Press, 1998.

Hurbon, Laënnec. *Culture et dictature en Haïti: L'imaginaire sous contrôle*. Paris: Librairie-Éditions l'Harmattan, 1979.

———. *Le barbare imaginaire*. Port-au-Prince: Éditions Henri Deschamps, 1987.

———. *Comprendre Haïti: Essai sur l'état, la nation, la culture*. Port-au-Prince: Éditions Henri Deschamps, 1987.

———. *Dieu dans le vaudou haïtien*. Port-au-Prince: Éditions Deschamps, 1987.

———. "American Fantasy and Haitian Vodou." In *Sacred Arts of Haitian Vodou*, edited by Donald J. Cosentino, 181–197. Los Angeles: Fowler Museum of Cultural History, 1995.

———, ed. *L'insurrection des esclaves de Saint-Domingue, 22–23 août 1791*. Paris: Éditions Karthala, 2000.

———. *Religions et lien social: L'église et l'état moderne en Haïti*. Paris: Les Éditions du Cerf, 2004.

———. "Le statut du vodou et l'histoire de l'anthropologie." *Gradhiva* 1, n.s. (2005): 153–164.

Hurston, Zora Neale. *Tell My Horse: Voodoo and Life in Haiti and Jamaica*. 1938. New York: Harper & Row, 1990.

Huxley, Francis. *The Invisibles*. London: Rupert Hart-Davis, 1966.

Hyppolite, Michelson Paul. *Une étude sur le folklore haïtien*. Port-au-Prince: Imprimerie d'État, 1954.

Inginac, Joseph Balthazar. *Mémoires de Joseph Balthazar Inginac, Général de Division, Ex-Secrétaire-Général près S. E. L'Ex-Président d'Haïti, depuis 1797 jusqu'à 1843*. Kingston, Jamaica: Imprimé par J. R. De Cordova, 1843.

Inman, Samuel Guy. *Through Santo Domingo and Haiti: A Cruise with the Marines*. New York: Committee on Co-operation in Latin America, 1920.

———. *Trailing the Conquistadores*. New York: Friendship Press, 1930.

Innocent, Antoine. *Mimola, ou l'histoire d'une cassette: Petit tableau de mœurs locales*. 1906. Port-au-Prince: V. Valcin, Imprimeur, 1935.

Inquiry into Occupation and Administration of Haiti and Santo Domingo; Hearings before a Select Committee on Haiti and Santo Domingo, United States Senate, Sixty-Seventh Congress, First and Second Sessions, pursuant to S. Res. 112 Authorizing a Special Committee to Inquire into the Occupation and Administration of the Territories of the Republic of Haiti and the Dominican Republic. Washington, DC: Government Printing Office, 1922.

James, C. L. R. *The Black Jacobins: Toussaint L'Ouverture and the San Domingo Revolution*. 1938. 2nd ed. New York: Vintage Books, 1963.

Jan, J. M. *Histoire religieuse du Cap: "Notes et documents."* Port-au-Prince: Éditions Henri Deschamps, 1949.

———. *Monographie religieuse des paroisses du Cap-Haïtien*. Port-au-Prince: Éditions Henri Deschamps, 1950.

———. *Collecta*. Vol. 1. Port-au-Prince: Éditions Henri Deschamps, 1955.

———. *Collecta III: Pour l'histoire religieuse du diocèse du Cap-Haïtien*. Port-au-Prince: Éditions Henri Deschamps, 1958.

———. *Le Cap-Haïtien, 1860–1966: Documentation religieuse*. Port-au-Prince: Éditions Henri Deschamps, 1972.

Janvier, Louis-Joseph. *La République d'Haïti et ses visiteurs, 1840–1882: Un peuple noir devant les peuples blancs*. Vol. 1. 1883. Port-au-Prince: Les Éditions Fardin, 1979.

Jean-Jacques, Thalès. *Histoire du droit haïtien*. Port-au-Prince: Imprimerie Nemours Telhomme, 1933.

Johnson, James Weldon. "Self-Determining Haiti, Part 1: The American Occupation." *Nation*, 28 August 1920, 236–238.

———. "Self-Determining Haiti, Part 2: What the United States Has Accomplished." *Nation*, 4 September 1920, 265–267.

———. *Along This Way*. 1933. New York: Viking Press, 1968.

Johnson, Paul Christopher. "Three Paths to Legal Legitimacy: African Diaspora Religions and the State." *Culture and Religion* 6, no. 1 (2005): 79–105.

———. "Secretism and the Apotheosis of Duvalier." *Journal of the American Academy of Religion* 74, no. 2 (2006): 420–445.

Joinville-Gauban, Pierre. *Voyage d'outre-mer et infortunes les plus accablantes de la vie de M. Joinville-Gauban*. . . . Bordeaux: Imprimerie de H. Faye fils, n.d.

Jordan, W. F. *Crusading in the West Indies*. New York: Fleming H. Revell, 1922.

Kaussen, Valerie. *Migrant Revolutions: Haitian Literature, Globalization, and U.S. Imperialism*. Lanham, MD: Lexington Books, 2008.

Kelsey, Carl. *The American Intervention in Haiti and the Dominican Republic*. Philadelphia, PA: Annals of the American Academy of Political and Social Sciences, 1922.

Kerboull, Jean. *Le vaudou: Magie ou religion?* N.p.: Éditions Robert Laffont, 1973.
————. *Voodoo and Magic Practices.* Translated by John Shaw. London: Barrie & Jenkins, 1977.

Kernisan, Clovis. *La vérité ou la mort.* Port-au-Prince: Imprimerie Modèle, 1933.

Kersuzan, François-Marie. *Conférence populaire sur le vaudoux donnée par Monseigneur l'Évêque du Cap-Haïtien, le 2 août, 1896.* Port-au-Prince: Imprimerie H. Amblard, 1896.

Kiernan, Frances. *The Last Mrs. Astor: A New York Story.* New York: W. W. Norton, 2007.

Kirshenblatt-Gimblett, Barbara. *Destination Culture: Tourism, Museums, and Heritage.* Berkeley and Los Angeles: University of California Press, 1998.

Kuser, J. Dryden. *Haiti: Its Dawn of Progress after Years in a Night of Revolution.* 1921. Westport, CT: Negro Universities Press, 1970.

Labat, R. P. Jean Baptiste. *Nouveau voyage aux îles de l'Amérique.* Vol. 2. 1742. Réédition Fort-de-France, 1972.

Laforestrie, Léon. *Cours de droit pénal à l'usage des agents de la police judiciaire.* Port-au-Prince: N.p., n.d.

Laguerre, Michel S. "Bizango: A Voodoo Secret Society in Haiti." In *Secrecy: A Cross-Cultural Perspective*, edited by Stanton K. Tefft, 147–160. New York: Human Sciences Press, 1980.

————. *Urban Life in the Caribbean: A Study of a Haitian Urban Community.* Cambridge, MA: Schenkman, 1983.

————. *Voodoo and Politics in Haiti.* New York: St. Martin's, 1989.

————. *The Military and Society in Haiti.* Knoxville: University of Tennessee Press, 1993.

————. "The Voodooization of Politics in Haiti." In *Blackness in Latin America and the Caribbean: Social Dynamics and Cultural Transformations*, edited by Arlene Torres and Norman E. Whitten, Jr., 2:495–539. 2 vols. Bloomington: Indiana University Press, 1998.

Lahav, Pnina. "The Chef de Section: Structure and Functions of Haiti's Basic Administrative Institution." In *Working Papers in Haitian Society and Culture*, edited by Sidney W. Mintz, 51–83. New Haven, CT: Antilles Research Program, Yale University, 1975.

Lane, Kris E. *Pillaging the Empire: Piracy in the Americas, 1500–1750.* Armonk, NY: M. E. Sharpe, 1998.

Largey, Michael. "Ethnographic Transcription and Music Ideology in Haiti: The Music of Werner A. Jaegerhuber." *Latin American Music Review* 25, no. 1 (2004): 1–31.

————. *Vodou Nation: Haitian Art Music and Cultural Nationalism.* Chicago: University of Chicago Press, 2006.

Larose, Serge. "The Haitian *Lakou*: Land, Family and Ritual." In *Family and Kinship in Middle America and the Caribbean*, edited by Arnaud F. Marks and René A. Rômer, 482–512. Curaçao: Insitute of Higher Studies and Leiden, Netherlands: Royal Institute of Linguistics and Anthropology, 1975.

———. "The Meaning of Africa in Haitian Vodu." In *Symbols and Sentiments: Cross-Cultural Studies in Symbolism*, edited by Ioan Lewis, 85–116. London: Academic Press, 1977.

Laurière, Christine. "D'une île à l'autre: Alfred Métraux en Haïti." *Gradhiva* 1, n.s. (2005): 181–207.

Law, Robin. "La cérémonie du Bois Caïman et le 'pacte de sang' dahoméen." Translated by Maryse Villard. In *L'insurrection des esclaves de Saint-Domingue, 22–23 août 1791*, edited by Laënnec Hurbon, 131–147. Paris: Éditions Karthala, 2000.

Lazarus-Black, Mindie. *Legitimate Acts and Illegal Encounters: Law and Society in Antigua and Barbuda*. Washington, DC: Smithsonian Institution Press, 1994.

Leaf, Earl. *Isles of Rhythm*. New York: A. S. Barnes, 1948.

Leconte, Vergniaud. *Henri Christophe dans l'histoire d'Haïti*. Paris: Éditions Berger-Levrault, 1931.

Le Gouaze, Joseph, Jean-Marie Jan, Paul Robert, and Albert Guiot. *Apostolat de quatre vingts ans*. Cap-Haïtien: Presse Almonacy, 1942.

Lescot, Élie. *Avant l'oubli: Christianisme et paganisme en Haïti et autres lieux*. Port-au-Prince: Imprimerie H. Deschamps, 1974.

Lescot, Élie, Jr. "Une page d'histoire mise à l'endroit ou les dessous de la campagne anti-superstitieuse de 1941–1942." *Pour Haïti* 45 (3rd trimester 2003): 16–17.

Lettre annuelle de l'Ordre de Nôtre Dame. Bordeaux: Imprimerie B. Coussan & F. Constalet, 1880.

Levack, Brian P. "The Decline and End of Witchcraft Prosecutions." In *Witchcraft and Magic in Europe: The Eighteenth and Nineteenth Centuries*, edited by Bengt Ankarloo and Stuart Clark, 7–47. Philadelphia: University of Pennsylvania Press, 1999.

Lewis, Laura. *Hall of Mirrors: Power, Witchcraft, and Caste in Colonial Mexico*. Durham, NC: Duke University Press, 2003.

Lhérisson, Élie. "Du vaudou: Étude de quelques manifestations psychiques et somatiques observées chez les danseuses." *La Lanterne médicale* 2, no. 3 (20 March 1899): 19–23.

Lichtenstein, Alex. *Twice the Work of Free Labor: The Political Economy of Convict Labor in the New South*. London: Verso, 1996.

Linebaugh, Peter, and Marcus Rediker. *The Many-Headed Hydra: The Hidden History of the Revolutionary Atlantic*. London: Verso, 2000.

Loederer, Richard A. *Voodoo Fire in Haiti*. Translated by Desmond Ivo Vesey. New York: Literary Guild, 1935.

Lovejoy, Paul E. *Transformations in Slavery: A History of Slavery in Africa*. 2nd ed. 1983. Cambridge: Cambridge University Press, 2000.

———. "Ethnic Designations of the Slave Trade and the Reconstruction of the History of Trans-Atlantic Slavery." In *Trans-Atlantic Dimensions of Ethnicity in the African Diaspora*, edited by Paul E. Lovejoy and David V. Trotman, 4–42. London: Continuum, 2003.

Lovelace, Earl. *The Wine of Astonishment*. 1982. New York: Vintage Books, 1984.

Lowenthal, Ira P. "Ritual Performance and Religious Experience: A Service for the Gods in Southern Haiti." *Journal of Anthropological Research* 34, no. 3 (Autumn 1978): 392–414.

————. "'Marriage Is 20, Children Are 21': The Cultural Construction of Conjugality and the Family in Rural Haiti." Ph.D. diss., John Hopkins University, 1987.

Lundahl, Mats. *The Haitian Economy: Man, Land and Markets*. New York: St. Martin's, 1983.

MacGaffey, Wyatt. *Religion and Society in Central Africa: The BaKongo of Lower Zaire*. Chicago: University of Chicago Press, 1986.

MacLeod, Murdo J. "The Soulouque Regime in Haiti, 1847–1859: A Reevaluation." *Caribbean Studies* 10, no. 3 (1971): 35–48.

Madiou, Thomas. *Histoire d'Haïti*. Vol. 1, *1492–1799*. Port-au-Prince: Éditions Henri Deschamps, 1989.

————. *Histoire d'Haïti*. Vol. 2, *1799–1803*. Port-au-Prince: Éditions Henri Deschamps, 1989.

————. *Histoire d'Haïti*. Vol. 6, *1819–26*. Port-au-Prince: Éditions Henri Deschamps, 1988.

————. *Histoire d'Haïti, années 1843–1846*. Port-au-Prince: Imprimerie J. Verrollot, 1904.

————. *Histoire d'Haïti*. Vol. 8, *1843–1846*. Port-au-Prince: Éditions Henri Deschamps, 1991.

Magloire, Félix, and Félix Soray. "The Legal System of Haiti." Translated by Carlos M. Sandoval. *Law Notes* 48, no. 1 (February 1944): 4–13.

Magloire, Gérarde. "Haitian-ness, Frenchness and History: Historicizing the French Component of Haitian National Identity." *Pouvoirs dans la Caraïbe* (1998): 18–37.

Magloire, Gérarde, and Kevin A. Yelvington. "Haiti and the Anthropological Imagination." *Gradhiva* 1, n.s. (2005): 127–152.

Magloire-Danton, Gérarde. "Anténor Firmin and Jean Price-Mars: Revolution, Memory, Humanism." *Small Axe* 18 (September 2005): 150–170.

Malenfant, Colonel. *Des colonies, et particulièrement de celle de Saint-Domingue: Mémoire historique et politique*. Paris: Chez Audibert, 1814.

Malinowski, Bronislaw. *The Sexual Life of Savages in North Western Melanesia*. New York: Harcourt Brace, 1929.

Mallon, Florencia. "The Promise and Dilemma of Subaltern Studies: Perspectives from Latin American History." *American Historical Review* 99, no. 5 (1994): 1491–1515.

Mandrou, Robert. *Magistrats et sorciers en France au XVIIe siècle: Une analyse de psychologie historique*. Paris: Plon, 1968.

Mangones, Edmond, and Louis Maximilien. *L'art précolombien d'Haïti: Catalogue de l'exposition précolombienne organisée à l'occasion du IIIe Congrès des Caraïbes sous le haut patronage de Son Excellence M. Sténio Vincent*. Port-au-Prince: Imprimerie de l'État, 1941.

Manigat, J. F. Thalès. *Conférence sur le vaudoux*. Cap-Haïtien: Imprimerie La Conscience, 1897.

Manigat, Leslie F. *La révolution de 1843: Essai d'analyse historique d'une conjoncture de crise*. Port-au-Prince: Édition Le Normalien, 1959.

———. *La politique agraire du gouvernement d'Alexandre Pétion, 1807–1818*. Port-au-Prince: Imprimerie La Phalange, 1962.

———. *Haiti of the Sixties: Object of International Concern*. Washington, DC: Washington Center of Foreign Policy Research, 1964.

Manigat, Max. *Mots créoles du nord d'Haïti: Origines, histoire, souvenirs*. Coconut Creek, FL: Educa Vision, 2007.

Marcelin, Louis Herns. "Haiti." In *Encyclopedia of Anthropology*, edited by H. James Birx, 3:1134–1137. 5 vols. Thousand Oaks, CA: Sage, 2005.

Matory, J. Lorand. *Black Atlantic Religion: Tradition, Transnationalism, and Matriarchy in the Afro-Brazilian Candomblé*. Princeton, NJ: Princeton University Press, 2005.

Maximilien, Louis. *Le vodou haïtien: Rites Rada-Canzo*. Port-au-Prince: Imprimerie de l'État, 1945.

McAlister, Elizabeth A. "A Sorcerer's Bottle: The Visual Art of Magic in Haiti." In *Sacred Arts of Haitian Vodou*, edited by Donald J. Cosentino, 305–321. Los Angeles: Fowler Museum of Cultural History, 1995.

———. "'The Jew' in the Haitian Imagination: Pre-Modern Anti-Judaism in the Postmodern Caribbean." In *Black Zion: African American Religious Encounters with Judaism*, edited by Yvonne Chireau and Nathaniel Deutsch, 203–227. New York: Oxford University Press, 2000.

———. *Rara! Vodou, Power, and Performance in Haiti and Its Diaspora*. Berkeley and Los Angeles: University of California Press, 2002.

McClellan, James E. III. *Colonialism and Science: Saint Domingue in the Old Regime*. Baltimore, MD: Johns Hopkins University Press, 1992.

McConnell, H. Ormonde. *Haiti Diary, 1933–1970: Mission Extraordinary*. N.p.: United Methodist Committee on Relief, n.d.

McCrocklin, James H. *Garde d'Haïti, 1915–1934*. Annapolis, MD: United States Naval Institute, 1956.

McGee, Adam. "Constructing Africa: Authenticity and Gine in Haitian Vodou." *Journal of Haitian Studies* 14, no. 2 (2008): 30–51.

Mennesson-Rigaud, Odette M. "The Feasting of the Gods in Haitian Vodu." Translated by Alfred Métraux and Rhoda Métraux. *Primitive Man* 19, nos. 1–2 (January and April 1946): 1–58.

———. "Le rôle du vaudou dans l'indépendance d'Haïti." *Présence africaine* (February 1958): 43–67.

Merwin, Bruce W. "A Voodoo Drum from Hayti." *Museum Journal* 8, no. 2 (June 1917): 123–125.

Métraux, Alfred. "Jacques Roumain, archéologue et ethnographe." *Cahiers d'Haïti* (November 1944): 23–24.

———. "Droit et coutume en matière successorale dans la paysannerie haïtienne." *Zaïre: Revue congolaise* (April 1951): 339–349.

————. *Making a Living in the Marbial Valley (Haiti)*. Paris: UNESCO, 1951.

————. "Croyances et pratiques magiques dans la vallée de Marbial, Haïti." *Journal de la Société des américanistes* 47 (1953): 135–198.

————. "Réactions psychologiques à la christianisation de la vallée de Marbial (Haïti)." *Revue de psychologie des peuples* 3 (1953): 250–267.

————. "Divinités et cultes vodou dans la vallée de Marbial (Haïti)." *Zaïre* 7 (1954): 675–707.

————. *Le vaudou haïtien*. Paris: Éditions Gallimard, 1958.

————. *Voodoo in Haiti*. Translated by Hugo Charteris. New York: Schocken Books, 1972.

————. *Itinéraires 1, 1935–1953: Carnets de notes et journaux de voyage*. Paris: Payot, 1978.

Métraux, Rhoda Bubendey. "Kith and Kin: A Study of Créole Social Structure in Marbial, Haiti." Ph.D. diss., Columbia University, 1951.

Midy, Franklin. "Un document historique pour la généalogie du vaudou haïtien." *Chemins critiques* 1, no. 1 (March 1989): 135–142.

Miller, Joseph C. "Central Africa during the Era of the Slave Trade, c. 1490s–1850s." In *Central Africans and Cultural Transformations in the American Diaspora*, edited by Linda M. Heywood, 21–69. Cambridge: Cambridge University Press, 2002.

Millet, Kethly. *Les paysans haïtiens et l'occupation américaine d'Haïti, 1915–1930*. La Salle, Quebec: Collectif Paroles, 1978.

Millspaugh, Arthur C. *Haiti under American Control, 1915–1930*. Boston: World Peace Foundation, 1931.

Mintz, Sidney. *Caribbean Transformations*. 1974. New York: Columbia University Press, 1989.

————. *Sweetness and Power: The Place of Sugar in Modern History*. New York: Penguin, 1985.

Mintz, Sidney, and Michel-Rolph Trouillot. "The Social History of Haitian Vodou." In *Sacred Arts of Haitian Vodou*, edited by Donald J. Cosentino, 123–147. Los Angeles: Fowler Museum of Cultural History, 1995.

Moïse, Claude. *Le projet national de Toussaint Louverture et la Constitution de 1801*. Port-au-Prince: Les Éditions Mémoire, 2001.

Montalvo-Despeignes, Jacquelin. *Le droit informel haïtien: Approche socio-ethnographique*. Paris: Presses Universitaires de France, 1976.

Montilus, Guerin C. "Haïti: Un cas témoin de la vivacité des religions africaines en Amérique et pourquoi." In Société Africaine de Culture, *Les religions africaines comme source de valeurs de civilisation: Colloque de Cotonou, 16–22 août 1970*, 287–309. Paris: Présence Africaine, 1972.

————. "Africa in Diaspora: The Myth of Dahomey in Haiti." *Journal of Caribbean Studies* 2, no. 1 (Spring 1981): 73–84.

Moore, Robin. *Nationalizing Blackness: Afrocubanismo and Artistic Revolution in Havana, 1920–1940*. Pittsburgh: University of Pittsburgh Press, 1997.

Moral, Paul. *Le paysan haïtien: Étude sur la vie rurale en Haïti*. Port-au-Prince: Les Éditions Fardin, 1978.

Moreau de Saint-Méry, Médéric-Louis-Élie. *Description topographique, physique, civile, politique et historique de la partie française de l'isle Saint-Domingue.* Vol. 1. Edited by Blanche Maurel and Étienne Taillemite. 1797. Paris: Société de l'Histoire des Colonies Françaises and Librairie Larose, 1958.

———, ed. *Loix et constitutions des colonies françoises de l'Amérique sous le vent.* 6 vols. Paris: Chez l'auteur, etc., n.d.

Morris, Rosalind. *In the Place of Origins: Modernity and Its Mediums in Northern Thailand.* Durham, NC: Duke University Press, 2000.

Mullaney, Steven. *The Place of the Stage: License, Play, and Power in Renaissance England.* Chicago: University of Chicago Press, 1988.

Murray, Gerald F. "The Evolution of Haitian Peasant Land Tenure: A Case Study in Agrarian Adaptation to Population Growth." Ph.D. diss., Columbia University, 1977.

———. "Population Pressure, Land Tenure, and Voodoo: The Economics of Haitian Peasant Ritual." In *Beyond the Myths of Culture: Essays in Cultural Materialism,* edited by Eric B. Ross, 295–321. New York: Academic Press, 1980.

Nalty, Bernard C., and Morris J. MacGregor, eds. *Blacks in the Military: Essential Documents.* Wilmington, DE: Scholarly Resources, 1981.

Nascimento, Elisa Larkin. *The Sorcery of Color: Identity, Race, and Gender in Brazil.* Philadelphia: Temple University Press, 2003.

Nau, Léon, ed. *Les codes haïtiens: Code d'instruction criminelle et Code pénal annotés avec annexes.* Paris: Librairie Générale de Droit et de Jurisprudence, 1909.

———. *Les codes haïtiens: Code d'instruction criminelle et Code pénal annotés avec annexes.* Paris: Librairie Générale de Droit et de Jurisprudence, 1914.

Nérestant, Micial M. *Religions et politique en Haïti.* Paris: Karthala, 1994.

Newell, William W. "Myths of Voodoo Worship and Child Sacrifice in Hayti." *Journal of American Folk-Lore* 1, no. 1 (April–June 1888): 16–30.

Nicholls, David. *Economic Dependence and Political Autonomy: The Haitian Experience.* Montreal: McGill University, Centre for Developing Area Studies, 1974.

———. "The Wisdom of Salomon: Myth or Reality." *Journal of Interamerican Studies and World Affairs* 20, no. 4 (November 1978): 377–392.

———. *From Dessalines to Duvalier: Race, Colour and National Independence in Haiti.* 1979. New Brunswick, NJ: Rutgers University Press, 1996.

Niles, Blair. *Black Haiti: A Biography of Africa's Eldest Daughter.* New York: Grosset & Dunlap, 1926.

Novack, Cynthia J. "Looking at Movement as Culture." *TDR* 32, no. 4 (Winter 1988): 102–119.

Ogle, Gene E. "'The Eternal Power of Reason' and 'The Superiority of Whites': Hilliard D'Auberteuil's Colonial Enlightenment." *French Colonial History* 3 (2003): 35–50.

O'Neill, Eugene. *The Emperor Jones, Anna Christie, The Hairy Ape.* New York: Modern Library, 1937.

Oriol, Jacques. "In Memoriam: Lorimer Denis." *Bulletin du Bureau d'ethnologie,* ser. 3, no. 14 (January 1958): 3–13.

Oriol, Jacques, Léonce Viaud, and Michel Aubourg. *Le mouvement folklorique en Haïti*. Port-au-Prince: Imprimerie de l'État, 1952.

Ortner, Sherry B. "Resistance and the Problem of Ethnographic Refusal." *Comparative Studies in Society and History* 37, no. 1 (January 1995): 173–193.

Palmer, Vernon V. "The Origins and Authors of the Code Noir." In *An Uncommon Experience: Law and Judicial Institutions in Louisiana, 1803–2003*, 331–359. Lafayette: Center for Louisiana Studies, University of Southwestern Louisiana, 1997.

Palmié, Stephan. "Which Centre, Whose Margin? Notes towards an Archaeology of US Supreme Court Case 91-948, 1993 (Church of the Lukumí vs. City of Hialeah, South Florida)." In *Inside and Outside the Law: Anthropological Studies of Authority and Ambiguity*, edited by Olivia Harris, 184–209. London: Routledge, 1996.

———. "Conventionalization, Distortion, and Plagiarism in the Historiography of Afro-Caribbean Religion in New Orleans." In *Creoles and Cajuns: French Louisiana—La Louisiane Française*, edited by Wolfgang Binder, 315–344. Frankfurt: Peter Lang, 1998.

———. *Wizards and Scientists: Explorations in Afro-Cuban Modernity and Tradition*. Durham, NC: Duke University Press, 2002.

Pamphile, Léon Denius. *La croix et le glaive: L'église catholique et l'occupation américaine d'Haiti, 1915–1934*. Port-au-Prince: Éditions des Antilles, 1991.

Paper Laws, Steel Bayonets: Breakdown of the Rule of Law in Haiti. New York: Lawyers Committee for Human Rights, 1990.

Parham, Althéa de Puech, trans. and ed. *My Odyssey: Experiences of a Young Refugee from Two Revolutions, by a Creole of Saint-Domingue*. Baton Rouge: Louisiana State University Press, 1959.

Parichy, Esselle. "Marine Sergeant Turns Adventurer: Faustin Wirkus Only White Ever Crowned King of Haitian Blacks by Popular Consent—Films Will Illustrate Lecture." *International Photographer* (November 1931): 4–5.

Parsons, Elsie Clews. "Spirit Cult in Hayti." *Journal de la Société des américanistes de Paris* 20 (1928): 157–179.

Parsons, Robert P. *History of Haitian Medicine*. New York: Paul B. Hoeber, 1930.

Paton, Diana. *No Bond but the Law: Punishment, Race, and Gender in Jamaican State Formation, 1780–1870*. Durham, NC: Duke University Press, 2004.

Paul, Emmanuel. *L'ethnographie en Haïti: Ses initiateurs, son état actuel, ses tâches, et son avenir*. Port-au-Prince: Imprimerie de l'État, 1949.

———. "Folklore du militarism." *Optique* 6 (1954): 24–27.

———. "Tâches et responsabilités de l'ethnologie." *Bulletin du Bureau national d'ethnologie*, sér. 3, nos. 17–19 (December 1958–March 1959): 11–19.

———. *Panorama du folklore haïtien: Présence africaine en Haiti*. Port-au-Prince: Imprimerie de l'État, 1962.

Peabody, Sue. "'A Dangerous Zeal': Catholic Missions to Slaves in the French Antilles, 1635–1800." *French Historical Studies* 25, no. 1 (Winter 2002): 53–90.

Péan, Marc. *L'illusion héroïque: 25 ans de vie capoise, 1890–1915*, vol. 1, *1890–1902*. Port-au-Prince: Imprimerie Henri Deschamps, 1977.

Peters, Carl Edward. *Lumière sur le humfort*. Port-au-Prince: Chéraquit, Imprimeur-Éditeur, 1941.

—————. *La croix contre l'asson*. Port-au-Prince: Imprimerie la Phalange, 1960.

Peters, Edward. *The Magician, the Witch, and the Law*. Philadelphia: University of Pennsylvania Press, 1978.

Petit-Frère, Roger. *Code rural de Boyer, 1826*. Archives Nationales d'Haïti/Maison H. Deschamps, 1992.

Pettinger, Alasdair. "From Vaudoux to Voodoo." *Forum of Modern Language Studies* 40, no. 4 (2004): 415–425.

Pierre, Hyppolite. *Haiti: Rising Flames from Burning Ashes; Haiti the Phoenix*. Lanham, MD: University Press of America, 2006.

Pierre-Charles, Gérard. *Radiographie d'une dictature*. Montreal: Éditions Nouvelle Optique, 1973.

Pietz, William. "The Problem of the Fetish, II: The Origin of the Fetish." *Res* 13 (Spring 1987): 23–45.

Piquion, René. *Manuel de négritude*. Port-au-Prince: Éditions Henri Deschamps, 1966.

Pluchon, Pierre. *Vaudou, sorciers, empoisonneurs de Saint-Domingue à Haïti*. Paris: Éditions Karthala, 1987.

Plummer, Brenda Gayle. "The Metropolitan Connection: Foreign and Semiforeign Elites in Haiti, 1900–1915." *Latin American Research Review* 19, no. 2 (1984): 119–142.

—————. *Haiti and the Great Powers, 1902–1915*. Baton Rouge: Louisiana State University Press, 1988.

—————. *Haiti and the United States: The Psychological Moment*. Athens: University of Georgia Press, 1992.

Polyné, Millery. "'To Carry the Dance of the People Beyond': Jean Léon Destiné, Lavinia Williams, and Danse Folklorique Haïtienne." *Journal of Haitian Studies* 10, no. 2 (2004): 33–51.

—————. "Expansion Now! Haiti, 'Santo Domingo,' and Frederick Douglass at the Intersection of U.S. and Caribbean Pan-Americanism." *Caribbean Studies* 34, no. 2 (July–December 2006): 3–46.

Pompilus, Pradel, and Frères de l'Instruction Chrétienne. *Manuel illustré d'histoire de la littérature haïtienne*. Port-au-Prince: Éditions Henri Deschamps, 1961.

Pons, Frank Moya. *History of the Caribbean: Plantations, Trade, and War in the Atlantic World*. Princeton, NJ: Markus Wiener, 2007.

Popkin, Jeremy D. *Facing Racial Revolution: Eyewitness Accounts of the Haitian Insurrection*. Chicago: University of Chicago Press, 2007.

Port-au-Prince et quelques autres villes d'Haïti. Port-au-Prince: Imprimerie de l'État, 1934.

Pradine, Linstant, ed. *Recueil général des lois et actes du gouvernement d'Haïti depuis la proclamation de son indépendance jusqu'à nos jours*. Vol. 4, *1824–1826*. Paris: Auguste Durand, 1865.

—————, annotator. *Code d'instruction criminelle et Code pénal*. Paris: A. Durand & Pedone-Lauriel, 1883.

Pressoir, Catts. *La médecine en Haïti*. Port-au-Prince: Imprimerie Modèle, 1927.

———. "Le protestantisme en Haïti." *Les Griots: La revue scientifique et littéraire d'Haïti* 3, no. 3 (January–February–March 1939): 384–397.

———. *Le protestantisme haïtien*. Vol. 1, pt. 1. Port-au-Prince: Imprimerie de la Société Biblique et des Livres Religieux d'Haïti, 1945.

———. *Le protestantisme haïtien*. Vol. 1, pt. 2. Port-au-Prince: Imprimerie de la Société Biblique et des Livres Religieux d'Haïti, 1946.

———. *Le protestantisme haïtien*. Vol. 2. Port-au-Prince: Imprimerie du Séminaire Adventiste, 1976.

Price, Hannibal. *De la réhabilitation de la race noire par la République d'Haïti*. Port-au-Prince: Imprimerie J. Verrollot, 1900.

Price, Richard. *The Convict and the Colonel: A Story of Colonialism and Resistance in the Caribbean*. Durham, NC: Duke University Press, 2006.

Price-Mars, Jean. *Une étape de l'évolution haïtienne*. Port-au-Prince: Imprimerie "La Presse," 1929.

———. "Lemba-Pétro: Un culte secret; Son histoire, sa localisation géographique, son symbolisme." *Revue de la Société haïtienne d'histoire et de géographie* 28 (1938): 12–31.

———. *Folklore et patriotisme: Conférence prononcée sous les auspices de l'Alliance Française, le 24 novembre 1951*. Port-au-Prince: Imprimerie "Les Presses Libres," 1951.

———. "Antoine Innocent, Ethnographe." *Conjonction* 48 (December 1953): 49–55.

———. *Lettre ouverte, au Dr. René Piquion: Le préjugé de couleur, est-il la question sociale?* Port-au-Prince: Éditions des Antilles, 1967.

———. *Ainsi parla l'oncle*. 1928. Ottawa: Éditions Leméac, 1973.

———. *La vocation de l'élite*. 1919. Port-au-Prince: Ateliers Fardin, 1976–1977.

———. *So Spoke the Uncle*. Translated by Magdaline W. Shannon. Washington, DC: Three Continents, 1983.

Ramsey, Kate. "Melville Herskovits, Katherine Dunham, and the Politics of African Diasporic Dance Anthropology." In *Dancing Bodies, Living Histories: New Writings about Dance and Culture*, edited by Anne Flynn and Lisa Doolittle, 196–216. Banff, Alberta: Banff Centre Press, 2000.

———. "Without One Ritual Note: Folklore Performance and the Haitian State, 1935–1946." *Radical History Review* 84 (Fall 2002): 7–42.

———. "Legislating 'Civilization' in Post-Revolutionary Haiti." In *Race, Nation, and Religion in the Americas*, edited by Henry Goldschmidt and Elizabeth McAlister, 231–258. New York: Oxford University Press, 2004.

———. "Prohibition, Persecution, Performance: Anthropology and the Penalization of Vodou in Mid-20th-Century Haiti." *Gradhiva* 1, n.s. (2005): 165–179.

Ranger, Terence. "The Invention of Tradition in Colonial Africa." In *The Invention of Tradition*, edited by Eric Hobsbawm and Terence Ranger, 211–262. Cambridge: Cambridge University Press, 1983.

Raymond, Louis. *Manuel des officiers de police judiciaire et des juges de paix*. Port-au-Prince: Imprimerie de l'État, 1935.

Regourd, François. "Mesmerism in Saint Domingue: Occult Knowledge and Vodou on the Eve of the Haitian Revolution." In *Science and Empire in the Atlantic World*, edited by James Delbourgo and Nicholas Dew, 311–332. New York: Routledge, 2008.

Renda, Mary A. *Taking Haiti: Military Occupation and the Culture of U.S. Imperialism, 1915–1940*. Chapel Hill: University of North Carolina Press, 2001.

René, Georges, and Marilyn Houlberg. "My Double Mystic Marriages to Two Goddesses of Love: An Interview." In *Sacred Arts of Haitian Vodou*, edited by Donald J. Cosentino, 287–299. Los Angeles: Fowler Museum of Cultural History, 1995.

"Resolution sur le folklore, approuvée à l'assemblée des ministres et directeurs d'éducation des républiques américaines réunie à Panama du 27 septembre au 4 octobre." 1943. Reprinted in *Bulletin du Bureau d'ethnologie* (March 1947): 39–40.

Rey, Terry. "The Virgin Mary and Revolution in Saint-Domingue: The Charisma of Romaine-la-Prophétesse." *Journal of Historical Sociology* 11, no. 3 (September 1998): 341–369.

———. *Our Lady of Class Struggle: The Cult of the Virgin Mary in Haiti*. Trenton, NJ: Africa World Press, 1999.

———. "Kongolese Catholic Influences on Haitian Popular Catholicism: A Sociohistorical Exploration." In *Central Africans and Cultural Transformation in the American Diaspora*, edited by Linda M. Heywood, 265–285. Cambridge: Cambridge University Press, 2002.

———. "The Politics of Patron Sainthood in Haiti: 500 Years of Iconic Struggle." *Catholic Historical Review* 88, no. 3 (July 2002): 519–545.

Rhodes, Gary D. *White Zombie: Anatomy of a Horror Film*. Jefferson, NC: McFarland, 2001.

Richman, Karen E. "They Will Remember Me in the House: The *Pwen* of Haitian Transnational Migration." Ph.D. diss., University of Virginia, 1992.

———. *Migration and Vodou*. Gainesville: University Press of Florida, 2005.

———. "Innocent Imitations? Authenticity and Mimesis in Haitian Vodou Art, Tourism, and Anthropology." *Ethnohistory* 55, no. 2 (2008): 203–227.

———. "Peasants, Migrants and the Discovery of African Traditions: Ritual and Social Change in Lowland Haiti." *Journal of Religion in Africa* 37, no. 3 (2007): 371–397.

Rigaud, Candelon. *Promenades dans les campagnes d'Haïti: La plaine de la Croix des Bouquets (Cul-de-Sac), 1789–1928*. Paris: L'Édition Française Universelle, 193-.

Rigaud, Milo. *La tradition voudoo et le voudoo haïtien: Son temple, ses mystères, sa magie*. Paris: Éditions Niclaus, 1953.

Riou, Roger. *The Island of My Life: From Petty Crime to Priestly Mission*. Translated by Martin Sokolinsky. New York: Delacorte Press, 1975.

Rivière, H. F., ed. *Codes français*. Paris: Librairie A. Marescq Aîné, 1882.

Roach, Joseph. *Cities of the Dead: Circum-Atlantic Performance.* New York: Columbia University Press, 1996.

Robert, Paul. *L'église et la première république noire.* Rennes: Imprimeries Simon, 1964.

Rodman, Selden. *Haiti: The Black Republic.* 1954. New York: Devin-Adair, 1961.

Rogozinski, Jan. *A Brief History of the Caribbean: From the Arawak and Carib to the Present.* New York: Plume/Penguin, 1999.

Romain, J. B. *Quelques mœurs et coutumes des paysans haïtiens: Travaux pratiques d'ethnographie sur la région de Milot à l'usage des étudiants.* 1959. Folcroft, PA: Folcroft Library Editions, 1974.

Román, Reinaldo. *Governing Spirits: Religion, Miracles, and Spectacles in Cuba and Puerto Rico, 1898–1956.* Chapel Hill: University of North Carolina Press, 2007.

Rony, Fatimah Tobing. *The Third Eye: Race, Cinema, and Ethnographic Spectacle.* Durham, NC: Duke University Press, 1996.

Roosevelt, Theodore. "Annual Message to Congress, 6 December, 1904." In *Encyclopedia of American Foreign Policy*, vol. 1, edited by Alexander DeConde, Richard Dean Burns, and Fredrik Logevall, 221. New York: Charles Scribner, 1978.

Rosemond, René J. *L'énergie nationale: "Les précurseurs."* Port-au-Prince: Imprimerie du College Vertières, 1942.

Roumain, Jacques. *À propos de la campagne "anti-superstitieuse"/Las Supersticiones.* Port-au-Prince: Imprimerie de l'État, 1942.

———. *Le sacrifice du tambour-assoto(r).* Port-au-Prince: Imprimerie de l'État, 1943.

———. *Oeuvres complètes.* Edited by Léon-François Hoffmann. Madrid: Allca XX-UNESCO ("Archivos" 58), 2003.

Rural Code of Haiti, Gendarmerie d'Haïti. Translated by R. S. Hooker. Port-au-Prince: Imprimerie Edm. Chenet, 1916.

Sagás, Ernesto. *Race and Politics in the Dominican Republic.* Gainesville: University Press of Florida, 2000.

Saint-Armand, J. *Le Code rural d'Haïti, publié avec commentaires et formulaire, notes et annexes à l'usage des fonctionnaires, officiers et agents de la police rurale.* Port-au-Prince: Imprimerie Vve J. Chenet, 1903.

St. John, Spenser. *Hayti, or The Black Republic.* 1889. London: Frank Cass, 1971.

Sala-Molins, Louis. *Le Code noir, ou Le calvaire de Canaan.* Paris: Presses Universitaires de France, 1987.

Sannon, H. Pauleus. *Essai historique sur la révolution de 1843.* Cayes: Imprimerie Bonnefil, 1905.

Schmidt, Hans. *The United States Occupation of Haiti, 1915–1934.* 1971. New Brunswick, NJ: Rutgers University Press, 1995.

Schoelcher, Victor. *Colonies étrangères et Haïti: Résultats de l'émancipation anglaise.* Vol. 1. Paris: Pagnerre, 1843.

———. *Colonies étrangères et Haïti: Résultats de l'émancipation anglaise.* Vol. 2. Paris: Pagnerre, 1843.

Scott, David. *Formations of Ritual: Colonial and Anthropological Discourses on the Sinhala Yaktovil.* [Minneapolis]: University of Minnesota Press, 1994.

———. *Refashioning Futures: Criticism after Postcoloniality.* Princeton, NJ: Princeton University Press, 1999.

———. *Conscripts of Modernity: The Tragedy of Colonial Enlightenment.* Durham, NC: Duke University Press, 2004.

Scott, Rebecca J. *Slave Emancipation in Cuba: The Transition to Free Labor, 1860–1899.* Princeton, NJ: Princeton University Press, 1985.

Scott, Rebecca J., and Jean M. Hébrard. "Servitude, liberté et citoyenneté dans le monde atlantique des XVIIIe et XIXe siècles: Rosalie de nation Poulard. . . ." *Revue de la Société haïtienne d'histoire et de géographie* 234 (2008): 1–52.

Seabrook, W. B. *The Magic Island.* New York: Harcourt, Brace, 1920.

Seabrook, William B. Introduction to Faustin Wirkus and Taney Dudley, *The White King of La Gonave*, xi–xv. Garden City, NY: Doubleday, Doran, 1931.

Sébillot, Paul. *Le folk-lore: Littérature orale et ethnographique traditionnelle.* Paris: O. Doin et fils, 1913.

Senn, Bryan. *Golden Horrors: An Illustrated Critical Filmography of Terror Cinema, 1931–1939.* Jefferson, NC: McFarland, 1996.

Shannon, Magdaline W. *Jean Price-Mars, the Haitian Elite and the American Occupation, 1915–1935.* New York: St. Martin's, 1996.

Sheller, Mimi. *Democracy after Slavery: Black Publics and Peasant Radicalism in Haiti and Jamaica.* Gainesville: University Press of Florida, 2001.

Simpson, George Eaton. "Haitian Magic." *Social Forces* 19, no. 1 (1940): 95–100.

———. "The Vodun Service in Northern Haiti." *American Anthropologist* 42, no. 2 (April–June 1940): 236–254.

———. "The Belief System of Haitian Vodun." *American Anthropologist* 47, no. 1 (January–March 1945): 37–59.

———. "Four Vodun Ceremonies." *Journal of American Folklore*, 59, no. 232 (April–June 1946): 154–167.

———. "Two Vodun-Related Ceremonies." *Journal of American Folklore* 61, no. 239 (January–March 1948): 49–52.

———. *Religious Cults of the Caribbean: Trinidad, Jamaica, and Haiti.* Rio Piedras, Puerto Rico: Institute of Caribbean Studies, 1970.

Smith, Jennie. *When the Hands Are Many: Community Organization and Social Change in Rural Haiti.* Ithaca, NY: Cornell University Press, 2001.

Smith, Matthew J. *Red and Black in Haiti: Radicalism, Conflict, and Political Change, 1934–1957.* Chapel Hill: University of North Carolina Press, 2009.

Smith, Theophus H. *Conjuring Culture: Biblical Formations of Black America.* New York: Oxford University Press, 1994.

Smith, Wilfred Cantwell. *The Meaning and End of Religion: A New Approach to the Religious Traditions of Mankind.* 1962. Minneapolis, MN: Fortress Press, 1991.

Smucker, Glenn R. "The Social Character of Religion in Rural Haiti." In *Haiti—Today and Tomorrow: An Interdisciplinary Study*, edited by Charles R. Foster and Albert Valdman, 35–56. Lanham, MD: University Press of America, 1984.

Sosis, Howard Justin. "The Colonial Environment and Religion in Haiti: An Introduction to the Black Slave Cults in Eighteenth Century Saint-Domingue." Ph.D. diss., Columbia University, 1971.

Spivak, Gayatri Chakravorty. "Subaltern Studies: Deconstructing Historiography." In Spivak, *In Other Worlds: Essays in Cultural Politics*, 197–221. New York: Routledge, 1988.

Starobinski, Jean. *Blessings in Disguise; or, The Morality of Evil*. Translated by Arthur Goldhammer. 1989. Cambridge, MA: Harvard University Press, 1993.

Stein, Robert Louis. *Léger Félicité Sonthonax: The Lost Sentinel of the Republic*. Rutherford, NJ: Farleigh Dickinson University Press, 1985.

Stewart, Dianne M. *Three Eyes for the Journey: African Dimensions of the Jamaican Religious Experience*. Oxford: Oxford University Pres, 2005.

Stuckey, Sterling. *Slave Culture: Nationalist Theory and the Foundations of Black America*. New York: Oxford University Press, 1987.

———. *Going Through the Storm: The Influence of African American Art in History*. New York: Oxford University Press, 1994.

Supplice, Daniel. *Dictionnaire biographique des personnalités politiques de la République d'Haïti, 1804–2001*. Belgium: Lannoo Imprimerie, 2001.

Taussig, Michael. *The Devil and Commodity Fetishism in South America*. Chapel Hill: University of North Carolina Press, 1980.

———. *Shamanism, Colonialism, and the Wild Man: A Study in Terror and Healing*. Chicago: University of Chicago Press, 1987.

———. *Mimesis and Alterity: A Particular History of the Senses*. New York: Routledge, 1993.

———. *Defacement: Public Secrecy and the Labor of the Negative*. Stanford, CA: Stanford University Press, 1999.

———. "Viscerality, Faith, and Skepticism: Another Theory of Magic." In *Magic and Modernity: Interfaces of Revelation and Concealment*, edited by Birgit Meyer and Peter Pels, 272–306. Stanford, CA: Stanford University Press, 2003.

———. *My Cocaine Museum*. Chicago: University of Chicago Press, 2004.

Terlonge, Henri. "Sociologie juridique: Institutions et lois haïtiennes." *Les Griots* 2, no. 2 (October–December 1938): 177–180.

Thoby-Marcelin, Philippe, and Pierre Marcelin. *All Men Are Mad*. New York: Farrar, Straus, & Giroux, 1970.

Thomas, Deborah. *Modern Blackness: Nationalism, Globalization, and the Politics of Culture in Jamaica*. Durham, NC: Duke University Press, 2004.

Thompson, Robert Farris. "From the Isle beneath the Sea: Haiti's Africanizing Vodou Art." In *Sacred Arts of Haitian Vodou*, edited by Donald J. Cosentino, 91–119. Los Angeles: Fowler Museum of Cultural History, 1995.

Thornton, John K. "'I Am the Subject of the King of Congo': African Political Ideology and the Haitian Revolution." *Journal of World History* 4, no. 2 (1993): 181–214.

———. "Les racines du vaudou: Religion africaine et société haïtienne dans la

Saint-Domingue prérévolutionnaire." *Anthropologie et sociétés* 22, no. 1 (1998): 85–103.

Thomas, Lowell. *Old Gimlet Eye: The Adventures of Smedley D. Butler*. New York: Farrar & Rinehart, 1933.

Torres-Saillant, Silvio. *An Intellectual History of the Caribbean*. New York: Palgrave Macmillan, 2006.

Trouillot, Duverneau. *Esquisse ethnographique: Le vaudoun; Aperçu historique et évolutions*. Port-au-Prince: Imprimerie R. Ethéart, 1885.

Trouillot, Hénock. *Introduction à une histoire du vaudou*. 1970. Port-au-Prince: Éditions Fardin, 1983.

———. "La guerre de l'indépendance d'Haïti: Les grands prêtres du vodou contre l'armée française." *Revista de historia de América* 72, no. 2 (1971): 259–327.

Trouillot, Michel-Rolph. *Ti difé boulé sou istoua ayiti*. Brooklyn: Koléksion Lakensièl, 1977.

———. *Haiti, State against Nation: The Origins and Legacy of Duvalierism*. New York: Monthly Review Press, 1990.

———. "Jeux de mots, jeux de classe: Les mouvances de l'indigénisme." *Conjonction* 197 (1993): 29–41.

———. *Silencing the Past: Power and the Production of History*. Boston: Beacon Press, 1995.

———. "Historiography of Haiti." In *General History of the Caribbean*, vol. 6, *Methodology and Historiography of the Caribbean*, edited by B. W. Higman, 451–477. London: UNESCO/ Macmillan, 1999.

Turits, Richard Lee. *Foundations of Despotism: Peasants, the Trujillo Regime, and Modernity in Dominican History*. Stanford, CA: Stanford University Press, 2003.

Turner, George E., and Michael H. Price. *Forgotten Horrors: Early Talkie Chillers from Poverty Row*. South Brunswick, NJ: A. S. Barnes, 1979.

Tylor, Edward. *Primitive Culture*. Vol. 1. London: John Murray, 1920.

Ulysse, Gina Athena. "Papa, Patriarchy and Power: Snapshots of a Good Haitian Girl, Feminism, and Dyasporic Dreams." *Journal of Haitian Studies* 12, no. 1 (2006): 24–47.

———. "The Spirits in My Mother's Head." *Poemmemoirstory* 8 (2008): 113–119.

———. "Why Representations of Haiti Matter Now More Than Ever." *NACLA: Report on the Americas* 43, no. 4 (July–August 2010): 37–43.

Vaissière, Pierre de. *Saint-Domingue, 1629–1789: La société et la vie créole sous l'ancien régime*. Paris: Perrin, 1909.

Valdman, Albert, Sarah Yoder, Craige Roberts, and Yves Joseph, eds. *Haitian-Creole-English-French Dictionary*. 2 vols. Bloomington: Indiana University, Creole Institute, 1981.

Vanhee, Hein. "Central African Popular Christianity and the Making of the Haitian Vodou Religion." In *Central Africans and Cultural Transformations in the American Diaspora*, edited by Linda M. Heywood, 243–264. Cambridge: Cambridge University Press, 2002.

Verna, Chantalle. "Maurice Dartigue and Educational Reform as a Strategy for Haitian National Development, 1930–46." *Journal of Haitian Studies* 13, no. 2 (Fall 1997): 24–38.

Vincent, Sténio. *La République d'Haïti: Telle qu'elle est.* Brussels: Société Anonyme Belge d'Imprimerie, 1910.

———. *Efforts et résultats.* Port-au-Prince: Imprimerie de l'État, 1938.

Voltaire, Frantz. *Pouvoir noir en Haïti: L'explosion de 1946.* Montreal: Éditions du CIDIHCA, 1988.

Weaver, Karol K. *Medical Revolutionaries: The Enslaved Healers of Eighteenth-Century Saint Domingue.* Urbana: University of Illinois Press, 2006.

Wexler, Anna. "Fictional Oungan: In the Long Shadow of the Fetish." *Research in African Literature* 32, no. 1 (2001): 83–97.

White, Ashli. *Encountering Revolution: Haiti and the Making of the Early Republic.* Baltimore, MD: Johns Hopkins University Press, 2010.

Wilcken, Lois. "Music Folklore among Haitians in New York: Staged Representations and the Negotiation of Identity." Ph.D. diss., Columbia University, 1991.

Wilcken, Lois, featuring Frisner Augustin. *The Drums of Vodou.* Tempe, AZ: White Cliffs Media, 1992.

Williams, Eric. *Capitalism and Slavery.* 1944. Chapel Hill: University of North Carolina Press, 1994.

Williams, Joseph J. *Voodoos and Obeahs: Phases of West Indian Witchcraft.* New York: Dial Press, 1932.

Williams, Tony. "White Zombie: Haitian Horror." *Jump Cut* 28 (Spring 1983): 18–20.

Wilson, Theodore Brantner. *The Black Codes of the South.* Southern Historical Publications 6. Birmingham: University of Alabama Press, 1965.

Wirkus, Faustin. "The Black Pope of Voodoo, Part 1." *Harper's*, December 1933, 38–49.

———. "The Black Pope of Voodoo, Part 2." *Harper's*, January 1934, 189–198.

Wirkus, Faustin, and Taney Dudley. *The White King of La Gonave.* Garden City, NY: Doubleday, Doran, 1931.

Wirtz, Kristina. *Ritual, Discourse, and Community in Cuban Santería: Speaking a Sacred World.* Gainesville: University Press of Florida, 2007.

Wise, Frederic May, and Meigs O. Frost. *A Marine Tells It to You.* New York: J. H. Sears, 1929.

Woodson, Drexel G. "Tout Mounn Se Mounn, Men Tout Mounn pa Menm: Microlevel Sociocultural Aspects of Land Tenure in a Northern Haitian Locality." Ph.D. diss., University of Chicago, 1990.

Yarborough, Lavinia Williams. *Haiti-Dance.* Frankfurt: Brönners Druckerei, 1959.

Yelvington, Kevin A. "The Invention of Africa in Latin America and the Caribbean: Political Discourse and Anthropological Praxis, 1920–1940." In *Afro-*

Atlantic Dialogues: Anthropology in the Diaspora, edited by Kevin A. Yelvington, 35–82. Santa Fe, NM: School of American Research Press, 2006.

Yih, Yuen-Ming David. "Music and Dance of Haitian Vodou: Diversity and Unity in Regional Repertoires." Ph.D. diss., Wesleyan University, 1995.

Zacaïr, Philippe. "Représentations d'Haïti dans la presse française du dix-neuvième siècle." *French Colonial History* 6 (2005): 103–118.

Abraham, Saint Erlonge, 224, 358n214, 358n215

Acaau, Louis Jean-Jacques, 72–73, 80

affaire de Bizoton, 83–86, 90

Africa. *See* Allada (Arada); Dahomey, in etymology of "Vodou"; Ginen; Kongo; slavery; Witchcraft Ordinance in Malawi and Zambia (1914)

African Americans, 78, 80, 128, 294n130, 310n26, 335, 343n84

African Methodist Episcopal (A.M.E.) Church, 103, 197, 198, 343n84

afrocubanismo, 178, 180, 335, 337, 362n254

Aguirre, Carlos, 64

Ainsi parla l'oncle (Price-Mars), 6, 19, 178, 179, 180, 181, 186, 202–3, 215, 242, 264–65n66, 336n9, 336n11, 336n13, 342n66, 359n222

Alix, Juan Antonio, 295n138

Allada (Arada), 29, 40, 80, 95, 274n81, 275n83, 275n85

Alphonse, Alexis, 104, 105

Angell, Ernest, 135, 139–40

animals: sacrifice, 8, 15, 74, 103, 104, 159, 166, 184–85, 188, 190, 191, 192, 205, 206, 221, 222, 239, 240–41, 242, 243, 291n91, 338n30, 339n34; transformation of humans into, 76, 205

anthropology. *See* ethnology

anthropophagy. *See* cannibalism

antisuperstition campaign. See *campagne antisuperstitieuse,* 1940–42

Antoine, Jacques Carmeleau, 336n16

À propos de la campagne "anti-superstitieuse"/ Las supersticiones (Roumain), 204, 210, 346n117

Apter, Andrew, 259n19, 259n24, 260n29

Arada, 29, 40, 80, 95, 274n81, 275n83, 275n85

Ardouin, Beaubrun, 52, 77, 294n131

Ardouin, Céligny, 44–45, 77, 276n94, 293n120

Aristide, Jean-Bertrand, 13, 262n45, 368n29

Armée Souffrante, 72–73

Armour, Norman, 220, 355n191

Article 30 (Haitian Constitution of 1987), 13

Article 297 (Haitian Constitution of 1987), 13, 262n44

art naïf movement, 218, 353n176

Ashton, Horace, 230

Assam (enslaved woman), 37, 272n60

Assembly of Ministers and Directors of Education of the American Republics, 230

Association des Vodouisants et Défenseurs du Vodou, 12

Aubourg, Michel, 301n221, 359n223

Audain, Léon, 103, 189, 235, 303n245

Auguste, J. Adhémar, 102, 104, 111

Augustin, Marthe, 240–41, 243, 363n262, 364n273

Augustin, Rémy, 202–3, 207, 340n46

Austin, J. L., 299n192

Azaka, 8, 251

Baker, Frederick C., 312n52, 328n212

Balch, Emily Greene, 121, 123, 309n14

Banque Nationale de la République d'Haïti, 118, 143

Baptiste, Alexandre, 198, 344n92

Baptists, 103, 127, 197, 198, 200, 304n248, 316n90, 343n84, 344n92

Barbados, 59

Barnett, George, 133, 134, 135–36, 137, 141–42, 314n77, 318n113

Bastien, Rémy, 69, 289n81
batá drums, 164
Batraville, Benoît, 132, 141, 143, 145, 314n72, 318n109
Bawon Samdi, 250
Beaubrun, Théodore, 239
Beauvoir-Dominique, Rachel, 7, 12, 17, 43–44, 52, 185, 258n11, 259n17, 261n43, 264n59, 273n62, 285n34, 285n37, 293n129
Béliard, Annibal, 111
Bellegarde, Cadeus, 19, 145–47, 265n70, 320n139, 324n179
Bellegarde, Dantès, 125, 142, *214*, 276n91
Bellegarde-Smith, Patrick, 262n48, 293n122
Benjamin, Élie, 104
Benoit, Clément, 228–29, 239–42, 243, 245, 359n223
Bertin, Father, 113, 117
Bervin, Antoine, 234
Biassou, Georges, 45, 46
bila, 38, 39, 41, 274n75
Bizoton, affaire de, 83–86, 90
Black Bagdad (Craige), 152, 163, 166, 328n217, 329n226, 330n228
Black Democracy: The Story of Haiti (Davis), 186
Black Haiti: A Biography of Africa's Eldest Daughter (Niles), 157, 218–19, *219*
Black Jacobins, The (James), 20, 50–51
Blaise, Lieutenant, 220
Blancpain, François, 286n49, 290n86
Blier, Suzanne Preston, 258n15
Bobo, Rosalvo, 119
Bòde Nasyonal, 12
Bois Caïman (Bwa Kayiman) ceremony, 42–45, 75, 276n97
bòkò: identity of, 12; *oungan* conflated with in Catholic literature, 104, 108, 208, 304n253, 342n73; popular insurgency of 1918–20 associated with, 139; Protestants compared with, 197; in *tonton makout,* 12, 251
Bolívar, Simón, 63
Bonaparte, Napoleon, 49, 50, 279n133
Bondye, 7, 259n20
Bonnet, Guy Joseph, 63–64, 280n138
Borges, Dain, 102
Borno, Louis, 136, 152, 198, 316n87, 344n91
Boukman, 42, 43, 44, 276n97, 277n104
Bouzon, Justin, 77
Boyer, Jean-Pierre: Code Pénal of 1835 of, 14, 55, 58–62, 65–67, 70, 72, 73; Code Rural of 1826 of, 57, 67, 69–70, 72, 124,

290n86; in consolidation of Haitian law, 56, 57, 58, 60, 64; Haiti reunited by, 57; and Haiti's diplomatic isolation, 63, 286n43; indemnity promised to France by, 63–64, 286n49; land tenure policies of, 68; liberal opposition to, 72, 282n12; negotiations with Vatican of, 78; overthrow of, 72; and Protestantism, 78, 294n130; Santo Domingo see taken over by, 78; Schoelcher's criticism of, 65
Bracken, Christopher, 185, 339n34
Brazil, campaign against "witchcraft" in, 102
Brelle, Corneille, 78
Brodwin, Paul, 38
Brokaw, Louis A., 133, 138
Brooks, David, 21, 22
Brouard, Carl, 178, 215
Brouard, Carmen, 227
Brown, John, 343n84
Brown, Jonathan, 65–66
Brown, Karen McCarthy, 8, 9, 13, 334n266
Brown, Vincent, 270n42, 283n27
brujería, 102–3, 315n85, 327n203
buccaneers, 27–28, 267n13
Bureau d'Ethnologie de la République d'Haïti: Denis as director of, 223, 353n178; Duvalier and Denis publish in *Bulletin* of, 250; Duvalier neglects, 366n8; ethnographic accounts of *sèvis* in, 238; lack of attention to visual art at, 353n176; mission of, 213–14, 353n173; performative orientation of programming, 222–25; as repository for objects salvaged from 1940–42 *campagne anti-superstitieuse,* 213, 351n168; Roumain as founding director of, 194, 210, 212–13, 351n162
Bureau d'Information à la Presse (B.I.P.), 244–45, 365n282
Buteau, General, 105, 113
Buteau, Pierre, 90, 178
Butler, Smedley D., 121, 125–26, 136–37, 140, 142, 143–44, 315n82, 319n128
Bwa Kayiman (Bois Caïman) ceremony, 42–45, 75, 276n97

Cabon, Adolphe, 73–75, 78, 293n129
caco. See kako
calenda (kalenda), 36, 38, 272n54, 272n55, 275n88
Camille, Roussan, 244
campagne anti-superstitieuse, 1940–42: 1935

penal law as authorizing legal basis for, 193; anti-Protestantism of, 197–200; destruction of sacred objects and sites during, 200–204, 211–12; 213; discourse of *le mélange,* 194, 203; explanations for why it was launched by the Catholic Church at this time, 193–95; interpreted as attack on malicious magic, 205; Lescot government withdraws support for, 207, 209–10; Lescot's endorsement of, 196; relation to popular *rejete* movement, 194–96; requirement of oath, 196; resistance to and protest against, 206–9. *See also* Roman Catholic Church; "superstition"; Vodou

Campagne anti-superstitieuse: Documentation (handbook), 194, 203, 204

Candler, John, 66, 290n84

Canez, Valério, 216

Cannibal Cousins (Craige), 166

cannibalism: accusations in *saints-guyons* conflict, 74; alleged in *affaire de Bizoton,* 83–86, 90; Bellegarde accused of, 145, 146; Caribbean associated with, 132; contrasted with "essential goodness" of Haitian peasantry, 143; European colonialism as context of term, 314n70; European detractors of Haiti literalize discourse of, 76; late medieval Vaudois accused of, 6; marines attribute to Haitian peasantry, 159; Senate hearings emphasize, 133

Caperton, William B., 142, 320n139

Cap-Haïtien: anti-Vaudoux campaign of 1896–1900 in, 21, 106, 110–11, 112; modernizing drive in fin-de-siècle, 102–3; Roosevelt's goodwill visit to Cap-Haïtien in July 1934, 229

caprelata, 58, 59, 60, 108, 184, 283n22, 284n32

Casimir, Jean, 68, 290n89, 312n51

Casseus, Maurice, 228

Castor, Kesner, 16

Castor, Suzy, 141, 318n109

Catholic Church. *See* Roman Catholic Church

Catts, James, 343n84

Celestin, Martial, 16, 263n52

Célius, Carlo A., 279n127, 280n135, 288n67, 335n6

Césaire, Simon (Père Simon), 195, 196

Chalbert camp, 126

chanpèt, 70, 151, 154–55

Chanpwèl, 17, 52, 264n59

Chants sauvages (Benoit), 239

charlatanism, discourses of, 5, 39, 40, 60, 98, 253, 270n40, 274n79

Charlier, Étienne, 75, 292n111

Charlier-Doucet, Rachelle, 354n181, 366n8

chèf seksyon, 70, 191, 290n88; abuses by, 341n61; income derived from fees, 291n92; as involved in Catholic Church's 1940–42 *campagne anti-superstitieuse,* 196, 199, 212; permits for rituals sold by, 192, 250, 290n91, 356n200; potential for graft by, 252; under pressure to enforce law against Vodou during 1915–34 U.S. occupation, 154–55; religious leaders as, 152; as the state within the section, 70

Cherisier, Vernélie, 157

Chidester, David, 25

Christophe, Henry: Code Henry, 67; defects from Toussaint Louverture, 50; land policies of, 67–68, 288n73; militarized agriculture under, 67; new church hierarchy established by, 78; northern Haiti ruled by, 57; policy toward popular religion, 14, 51; suicide of, 57

Churchstone-Lord, S. E., 198, 344n86

Cinéas, J. B., 221

civilization: blacks seen as incapable of, 94; Catholic Church seen as agent of, 85; Code Pénal of 1835 justified in terms of, 62–67; Code Pénal of 1864 as signal of, 90, 91; Concordat with Catholic Church seen as sign of, 79; development of modern sense of, 54–55; seen as façade in Haiti, 92; vindicationist writings on, by Haitian authors, 92–100

Cochinat, Victor, 95, 97

Code Henry, 67

Code Noir (1685), 24–25; interdiction of African-based ritual practices absent in, 24–25, 31; manumission likened to free birth in, 37; ostensibly protective provisions of, 30, 269n28; and reforms of 1784, 30; slave gatherings prohibited by, 14, 25, 31, 34–36, 37

Code Pénal
—Article 246, 89, 160, 172
—Article 405, 58, 59–62, 64–65, 66, 71, 75, 76, 79–80, 89, 90, 98, 109, 112, 120, 129, 131, 148, 152–53, 155, 156, 181, 182, 183, 187, 218, 283n22, 284n28, 298n181, 338n25
—Article 406, 58, 59, 71, 76, 80, 89, 90, 98, 112, 120, 129, 131, 148, 152–53, 155, 156, 183, 218, 283n22, 284n28, 338n25

Code Pénal (*continued*)
—Article 407, 59, 71, 76, 80, 89, 90, 98, 112,
120, 129, 131, 148, 152–53, 155, 156, 162,
183, 187, 218, 283n22, 284n28, 340n51
—law of 1826 against the "*métier* of Macandals," 57, 59, 60, 72, 283n25, 284n28
—law of 1835 against *les sortilèges,* 58–67; abrogation of, in 1843, 72; and *affaire de Bizoton,* 85; antecedents of, 59; "civilization" as rationale for, 1, 62–67; *La Croix*
on failure to enforce, 109–10; in Geffrard's campaign of 1864, 86; implicated
in logic of sorcery, 71; passage of, 14, 55;
and popular political and religious mobilizations of 1840s, 72–76; popular pressure and enforcement of, 70–71, 75; prohibiting *vaudoux,* 58, 59–60, 64–65, 85;
referential uncertainty in, 60, 62, 184–85;
reimposition in 1845, 73; Riché's enforcement of, 76–77; role in politically
marginalizing Haitian majority, 3, 10,
55–56, 250, 365n284; during Soulouque
regime, 79–80
—law of 1864 against *les sortilèges,* 89–91; as
in force under U.S. occupation, 128–
30, 181; implicated in logic of sorcery,
157, 255; increased penalties in, 181, 184,
298n181, 299n185; popular pressure and
enforcement of, 89, 156–57; read by
Haiti's detractors as proof of decline of
civilization, 91–92; referential uncertainty in, 184–85; U.S. occupation enforces to exact labor, 128–30
—law of 1935 against *les pratiques superstitieuses,* 181–91; abrogation of, 12–13,
254–55, 337n19; animal sacrifice as focus
of, 15, 185, 190, 243; calls for repeal of,
12–13, 243, 254; Catholic Church's antisuperstition campaign of 1940–42 sanctioned by, 193, 346n109; defense of
Haiti's reputation as justification for, 187,
248; Duvalier regimes maintain, 252;
enforcement of, 191–93; ethnological
studies inaugurated at time of passage
of, 242; folklore performances stage acts
prohibited by, 242, 244–45; material
consequences for peasantry of, 1–2, 246;
popular dance permitted by, 177, 188–91,
217, 238, 245, 246; as pretext for force,
193; prologue of, 15–16, 187, 188
—Price-Mars on function of, 181
—U.S. enforcement of, 15, 120, 128, 131,
135, 145, 152, 153, 155, 162, 181

Code Rural (1826), 57, 67, 69–70, 72, 124,
282n15, 290n86
Code Rural (1864), 89, 124, 125–26, 128, 148,
151, 160, 191, 310n34, 311n35, 311n42,
337n18, 341n61
Code Rural, English translation (1916), 128,
129, 148, 151, 160
Colbert, Jean-Baptiste, 24, 266n1, 270n40
Cole, Eli K., 130, 311n41
Comaroff, Jean and John, 333n258
"comédie rituelle dans la possession, La"
(Métraux), 302n227
Comhaire, Jean L., 61, 70, 75, 284n32,
290n87, 323n165
Comhaire-Sylvain, Suzanne, 61, 214, 265n71,
284n32
Comte, Auguste, 94
Congrès des Rejetés (1942), 207
*Conjuring Culture: Biblical Formations of Black
America* (Smith), 6
Conseils Supérieurs, 28–29
Coombes, Rosemary, 190
corvée. See *kòve*
Coulanges, Jean, 227, 354n184, 358n220
Courlander, Harold, 150, 165, 305n258,
322n158, 351n167, 354n185, 356n201
Courrier haïtien, Le (newspaper), 159, 162
*Cours de droit pénal à l'usage des agents de la police
judiciaire* (Laforestrie), 187
Courtin, Sébastien, 35
Corvington, Georges, 332n250, 345n97,
345n99, 363n262
Craige, John Houston: *Black Bagdad,* 152,
163, 166, 328n217, 330n228; *Cannibal Cousins,* 166; correspondence with
Herskovits, 166; describing self as amateur anthropologist, 166; on maddening effect of drumming, 328n217; on
religious elders in police ranks, 152,
323n169; sacred objects confiscated by,
163, 328n213; on Seabrook having confidential information, 326n199; on wish-
ing to learn about prohibited ritual practices, 161
Croix, La (weekly), 103, 106, 108, 109–11,
113, 304n247
croix contre l'asson, La (Peters), 195, 206
Cromer, Lord, 325n185
Cuba: African diasporic religious practices
pathologized in, 102; *afrocubanismo,* 178,
180, 362n254; *brujería,* 103, 315n85; confiscation of *batá* drums, 164; Haitian
migration to, 8, 173, 311n41, 335n4; Ortiz

on "racial atavisms" in, 180; U.S. occupations of, 118, 164
Cukela, Louis, 146
Cumberland, W. W., 316n87
curé des nègres, 36, 37

Dahomey, in etymology of "Vodou," 7, 258n15
daïmons du culte vodu, Les (Holly), 162, 335n6
d'Alaux, Gustave (Maxime Raybaud), 72–73, 79–80, 97, 291n101, 294n138
Dalencourt, Carmen, 361n243
Dalmas, Antoine, 42–43, 276n94
dance. *See* popular dance
Dandin, Marvel, 264n65
Dandin, Yanick Guiteau, 91
Daniels, Josephus, 134, 320n139
d'Ans, André-Marcel, 213, 350n160
Danse rituel du feu (Falla), 227
Dartiguenave, Philippe Sudre, 122, 145, 147, 148, 151
Dash, J. Michael, 92–93, 300n197, 319n128, 335n2, 335n5
Davis, H. P., 186, 327n199, 360n232
Day, Martial, 361n243
Dayan, Joan/Colin, 19, 24, 30, 36, 49, 260n27, 271n52, 294n133, 296n157
de Bercy, Drouin, 60, 65, 284n32
dechoukaj, 11–12, 254
Declaration of the Rights of Man, 45
Dehoux, J. B., 303n242
Déita (Mercédes Foucard Guignard), 334
Déjean, Jacqueline, 361n243
De la réhabilitation de la race noire par la République d'Haïti (Price), 83
Delatour, Ferdinand, 253, 257n3, 368n28
De l'égalité des races humaines (anthropologie positive) (Firmin), 55, 93, 300n204
"De l'évolution stadiale du vodou" (Denis and Duvalier), 224
De l'inégalité des races humaines (Gobineau), 55, 79, 93–95
Delmas disturbance (1942), 207, 210
Delorge, Lorgina, 233, 361n240
Delorme, Démesvar, 300n204
de Man, Paul, 91–92, 300n193
demanbre, 69
demwatye system, 68, 173, 289n76
Denby, Edwin, 197
Denis, Lorimer, 215, 223, 224, 243, 244, 250, 353n178, 358n214
"De Paris à Haïti" (Cochinat), 95
Derby, Lauren, 309n10

Derrida, Jacques, 4, 91, 193, 246
Des colonies, et particulièrement de celle de Saint-Domingue (Malenfant), 65
Descourtilz, Michel Étienne, 65, 272n54, 277n105
Description (Moreau de Saint-Méry), 36, 40, 41, 47, 274n76
Desmangles, Leslie G., 263n51, 327n201
Desquiron, Lilas, 260n25
Desrameaux, Pierre, 241, 364n266
Dessalines, Jean-Jacques: assassination of, 52, 56, 78; Constitution of 1805 of, 51, 77–78; defects from Toussaint Louverture, 50; independent Haiti proclaimed by, 51; "indigenous army" led by, 50; Kersuzan on attitude toward Vodou of, 107; militarization of agriculture under, 67; motivates his troops, 277n105; policy toward popular religion, 14, 49, 51; remembered in Vodou, 49; "share system" under, 289n76
Destiné, Jean-Léon: arrest at Vodou *sèvis,* 233; on Benoit, 229; on Benoit's theatrical representation of Vodou, 240, 241; on Dunham, 359n221; on Fussman-Mathon, 228, 229, 359n224; in National Folk Festival of 1941, 232–33, *233,* 234, *234,* 235, 236, 361n243, 362n246; on performative orientation of Institut d'Ethnologie classes, 222–23; photographs of, *225, 233, 234;* on ritual versus theatrical contexts, 241
Devésin, Kébreau, 151
Diaquoi, Louis, 215
Diederich, Bernard, 325n180, 346n112, 367n19
Discipline and Punish (Foucault), 88
divination, 33, 59, 65, 77, 106
divorce, legalization of under Dessalines, 78
doktè fey, 150, 367n23
Dominican Republic: independence of, 73; massacre of Haitians in, 209, 348n145; Roumain arrested at insistence of, 211; Silvani contrasts Haiti with, 208–9; Trujillo, 209, 211, 348n145, 366n11; U.S. occupation of, 118, 120, 134, 136, 309n10
Dominicans, 36, 37
Dominique, Didier, 7, 12, 17, 52, 185
donpèdre, 58, 59, 80, 183, 184, 274n76
Dornéval, Étienne, 148
Dorsainvil, J. C., 202, 209, 248, 249, 303n242, 335n6
Doxey, John L., 318n109

Dra-Po (Holly), 1–2, 242, 335n6
drums: *asòtò,* 149, 156, 224, 328n213; in
    Catholic Church's anti-Vaudoux cam-
    paign of 1896–1900, 109, 110; confisca-
    tion of, 129, 131, 162–64, *163,* 327n207;
    Craige on maddening effect of drum-
    ming on whites, 328n217; Herskovits on
    Haitian drumming, 361n238; marines
    take, as souvenirs, 162, 323n173; muf-
    fling with cotton fiber, 149, 322n155;
    at National Folk Festival of 1941, 234;
    piano replaces, 216, 229; puncturing of
    drumheads, 164; repression leads to in-
    novations in ritual uses of, 149–50, 154;
    as sacred objects, 164–65; spirits invited
    through rhythms of, 8; used for commu-
    nication, 132–33
Dubois, Laurent, 42, 51, 273n3, 276n90
Du Bois, W. E. B., 6
Du Casse, Jean-Baptiste, 27
Dudley, Taney, 167
Dumesle, Hérard, 276n94
Dunham, Katherine: Coulanges on, 227; de-
    nied permission to work at Rex Theatre
    with Cul-de-Sac friends, 240; Destiné
    on, 359n221; influenced by Haitian re-
    search, 227–28, 358n219; interest in Hai-
    tian culture inspired by, 359n220; *Island
    Possessed,* 226; *lave tèt* undergone by, 227,
    228; performs at Rex Theatre, 225–27,
    358n218; photograph of, *227;* and Code
    Pénal of 1935, 187–88; researches dance
    in Haiti, 187–88, 225–26, 356n201
Duplessis, Chaton, 361n243
Duplessis, Félix, 361n243
Dupuy, Alex, 281n11, 291n92
Duquesnoy, Father, 37
Duré, Carline, 361n243
Duré, Lucienne, 361n243
Durkheim, Émile, 179, 336n9
Duvalier, François: Bureau d'Ethnologie
    neglected by, 366n8; death of, 253; "De
    l'évolution stadiale du vodou," 224; and
    Denis, 250, 353n178; in Griots group,
    215; legal prohibition of Vodou ignored
    in ethnographic work of, 243; official
    prohibition of *pratiques superstitieuses*
    maintained by, 252; as "Papa Doc," 250;
    regulation of Vodou under, 250–54;
    sought to appropriate popular power
    of Vodou, 12, 250–51; *tonton makout,* 12,
    250, 252
Duvalier, Jean-Claude, 11–12, 252, 253, 254

Efforts et résultats (Vincent), 182
Elie, Justin, 228
Empereur Soulouque et son empire, L' (d'Alaux),
    79
Emperor Jones, The (O'Neill), 167
Episcopal Church, 197, 198, 199, 343n84
eritaj, 69, 289n79
Esquisse ethnographique (Trouillot), 60, 98–99,
    302n227
Estimé, Dumarsais, 250, 253
ethnology: Haitian school of, 178; Institut
    d'Ethnologie, 214–15, 222–23, 353n175,
    353n176; Jean Price-Mars as pioneer of,
    178–81; little attention paid to ques-
    tions of law in, 243; and *noirisme,* 215;
    on Vodou as locus of Haitian identity
    and culture, 248–49. *See also* Bureau
    d'Ethnologie de la République d'Haïti
Evans, L. Ton, 127, 137, 198–99, 200, 201,
    316n90, 344n86
Ezili Dantò, 8, 155, 296n151
Ezili Frida, 8; historical associations of,
    260n27
Ezili Kawoulo, 43

Falla, Manuel de, 227
Farmer, Paul, 266n82
Farnham, Roger, 143
Fatiman, Cécile, 75, 292n111
Fick, Carolyn E., 269n25, 271n52
Fields, Karen, 158
Firmin, Anténor, 55, 93–95, 99, 103, 107–8,
    300n204
First National Congress of the Eucharistic
    Crusade, 195
Fischer, Sibylle, 286n43, 295n138
Fisher, Kurt, 350n160
Fleurant, Gerdès, 9, 165, 258n11
Foisset, Père, 210
Folk Festival Association, 231
folklore, 210–47; Assembly of Ministers and
    Directors of Education of the American
    Republics resolution on, 230; Comité
    d'Anthropologie highlights, 230; con-
    testation surrounding performance of,
    216–17, 228–29, 231–32, 236–38, 241–
    45; "folkloricization," 247, 365n285,
    365n286; and Good Neighbor Policy,
    230; law of 1935 and performance of,
    218; law of 1935 influenced by concep-
    tion of, 190; Mater Dolorosa troupe, 8,
    223–25, *226,* 240, 358n214, 358n215; mis-
    taken for actual ritual, 237–38; *mouve-*

ment folklorique, 177, 215–16, 241, 244,
248–49; as national culture, 218, 232, 235;
National Folk Festival of 1941, 230–38;
policing of independent staging of in
early 1940s, 238–45; Price-Mars on, 179,
181, 336n11; theatrical staging during and
after U.S. occupation, 218–25; Troupe
Folklorique Nationale, 229, 361n240;
urban performances of, 225–30
Folklore et patriotisme (Price-Mars), 10,
364n267
folk songs, 216
"Force of Law: The 'Mystical Foundation of
Authority'" (Derrida), 193
Foucault, Michel, 88, 89, 290n90
Fouchard, Jean, 275n83
"Four Vodun Ceremonies" (Simpson), 221–
22
Fowler, Carolyn, 357n210
Franklin, James, 65, 287n59, 288n60
free people of color: French attempt to
make alliance with, 45–46; legislation directed against, 37–38, 41; in military and
police, 38
Frère Joseph, 73–74, 75, 80, 82, 292n106,
294n136
Froude, James Anthony, 91, 92, 300n194
Fussman-Mathon, Lina, 228–29; arrest at
Vodou *sèvis,* 233; collaboration with
Jaegerhuber, 216; and difficulties for
women performers, 359n224; folklore
troupe of, 228, 232–36; at informal dance
performance, 217; and Lorgina Delorge,
361n240; in National Folk Festival of
1941, 232–33, 234, 237, 238; as pioneer in
folklore performance, 229, 359n223

"Gabélus" (song), 240–42, 363n262
Gaillard, Roger, 126, 127, 150, 174, 311n41,
312n44, 314n72
ganbo, 150, 322n158
garde-corps, 35, 39
Garde d'Haïti, 180, 191, 212
Garraway, Doris, 267n5, 270n43, 273n66
Garrigus, John D., 267n13
Gautier, Stéphen, 127
Gede *lwa,* 250
Geffrard, Fabre Nicolas: campaign against
Vodou of 1864, 86–89, 90, 97–98, 116,
117, 148, 160; Code Pénal of 1835 re-
vised by, 15, 55, 89–91, 181, 184, 293n120;
Code Rural of, 89, 124; Concordat with
Catholic Church negotiated by, 81–82;

on following public outcry in enforcing
laws against *les sortilèges,* 88, 254
Geggus, David, 42–43, 44, 48, 274n81,
275n83, 276n94, 278n106, 278n111,
279n121
Gendarmerie d'Haïti, 121–24, 150–51
Georges-Jacob, Kléber, 242, 257n3, 364n271
Germain, Étienne, 129
Ghachem, Malick, 24, 29, 30, 273n65
Ginen: as analyzed by Serge Larose, 61–62,
100; law and ethos of, 16–20; malevolent
magic opposed by, 9–10, 14, 61–62, 176,
261n31; as moral philosophy and ethical
code, 7; as originary tradition, 100; other
meanings of, 259n18. *See also* Vodou
Gobineau, Joseph Arthur de, 79, 92, 93
Goman (Jean-Baptiste Perrier), 282n11
Good Neighbor Policy, 229–30, 360n232
Goveia, Elsa, 269n28
Gran Mèt, 7
Gressier de la Jalousière (colonist), 40
Griots, Les (journal), 215, 250
Groupe des Griots, 215–16, 242, 364n271
Gruening, Ernest, 134, 168, 330n235
Guerrier, Philippe, 73
Guide économique de la République d'Haïti, 253
Guillén, Nicolás, 211, 359n220
Guilloux, Monsignor, 111
guyons, 73–76

Haiti: called the "Black Republic," 1, 76,
249; Code Civil of 1825, 57; codification of law under Boyer, 56–57, 60, 64,
66; Concordat with Catholic Church, 4,
15, 56, 78–79, 81–82, 107, 191; Constitution of 1805, 51, 77–78; Constitution of
1918, 119; Constitution of 1987, 13, 252,
254, 262n44, 337n19; cultural nationalist policy in post-occupation, 177–247;
defensive militarization of, 286n45; demise of civilization associated with, 54–
55, 64, 76, 79, 80, 92–100, 101; diplomatic
isolation of, 51, 62–63, 79; earthquake
of 2010, 20–23, 265n73; establishment of
independent, 3, 51; export crops of, 68,
308n6; foreign indebtedness of, 63, 118,
308n2; judicial system of, 16–17, 144–45,
147; locus for debate about capacity for
self-government of peoples of African
descent, 1, 95, 142–43, 319n121; map of,
3; National Party, 106–7; political sub-
divisions of, 191, 341n55; and popular
political and religious mobilizations

Haiti (*continued*)
of 1840s, 72–76; popular spirituality in
nineteenth-century, 54–117; poverty
of, 21–23; as refuge for enslaved and oppressed, 55, 281n7, 286n43; in rehabilitation of Africa, 94–95; Revolution as
supplementing and transforming Enlightenment modernity, 20; slave revolt feared from, 63; tourist industry,
360n236; U.S. anthropological interest
in, 165–66; U.S. involvement in, after
end of occupation, 229–30, 360n236;
weakness of judiciary and rule of law in,
16–17. *See also* Code Pénal; Code Rural
(1826); Code Rural (1864); Code Rural,
English translation (1916); U.S. occupation of, 1915–34; *and heads of state by name*
Haitian Revolution, 42–51; interpretations
of, 20, 51, 54–55. *See also* Haiti; Saint-
Domingue; Vodou
Haitian school of ethnology, 178
"Haïti, champion du Panaméricanisme"
(Benoit), 229
*Haiti: Its Dawn of Progress after Years in a Night
of Revolution* (Kuser), 138
Haiti–Santo Domingo Independence So-
ciety, 135
Hall, Robert Burnett, 329n224
Halperin, Edward, 170, 172
Halperin, Victor, 170, 172
Harding, Warren G., 134
Harrison, Lawrence, 21, 22
Hart, Franklin A., 124–25
HASCO (Haytian American Sugar Com-
pany), 143, 172–76, 332n251, 333n256
Hayti, or The Black Republic (St. John), 84,
132
Haytian American Sugar Company
(HASCO), 143, 172–76, 332n251,
333n256
healing, 1, 7, 16, 25, 31, 38, 39, 45, 77, 195,
271n51, 314n72, 321n144
Herskovits, Frances, 165–66, 219, 329n224
Herskovits, Melville J.: on conflicts dur-
ing pilgrimage to sacred falls of Sodo,
155; correspondence with Craige, 166,
329n226, 330n228; dance as interest of,
355n193; on destruction of sacred objects during U.S. occupation, 345n103;
Dunham's research directed by, 187–88,
356n201; first visit to Haiti of, 165–66,
329n224; on Haitianizing the Catholic
Church, 341n57; intervenes to have

Vodou ceremony performed, 219–21,
355n191, 356n200; *Life In a Haitian Valley*,
221; *Life In a Haitian Valley Film Study,
1934*, 355n193; on *loa (lwa)*, 19; on local
regulation of popular rituals, 191; and
Métraux, 211; on National Folk Festival
of 1941, 231–32, 361n238
Heure de l'art haïtien, L' (radio program), 228,
238–42, 243, 363n255
Hispaniola: Boyer invades and takes over
eastern, 57; French acquisition of
Western, 26–28. *See also* Dominican Re-
public; Haiti; Saint-Domingue; Santo
Domingo
*History and Present Condition of St. Domingo,
The* (Brown), 65–66
Hoffmann, Léon-François, 42, 84, 159,
257n3, 325n182, 340n51
Holly, Arthur, 1–2, 162, 242, 335n6, 364n268
Holly, James Theodore, 335n6, 343n84
Honorat, Michel Lamartinière, 212, 215, 242,
243, 357n207, 358n214, 359n223
Hooker, Richard S., 128, 129, 326n193
Hoover, Herbert, 125, 229
Howe, Walter Bruce, 131, 165
Hull, Cordell, 209, 238
Hulme, Peter, 132, 314n70
Hurbon, Laënnec: on the *affaire de Bizoton*,
86; on Catholic Church's antisuperstition campaigns, 295n146, 305n256,
347n122; on Code Pénal of 1935, 188,
189, 246; on Concordat of 1860, 81–82;
on Duvalier, 250, 251, 252; on European
roots of rumors of sorcery and cannibalism, 75–76; on Haitian state's fear of
parallel powers, 52, 66; influence on this
study, 3; on osmosis of Catholicism into
services for *lwa*, 116; on *oungan, manbo*,
and *bòkò* as targets during *dechoukaj*, 12;
on repression of sorcery intensifying rumors of malicious magic, 176; on section
chiefs authorizing Vodou ceremonies,
264n63; on sorcery and Vodou, 286n40;
on *sosyete sekrè*, 17; on state keeping peasantry closed in on itself, 246, 365n284;
on *zonbi*, 333n258
Hurston, Zora Neale, 325n180, 356n201,
359n220
Huxley, Francis, 252
Hyppolite, Florvil, 99, 105, 114, 305n256,
305n258, 307n302
Hyppolite, Gladys, *234, 235*, 361n243,
362n246

indentured servants, 29
indigénisme: as cosmopolitan modernism, 335n4; and Dunham, 226, 228; exception for popular dance in 1935 law as concession to, 190; on popular culture and national literature, 178; and post-occupation promotion of folklore, 181, 235; relationship to contemporaneous movements, 178, 180; *La Revue indigène,* 178, 215, 337n23; Vincent opposed by proponents of, 182; on Vodou as locus of Haitian identity and culture, 248–49
Inginac, Joseph Balthazar, 57, 64, 66, 282n14, 294n131
Inman, Samuel Guy, 344n86
Inquiry into the Occupation and Administration of Haiti and Santo Domingo, 120, 309n11
Institut d'Ethnologie, 214–15, 222–23, 353n175, 353n176
Institut Haïtiano-Américain, 230
International Civilian Mission in Haiti (MICIVIH), 254, 368n29
Invisibles, The (Huxley), 252
Isambert, M. J., 287n53
Island Possessed (Dunham), 226

Jaegerhuber, Werner A., 216, 232, 354n185, 355n187
Jamaica, 17–18, 59, 263n54, 283n27, 298n179
James, C. L. R., 20, 51, 279n128
Jan, J. M., 105, 113, 114, 115, 148, 317n101
Janvier, André, *234,* 236, 237, 247, 361n243
Janvier, Louis-Joseph, 55, 95–96, 103, 107, 300n204, 301n207
Jean, Alphonse, 192, 206, 250, 252, 291n91, 343n79, 349n151
Jean, Destine, 138, 175
Jean-Baptiste, Luc, 363n262
Jean-François (rebel leader), 45, 46
Jean-Jacques, Thalès, 56, 57–58, 60, 282n14, 286n45, 293n120
Jeannis, Mérisier, 305n258
Jeanty, Occide, 228
Jesuits, 34, 36, 37, 272n59, 272n61
Joachim, Léonce, 221
Johnson, James Weldon, 123, 126–27, 130, 134
Johnson, Walter E., 133, 134, 138, 139, 317n99
Joinville-Gauban, Pierre, 44
Jonas (drummer), *234*
Jordan, W. F., 197–98, 344n92
Journal of American Folk-lore, 6

kako, 127, 138, 142, 161, 175, 251, 312n51, 326n193
kalenda (calenda), 36, 38, 272n54, 272n55, 275n88
kanpay rejete, 195–97
Kaussen, Valerie, 335n4, 353n177
Kelsey, Carl, 319n121
Kerboull, Jean, 33, 205, 206, 252, 342n72, 367n18
Kernisan, Clovis, 57, 282n15
Kersuzan, François-Marie: and breaking of St. Jacques statue, 114, 115; initiates Catholic Church's anti-Vaudoux campaign of 1896–1900, 55, 101–2, 103, 104–7, 112, 116, 194, 302n238; in Ligue Contre le Vaudoux, 111; on Vodou affecting worker productivity, 96
King, William, 135–36, 316n87
Kirshenblatt-Gimblett, Barbara, 247, 365n285
"Kith and Kin: A Study of Creole Social Structure in Marbial, Haiti" (Métraux), 211
Knapp, H. S., 147, 159
Knott, Sarah Gertrude, 231–32, 234, 236, 361n238
Kongo: Petwo spirits' roots in, 9, 39, 61, 285n34; and Romaine Rivière, 45; Roman Catholic Church in kingdom of, 33, 82, 270n41
kòve, 120, 124–28, 135, 164, 310n34
Krieger, Herbert W., 329n224
Kuser, J. Dryden, 138, 144, 317n100

Lacombe, Joseph, 308n7
Laforestrie, Léon, 187, 339n32
La Gorce, John Oliver, 328n216
Laguerre, Michel, 251, 252, 264n62, 323n169, 367n21
lakou, 68–69, 289n81
lalwa, 264n65
Lamothe, Ludovic, 216, 354n186
land tenure, 67–69
Lang, Freeman, 315n82
Lansing, Robert, 141
laplas, 52
Largey, Michael, 216, 354n185, 354n187
Larose, Serge, 61–62, 69, 99–100, 285n36, 302n227
Lavoie, Ernest, 315n82
law: "always has a trap in it," 5, 91–92; codification of Haitian under Boyer, 56–57, 60, 64, 66; force of, 193; *lwa/loi* homol-

law (*continued*)
ogy, 19–20; magic's commonality with, 6; Napoleonic Code, 57–58; as performative, 91–92; as repository of social performances, 83; "trickery" of, 5–6; and Vodou legal processes, 16–20. *See also* legal prohibitions of popular religious and healing practices

Lechtenberg, Sara, 368n31

Leclerc, Charles Victor Emmanuel, 50–51

Leconte, Cincinnatus, 111, 115–16, 148, 321n147

legal prohibitions of popular religious and healing practices: aimed at reforming popular "backwardness," 14, 108; anthropology and ethnology pay little attention to, 3–4, 221, 242–43; campaigns against Vodou authorized by, 4, 12, 15, 82, 105, 128–33, 193; Catholic and Protestant clergy support repression of Vodou during U.S. occupation, 148; clerics exhort authorities to enforce, 108–9; conviction rates during occupation, 154–55, 324n177; under Duvalier regime, 250–54; evasion of and resistance to enforcement during occupation, 147–56; incommensurability of laws and their purported objects, 10, 14, 60–62, 116, 184–85; *les lois divines et humaines,* 56, 77–83, 111–13, 116; local communities shape enforcement of, 14–15, 70–71, 75, 87–89, 156–57; Louverture's ordinance of January 1800, 14, 48–49; after mid-1940s, 250–56; motivated by colonial and imperial representations of Vodou, 2, 63–64, 185–87, 249; national honor as rationale for, 81, 106, 107, 109, 110; in nineteenth-century, 54–117; peasantry and urban poor marginalized by, 3, 10–11, 246, 250; penalties for transgressing, 47, 58–59, 89, 900, 157, 243; Pétion's proclamation of February 1814, 51–52; political stakes of, 2–3; popular influence on local enforcement of, 4–5, 71, 88, 116–17, 156–65, 175, 249–50, 254–55; as pretext for graft, 193, 252–53; as pretext for voyeurism and appropriation during U.S. occupation, 161; promulgated to check potential political threat of popular religious organization, 14; prosecutions after 1987 abrogation, 254–55, 368n31; read by Haiti's detractors as proof of barbarism, 5, 91–92; as reinforc-ing beliefs they were meant to eliminate, 5, 91–92, 157, 158–70, 254, 255; render practitioners perennially delinquent before the law, 11. *See also* Code Pénal

Legba, 8

Le Gouaze, Joseph, 81, 347n117, 349n152, 351n168

Lejeune, John A., 134, 136–37, 315n82

Le Jeune, Nicolas, 30, 269n32

Lescot, Élie: and Bureau d'Ethnologie, 213; Catholic Church's antisuperstition campaign of 1940–42 criticized by, 209–10; Catholic Church's antisuperstition campaign of 1940–42 supported by, 16, 193, 194, 196, 207, 217, 238, 248; and Delmas disturbance of 1942, 210; exiles return under, 211; on felling of Mapou Dampus, 347n117; folklore performance encouraged by, 218; *L'heure de l'art haïtien* endorsed by, 239; informal regulation of ritual practices under, 250; *mouvement folklorique* takes off under, 177; and National Folk Festival of 1941, 231, 232, 234–35, 236, 247; Rara bands banned by, 210, 349n151; school for *chèf seksyon* under, 341n61; Silvani opposed by, 209, 349n146; war exploited to curtail civil liberties, 245

Lesser, Julian, 331n238

Lhérisson, Camille, 213, 214, *214*

Lhérisson, Élie, 102, 303n242

Lhérisson, Justin, 364n274

Lhérisson, Nosirel, 198, 200, 344n92

Lichtenstein, Alex, 313n56

Life In a Haitian Valley (Herskovits), 221

Life In a Haitian Valley Film Study, 1934 (Herskovits), 355n193

Ligue Contre le Vaudoux, 111–16, 194

Linebaugh, Peter, 28

Little, L. McCarty, 317n99

loa. See lwa

Loederer, Richard A., 186–87

Loix et constitutions des colonies françoises de l'Amérique sous le vent (Moreau de Saint-Méry), 41

Lomax, Alan, 325n180, 356n201

London Methodist Missionary Society, 200

Lott Carey Mission Society, 198

lougawou, 157, 205, 254, 296n149, 323n172

Louinis, Louines, 358n214, 361n240

Louverture, Toussaint, 46–50; consolidates political power, 48; Constitution of 1801, 49–50; Kersuzan on attitude toward Vodou of, 107; militarization of agriculture under, 49, 67; policy toward popular religion, 14, 48–49; *Règlement de culture* of 1800, 49, 67; surrenders to French, 50; takes over Spanish part of island, 50

Lovelace, Earl, 11, 13

Lowenthal, Ira, 263n52, 288n73, 289n79, 301n218

Lubin, Antoine, 365n277

Lubin, Eddy, 43–44

Lumière sur le humfort (Peters), 202–3, 206

Lunique, Léandre, *234*, 361n243

lwa: in Catholic Church's antisuperstition campaign of 1940–42, 200, 202, 203, 204, 205–6; Catholic saints associated with, 8, 203; ceremonies in honor of, 8, 43; dance in rituals serving, 188; etymology of, 19–20, 265n71; and family, 100; and historical interpretation, 9, 260n27; invited to ceremonies, 8; *loi* homology, 19–20; mounting a horse, 8–9; nations of, 7; Protestantism seen as refuge from angry, 199, 204; of same "family," 8; songs honoring, 216; spirit of baptized drums compared with, 165

lwa zandò, 260n30, 285n37

MacArthur, Bruce B., 145–46

madanm sara, 141

Madiou, Thomas, 45, 49, 63–64, 73–75

magic (*maji*): category of *sortilèges* and, 60–62, 284n31; commonality of law with, 6; on enforcement of law against *sortilèges* inciting rumors of malicious, 154, 176; moral opposition to, 9–10, 61–62, 74, 100; outsiders associate Vodou with, 9–10, 62, 80; popular pressure for enforcement of laws against malicious, 71, 117, 156–58, 254–55. *See also* sorcery; *sortilèges*

Magic Island, The (Seabrook), 128–29, 149–50, 160–61, 166, 172, 186, 318n114, 326n196, 326n197, 330n229

Magloire, Félix, 282n17, 283n21, 353n172

Magloire *fils,* Clément (Magloire Saint Aude), 215

Magloire, Paul, 250, 253, 368n25

Magloire-Danton, Gérarde, 300n204, 336n13

magnétisme, 38–39

Makandal, François, 33, 34, 35, 41, 42, 61, 77, 271n46, 285n33

makandal (macandal), 34, 35, 41, 58, 59, 60–61, 64, 183, 184

Makaya (rebel leader), 50

Making a Living in the Marbial Valley, Haiti (Métraux), 211

mal d'Haïti, Le: Ses causes et son traitement (Audain), 103, 235

Malenfant, Charles, 44, 65, 275n86, 287n56

maman-bila, 39–40

Maman Dio, 48

Mambo-chérie (Rosemond), 244

manbo: attacked after fall of Duvalier regime, 12, 254; Benoit's theatrical representation of, 240; called *mamaloi,* 87, 138, 139, 147, 152, 323n172; in Catholic Church's anti-Vaudoux campaign of 1896–1900, 109; Catholic Church's ordinances against, 82; in census of 1924, 152, 323n172; contributions to Haiti's gross domestic product, 253–54; displacement of, 153; and healing, 7; identity of, 7; portrayed as charlatans, 98, 253; purchasing permits for ceremonies, 192; resistance during Catholic Church's antisuperstition campaign of 1940–42, 206; Riché's campaign against, 77; in *tonton makout,* 12, 250; uprising of 1918–1920 associated with, 139; Vodouizan incorporated in fictive kinship networks with, 8

Mangones, Edmond, 351n166

Manigat, J. F. Thalès, 104, 111

Manigat, Leslie, 72, 291n99

Manigat, Max, 306n276

Mapou Dampus, 346n117

Marc, Elie, 304n248

Marmelade, 38–40

marriage, 78

marronage, 17, 18, 33, 38, 40, 47, 67

Mars, Louis, 214

Mater Dolorosa (folklore troupe), 8, 223–25, *226,* 240, 358n214, 358n215

Mathon Blanchet, Lina. *See* Fussman-Mathon, Lina

Maximilien, Louis, 351n166, 354n185

Mayard, Pierre, 244, 364n274

Mayo, Henry, 134, 159, 315n83

mayombo, 39, 40, 41

McAlister, Elizabeth, 260n28, 295n146, 349n151

McConnell, H. Ormonde, 200, 201

McCrocklin, James, 121, 151, 152, 309n15, 318n108

McDougal, Douglas C., 152–53

McQuilkin, John, Jr., 133, 134, 138

"Meaning of Africa in Haitian Vodu, The"
(Larose), 61–62, 99–100, 302n227

mélange, le, 5, 194, 196, 197, 203, 204, 208, 211,
342n66

Melhorn, Kent, 321n144

Mennesson-Rigaud, Odette, 49, 361n240

mesmerism, 39

Methodists, 103, 197, 198, 200, 343n84

Métraux, Alfred: on *affaire de Bizoton,* 83; on
calenda, 275n88; on "Captain Daybas,"
156; on Catholic Church's antisuperstition campaign of 1940–42, 194, 201,
204–6, 208, 345n106, 357n207; on ceremonies at Christmas, 1947, 321n150; "La
comédie rituelle dans la possession,"
302n227; confiscated objects shipped to
Smithsonian Institution by, 213, 350n160,
352n168; and Herskovits, 211; on *laplas,*
52; *Making a Living in the Marbial Valley,
Haiti,* 211; on penal code article 405, 90;
on Pentecostalism, 200; predicting Vodou's inevitable decline, 212, 351n164;
on priests' conceptions of *lwa,* 204; and
Roumain, 212, 350n162; on Roumain's
Le Sacrifice du tambour-assoto(r), 357n213;
on sacredness of Haitian drums, 164; on
Seabrook, 174; on taxation of Vodou
ceremonies, 193; trip to Haiti of 1941,
211, 212, 350n161; *Le vaudou haïtien,* 194,
204, 211, 212, 357n207, 361n240; at Yale
Institute of Human Relations, 211

Métraux, Rhoda, 211, 212, 350n161

Michaud, Valéra, 314n72

MICIVIH (International Civilian Mission in
Haiti), 254, 368n29

Miller, Adolph B., 162, 328n217

Miller, Gerrit S., Jr., 322n158, 329n224

Millet, Kethly, 119, 123–24, 126, 141

Millspaugh, Arthur, 333n254

min'kisi, 274n74

Mintz, Sidney, 284n30, 286n41, 288n73

Monfleury (journalist), 84–85

Mongin, R. P., 275n85

Moniteur, Le, 84–85

Monroe Doctrine, 118

Montalvo-Despeignes, Jacquelin, 16

Montas, August, 147

Montesquieu, Baron de, 49

Montilus, Guerin C., 257n3

Moore, Robin, 362n254

Moral, Paul, 67–68, 69, 289n81, 308n7,
333n256

Moreau de Saint-Méry, Médéric-Louis-Élie:

as apologist for slavery, 49; on *calenda,*
36; on case of Jean, Jérôme, and Télémaque, 40, 274n79; on *danse à Dom Pèdre,*
61, 274n76; *Description,* 36, 40, 41, 47,
274n76; *Loix et constitutions des colonies
françoises de l'Amérique sous le vent,* 41; on
macandal, 61; on *mayombo,* 39; on *Vaudoux,* 40–42, 47, 52, 64–65, 79, 275n82,
366n3

Morris, Mike, 316n89

Morris, Rosalind, 237, 362n251

Moscoso, Maritou Chenêt, 334n1

mouvement folklorique, 177, 215–16, 241, 244,
248–49

Mullaney, Steven, 346n113

Murray, Gerald F., 263n52, 333n256

Museum Journal (University of Pennsylvania
Museum), 164

Muth, Lawrence, 316n89

NAACP, 135

Nan Kanpèch (Nan Campeche), 43, 105

Napoleonic Code, 57–58

Nation (magazine), 134, 166, 318n116

National Folk Festival (1941), 230–38,
361n243

National Geographic (magazine), 314n66,
328n216

National Geographic Society, 166–67, 168

National Party, 106–7

Nau, Émile, 178

Nau, Léon, 59

Negro Church, The (Du Bois), 6

Negros brujos, Los (Ortiz), 180

Nérestant, Micial M., 304n249

Newell, William W., 6, 259n16

"New Negro" movement, 228

Nicaragua, 118, 136

Nicholls, David, 286n46

Nicolas, Pierre, 198

Niles, Blair, 156–57, 218–19, 314n69

Nina Rodrigues, Raimundo, 180, 336n15

Nine Years' War, 27

Noël, Marie, 358n215

Noires, Massillon, 317n101

noirisme, 215

Nord Alexis, Pierre, 111, 112, 114, 115, 116

Notes sur le vaudou (Augustin), 202

Notes sur l'histoire religieuse d'Haïti (Cabon), 73

Notre-Dame de l'Assomption, feast of, 43

Noustas, Elias, 248, 249, 365n1

obeah, 17–18, 59, 64, 283n27, 298n179

Oblates of Mary Immaculate, 194, 209, 349n146
occupation of Haiti, U.S. *See* U.S. occupation of Haiti, 1915–34
Occupied Haiti (Balch), 121
Ogou, 114, 117, 307n305
Ogou Panama, 307n302
O'Neill, Eugene, 167
Oriol, Jacques, 301n221
Ortiz, Fernando, 180, 336n15, 336n16
Ortner, Sherry, 89, 298n178
ouanga (*wanga*), 58, 59, 60, 65, 77, 161, 183, 184
oungan: appointed to positions of local authority, 70; attacked after fall of Duvalier regime, 12, 254; Bellegarde reputed to be, 145; called *papaloi*, 152, 175, 323n172; in Catholic Church's anti-Vaudoux campaign of 1896–1900, 109; Catholic Church's ordinances against, 82; in census of 1924, 152, 323n172; clergy deny Catholic burial to, 343n79; conflated with *bòkò* in Catholic literature, 108, 208, 342n73; contributions to Haiti's gross domestic product, 253–54; displacement of, 153; Duvalier associates himself with, 250; in Geffrard's anti-Vodou campaign, 87; in gendarmerie, 150–52; healing and, 7; identity of, 7; marines target reputed, 138; and National Folk Festival of 1941, 231; portrayed as charlatans, 98, 104, 253; purchasing permits for rituals, 192; resistance during Catholic Church's antisuperstition campaign of 1940–42, 206; Riché's campaign against, 77; Russell on peasants as prey of, 145, 147; St. John on, 97, 98; in *tonton makout*, 12, 250; uprising of 1918–1920 associated with, 139; in U.S. military intelligence network, 150–52, 323n169; U.S. occupiers' campaign against, 137, 138, 139, 147; worshippers incorporated in fictive kinship networks with, 8
outò, 164–65
Overley, Homer, 148

Palmer, Vernon V., 266n1
Palmié, Stephan, 22, 103, 164, 174–75, 266n80, 327n203
Panama, 118
Panama Congress (1826), 63
pan-Americanism, 229–30, 235
Papillon (insurgent), 141, 143

Parrish, Lydia, 356n201
Parsons, Elsie Clews, 312n53, 329n224, 356n201
Paton, Diana, 17–18, 59, 263n54, 298n179
Paul, Emmanuel C., 243, 301n221, 341n61
Péan, Marc, 102, 104, 112, 113, 114, 116, 305n256
peasant novel, 238
peasantry: displaced by American-owned enterprises, 173; double-sided nature attributed to, 141–44; during U.S. occupation of Haiti, 119–20, 124, 128, 129–30; forced to work on the *kòve* during U.S. occupation, 125, 126, 311n42; in Gendarmerie d'Haïti, 122; Janvier on evolution of, 95; legal prohibition of Vodou as pretext for everyday forms of exploitation of, 250; local hierarchies of, 69, 71, 75, 89, 289n83, 292n112, 298n178; marginalized by criminalization of Vodou, 10–11, 250; migrations, 8, 119, 240; and National Folk Festival of 1941, 231; popular insurgency during 1915–34 U.S. occupation, 127, 132–33, 136–37, 140–41; portrayed as cultural agents of own immiseration, 22, 255–56; portrayed as exploited by popular ritual specialists, 145, 147; rural law and customary order, 67–71; shaped local enforcement of law against *sortilèges*, 4–5, 75, 88–89, 156–57, 254–55; trauma of Catholic Church's antisuperstition campaign of 1940–42 for, 205–6; in uprising of 1918–1920, 141, 142; U.S. occupation disrupted customary laws that protected, 124; Vincent portrays himself as champion of, 182; in Volontaires de la Sécurité Nationale, 251
Pélé, Congo, 83
Pélé, Jeanne, 83, 84–85
penal code. *See* Code Pénal
Pentecostalism, 197, 200, 345n97
Péralte, Charlemagne, 141, 143, 318n109
Père Simon (Simon Césaire), 195, 196
Perrier, Jean-Baptiste (Goman), 282n11
Peters, Carl Edward: on antisuperstition campaign of 1940–42, 195, 207, 213, 342n75, 351n168; on Concordat of 1860, 82; on counter-oaths during 1940–42 campaign, 206; *La croix contre l'asson*, 195, 206; on felling of the Mapou Dampus, 347n117; *Lumière sur le humfort*, 202–3, 206
Peters, Dewitt, 353n176

Pétion, Alexandre: Bolívar given refuge by, 63; Constitution of 1816 of, 286n43; as free person of color, 67; in "indigenous army," 50; land and labor policies of, 67–68; on Napoleonic Code and Haitian law, 57; new church hierarchy established by, 78; as *papa bon kè,* 68; proclamation of February 1814 of, 51–52; southern republic ruled by, 57

Pettinger, Alasdair, 65

Petwo spirits: in Dahomean-Yoruban cosmological schema, 260n29; and Ginen, 7; and historical interpretation, 9; and indictment of Jérôme, Télémaque, and Jean, 39–40; Kongo roots of, 9, 39, 61; and magical identification, 8, 61, 285n34; Rada spirits contrasted with, 8

Pierre, Olivine, 110, 306n284

Pierre-Charles, Gérard, 251, 252

Pierre Damballah (folklore troupe), 243

Pierrot, Jean-Louis, 73, 75, 80

Piquet Rebellion, 72–73

Piquion, René, 227, 358n218

Pius IX, Pope, 81

Placide, Leonard, 138, 175

Plaine-du-Nord, 114–16

Pluchon, Pierre, 41, 44, 271n51

poisoning: in 1835 and 1864 penal codes, 89, 128; colonial association of healing with, 38, 271n51; in English translation of 1864 Code Rural, 128, 160; healing associated with, 38, 271n51; Makandal case, 33–34, 35

policé, 54, 55

politique de doublure, 73, 77, 79

Polverel, Étienne, 46, 49, 67

Polynice, Constant, 172, 332n249

popular dance: *calenda (kalenda),* 36, 38, 272n54, 272n55, 275n88; law of 1935 affirms right of, 177, 188–91, 217, 238, 245, 246; as national culture, 189, 190, 217, 218; stigmatization of, 95–97; Vodou seen as, 7, 21, 40, 47, 80, 98, 103, 159, 189–90, 235, 301n218

Port-au-Prince: becomes capital, 28; Catholic Church's antisuperstition campaign of 1940–42 in, 202, 207, 209, 210, 349n152; folklore performances in, 225–30; police in, 38, 152; Rex Theatre, 225–27, 239, 244, 245

Porter, Cole, 249

potlatch, 185

Pradines, Emerante de, 364n274

pratiques superstitieuses: abrogation of law of 1935, 12–13, 254–55, 337n119; animal sacrifice becomes definitive mark of, 15, 185; arrests for, after 1987 abrogation of 1935 law, 254–55, 368n31; and Catholic Church's anti-Vaudoux campaign of 1896–1900, 101; as constructed during Catholic Church's antisuperstition campaign of 1940–42, 202–3; as defined in law of 1935, 184; laws as performative texts signaling state's will to eliminate, 92; Vincent's law of 1935 against, 14, 15–16, 177, 181–93, 242, 243, 245, 248, 252. *See also* "superstition"

Première Légion de Saint-Domingue, 272n55

Present State of Hayti, The (Franklin), 65

Pressoir, Catts, 214, 294n130, 303n242, 344n90, 344n92

Pressoir, Malherbe, 344n90

Préval, René, 276n97

Prezeau, Zule, 152

Price, Hannibal: on *affaire de Bizoton,* 83; on *caplata,* 284n32; critique of Haiti's detractors, 96–98; on decline of African dances, 96–97; *De la réhabilitation de la race noire par la République d'Haïti,* 83; on Geffrard's campaign against Vodou of 1864, 87; on Haiti as exemplary, 95; on misunderstandings of Haiti springing from *vaudoux,* 2; Trouillot compared with, 100; on Vodou, 97, 98, 99, 300n204, 301n220

Price-Mars, Jean, 178–81; on African beliefs in Haitian liberation, 51; *Ainsi parla l'oncle,* 6, 19, 178, 179, 180, 181, 186, 202–3, 215, 242, 264–65n66, 336n9, 336n11, 336n13, 342n66, 359n222; argues for status of Vodou as religion, 13, 179–80, 242; arrest in 1918, 126; civil ethics project of, 336n9; on Code Rural, 337n18; on colonial use of word *vaudoux,* 41; on conflict during pilgrimage to Sodo, 155; on criminalization of Vodou and marginalization of peasantry, 10; on etymology of Vodou, 6–7; on folklore, 179, 181, 336n11; *Folklore et patriotisme,* 10, 364n267; influence on this study, 3; Institut d'Ethnologie founded by, 214, 353n175; as Institut Haïtiano-Américain president, 230; legal prohibition of Vodou challenged by, 10, 242, 364n267; on *lwa/loi,* 19, 264n66; on *le mélange,*

342n66; ousted from National Assembly, 337n23; photograph of, *179;* in presidential election of 1930, 337n21; in resignification of Vodou, 13; on popular themes in theatrical and musical performances, 228; on reform of regime against Vodou necessary for empowerment of the Haitian majority, 10–11; Seabrook asks him to show him a ceremony, 218, 355n188; on Seabrook's *The Magic Island,* 326n197; *Une étape de l'évolution haïtienne,* 336n13; *La vocation de l'élite,* 337n18; on Vodou, 16, 179–80, 336n13

"profanations," 32–33, 34, 35, 38, 59

progress: lay support for anti-Vaudoux campaign of 1896–1900 focused on, 102; Vodou portrayed as impeding, 21–23

Protestantism: Boyer's sometime openness to missionaries, 78, 294n130; Catholic Church opposes activity of, 103–4, 197–200, 304n247, 304n249; grows in Haiti during and after 1915–34 U.S. occupation, 197–99; missionary activity in Haiti, 103–4, 197–98, 304n248, 343n84; repression of Vodou during U.S. occupation supported by clergy, 148; seen as refuge from angry *lwa,* 199, 204

pwen, 132, 176, 334n266

pyè-tonnè, 213, 351n167

Quatrefages, Armand de, 99

Quelques mœurs et coutumes des paysans haïtiens (Romain), 91

Rada spirits: *arada,* 80; and Ginen, 7; and historical interpretation, 9; Petwo spirits contrasted with, 8; Pierrot and, 75; Rada drums, 156, 162, 229; West African roots of, 7

rad penitans, 82–83

Rameau, Pierrot Benoit, 292n111

Raymond, Louis, 183–84

Rediker, Marcus, 28

registration of royal laws, 29

regleman, 8

Règlement de culture (1800), 49, 67

rejetés (rejete), 194–97, 199, 202, 205, 207, 209, 212, 349n147

religion: in Haitian Constitution of 1805, 51, 77–78; invention of concept of, 262n49; people of African descent portrayed as incapable of true, 55; Price-Mars argues Vodou should be considered a, 13, 179–

80, 242. *See also* Ginen; Protestantism; Roman Catholic Church; Vodou

Renda, Mary A., 140, 170, 316n89, 332n245, 334n263

repozwa, 200, 203, 205

République d'Haïti, La: Telle qu'elle est (Vincent), 189

République d'Haïti et ses visiteurs, 1840–1882, La (Janvier), 55, 95

Reser, Stanley ("Doc"), 325n180

Résil, Gerard, 359n224

Revival and Rebellion in Colonial Central Africa (Fields), 158

Revue de la Société de législation (journal), 103

Revue indigène, La, 178, 215, 337n23

Rex Theatre (Port-au-Prince), 225–27, 239, 244, 245

Rey, Terry, 45, 82, 301n218

Rhodes, Gary D., 331n238, 331n241, 334n263

Richman, Karen, 9, 62, 173, 174, 176, 261n31, 285n37, 285n39, 308n7, 333n256, 334n266

Rigaud, André, 46, 48

Rigaud, Candelon, 173–74, 332n251

Rigaud, Milo, 156, 165, 193, 243, 257n3, 325n180

Riou, Roger, 201, 203, 352n168, 352n170

Rivière, Romaine (Romaine la Prophétesse), 45, 278n106

Rivière-Hérard, Charles, 72

Roach, Joseph, 83, 189

Robert, Paul, 195, 348n133

Robertson, Pat, 21

Rochambeau, Donatien-Marie-Joseph de Vimeur, comte de, 50, 51

Rodman, Selden, 218

Romain, J. B., 91

Romaine la Prophétesse (Romaine Rivière), 45, 278n106

Román, Reinaldo, 297n167, 363n254

Roman Catholic Church: antisuperstition campaign of 1940–42, 16, 165, 177, 193–213, 238, 246, 248, 347n122; antisuperstition campaigns of, 16, 18, 56, 82, 258n6; anti-Vaudoux campaign of 1896–1900, 55, 101–17, 148, 347n122; Boyer negotiates with Vatican, 78; church hierarchy in 1934, 341n56; clergy arrive in Haiti in 1864, 83, 296n158; in Code Noir of 1685, 24–25; Concordat with Haitian state, 4, 15, 56, 78–79, 81–82, 107, 191; in Constitution of 1801, 50; Constitution of 1805 and, 77–78; cult of the Virgin,

Roman Catholic Church (*continued*)
43, 45, 73, 82, 114, 155–56, 296n151; defining itself in opposition to "superstition," 81, 295n146; Dominicans, 36, 37; feast of Notre-Dame de l'Assomption, 43; Jesuits, 34, 36, 37, 272n59, 272n61; in kingdom of Kongo, 33, 82, 270n41; law of 1935 used as sanction for antisuperstition campaign of 1940–42, 202; material culture of Vodou destroyed during campaign of 1940–42, 200–204; Oblates of Mary Immaculate, 194, 209, 349n146; as official religion, 78; parishes, 191; Protestant activity opposed by, 103–4, 197–200; repression of Vodou during U.S. occupation supported by, 148; in repression of Vodou practices, 4, 5, 10, 15; resistance to antisuperstition campaign of 1940–42, 204–10; Romanizing popular Catholicism, 102; Schoelcher on clergy, 296n149; seen as agent of civilization, 85; seen as cover for slave resistance, 36–37; Vodou and, 5, 8, 82–83, 101, 114–16, 194, 199, 203

Rony, Fatimah Tobing, 170

Roosevelt, Franklin D., 125–26, 229, 360n232

Roosevelt, Theodore, 118

Rosemond, René, 244, 365n277

Rosenbère, Philoclès, 165

Roumain, Jacques: *À propos de la campagne "anti-superstitieuse"/Las supersticiones,* 204, 210, 346n117; Bureau d'Ethnologie founded by, 194, 210, 212–13; on Catholic Church's antisuperstition campaign of 1940–42, 194, 203–4, 212, 213; as chargé d'affaires to Mexico, 223, 357n210; as communist, 194, 210, 215, 337n23; foreign travels and study of, 210–11; and the Griots, 215–16; at Institut d'Ethnologie, 214; and Métraux, 212, 350n162; and *mouvement folklorique,* 215; photograph of, *214;* pre-Columbian archaeology as interest of, 213, 351n166; *Le Sacrifice du tambour-assoto(r),* 224, 357n213; views on Vodou, 212

Rouzier, Gontran, 213

Roy, Denise, 361n243

Roy, Marie-Thérèse, 361n243

Roy, Max, 361n243

Russell, John H.: on British occupation of Egypt, 325n185; on Haitian judicial system, 147, 175; on Haytian American

Sugar Company hiring former insurgents, 143; and Kuser's travelogue, 138, 317n100; on pernicious effects of "Vaudoism," 144–45; on Protestant missionary activity, 198

Sacrifice du tambour-assoto(r), Le (Roumain), 224, 357n213

Saint-Armand, J., 311n35

Saint-Domingue, 24–53; ban of slave assemblies, 25, 31, 35, 38, 41, 43; British occupation of, 48; colonial administration of, 28–29; commodities produced in, 28; Constitution of 1801, 49–50, 279n127; exiles in U.S., 287n57; feast of Notre-Dame de l'Assomption, 43; forced migration of enslaved West and West Central Africans to, 29; insurrection of 1791, 3, 14, 21, 42–45; Jesuits expelled from, 37; law and labor in eighteenth-century, 26–30; Leclerc's expedition to, 50–51; map of, *2;* ordinances against black healers, diviners, and "sorcerers," 31–42; provinces of, 28; role of African-based spiritual practice, organization, leadership in Haitian Revolution, 3, 42–51; slavery in, 25, 29–30, 268n24, 269n25; under Spanish rule, 26–27. *See also* Haiti

Saint-Jacques, 114–16, 117, 307n305

saints (and *guyons*), 73–76

Sala-Molins, Louis, 24, 31

Salnave, Albert, 111, 112

Salomon family, 72

Salvatore, Ricardo, 64

Sam, Tirésias Simon, 105, 115, 148

Sam, Vilbrun Guillaume, 119

Sans Souci, Jean-Baptiste, 50, 279n132

Santo Domingo, 26, 27, 57, 78. *See also* Dominican Republic

Savalou E (Beauvoir and Dominique), 12, 259n17

Schmidt, Hans, 174, 308n2, 318n113, 320n141, 325n185

Schoelcher, Victor, 65, 296n149

scientific racism, 93, 95

Scott, David, 80

Seabrook, W. B.: asks Price-Mars to show him a ceremony, 218, 355n188; on bamboo drums, 149–50; Craige and Herskovits criticize, 166; Craige on confidential information obtained by, 326n199; and Haitian law on *zonbi,* 160–61; *The Magic Island,* 128–29, 149–50,

160–61, 166, 172, 186, 318n114, 326n196, 326n197, 330n229; on peasants as double-natured, 318n114; on police tolerance of Vodou practices, 151; on rumors of *zonbi* working at Haytian American Sugar Company (HASCO), 172–73, 174; on U.S. enforcement of legal prohibition of Vodou, 323n173; on Wirkus, 128–29, 167

Sébillot, Paul, 179, 336n11

Seligmann, Herbert, 134

sénéchaussées, 29

Senn, Bryan, 170, 172

Service d'Hygiène Nationale, 321n144

Seventh-Day Adventists, 197, 198

Seven Years' War, 37

Seward, Julian, 352n170

SHADA (Société Haïtiano-Américaine de Développement Agricole), 240, 363n260

Sheller, Mimi, 63, 73, 281n7, 291n97

Silvani, Monsignor, 195, 208–9, 349n146

Silverthorn, Merwin H., 150, 161–62, 320n134

Simpson, George Eaton, 19, 150, 188–89, 191, 221–22, 351n164, 356n201

slavery: abolition in French territories, 46; children of planters and enslaved women, 37; Haiti suspected of inciting slave revolts elsewhere, 63; *kòve* compared with, 127; Napoleon and, 49; ordinances against black healers, diviners, and "sorcerers" in Saint-Domingue, 31–42; penal, 313n56; persons of color prohibited from practicing medicine, 38, 273n68; poisonings of slaves, 33–34; recourse to obeah in Jamaica, 17–18; religious orders as slaveholders, 37, 272n61; restoration in Guadeloupe and French Guiana, 50; in Saint-Domingue, 25, 29–30, 268n24, 269n25; Saint-Domingue insurrection of 1791, 3, 14, 21, 42–45; slaves as healers, 38; in Spanish Hispaniola, 26; transforming former slaves into republican citizens, 47; Vodou associated with, 106. *See also* Code Noir (1685)

Smith, Jennie M., 17, 52, 76, 266n81, 310n34

Smith, Matthew, 343n77

Smith, Theophus, 6

Smithsonian Institution, 162–63, 164, 212, 213, 329n224, 350n160, 352n168, 352n170

Sodo, pilgrimage to, 155–56, 296n151

Sonthonax, Léger-Félicité, 45–46, 47, 48, 49, 67, 278n115

Soray, Félix, 282n17, 283n21, 353n172

sorcery: decriminalization in France, 32, 270n40; European roots of such beliefs, 33, 76, 100; Ginen and, 61–62; *guyons* seen as malevolent sorcerers, 74, 75–76; "holy things" used in, 32–33, 34; law against *sortilèges* implicated in logic of, 71, 157, 255; legal action used by those who believed themselves victimized by, 71, 156–57, 254–55; no generalized word in Kreyòl for, 284n30; outsiders associate with Vodou, 9–10, 13, 15, 62, 80; popular linkage between political power and, 71, 105, 251; prosecutions after 1987 abrogation, 254–55, 368n31; sedition associated with, 15, 148; Trouillot on, 100. *See also* sortilèges

sortilèges: law against in Code Pénal of 1835, 1, 14, 55, 58–67, 70–77, 82, 85, 89, 90, 181, 283n23, 284n28, 298n181, 299n185, 346n109; law against in Code Pénal of 1864, 14, 90, 128, 148, 181, 184, 293n120, 298n181, 299n183, 299n185, 346n109; legal prohibition as affirming what it negates, 5, 91–92, 157, 160, 184, 254, 255; and magic, 60–62, 284n31; meanings of, 284n29; as not a popular category, 60; popular investment in laws against, 71, 117, 254–55; Schoelcher on, 65; U.S. occupation enforces laws against, 128, 129–30, 133, 147; Vincent's government abrogates prohibition against, 15, 177, 183

sosyete kongo, 167, 169, 313n57

sosyete sekrè: dread associated with, 17; judicial processes and punitive actions of, 18; legal action versus recourse to, 18, 71; obeah compared with, 18; passports issued by, 17; and *tonton makout,* 251; women in, 264n59

Soulouque, Faustin (Faustin I), 79–81; and apparitions of the Virgin, 296n151; circular affirming legality of "arada" dances, 80; Frère Joseph associated with, 80, 294n136; Louis Napoleon compared with, 294n133; open association with popular religious practice and organization, 79–80

Spear, Frederick L., 134, 137, 139–40, 317n99

spells. See *sortilèges*

Spiritual Baptists, 11

Starobinski, Jean, 54

St. Aude, Cicéron, 233, 361n240

Stein, Robert Louis, 47

St. John, Spenser: on *affaire de Bizoton,* 84, 86, 297n167; critiqued by Price, 98, 301n220; Haitian legal discourses read as evidence of barbarism by, 91, 92, 97; *Hayti, or The Black Republic,* 84, 132; on Testard Du Cosquer's arrival in Haiti, 296n158

Suméra, Roséïde, 84

"superstition": Catholic Church's antisuperstition campaign of 1940–42, 16, 165, 177, 193–213, 238, 246, 248, 347n122; Catholic Church's antisuperstition campaigns, 16, 18, 56, 82, 165, 177, 258n6; Catholic Church's anti-Vaudoux campaign of 1896–1900, 55, 101–17, 148, 347n122; Dartiguenave government calls for repression of, 148; enforcement of laws against *sortilèges* seen as reinforcing, 156, 157; Kersuzan's survey on, 101; material culture of Vodou destroyed during campaign of 1940–42, 200–204; Protestantism portrayed as way of extricating oneself from, 199; U.S. campaign against, 147, 321n144. See also *pratiques superstitieuses*

Sylla (rebel leader), 50

Taussig, Michael, 140, 174, 189, 258n9, 333n258, 334n261

tax collection, 124, 172, 193, 252, 367n18, 367n19

temple Vodou: becomes more common in countryside, 8; *laplas* in, 52; popular protests against prohibition of, 254; relationship to *sosyete sekrè,* 17; taxation of, 252

Terlonge, Henri, 364n271

Testard Du Cosquer, Martial-Guillaume-Marie, 296n158

Thornton, John, 274n74, 280n140

Tighe, Thomas A., 328n212

Ti Joseph, 172, 174

Ti-Jules, 195, 196, 342n72

Ti Memenne, 167, *168*

Ti-Nomme, Mme, 222, *223,* 224

tonton makout, 12, 250, 252

tradition voudoo et le voodoo haïtien, La (Rigaud), 193, 243

Trouillot, Duverneau, 60, 97, 98–99, 100, 103, 257n3, 301n221, 302n227

Trouillot, Hénock, 76, 86, 280n144, 297n169

Trouillot, Michel-Rolph, 25, 33, 50, 51, 124, 250, 251, 261n39, 284n30, 288n65, 309n9, 336n9

Troupe Folklorique Nationale, 229, 361n240

Trujillo, Rafael Leonidas, 209, 211, 348n145, 366n11

Turner, George E., 168

Underwood, R. O., 162

Une étape de l'évolution haïtienne (Price-Mars), 336n13

Union Patriotique d'Haïti, 135, 182

United States: in campaigns against Vodou, 4, 5, 15, 130–58, 246; Good Neighbor Policy, 229–30, 360n232; Haiti denied diplomatic recognition by, 63; interventions in Pacific, Caribbean, and Latin America, 118; involvement in Haiti after end of occupation, 229–30, 360n236; Monroe Doctrine, 118; pan-Americanism sought during World War II, 229–30. See also U.S. occupation of Haiti, 1915–34

University of Pennsylvania Museum, 163, 164

urban poor: criminalization of Vodou marginalized, 10–11; in Gendarmerie d'Haïti, 122; U.S. occupation disrupted customary laws that protected, 124; Vincent portrays himself as champion of, 182; in Volontaires de la Sécurité Nationale, 251

U.S. occupation of Haiti, 1915–34, 118–76; agroindustrial land takeovers during, 62, 145, 173; atrocities against Haitians reported, 120, 127, 133–39, 316n88; atrocities against marines reported, 134–35, 143, 144, 159; campaign against "voodoo" during, 4, 130–58, 246; Catholic and Protestant clergy support repression of Vodou during, 148; charges of indiscriminate killing of Haitians during, 133–39; Constitution of 1918, 119, 308n5; elite opposition to, 120; end of, 229, 360n232; evasion of and resistance to regime against Vodou, 147–56; Haitian-American Treaty of 1915, 121, 146; Haitian courts seen as opposed to, 144–45; insurgency of 1918–1920, 132–33, 137, 139–47, 148, 161; justifications of, 15, 120, 123, 130, 136, 147, 167, 313n64; *kòve* during, 120, 124–27; laws altered during, 119, 308n6; marines seen as experts on "voodoo" in U.S., 165–70; naval court of inquiry, 134–35, 315n83; paternalism of, 15, 21, 22, 125, 130, 140,

142; pretexts for, 118–19; racial discrimination of Marine Corps, 310n26; selective enforcement of Haitian laws during, 121, 124, 125, 128–30; Senate inquiry into, 120, 131–32, 133, 135–36, 137, 139–40, 165, 182, 199; "superstitious" beliefs confirmed rather than undermined during, 5, 157, 158–70, 254; tax collection during, 124; as U.S. presidential election issue in 1920, 134; Vodou seen as obstacle during, 21–22, 130–33

vagrancy, 59, 70, 89, 128–29, 183
Valera, Pedro, 78
Vanhee, Hein, 82, 271n46, 285n33
Vaudois, 6, 259n16
vaudou haïtien, Le (Métraux), 194, 204, 211, 212, 357n207, 361n240
vaudoux: Code Pénal of 1835 on, 58, 59–60, 64–65, 85, 120, 183, 184; etymology of, 6; taken by foreigners as name for Haitian "sorcery," 7, 13, 80; "voodoo" as English for, 120. *See also* Vodou
vèvè, 8
Viaud, Léonce, 301n221
Victor, René, 223
Viejo (Casseus), 228
Villiers, Antoine, 160
Vincent, Sténio: *Efforts et résultats,* 182; informal regulation of ritual practices under, 250; law against *pratiques superstitieuses* (1935), 14, 15–16, 177, 181–91, 217, 246; negotiates end of U.S. occupation, 360n232; populism of, 182; presidency of, 182; in presidential election of 1930, 337n21; *La République d'Haïti: Telle qu'elle est,* 189; Roumain imprisoned under, 210; on *vaudou* as popular dance, 189–90
Virgin, cult of the, 43, 45, 73, 82, 114, 155–56, 296n151
vocation de l'élite, La (Price-Mars), 337n18
Vodou
—beliefs and practices: cultural origins of, 6–7, 9, 29, 39, 40, 80, 258n15, 260n29; founding of family *lakou* remembered in, 7, 69; Ginen, 7, 9–10, 16, 17, 61–62, 100, 176, 259n18, 260n30, 261n31; in Haitian economy, 193, 253–54; and healing, 1, 7, 16, 77, 195; land tenure and spiritual inheritance in, 69, 263n52; as locus of embodied history, 9, 83, 296n157; moral ethos of akin to law, 16; moral opposition to malicious magic in, 9–10, 61–62, 74; permits to practice, 70, 193, 250, 252, 290n91; relationship to Catholicism, 5, 8, 82–83, 101, 114–16, 194, 199, 203; taxation of, 70, 192–93, 252, 367n19
—in colonial and revolutionary Saint-Domingue, 24–53; Bwa Kayiman ceremony, 42–44; Dessalines' policy toward, 14, 49, 107; during revolutionary struggle, 14, 42–45, 66; juridical silence about, in eighteenth century, 40–41, 275n83; law of 21 November 1796 banning, 21, 47; Louverture's policy toward, 14, 48–49, 107; problem with assuming transhistorical identity of, 7, 275n88
—negative associations with: seen as antimodern and/or progress-impeding, 21–23, 147, 245; seen as proof of decline of "civilization" in Haiti after 1804, 2, 14, 55, 66, 76, 80, 84, 98, 101, 106, 146, 249; seen as proof of Haitians' incapacity for self-government, 1, 55, 249; seen as sorcery, 9–10, 13, 15, 62, 80; seen as superstition, 6, 40, 85, 87
—in nineteenth-century Haiti: Catholic Church's anti-Vaudoux campaign of 1896–1900, 55, 101–17, 148; and the formation of *lakou,* 68–69; Geffrard's campaign of 1864 against, 86–89, 90, 97–98, 116, 117, 148, 160; legal studies at turn-of-the-century, 103; Ligue Contre le Vaudoux, 111–16; medical study of, 102–3; prohibited as form of *sortilège* in 1835 and 1864 penal codes, 58, 61–62, 90; *saints* and *guyons,* 72–75; seen by state as potential parallel political power, 52, 66; Soulouque associated with, 79; term infrequently used by foreigners before Soulouque, 80; Vodouizan shaped enforcement of law against *sortilèges,* 70–71, 75, 87–89; worker productivity said to be affected by, 67, 96
—outsider discourses on: foreigners in campaigns against, 4, 101–16, 128–70; 193–210, 246; French authors on *vaudoux* in early nineteenth century, 65–66; Haitians problematize foreign constructions of, 97–99; maligning and misinterpretation by outsiders, 1–2; objectification of, 6, 10, 13–14, 47, 80, 262n48; as primary object of foreign ethnographers, 249

Vodou (*continued*)
—in post-occupation Haiti: Catholic
  Church's *campagne anti-superstitieuse* and
  Vodouizan resistance, 193–210; informal
  regulation, 191–93; as locus of Haitian
  identity and culture, 248–49; passage
  of 1935 law against *pratiques superstitieuses,* 183–90; popular *rejete* movement,
  194–96; radio broadcast of rhythms and
  songs, 238–39; as reevaluated in work
  of Jean Price-Mars, 178–81; represented
  at National Folk Festival of 1941, 231–
  38; theatrical staging of during and after
  U.S. occupation, 218–25; "Voodoo" as
  brand, 248, 249, 366n4
—since mid-twentieth century: abrogation of 1935 law against *pratiques superstitieuses,* 13, 254; official acknowledge-
  ment of contribution to gross domestic
  product, 253–54; official recognition of,
  13, 262n45; penal regime between 1946–
  1957, 250; penal regime under François
  Duvalier, 250–52; spectral life of 1935
  law after repeal, 254–55; Vodouizan attacked during *dechoukaj,* 12; Vodouizan
  in *tonton makout,* 12, 250, 252
—terminological and conceptual considerations: as a dance, 7, 21, 40, 47, 80,
  98, 103, 159, 189–90, 235, 240, 301n218;
  English-language references to *vaudoux*
  proliferate, 80–81; etymological debate
  about, 6–7; orthographies of "Vodou,"
  257n2, 258n11; popular versus official/
  ecclesiastical constructions of the term
  vaudoux, 56, 62, 116–17; referential uncertainties and ambiguities, 26; significance of "Vodou" in Haiti, 7; *vaudoux*
  and its cognates as signs, 249; Vodouizan
  tend not to objectify religion as such, 6;
  as "voodoo" in English, 120
—and U.S. occupation of Haiti (1915–34),
  118–76; census of 1924–25, 152–54; construction of "voodoo" during and after
  U.S. occupation, 159–70, 248–49; insurgency of 1918–1920 associated with,
  138–39, 143, 144–47; as justifying occupation, 21–22, 130–33; marines initiated
  into, 156, 325n180; marines seen as experts on, 165–70; relationship of regime
  against Vodou to imperial construction
  of "voodoo," 130–44, 158–70; stories of
  the ascendance of *lwa* over the law, 155–
  56; Vodouizan integrated into military

and police structures, 159; Vodouizan
  resistance to and evasion of marine regime, 128, 132–33, 147, 149–52, 155–56;
  Vodouizan shaped enforcement of law
  against *sortilèges,* 156–57
Vodou et névrose (Dorsainvil), 202, 248, 335n6
"Vodun Service in Northern Haiti, The"
  (Simpson), 221
Vogel, Clayton, 220
"voix des nos rues, Les" (Victor), 223
Volontaires de la Sécurité Nationale (VSN),
  251
"voodoo": as brand, 248, 249, 366n4; con-
  struction during and after U.S. occupa-
  tion, 130–70; as English for *le vaudoux,*
  120; as verb, 80. See also *vaudoux;* Vodou
Voodoo (film), 168–70, 331n238, 331n241
Voodoo Fire in Haiti (Loederer), 186–87
Voyages d'un naturaliste en Haïti, 1799–1803
  (Descourtilz), 65

Walker, Léon, 361n243
Waller, Littleton, 131–32, 164, 165
wanga (ouanga), 58, 59, 60, 65, 77, 161, 183, 184
Washington Post (newspaper), 231, 235–37
Weaver, Karol K., 39
Welles, Benjamin Sumner, 235
Wells, Clarke H., 127, 315n82
White, Ashli, 287n57
White, J. C., 209, 238, 241, 349n149
White Zombie (film), 160, 170–72, 334n263
Williams, Alexander S., 126, 137–38, 163–
  64, 315n82
Williams, Dorcas L., 315n82
Williams, Tony, 332n248
Wilson, Woodrow, 118–19, 134
Wine of Astonishment, The (Lovelace), 11
Wirkus, Faustin: on Cherisier *lougawou* case,
  157; on desire to learn about "voodoo,"
  161; on drums used for communication,
  132–33; on enforcing laws against vagrancy and *vaudoux* to exact labor, 128–
  30; good relations with female leadership
  of *sosyete kongo,* 167; as international celebrity, 167; and La Gonâve's *sosyete kongo,*
  167, 169, 313n57; lecturing and writing
  by, 168, 330n236; on muffling drums with
  cotton fiber, 149, 322n155; O'Neill's *Emperor Jones* compared with, 167; on raid
  on Vodou ceremony, 148–49; on rebels
  becoming wage workers, 319n123; on religious elders appointed police officers,
  151–52; and Ti Memenne, 167, *168;* on

Vodouizan strategies for evading repression, 149; *Voodoo* film of, 168–70, 331n238, 331n241
Wirtz, Kristina, 362n254
Wise, Frederic May, 123, 137–38, 141, 142, 143
Witchcraft Ordinance in Malawi and Zambia (1914), 158
Woodson, Drexel, 68, 289n76

Yelvington, Kevin A., 356n199
"You Do Something to Me" (Porter), 249

Zacaïr, Philippe, 294n138
Zamor, Oreste, 110, 306n282
Zantray, 12, 277n97
Zombie (play), 172
zonbi: and capitalist development, 174–75; in Catholic Church's antisuperstition campaign of 1940–42, 205; Code Pénal seen as verifying existence of, 160; rumored to work at the Haytian American Sugar Company (HASCO), 172–76; *sosyete sekrè* and, 17; *White Zombie* film, 160, 170–72, 334n263